37

Consumer Economic Problems

Seventh edition

W. ~~HARMON~~ WILSON

Rickie

President
South-Western Publishing Co.

AND

ELVIN S. EYSTER

Chairman, Department of Business Education,
School of Business, Indiana University

SOUTH-WESTERN PUBLISHING CO.

Cincinnati   Chicago   Burlingame, Calif.   New Rochelle, N. Y.   Dallas

H31

Preface

The Seventh Edition of *Consumer Economic Problems* is based upon a successful history of thirty years. It has moved with the times, gradually blending new objectives and new emphasis with the old.

Consumer Economic Problems is a living, moving, dynamic treatment of the forces and influences that surround all of us in our daily lives. It deals with the essentials of economic principles and business relations woven into a fabric of experience that moves from student experiences to the responsible experiences of an adult life of earning, spending, voting, and managing money.

Consumer Economic Problems, Seventh Edition, has grown out of its successful use in the hands of students and teachers. Hundreds of suggestions have contributed to the development of this book into its present form, content, emphasis, balance, and relation to vital daily problems.

In line with the current concepts of economic education, the subject matter of *Consumer Economic Problems* is presented to attain the following objectives:

1. To understand the concept of free enterprise, how the American economic system operates, and how dependent we are upon business to satisfy our economic wants and needs.
2. To understand the economic principles that are essential for participation as a citizen and voter in resolving economic issues of local, state, and national importance; for wise management of one's economic affairs; and for performance as an efficient producer in one's occupation and profession.
3. To understand the application of the principles and procedures of business to personal and family problems relating to earning an income; to wise management of money and savings; to protection from loss through insurance; to procurement of a home; and to personal expenditures.

If you are looking for a treatment of economics with emphasis on theory and rules, you will not find it in this book. The emphasis is placed upon the analysis, interpretation, and application of economic principles to the solution of the problems of individuals and of society in general. Enough facts, procedures, and practices are used to emphasize realism and to lead the student through the experiences of using the mechanics of our society in solving vital problems.

iii

The subject matter of *Consumer Economic Problems* is highly integrated so that the student gets a total, workable pattern of the forces of economic society. For example, the student learns about credit not only in its economic function, but also in its relation to law, business practice, management of income and spending, and government. Certain chapters have a primarily economic emphasis, but may also include legal and business applications where they apply. Certain chapters deal more specifically with business practices and procedures, but include economic emphasis where it applies.

Although the title of this book emphasizes the consumer aspects of economics, this personal-interest approach is used to develop basic economic reasoning to help the student to operate intelligently and efficiently as a member of society and to understand free enterprise and the interrelationships of the individual with business and government. It is hoped that the study of this book will help the student become more efficient in handling his personal business affairs and that he may be guided intelligently in solving the economic problems of society through intelligently voting on economic issues.

In this volume there is an adequate range of subject matter and problem material to enable the teacher to appeal to students of a wide range of abilities. There is adequate material for a full year of work, but the flexibility of the organization makes it feasible to select subject matter content and problems for a one-semester course. *Buying Guides for Consumer Economic Problems,* a supplement, is available for students and teachers if special emphasis on buying is desired.

It would be impossible to thank individually the hundreds of teachers and students who have contributed directly and indirectly to the development and improvement of this book. However, in the preparation of the Seventh Edition of *Consumer Economic Problems,* we offer special acknowledgment to the following persons for the specific contributions they made: Dr. Harlan B. Miller, Dr. Earl Nicks, Dr. Gerald A. Porter, Dr. Eugene D. Wyllie, Dr. H. Donald David, and to the numerous teachers, economists, bankers, businessmen, and other authorities.

W. HARMON WILSON
ELVIN S. EYSTER

Table of contents

Chapter   **Page**

Part I • The American economic system and the consumer

1 Some simple truths of economics   1
2 The American free-enterprise system   19

Part II • The operation of American business

3 Our production system   35
4 The marketing distribution system   61
5 Labor, management, and government   79
6 Jobs, productivity, and level of living 101
7 The organization of business enterprise 125
8 The role of government in our economic system 143

Part III • National income, money, and banks

9 National income and its distribution 156
10 Money and credit 181
11 Banks and the banking system 199

Part IV • Prices and economic stabilization

12 Price, demand, and supply 215
13 Economic changes, fluctuations, and stabilization 235
14 Economic stability and government finance 255

Part V • Taxation and international trade

15 Taxation 275
16 International trade, balance of payments, and tariffs 293

Chapter		Page

Part VI · Financial and credit services

17	Bank services and loans	317
18	Understanding and using credit	343
19	Using installment credit	361

Part VII · The consumer and the market

20	Advertising and the consumer	383
21	Aids and protection for consumers	398
22	Legal relations important to consumers	423
23	Buying and spending wisely	446

Part VIII · A financial management plan

| 24 | Managing our finances | 463 |
| 25 | Principles and procedures of investing | 481 |

Part IX · Protection through insurance

26	Protection through property and liability insurance	505
27	Protection through life and health insurance	525
28	Buying life insurance	545
29	Individual and family security through social insurance	563

Part X · Problems of obtaining a home

30	Providing housing for the family	581
31	Financing the purchase of a home	602
32	Legal problems of obtaining a home	621

| Index | | 641 |

Chapter 1

Some simple truths of economics

PURPOSE OF THE CHAPTER

Our wants and needs must be satisfied through our mental and physical efforts—individually and as a group. To reach our goals we must make choices. These require personal and group decisions. This textbook and specifically this chapter help you to understand some of the problems of satisfying our wants and needs.

You will find answers to these questions:

1. What is the nature of our wants and needs?
2. What is economics?
3. What is meant by scarcity?
4. What are some desirable economic goals?

A. Wants and their satisfaction

WHY WE WORK AND EARN

Most of us work and earn so that we can buy the goods and services we want and need in order to live as nearly as we can in the manner we want to live. We want many things—necessary items, such as food,

clothing, and shelter; desirable things, such as education and the professional services of physicians and attorneys; and personal convenience services, such as dry cleaning, beauty and barber services, and repairing of automobiles and home appliances. The materials and services required to satisfy these wants and needs are known as *economic goods and services.*

If all items of goods and all kinds of services were available free of cost and in unlimited quantity, working and earning would not be necessary except to satisfy our inner desires to achieve and to accomplish something worthwhile. We would have no wants and needs for goods and services. But, who would want to live in such a world? A great portion of the real enjoyment and satisfaction we get from life comes from working and earning and from making worthy contributions to other people through our work.

Economic goods and services. An *economic good* is any material object that is useful to man in satisfying his wants or needs and that is scarce enough that he is willing to pay for it. Almost everything you own is an economic good. A material object must be useful, and it must have monetary value in order to qualify as an economic good. This ordinarily means that it is scarce, that is, it is not free. Your ballpoint pen meets the requirements of an economic good.

A person may be able to perform a personal service such as cutting your hair or a health service such as your physician provides. This service satisfies a want or need and it has monetary value. Usually it is classified as an *economic service* rather than an economic good because it is not tangible and is not an object.

Economic goods are classified as consumer goods or capital goods or producer goods according to their use. *Consumer goods* and *services* are those used or consumed directly by people. They include such items as clothing, food, shelter, medicine, furniture, and carpets. *Capital goods*, or *producer goods* as they are sometimes referred to, are those used by manufacturers, farmers, transportation companies, and others who produce consumer goods or who produce goods for other producers. Farms, buildings, machinery, equipment, and raw materials are examples of capital goods.

In addition to economic goods, some of the wants and needs of man may be satisfied by free goods. A *free good* is one that has no monetary price to the user, and it is not scarce. An example of a free good is the air we breathe or the drinking water flowing from a spring in the mountains of a national park.

THE NATURE OF OUR WANTS

Our wants are of two kinds—intangible and tangible. The *intangible wants* include the desires for love and affection of our family, respect and admiration of our friends and acquaintances, recognition of our achievements, and freedom from worry and anxiety and other things that take away the joy of living. *Tangible wants* consist of our desires and needs for the other necessities of life, such as clothes, food, and shelter. We also want such other tangible things as athletic and sporting goods, hi-fi sets, sports cars, books, and magazines. We want money income regularly to provide the tangible things we want. These tangible wants can be evaluated in terms of money. They are, therefore, the *economic wants* of man.

Clothing, record player, sports equipment, furniture, and food are the kind of tangible or economic wants for which we must earn money to obtain.

Sometimes we classify wants as *primary wants* or *essential wants* (those which must be satisfied for a person to live, such as food, clothing, shelter, and medicine) and *secondary wants* or *nonessential wants* (those which may be satisfied for pleasure or comfort, such as cosmetics, special foods, stylish clothes, or even an automobile). Of course, some of us would consider many nonessential goods to be very important, but in terms of economics they would not be essential.

THE PROBLEM OF SCARCITY

Economics is a study of how man satisfies his wants and needs for material goods and services through the use of his mental and physical efforts. The proper function of a society is to satisfy the wants and needs of people for goods and services. There would be no economic problem if everyone could satisfy his wants (demand) and if there were enough goods and services available (supply) to satisfy demand at prices people are willing and able to pay.

Many wants but limited supply. Our major economic problem arises from *scarcity*, which means there is a limited supply. If everything were free and as plentiful as the air we breathe, there would be no scarcity and no economic problem of fulfilling wants. Actually, some parts of the air are scarce. Air is composed mainly of oxygen and hydrogen, which are scarce and have special uses and values. These, then, are economic goods. Supplying the wants for these goods is an economic problem of production. Under some circumstances even air is an economic good. Air is scarce in a deep mine. Pumps that supply air are providing an economic good.

Land, minerals, and water suitable and available for use are scarce. There is a limited supply in terms of wants. Clothing and houses are scarce in terms of wants. They are not free. They must be produced.

There is usually less of everything readily available than we want. Most of us have fewer goods and services than we want and less purchasing power to purchase what we want. Our purchasing power in terms of money is usually limited or determined by our own ability to produce. So the key problem for each of us is to produce enough so that we can satisfy our wants by purchasing with money we earn or by trading our services for goods and services produced by others.

Choices must be made. Part of our problem of satisfying our wants for scarce items is the price that must be paid and our ability to buy. The price may be too high for people to be willing and able to pay. The want is still there, but people must make choices as to how they will spend the limited resources they have for their many wants. If the price can be reduced by efficient production, people may then choose to buy.

Is there a surplus? There apparently is an oversupply or surplus of some items at certain times and certain places in terms of what people will and can buy. Someone wants and needs these items but cannot buy them, so they are scarce to that person.

Some items are plentiful in certain places and scarce in others. Scarcity may be met by transporting coal, oil, water, and other items from locations of plenty to locations of scarcity, thereby fulfilling wants. This process is a part of what we call production.

Even when the showrooms of auto dealers are filled with cars they cannot sell, there are unfulfilled wants for cars. There are people who want cars who do not have them, those who would trade in an old car for a new one, and those who would like to have a second car, but not at the price offered. They must make a choice of buying a car or buying bread, clothing, or something else.

We read much about the surplus of wheat that is stored by our government. Certainly we have more wheat than appears to be needed, but there are still hungry people who could use this wheat if it were available to them. Part of the problem of apparent overproduction and oversupply of wheat arises from the activities of our government, which will be discussed later.

---

1. Most of us have unfulfilled wants.
2. Satisfying our wants is our main economic problem.
3. There are unfulfilled wants even when there appears to be a surplus.
4. Business is the main means of our society in fulfilling wants.

SATISFYING OUR ECONOMIC WANTS

It is necessary for most of us to work in order to satisfy our wants. Almost everything we have and use has come to us because of work that we or others have done. By working we earn, and with the money we earn, we buy the things we want and need. Sometimes we do not spend the money we have earned but save it to buy things we will need at a later time.

In a lifetime we use or consume many economic goods and services. It is the responsibility of each of us during the working period of our lives to work and to produce at least as much as we will use or will consume during our whole lives. And if we are to contribute toward better living for the nation as a whole, we shall have to produce more in our lives than we use.

To save for future economic wants and to contribute to the betterment of society, we must produce more than we use.

Our wants change as education and income increase. Many of our wants are to experience satisfaction as in the use of cosmetics, style in clothes, or taste in food. Even to satisfy hunger wants there are many kinds and varieties of foods to please various tastes. These differences are not only in taste but also in color, packaging, and preparation for use, such as frozen, canned, or dried. Many are identified by brands to guide buyers in making choices.

To satisfy wants for scarce items, each person would like to find a way to earn enough to fulfill his wants. In some cases, labor unions have created a scarcity by limiting the admission of new workers, by attempting to prevent nonmembers from working, by restricting hours of work, by restricting or limiting production, and by demanding higher wages.

Businessmen attempt to fulfill or satisfy the wants of people and to compete with other businesses in doing so. One of the methods used by business in creating demand for its product and getting its price is through the advertising of brands and satisfying the wants of consumers as indicated above. Businessmen also try to develop new services and new products that are better than those of competitors and thereby demand higher prices and make more profit. Competition helps all of us to fulfill our wants.

The answer to the problem of satisfying wants by eliminating scarcity is through efficient production of goods and services. In a sense, each of us trades goods and services to others for the goods and services they produce. If you were making shoes and could trade two pairs of shoes for a suit of clothes, you would satisfy your wants better if you could produce four pairs of shoes (or equivalent amount in money) to trade for two suits of clothes.

To raise the level of living, everyone must produce sufficient goods or services to earn enough to satisfy his wants. Efficient production is, therefore, the key to solving the problem of scarcity. Production in its broad sense, as we shall learn more about later, also includes communication (telephone), transportation (trucks), storing, distributing, and many other factors. The more we produce, the more purchasing power we have, and the greater ability we have to fulfill our wants and to solve the problem of scarcity.

ECONOMIC ACTIVITY

Economics was defined as a study of how man satisfies his wants and needs for economic goods and services. The study of economics is concerned with the production, distribution, and consumption of those goods and services. Economic activity at a given time includes everything that is being done to satisfy man's wants and needs through production, distribution, and consumption. Management, labor, and government all contribute to economic activity through which man's wants and needs are satisfied. The end results sought through economic activity are twofold: first, the creating of economic goods and services for man's use; and second, the providing of opportunities for man to earn a reasonable income so he can acquire and consume the goods and services he wants and needs.

B. Our economic goals

OUR GOALS IN AMERICA

We differ widely as to our specific preferences and choices of an occupation, a place to live, the clothes we wear, the food we eat, the college we want to attend, the kind of recreation we enjoy most, and in many other things that contribute a great deal to the satisfaction and contentment we have in life. Because each of us is different from others, our personal goals in these matters are different. But, there are some major goals that are common to almost all people.

What is an economic goal? Our economic wants are not satisfied automatically, however. To get the goods and services we want, we need to plan and manage. Otherwise our wants will not be satisfied. Getting the economic goods and services we want requires both thought and effort. This planning and management involves work or production on our part. It involves earning so that we can acquire what we want. It also involves making decisions as to how to spend our earnings so that our economic wants and needs are satisfied in a manner that is most pleasing to us. Saving and investing a part of our earnings enables us to satisfy some of our economic wants in the future. Some of our wants for goods and services are provided by local, state, and federal governments rather than by ourselves individually. Hence, buying goods and services through taxes, licenses, and fees is also a means of satisfying our wants.

Personal economic goals. Each person must make choices. We must decide what we want and set a goal. The cost of any choice to you is what you must give up to gain what you want. You must decide whether to spend your money for a vacation or for more education; to buy shoes or a suit if you cannot buy both; to make a down payment on a house or to buy a new car; or whether to save or to spend. If we are to make wise decisions, we must think carefully about the value of each choice.

Choice and real cost. Many times you must make a decision between two things, both of which you want. For example, you may anticipate having earned and saved $2,500 by the time you complete your present school program. You want a car and you also want to go to college or to take a technical course. You know you cannot afford both. Hence, you must decide which one will help you most to achieve your long-range goal and which one will give you the greatest pleasure over a long period of time. If you choose to save the money for further education and do not buy the car, you forego the pleasure and satisfaction you would have derived from the car; if you decide to buy the car, you forego the value you would have derived from further education. The value of that which you had to give up by making your decision is referred to in economics as the *real cost* of the thing you choose. We cannot usually satisfy all our wants; hence we must choose which ones to satisfy. In order to choose wisely, we must know what our goals are and then use common sense and good judgment in making the decision.

In a practical sense, economics involves (1) determining our goals, that is, what will give us the greatest satisfaction and pleasure; and (2) making decisions as to how to obtain, to choose, and to use economic goods and services to the greatest advantage in attaining those goals. The basic economic principles applicable to satisfying our personal wants and needs are also applicable to a business firm, to an industry, and to the nation. As citizens we have a vital stake in the economic decisions made for the nation as a whole. As individuals we are concerned with obtaining and using the economic goods and services that will satisfy our wants.

Income as a goal. Our desires for goods and services are really never fully satisfied. Seemingly we always want more and different kinds of commodities from those we now have. For example, you may have plenty of food, but you always would enjoy something new and different; your family may have one automobile but would like to have two; or you may spend your vacation at nearby lakes or mountains but would like to take a trip abroad. In general, all of us want an ever-increasing standard of living.

The increase in two-car families provides one example of our continuous desire to have more in kind and quantity of various goods and services.

An adequate income to satisfy our standard of living and to provide for some savings is a goal sought by all. The opportunity to work and thus to earn income is a privilege and a right that in America we believe every person should have. The particular economic system that a country may have affects the opportunity of its citizens to work and to earn an income. The *free-enterprise system,* sometimes referred to as the American economic system and as the American capitalistic system, has provided better than the system in any other nation the opportunity for its citizens to earn an income.

National economic goals. In any society (communist, socialist, or a free society such as ours) the economic goals are the same—to fulfill the wants of people.

In a government-controlled society, such as communist or socialist, the productive resources are owned and directed by government. They are owned by the group (all citizens combined) and not by individuals. The leaders set the goals. Thousands of decisions must be made by the leaders, and they may be right or wrong. Great power is in the hands of a few who decide how resources will be used to fulfill wants and how each will share in production. In a free society millions of people decide their goals. Through elected officials or representatives decisions are made as to the goals that will be directed by government. Individuals, however, are free to use their labor, their savings, and other resources to set their own goals and to produce to fulfill their own wants and the wants of others.

National goals, as a result of choices, are political decisions. They may be economic in nature and each of us shares in the decisions, but the decisions are made through democratic political processes. It is through these processes that the wishes of the majority are expressed.

In our society (our nation), we individually and as a group must set our goals and make our choices based upon careful reasoning. We cannot have everything we want. We cannot have all our personal pleasures, leisure, security, plenty of food and clothing, good highways, good police protection, and government controls without making choices. We must decide how much freedom we want and how much freedom we are willing to lose if decisions are made for us by our government.

How much of our limited income are we willing to give up for a government service? Should we give money to help foreign countries, or should we spend it on our own schools? Should we spend billions of dollars to send a man on a trip to the moon, or should we spend more for health and welfare? Shall we spend billions of dollars for guns and missiles or more for bread and butter? These are some of the many basic questions which each of us must face as consumers and citizens.

Civil liberties and political freedoms as goals. As American citizens we have personal liberties and freedoms that are enjoyed by very few other people of the world. Although we are grateful for these liberties and freedoms, we may not be keenly sensitive to their full meaning to us, for our lives have never been controlled by a government or by a dictator. We have never been slaves subject to the tyrannical power of an unjustly severe, powerful ruler.

Let us consider the nature of the personal liberties and freedoms that we enjoy. In a sense, we may say that our liberties and freedoms are of two distinct, yet closely related, kinds. One kind is comprised of what we shall refer to as our *civil liberties* and *political freedoms* and the other as our *economic freedoms*. Like the air we breathe and the water we drink, as long as we have our personal liberties and freedoms, we are scarcely conscious of how impossible the life we live would be without them.

What are some of the civil liberties and political freedoms that are so greatly a part of our existence? Because you already have an understanding of them from your study of history and government, let us merely list, without explanation, some of those that mean the most to us.

Many of these liberties and freedoms do not exist at all in countries in which the state (and its rulers) is considered more important than the freedom of the individual. Here in America we think of government as protecting the rights and privileges of people—not as curbing

Civil liberties and political freedoms of citizens in a democracy

1. Right to personal privacy; our home is our castle.
2. Right to voice our opinions, points of view, and beliefs in conversation, in the press, or in public lecture.
3. Right to disagree with another person and tell not only him but also the whole world that we disagree.
4. Right to own property—land, houses, automobiles, clothes, books, hi-fi sets—and to have that right protected.
5. Right to worship as we choose, or not to worship at all, if we so choose.
6. Right to trial by an impartial jury and a fair judge, if accused of a misdemeanor or crime.
7. Right to read, study, and learn whatever we wish as long as it interests us; right to grow and advance.
8. Right, in general, to do as we wish, as long as it does not infringe upon the rights of other persons.
9. Right to participate in government through voting.

them. The Bill of Rights, contained in the first ten amendments to the Constitution, in reality assures people that government will not interfere with but will protect the basic political and civil rights of man.

A distinguishing characteristic of a democracy is the right of citizens to control and govern themselves. In a democracy people elect their officers and delegate to them certain powers. They vote on matters affecting their civic and political lives.

We are said to be free people because we have the privilege of controlling our own destiny both indirectly and directly through our

The right to select one public official and reject or remove another is a basic democratic political right that also affects our economic choices.

ballots for candidates. Government protects our rights. Being free, we are not slaves. Collectively, we make our own decisions. A goal of every American citizen from 1776 to the present has been to preserve and maintain our political and civil freedoms.

Economic freedoms as goals. Just as we have seen that our political and civil freedoms and liberties provide foundational pillars for the lives we want to live, so do economic freedom and liberty provide an equally essential foundation.

Economic freedoms of citizens under a free-enterprise system

1. Right to work and earn an income.
2. Right to make a profit.
3. Right to choose our vocation or profession by which we earn a living and to pursue our ambitions in accordance with our abilities.
4. Right to change one's vocation and right to change jobs.
5. Right to engage in business for ourselves.
6. Right to spend savings and earnings as we choose.
7. Right to offer our products or services at any price we may name; to reject or accept prices on products and services we want to buy.
8. Right to use our properties to increase themselves or to produce income.
9. Right to select and buy what will best satisfy our needs.
10. Right to compete in prices and in quality of product or service.

Imagine what life would be like if our economic freedoms were removed. Think what it would mean if we were assigned to jobs without our preferences being considered, if we were forced to work whether or not we wanted to, if we were not permitted to use the properties we have to earn more money, if businesses were not permitted to make a profit, or if all prices were set. Countries under dictatorial rule do not have these economic freedoms.

As stated earlier, civil liberties and political freedoms are the products of a democracy in which citizens cast ballots; economic freedoms are also the products of a free-enterprise system. Consumers' votes control free enterprise just as much as citizens' ballots control democracy.

ECONOMIC VOTING

People who buy and use economic goods and services have a powerful influence on the nature of the goods and services that are

Every economic choice made is an economic vote.

The Kroger Company

made available and also to some extent on the prices at which they are offered. Actually, every time you make a choice between two articles or two services on the basis of their qualities or the prices asked for them, you have cast an *economic vote*. The economic votes from all the people collectively determine the nature and the prices of the goods and services that will be offered for us to buy.

Every economic choice you make is an economic vote. You are really serving as one of the final judges as to whether or not a commodity shall remain on the market in its present form and at its present price. The manufacturer and the merchant try to determine what customers will buy, but they may guess wrong. Customers not only have the power to determine what goods and services will be offered to them, but also they indicate what prices they are willing to pay.

INCOME, WEALTH, AND PRODUCTION

Income is the total value of the goods and services produced in a given period of time, such as a month or a year. *Wealth* is the total value of the things we own at a given time. The wealth of a person is increased only when he has income left over after all his expenditures have been made. The same is true for a nation.

13

Our wealth consists of things we own.

Income results from the production of economic goods and the performance of economic services for the satisfaction of desires. One may think of income as one's share of new wealth that he has helped to create by using his labor. One may also think of income as the reward for performing economic services, or as amounts received for the use of savings and other tangible property.

The baker, through his labor and by use of his equipment, converts flour and other ingredients into bread. People want bread; therefore, the baker, by satisfying the desire of people for bread, earns income. He has produced an economic good. The barber, through his labor and by use of his equipment, satisfies a desire. He has earned income through his performance of an economic service. Both the baker and the barber may have accumulated savings that they have loaned to others. From lending they receive additional income.

Thus, income arises from manual or professional labor; from the use of savings from which dividends or interest are received; from the use of tangible property for which rent is earned; or from business operations resulting in the production and distribution of goods.

Relation between income and wealth. We should keep in mind that wealth is comprised of tangible goods that have a money value because they are relatively scarce, useful, and people want them; and that income, which usually is measured in money, is one's reward for his share in producing those goods, in rendering services, and in lending funds and the use of tangible property to others.

Now, all of us as individuals want more wealth—we want to own more land, buildings, stocks in corporations, and personal possessions, such as automobiles and good clothes. Income enables us to get these things. Income, we have learned, however, is our share for having produced. Therefore, how do we become more wealthy? By working and by producing. In other words, the more one produces, the greater his income is, and hence the greater his wealth becomes.

A few people think it is evidence of cleverness to turn out as little work as possible for the pay they receive. They really are curtailing production which means that, in accordance with their pay, they are not doing their share in creating new wealth. Our level of living for all people together increases only as new wealth is created. Hence, if everyone did as these few people do, there would be no improvement; and perhaps we would slip backward in living standards. Actually, everyone of us is affected adversely by those people who get pay for more than they contribute.

Some simple truths everyone should know about economics

1. Economics is a study of how we fulfill our wants.
2. We have many wants.
3. Goods and services that fulfill wants are scarce.
4. Some wants are essential; some are nonessential.
5. We must make choices in fulfilling our wants.
6. An economic good is something that has value.
7. Capital goods are those used to produce more goods.
8. Our goals determine how we fulfill our wants.
9. Because of scarcity we have to give up something to satisfy our wants. This is the real cost.
10. In a democracy we have many economic freedoms that are not enjoyed in some nations.
11. Economic voting is choice making, and it determines what is produced.
12. Income produces wealth.

■ QUESTIONS ON THE TEXT

1. What are economic goods and services?
2. Which of our wants are tangible? Which are intangible?
3. Explain the difference between a primary or essential want and a secondary or nonessential want.
4. What is economics?
5. How does scarcity of goods and services create an economic problem?
6. Why must we usually make choices in what we buy?
7. Indicate some of the choices that must be made in satisfying wants for food.
8. How do businessmen attempt to satisfy wants of people?

9. Explain what is meant by capital goods.
10. What is meant by an economic goal?
11. In a democratic society how do people determine their economic goals?
12. What is meant by the real cost in making an economic choice?
13. Name some economic freedoms that we enjoy as part of our goals.
14. What is meant by economic voting?
15. How is income created?
16. What is economic wealth?

▪ QUESTIONS FOR DISCUSSION

1. Explain how one item might be a primary or essential want for one person but a secondary or nonessential want for another.
2. Explain how one item might not be an economic good in some cases because it is free but would be an economic good in a different situation.
3. Because a dealer or a manufacturer of automobiles is not able to sell the cars that have been produced, does this mean that there is no scarcity and no unfulfilled wants?
4. We read about the surplus of agricultural products such as wheat. Is there really a surplus?
5. Explain how our wants sometimes change and increase.
6. Explain how production is the key to satisfying our wants.
7. Try to name something that is not an economic good.
8. Explain how a machine might be either a capital good or a consumer good.
9. Explain the difference in the way a government controls society and a free democratic society determines and directs national goals.
10. Explain in what way some of our civil liberties also are examples of economic freedoms.
11. Explain some of the economic freedoms you think we have which do not exist under communism.
12. Explain how you feel that citizens in the United States determine through economic voting what is produced and the price at which it is sold.

▪ PROBLEMS TO SOLVE

1. Prepare a priority list of 10 secondary or nonessential wants and the approximate dollar cost of these wants that you would like to have satisfied or fulfilled by the time you are graduated from high school. Ask one or both your parents to check your list and indicate those wants which are identical to theirs. What reasons can you give for the differences? If you were able to have fulfilled only one of the wants from your list, which one would you choose? Why did you make this choice?

2. From one of the statistical reference books (*Information Please Almanac, Statesman's Yearbook, World Almanac and Book of Facts*) in your library, collect figures and prepare a chart that compares the United States with the rest of the world as to the amount of economic goods possessed (such as automobiles, telephones, radios, refrigerators, and TV sets). What reasons would you propose for the higher standard of living in the United States as indicated by the amount of economic goods possessed by its people as compared with the rest of the people of the world?

3. Nine personal rights were listed in the chapter as civil liberties and political freedoms. These, in a sense, are principles that protect us as individuals in our relations with others. In school you are with others all the time. Explain and discuss how each of the nine personal rights applies to your life in school. For example, you have space in a desk or cabinet in a typing or science room in which to keep your supplies and equipment; you have a desk or locker for your books and personal belongings; and by placing your name in your books and notebooks, you claim them as your own.

▪ COMMUNITY PROBLEMS AND PROJECTS

1. Prepare a paper in which you stress the nation's problem in the scarcity of natural resources over a half century ago and the role Theodore Roosevelt and Gifford Pinchot played in leading America into a program of conservation of natural resources.

2. Scarcity of raw materials and natural resources is still very much a problem facing Americans in the second half of the twentieth century. This is a problem being attacked not only by our federal government but also by our state and local governments.

   Prepare a paper that points out and describes conservation measures (projects) which have been started recently in your state (or, say, within a radius of 100 miles of your home) and what such projects are designed to conserve or preserve, what effects such projects will have on your life in the state or area, and what causes led to the undertaking of such projects.

3. Prepare a paper in which you compare the civil liberties and political freedoms of the people of any country that you may select which is under communistic rule and the civil liberties and political freedoms of the people of the United States.

   Your school or city librarian and your teacher will acquaint you with references that will give you information about the freedoms and liberties of peoples in other countries.

4. Ten economic freedoms of citizens were given in the chapter. These are the principles that protect our rights to earn and to acquire and use property. You have certain plans or hopes as to the work you would like to do in the future. You may hope to work in a factory or store, operate a service business, give a professional service, or engage in some other activity by which you will earn a living. Progress in the community is dependent upon the ability of individuals to carry out their personal plans.

Prepare a paper on the value and importance of these economic freedoms to you and to the community in carrying out your plans.

Chapter 2

The American free-enterprise system

PURPOSE OF THE CHAPTER

The American enterprise system is not completely a free-enterprise system since government to some extent regulates it. In this chapter you will learn about the essential characteristics of this system through which our wants and needs are satisfied.

You will find answers to these questions:

1. What are the essentials of free enterprise?
2. How is free enterprise related to democracy?
3. What is the free-market system?
4. How does government interfere?

A. The nature of the free-enterprise system

ESSENTIAL CHARACTERISTICS OF FREE ENTERPRISE

How does the free-enterprise system give us our economic freedoms and liberties? How does free enterprise operate? What are the essen-

tial characteristics of the free-enterprise system through which our economic freedoms are attained? In answer to these questions, let us now study the essential ingredients of which free enterprise is comprised.

Private property.   The sources of our personal income are wages for the work we do, profits from business transactions, interest for money we have loaned, and rent for the use of buildings or land. After local, state, and federal taxes are paid, our American economic system permits us to spend or to keep as much of our income as we wish. This privilege is based upon the belief that people are entitled to keep the rewards from their labor or their business. The portion of your income that you keep, regardless of whether it is kept in money, invested in bonds, or held in the form of material assets, is known as *private property*. By saving some of their income, people buy land, buildings, and other things. This private property may then be used to earn more income. Thus, we can see that the right to own private property is very important to us.

Let us assume for a moment that the government owned all property. This would mean that the government would have to produce the economic goods needed by us to live. There would be no profit, hence no incentive to improve a product. Government ownership of property and hence of the means of producing economic goods would mean that you would receive goods as the government chose to allocate them to you. You would have little, if any, choice among products. Such a plan of ownership of property would make most of our economic freedoms impossible. The right to own property and to use it in making a profit provides the incentive to establish and operate business enterprises.

One of the essential characteristics of free enterprise is that substantially all property is privately owned, especially property that is

Individual ownership of a home and other private property is an essential characteristic of the free-enterprise system.

Ewing Galloway

used in the production of goods and services. Examples of *public property* are public buildings, schools, and other facilities that can be provided by local, state, or federal governments but that would be impractical, if not impossible, to provide through private ownership.

Free markets. The 195 million people in America want, need, and demand many economic products and services. These products and services are provided for consumers through business. But, how does business know what products and services consumers want? How does business know how much of each product or service to provide? How can the demands of 195 million people for goods and services be satisfied at prices they are able and willing to pay?

These economic questions are answered in the United States through a *free-market system,* which is really a system of freedom of choice. Under a free-market system, no person or bureau or government agency makes arbitrary decisions to answer the questions for the country as a whole as to what consumer needs shall be satisfied or the way in which those needs shall be satisfied. Rather, the decisions made by individual consumers, workers, and owner-managers collectively provide the answers to such questions as what needs for goods and services shall be satisfied, who shall produce specific products, and who shall be employed in certain businesses. One might say that free markets are *self-regulated* and *self-controlled.* This means that the decisions as to the basic economic questions regarding the satisfaction of consumers' economic needs are outgrowths of the operation of the free-market system. The main regulating or controlling factors are profits and competition, which are discussed later in this chapter.

Free markets mean that consumers have freedom of choice and that their choices determine what shall be made, how much of each product is needed, and the price that will be paid for it. To producers and manufacturers, free markets mean that they are free to engage in any lawful business from which they believe they can make a profit. Free markets mean to the individual that he may live where he wishes to live, work at what he prefers to work, ask whatever wage or salary he wishes, and select (buy) whatever goods and services he wishes.

Under a free-market system, everyone—the businessman who wishes to engage in business, the worker, and the consumer—has freedom of choice. Under communism, fascism, and socialism, however, the decisions as to how peoples' economic needs shall be satisfied are controlled by government. Under a free-enterprise system, these decisions are made by the consumers themselves. The heart of free enterprise is free markets. Every decision you make to buy or not to buy a particular article or the decision whether to keep your savings or use them to buy an automobile is a choice in the free-market system. In fact, you and every other consumer cast many economic votes in the free-market system every day.

Profit motivation. Although most people get enjoyment and satisfaction from their occupation or profession, very few work just because they like to work. Certainly, very few people would maintain a rigorous work schedule day by day if there were not some incentive or some driving force that makes them want to work. Slaves work because of fear of physical punishment or fear of starvation if they do not work. Free men, however, have incentives to work. They get satisfaction from accomplishment; they have a desire to help mankind by making a product or giving a service that men need; and last, but certainly not least, they work in order to earn an income. The income enables them to maintain their level of living, and the part that is left over may be invested in private property which, in turn, may be used to produce a profit.

Free men work for an income to attain the standard of living they desire.

We learned earlier in the chapter that to own private property is a right and privilege under democracy and free enterprise. The right to use private property in a manner that will result in a profit is an equally important right and privilege. We obtain private property either by gift from someone else or by saving a part of our income. The part of our income that we save may be deposited in a bank or invested in real estate or other property from which we hope to receive an income. But, there is another way we can invest our savings in which the risk of losing our investment is greater than in those ways just mentioned, but also in which the chances of a greater return are

---

Even socialists turn to the profit system

There is ample evidence that the ideals of socialism or communism as they relate to centralized government planning are not so successful as the profit system that is guided by consumer demand. Here is a portion of a 1964 news report from Russia:

MOSCOW—The new Soviet regime acknowledged Sunday that a modified free-enterprise system is the best way to produce consumer goods, thus endorsing reforms by Nikita Khrushchev.

A front-page editorial in Pravda, organ of the Soviet Communist party, called for less central planning in light industries. It urged consumer industries to plan their own production on a profit basis.

The Pravda editorial said, "It is time to give more independence to the (consumer) enterprises so that they will be economically interested in producing high-quality goods popular among the customers."

---

possible. This opportunity is to invest our savings in a business enterprise which we plan to operate ourselves. It may be a privately owned and operated business like an appliance repair shop, a lunch counter, a poultry farm, or any other business that provides consumers with some goods or services that they want and need. The income from such a business must first be applied to the costs of the business; the portion left over is profit.

One's judgment would be considered very unsound if he invested his savings in a business if there were no chance to make a profit. Furthermore, one's business could not continue to operate long if the income were only great enough to meet costs. Corporations like General Motors, Standard Oil Company of New Jersey, Ford Motor Company, and United States Steel are no different in this respect than are business enterprises owned and operated by a single individual. They, too, must make a profit in order to remain in operation.

The more efficient a business is, the greater its profits will be. Likewise, a business increases its own chances for greater profits by giving consumers better products, lower prices, and better services than they receive from competing business firms. Consumers are always looking for better products and services and for lower prices. Only businesses that give consumers products and services that rate favorably with the products and services of other business firms can stay in business. Thus, the business owner, in his efforts to make a greater profit by making his business more efficient and by serving consumers better, indirectly benefits consumers.

What entitles an owner to profit?

1. Risk of losing the money he invests.
2. Ideas he originates that are used by the business in producing products and services that will be useful to consumers.
3. Ability, skill, and experience that enable him to manage and operate the business.
4. Time and work expended in managing and operating the business.*
5. Use of the money invested.

*To manage and operate the business, some firms employ men whose salaries are paid before profits are computed.

Almost half of the profits of business corporations are retained within the business to be used to pay expenses in years when business is not good, to build new buildings, and to buy machines, equipment, and materials. Thus, profits are used to expand, thereby creating more jobs for more people.

Few, if any, businesses would be started if it were not for the chance of making a profit. Businesses are spurred on in their efforts to develop new products and to improve present products by the chance of making greater profit. Many of the new ideas and improvements in goods that consumers want and use have been stimulated by business owners who believed that such new ideas and improvements would result in greater profit for their firms. In fact, the businesses that provide the many products and services consumers use would not exist were it not for the profit motive. If these businesses did not exist, not only would consumer goods and services not be produced but also jobs created by those businesses would not exist.

Profit creates jobs

No Profits = No Capital

No Capital = No Tools   Therefore   No Profits = No Jobs

No Tools = No Jobs

Competition. Since the motive of business is to make as large a profit as possible, what prevents a business firm from demanding excessively high prices for its products and services? Why cannot business set its prices as high as it wishes?

A business would have practically no limits on how high prices might be set if it were the only business firm that could supply consumers with a particular product. But, when two or more business firms offer the same or similar products or services, they attempt to attract consumers by offering their products and services at prices that either are lower or that compare favorably with those of other business firms serving the same consumers. These business firms are said to be competitors. *Competition* is the effort of two or more business firms or individuals acting independently to attract a customer. A business firm may compete with its rivals in several ways. It may lower prices or give more favorable terms; it may improve its product or create a new one that will better satisfy consumer needs; or it may vary its product so that it has features that competing products do not have, thus making it more attractive to consumers.

Competition exists when there are many buyers and many producers or sellers of each product and when no single producer or seller can control the market price. In a sense, the price of a product or service is not controlled by competition, but rather each producer or seller is controlled or limited by the market price. Thus, by controlling or limiting the prices that business firms may demand for their products or services, competition in effect controls or limits the profits that business firms make. Competition among business firms ordinarily results in benefits to consumers through lower prices, better services, improved products, and new products that better satisfy needs.

Competition encourages business firms to conduct research to improve the products offered to consumers.

The Kroger Company

The right to compete is one of our economic freedoms. Everyone is free to enter any trade or business and to compete with anyone else. This freedom gives every person in America a chance to use his talents, to try out his ideas, and to prove what he can do. In practice, this means that a worker seeking the best opportunity also is free to change from job to job. Thus, in a sense, business firms compete for workers' services.

In order to assure unrestricted but fair competition, several federal laws have been passed to prevent business firms from agreeing upon prices to be charged for a product, and thus eliminate the effect of competition. In the field of public utilities, such as water, electricity, and transportation, competition does not operate in the same manner as in other types of enterprise. Public utilities usually have exclusive rights to provide service to a community; hence, they are said to be a *monopoly* since there are no competing firms. But, in order to assure reasonable prices, utility rates are controlled by public commissions.

Essential characteristics of a free-enterprise system

1. Property is privately owned, with the exception of certain facilities, such as schools and public buildings.
2. A free-market system operates, assuring practically unrestricted opportunity for individuals and business firms.
3. The right to profit provides the incentive to enter and operate business.
4. Competition acts as an automatic control on the quality and kind of product or service and the price of goods and services offered by a business firm.

B. The free-market system

PRODUCTION AND DISTRIBUTION IN THE FREE-MARKET SYSTEM

We have learned that the goods and the services available to us are limited (scarce) and are determined by the ability of all of us to produce. In any nation—communist or free—decisions must be made as to:

(1) What shall be produced?
(2) How much shall be produced?
(3) How shall it be produced?
(4) Who shall get the shares of goods and services and how much?

In a free society, such as ours, how are these decisions made? Before we answer this question, let us examine the nature of our society. Actually, our society is not completely a free-enterprise system, nor is it completely government directed. In our society we believe in the right of private ownership or property. People are not only free to choose what they want, but the owners of property also are free to decide what to produce, how much to produce, how to produce it, and for whom to produce it.

In a communist or socialist nation or society the resources are owned by the total society or the group, not by individuals. The individual does not determine how the property is to be used, even his own labor. Decisions are made by the group, but actually in a communist or socialist society the leaders make the decisions for everyone in regard to the four questions previously mentioned.

What to produce. In our society, the owner of property, including a factory, a farm, or materials, is free to produce what he wants for himself, or to produce what others want and are willing to buy or trade for. Few of us could produce all the goods and services we need; therefore, we use our resources to produce for others those items that will make it possible to obtain the most that we want—in other words, each of us produces those items that are most profitable to us.

In the illustration on page 28, the individual who has the economic vote (free choice) (1) directs business by his demand (purchases) as to what to produce. The individual furnishes (2) labor, land, money, and other resources with which the firm produces (through management) the goods and services needed to satisfy the demand of consumers. These goods and services are (3) delivered in quantities needed to consumers who pay for them and furnish the income for the firm. (4) The various individuals are paid for their contributions in proportion to their competitive values. Unless the management of the business can combine resources successfully enough to make a profit, the firm must go out of business or make some other goods or services that will produce a profit. Profit is necessary to make it possible to divide the shares of production with all those who contributed (wages for labor and management, rent for land and machines, interest on borrowed money, profits to those who took the risk by investing their money).

Firms have resources that they use to produce goods. Consumers also have resources that they lend to or invest in firms to produce goods. Firms hire workers to whom they pay wages. These workers

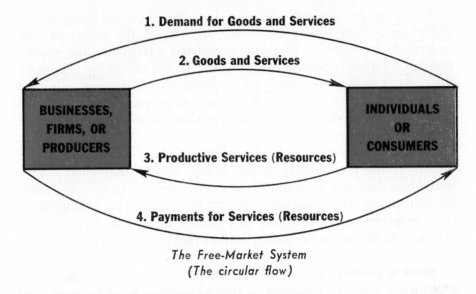

1. Demand for Goods and Services

2. Goods and Services

| BUSINESSES, FIRMS, OR PRODUCERS | | INDIVIDUALS OR CONSUMERS |

3. Productive Services (Resources)

4. Payments for Services (Resources)

The Free-Market System
(The circular flow)

Explanation of chart

1. *What to Produce.* The demand for or purchases of goods and services (representing income to producers).
2. *How Much to Produce.* The delivery of goods and services produced for and purchased by consumers at the prices offered.
3. *How to Produce.* The furnishing of and use of resources (goods and services) in a production process to satisfy wants.
4. *How Production Is Shared.* Payments for use of resources in the form of wages, rent, interest, profits.

---

are the consumers who buy the goods. In almost every case the consumer is also a producer and the producer is a consumer.

Every producer is producing something for a consumer, even the producer of guns. He is making guns for someone to use. The producer of equipment is making the equipment for another kind of producer who will use the equipment to produce something for another kind of consumer.

How much to produce. The amount of goods and services produced is determined by how much consumers are willing to buy at the price that is offered. If people do not like the good or the service, or the price is too high, the producer quits making it. If the producer makes a good product that everyone likes and it can be sold at a profit, he will probably expand his business and make more goods. If a competitor offers a new product that is cheaper or that consumers like better, the first producer will have difficulty selling his good or service.

In a free-market economy, the consumer is "king." He decides what will be produced and how much he will buy. Of course businessmen try to influence the demand of consumers through advertising and other selling activities, but the final decision is made by the consumer. He decides whether he will buy or will not buy and in what quantities and at what price. Because of the competitive nature of business, if the consumer cannot obtain what he wants from one producer, there is always another producer from which he can buy.

How to produce. The profit motive is the incentive for the owner or manager of a business to satisfy the wants of consumers in the most efficient manner. He should always keep in mind that he must compete with other producers. In our free society, the owner of property (resources) is free to determine how he can most efficiently use resources available to him. This function is part of management. It is a great responsibility, and for that reason managers are paid good wages if they are successful.

The producer may use some of his own property, hire labor, borrow money, buy materials, rent or buy land, and buy or lease equipment to produce in the most efficient manner. In this process of production, the producer pays out income to workers, landowners, and suppliers of other materials and services. These incomes that are paid out become a part of the circular flow of money that makes it possible for consumers to buy goods.

All the factors that enter into production must be put together by the manager in a pattern that will enable the producer to make the best product possible at the lowest possible price and still make the highest profit possible for the producer. His choice of materials may determine cost and quality. He must decide how to use labor and machines to reduce cost, speed production, and improve quality. He must also satisfy the customer as to design, color, and other characteristics because he must compete with other producers.

How production is shared. In a free society, there are different values placed upon goods and services. These are values, determined competitively, by the people who buy the goods and services. There are many types of people with many types of abilities, and there are many goods and services involved in producing goods and services.

How much we share in production is determined by the relative scarcity of what we have to offer and the productivity of our resources.

The well-educated and well-trained worker earns more than a worker with no skill. The efficient worker produces more goods than the inefficient worker and is paid higher wages because he is more productive. Highly skilled managers receive more compensation than those with less ability. Goods and services of high quality sell for higher prices than those of low quality. In other words, in a competitive free society, we are paid for our resources, whether labor or materials, according to how they satisfy wants.

How government influences the free-market system

(a few examples)

1. What to produce.

> Collects taxes to produce guns and missiles.
> Places special taxes on luxuries.
> Pays farmers more than market price.
> Pays a subsidy (part of cost) to build ships.
> Sets a high price for uranium ore.
> Makes production of narcotics illegal except as controlled.

2. How much to produce.

> Pays farmers not to use land.
> Pays subsidy to airlines.
> Regulates rates and competition of public utilities and public transportation.
> Gives special tax inducements to business for expansion.
> Controls interest rates.
> Lowers taxes to increase spending.

3. How to produce.

> Regulates rates and competition of public utilities and public transportation.
> Controls working conditions of women and children.
> Regulates use of resources, such as oil, gas, and water.
> Controls public education.

4. How production is shared.

> Legislates hours of work, overtime, minimum wages.
> Taxes profits and income.
> Controls employment practices.
> Controls monopolies, such as public utilities and transportation.
> Regulates use of certain resources, such as land, oil, gas, and water.
> Operates businesses in competition with private businesses.

The results of production are distributed according to the value of the contributions made to production and the scarcity of each. For example, wages may be high for a skilled worker or low for an unskilled worker; interest may be high on borrowed money if money is scarce or if the risk is high; salaries of managers may be high if they are successful but low if the profits are low; rent on land and buildings may be high if they are scarce but low if not scarce; a good building will demand higher rent than a poor building; a building in a good location will command higher rent than in a poor location; the investors and owners may earn high profits if their ideas and products are good and production is efficient but low profits or no profits if their ideas and efficiency are not good.

Distribution will be discussed further in Chapter 9.

The government influences the free-market system. In our previous discussions of scarcity, the free-market system, competition, and productivity as factors that determine what each one receives from his productive efforts, we have been talking in terms of a completely free enterprise system.

If we had a completely free enterprise system, without any interference by government, the income from production would be distributed in proportion to the productivity or the value of the contribution to production. In other words, the greater contribution one makes to the production of goods and services, the larger will be his income. But we do not have a completely free enterprise society.

There are those who believe that everyone in our society, regardless of his ability to produce goods and services, should have a fair or reasonable standard of living. Since we live in a democracy, if the majority of people believe that this should be our goal, the government will often interfere to distribute more evenly the shares in our production. Examples of the ways in which this purpose is accomplished by our government are: (1) To place high rates of taxation on those with high incomes and low rates on those with low incomes. (2) To establish minimum wage rates. (3) To tax everyone in order to support those who produce such goods as cotton and wheat. (4) To tax everyone in order to provide an education for those who otherwise might not be able to afford it.

Under this system of government interference, we still have a marketing system through which demand and supply are operating, but government interferes with this marketing system in some respects. For example, in the case of minimum wages, if a person who is covered by minimum wages is able to obtain a job, he will earn at least a minimum wage; but if the employer cannot hire this person at a minimum wage and make a profit, the person will not obtain a job with that employer.

Let us take another example—the government support of prices of farm products such as wheat. If producers of wheat had to depend upon the free market, they would quit producing wheat and would use land for some other purposes. Since the farmer is guaranteed a certain price for wheat, which is above the normal market price, he continues to produce wheat even though there is no scarcity and it is not needed.

Right or wrong, these are some of the examples of the interference of government in the free market system.

Facts everyone should know about how free enterprise affects consumers

Characteristic	Effect on consumer
Private property	Savings (part of income not spent) may be invested in property, which in turn produces an income; thus, private property increases ability of consumers to maintain a high level of living.
Free markets	Balance between supply and demand of goods and services wanted by consumers at prices consumers can pay is maintained through consumers exercising their economic freedoms in the form of "economic voting." Markets are sensitive to consumers' economic votes. All goods and services consumers want and demand are the products of free enterprise.
Profit motivation	Without the possibility of making profit, businesses that produce the products and services that consumers want and need would not be started; hence, the products and services would not be available, and the jobs in business on which consumers are employed would not exist. Businesses, spurred by the hope of greater profit, improve present products and services and develop new ones, which indirectly benefit consumers.
Competition	Producers and sellers are automatically limited by competition in the prices they demand from consumers. Thus, unrestricted but fair competition among producers and sellers results in reasonable prices and better products and services for consumers.

▪ QUESTIONS ON THE TEXT

1. What is meant by private property?
2. What is public property?
3. What is the essential characteristic of the free-market system?
4. How do consumers influence what is done under the free-market system?
5. What kind of incentive is offered under the free-market system?
6. What determines how much profit a business can make?
7. What are some of the justifications for profits?
8. What do profits create?
9. What prevents one business from charging prices that are too high?
10. Under a free-market system what determines what each of us produces?
11. Under a free-market system what determines how much is produced?
12. Under a free-market system what factors must be considered in determining how to produce?
13. Under a free-market system what are the factors that determine how the results of production are shared?
14. Give some examples of how government influences or interferes with the free-market system.

▪ QUESTIONS FOR DISCUSSION

1. Why is the use of private property discouraged or prohibited in a state-controlled society such as socialism or communism?
2. If you lived under a government that owned all property, what are some of the freedoms that you would lose?
3. Explain how you think your local store determines what to sell and at what price.
4. How does profit determine whether a product will or will not be produced?
5. How does the free-market system help the consumer?
6. Give some reasons why profit is necessary to encourage someone to take a risk.
7. What do we mean when we say profit is necessary to create new jobs?
8. What would happen to the consumer if there were no competition?
9. It is sometimes said that the consumer is king. What is meant by this statement?
10. What is the function of the factory manager in determining how goods and services are produced?

▪ PROBLEMS TO SOLVE

1. You made several decisions today that express your preference, such as your choice of a cold drink or a candy bar, or you may have decided to save some of last week's income for future use. These are economic

votes. Make a list of the choices and decisions which you have made in the past week that are really economic votes. How seriously would you be affected if there had been no alternatives between which to choose, or if someone else had made the decision for you?

2. Prepare a chart or poster depicting the aids and services government provides producers of economic goods and services.

3. Prepare a written report showing the historical record of governmental action to aid business by expanding markets or by preserving free competition. Point out any instances where such action did not prove to be an aid to business.

▪ COMMUNITY PROBLEMS AND PROJECTS

1. In this chapter we have learned that there are four essential characteristics of the free-enterprise system. It is sometimes said that people generally do not know enough about our economic system and how it operates.

Let us find out what people know and believe about the free-enterprise system. Inquire what the essential features and characteristics of the free-enterprise system are from five students who are not taking this course, five teachers in your school, five neighbors in the community who work in stores or factories, and five persons who own or manage a business enterprise.

Prepare a report in outline form, omitting the names of the persons you interviewed, in which you give the composite ideas that each of the four groups has about free enterprise.

2. In this chapter you have seen examples of how the federal government interferes in the free-market system. There are equally as many examples of local (community, village, city) government influence. Identify as many instances as possible where the local government in your city interferes in the free-market system and the reasons given for such interference. Could you classify any of the examples as being unfair in the free-enterprise system?

3. Investigate your local light and power company, the water and gas company, a local insurance company, city transportation company, telephone company, and a small loan company to find out how prices for rates and fees are determined and who determines the rates. What conclusions can you draw from your investigation?

Chapter 3

Our production system

PURPOSE OF THE CHAPTER

Many factors contribute to the production of goods and services to satisfy the wants and needs of people. The effective use of these resources is largely through business and agriculture.

You will find answers to these questions:

1. What are the factors of production?
2. How do we choose the way to use resources?
3. What functions are performed by business?
4. What are the special problems of farm production?

A. The elements and functions of production

Factors of production. In thinking about economics, we have in the past considered the factors (resources) that contribute to production to consist of (1) labor, (2) land (natural resources), (3) capi-

tal, and (4) the entrepreneur. *Labor* means all forms of physical and mental effort. *Land* in its broad economic sense means land, minerals, water, oil, and all other *natural resources*. *Capital* means machines and buildings. The *entrepreneur* is the person who furnishes the idea and takes the risk of investing and borrowing money to put all factors to work so that a profit can be made.

In modern practice one person may start a business and become an entrepreneur, but in a large corporation there are many investors who own the business and share the risk but take little or no part in the affairs of the business. They hire a manager to run the business for them. The manager becomes the agent of the investors and may also be one of the owners. Now we generally think of the manager as one who takes the place of or represents the entrepreneur, so the investor (owner), manager, or entrepreneur may mean one and the same thing.

Since the manager, either a hired manager or a sole owner, of the business performs mental and physical work, his services are a special form of labor. So the manager or entrepreneur may serve more than one economic function.

Some economists also consider government to be a factor in production because of the services it performs and the taxes it collects as its share of production.

All these factors of production are also called *resources*.

We can broaden our ideas about the factors or resources that contribute to production by saying that they consist of (1) labor, (2) land (natural resources), (3) capital, (4) management (entrepreneur), and (5) government.

Labor. *Labor* is manpower in its broadest sense, including physical effort, mental effort, and use of technical skills. Labor in the United States is performed by free men who choose whether or not they want to work, where they want to work, and in what kind of business activity they want to work. They also decide how long they will work and for what wages they will work. One of the essential characteristics of democracy and our free-enterprise system is man's freedom to plan his own work career.

Land or natural resources. *Natural resources* are materials supplied by nature. Man had nothing to do with their production or existence, although he may have had to work to extract them from the earth or to put them in a form that he can use. Tangible economic goods, such

Modern plants are essential to successful competition. Much of a company's retained profits is used for new plants and equipment.

as foods, fabrics, machines, and houses, all had their origin in the earth; hence they come from natural resources. Fabrics, for example, may be made either from natural fibers, such as wool or cotton, or from man-made fibers, such as dacron or rayon. But, regardless of the kind of fiber, the materials from which the fibers originated were natural resources. Most of our wants and needs for economic goods could not be satisfied without natural resources. They comprise the basic element for the production of tangible goods. One of our greatest economic problems is the conservation and wise use of natural resources.

Capital. In an economic sense, *capital* refers to any buildings, equipment, or other physical property other than raw materials used in a business. Goods used for productive purposes in a business are known as *capital goods.* One of the most important among capital goods is machinery. Machinery and other forms of equipment have not only contributed greatly to the prosperity of the United States by increasing our productivity but also have made man's work more pleasant and less burdensome. According to a *Twentieth Century Fund* report, man supplies less than 6 percent of the energy, that is the power, used to produce all our economic goods, 94 percent being supplied by energy or power applied to machines. In other words, tools and machines make it possible to produce about sixteen times as much goods as could be produced without them.

Management. *Management* of business involves the development of ideas for the production of goods and services that man wants, planning and operating the business, establishing policies, and making decisions. Management is the key to a successful business operation. Even if we had the most modern buildings and equipment and the most intelligent and industrious labor, there could not be a successful business without good organization and management. In a sense,

37

management supplies business with human judgment without which no business would ever be started or operated.

The same principles of management apply in a one-man business and in a large business, but management becomes more complicated in a large business. In all businesses plans must be made, workers hired in some instances, raw materials obtained, and equipment purchased or built. Putting all these factors together in the operation of a business is the function of management.

Government. Under very simple and uncomplicated economic conditions, the main factors of production are probably limited to natural resources, labor, capital, and management. But where the number of business firms is very large, where competition is great, and where the economic structure is very complex, such as in the United States, a fifth factor of production is present. This factor is *government.* Business is dependent upon government for protection from unfair competition, development of standards, statistical information of aid to management, and establishment of favorable conditions for foreign trade. On the other hand, business is regulated and in some respects controlled by government. Government regulations pertain to markets and prices; labor, hours, wages, and employee-employer rights; financing; and similar aspects of business operations.

Performing economic services. Another type of producer is one who performs services that satisfy human wants directly, but has no connection with the creation of goods. These people are, therefore, producing economic services. An opera singer is a producer because he satisfies a human want directly. Teachers, lawyers, physicians, and actors are also producers because they satisfy human wants directly. A stenographer who works for a doctor is performing an economic service that indirectly satisfies a human want.

Choices in the use of resources. If the resources that we have as individuals and as a nation are used to satisfy one want, they cannot be used for another. The giving up of a choice of the use of resources for filling one want is the cost of filling the want for which the resource is used. For example, if a factory uses labor and machines to make guns, it cannot use the same labor and machines to make refrigerators. If a nation uses its resources for an army and the manufacture of guns, it cannot use the same resources for education or for producing goods and services for consumers to use.

The same principle applies to the individual. Very few people have enough income to satisfy all their wants. If a family buys a new refrigerator, it may not be able to buy clothes.

When, as a nation or as a society, we fail to use all our productive resources such as men and machines, we create a scarcity for everyone. Failure to use men and machines available reduces the total goods and services that could have been produced.

Changes in the use of resources. A good example of the problem of using resources is what happens to a community that depends upon an industry created by needs that suddenly change. Take the case of the production of aircraft. The government taxed people and used tax funds to create a great aircraft manufacturing plant employing many people. Suddenly the government decided that it did not need enough new airplanes to keep the plant running. All the resources of production in this case are available, but there is no demand for the product. It is not easy to change quickly the use of all the resources to the production of other goods. There will be idle resources until new ways can be found to use (allocate) them for other production for which a demand can be found. Workers may have to move, and new equipment (capital) will have to be provided before new jobs can be created and new goods produced.

Government decisions in the use of resources. Sometimes we create a surplus of one commodity because of failure to use resources properly. Because of the government's support of wheat prices, a surplus of wheat was created. Taxpayers provided the funds to buy the surplus wheat. Both the taxpayers and the government could have used this money for other purposes. Land that is used for wheat cannot be used for other purposes at the same time. If the land, labor, and other resources used in growing wheat were used for producing other goods and services, we could satisfy other unfulfilled wants.

Demand determines production. Human wants and needs are not the same as demand or consumer demand. You may want something or need something, but in the marketplace there is no *effective demand* unless you are both willing and able (have the money) to buy. When wants become demand, we have *consumption*. The consumer buys and uses or consumes.

There will be no production without demand. The demand is determined by the consumer. As we shall see later, business may stimulate demand by creating a product or a service and convincing the consumer he should buy it.

Production must create value or utility. Production involves creating value, which we call *utility—form utility* by changing the form, *time utility* by making it available when needed, *place utility* by making it available where needed, and *possession utility* by placing it under the control of the person who wants it.

Needs, wants, demand, consumption. Needs and wants may not be the same. One may apparently need a new suit, but he may not really want or desire it because he is happy and satisfied with the old one, so there is no want in terms of economics. When he wants a suit and has the money to buy it, there is no demand for it in terms of economics unless he actually buys a suit. He may make a choice and either keep the money or spend it for something else. He may want a suit very badly but not have the money to buy it; therefore, there is no demand. But he may borrow the money or buy the suit on credit. Then, the want becomes a demand. In this case borrowing (one form of credit) or buying on credit increases demand.

The actions by which needs and wants become demand are called consumption (use). Demand that results in consumption occurs when a person with a want is willing and able to buy and does buy what he wants.

Consumption of goods and services is the ultimate goal of all production. Consumption means buying and using or consuming. In our economic system the consumer is king because he is the one who determines what he will buy. Unless he does buy, there is no need for or demand for production. Of course, consumers are influenced by producers in their buying, but still the consumer must make his choice and actually buy before there can be any consumption.

B. Business in the production process

FUNCTIONS OF BUSINESS

Many consumer wants can be fulfilled by materials that may be seen, weighed, or measured. Some wants can be satisfied only by the labor or the skill or the knowledge of other people. Fulfilling wants for material things often involves several steps, such as obtaining the raw materials of which a product is made, processing or changing the form of the materials, and assembling or putting together the various materials or parts into a form that will serve the needs of the consumer. The wants of consumers for service usually are satisfied primarily by the expenditure of human effort of some kind.

Business makes materials useful. Essentially what business does is to change, process, modify, or organize things that already exist, thus converting them in such a manner that they will be useful to consumers. Business makes materials useful to consumers by collecting raw materials, changing their form through manufacturing and other processes, moving or transporting them where the consumer wants them, and by having them available when the consumer wants to use them.

Let us use the making and selling of a wristwatch as an illustration of what business does to satisfy our wants. Metals, minerals, and precious stones of various kinds are used in making a watch. A mining company extracts these materials from the earth, and manufacturers, through various processes, change the form of the materials many times until ultimately a wristwatch is produced. The raw materials have little usefulness to a consumer in satisfying his wants for a wristwatch until they have been through the many processes that change their form. But a wristwatch, which the consumer does not know exists, in the stock room of a watch manufacturer in Illinois or in Switzerland or in France will not satisfy his want for a watch. It has to be transported to a place such as a jewelry store in his hometown so he can see and examine it. Another factor in satisfying the con-

Molten steel flows from one of the open-hearth furnaces of U. S. Steel Corporation. A function of business is to change raw materials into useful form.

U.S. Steel Corporation

sumer's want for a new watch is having it available at the time he wants it. Thus, business serves by making materials available in a form useful to consumers, at a place the consumer can use the product, and at the time the product is needed.

Business performs complex tasks for consumers. Satisfying the economic wants of people is a complex process. Some products go through many hands. For example, the milk you use on your cereal is the product of many steps. First, a farmer raised a calf and fed and cared for it until it became a cow; the cow is then milked at least twice a day. The milk is cooled and sent by truck to a market. When the milk reaches a dairy processing plant, it is pasteurized and bottled. Then a deliveryman takes it either directly to your home or to a retail grocery store where you purchase it, and finally it is placed on the table for your use. These steps are complex, and no one of us as a consumer would perform all of them. All of these steps were taken by business, however, to satisfy your need for food. The activities involved in satisfying your wants are business activities. Other economic necessities, such as shelter and clothing, are provided in a similar manner.

Business raises the level of living. Imagine how different our lives would be if there were no business organizations to prepare goods or provide services for the satisfaction of our economic wants. We would have to do everything ourselves as primitive man did. Our level of living, which now is the best man has ever had, would be at the low end of the scale. Business makes our high level of living possible by making goods and services available to us in useful form to meet our needs and to satisfy our wants.

Business develops new products. In their continuous attempt to satisfy consumer needs in better and more satisfactory ways, business organizations improve many currently existing products and develop new ones. Inventions and improvements in production methods are constantly stimulated by the desire of business to serve consumers in a more satisfactory manner. Great sums of money are spent annually by business organizations on research directed toward the discovery or invention of new and better products.

Almost everything we use has been either invented or improved through the efforts of business. It would be difficult to imagine how different life would be if all the economic goods and services that have been originated or improved by business were to be removed. We are much more dependent upon business than most of us realize.

Through research, business firms improve old products and develop new ones for consumer use.

Ford Motor Company

Business creates jobs. If each person provided his own shelter, tools, and appliances; made his own clothes; produced and prepared his own food; gave himself his own haircuts; and provided all other services he uses; there would, of course, be no business. Hence, there would be no jobs. Probably a person would be busy most of the time struggling for food, clothing, and shelter much as early man did, and his level of living would likewise be similar to that of early man.

Most of us today prefer to have a job from which we secure regular earnings and then have the freedom to use the earnings to buy the economic goods and services that will best satisfy our wants and needs. Through the process of producing the economic goods and services that we want and need to maintain our level of living, business creates jobs. The greater business activity is, the more jobs there are available. These jobs give us an opportunity to earn so we can pay for the goods and services we use.

The many different kinds of jobs created by business give an individual the opportunity to choose one that he likes and for which he is best fitted. There would be no choice of occupations if business did not create jobs from which to choose.

Business provides tools and equipment for production. When a stenographer is employed, the personnel manager does not tell her to bring her typewriter and report for work. Rather, the business firm provides the machine. Likewise in manufacturing, the business provides the tools and equipment that are necessary for production. Although the

43

Business provides tools and equipment averaging about $15,000 an employee to enable workers to produce more and thus to earn more wages.

Aluminum Company of America

amount varies from one kind of firm to another, the average investment in plant and equipment for each worker is approximately $15,000.

The greater output that the tools and equipment make possible reduces the cost of production per unit, which should mean lower prices for the consumer. It is estimated that it would cost $40,000 to make by manual methods, that is, without the use of modern presses and other tools used in factories, an automobile that now costs $3,500 to make. This cost would be prohibitive for most buyers. The lower cost per unit of production not only lowers the price of the commodity for consumers but also makes it possible to pay higher wage rates to the workers who produce the item than if their output per day were lower.

Business assists in paying the cost of government. The cost of government and the many services performed for special groups by government is borne through taxes of various kinds. It is estimated that 30 percent of the federal income is secured from corporation income taxes. The owners of single proprietorship and partnership business enterprises also pay federal income taxes. All forms of business organizations pay local and state taxes.

It is clearly apparent that local, state, and federal taxes paid by business firms represent a great portion of the total income of those governmental units. Without the benefit of the taxes paid by business, either government expenditures would have to be curtailed drastically or the taxes paid by individuals greatly increased. In other words, American business supports financially the cost of local, state, and federal government to the extent that it would be impossible to continue government operations even at a greatly reduced level without that support. Although taxes paid by business are reflected in the cost of goods and services purchased by consumers, the business taxes paid annually contribute materially to a reduction in the taxes paid by individuals.

Business provides organized markets. Imagine how difficult it would be for each of us to obtain the food, clothing, and other things we need directly from their producers. Our marketing system performs

Our marketing system brings products and consumers together, thus saving both time and money for producers and consumers.

that transfer service for us and also, through advertising, acquaints us with products and services for sale. Perhaps you think the marketing system costs too much and is wasteful in some instances. It must be remembered, however, that the functions performed are essential. Since the field of marketing is competitive, only the most efficient firms can survive in the long run.

Our marketing system makes it possible for us to buy almost anything we want if we have the money to pay for it. This magic has been brought about by a complicated system that will be discussed in detail in Chapter 4.

SOME CHARACTERISTICS OF OUR PRODUCTION

Let us not overlook the fact that production includes many types of effort, such as farming, financing, transporting, storing, and selling. Efficiency determines how well a producer can compete with other producers and make a profit. Efficiency also determines how well we can increase our production and reduce our costs. By reducing our costs everyone can buy more with the money he earns.

Production efficiency. Efficiency is brought about in many ways. In manufacturing efficiency is gained through management, skill of workers, modern machines, mass production, and specialization.

American industry has increased its efficiency greatly by skilled managers and workers. Modern machines increase the amount and quality of goods that a worker can produce, usually with less effort. Of course, machines cost money, but the worker and the machine together reduce cost.

The principle of mass production. The principle of *mass production* is that greater efficiency in business operation is attained by making one or, at the most, a few products in large quantity rather than by making a smaller quantity of many products. For example, one business organization, employing a thousand people, may produce perhaps 100 fabricated metal products ranging from the chrome trim for automobiles to ironing boards. It divides its productive efforts among the 100 items. Another business organization also may produce fabricated metal products, but it limits its production to metal step-stool ladders for household use, metal kitchen and breakfast furniture, and metal ironing boards. It, too, employs 1,000 people. It produces the three items in large quantities. Both businesses make step-stool ladders, metal kitchen furniture, and metal ironing boards. In which business firm will the cost of production of each of these three items be the lower? The answer, of course, is easy. The business limiting its production to three items, but producing them in large quantities, probably will have a considerably lower unit cost. The firm limiting its production has employed mass-production methods.

Mass-production methods lower production costs per unit. The abundance of power and the use of machines have made mass production possible. Production costs are lowered by the use of power and tools. Science has helped improve manufacturing processes and products. New machinery has been developed. New uses have been found for many raw materials that formerly were not used.

The principle of specialization. One of the operational techniques developed by business is based on the *principle of specialization*. This principle means that greater efficiency results from the assignment of an employee to the performance of a particular task rather than to the performance of all tasks pertaining to an operation. For example, in the making of shoes, a worker could be assigned to the whole job of making a shoe, which would involve performing all the tasks that are required in its production; or he could be assigned to one of the tasks in making a shoe, such as stitching or cementing the sole to the upper. In the latter assignment, the worker's job is said to be specialized.

Specialization is sometimes referred to as *division of labor*. Specialization benefits both the worker and the consumer. When the worker performed every task necessary to make an article, production was low and consequently the costs of production were high. With specialization, however, production is high and workers can be paid greater wages; costs are low and thus consumers can buy more.

Specialization also permits the assignment of workers to the kind of work for which they are best fitted. Usually we enjoy doing the things we can do well. Furthermore, ordinarily the quality of a person's work is better if he is well qualified for his job than if he is not so well fitted to it.

Advantages of specialization. Some of the advantages of specialization are: (a) it increases production, hence the amount of wealth and income; (b) it encourages the development of greater skill; (c) it saves time; (d) it lowers production costs; (e) it makes possible the employment of persons who may otherwise be unemployable; (f) it permits the continuous and economical use of tools and equipment; and (g) it develops a spirit of interdependence.

Disadvantages of specialization. Some of the disadvantages of specialization are serious, but they do not necessarily affect the production of wealth. Among the disadvantages are: (a) workers become greatly dependent upon one another; (b) work may become monotonous and deadening to the worker; (c) a worker may not have as much pride in his workmanship; (d) because he is efficient, a worker may not be given an opportunity to change to another job; whereas in seeking to find the best assignment for an inefficient worker, the inefficient worker may be given an opportunity to try other jobs; and (e) a worker who loses his position may have difficulty finding or adjusting to another job because other jobs may require skills and knowledge he has not acquired.

MACHINES, POWER, AND PRODUCTIVITY

In man's struggle to overcome scarcity by more efficient production, he has gone through various stages as follows:

Stage 1—Man produced with his own hands and power.
Stage 2—Man used tools.

Stage 3—Man used tools and animals which supplied part of the power.

Stage 4—Man used better tools called machines and used the wind and water to supply power.

Stage 5—Man used still better tools and machines with electric power.

Stage 6—Now man uses many machines some of which are automatic (automation) and great amounts of electric power.

We sometimes give most of the credit for production efficiency to well-trained workers, good management, and modern machines, but we often ignore the great importance of electric power that makes the use of machines possible and work easier. If electric power is scarce and costly, production costs will be high. Some nations suffer from a lack of cheap power because they lack water supply resources and fuel resources from which electric power can be made. Now we have atomic power coming into use. At some time in the future it may very well help solve the problem of scarce and costly electric power.

Productivity is the key to prosperity since a nation improves its standard of living through increases in productivity. Future progress depends upon raising the output of each man, and greater production for each man-hour is possible through increased use of machine power. Machines are now the helping hand of man in modern industry. A man with his hands alone can make only a very limited quantity of any product. With the aid of a few tools, however, he can increase his production. With the aid of machinery and power he is often able to multiply his production ten or twenty times or more.

Machines multiply man's productivity many times.

Increased output or production per man per day by using machines and power has two distinctly favorable results:

1. *Workers have more leisure time.* They can produce more per hour, hence the number of hours of work per week can be reduced without curtailing production.
2. *The worker's daily wage tends to be increased.* The increased output makes goods available to more people at lower cost, hence the standard of living is improved.

Many products that we use today could not be produced at any price if it were not for modern machinery and power. Machines are definitely the muscles of business which lighten the burdens of workers and increase their efficiency so that we all have more and better things for lower prices. Business firms provide the machines that enable employees to produce more than they could produce by manual methods.

Effects of new machinery. New machines and new processes invented and discovered, especially during the past thirty years, are great aids to workers, enabling them to produce more per day and often with less effort. This development in industry is referred to as *technology*. With the introduction of automatic machines and processes to factory and office operations, technology has progressed to a new stage known as automation. *Automation* generally is accepted to mean a continuous operation in production, such as the assembly line, through the use of automatic equipment. This equipment automatically performs routine operations, regulates the flow of materials being processed, and controls the quality of production.

As the effects of technology resulted in many changes in routine operations in factories, some workers were fearful of technological unemployment. They felt that machines would be substituted for men or that machines aiding workers would increase the output per man to the extent that the number of workers would be reduced. These fears have been proved largely ungrounded.

Before one jumps to the conclusion that machines create unemployment, one should ask himself some of these questions: Would I want to give up the use of a shovel and use my hands? Would I want to give up the use of a lawn mower? Would I want to give up the use of a vacuum sweeper? Would I want to give up the use of an automobile and walk instead of ride? Would the worker want to give up an electric drill or drilling machine and use manual labor? All of these items are machines, and they are made by machines.

Many workers now look upon automation in the factory as a competitor to labor. Again there is fear of technological unemployment. Undoubtedly there will be temporary dislocation of labor, and readjustment of workers to new jobs will be necessary. In taking a larger view of industry, however, we find that machines are not competitors of man, and automation is not a threat to the security of labor. Rather, machines are man's helpers. They enable him to produce more in a shorter period of time with less physical discomfort and strain. In individual cases a machine may be a competitor of man for a particular job. Automation may affect a particular worker adversely by eliminating his job entirely. In the long run, however, technology and automation will reduce the number of hours a week a man will need to work to earn the same amount he earned before the changes took place.

How we benefit from business. Because the people of America are accustomed to a high level of living, they may in a measure fail to recognize and to appreciate the important role of business in their lives. It becomes easy to take for granted that the benefits coming to us through business are commonplace and are our inherent rights. If we would preserve the American business system and the benefits accruing from it, we, the people, must recognize and appreciate what it means to us. We must also understand what American business is, what its objectives and motives are, and how it benefits all people. The first requisite for the protection of the American business system is for the people to understand it.

How we benefit from business

1. The economic goods and services that we want and need are provided through American business.
2. Business has given us the highest level of living known to man, and it is still improving.
3. Business converts raw materials into products that are useful to us.
4. Through research, business develops and improves goods that make life easier and more pleasant for us.
5. Business makes jobs for us.
6. Through specialization and mass-production methods, business produces goods at a price we can afford to pay.
7. We pay lower prices for goods because business provides tools and equipment that increase output per employee.
8. We have available many public services and benefits such as expressways, bridges, schools, and police protection because business contributes to government through taxes.

C. Special problems of agricultural production

FARM PRODUCTION PROBLEMS

Almost everybody believes that there is a farm or agricultural problem, and almost everybody seems to believe that he has a solution to the farm problem. Actually, there are many farm problems.

Farming is production just as it is in the factory except that different labor, different tools, and other different resources are used for production; but the farmer has some production and marketing problems that are different from those of other producers.

Farm efficiency. Early in the history of the United States most farms were small; at least they were small in comparison with some of the farms today. Farmers worked their land themselves or with workers directly under their supervision with relatively simple tools and machines. As new farm machines were developed, they gradually took the place of human labor and work performed by horses. As larger and better equipment for farms was produced, small farms were combined into large farms so that the equipment could be used efficiently. Many types of expensive farm equipment cannot be used efficiently on a small farm, and a small farmer cannot afford to buy some of this new equipment.

In many parts of the country, the land is so rough that modern equipment cannot be used on it. In other parts of the country, the land is so poor that it is not productive. On land of this type we find many of the small farms. It has been estimated that 50 percent of the owners or operators of these small farms have a very low average

Farms classified by acreage					
Size of farm	Number of Farms				
	1900	1925	1950	1954	1959
	Thousands				
TOTAL	5,737	6,372	5,381	4,782	3,703
Under 10 acres	267	379	485	484	241
10-49 acres	1,664	2,039	1,478	1,213	811
50-99 acres	1,366	1,421	1,048	864	658
100-259 acres	1,912	1,887	1,589	1,417	1,186
260-999 acres	481	583	660	674	671
1,000 acres and over	47	63	121	130	136

Source: *Statistical Abstract of the United States,* 1965.

income of approximately $2,000 a year. So we have rural poverty even with government assistance.

Besides the increased efficiency of farming because of new equipment, there is also greater productivity because of better seeds, better and more generous use of fertilizers, the use of insecticides to kill insects that destroy crops, and better methods of farming. Besides all these factors that have tended to increase production and to make it more efficient, the government has brought into new production thousands of acres of land through irrigation of dry land and draining of wet land.

Supply, demand, and price. A farmer is constantly aggravated with the problems of supply, demand, and prices. The farmer provides products that are used in industry, but most of these products are consumed by individuals as some kind of food. Demand for food does not change much, regardless of the price, because people usually buy food before they buy anything else. Therefore, if the farmers produce more hogs, they cannot increase their sales by increasing the consumption of hogs because consumers cannot and will not eat much more than they have been eating. Even if the farmer reduces his prices, he is not always able to increase his sales to any great extent except in competition with other goods. For example, if beef prices are high when pork prices are low, consumers may eat more pork and less beef.

The farmer has difficulty adjusting his production to demand. There are thousands of farmers and they like to be independent. If there is an oversupply of manufactured products, the manufacturer responds rather quickly and reduces production. It may be done in a day's time, but the farmer is working on a yearly basis. He has to plan ahead and take a chance, and there are thousands of competing farmers who are doing the same thing.

If there is an oversupply of a farm product and the prices are low, the tendency of the farmer, if he has enough land to do so, is to raise more of the same product so that his income will be the same at the low price as it would be at a high price. If all farmers do this, you can easily see what happens. There will be a greater supply and, in a free market, the prices would fall.

Farm prices and prosperity on the farm do not always follow the same patterns as in other forms of production. While people in the city are enjoying prosperity, the farmer may be in a reverse situation. He may have to pay increasing prices for the items he buys and for labor, but he may receive less for his goods in a free market because of overproduction. Because of this cost squeeze he may not be able to make a profit.

The farmer competes with all other farmers producing the same product because farm products are essentially the same. There may be some slight differences in quality, but a farmer has to sell his wheat or his cattle along with all other wheat and cattle at competitive prices. He cannot advertise it and sell it as a special product under a brand name and cause people to buy his product in preference to another as the manufacturer does.

The soil and climate problem. There is another problem which is very serious for many farmers. On some farms in certain climates with certain types of soil, the farmer has a choice of raising any one of several choices of products. The owner of such a farm is very fortunate because he can *diversify*, that is, he can produce several products and not be dependent upon what happens to the price of just one of his products. If he chooses, he may grow just one product at a time; but if he thinks the prices are going to be low, he can shift to another product that he thinks may be more profitable. Other farmers are not so fortunate. They live in parts of the country where the land and the climate will not permit them to use their farms for a variety of products. These are the farmers who have one of the greatest problems if their product is highly competitive.

The differences in climate and soil also make a difference in the cost of production. It is estimated that in cotton-producing areas with poor soil and rough land where modern equipment cannot be used, the cost of producing cotton is more than four times as much as it is in other locations where soil and climate factors are more favorable to production.

Natural hazards. There are problems arising from weather that are called natural hazards. There may be too much rain or not enough rain. There may be floods or droughts. There may be tornadoes and hailstorms that destroy crops. New pests and diseases may also injure or destroy crops. Freezing temperatures may kill crops.

Farm aids and controls. Up to this point we have been talking largely about farm production and its problems in a free competitive market. If we had a free competitive market for farm products, thousands of small farmers would have to leave their farms. In fact, many of them have. Regularly our farm population has decreased, while our city population has increased. Fewer farms are producing more farm products with less labor.

Because of the difficulty of adjusting the supply of farm products to the demand for them, the farm economic problems have become political problems. Numerous attempts have been made since 1930 to solve these problems. The most important of these solutions that have been used or have been proposed, either alone or in combination, are as follows:

(1) A minimum price, called a *parity price*, is established for a farm product. This is also called a support price and is considered to be the price that the farmer must receive in order to make a profit. It is determined by figuring what he has to pay for what he buys and then determining the price at which he can sell to make a profit. Parity or support prices have been used for about 15 different agricultural products.

(2) When parity prices are established, the farmer can obtain a federal loan to finance his crop. If he can sell his crop in the free market for more than the loan, he can do so and pay off the loan and keep the difference. If he cannot sell at a price higher than the support price, the government will take the crop and cancel the loan. These crops must be stored under government supervision.

(3) The federal government sometimes bids on the free market to keep prices at a desired level. The crops that are bought must be stored under government supervision.

(4) Some programs restrict production. Farmers are paid not to plant crops or, in other words, to withdraw land from production or

Examples of market prices and parity or support prices (March, 1965)			
Product	Unit	Market Price	Parity or Support Price
Wheat	bushel	$1.36	$2.53
Rice	100 pounds	5.23	6.52
Peanuts	pound	.116	.143
Potatoes	100 pounds	4.19	2.56
Milk	100 pounds	4.15	5.53
Eggs	dozen	.307	.474
Turkeys	pound	.226	.318
Lemons	box	2.83	2.31

Source: *Statistical Abstract of the United States, 1965.*

to use it for some product that is not involved in the farm supports. This type of program may be voluntary or required by law.

The poorest land is always withdrawn first. The remaining land is farmed more efficiently. Production is increased per acre and the total production is increased through better seeds, more fertilizer, better methods, and better equipment.

It has been interesting for many people to observe that while farmers are being encouraged to take land out of production, our government is building new irrigation dams to bring new land into production. The taxpayer is asked to pay some farmers not to produce and at the same time to help other farmers to produce.

(5) The acreage allotment system is similar to the acreage reduction system. For example, a farmer may be allotted a certain number of acres to be planted in wheat or tobacco. If he plants more than is allowed, he must pay a penalty or he is not entitled to any loan or other price support.

(6) Through marketing agreements with farmers, usually with associations such as farm cooperatives, the government helps to control free market prices by reducing the harvest or controlling the amount or the rate at which the crop is offered on the market. This practice is common in fruits and vegetables.

(7) Part of our farm problem has always had a relation to foreign trade. Foreign trade is both political and economic and depends upon the policies of our government. Much of our wheat and many other farm products sold for export to foreign countries is by government agreement at special prices, which are often below the regular competitive prices in the United States. In other words, people in foreign countries can buy some of our products cheaper than we can buy them here. This situation has been rather disturbing in some instances

Wheat planting and wheat production (Selected years)			
	1941-43	1949-50	1965
Acres planted (in millions)	57.2	77.8	44.7
Bushels produced (in millions)	918.4	1,058.9	1,354

Source: U.S. Department of Agriculture, July, 1965.

when, for example, cotton sold to foreign countries below the price in the United States has been manufactured into goods and shipped back into the United States in competition with goods manufactured in the United States.

(8) Our government has acquired tremendous surpluses of farm products that are stored at great expense. Some of these spoil and some have to be sold for animal food because they have been kept too long and are not good for human food. Our government has attempted to find some way to dispose of these foods, especially perishable foods, because if they were sold on the open market, they would be in competition with new foods being produced. One solution to the problem has been to make them available at no cost or at low cost for use in school lunch programs.

(9) Surplus grains, especially those of poor quality or those that have been stored long, are offered to farmers at a reduced price below normal market price for animal food. This plan is called the feed-grain program. The lower cost of feed grain makes it possible to lower the cost of producing meat and tends to keep the free market price of meat from rising.

(10) Attempts have been made to increase the consumption of farm products, but as already indicated, the demand for farm products is not very elastic. In other words, people will not increase their consumption of farm products very much even though prices may be reduced.

(11) There has been considerable study to create new uses for farm products, and some of this research has been successful. For example, oil from soybeans has found many uses in paints and in other industrial products. It is also used in food products, such as margarine or cooking oils. Corn oil and peanut oil are also used for the same purposes. Margarine has become so popular that its use has created another farm problem; there is a surplus of butter because it competes with margarine. Vegetable fats and oils also compete with animal fat such as lard. It is interesting to note that our government has had a support price for butter (a direct farm product); but there is not a support price for margarine, which is a manufactured product. It seems that solving some problems creates others.

These are the main solutions that have been used to attempt to solve the farm problem, but they are much more complicated than described here. They never seem to work completely successfully. Take just the one example of wheat. Between 1950 and 1961 there were more than 22 million acres of wheat land taken out of production, but the remaining acres that were planted produced over 170 million bushels more than were produced on the larger acreage in 1950. This increase in production on less land came about through better fertilizer, seeds, farming methods, equipment, and weather.

Facts everyone should know about production

1. Factors or resources of production are labor, land, capital, management, and government.
2. Capital is mainly equipment, buildings, and machines used in production.
3. Teachers, lawyers, doctors, and others provide economic services.
4. We must choose how we use our resources.
5. Government sometimes determines how resources are used.
6. There is no demand until there is a purchase.
7. Production creates form, time, place, and possession utility.
8. Consumption is use.
9. Business creates jobs.
10. Mass production helps the consumer through efficiency.
11. Specialization helps consumers through efficiency.
12. Tools and electric power increase production.
13. Good equipment, seed, and fertilizer increase farm production.
14. Gradually, fewer workers on farms are needed to produce the food we need.
15. Usually a reduction in farm prices does not increase consumption very much.
16. It is difficult to regulate the supply of farm products in relation to demand.
17. There are many attempts by government to regulate farm production and protect the farmer.

▪ QUESTIONS ON THE TEXT

1. What are the factors of production?

2. What are all the factors of production also called?

3. In economics, what do the following terms mean?
   (a) labor
   (b) land *or* natural resources
   (c) capital
   (d) management (entrepreneur)
   (e) government

4. Name some producers of services who do not produce goods but satisfy wants.

5. Explain what is meant when we say that a nation must make a choice whether to produce guns or butter.
6. Explain how the government sometimes makes decisions as to how our resources are used in farming.
7. What is meant by:
    (a) effective demand?
    (b) consumption?
8. What four forms of utility are created by production?
9. Explain the difference between a want and a demand.
10. How does business contribute to raising the level of living for people generally?
11. What part does research play in the activities of business?
12. Why is business interested in developing new products?
13. How does business create jobs?
14. Why do manufacturers limit their production to a few products?
15. (a) What is meant by mass production?
    (b) What is the objective sought in mass production?
16. (a) Why does business provide the tools, machines, and other equipment that employees need in their work?
    (b) Who benefits from the use of tools and equipment in production?
17. To what extent does business pay the cost of the federal government?
18. Why is our organized market system important to the consumer?
19. Why is specialization important in helping us to produce effectively?
20. Explain the importance of machines and electrical power in our production system.
21. What is meant by:
    (a) technology?
    (b) automation?
22. How may machines and automation result in technological unemployment?
23. Explain why farm efficiency has increased and caused a decrease in the need for farm workers.
24. What has happened to the average size of farms and why?
25. Why are the problems of supply, demand, and price so difficult in agriculture?
26. Why does climate have an important influence on whether a farmer makes a profit?
27. Why is it impossible for all farmers to diversify their crops?
28. Name some ways in which government attempts to aid the farmer.

▪ QUESTIONS FOR DISCUSSION

1. Who is the entrepreneur in a large corporation?
2. Explain why the government is sometimes considered a factor of production.

3. On a national scale when a government makes decisions on how to use resources in production of missiles, atomic energy, and rockets to send to the moon, how is the consumer affected?

4. What happens in a community when the resources being used for one purpose are no longer needed?

5. From your own experience, give an example of how demand has determined production.

6. Why does a clothing manufacturer find it necessary to change styles and designs frequently?

7. It is still possible for an individual to make cloth and to prepare some of his food. For instance, one could buy a bushel of oats and make rolled oats for breakfast cereal. Rolled oats that you buy in a package in a store cost about ten times as much as the raw oats from which they are made. Would you recommend that every family prepare its own rolled oats? Why?

8. (a) Explain what is meant by the statement that business creates jobs. (b) What happens to a business if there is no profit?

9. In the United States there are many products of high quality available in good supply and at more reasonable prices than in many other countries. Explain why this is true.

10. It is sometimes said that electrical power is an index or an indication of the productivity of a nation. Explain why this may be true.

11. From the point of view of economics, what is your argument for or against the protection of the small farmer against the large farmer?

12. What are your arguments for or against farm price supports?

▪ PROBLEMS TO SOLVE

1. Prepare a two-part report on (a) the life and (b) the contributions to the economic development of the United States of one of the following men: Henry Ford, Cyrus McCormick, or Eli Whitney.

2. Prepare a report on one of the following topics: (a) The Effect of Acreage Restriction on Production and Farm Income, (b) The Problem of Agricultural Surpluses and Some Suggested Solutions, and (c) Our Declining Farm Population: Its Effect on Our Economy.

3. Construct a series of graphs to show the following information:
   (a) Population on Farms Compared with Population of the United States (1900 and the present)
   (b) Trends in Acreage Production (1900 to the present)
   (c) The Importing and Exporting of Agricultural Produce
   (d) Farm Income's Share of Gross National Income

4. In the form of a report, trace each of the basic materials from its probable origin through the various processing steps that are used in the making of an ordinary wooden lead pencil that has an eraser. In tracing the basic materials consider the following: (a) how the

form of each basic material was changed to make it useful in the manufacture of the pencil; (b) the changes in location of the materials necessary to get them to the manufacturer; (c) the kinds of machinery and tools used in making the pencil; (d) the kinds of operations that workers performed on the materials; and (e) the steps that were taken to get the pencil to you from the manufacturer.

5. Give your own definition of mass production. Support your definition by statements as to the essential characteristics of mass production.

▪ COMMUNITY PROBLEMS AND PROJECTS

1. Select a business firm in your city and identify specifically the person or persons who represent each of the five factors of production in the business and the economic returns that each receives for his part in production.

2. Select any business in your community with which you are familiar. It may be a business that offers a service, sells merchandise, or makes something that people want.

   Make a complete study of the business you have selected, analyzing what the business *does* in light of the topics you have studied. Some of the topics will not apply to some types of business as well as to other types, but all topics should be considered in the analysis of what the selected business firm does. Write a report of the analysis you make covering the following items:

   (a) In what way does the business change the form or place of materials making them more useful to consumers?

   (b) What tasks does the business perform in connection with its products or services for consumers?

   (c) How does the product or service offered by the business contribute to raising the level of living?

   (d) Has the business developed new products or services recently? What opportunities does it have to develop new products or services?

   (e) How many jobs does the business provide?

   (f) Through what means does the business strive for greater efficiency and for lower costs of production?

   (g) To what extent does the business provide tools, equipment, and machinery that employees use? Can you estimate how much per employee is invested in tools and equipment?

   (h) Estimate how much the business pays in local and state taxes and in federal income taxes.

   (i) Summarize the effect the business has on consumers, on labor, and on the community.

Chapter 4

The marketing distribution system

PURPOSE OF THE CHAPTER

The marketing system or the marketing distribution system is the phase of production through which goods and services reach the consumer. Since most of your relations with business pertain to selecting and buying goods and services, you need to understand the marketing system, its functions, its services, and the role it plays in production.

You will find answers to these questions:

1. Why is marketing a phase of production?
2. What functions are performed in marketing?
3. What is the problem of costs in marketing?

A. The economic functions of marketing

THE ECONOMICS OF MARKETING

We have previously learned that marketing services are a part of production, but let us not confuse some economic terms. The term

"distribution" as previously used in economics refers to the distribution of production among the various factors of production. *Marketing distribution* refers to the function of distributing goods and services.

The significance of marketing. Marketing not only plays the very important role of getting goods from producer to consumer, but it also is important to us in several other ways.

Approximately one in every six gainfully employed persons is engaged directly in wholesaling or retailing activities. This ratio does not take into account other persons who are serving marketing through transportation, communication, and office jobs.

Marketing provides opportunities for many kinds of jobs requiring a wide range of skills and abilities. Although we naturally think of selling as being the primary occupation in marketing, there are opportunities in management, advertising, market and product research, and buying.

The economic well-being of our country is determined largely by productivity, consumption, and employment. The efficiency of the marketing process affects all three. If marketing stimulates demand, people will consume goods at a high rate. High consumption requires high productivity to meet the wants of people, and high productivity and high-level activity in marketing combined result in high employment. Indirectly, marketing is a key to a high level of economic living for the people.

Marketing services and utility. Some people assume that the many services performed between the producer and the consumer are unnecessary. In some cases the costs may be too high because of inefficiency or lack of competition. All the services, however, are necessary and cannot be avoided. The only way that the situation can be improved is through greater efficiency and savings in cost. Sometimes there are savings when one person performs more than one service, or new methods make it possible to save costs. In order to illustrate these marketing services, let us think in terms of a practical situation in Alaska. Wheat is not grown in Alaska. Therefore, in order to obtain flour to make bread, it has to be shipped from some other source. In other words, it has to be available in a certain place (Alaska); and to make it available in this place, the services performed (which add value) are called place utility. It also has to be available at a certain time in order to have value. This value is called time utility.

Besides time and place utility that are created by the marketing distribution system, there is possession utility. The fact that goods exist or are even displayed and made available at the proper time and place does not cause a demand or create consumption or use. The salesman who induces and arranges for the buyer to possess the goods is creating possession utility.

The farmer in Kansas grows wheat. This wheat is assembled, stored, graded, financed, transported, insured, and ground into flour. People have to be paid for these services. The person who grinds it must have equipment and labor. He has to pay for insurance and has to package the flour and store it. He has to advertise it and sell it, and, of course, he needs to make a profit.

Now let us examine the situation in Alaska. A family living on the edge of a wilderness wants ten pounds of flour. This family cannot stop work and go to Kansas, buy the flour, and take it back to Alaska. This family has to depend upon a retail store, and the retailer has to depend on the wholesaler who will import the flour from Kansas or some other state.

The wholesaler purchases flour from a miller who arranges for shipping it by rail to the West Coast and then by boat. The railroad will make a charge for its services, including labor, equipment, insurance, and other items. The operator of a ship has to pay the crew, charge something for the use of the ship, and pay for insurance and other operating costs. Of course, the flour has to be packaged carefully so that it will not be damaged. It will take considerable time to transport the flour, so there is money invested in it during all this time. A certain amount of risk is involved because of possible damage or spoilage. Naturally, the shipper hopes to make a profit on his services.

The flour has to be unloaded and transported to the wholesaler who will store it. He has to transport it by road to the retailers in small quantities. He has various costs of operation for which he has to pay. He has certain risks and expects to make a profit. The retailer and the wholesaler have to keep records and collect the money for the flour that they sell.

We could not perform all of these services for ourselves. We have to depend upon specialists all along the line. These specialists perform all kinds of services and take all sorts of risks for which they must be paid. Even with all these helpers who are being paid, it is cheaper to obtain the goods in this manner than for each individual to attempt to obtain his own goods and perform his own services.

WHAT MARKETING IS AND DOES

All people have economic wants. The purpose of economic goods and services is to satisfy those wants. The act of using goods and services to satisfy our wants is known as *consumption*.

Consumption does not take place unless two conditions are met. First, we must know that goods suitable and appropriate for satisfying our wants exist and that they are being produced, thus, that they are available to us. And, second, the goods must in some way reach us at a time and place that we can use them. For example, if a scientist in a foreign country were to produce a drug that would cure cancer, it could not be used to cure a cancerous condition that we might have unless we or our physician knew that such a drug had been discovered and that it was being produced. But knowledge of the drug and its production would not satisfy our want and need for it unless through some process we could obtain it. Marketing fulfills these two conditions. It may be said that *marketing* consists of most of the activities that occur in placing tangible goods in consumers' hands. Marketing does not include, however, those activities that change the form of goods. Thus, agricultural productive activities and manufacturing processes are not included in marketing.

Marketing makes consumption possible by telling us that products are available and where they can be bought.

FUNCTIONS OF MARKETING

The marketing process is sometimes called marketing distribution or the distributive system. Some of the functions of the system involve the physical handling of goods, and others involve the rendering of services. These functions are as follows:

Functions of marketing

1. Assembling and buying	5. Merchandising
2. Storing	6. Transporting and communicating
3. Grading and standardizing	7. Financing
4. Selling	8. Risk taking

Each of these functions is necessary and must be performed by someone if the marketing task is to be fulfilled; that is, if goods are to reach the consumer.

Assembling and buying. The assembling of goods is one of the first steps in marketing. *Assembling* means accumulating or gathering goods from various sources. Wholesalers assemble many types of manufactured goods from many different manufacturers located in many different places and make these available for the retailer. The retailer assembles a considerable variety of goods from different wholesalers. Cream stations, grain elevators, and stockyards are also important agencies in the assembling of products for consumers.

Buying consists of activities pertaining to: (1) agreement on prices and terms of purchase, date of shipment or delivery, and transfer of title; (2) careful determination of needs; (3) selection of sources of supply, that is, from whom to purchase; and (4) determination of the quality and suitability of the goods. Each of these activities is an essential aspect of the assembling and buying function of marketing.

Storing. At all stages in the distribution process, it becomes necessary to hold goods for varying periods of time. For some goods, production may be geared to demand, thereby reducing the need for storage to a minimum. Goods having a fairly steady demand and a very seasonal production, such as wheat, call for storage, however.

Providing a physical supply of manufactured and processed goods to assure delivery to customers within a reasonable time requires storage by manufacturers, wholesalers, and retailers. Goods such as room air-conditioners and circulation fans that are used during only a few months of each year require storage because the manufacturing of them must be continuous throughout the year. Also, the storage of many manufactured goods is necessary to prevent unavoidable delays in delivery and to make shipping in larger units such as by truckload or carload possible. Perishable foods and other products require freezing and cold-storage facilities.

Storing a product until needed is a function of marketing.

Grading and standardizing. *Grading* is the process of separating the supply of a commodity into classes according to established standards. For example, eggs are separated into Grades A, B, and C according to quality. Grading has rapidly become an important function of distribution. Tobacco, wheat, corn, and other agricultural products are carefully graded as they are assembled and marketed. For example, the standards set up by the federal government for wheat include classes or kinds of wheat, amount of moisture present, and percentage of damaged kernels and foreign matter. Most farm products are sold in large lots on the basis of grade. Meat, for instance, is marketed on the basis of inspection and grading.

Standardizing is the process of preparing a definition or description of the various qualities of a commodity. For example, a No. 1 apple is well-colored, without blemishes, and mature. The federal government and many associations cooperate in promoting the development of standards. Thus, customers are enabled to buy a commodity again and again with the assurance that the quality of each purchase will meet certain minimum specifications.

Grading facilitates selection and purchase of goods.

66

Selling. The preceding functions deal with the accumulation and preparation of goods for distribution through the various channels on their way to the consumer. Those who have collected goods, stored them, and graded them cannot assume that people who want these goods will seek them. It is an entirely false assumption that if you have a good product, "customers will beat a path to your door." One of the primary functions of *selling* is to create or stimulate demand for goods. Stimulation of demand involves informing people that products are available, teaching them how the goods will satisfy their wants, and persuading them to buy.

Elias Howe, inventor of the sewing machine, died a poor man because he could not sell his sewing machine. This happened because selling and advertising were not used to tell women about it and to educate them to its use. Similar stories are frequent in our history. Do you suppose, for instance, that practically every home would have one or more television sets today if it had not been for the force of selling and advertising which taught people about television and that sets were available?

Demand is stimulated in two ways, through personal selling and through advertising. The most common type of *personal selling* is practiced by the retail salesperson who serves the customer both by providing information and demonstrating the product and also by attempting to convince him that the product or service should be bought. Personal selling is being practiced every day by thousands of people. Technical engineers sell when they try to show manufacturers how new, expensive equipment will enable them to reduce manufacturing costs and to produce better products. The manufacturer has salesmen to sell his product. Salespeople sell goods to consumers over the counter, and some salesmen sell from door to door.

In addition to personal selling, *advertising* is used to stimulate consumer demand. Under this plan the manufacturer buys advertising space in newspapers and magazines, buys time on radio and television, and uses various other media of mass advertising to tell consumers about his goods, thus causing them to want his goods in preference to others.

In actual practice, the two methods of stimulating customer demand are always intermingled; the manufacturer advertises to the public, but he also has salesmen to call on wholesale dealers. The wholesaler or manufacturer, in turn, may advertise to the public; but he will also send salesmen to call on retailers. In recent years, however, manufacturers have tended to use the mass advertising message, such as television and magazine advertising, alone in creating customer demand. Creating consumer demand directly through mass advertising gives the manufacturer better control over the manner in which his product is presented to the public than is possible when the information about it is passed on to prospective consumers by salesmen for wholesale and retail firms.

Selling includes not only creating and stimulating demand but also finding buyers; arriving at terms of sale; determining prices; agreeing upon delivery dates; and finally, of course, providing for a method of payment and transfer of title.

Merchandising. After demand has been created, it must be satisfied. *Merchandising* is the process of actually filling demands for products. It is particularly important in retail stores, and in such cases includes the following:

1. Arrangement of counters and other store facilities.
2. Display of goods.
3. Window displays.
4. Procedure and personnel for showing and demonstrating goods to prospective customers.
5. Delivery service.
6. Systematic credit policy.
7. Installation and repair service for goods.

Not every retailer performs all these functions, but he must perform some of them. For instance, a retailer may have no delivery service, and he may not need to perform installation and repair service; but he probably does have to perform the other functions.

The merchandising function just described deals with the relationship between retailers and consumers. An equally important merchandising relation exists between manufacturers and wholesalers and retailers. As markets have expanded and the marketing process has become more complex, there is an increasing need on the part of wholesalers and retailers for market information. Much of this information is collected by manufacturers and by producers' associations and is sent on to wholesalers and retailers. An example of information useful to wholesalers and retailers is the probable future supply of a commodity such as wool or citrus fruits. Another example is the trend in fashions and styles of clothing that may affect the inventory and buying practices of wholesalers and retailers. The possibility of work stoppages due to impending labor-management disputes may affect

Communication is an essential factor in marketing.

The Western Union Telegraph Company

production, and, in turn, the supply and delivery dates of many products. Market information may be as helpful to wholesalers and retailers as credit and installation services are to consumers.

Transporting and communicating. Usually when ownership of goods is transferred from seller to buyer, there is also a change in the location of the goods. Thus, as goods are sold and transferred from manufacturers to wholesaler, from wholesaler to retailer, and from retailer to consumer, *transportation* is involved. The airlines, railroads, trucklines, pipelines, ships and barges, and other transportation facilities play an important role in our marketing process. Pipelines now transport such items as coal, chemicals, and other products besides oil, gas, and water. This method has reduced the cost of transportation to the benefit of all. Modern rapid transportation facilities expand tremendously the markets for fresh foods and many other perishable products.

Telephone, telegraph, radiotelephone, and postal services provide the *communication* links between sellers and buyers of commodities and hence, like transportation, play an important role in marketing. For example, orchids ordered by cablegram from Hawaii may be delivered by air in Chicago within 24 hours.

As the distance between the supplier and the consumer increases, the economic significance of transportation and communication in the marketing process also increases.

69

Financing. The movement of goods from producer to consumer requires considerable time. The manufacturer may have to store the goods in a warehouse, subject to their sale to wholesalers; likewise, wholesalers and retailers must keep in storage an ample supply of goods to meet customer demands promptly. Furthermore, time in transit from one location to another is required. During the time that goods are in the process of moving to the consumer and while they are in storage, someone owns them. Consequently, someone has money invested in the goods that cannot be recovered until they are sold. At the same time, the person who owns them needs money to buy more goods and to operate his business. This may mean that he must obtain a loan. Hence, *financing*, that is, providing for the money that is invested in the goods while they move to the consumer, is an important aspect of the marketing process.

Financing is involved also when the retailer sells goods to customers on credit. He may in part shift this financial responsibility by purchasing goods from the wholesaler on credit, and the wholesaler in turn may pass part of the credit extension back to the manufacturer of the goods.

Risk taking. Unavoidable risks of taking a loss occur all along the line of distribution. These risks include fire, theft, breakage, physical deterioration, obsolescence, changes in the price level, and changes in customers' wants and demands.

Speculation on our organized markets is one form of risk taking that is important in our distribution system. Speculators are willing to offer a purchase price on a commodity months in advance, even before it is produced. They believe that the price of the commodity will increase, and hence they are willing to buy at present prices with the hope of making a profit. Other speculators are willing to sell for future delivery goods that they do not yet have. They believe that the purchase price of the commodity may decrease; hence, they hope that they may make a profit.

Some risks, such as loss from fire and theft, can be covered by insurance. Other types of risk may be reduced or eliminated through good management practices. Regardless of insurance coverage and good management, however, some losses will occur. For that reason, owners and operators of businesses are entitled to the opportunity to make a profit in periods when losses do not occur in order to compensate for losses that do occur in other periods.

B. The nature and costs of marketing

KINDS OF MARKETS

In the preceding discussion, we have used the term marketing to include most of the processes involved in the movement of goods and services from producers to consumers. To the businessman, *market* also means the demand that there is for his goods. He says that there is a "good" market if the demand for his merchandise is good.

The term market may also refer to a place used for buying and selling. In many cities there are public market squares where produce merchants and farmers gather to sell their products. Exchanges are markets. The New York Stock Exchange, for instance, is a security market. The Chicago Board of Trade is a grain market. In many cities, livestock markets are operated. If a person says, "How is the stock market today?" he has reference to the trend of prices and conditions in the entire United States as reflected by the current selling prices of shares of stock on the stock exchange.

Certain kinds of markets, sometimes called *marketing institutions,* have been formed to serve special purposes in the distribution process. Let us examine some of the most common of them.

Wholesale market. A *wholesale market* is distinguished by its practice of trading only in large lots. A large lot may be one hundred cases, a carload, or an entire shipload of goods. A wholesale market ordinarily accommodates all producers and manufacturers in the entire range of commodities in a particular industry. For example, a wholesale market for women's ready-to-wear clothing and accessories may serve all manufacturers who produce merchandise in this line. Another illustration is the Furniture Mart in Chicago, which is a wholesale market forming the connecting link between manufacturers and wholesalers and retailers of all kinds of household furniture and furnishings.

Dealers and brokers operate in all kinds of markets. A *dealer* buys goods with the hope of selling at a profit. He takes the title to goods and sells them in smaller quantities to other wholesalers or directly to consumers. For example, dealers may buy hogs and cattle that have been brought to a central marketing place and sell them to packing houses, who are the wholesalers. These wholesalers then sell the meat to retail stores, and the retail stores sell the meat to consumers.

A *broker* acts as agent in buying or selling for someone else; he does not take title to the goods but assists in the transaction between the buyer and the seller.

Commission market. A *commission market* usually is a wholesale market in which commission men operate. A *commission man*, acting as an agent, takes physical possession of the goods offered by a producer and handles the sale of them to wholesalers or retailers. He usually does not actually own the goods. In some markets, however, he may buy the goods instead of acting as agent for the seller. He attempts to sell the product entrusted to him at the highest price he can secure, although he sometimes follows special instructions from the seller as to the price he should obtain. For his services he obtains a fee known as a *commission*. There are commission markets in all large cities. Products that are commonly sold on these markets are fruits, vegetables, and poultry.

Suppose, for example, a farmer brings fifty sacks of potatoes to a commission merchant in Cincinnati. In the absence of specific instructions with regard to the selling price to be accepted, the commission man will sell the potatoes at the highest price that he can obtain on the basis of offers by buyers. For his services he will charge either a percentage of the sale or a fixed amount.

Auction market. An *auction market* is one in which buyers congregate and bid for products that are offered for sale. An *auctioneer* sells one lot of goods at a time, seeking the highest possible bid from the buyers present. Fruits, tobacco, and furs are frequently sold in this manner. Important tobacco auction markets are located in Lexington and Louisville, Kentucky. Important fur markets are located in St. Louis and New York.

Auction markets for agricultural products, especially livestock, have been established in many farm communities. The bidders may be local retailers, wholesalers, or the agents for large food processors. Auction markets for used automobiles also operate in many large metropolitan areas. Both individuals and automobile sales firms may offer used automobiles for sale.

Retail market. A *retail market* is the final outlet in the distributing system—the final link in the chain between the producer and the consumer. There are more retailers than any other type of business proprietor. Grocery stores, department stores, service stations, meat markets, shoe stores, and clothing stores are representative types of retail markets.

Organized market. An *organized market* is a place where buyers and sellers congregate for the purpose of trading in securities or products. Such a market is commonly referred to as an *exchange*.

Organized security markets are located in New York, Chicago, and San Francisco. Security brokers in all cities may obtain telegraphed, or ticker tape, price reports throughout the period of each day that the markets are open. Common stocks, preferred stocks, bonds, and other types of securities are bought and sold on the exchanges.

Organized commodity markets are located in many parts of the country. Some of the smaller exchanges maintain close contact with the larger exchanges. Canned food, cottonseed, grains, feed, eggs, hides, lard, lead, potatoes, rubber, silk, minerals, sugar, tobacco, wool, and many other products are sold on organized exchanges in various parts of the country. Products are sold on the basis of grades and frequently by use of samples.

Exchanges provide a means of local, regional, or national buying and selling. They benefit the seller by providing an assured market of a wide scope so that he does not have to depend solely upon the local sale of his products. Organized markets benefit the buyer by providing a relatively sure and constant supply of goods. They also tend to establish and to stabilize prices. For instance, one can quickly determine the price of a commodity by checking the latest market quotations which are published in newspapers and often broadcast over radio and television.

GEOGRAPHICAL RANGE OF MARKETS

In general, markets are considered to be (a) *local,* (b) *regional,* (c) *national,* or (d) *international.* International markets are frequently referred to as *world markets.*

A large national market encourages production in large quantities. As large-scale production is usually economical, the consumer benefits. For instance, if an automobile manufacturer were limited to a market the size of Michigan, the company could not produce automobiles in large numbers. Both the cost of production and the price to the consumer would therefore be high. Automobile manufacturers, however, have a national market, and some have international markets.

Not all products or services can reach out into the national market. The nature of the product or the service and various other influences tend to restrict the market. Laundries, for instance, are usually con-

Modern transportation facilities expand markets.

The N.Y.N.H. & H.R.R. Company

fined to local communities. Without establishing branches, a laundry seldom finds it profitable to solicit business at greater distances than twenty or thirty miles. A single retail meat market is necessarily confined to its own neighborhood, although it sometimes enlarges its territory by providing delivery service.

The marketing of vegetables at one time was confined to areas close to the points of production. The marketing areas for these products have, however, been greatly extended through the use of transportation and storage facilities. For example, certain regions, such as the South and the West Coast, have national markets for fresh fruits and vegetables during the seasons when other regions cannot produce these foods.

THE PLACE OF MIDDLEMEN

Any person or business concern that performs one or more of the eight marketing functions explained earlier in this chapter is a *middleman*. This means that retailers as well as wholesalers, jobbers, agents of all kinds, brokers, and commission men are middlemen. We have discussed the function of each of these middlemen, with the exception of the jobber. The term *jobber* arose out of the custom of certain dealers to buy from producers in quantities called "job lots." Jobbers and wholesalers are now almost the same because they serve essentially the same purpose.

Many criticisms are directed at the middlemen. Some of the criticism stems from the increase in the cost of a commodity as it moves from the producer to the ultimate consumer. Criticism of the middleman may be attributed largely to a lack of understanding of the functions he performs. Many buyers fail to realize that after goods are produced, many additional services are required before consumers can enjoy these goods.

METHODS OF MARKETING

As we have already learned, goods move en route from the producer to the ultimate consumer through various middlemen. The route taken by the goods is known as the *method of marketing*. It also is sometimes known as a *channel of distribution* or a *trade channel*. The route is not the same for all goods, and it is not necessarily the same for all goods of the same kind.

When goods flow from producer to consumer through a wholesaler and a retailer, or through other combinations of middlemen, the method is frequently referred to as *indirect marketing.* This term is used because the products pass through several hands in going from a producer to a consumer.

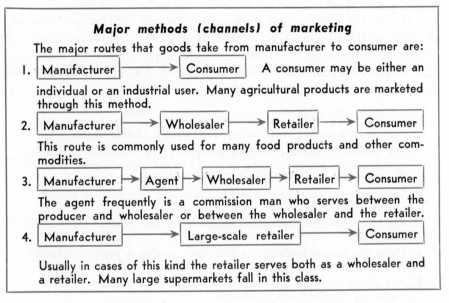

Direct marketing is any process by which the producer sells to the consumer directly or through his representative. The Fuller Brush Company, distributing its products by house-to-house selling, is an example of direct marketing. Several other well-known manufacturers sell directly to the consumer.

The producer ordinarily controls the first steps in the marketing process; that is, he decides whether his product shall be sold directly to consumers or sold to wholesalers and jobbers who will control the marketing process from that point forward. The numerous methods of marketing may be grouped into four major classes as shown in the illustration above.

THE COST OF DISTRIBUTION

It is difficult, if not impossible, to determine what part of the dollars spent annually at retail represents the cost of producing or manufacturing the goods, what part represents the costs of marketing, and what part is the middlemen's profits. Undoubtedly more reliable estimates could be made for certain commodities than for all commodities combined. According to the estimates that have been made, the costs of distribution generally exceed the production costs. Several years ago, the Twentieth Century Fund reported that, on an average, about 41 cents of a retail dollar is accounted for by production costs and 59 cents by distribution costs. Only a small portion of the 59 cents is profit, for on the average, wholesale and retail firms realize a profit of 3 to 10 percent on net sales.

The cost of distribution is thought to be too high by many people. A study of the functions performed by marketing, however, indicates that none of them can be eliminated. The hope of reducing marketing costs lies not in eliminating marketing services, but in devising methods of operation that will be more efficient.

Facts about marketing everybody should know

1. The marketing process includes everything that happens to tangible goods as they move from the producer to the ultimate consumer, with the exception of any significant change in their form.
2. Satisfaction of consumers' wants is dependent equally upon production and distribution of goods.
3. The functions of marketing can be combined, but none of them can be eliminated.
4. There are several kinds of markets, each serving a particular function in the distribution of goods.
5. Any person or business concern who performs one or more of the eight marketing functions is a middleman.
6. Middlemen perform necessary marketing services somewhere between the producer and the consumer.
7. Costs of marketing generally are as large as or larger than costs of production. Reduction of marketing costs cannot come from eliminating marketing services but rather will come from increased efficiency.
8. Marketing is one of the most important factors in the American Economic System; it is one of the keys to a high level of economic living.

▪ QUESTIONS ON THE TEXT

1. Distinguish between distribution and marketing distribution.
2. What proportion of all workers is engaged in wholesaling or retailing?
3. How does efficient marketing help to raise our economic level of living?
4. What types of economic utility are created by marketing distribution?
5. What marketing services are unnecessary?
6. If marketing costs are too high, what is the remedy?

7. (a) What is consumption?
   (b) What two conditions must be met before a consumer can obtain and use economic goods?
8. How is marketing defined?
9. Name and explain the functions of marketing.
10. What is meant by standardizing? by grading?
11. How is demand for goods and services created or stimulated?
12. Explain what is meant by merchandising. What does it include?
13. What is the importance of financing in the marketing process?
14. What is a wholesale market?
15. Explain the difference between a dealer and a broker.
16. What is meant by the term "middleman"? Give examples.
17. Describe the major channels of distribution.
18. What is direct marketing?

▪ QUESTIONS FOR DISCUSSION

1. Give some examples from your observations as to how marketing creates utility.
2. Explain why possession utility is essentially the same as demand.
3. Using the example of flour consumed in Alaska, give another example of the marketing distribution problem and explain the functions performed.
4. Do you think we could get along without the services of the wholesaler? Explain your answer.
5. The primary function of selling is to create demand. Explain what is involved in creating demand and how it is accomplished.
6. Explain the function of transportation in the marketing of citrus fruits.
7. Explain some of the various meanings of the term "market."
8. Of what value to the consumer is the marketing function of standardization and grading? Illustrate by examples.
9. Explain the geographical range of markets and some of the products which usually are found in each range.
10. Criticism is often leveled at the middleman. Give the reasons for this criticism and state whether or not you think it is justified.

▪ PROBLEMS TO SOLVE

1. The Mareck Bicycle Repair Shop specializes in repairs and has only a few bicycles for sale. The retail price of one of them is $75. The cost items related to it are:

Financing of purchase from manufacturer	$ .50
Cost of manufacture	59.50
Transportation	1.50
Uncrating and assembling in shop	1.00

Manufacturer's selling cost (national advertising) 3.00
Insurance in transit .... .25
General repair shop operating costs 1.00
Manufacturer's profit 5.00
Advertising in the local newspaper .... .25

(a) What is the total of the cost items that are functions of production?
(b) What percent of the retail price is this production cost?
(c) What is the total of the cost items that are functions of marketing?
(d) What percent of the retail price is this marketing cost?
(e) Assuming that the items listed are all of Mr. Mareck's costs for the bicycle, what is the amount of his profit if he sells it for $75?
(f) What percent of the retail price is his profit?
(g) To which of the eight functions of marketing should the profit figure be assigned?

2. Prepare a list of 10 products that ordinarily are marketed nationally or internationally. Then prepare another list of 10 products that usually are marketed on a local (state) or regional basis. Indicate a conclusion you reached while preparing the two lists.

▪ COMMUNITY PROBLEMS AND PROJECTS

1. With the approval of your teacher, select for study one of the five kinds of markets described in this chapter. Begin your study with library materials and information, then extend it with an interview with a businessman in your community who is engaged in the operation of that particular kind of market. Write a report that indicates your understanding of the kind of market you chose and the special purposes it serves in the distribution process.

2. Newspapers and periodicals sometimes carry advertisements in which the statement is made that the product is offered to the consumer by the producer himself. Select from these advertisements two or more direct-to-consumer offers. Try to determine if the business firm offering the goods for sale is the firm that made or produced the goods. Visit one of the local stores or markets, if there is one in your community, that claims to engage in direct marketing. Interview the manager to determine if he is a representative of the manufacturer who produced the goods offered for sale.

3. Make a study of the steps in the process of getting a pair of shoes from the shoe manufacturer to you. Consider what marketing functions have been performed and by whom they were performed, the kinds of markets that were concerned in the process, the method or channel of distribution that was used, and if possible the probable total cost of the marketing process.

Chapter 5

Labor, management, and government

PURPOSE OF THE CHAPTER

Labor and management are two of the most important factors in the successful operation of a free-enterprise system. The success with which they work together will largely determine how well we can all live and have the goods and services we want.

You will find answers to these questions:

1. What do we mean by labor?
2. What are the purposes of unions?
3. How do labor and management settle their differences?
4. What is collective bargaining?

A. The labor movement

SOME CENTRAL IDEAS ABOUT LABOR

There are many ideas about what labor really means. When one first thinks about this subject, he probably assumes that labor means

physical labor, that is, working with one's hands. In economics, the term *labor* has a very broad meaning. It means all forms of human effort, physical and mental, that provide a service or directly or indirectly add value or utility to goods. When we think of labor in these terms, we realize that it includes the services performed by managers, engineers, mechanics, skilled factory workers, unskilled factory workers, stenographers, bookkeepers, truckers, buyers, salesmen, and many others.

Besides producing goods or adding value or utility to goods, labor also performs important economic services that are not directly related to the production of physical goods. In this category we have such workers as lawyers, doctors, teachers, and many others. Each type of labor in its own special way is very important. Most workers are employed by others and are paid wages. Workers are classified in several thousand types of jobs. Some workers are self-employed. They own their own businesses and perform work in those businesses. Some workers are professional managers. They manage businesses for the owners, and they hire additional workers to perform the various tasks. The manager is an employee in the same way that a factory worker is an employee, but he is simply working on a different kind of job.

A RESTRICTED DEFINITION OF LABOR

As you study economics, you should always remember the broad definition of labor. There is another definition of labor, however, that has a restricted meaning. It is pretty hard to define, but it generally refers to the kind of labor that is commonly found in organized labor unions. It is the labor involved in the so-called labor movement. It is that group in our society which is paid wages or other compensation for the creation or distribution of goods and services. Generally, the workers in this group are not the owners of the goods they produce or the business in which they work. But many do own, directly or indirectly, an interest in business. They own shares of corporation stocks, and their unions own stocks. Some corporations have encouraged workers to own stock in the companies in which they work.

LABOR MOVEMENT

The term *labor movement* is a general term applied to an organization of workers for the purpose of improving their wages and the conditions under which they work. The term "labor movement" also refers to a whole series of unrelated attempts by organized workers to achieve their goals. A labor movement is limited to employees.

Unions, as we know them today, are a part of the labor movement. We have gradually accepted the meaning of the labor movement to mean the organization and the activities of labor unions.

The labor movement is very old. More than 300 years ago, there were organizations of employees in the simple small shops of England and Europe. The paid helpers in these small shops formed organizations to bargain with the owners in regard to wages and working conditions.

As the labor movement progressed, the objectives became greater than simply bargaining with employers. Labor unions sought and succeeded in obtaining political action to gain certain protection and advantages by law. Some of these objectives obtained by law have involved working conditions, hours of work, and certain other advantages that will be discussed later in this chapter.

EARLY UNIONS, THE GUILD SYSTEM

Our unions in this country and those of western European nations date back to the stage of industrialization generally described as the guild system. As the agricultural system of large estates gave way to the system of home workshops in England and western Europe, these guild organizations developed and gained wide acceptance. There were two types, one composed of shopkeepers or retailers and known as *merchant guild* and the other made up of handicraft workers called *craft guild.* Craft guilds included three types of members: older craftsmen in whose homes the work was performed were the *masters*; the craftsmen they employed on a day-wage basis were known as *journeymen*; young beginners in the craft, who worked for their board and room while they were learning the trade, were called *apprentices.* An apprentice became a journeyman after a period of training. He could then work for wages in the same shop or in other shops; and when he had accumulated sufficient capital, he could set himself up as a master. Journeymen later formed their own guilds to secure better wages and working conditions from the masters.

CRAFT OR TRADE UNIONS

In a *craft* or *trade union* the members are usually workers in a single occupation or in closely related occupations. Plumbers, carpenters, painters, airline pilots, and welders are examples of this type of union. The main advantage claimed for the craft type of organization is that the common interest of members makes for strength and stability.

UNION MEMBERSHIP

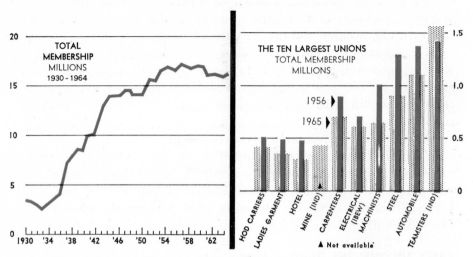

Adapted from Road Maps of Industry, National Industrial Conference Board, Inc., 1964

INDUSTRIAL UNIONS

An *industrial union* is composed of all classes of workers in an industry. Illustrations of this type of union are mine workers, automobile workers, and electrical workers (all types). Industrial unions stress the importance of the underlying interests of all kinds and classes of workers in an industry.

DEVELOPMENT OF NATIONAL ORGANIZATIONS

The first permanent national labor organization, the International Typographical Union, was formed in 1850. It set an example that was soon followed by unions of stonecutters, molders, locomotive engineers, machinists, hatters, and blacksmiths. One of the principal aims of these organizations was to control the supply of workers in the industries represented by the unions.

The formation of unions that developed during the Civil War continued after the war. Many locals were established in industrial areas. Additional city federations were organized. Several national organizations were established from 1866 to 1881.

AFL, a federation of trade unions. For half a century the underlying ideas of the American Federation of Labor (AFL) and that of the railroad brotherhoods (engineers, conductors, firemen, and trainmen) directed and controlled the nature and aims of American unions. This federation of trade unions accepted the idea of free enterprise and did not question the ethical foundations of free enterprise. Except in an incidental way, the Federation and the brotherhoods did not concern themselves much with the social and political welfare of their workers and their families, nor were they concerned about the welfare of all workers in general. The Federation sought to further the interests of skilled workers in certain specific occupations. The railway brotherhoods restricted their interests to particular groups of workers. Seldom did they admit to their membership unskilled workers.

Formation of the CIO industrial unions. For many years there was a division of opinion among leaders in the American Federation of Labor over the desirability of promoting unions on an industry-wide basis (industrial unions). There were those who insisted that in the organization of unions the nature and characteristics of an industry, and not workers with certain skills, should be the guiding considerations. For example, in the automotive industry, it was said that organization activity should not be directed to forming separate unions of machinists, patternmakers, molders, chemists, and toolmakers, but instead there should be a union consisting of all workers in the automotive industry.

Because of a lack of interest on the part of the American Federation of Labor to give more attention to the organization of industrial unions, a committee was formed to organize the mass-production industries. The committee was known as the Committee on Industrial Organization (CIO). It immediately began a campaign to organize the workers in several very important industries. The attempt to organize the great automotive, steel, and other industries was successful. Due to a difference regarding organizational policy, the CIO leaders and their unions were expelled from the AFL in 1938. At this point the committee established an independent federation, which became known as the Congress of Industrial Organizations.

Merger of AFL and CIO. The formation of the CIO in 1938 had several important effects, both on the labor movement and on the public. It caused some of the craft unions in the AFL to liberalize their requirements for admission to these unions. Rivalry between the AFL and CIO caused the leaders of the unions to compete with each other in attempting to win benefits from employers. It resulted in jurisdictional disputes (arguments as to which union's members should be permitted to do certain types of work) between unions that led to strikes, even though no issue between a union and an employer was involved.

STRUCTURAL ORGANIZATION OF THE AMERICAN FEDERATION OF LABOR AND CONGRESS OF INDUSTRIAL ORGANIZATIONS

EXECUTIVE COMMITTEE
President, Secretary-Treasurer, 6 Vice-Presidents

STANDING COMMITTEES
Civil Rights
Community Services
Economic Policy
Education
Ethical Practices
Housing
International Affairs
Legislation
Organization
Political Education
Public Relations
Research
Safety and Occu- pational Health
Social Security
Veterans Affairs

STATE CENTRAL BODIES
in 50 States and 1 Commonwealth

LOCAL CENTRAL BODIES
in over 774 Communities

NATIONAL CONVENTION
(EVERY 2 YEARS)

EXECUTIVE COUNCIL
PRESIDENT, SECRETARY-TREAS., 27 VICE-PRESIDENTS

OFFICERS
PRESIDENT AND SECRETARY-TREAS.
HEADQUARTERS, WASHINGTON, D.C.

130 NATIONAL AND INTERNATIONAL UNIONS

60,000 LOCAL UNIONS OF NATIONAL AND INTERNA- TIONAL UNIONS

332 LOCAL UNIONS DIRECTLY AFFILIATED WITH AFL-CIO

MEMBERSHIP OF THE AFL-CIO, JANUARY 1, 1964

13,500,000

GENERAL BOARD
Executive Council and one principal officer of each international union and affiliated Department

STAFF
Accounting
Civil Rights
Community Services
Education
International Affairs
Investment
Legislation
Library
Organization
Political Education
Publications
Public Relations
Religious Relations
Purchasing
Research
Social Security
State and Local Central Bodies

TRADE AND INDUSTRIAL DEPARTMENTS
Building Trades
Food and Beverage
Industrial Union
Label Trades
Maritime Employees
Metal Trades
Railway Employees

922 Local Department Councils

Leaders of both sides recognized that this division among labor unions weakened the strength and progress of the organized labor movement. After a long period of negotiations, a merger of the American Federation of Labor and the Congress of Industrial Organizations was completed, December 5, 1955. The "raiding" of members from one union by another and jurisdictional disputes were discouraged. A declared purpose of the AFL-CIO is "to protect the labor movement" from corrupt influence and practices of all kinds, including the efforts of communists to gain control of the unions. The federation has adopted six Codes of Ethical Practices that apply to the following matters: the issuance of charters to local unions; the handling of health and welfare funds; labor racketeers and communists and fascists in unions; and the practice of democracy in union affairs.

On the whole, American unions rely on collective bargaining with employers to achieve their objectives. As to political practices, unions appear to follow the policy of rewarding their friends and punishing their enemies.

LOCAL, NATIONAL, AND INTERNATIONAL UNIONS

Labor unions are classified not only as trade or industrial unions but also as local, national or international, and federated unions.

Individual members of labor organizations belong to local unions and only indirectly to national and federated unions. Some of the large locals include most of the workers in a number of different plants. Many unions employ a *business agent*, who is a full-time employee of the local. Where a business agent is employed, he is the general business manager of the local. *Shop stewards* are usually elected by the departments in unionized establishments. They are not officers of the union. Their chief function is to handle grievances of members with the employer.

Most local units are units in national or international unions. A local union which is a part of the larger union does not have the right of autonomy (independence) that it would otherwise have. The national unions and the federations often take the lead in organizing local unions. The constitution and the regulations of the locals must observe the general and specific regulations prescribed by the national union. The main functions of the national unions are: (1) to promote and extend union organization by securing additional members for existing locals and to organize new locals; (2) to aid locals in their negotiations with employers; and (3) to represent the local union in the national federation with which they are affiliated. Some international unions include locals in the United States, Canada, Puerto Rico, and the Canal Zone.

B. Management and labor relations

COLLECTIVE BARGAINING

Collective bargaining means bargaining as to wages and matters relating to working conditions with employers by representatives of organized groups of workers. Such agreements, if lawful, become binding to a certain extent on all individuals concerned. Collective bargaining is the central objective of labor unions.

COLLECTIVE BARGAINING

The core of industrial relations in our country is collective bargaining between employer and union.

National Labor Relations Act. It was not until the passage of the National Industrial Recovery Act in 1933 that our government gave approval to collective bargaining. The Act contained many provisions; collective bargaining was only one. When the Supreme Court ruled that one section of the Act was unconstitutional, the whole measure became invalid.

In 1935, Congress passed the National Labor Relations Act, which guarantees the right of collective bargaining. The Act provides that, if a majority of the workers state a desire to bargain collectively, the employer must deal with the duly selected representatives of the group. The Act states that employers may not "interfere with, restrain, or coerce employees," or "dominate or interfere with the formation or administration of any labor organization or contribute financial support to it." Under the law employers are forbidden to "encourage or discourage membership in any labor organization."

To carry out the intention of the Act, a National Labor Relations Board was established. It has the power to supervise elections in

Labor-Management Relations Act
(Taft-Hartley Act)

1. Lists unfair union practices.
2. Prohibits closed shop agreements.
3. Puts restrictions on strikes, boycotts, and picketing.
4. Revives the use of injunctions where strikes threaten national security.

In 1947 Congress passed the Labor Management Relations Act, commonly called the Taft-Hartley Act. The intent was to balance the interests of labor, management, and the public interest.

situations where there is a dispute as to whether a majority of a group of employees desires that a particular union should represent them in negotiating with the employer. It may investigate charges of unfair practices by an employer. It has the power to call upon employers to "cease and desist" from "unfair" labor practices. The Act, of course, was a great help to the unions in their efforts to organize labor.

Arguments for collective bargaining

1. Only by collective agreements can workers have equality of bargaining power with employers.
2. When individuals bargain, wages for the entire group tend to be set by workers who will accept wages that may have no relation to productivity.
3. Since the supply of labor usually is greater than the demand, collective bargaining is necessary to obtain fair wages.
4. Strikes are prevented if both parties do not violate the contract.
5. A long-term contract makes it possible for an employer to know what his labor costs will be and gives employees job or wage security.

Arguments against collective bargaining

1. Employers contend that unions demand too much and threaten to destroy profits.
2. Unions interfere with the decision-making authority of management.
3. Unions tend to destroy loyalty of employees to the employer.
4. The employer considers himself generous and kind to his employees and considers it an insult for a union to want to speak for and negotiate for his employees.
5. The human aspects of management are being destroyed, and labor is being separated and divided from management because there are collective spokesmen.

COLLECTIVE BARGAINING AND INDUSTRIAL CONFLICT

Why do we have these sharp disagreements between employers and employees? Do they indicate a deep-seated, continuing class struggle between property owners and workers? Are they likely to disrupt our society? Who is to blame for them? Are they the result of collective bargaining?

Thousands of disputes and millions of man-days lost each year arise out of the negotiation or the interpretation of labor contracts. More than 100,000 collective agreements are negotiated each year, an average of almost 300 each day. More than 90 percent are signed without a work stoppage. The large majority of contracts are carried through to the end of their terms without a strike or a lockout.

Contract Between Labor and Management

1. Wages
2. Hours
3. Working Conditions
4. Fringe Benefits
5. Hiring, Firing
6. Procedures for Handling . . .
   A. Grievances
   B. Layoffs
   C. Disciplinary Problems
   D. Reinstatements
7. Contract Negotiations

A contract between labor and management contains specific statements of agreement relative to a number of points.

Union security. In order to deal effectively with employers in collective bargaining, unions insist that they must organize and maintain *union security*, which means acceptance and recognition of the union by the employer.

To achieve as high a degree of security as possible for themselves, unions employ several methods. These methods include: the open shop; the agency shop; the closed shop; the union shop; the preferential shop; the maintenance-of-membership provisions in contracts; and checkoff systems.

In earlier periods, what is now usually considered as union security was generally described as *recognition*. The most important of these patterns of recognition are discussed on the next page.

In some contracts the union is the *bargaining agent for members only*. The union of employees is accepted as representing only those employees who are members. The union is not regarded as speaking for other employees in the same shop or unit. The employer thus maintains his freedom to deal with other employees as individuals.

The union may be the *sole* or *exclusive bargaining agent*. In such cases, the union is accepted as the agent for all employees in the unit. While there may be no requirement that all employees join the union, the organization negotiates for all employees, including nonmembers.

Employers usually prefer the *open shop*, which means that the employer is free to hire employees without reference to union membership.

In an *agency shop*, all employees in the bargaining unit pay dues to the union, although they do not have to join it.

A *closed shop* is an establishment that operates under a collective-bargaining agreement not to employ nonunion workers. Before non-union workers are employed, they are required as a condition of employment to become and to remain members of the union with which the employer has an agreement.

A *union shop* closely resembles the closed shop in that a union-shop agreement requires any nonunion worker who secures employment in the establishment to become a member of the union at the end of a specified probationary period.

A *preferential shop* is one in which the union contract requires that the employer give special consideration to union employees. For example, the agreement may stipulate that, in hiring additional workers, preference be given to union members; or the agreement may provide that, in case of layoffs or promotions, union members shall be given preferential consideration.

Maintenance-of-membership arrangements require that employees who become members of a union must remain members for the duration of the union contract with the employer.

Under the *checkoff system*, the employer agrees with the union to deduct union dues from the pay of employees and to turn these funds over to the union treasurer.

WAGE PLANS

There are three basic methods of wage payment: (1) timework; (2) piecework; and (3) some form of incentive wage payment that frequently takes the form of a combination of timework and piecework.

Under the timework method the worker is paid wages at a stated rate of so much an hour, a day, a week, or other period of time. If he works on a piecework basis, he receives compensation for the number of units he produces or the number of processes or operations he completes. If the worker is paid on the basis of a combined time-piece method, he receives a basic time wage and an additional amount for production in excess of the standard output upon which the basic wage is based.

Labor unions usually demand that the rate be the same for each employee in a given class of workers, whatever the basis upon which the rate is calculated. When piecework rates exist, workers may increase their earnings by completing more units or operations.

When a combination of the two methods is employed, workers receive a minimum wage based on a standard day's work, and an incentive for greater production is offered by paying a higher piece rate for additional units after the worker has met the requirements for a standard day's work.

Another type of incentive wage rate exists when workers are paid a premium (extra pay) for completing the quantity required for a standard day's work in less time than the standard time.

Labor is generally suspicious of incentive wage systems, whether they take the form of piece rates or bonuses for faster work. Labor unions usually insist upon a "fair" wage for a "standard day's work." They contend that such an arrangement is necessary in order to protect employees from overwork.

REDUCTION OF HOURS OF WORK

Leaders of organized labor seek to justify a gradual decrease in the workday and the workweek with several arguments: (1) The rapidly increasing productivity of industry makes possible the production of more goods with less work than formerly. (2) Workers should have more time for their cultural improvement. (3) Increased leisure stimulates the demand for more and different goods. (4) Problems of the democratic way of life require workers to have time to study public problems and to participate intelligently in political efforts to solve these problems. (5) A reduction in the work period would result in an improvement in the health of the working population.

Can workers produce enough goods in a shorter period to enable employers to maintain or to increase wages? As a rule, employers have opposed any reduction in the work period without a corresponding reduction in the amount of wages that will be paid or an increase in the productivity of workers.

FRINGE BENEFITS

In addition to wages and salaries, employees may receive a wide range of additional benefits and services, generally described as *fringes* or *fringe benefits*. Most common among them are life insurance, pension systems, and hospitalization paid for by employers.

Fringes are no longer rare or unusual. They were and are widely described as "employee benefits" and "employee services." In some cases, they were established by employers who sought to gain the favor of employees or who regarded the provision of security for workers as an employer's responsibility. They have become a part of wages because employers, employees, and public policy favor them. Pensions and other welfare provisions, for example, meet public and individual demands for economic security.

The number and the variety of these fringes has grown rapidly. This development has been speeded because unions have recognized a chance to get "bargains" in these benefits and have made them a favorite subject for collective bargaining. Employees can get more for their money by purchasing life insurance or hospitalization or other such benefits on a group basis. Their interests may be better served

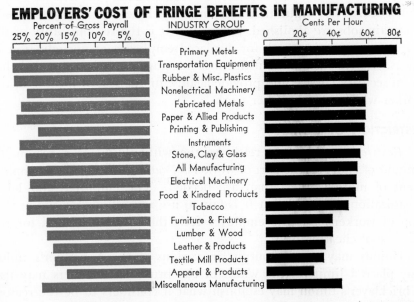

EMPLOYERS' COST OF FRINGE BENEFITS IN MANUFACTURING

Percent of Gross Payroll	INDUSTRY GROUP	Cents Per Hour
25% 20% 15% 10% 5% 0		0 20¢ 40¢ 60¢ 80¢
	Primary Metals	
	Transportation Equipment	
	Rubber & Misc. Plastics	
	Nonelectrical Machinery	
	Fabricated Metals	
	Paper & Allied Products	
	Printing & Publishing	
	Instruments	
	Stone, Clay & Glass	
	All Manufacturing	
	Electrical Machinery	
	Food & Kindred Products	
	Tobacco	
	Furniture & Fixtures	
	Lumber & Wood	
	Leather & Products	
	Textile Mill Products	
	Apparel & Products	
	Miscellaneous Manufacturing	

Adapted from *Road Maps of Industry*, National Industrial Conference Board, Inc., 1964.

by having a 5-cent increase expended for a medical care plan than by taking the same increase in cash.

Studies have calculated the cost of these supplements to wages and salaries. Most recent surveys have found that, on the average, they represent an added cost to employers amounting to about 20 percent of the total payroll.

USE OF LABORSAVING MACHINES

In the early days of factories the introduction of laborsaving devices by an employer often met with opposition from employees. Workers in factories felt the use of new machines would eliminate their jobs.

Gradually the objection of workers to the use of laborsaving machines and processes has decreased. Unions still recognize the fact that the loss of jobs and unemployment because of improvements in productive processes will result unless it is possible to find work opportunities for workers displaced by machines. The unions usually agree that in the long run new inventions and improved processes in production cause a greater demand for labor from a greater number of industries.

Generally the unions agree that all new improvements in productive processes should be used immediately by employers, but not at the expense of workers whose services in their present jobs will no longer be needed. They argue that every new machine should pay for itself. If certain jobs are abolished, unions feel it is the responsibility of the employer to provide work for displaced employees at no reduction in wages. Where such an adjustment is not possible, it is contended that social security laws should provide against undue loss of income to the worker while he seeks other work.

RESTRICTION OF OUTPUT

Restriction of output refers to the withholding of a reasonable amount of effort on the part of workers. *Featherbedding* is the employment of more workers than are needed. The employee and labor organizations may feel that it is fair to use restrictions for the protection of workers, but the employer feels the practice is used for the purpose of cheating him.

Unions may restrict output in various ways. A painter's union may place a limit on the width of the brush its members may use. A bricklayer's union may establish what it considers to be the reasonable number of bricks that a member may lay in a given time.

Occasionally the failure of union and management to reach agreement results in a strike accompanied by picketing.

Ewing Galloway

From the standpoint of the welfare of our total society, it is difficult to justify a policy of restricting output or employing someone not needed.

METHODS USED BY ORGANIZED LABOR

The employment relation between unions and management is friendly most of the time, and differences of opinion are settled by peaceful negotiation. Sometimes the failure of unions and management to reach an agreement results in the use of drastic methods by one or both sides. Both unions and employers have used a number of methods to gain their goals. The methods that have been used by organized labor include: (1) strikes, (2) picketing, (3) boycotts, (4) sabotage, and (5) propaganda and political pressure.[1]

A *strike* is a temporary stoppage of work by a group of employees for the purpose of compelling an employer to agree to their demands. By stopping work, strikers feel that they do not cease to occupy the status of employees and that they do not forfeit the right to return to their jobs when the dispute which induced them to strike has been settled. Employers often feel that when an employee leaves his job, he quits his job and that they should be free to fill the position with a new employee. Any attempt by employers to fill positions vacated by strikers, of course, is opposed by the striking employees.

A *direct strike* is against the employer and does not involve a third party. A *sympathetic strike* is one that does not arise from a grievance of the employees against their employer; its purpose is to assist other employees in a dispute with their employer.

A *general strike* is one that involves the workers in all industries in a city, region, or other large area, but they should be distinguished from strikes that are *industry-wide* in their scope. The general strike is in the nature of a sympathetic strike to achieve the common aims of workers in different industries, while the industry-wide strike is for

---

[1] Under certain conditions sympathetic strikes, general strikes, mass or coercive picketing, sit-down strikes, sabotage, and certain types of boycotts are illegal.

the purpose of achieving or of maintaining a system of collective bargaining on some issue in a given industry.

Jurisdictional strikes arise out of a dispute between rival unions, and not because of a demand upon the employer. For example, a dispute between carpenters and steelworkers belonging to different unions may arise as to which union is entitled to perform a certain kind of work. A *wildcat strike* occurs when the members of a local union quit work without authorization by the national union with which the local is affiliated.

A *sit-down strike* is one in which the striking workers cease work but remain on the premises of the employer for the purpose of preventing others from taking their jobs. The sit-down strike has been declared unlawful by the United States Supreme Court.

A *slowdown* is a form of strike that occurs when employees stay on the job but agree among themselves to restrict the amount of work they perform.

Upon the expiration of a contract between the union and the employer, the union may adopt the method of "no contract—no work" and refuse to permit its members to work until the employer renews the contract or signs a new one. The union in this case is likely to argue that the work stoppage is not a strike.

A *union picket* is a person stationed near the entrance of a place of employment by a labor organization during a dispute with the employer. The process is called *picketing*. The usual functions of pickets are to inform other employees, any prospective employees, and the public that a dispute exists; to persuade nonstrikers to join in the strike; and to discourage anyone from entering the place for the purpose of working.

Mass picketing is the parading or assembling of a considerable number of strikers before the work place for the same purposes as indicated above and in order to emphasize the strike or to provide a display of strength in opposition to workers who refuse to recognize the strike. *Cross picketing* occurs when pickets of rival unions claim to represent a majority of the workers in a struck plant. *Secondary picketing* is the picketing of an employer who may be engaged in business transactions with the employer against whom the employees are striking.

A *boycott* is defined as a mass effort to withdraw and to induce others to withdraw from economic or business relations with the employer against whom the boycott is directed. Sometimes a distinction is made between a primary and a secondary boycott. The *primary boycott* is one in which the workers agree not to patronize a firm because of their own complaint against the management. The *secondary boycott* is an action by a labor union whereby the union (not involved in the dispute) forbids its members to work for or to have any dealings with a concern whose employees are on strike.

The term *sabotage* has been commonly used to refer to various kinds of actions by employees intended to restrict production or to inflict damage on an employer's property or his business.

Labor unions make every effort to create public opinion favorable to unions, especially in any specific labor dispute. Picketing is one device used, plus public statements, radio and television programs, and handbills. Only when the public suffers inconvenience from a dispute between employers and employees is it greatly concerned. Even then, the primary interest of the public may not be in the cause of the difficulty or in the way the dispute should be settled.

In common with other organized groups, unions attempt to secure the passage of laws that will give labor the legal rights and protection which the unions feel are needed. Both in Congress and in the state legislatures organized labor has striven for the enactment of laws that would guarantee the right of collective bargaining and of engaging in certain labor-union activities.

METHODS USED BY EMPLOYERS

The methods that may be used by employers in disputes with unions include: (1) injunctions, (2) lockouts, (3) strikebreakers, (4) company unions, and (5) propaganda and political pressure.[2]

An *injunction* is an order from a court commanding an individual or a group of individuals to do or to refrain from doing an act or acts. According to the theory of the injunction, damage may result from the acts of individuals or groups for which there would be no adequate remedy, such as money damages. One who disobeys an injunction is also liable for prosecution (sued) for any damages to property that he may have caused. The injunction is used when an employer feels the union is doing or is about to do something that is illegal and will result in damage to the employer.

A *lockout* is a temporary stopping of the operation of his business by an employer in an attempt to win a dispute with his employees. It is the employer's equivalent of the strike. In terms of the number of

---

[2] The blacklist, yellow-dog contract, and industrial espionage, which were formerly used by employers, are not considered because they have been declared clearly illegal.

occurrences, the lockout is a relatively unimportant device for use in conflict with employees because employers seldom shut down their plants in order to force a settlement with labor.

A *strikebreaker* is a person hired by an employer to replace a striking employee. Some states have laws that establish certain conditions under which employees may be hired to take the place of striking workers. Under federal law it is illegal to transport strikebreakers across state boundaries.

A *company union* is an organization of employees of a particular employer that is not affiliated with any other labor group.

Employers and employers' associations seek the help of public opinion in the settlement of industrial disputes. They also seek to secure the passage of laws that will not discriminate against them in their relations with their employees. In the case of a strike that affects a whole community or interrupts business to a considerable extent, employers and associations to which they may belong are likely to place their case before the public in newspaper advertisements.

To secure the enactment or retention of laws, employer groups often distribute printed materials that set forth arguments for or against laws pertaining to labor relations in industry. Like the large labor organizations, employer groups attempt to prevent the enactment of laws that are considered unfavorable to their own interests and to enact laws that are favorable.

PUBLIC POLICY ON LABOR AND MANAGEMENT

In our nation, we have recognized the danger that some of the issues arising out of employment might divide our citizens, create lawlessness and violence, and thus threaten the peace and security of our society. We are trying through collective bargaining to develop procedures for settling most differences. Conciliation, mediation, cooling-off periods, arbitration, and formal grievance procedures are examples of these methods. We have tried to minimize the part that government agencies play in actually deciding issues.

To prevent unrest and misunderstanding, there is a procedure for handling complaints and disputes originated by workers or unions. This is called a *grievance procedure*. It is usually a carefully written procedure and often is a part of a union contract between the employer and the union.

When disputes cannot be settled by mutual agreement or negotiation, the next step is often *arbitration*. In this process the dispute is submitted to a third person or group of persons agreed upon. Such a

TYPICAL GRIEVANCE PROCEDURE UNDER UNION CONTRACTS		
	8	A GOVERNMENT MEDIATOR OR AN ARBITRATOR MAY HELP SETTLE DISPUTE
	7	THE NEXT STEP IS TO HIGHER UNION AND COMPANY OFFICIALS
	6	NATIONAL UNION AGENT MAY NEGOTIATE WITH GRIEVANCE COMMITTEE
	5	THE NEXT STEP IS TO HIGHER AUTHORITY SUCH AS PERSONNEL MANAGER
	4	IF PROBLEM IS NOT SETTLED, STEWARD GOES TO MANAGEMENT, CHIEF PLANT STEWARD OR GRIEVANCE COMMITTEE
	3	STEWARD AND EMPLOYEE TALK TO FOREMAN
	2	STEWARD TALKS TO SHOP FOREMAN
	1	EMPLOYEE REPORTS ON COMPLAINTS TO SHOP STEWARD

person is called an *arbitrator*. His decision must be accepted by both parties, labor and management.

In some labor disputes, a government agent, called a *mediator*, meets with labor and management to help reach an agreement. This procedure is called *conciliation* or *mediation*. The mediator has no power but merely attempts to bring both parties into agreement. The federal government, however, in some situations, has the legal power to require a *cooling-off period* (delay) before a strike.

To encourage negotiation and reduce conflict, society has tried to narrow the area of possible disagreement between the parties in collective bargaining. We maintain public agencies to establish the general rules and to answer certain types of questions for the parties.

Public agencies are taking an active part in many employment relationships. Representatives of the federal agencies are checking on hours of work and wage rates. State agencies are checking working conditions and the jobs held by young workers and women. Federal, state, and local fair-employment-practice commissions are seeking to prevent discrimination in employment based on race, nationality, or religion.

Role of government in labor-management relations

(1) Setting and maintaining standards of safety and health in working conditions by such means as factory inspection and safety programs.

(2) Setting standards of minimum wages and maximum hours in both public and private employment.

(3) Preventing child labor and hazardous employment of women.

(4) Enforcing standards of training for apprentices and assisting in apprenticeship programs.

(5) Preventing discrimination based on race, religion, or nationality.

(6) Assisting in the prevention and settlement of labor-management disputes through conciliation and mediation.

(7) Interpreting and enforcing the rules of collective bargaining.

■ QUESTIONS ON THE TEXT

1. In economics, what is the broad meaning of labor?
2. Is a manager a part of labor?
3. Does a doctor perform labor?
4. What is the restricted meaning of labor in relation to the labor movement?
5. What is meant by the labor movement?
6. What are some of the gains made by labor unions and by political action?
7. What is meant by:
   (a) masters
   (b) journeymen
   (c) apprentices
8. (a) What is a craft or trade union?
   (b) What is an industrial union?
9. What is a labor federation?
10. What is:
    (a) a business agent?
    (b) a shop steward?
11. What are the main functions of national unions?
12. What is collective bargaining?
13. What is the function of the National Labor Relations Board regarding elections to determine union representation?
14. What are some of the arguments
    (a) for collective bargaining?
    (b) against collective bargaining?
15. (a) What is meant by union security?
    (b) What are some objectives and devices for obtaining security?
16. What is meant by piecework in paying wages?

17. What are some arguments of unions for reducing the length of the workday or the workweek?
18. (a) What is a fringe benefit?
    (b) What is the estimated cost of fringe benefits?
19. What does the term "featherbedding" mean?
20. What are some of the methods used by organized labor to gain objectives?
21. What are the methods used by employers to oppose unions in disputes?
22. What is an injunction?
23. What are the procedures used by society in labor disputes under what are called grievance procedures?

□ QUESTIONS FOR DISCUSSION

1. Explain the difference between the broad term "labor" and the term "labor movement."
2. Is there any organization in existence today that might be considered similar to the old craft guild?
3. Explain the main differences that existed between the American Federation of Labor and the Committee on Industrial Organization.
4. Explain how jurisdictional disputes hurt almost everyone in society.
5. Assume that an employer talks to an employee and offers him an inducement not to join a labor union. Is this a legal act?
6. One of the arguments against collective bargaining is that unions tend to destroy loyalty of employees to the employer. What is your opinion?
7. What are your arguments for or against the union shop?
8. Under many union contracts all workers are paid the same wage in each classification even though their abilities and productivity may not be the same. What do you think of this practice?
9. From the point of view of economics, is it sound to continue to reduce the length of the workday and the workweek?
10. Who pays the cost of fringe benefits?
11. What is your opinion in regard to arguments against laborsaving machines?
12. Give your justifications for or your arguments against featherbedding.
13. Compare a strike with a lockout. Indicate the fairness of each.
14. (a) What are some of the advantages of arbitration?
    (b) What are some of the disadvantages of arbitration?

■ PROBLEMS TO SOLVE

1. A machine operator making one small part of a larger product is paid at the hourly rate of $2.50 per hour for an eight-hour day. His employer plans to establish a piecework wage plan whereby the machine operator would receive $.075 for each piece he produces. If he produces an average of 300 pieces a day, and thinking only in terms of

income, is it probable that he will be happy or unhappy about the change? Why?

2. Labor turnover is the ratio of the number of persons quitting and being discharged from their jobs to the total number of workers employed by a firm. Normally, the Hammer Manufacturing Company employs 50 women and 150 men. During the past year, 10 women and 15 men left the company and were replaced by other workers. What was the labor turnover for the year? Was the turnover for women higher or lower than that for the men? Is the difference about what you think should be expected? Why?

3. In a recent year 1,590,000 workers were involved in strikes or other work stoppages related to labor disputes. The man-days lost were 22,700,000.
   (a) If the working day is 8 hours, how many hours were lost?
   (b) If the average wage is $2.20 per hour, how much in wages did the workers lose?
   (c) How much did each worker lose (average) based upon the previous figures?
   (d) If each worker gained an increase of 10 cents an hour as a result of the strike, how long must he work to gain back what he lost?
   (e) From the figures available for the latest year (if directed by your teacher) compute a, b, c, d above for the latest year.

4. In the American Wire Fence Company the fringe benefits average 28 cents an hour for vacations, holidays, and sick leave; Christmas bonus, 1.7 cents an hour; social security and state benefit programs, 17.8 cents an hour; insurance, pensions, and other welfare programs, 13 cents an hour.
   (a) What is the cost per hour to the employer?
   (b) If the average wage is $2.00 per hour, what is the percentage of wages paid in benefits?

▪ COMMUNITY PROBLEMS AND PROJECTS

1. Most workers are at times uncertain about their ability to make progress in their jobs or even of keeping them. Interview two or more workers you know and question them to find out why this is true. Prepare a list of the reasons given.

2. With the help of your teacher, select a business firm in your community that offers fringe benefits to its employees. From the owner, manager, or personnel director of that firm obtain information about the kinds of benefits provided for its employees. Write a report in which you show how the fringe benefits offered would influence your decision to work or not to work for that firm.

Chapter 6

Jobs, productivity, and level of living

PURPOSE OF THE CHAPTER

Most people would like an income that will satisfy their wants, and most people are disturbed when others cannot find a job to earn a decent income. In this chapter we shall study some of the difficult problems of providing jobs and giving all of us a satisfactory level of living.

You will find answers to these questions:

1. How do we attempt to provide jobs?
2. What is capital? How is capital created?
3. How do prices affect the level of living?
4. How does increased production help us?

A. Employment and unemployment

THE EMPLOYMENT PROBLEM

The civilian labor force. The *civilian labor force*, with certain exceptions, means all those who are willing and able to work and are

employed or are seeking employment. It includes self-employed persons, but does not include students while in school, unpaid family workers, those in the armed services, retired persons, or those not able to work because of physical or mental problems.

The *work force* is the term applied to persons actually employed, but does not include those unemployed.

Another term that is often used is *manpower* or *manpower resources.* It does not refer to the number of persons available in the labor force, but simply means the combined ability or capacity of labor and management to produce goods and services.

The unemployment problem. In any society there is a serious problem when people do not have work; they cannot buy goods and services, but they must live by some means—by public charity usually. Public charity is a burden on all other workers and taxpayers. Unemployment also leads to crime; therefore, it is important to everyone that unemployment be kept at a minimum.

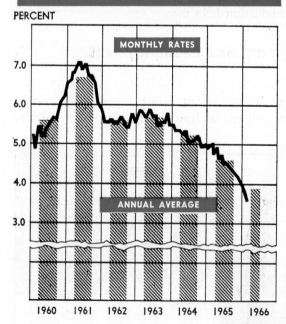

PERCENT OF THE CIVILIAN LABOR FORCE UNEMPLOYED

MONTHLY FIGURES SEASONALLY ADJUSTED

PERCENT

MONTHLY RATES

7.0

6.0

5.0

4.0

ANNUAL AVERAGE

3.0

1960   1961   1962   1963   1964   1965   1966

SOURCE: Bureau of Labor Statistics

Finance Facts, April, 1966.

Full employment. The ideal situation is *full employment*, which means full or maximum use of all productive resources, including labor. Usually, however, we tend to think of it as meaning labor. Even in periods of full employment there will be 2 to 4 percent of the civilian labor force who are not working. These are the workers who are changing jobs or who are in between jobs (labor turnover) plus new workers who have not yet found jobs.

The situation called *underemployment* means part-time work for those wanting full-time work or persons working on jobs that do not use their full abilities. For example, a carpenter working as a common laborer is underemployed. Underemployment is a part of the total problem of unemployment. For example, a person who is employed only 20 hours a week is partially unemployed. Any worker not earning enough to live on is underemployed.

Supply and demand determine unemployment. The unemployment problem is a matter of demand and supply of labor. There is not enough demand for the persons whose skills and knowledge are offered for employment. Demand does not always match supply, either as to numbers of workers or types of workers. For example, even in periods of great unemployment the newspaper advertisements in large cities may show considerable demand for certain types of skilled workers.

In almost all working situations—factories, offices, transportation, communication, farming—jobs have become more complicated because of new machines and processes. Many workers are needed with more education and skills. As machines replace common labor, it becomes increasingly difficult for workers without skills to obtain jobs.

One economic problem of unemployment is also a social problem. There is a higher degree of unemployment among some racial groups because of discrimination in hiring. Failure to obtain a job or to obtain wages comparable to those of others is not always because of a lack of education and skill.

General solutions to unemployment. There are two major points of view as to the general solution to the problem of unemployment:

(a) When employers cannot hire and use profitably the many workers available who lack skills and proper education, the solution is to educate these people and prepare them for the better jobs that are available.

(b) When there are not enough jobs available, the way to solve unemployment is to encourage the expansion of business through investment of savings in business enterprises, thus creating more jobs. If there are more jobs, there will be more demand for workers, even if they do not possess all the skills and education desired.

There is considerable merit in both points of view. It should be easy to see, however, that the persons with the least to offer in skill and education will understandably be the last to be hired and first to be unemployed.

Some proposed specific solutions to unemployment. Many different ways have been tried and are being tried to prevent or to eliminate unemployment. Some of these methods are:

Solutions directed primarily by business and individuals

1. Retraining by industry of workers displaced by machines so that these displaced workers can fill new jobs.
2. Apprentice training plans (learning while working) with the cooperation of labor unions and employers to develop skilled workmen for special trades such as carpenter, electrician, or machinist.
3. Creation of greater consumption (buying) through easy credit terms, greater advertising and sales effort, and development of new products.
4. Elimination of seasonal unemployment. To avoid seasonal unemployment, some employers have found new methods and new products to keep workers employed steadily. For example, a factory may produce and store goods in a period of low sales for use in a later period of higher sales.
5. New investment by individuals and companies in plant and equipment to increase production and create jobs. New investment depends upon the opportunity to make a profit.
6. Reduction of costs. In some cases wages and other operating costs have become so high that a producer could not make a profit. The only way for the firm to stay in business and provide jobs is to reduce costs. Producers sometimes move to a more favorable location, leaving workers without jobs. In some of these situations, labor and management have been able to reach an agreement on reduced wages and improvements in production so that operations can continue in the old location at a profit.

Solutions directed primarily by government

1. Provision of more and better technical and vocational education and keeping students in school until they are qualified to fill jobs in modern industry.

2. Provision of vocational training for school dropouts and other unemployed persons so that they have sufficient skill and education to fill the types of jobs available.

3. Reduction of interest rates through federal reserve bank policies to encourage borrowing and the expansion of business and to make it easier for persons to buy on credit.

4. Reduction of taxes to create more demand (spending) for and consumption of goods and services.

5. Stimulation of more savings and investments for the purchase of capital goods to create new jobs by expanding industry. Tax reduction is one method used.

6. Government spending, called *pump priming*, by borrowing and spending instead of increasing taxes. This method stimulates buying because the government spending causes new jobs to be created, even though temporary. The idea is to stimulate business so that it can then carry on without help. If taxes are increased to make government spending possible, however, taxpayers will have less money to spend.

7. Establishment of minimum wages. One purpose of the minimum-wage law is to help assure each worker enough income to live on. In some cases the worker is not helped by this law. It may have the opposite effect intended. If the employer cannot use labor profitably at the minimum wage, the worker will not be hired.

8. Unemployment insurance. The payment of unemployment insurance benefits (explained in Chapter 29) helps those who are unemployed until they can find jobs. Unemployed workers without money to spend cannot buy goods and services produced by other workers; therefore, if many workers are unemployed for any great length of time without money to spend, other workers will also lose their jobs because of a lack of demand for goods and services. The fact that employers must pay for unemployment insurance causes them to attempt to provide steady employment since their costs of insurance go up if their employees become unemployed.

9. Establishment of state and federal employment offices to help persons find jobs and to help employers find workers.
10. Government has attempted to solve some of the unemployment problems caused by discrimination in employment by civil rights laws prohibiting an employer from refusing to hire a person because of his race.
11. Control of immigration of workers and prohibiting temporary workers from coming in from such countries as Mexico, Japan, and Canada.

Technology and employment. The U. S. civilian work force (those actually working) averages about 74 million people. In the 1950's, the net growth in the labor force (new workers available and willing to work) averaged some 750,000 a year (newcomers less replacements for workers who died, retired, or otherwise left the labor force). The growth rate averaged 1,200,000 from 1960 to 1965, and it continues to increase because of the increasing birth rate in previous years.

What about the demand for manpower? Two economic factors are largely responsible for determining the number of workers required: (1) The demand for goods and services, and (2) the extent of our *technology* (the extent to which machines or laborsaving methods rather than manpower can be used to produce goods and services). As demand for goods and services has risen because of more workers and increased earnings, the number of people employed has risen; but progress in technology has caused some of the increase in demand to be met through increased productivity of workers already employed rather than through new workers.

These facts and figures do not tell the entire story. We often have unemployed workers and unfilled jobs at the same time and in the same place because workers do not have the skills and the knowledge required for the available jobs.

It is hard to measure the effect of technology on the total demand for manpower and to determine whether new technology creates more jobs than it eliminates. There is no argument that new technology is changing the types of manpower skills and knowledge required. The demand for agricultural skills, for example, has been both reduced and changed. New farm machinery and methods (plus the increase in the size of many farms) have steadily cut the proportion of our manpower required to produce our farm products. In manufacturing there are several other trends. In the 1920's new technology developed mass-production and assembly-line methods requiring unskilled and semiskilled workers who could learn the necessary skills while working on the assembly line.

The new production technology of recent years provides for automatic assembly (automation); it replaces many hand functions and reduces the need for semiskilled or unskilled workers. The shift from hand and machine production to automatic machine production is illustrated in employment and production figures. Total employment in manufacturing in 1964 was about equal to that in 1956, but production output was about 30 percent higher.

Technology is changing job opportunities and occupational trends. Blue-collar employment (production worker jobs) declined during the period of 1956 to 1964 by about 600,000 (5 percent), but employment in nonproduction, white-collar jobs (clerical, scientific and technical, sales and supervisory workers) increased by more than 600,000 (a 17 percent increase).

This shift in occupational requirements is apparent in the total of job opportunities. Since 1947, employment in white-collar occupations has increased by more than 50 percent, while that in blue-collar occupations has increased only about 10 percent. It is clear that demand for workers is increasing most in those occupations that require skill and preparation through longer periods of education and training, while the unskilled occupations that require only limited educational qualifications are decreasing or show little if any increase. The decline in need for manpower on the farm, for instance, has caused underemployment of farm workers and has caused a movement of farm workers to city areas. This movement because of lack of jobs is called *dislocation*. Many of those leaving farm areas are not trained for city employment.

The previous discussion of the labor force and the work force points up the necessity for constantly increasing investment in business to create new jobs so that new workers entering the labor force can find jobs, earn money, and consume the goods and services that are produced. The increased efficiency through better machines and methods will not help us unless people have jobs.

The changing nature of business through technology also points up the fact that workers must have better training, and often a new type of training, to fill new types of jobs.

Is the shorter workweek the answer? Some proposals have also been made to reduce the length of the workweek and spread the work among more workers, and, of course, at the same weekly pay as for the longer week. Without increased efficiency, such a plan raises the cost of production and raises prices for everyone if the practice is widespread.

It is argued that employers should be required to hire more people instead of working their regular employees overtime at a higher rate. If the workweek were shorter, the overtime rate would begin earlier and, therefore, the employer would find it cheaper to hire more workers than to pay overtime.

Solving unemployment is not that simple. A shorter workweek may not result in hiring more workers if workers with skills are not available and if work schedules cannot be arranged to fit the reduced workweek. It still may be cheaper to pay overtime than to hire new workers. If the result is higher prices of goods produced, everyone loses.

The need for better education and training of workers, plus the creation of job opportunities, seems to be the permanent basis for solving unemployment. Two situations emphasize this conclusion:

1. While there are workers unemployed in a community, there are unfilled jobs for which qualified workers cannot be found.
2. While there are unemployed workers in a community, there are workers holding two jobs. This practice is called *moonlighting*. In one community 15 percent of the workers in a major industry were found to be moonlighting. The average hours worked a week on the second job were 21. In May, 1963, the total number of workers in the United States holding two jobs was almost four million.

We shall now study the ways in which jobs are created.

B. National economic growth

CAPITAL AND JOBS

Capital is needed to create jobs. An economic goal of our society is to have jobs for all who want to work for wages or other income that will permit them to fulfill their wants for scarce goods and services. We have learned that we can raise our level of living by increasing our production and by increasing our efficiency of production so that each of us has more goods to share.

To create jobs, there must constantly be new capital provided. *Capital* means buildings and equipment such as machines used by workers to make goods. It is estimated that the average amount of

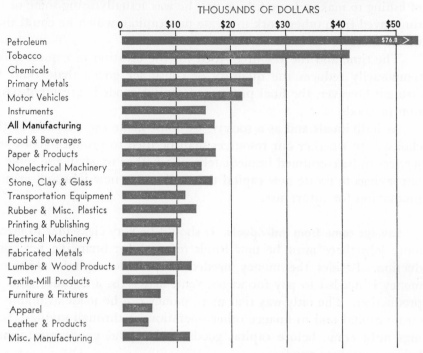

CAPITAL INVESTED PER EMPLOYEE IN MANUFACTURING
THOUSANDS OF DOLLARS

Petroleum — $76.8
Tobacco
Chemicals
Primary Metals
Motor Vehicles
Instruments
All Manufacturing
Food & Beverages
Paper & Products
Nonelectrical Machinery
Stone, Clay & Glass
Transportation Equipment
Rubber & Misc. Plastics
Printing & Publishing
Electrical Machinery
Fabricated Metals
Lumber & Wood Products
Textile-Mill Products
Furniture & Fixtures
Apparel
Leather & Products
Misc. Manufacturing

Adapted from *Road Maps of Industry*, National Industrial Conference Board, Inc., 1965.

new capital required to create a new job in industry is about $20,000. This capital investment per worker ranges from about $5,000 in some industries to $120,000 in others.

Another term used in business is *working capital*, which means money for day-to-day operations, such as wages, materials, and other expenses. Business needs working capital besides money that is invested in capital goods.

The function of capital goods. The function of capital is to assist labor in production. Capital goods make labor more efficient. These goods reduce the need for labor and make work easier. For example, the tractor and plow make farming easier and more productive. Machines and all types of power equipment in factories make work easier and more productive. More goods can be produced with less effort. The individual gains from capital, and we all gain from more efficient production.

In order to make these gains in the production of capital goods, we must save by temporarily giving up the use of some of our earnings.

For example, when a primitive man took time out from crude methods of fishing to make a large fishing net, he was actually using some of his time saved from other work to create new capital, which he could then use to increase his catch of fish.

The time and the resources used for the creation of capital goods temporarily reduces the quantity of consumer goods that could be created; however, the final purpose of capital goods is greater production of goods.

As individuals and as a society, we must make the decision or the choice as to whether our resources shall be used to produce goods and services to be consumed immediately, or whether we shall use some of our savings to create new capital that will create new jobs and greater production for future use.

Savings come from individuals. It should be very clear that to create more jobs there must be new funds (money) for financing new production. Besides the money needed to provide capital, additional money is needed to pay for wages, rent, materials, and other costs of production. The only way that more money can be made available to create capital and to finance other operations is through savings. Savings must come before capital goods, and capital goods must come before consumer goods.

In the final analysis, all savings that are available for the creation of new capital come from the savings of individuals. Even the profits of a corporation that are kept by the corporation for creating new capital really could have been paid out as dividends to stockholders. They are corporation earnings that have been saved. These savings retained by the corporation belong to the stockholders. The decision of the board of directors to keep some of the earnings for capital expansion is a sort of savings forced upon the stockholders.

People furnish money to business with which other resources needed in the business can be purchased. Even when banks lend money, this money belongs to the people—the investors in the bank and the depositors.

---

1. Savings and profits come before capital goods.
2. Capital goods come from savings.
3. Capital goods come before jobs.
4. Capital goods come before consumer goods.
5. Capital goods increase the ability to produce consumer goods.

Sources of new capital. Savings are used in two ways to create new capital. One way is to lend money to those who wish to create capital goods or for other business purposes. Savings available for loans to business are known as *loanable funds.* Interest is paid to those who lend money. The second way to use savings to create new capital is to invest in business. When one invests in a business, he takes a risk because he becomes one of the owners. He invests because he hopes to make a profit as a share in the successful operation of the business. Savings available to buy an interest in business are called *investment funds.*

The interest rates paid for the use of loanable funds are determined largely on the basis of supply and demand, just as in the case of goods and services. Sometimes funds are available for loans, but the owners of these funds will not use them for investment purposes. They feel that there is not sufficient chance for profit to take the risk of investing the funds and becoming the part owner of a business.

Even a single individual (which may be hard to understand) who owns a business by himself invests his money in the business, which is separate from him but is owned by him. Therefore, people or individuals in the final analysis provide the resources or the money needed to buy resources used by business. When we say business does something, we mean that it is the managers of the business who do it; and they do it with the resources furnished by others, including what the managers as individuals also furnish.

Taxes affect savings and new capital. Taxes have a great influence on savings; therefore, they have a great influence on the creation of new capital and the creation of new jobs for more people. Taxes reduce the amount of spendable income that people have and reduce the ability of people to save. Taxes also reduce the profits of corporations, leaving less profit to keep in the business for new capital or to divide with stockholders who could save or spend it. Taxes shift the use of savings from individuals to the use by government. Some taxes collected by government may be used for the creation of new capital, such as roads, bridges, and power dams.

1. Taxes reduce spendable income.
2. Taxes reduce ability of individuals to save.
3. Taxes reduce our ability to buy capital goods.
4. Taxes shift individual spending to government spending.

ECONOMIC GROWTH

Just as an individual or a business firm through proper records may determine the value of the economic goods and services it produced in a given year, so also may a nation determine the value of all of the goods and services produced by all of the people of the nation. The value of the goods and services produced is known as the *gross national product*, sometimes referred to as *national output*.

Meaning of economic growth. *Economic growth* is indicated by an increase in per capita (amount per person) output. An increase indicates economic progress or growth. In general this means an improvement in "economic conditions" for people and a rising standard of living. A decrease in per capita output may indicate that the economy is in a period of depression. Depression is explained in detail in Chapter 13.

In the United States there has usually been a good increase in per capita output of economic goods and services for each of several years. This increase has resulted in our standards of living rising to high levels. In many underdeveloped countries, the national output or production always has been low, and the increase per year, if any, is small. In these countries economic growth is taking place slowly or not at all, and the standard of living remains low.

Factors in economic growth. National economic growth is the result of the combined effect of many factors. Some of the factors may be controlled by government action; others are not subject to control. Hence national economic growth may be influenced only partially by the action of business firms, individuals, or government. Some of these factors will be discussed in this chapter and in later chapters.

Population. As population increases, the labor force also increases. It is estimated that the population of the United States will increase from an estimated 194 million in 1965 to approximately 235 million in 1975. Of the 42 million increase in population, an estimated 17 million will seek jobs. Thus an average of 1.7 million jobs for each of these ten years must be created through expansion of business and industry or unemployment will increase. The value of the goods and services produced each year by these additional people will increase the gross national product. If economic growth is to take place, the rate of increase in the gross national product per year must be greater than the increase in population.

THE COST OF ECONOMIC GROWTH

Economic growth does not just happen. It is not free. To get economic growth, other things of value and certain advantages must be given up. The growth may require sacrifices on the part of people. The benefits of economic growth must be considered in relation to the costs of obtaining growth at a desired rate.

Sacrifice of leisure. One way to increase the national per capita output or production is through making greater productive use of capital invested in facilities and equipment. This means that every worker would spend more hours per day in using the capital resources. Leisure time would have to be sacrificed for growth. The cost of increased economic growth is determined by the sacrifice of leisure. The price we pay for growth depends upon the value of the leisure time we forego in order to produce more.

Curtailment of consumption. One of the economic goals in America is to enable people to increase their consumption of goods and services thus raising their standard of living. But the more of our income we save for capital investment, the less of our income will be available for buying consumer goods. If nobody saved, there would be no funds to invest in capital. Hence, any increase in per capita output that is not the result of fuller use of existing capital resources comes from money that could be spent for consumption. A portion of the current income of individuals, business firms, and governments (through taxation) must be saved and invested.

Foregoing leisure and expenditures for current consumption are the two primary costs of economic growth. But these costs are only temporary, for the future benefits of economic growth that come from saving and investing in capital goods will enable people to increase again their leisure time and their consumption of consumer goods and services. The costs of economic growth are borne in the present, but the benefits come in the future.

C. Elements that determine the level of living

LEVEL OF LIVING

Most of us would like to buy more goods and to use more services than we are buying now. We would like for our money to go further. In other words, we would like to live on a higher economic level than we are at present. Our *level of living* is indicated by the quality of the home we live in, by the kind and to some extent the amount of food we use, by our ability to travel and to take vacations regularly, by the monthly accumulation of our insurance and investments, and by the other savings we are able to lay aside for a "rainy day." The level of living is much higher in some countries than in others; it is higher in some parts of this country than in other parts; and it is higher for some people within a community than for others in the same community.

The level of living consists of the goods and services that an individual or family regularly obtains. A *standard of living* is similar to a goal or a guide. Many of us set standards that we should like to attain. There really is no standard in the true sense of the word; but when we use this term, we usually are thinking of a certain degree of success in satisfying our needs and wants.

Our level of living depends not only upon the income we receive and upon our savings but also upon how wisely we spend our money in satisfying our wants. Other factors also affect our level of living. For example, if the supply of the goods you want is very limited, you may not be able to get what you want. Or, if prices in general are very high, your income may not be large enough to permit you to buy what you want. Our level of living is also influenced by inventions of such conveniences as automobiles, dishwashers, and power lawn mowers. Modern methods of manufacturing make many of these products available to us at a cost we can afford to pay. It is easily seen that how well our wants for goods and services are satisfied is dependent upon many factors.

We have some control over our income. In general, the harder one works or the better one serves in his job, the greater are his earnings. Of course, we have control over the spending of our income. Both our income and our expenditures affect our level of living.

Raising our level of living. Through our efforts and by our work we produce economic goods and services that people want and that they are willing to buy. The return we get for our work is in the form of wages and income. We use our income to obtain the things we need to maintain our level of living. Thus, our level of living is closely related to the work we do or, more accurately, to how much we produce individually. The main way we raise our level of living is by increasing our production—our output; hence, we earn more and can buy more.

If an employee receives a wage of $20 a day and gives service of equal value, he is helping to maintain the present level of living. But, if he receives a wage of $20 a day and produces less, he really is contributing to lowering our level of living. He may feel that temporarily he benefits from receiving more wages than he really earns, but in the long run the prices of the products he turns out or the service he gives will have to go up. Consequently, fewer people will be able to buy the goods and services they want and the level of living goes down.

If we want to raise our level of living, we must do it by increasing our individual production, which in turn will increase the total production of all people. This means that we must strive for the greatest efficiency. To do that we must have educated and skilled workers. We must take advantage of modern machinery, modern power, and modern science. It also means that we must not artificially restrict production except to avoid overproduction to the extent that there is more than can be consumed. These factors working together for greater efficiency and productivity result in making more goods that people want available at lower prices. This process helps raise our level of living.

Restriction of production may enable a producer to get a higher price for each unit of what he does produce. He may not increase his total income, however, because fewer people may be able to buy his product at the higher price. Restrictions on output or production, whether by labor or management, tend to lower the level of living for all people as a whole by forcing prices up.

Value of a dollar affects level of living. We are all acutely aware of the amount of our weekly or monthly earnings and of how much

The more we produce and the more efficiently we produce, the higher the level of living for all people.

Chrysler Corporation

we have saved. The amount of money we have saved or the amount we earn, however, is not so important as what it will buy. One's *wages* in dollars are indicated by the amount of his paycheck, but one's *real wages* are measured by the amount of goods and services his wages will buy. For example, if five years ago a dollar in wages would have bought six 24-ounce loaves of bread and now a dollar from your current wages will buy only four loaves, the purchasing power of the dollar for buying bread has decreased 33⅓ percent.

To illustrate further this economic principle, let us assume that Fred Smith was earning $50 a week ten years ago. By careful planning and economical living, he was able to save $10 a week. In the meantime, he gained experience and thus became a more valuable employee for which he was rewarded by a series of promotions and pay increases until now he receives $100 a week—twice the amount he received five years ago. During the ten-year period the rent on Fred's apartment has doubled, his clothes cost more, his food is more expensive, and everything Fred buys costs more. He is just as careful in spending as he was five years ago. Now, his living costs $85 a week for items comparable to those that cost $40 a week ten years ago. He is able to save $15 a week, but actually his financial situation is not as good as it was ten years ago. The $15 he saves now will buy only three fourths as much as the $10 he saved ten years ago would have bought at that time. In other words, the purchasing power of the dollar has decreased, and the decrease has actually resulted in a decrease in Fred's level of living.

Prices affect our real income. When the prices of goods and services generally increase, our dollars of income buy less; when prices decrease, our dollars buy more. Indirectly, then, the general price level affects our level of living.

Prices of goods and services wanted by consumers increased in general from 1940 to 1965. If all goods and services wanted by consumers are considered together, a dollar would buy 45 percent as much in 1965 as in 1940. This means that a person would have needed an income more than twice as large in 1965 as in 1940 in order to buy the same amount of goods and services.

Prices do not always go up, causing the purchasing power of the dollar to decrease. There are times when prices of goods and services go down. Under such conditions the purchasing power of the dollar increases; and as a result, one can maintain his level of living on less money than when prices were higher.

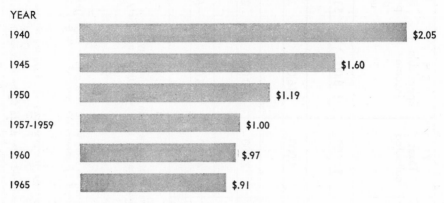

THE PURCHASING POWER OF THE CONSUMER'S DOLLAR
Based on the 1957-59 dollar

YEAR

1940	$2.05
1945	$1.60
1950	$1.19
1957-1959	$1.00
1960	$.97
1965	$.91

Source: Department of Labor.

PRODUCTION AND ITS DISTRIBUTION

We can do more to raise our level of living. In any way that it is measured, the United States is the richest nation in the world, and the average level of living is very high. Even with this wealth, we live under conditions of scarcity. We are still not producing or distributing enough goods and services for all families to enjoy a comfortable level of living. Almost every person has many unfulfilled wants. If our goal is for all people to dress well, to eat well, to live in a good home, to get a good education, to have good medical care, and to have their choices of many manufactured articles, we need much greater production of goods and services. We can increase production by greater efficiency and by using all available resources—labor, land, and machines.

Production solves the problem of scarcity. In order to understand some of the production problems of our nation, let us consider a very simple example. Let us assume that on a small island there are only three families. The Stern family makes shoes; the Jones family makes hats; and the Pulaski family makes hoes to cultivate the fields. Each family grows its own food and makes its own clothes. The only products that they buy and sell are shoes, hats, and hoes. The Stern family produces ten pairs of shoes a year; the Jones family produces five hats a year; and the Pulaski family produces five hoes a year. No one has enough of these three items. The old ones are always worn out before new ones are available. They trade among themselves. Two pairs of

PRODUCTIVITY AND REAL WAGES
(For simplicity all figures are assumed, not real)

1 Scarce units produced (Available to divide)	2 Total population	3 Units per person	4 Workers	5 Units per worker	6 Wages and other income earned	7 Taxes collected	8 Spendable income	9 Bid price per unit
(A) 2,400	1,200	2	1,000	2.4	$10,000	$2,000	$ 8,000	$3.33
(B) 4,800	1,200	4	1,000	4.8	20,000	4,000	16,000	3.33
(C) 4,800	1,200	4	1,000	4.8	12,000	2,000	10,000	2.08
(D) 2,400	1,200	2	1,000	2.4	20,000	4,000	16,000	6.67

(Numbers refer to the columns in table)

1. Assume that the 1,000 workers can produce this quantity, and it can be sold at the bid price that wage earners can and will pay.
2. The 200 nonwage earners (children and others who cannot work), get nothing unless individual wage earners share with them, or society (government) provides their needs through taxes.
3. These would be the shares if all units were divided equally among all people.
4. These would be the shares if only the workers with income divide the units equally.
5. The total persons contributing to production.
6. The assumption here is that all who contribute to production earn the same. Of course, they do not, so some would have greater shares than others.
7. Taxes taken out of earnings reduce the spendable income and divert earnings to purposes determined by government, some of which may be used to support nonwage earners.
8. The spendable income is what is left after taxes.
9. Assuming all spendable income is spent and that all scarce units are bid for and that all earn the same, the producers who have the income to spend would pay these unit prices.

Note that in B the production is doubled, income is also doubled. The price remains the same as compared with A. In C the increase in production is greater than in wages. Everyone gets more units, but the unit price is lower. In D the wages are increased, but production is not increased; therefore, the unit cost is higher because the persons with more spendable income have more money to bid up the prices of the scarce items.

shoes are traded for one hat or one hoe. One hat is traded for one hoe. If each family learns how to produce twice as much, each family will have twice as many items to trade and will have available for its own use twice as much as it formerly had.

The Jones family, the maker of hats, learns to produce more efficiently and is able to produce ten hats a year. Members of that family will share in production much better than the other families because it will have ten hats to trade for the hoes and shoes that are needed. However, there may be a point at which the wants for hats are satisfied. For example, the Jones family might find that if twenty hats a year are produced, the demand for them will be only fifteen, or it might even be necessary, for example, for them to trade two hats for one hoe.

Production must increase. We have a means of determining the effectiveness of our production. We calculate the total goods and services produced each year, and we call this the gross national product (or GNP). Because our population is increasing each year, our gross national product must increase each year or the citizens of the United States will have a lower level of living because there will be fewer goods and services to divide among the population. If we expect to have a higher level of living, the gross national product must increase faster than the population.

There is another way of measuring our productivity in relation to the gross national product. As the labor force grows (those available and willing to work), the gross national product must increase at the same rate just in order to maintain our same level of living. If we expect to have a higher level of living, the gross national product must grow faster than the labor force. The comparison of the labor force with the gross national product is a measure of our efficiency in production.

Productivity and wages. The problem of productivity of our resources is of great importance to all our leaders in government, and it is certainly important to every individual. Each of us has a selfish interest. We want to earn as much as we can, so that we can use our earnings to buy the things we want. From an individual point of view, increased earnings permit a higher level of living provided the prices of all goods and services remain the same. The only way that we can increase our level of living is to increase our efficiency in production and to increase our gross national product faster than the population. Wage increases, without similar increases in production, merely allow persons with increased wages to buy more compared with those who are not successful in obtaining increased wages.

If everyone has an increase in income, the prices of all goods and services will increase if the supply remains the same. When wages increase faster than production, those with money to spend bid for the scarce goods and services and cause prices to increase. This is the situation that we call *inflation*, which will be discussed in more detail in a later chapter.

The problem of distribution. While it is true that efficient production is the key to a high level of living for members of any society, we are still living in an economic society of scarcity. At least there is a scarcity of many items and services for many people. There are still many unfulfilled wants. From an individual point of view, the solution to this problem is to use one's resources to fulfill his wants. The productivity of the individual determines how well he will share in production. There are many who, because of a lack of education, poor health, old age, or location, do not have the resources or are not able to use their resources to provide a high level of living.

There are many factors that influence wages of individual workers at different times. But in the long run and for all workers, wages depend on the productivity of labor. Producers can pay only wages that are justified by the productivity of workers. Producers cannot continue to operate for any long period of time unless they can make reasonable profits. Therefore, they cannot pay wages that are higher than the productivity that will permit a profit.

Businesses compete for workers just as they compete for sales. Therefore, businesses bid for productive workers in competition with other businesses. The bidding for competent workers will cause wages to reach a level justified by the productivity of the workers.

Some types of workers (labor) are scarce. Since the supply is limited, they can demand high wages because of their education, experience, and special abilities. Some types of workers are plentiful and their productive ability is low because of lack of education, experience, and special skills. These workers are paid low wages because there are plenty of them to satisfy wants. If strong workers willing to do manual labor were limited (scarce), their wages would be higher.

American workers are the highest paid workers in the world. They are paid high wages because of their productivity. The productivity of American workers is high because of their superior education, their skill, their methods of working, the use of modern machines, and expert management. Under our American system, the workers, the managers, and those who have invested money to create the businesses share in production.

One of the great dangers in satisfying our selfish desire for a high income is that all of us may increase our money income, but we may not increase our real income. If prices and the cost of goods produced increase faster than wages, the wage earner loses; if wages and prices rise at the same rate, there is no gain in real wages; if wages rise faster than prices, there is a gain in real wages. Gain in real wages must come from increased efficiency in the productivity of labor.

Facts everyone should know about jobs and prosperity

1. The primary economic goals are to maintain a rising standard of living through full employment and a reasonable rate of growth.
2. Economic growth is measured by the increase in *per capita* gross national product for a given period of time.
3. Capital is comprised of savings of individuals, business firms, and government that are invested with the idea of producing something.
4. Economic growth is not free. Among the primary costs are the sacrificing of some leisure to provide more time to produce and the curtailment of consumption to increase savings for investment with the idea of producing something.
5. Economic growth creates jobs.
6. Greater production is the key to solving the problem of scarcity.
7. If we are to make gains in our level of living, production must increase faster than wages.
8. Productivity or efficiency in production comes from combining all resources so that there is more production per person and at a reduced cost.
9. Our share in production is measured by the goods and services that wages will buy.

▪ QUESTIONS ON THE TEXT

1. Define: (a) civilian labor force; (b) work force.
2. What is meant by full employment?
3. What is underemployment?
4. In what way can education help solve unemployment?
5. Give some examples of how business attempts to solve the unemployment problem.
6. Give some examples of how government attempts to prevent unemployment.
7. What is meant by technology in business?

8. Explain how technology in industry and agriculture have helped to improve our level of living.
9. What happens if workers receive the same pay for shorter workweeks?
10. Distinguish between capital and working capital.
11. Explain how savings are used by business to create new jobs.
12. Explain the two ways in which savings are used to create new capital.
13. How do taxes affect savings and the creation of new capital?
14. Explain briefly what is meant by gross national product.
15. When we speak of the cost of economic growth, what do we mean?
16. Distinguish between a standard of living and a level of living.
17. Do we all have the same standard of living? Why or why not?
18. Explain how our level of living is determined by efficient production.
19. What things must each individual do in order to raise his own and the nation's level of living?
20. How would slowing down or restricting production affect our level of living?
21. What is meant by real wages or real income?
22. What is meant by the purchasing power of the dollar and why does it vary?
23. Which is the more accurate measure of our level of living, real wages or money wages?
24. In this chapter on page 118, there is a table illustrating productivity and real wages. What happens to wage earners and consumers if the number of units of production remain the same but wages are doubled?
25. What is the basic way in which we can raise our level of living?
26. If you made one product that you could trade to someone else for a product that he makes, how could you obtain more of the other product?
27. For us to maintain our present level of living, why is it necessary for our gross national product to increase each year?
28. From the point of view of economics in a free society, what is the main factor in determining wages?

▪ QUESTIONS FOR DISCUSSION

1. Is a student ever included in the labor force?
2. Why is it impossible to have truly full employment?
3. Explain why education is becoming more and more important in the solution of our employment problem.
4. Give some examples that you have observed of the shortage of workers even when a considerable number of people are unemployed.
5. Give your views of the two general solutions mentioned on page 103 to the unemployment problem.
6. Give your explanation of how you think the system of government "pump priming" helps to create jobs.

7. Explain whether you feel the increased use of machines, or technology, in business is good or bad.

8. Many years ago some workers had a workweek of as much as 60 or 70 hours. A normal workweek now is 40 hours or less. From the point of view of your welfare and the welfare of everyone, what do you think of this trend and should it continue?

9. In many newspapers, magazines, and government reports there is a regular reference to the amount of new investment in capital equipment as an indication of our economic growth. Why do economists watch this trend carefully?

10. Explain the relationship between profits, savings, capital, and jobs.

11. Explain how taxes may affect both the creation of new capital and jobs.

12. If the population increases at the rate of 5 percent a year and the gross national product increases 2.5 percent a year, do we have a satisfactory economic growth? Explain your answer.

13. Under what circumstances may the temporary curtailment of consumption create an increase in later production?

14. (a) Are savings accumulated purchasing power?
    (b) How does the changing of the purchasing power of the dollar affect savings?

15. Explain why an increase in real prosperity cannot be measured in terms of wages.

16. One of the goals of almost every person is to have more income so he can live better economically, that is, so he can buy more of the goods and services he wants. (a) What does a person have to do in order to raise his level of living? (b) To what extent is every person responsible for his own level of economic living?

17. By referring to the table on productivity and real wages in this chapter, explain what happened that caused the price to remain at $3.33 in Example B.

18. Explain what can happen if everyone receives an increase in wages and there is no increase in efficiency or production.

19. There is always resistance to a minimum wage law. Explain any circumstances under which the minimum wage might hurt rather than help workers.

▪ PROBLEMS TO SOLVE

1. The Hastings Manufacturing Company borrowed $240,000 at 6 percent interest and spent all of it on tools and equipment with which to expand its production. As a result of this expansion, 10 new jobs were created.
   (a) What is the amount of capital used to create each of the new jobs?

(b) How much interest must be paid during the first year on the total investment in tools and equipment? How much must be paid on the investment for each new worker?

(c) Do you believe that this is the kind of expansion that the Hastings Manufacturing Company should expect to accomplish every two or three years? Why?

2. If the GNP (gross national product) was $570 billion and the population was 185 million one year, was there any economic growth five years later if the GNP was $650 billion and the population was 193 million? Explain your answer.

▪ COMMUNITY PROBLEMS AND PROJECTS

1. Assume that each of three men in Your Town took action that had something in common with what the other two men did. James Smallwood purchased a new pickup truck for use in his business. Henry Harlow deposited money in his savings account which the bank, in turn, loaned to a firm that was expanding its building. Lester Johnson paid taxes that were levied for the purpose of constructing a public library.

(a) What is the similarity that exists in the actions of Smallwood, Harlow, and Johnson?

(b) Prepare a list of 10 situations observable in your own community that illustrate further how people take action similar to that taken by the three men in this problem.

2. Study the classified advertising section of a newspaper in which job opportunities are listed. Analyze each of the statements about the jobs for which employees are being sought. Prepare a written report under the title, *Employment Opportunities.* Include in the report a list of the kinds or classifications of jobs that appear to be most readily available. End your report with two or more conclusions that you draw from this study.

3. Select a business in your community and interview the owner of it. Seek answers to such questions as: How much investment is needed to start such a business? How much money is needed to cover operating costs for one month? What emergency kinds of expenditures might arise? How much income can an individual expect from such a business each year? How long should one expect to have to operate such a business before it begins to return a profit?

Chapter 7

The organization
of business enterprise

PURPOSE OF THE CHAPTER

Business plays an important role in our lives. Business produces goods and services and provides job opportunities. Because of its great importance we need to know how it is organized.

You will find answers to these questions:

1. What is business?
2. What are the purposes of business?
3. What are the different types of business?
4. What are the legal types of organizations?
5. What is a monopoly?

A. Characteristics of business

WHAT BUSINESS IS

Organizations that produce and make available for us the economic goods and services that we want and need are known as *business*

organizations. From a consumer's point of view, *business* is any organized activity conducted either by a person or by an organization that in any way contributes to or assists in satisfying the wants and needs of people for economic goods and services.

One business may mine ores and minerals that are needed; another may make or produce goods such as hi-fi sets, corn flakes, or shoes; another may provide professional services such as those of your medical doctor and dentist; still another may offer repair and maintenance service on such items as home appliances and automobiles. Most business organizations provide only one or two of these economic goods that we want and need.

The purpose of owners and managers through business activity is to produce the goods and services that people want and need. The problem of business is to determine what the specific wants of people are and to determine what types or kinds of goods and services will fill those wants most satisfactorily.

Objective of business. The successful operation of any business is dependent upon how well its product or service really satisfies the needs and wants of people at a price they can and are willing to pay. Several business firms may attempt to satisfy a particular economic need. The products or services intended to meet that certain need probably vary from one business to another. Likewise the prices may vary. Any one of the business firms may offer goods and services that actually meet the economic need that people have, but the business that offers products and services that are the most pleasing and satisfactory to the consumer at the most reasonable price will be the most successful. Every business tries to please and to satisfy customers. It may be said, therefore, that the *objective of business* is to fulfill the needs and wants of people for economic goods and services in a manner that is the most pleasing and satisfactory to the consumers and at a price which they consider to be fair and reasonable.

Classes of business. Business firms may be grouped into four classes according to the kind of activity in which they engage. Each of these classes is highly important in producing the goods and services people need. The classes, which are intended to represent broad general categories of American business, are given on page 127.

Most business firms belong to only one of the four classes of businesses. However, some may engage in more than one class of activity. For example, a business may manufacture, sell, and service its product.

Classes of businesses by activity and approximate number of workers

1. Basic production—including such as farming, mining, fishing, and forestry. Approximately 7.5 million workers.
2. Processing—including such as manufacturing, construction, processing foods, oil refining, publishing, and printing. Approximately 20 million workers.
3. Distribution—including such as wholesale and retail trades, advertising, transportation, and some forms of communication and other public utility service. Approximately 15 million workers.
4. Service—including such as finance, insurance, real estate; professional services, as medicine and law; personal services, as beauty and barbershops; maintenance and repair; government service, local, state and federal; and amusement and sports. Approximately 18 million workers.

Some communities are essentially mining, some farming, and some manufacturing communities. Also, a community may be a trade center where the business firms engage principally in wholesaling and retailing.

IMPORTANT FACTS ABOUT BUSINESS

Business as a whole in the United States is highly complex. Certain general information and facts are essential to understanding how business is organized and operated.

Number of business establishments. The vast amount of business transacted daily requires the efforts of many business firms. Sometimes, the impression is gained that the business of the country is conducted by a relatively few business firms that are very large. Although we do have some business firms that employ thousands of people and are of tremendous size, the total amount of business transacted by small firms is also very great.

The number of business firms in operation fluctuates according to general business conditions and the prosperity of the people. Each month many new businesses are started and many are discontinued.

The life of business firms also varies widely. Only about three fourths are in operation a year after they started, about one fourth after five years, and one fifth after ten years.

People employed in business. In 1965 the estimated number of the civilian labor force was more than 70 million. Of this number about 66 million were employed in business and industry (not including agriculture).

Business size and growth. The table below shows the number of businesses. Each year new businesses are started, and others fail and cease operation. In 1964 there were 13,501 business failures.

As business expands, new jobs are created. In 1965 the cost of new plant and equipment for business amounted to $50 billion.

NUMBER OF BUSINESS ESTABLISHMENTS IN OPERATION IN 1962

(not including professional services)
(numbers in thousands)

Industry	Sole propri-etorships	Partner-ships	Corpora-tions
Agriculture, forestry, and fisheries	3,445	133	23
Mining	35	15	14
Construction	686	58	91
Manufacturing	180	43	183
Transportation, communication, etc. ...	284	17	53
Wholesale and retail trade	1,888	268	389
Finance, insurance, and real estate	473	229	359
Services	2,133	166	151
ALL INDUSTRIES	9,124	929	1,263

Source: Treasury Dept., Internal Revenue Service; *Statistics of Income, U. S. Business Tax Returns.*

Profits of business firms. In an earlier chapter, profit was stated to be the difference between the income received and the total cost, including taxes, of producing goods or services. It is not possible to determine how much profit is made collectively by the more than four million business organizations now in operation.

An example may serve to illustrate the rate of profit for a certain class of business firms. In a recent year, average profit after taxes per dollar of sales was 4.6 cents for all firms manufacturing durable goods, such as lumber products, furniture, stone and glass, steel, fabricated metals, and automobiles. The profit after taxes per dollar of sales varies among the types of businesses. Ordinarily the rate of profit is lower for those dealing with foods, textiles, and leather products than for those engaged in the manufacturing or processing of petroleum products or chemicals.

In general, the larger the size of the firm as indicated by the net assets, the greater the net profit on sales. From this it would seem that the larger the volume of business, the greater the chance of higher profit on sales, running from 1.4 percent of sales for smaller manufacturing companies to 7.0 percent for the largest.

B. Legal forms of business enterprise

LEGAL TYPES OF BUSINESS ORGANIZATIONS

The four principal types of business organizations are: (1) sole proprietorship, (2) partnership, (3) corporation, and (4) cooperative. The legal form of organization under which a business is organized automatically determines: (a) the laws to which the business will be subject, (b) the liability of the owners for debts of the business, (c) the specific taxes to which it will be subject, (d) the voice that each owner will have in management, and (e) the manner in which it may be financed.

Sole proprietorship. A *sole proprietorship* is sometimes called an *individual proprietorship* or an *individual enterprise.* Such an enterprise is one that is owned and managed by one person. That person is the only one who receives the profits. He is a *capitalist* because he owns the business and receives the profits (anyone who owns property from which he earns an income is a capitalist); he is a *laborer* because he performs some of the work and services. He may run the business in any way that he sees fit and make his own decisions provided that he follows the laws and regulations applicable to his business. The income that he receives from the business may be either very small or very great. It may be only a small payment for the time and effort he expends, or it may pay him well for his efforts, plus a good return on his investment.

The sole proprietorship is the oldest and the simplest form of business organization. It is the usual form of organization for small businesses. Very few large businesses are operated as sole proprietorships.

Characteristics of a sole proprietorship

1. Owner provides the money for investment in the business either from savings or by borrowing.
2. Owner manages.
3. Owner makes decisions of policy.
4. Owner usually works in the business.
5. Owner is responsible for acts of the business the same as an individual is responsible for what he does.
6. Owner is personally liable for all debts of the business.
7. Profit goes to the sole owner.

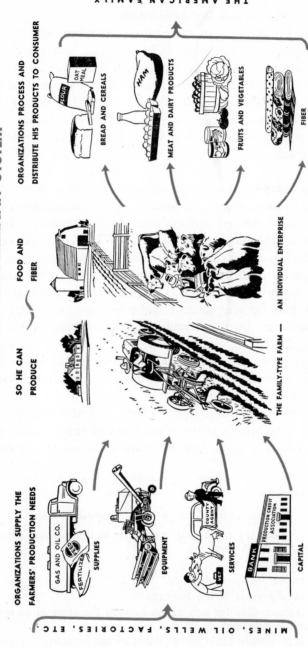

DIFFERENT KINDS OF BUSINESS ORGANIZATIONS
WORK TOGETHER IN THE AMERICAN SYSTEM

THE AMERICAN FAMILY

ORGANIZATIONS PROCESS AND
DISTRIBUTE HIS PRODUCTS TO CONSUMER

BREAD AND CEREALS

MEAT AND DAIRY PRODUCTS

FRUITS AND VEGETABLES

FIBER

FOOD AND
FIBER

SO HE CAN
PRODUCE

THE FAMILY-TYPE FARM — AN INDIVIDUAL ENTERPRISE

ORGANIZATIONS SUPPLY THE
FARMERS' PRODUCTION NEEDS

GAS AND OIL CO.

FERTILIZER

SUPPLIES

EQUIPMENT

COUNTY AGENT

SERVICES

BANK

PRODUCTION CREDIT ASSOCIATION

CAPITAL

MINES, OIL WELLS, FACTORIES, ETC.

American Institute of Cooperation and the National Education Association

The average farmer operates his farm as an individual enterprise. To do this successfully, he often cooperates with others to maintain an economic flow of goods and services to and products from his farm.

Partnership. A partnership is sometimes called a *copartnership*. It is formed, owned, and managed by two or more persons. Legally, a partnership is based upon an agreement which is really a contract.

Partners are subject to obtaining licenses or permits to do business the same as though they operated as individuals. Management usually is shared equally by the partners, although their investments in the business may not be equal. Profits may be divided among the partners in a predetermined ratio, or, if the partners wish, profits may be used to expand the business. In most states, each partner possesses *unlimited liability;* that is, each partner is liable for the total debts of the partnership regardless of the proportionate share that his investment may be of the total investment in the partnership. There are, however, special types of partnerships, referred to as *limited partnerships,* which permit a partner to participate without the usual liability for debts.

An advantage of a partnership is that it combines the talents, labor, experiences, and property of all partners, thus increasing the chance that each partner may earn a greater profit than he otherwise could earn alone. Another advantage of a partnership is that two or more people share in the management. Each may have special abilities, and these abilities may make the business more successful than one operated by one person.

Disadvantages of the partnership form of organization are the unlimited liability of each partner for the total debts of the partner-

---

Characteristics of a partnership

1. A partnership is based on a legal agreement or contract between the partners.
2. A partnership operates under state laws to protect both the partners and persons who do business with it.
3. Partners share equally in policy making and management.
4. Decisions are made by majority vote of partners.
5. Partners are joint owners and share in profits according to agreement.
6. Each partner is responsible for the things done or promised by any other partner in operating the business.
7. Each partner is legally liable for the total debt of the partnership regardless of his share in the investment.
8. A partnership is terminated automatically upon the death, retirement, or withdrawal of a partner.
9. Partnerships make it possible to combine the abilities of partners for better management.

ship, the limited financial resources, and the uncertain duration of the business due to the possibility of death, retirement, or withdrawal of a partner.

Corporation. An important form of business organization is the *corporation,* which is owned by *stockholders.* The ownership in a corporation is represented by *shares of stock.* Ownership of one or more shares of common stock in a corporation carries the privilege of sharing in selecting the members of the *board of directors,* who manage the corporation. The directors usually delegate much of the responsibility for the management of the business to *officers* and to career-management persons who are selected by the board of directors. The officers usually consist of the president, the treasurer, and the secretary. The chairman of the board of directors sometimes also serves as an active manager of the business.

A *charter* authorizing the formation and operation of a corporation is issued by the state in which the corporation is organized. It is common practice for a corporation to be authorized in one state but to extend its scope of activities to other states. A license to operate must be obtained to do business in states in addition to the one in which a corporation is chartered.

Besides the laws of the state and the privileges and limitations stated in the charter, there are other regulations that govern a corporation. The stockholders vote on and approve a set of *bylaws,* which

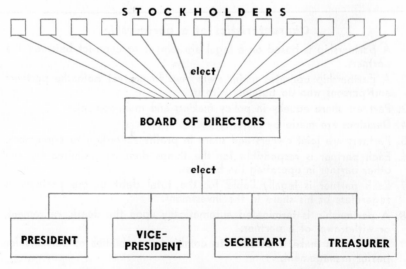

Chart of the organization of a corporation

The basic policy direction of a corporation is set by the board of directors who, in turn, usually delegate responsibility for the direct management of the business to officers selected by the board of directors.

Ewing Galloway

become additional regulations under which the board of directors, the officers, and the employees may operate the business.

Generally, a stockholders' meeting is held once a year at which time the directors are elected and major business of the corporation is voted upon (state laws provide that certain decisions must be made by stockholders). The law usually requires a corporation to send each stockholder, within a specified period in advance, a notice of the time and the place of the meeting. If the stockholder cannot attend the meeting personally, he may be represented by someone else. The written authority to allow someone else to represent a stockholder is called a *proxy*. Corporations normally mail proxy forms, with return envelopes, to stockholders along with their notices of the meeting.

Close corporation. A *close corporation* is one that does not offer its stock for public sale. All the ownership is frequently held by just a few stockholders, some of whom may be actively engaged in operating the business. A close corporation, under the laws of most states, does not need to make its investment activities known to the general public since its securities are not offered for general sale. It must, however, submit reports to stockholders and to the state from which it obtained its charter. A close corporation is also called a *closely held corporation.*

Open corporation. An *open corporation* is one that offers its stock for general sale to anyone who wishes to buy it. Stocks of open corporations may be listed and quoted for sale on organized *stock* *exchanges* or may be sold privately as unlisted securities by brokers and dealers. An open corporation is often called a *public corporation* or a *publicly held corporation.*

Large corporations, owned by thousands of individual stockholders, require many millions of dollars. It usually is impossible for a few individuals to provide personally the amount of money needed to start and to operate a large corporation. Therefore, banks and other dealers in securities take over the function of selling securities for a corporation. These securities may be in the form of common stock, preferred stock, bonds, or notes, which are discussed in detail in Chapter 25.

Advantages of the corporation. The corporate form of organization has several advantages. First, large amounts of capital may be obtained by issuing bonds and selling shares of stock, thus extending the possibilities for expansion and growth. Second, the duration or life of the organization is not affected by the death or withdrawal of an owner, that is, of a stockholder. The ownership of stock may be transferred to heirs at the death of a stockholder. Third, an owner may sell his share in the business without obtaining permission and without affecting the existence or the operation of the corporation. Fourth, the interests of both stockholders and the public are protected by state and federal laws and regulations. And, fifth, stockholders are not personally liable for the debts of a corporation, except in certain financial institutions in which a stockholder is liable for debts to the extent of an amount equal to the face value of the stock he owns.

The economic significance of the corporation is not to be overlooked. It has been primarily responsible for making mass production possible which, in turn, has resulted in "better things for better living." The American corporation has become the vehicle of expansion of the economic interests of the United States all over the world and is now fulfilling a leadership role in the area of scientific research and development.

The corporate form of business organization brings together capital for investment in gigantic factories.

North American Aviation

Disadvantages of the corporation. One of the major disadvantages of a large corporation is that management is often remote from ownership, except that stockholders do select the board of directors who in turn select officers and managers. Although stockholders have the right to vote, many do not attend stockholders' meetings and do not send proxies. Another disadvantage of the corporate form of organization is the limitations placed on its management and operation by laws and regulations of the various states in which it seeks to do business.

Characteristics of a corporation

1. The authority for the creation and operation of a corporation rests with the states.
2. The corporation operates within the provisions of its charter.
3. Management rests with officers who are appointed by a board of directors, which is the legal managerial body of a corporation.
4. Ownership is represented by shares of stock which are held by stockholders.
5. Stockholders elect the board of directors and vote on policy matters.
6. Profits may be paid to stockholders as dividends, or they may be reinvested in the business for expansion.
7. A stockholder has no personal liability for the debts of a corporation, except in the case of certain financial institutions.
8. Ownership of shares of stocks may be transferred without obtaining permission and without affecting the existence or operation of a corporation.
9. The corporate form of business organization is economically significant in the United States. It has been largely responsible for mass production which has made "better goods for better living."

Cooperative. A *cooperative* is a form of business organization in which individuals become members usually by depositing a nominal sum of money or by purchasing a share of stock. To be eligible for membership, ordinarily a person must be associated with or belong to the group of persons for whom the benefits of the cooperative are intended. For example, membership in a consumers' cooperative may be open to the employees of a certain manufacturing firm or to individuals who are actively engaged in farming. The purpose of a cooperative is to give members a financial advantage in buying the goods or services they want or in selling their products.

The charter of a cooperative specifies in what kinds of business activity it may engage and how its affairs may be conducted. An elected board of directors and officers manage the cooperative in

Rural electric cooperatives, like other business organizations, take pride in modern, functional headquarters buildings.

accordance with the provisions in the bylaws and charter. Each member ordinarily has one vote regardless of how many shares of stock he may own. The gain or margin (profit) from business operations is usually returned to the members of the cooperative at the end of the year and is called a *patronage dividend.*

Although the cooperative form of business organization is widely used in agricultural purchasing and marketing, it is also common in areas of business activity such as personal credit, housing, health protection, insurance, telephone and electricity lines, and newspapers. For example, the Associated Press is a world-wide news-gathering agency that serves member news publishers. Thousands of individually owned grocery stores, jewelry stores, drugstores, and other businesses unite and jointly form cooperatives which serve as their own wholesale houses. The credit union, which is the most common type of cooperative association, will be discussed in Chapters 17 and 24.

The advantage of the cooperative form of organization is the reduction of consumer costs for goods and services, since the association passes its gains on to the members. A disadvantage of the retail

Characteristics of a cooperative

1. The cooperative organization ordinarily is created by a state and operates under the provisions of a charter.
2. The management is by an elected board of directors and officers. Each member has one vote regardless of the number of shares he owns.
3. Capital is provided by sale of shares and by membership fees. Usually a fixed rate of return is set on shares.
4. Cooperatives operate on the principle that goods and services will be priced at cost to members; hence, there is no profit. An accumulation of funds resulting from operations is returned to members as patronage dividends.
5. Members are not liable for the debts of a cooperative.
6. Death or withdrawal of a member does not affect the operations of a cooperative. Usually shares are not transferable.

CONSUMER COOPERATIVES, BY TYPE OF ASSOCIATION

[Members in thousands; business in millions of dollars. Includes Alaska and Hawaii]

Type of association	1963		
	Associa-tions	Members	Business
Credit unions	21,380	14,583	6,171
Electric power cooperatives	890	4,749	696
Rural telephone cooperatives	209	432	40
Nonprofit voluntary prepayment health plans	(NA)	9,100	470
Community	(NA)	3,500	180
Employer-employee-union	(NA)	5,600	290
Housing	1,778	90	1,139
Farmer retail supply cooperatives	6,921	(NA)	2,704
Producers' goods	4,400+	(NA)	1,708
Petroleum products	2,782	(NA)	634
Meats and groceries	800	(NA)	55
Miscellaneous	4,600+	(NA)	308
Associations *principally* engaged in farm supply business	3,211	3,596	(NA)

NA Not available.

Source: Statistical Abstract of the United States, 1965.

cooperative is that, in order to benefit by the lower prices offered by the cooperative, a member must make his purchases from the goods the cooperative offers for sale. Many persons, however, like the freedom of wide selection afforded by shopping in many stores.

A common objection or criticism of retail cooperatives by owners and managers of competing business firms is that because a cooperative does not make a profit, most of them are exempt from paying federal income taxes.

PUBLIC UTILITIES

Such services as telephone, gas, water, electricity, and transportation are often provided by business firms that are known as *public utilities.* Some public utilities are owned by a government unit, such as a town, township, or city. These are said to be publicly owned. These companies usually are given the exclusive right to provide a service to the consumers of a certain geographical area. This right is granted to assure the utility company that no other company will be permitted to compete with it in providing the same kind of service to consumers in its territory. This protection is necessary because of the exceedingly high cost of laying water and gas mains and erecting electric and telephone lines.

The heavy investment in power stations by public utilities is protected by exclusive rights to provide service to a given geographic area.

The city, state, and in some instances the federal government have the power to give the public utility company the privilege to operate and to provide a particular service in the territory concerned. This privilege or right to operate is known as a *franchise*. In accepting a franchise, the public utility company assumes certain responsibilities and agrees to abide by certain regulations relative to its management, operation, and rates.

Most services of public utilities would be impossible for the consumer to provide for himself. Thus, public utilities are important in satisfying the wants and needs of consumers in modern life.

The provision of power, communication facilities, and transportation facilities to remote areas of the country has made it possible to build immense processing and manufacturing plants at or near the sources of raw materials. These plants have made it possible to utilize economically resources that otherwise could not have been used. Furthermore, in areas of the country where economic conditions were not conducive to a high level of living, the building of new industrial facilities has created jobs for labor, thus raising tremendously the economic level of the people in those areas. The facilities and services provided through public utilities are of great economic significance in the expansion and development of industrial America.

MONOPOLY

A *monopoly* exists in business when there is no competition. A lack of competition may permit a business to set its selling prices on products so high as to cause hardship to the buyer. In addition, the business may set its buying prices for materials and labor so low as to cause hardship to the supplier. In the early years of the twentieth century, monopolies provided the means of developing many natural resources and raised the level of living. Abuses of the noncompetitive position of monopolistic enterprises arose, for example, in the production and distribution of oil and other products. In 1915, Congress created the Federal Trade Commission to promote free and fair competition. Then followed a series of federal acts and rulings of the Supreme Court that curtailed the powers and activities of monopolies.

Though many public utilities are virtually monopolies because they are free from competition in their territories, the rates charged for their services are regulated and controlled by the city, the state, or the federal government. The rates are regulated to insure that consumers will receive the services at a fair and reasonable cost.

Facts that everyone should know about business organization and operation

1. More people are engaged in the manufacturing, construction, and processing of materials than in any other type of business activity.
2. More than 4½ million businesses are in operation. The typical business firm has small volume and employs only a few workers. Small business enterprises are important in our economy.
3. The life of the typical business firm is relatively short; only one of five survives ten years. Competition eliminates the less efficient.
4. Hourly wage rates are dependent upon knowledge, skill, experience, and productivity.
5. Approximately four of every ten persons are in the labor force, that is, they are employable by business.
6. The primary legal forms of business organization are sole proprietorship, partnership, corporation, and cooperative. Each form has distinct characteristics that must be thoroughly understood before starting a business enterprise, or investing in one.
7. Public utilities are the only real monopolies in the United States and they are controlled by government regulations for the protection of consumers.

▪ QUESTIONS ON THE TEXT

1. What do we mean by the term "business" in economics?
2. What is the objective of business?
3. Name and explain the four broad general classes of business according to their activities.
4. What is the relationship between the size of firm and the rate of profit on sales?
5. (a) Name the four principal legal forms of business organization.
   (b) In what respects does legal form affect the organization?
6. Name the primary characteristics of the sole proprietorship.
7. How are the profits of a partnership generally distributed?

8. What are the primary disadvantages of a partnership?
9. (a) What is the evidence of ownership of a corporation?
   (b) By whom is a corporation owned?
10. How is a corporation managed and operated?
11. How is a corporation authorized to do business?
12. (a) What is a close corporation?
    (b) What is an open corporation?
13. (a) What is the primary purpose of the cooperative form of business?
    (b) Who is eligible for membership in a cooperative?
    (c) What happens to the gain or margin from the operation of the cooperative?
14. (a) What objections to cooperatives do their members sometimes voice?
    (b) What objections do other businesses raise to the cooperative business form?
15. What are some of the business services that are usually organized as public utilities?
16. What is a franchise?
17. Why are monopolies regulated by government?

▪ QUESTIONS FOR DISCUSSION

1. If a business expects to be successful and make a profit, what is necessary?
2. Explain why there are so many business failures.
3. From the information in this chapter on profits of manufacturing companies, what is your conclusion as to the efficiency and success of a company based on profits and size?
4. If you were engaged in a business, indicate a possible (a) advantage of your having a partnership; (b) disadvantage of your having a partnership.
5. If you were trying to start a business and needed additional money to operate the business, give your reasons as to whether you think it would be easier to get someone to invest in the ownership of a partnership or a corporation.
6. What in your opinion are the advantages and disadvantages of a sole proprietorship?
7. Give your opinion as to why you think most large companies are organized as corporations.
8. Explain how a retail grocer could belong to a wholesale cooperative and how he would be affected.
9. Generally, cooperatives formed by consumers and farmers are not subject to the same taxes as other forms of business. There is considerable argument about this. Give your opinion on this subject.
10. Give your reasons as to why you feel monopolies should or should not be controlled by the government.

▪ PROBLEMS TO SOLVE

1. In your school or city library examine a copy of *The World Almanac and Book of Facts* for the current year to find the following facts: (a) the trend in business failures in the United States for the past five years, (b) trend of sales in retail stores by kinds of business for the two most recent years for which data are given, (c) trend in profits as a percent of sales before and after taxes for manufacturing corporations, (d) trend of hourly earnings of employees in the manufacturing industries for the two most recent years for which data are given, and (e) total number of employees and total number of production workers in all manufacturing industries combined.

   What general conclusions can be drawn from the facts you have found?

2. James Huneke and John Unger entered into a partnership for the purpose of building and equipping a dry cleaning and laundering establishment. Huneke invested $32,000 and Unger, $24,000. They agreed that each should draw a small monthly salary for his labor and that they would divide annual profits or losses on the basis of the ratios of their investments when the business was started.
   (a) At the end of the first year, their profit was $12,000. They used $5,000 to purchase additional equipment and divided the remainder. What was each partner's share?
   (b) In the second year, another cleaning establishment was started only one block away. As a result, Huneke and Unger suffered a loss of $3,500 for the year. What was each partner's share of that loss?

3. Assume that from your wages or salary you will have $100 a month to invest. After considering various types of investments, you decide that you want to invest in an active business firm; but, because of your plans for the immediate future, you will not be able to spend any time in managing or working in the business in which you invest. This eliminates the sole proprietorship, partnership, and cooperative forms of business. You, therefore, decide to invest in a corporation.

   How will you learn what corporation stock is available? To whom may you go to make the purchase? What procedure is followed in purchasing stock? Books in business law, pamphlets offered by investment companies, and financial pages of newspapers are possible sources of reference.

▪ COMMUNITY PROBLEMS AND PROJECTS

1. Interview one of the officers, preferably the president, of a consumer cooperative enterprise in your community. Prepare a report giving the nature of the cooperative enterprise, number of members, requirements for membership, how the cooperative is managed, the volume

of business and the savings for consumers during the past year, and the basis for distributing the savings to the members.

2. From your proper state official, a local bank, a lawyer, or some other source, obtain information as to the requirements in your state for organizing a corporation. Make a list of these requirements and procedures.

3. Make a list of the public utilities in your community, such as those providing water, gas, electricity, transportation, and telephone. Find out and report whether they are owned by individuals, partnerships, corporations, or the community, such as the city or any other public authority. If possible, find out how rates are established and regulated and report these facts.

4. Assume that the students in your class decide to start a sandwich shop across the street from the school; a new building and new equipment will be needed; the students in the class will invest as much as they can, but investment from other sources also will be needed.

   Study thoroughly each of the four main legal forms of business organization for this enterprise. List all advantages and disadvantages of each of the four. Reach a conclusion as to the legal form of organization you believe to be best adapted to this venture, and state your reasons.

5. Make a study of the business firms in your community, considering the following points for each: (a) how the business may be classified—basic production, processing, distribution, or service; (b) legal form of organization; (c) estimated number of employees; (d) number of years it has been in operation; (e) type of management, that is, by owners, employed managers, etc.; (f) nature of ownership—home owned, chain store, etc.

   If your town is small, include all business firms in the study; if your city is large, confine the study to the business firms in certain city blocks that are designated by your teacher.

   What general conclusions can be drawn about the general characteristics of business in your community?

Chapter 8

The role of government in our economic system

PURPOSE OF THE CHAPTER

Government plays an important role in our economic system. Although the role of government is treated in several other chapters, this chapter discusses the broad nature of government controls and services.

You will find answers to these questions:

1. Who pays for government services?
2. Who controls government services?
3. What services are for the common good?
4. What special groups receive special services?

A. The growth and nature of government's role

GROWTH OF GOVERNMENT SERVICES

When the federal government was established in 1776, its functions were limited primarily to the enactment of laws for the common good

of all people, protection of the individual rights of every person, maintenance of security through control of foreign affairs and national defense, control of interstate commerce, and coinage of money and establishment of its value. As the population increased and business activity grew, the demand increased on the part of relatively small groups of citizens for the government to provide special services for groups of people. Some groups wanted government financial aid; others wanted regulations to govern competitive practices; and some, other government services. Today both the federal government and the various state governments offer a wide range of services, some of which are for the benefit of all people and others primarily for the benefit of small groups of the population.

Who pays for government services? Some people assume that services provided by government are free because they do not specifically pay a certain amount of cash when they use a government service. But, are these services free? No, the cost of services provided must be paid from public income, which is comprised primarily of taxes paid by both business firms and individuals.

The more service we obtain at public expense, the higher the cost of government services; and the higher the cost of government services, the more taxes we pay. When we consider buying an article for personal use, we ask ourselves whether we need it and whether our budget can stand it. However, when we request our legislators to vote for another service or for a new building or bridge, do we consider the question of whether we and other consumers are willing and able to pay for it by paying higher taxes? Some elected legislators promote certain ideas, not because they have been requested to do so, but because of an attempt to get votes. This decision of buying government services faces the consumer directly when he votes on federal, state, and local tax issues.

Who controls government services? As citizens in a representative form of government, we have the privilege of participating in making the regulations and rules by which we are governed. We participate intelligently in government when we vote for the legislators whose points of view about government we know and approve.

Our interest is to see not only that our government provides services for the general good of people but also that the government does not provide services and special benefits that are nonessential. Once a

An essential government service such as Federal Aviation Agency's Air Route Traffic Control is provided through payment of taxes for the general good of the people.

Federal Aviation Agency

government service is provided at public expense, all consumers help pay for it through taxes and often through higher prices even though many of them may not need or want the service.

What are the issues? The majority of people believe that government should produce only those services that are not or cannot be provided by individuals and private enterprise. Illustrative of the services that are not usually provided by individuals and private enterprises are national defense, police and fire protection, conservation of natural resources, general hospitals, public health, education, and institutions for unfortunate people.

Those persons who lean strongly toward socialism, however, believe government should assume the responsibility for providing as many services and for producing as many commodities as possible. Under this plan, they assume that prices to consumers will be lower than under free enterprise. It is obvious that as more business is taken over by government, there is less opportunity for people to start private businesses and fewer businesses to pay taxes.

The issue of socialism centers on the extent to which the production and distribution of the goods and services we want and need should be taken away from private business and be provided by government.

The broad issues relate to the amount of freedom we want instead of controls, the amount of services and help we want instead of self-help, whether we want to decide how to spend our money or instead to let the government take it from us in taxes and decide for us how to spend it. Since we live in a democracy, we have the power to decide these issues for ourselves.

GOVERNMENT PERFORMS MANY SERVICES

If you were the only person who lived in the United States, you would be entirely independent; your work, your actions, and even your thoughts would not affect anyone else. At the same time you would be wholly dependent upon yourself. You would have to protect yourself. You could turn to no one for help, nor could you exchange commodities with others. No need would exist for laws or regulations. Likewise, there would be no need for government services.

Dependence upon government. In a society people help each other. They cooperate in making and doing things that would be difficult or impossible to accomplish alone. Under a system of specialization or division of labor, people become dependent upon one another and upon government to supply the services and the goods they want. The more complex the problems of working and living together, the greater is the need for government.

Government serves citizens in many ways. In addition to giving protection, government also renders other services needed by its citizens, such as are shown in the table on page 147.

Services for special groups. While all government services are intended to serve society in general, some groups of citizens benefit directly from certain services and others only indirectly. Old-age assistance, medicare, unemployment insurance, and price supports for eggs and cotton are examples of services or benefits to special groups of citizens. In some instances we have a moral obligation to take care of special groups of people, such as old people and people who for some legitimate reason do not have an income. As will be explained later in the chapter, aids by government to special groups of producers, like farmers, may be for the general economic welfare of the nation.

Services for the public. Some of the services provided by government are not necessarily for individuals but are provided for all of the people collectively. Inspection of food-processing plants to insure clean and wholesome food is an example of services for the good of all people. The use of many government services by consumers is voluntary; however, a few services, such as provisions for social security, are compulsory for those persons to whom the laws are applicable.

GOVERNMENT ENGAGES IN BUSINESS

Ordinarily we think of commodities and services as being produced under competitive conditions by individuals and by private enterprises

Services by local, state, and federal governments

1. Police, fire, military, and coast-guard service.
2. Legal title records.
3. Health and sanitation.
4. Garbage collection and sewage disposal.
5. Inspection of goods: weights, standards, quality.
6. Schools, universities, and research laboratories.
7. Legislative and executive services.
8. Postal service.
9. Transportation service.
10. Courts, prisons, and jails.
11. Welfare and relief agencies.
12. Mental hospitals and institutions for care of handicapped.
13. Water, electric, and gas systems.
14. Street lighting and cleaning.
15. Maintenance of streets, sidewalks, highways, bridges, and waterways.
16. Parks and recreational activities.
17. Civic museums, auditoriums, and libraries.
18. Harbor and terminal facilities.
19. Unemployment insurance and old-age pensions.
20. Inspection of building construction.
21. Licensing and regulating for consumer protection.
22. Forestry and reclamation service.
23. Employment service.
24. Price supports and subsidies.
25. Bank deposit insurance.
26. Information and consultation services.

for profit. Upon examination, however, we find that many services and some commodities are produced by the government without profit and under noncompetitive conditions. Whether consumers actually pay less through taxes for a service provided without profit by the government than they would pay for the same service provided by a private enterprise that makes a profit is an unsettled question.

In some instances private business is unable to finance the development of projects, such as the St. Lawrence Seaway or the International Bank. Thus, the development, ownership, and operation of some businesses and facilities is feasible only by the government. In other cases the cost of operation makes private ownership impossible. The United States Postal Service is an example of a highly valuable service that operates at a loss which is paid for out of taxes.

Our federal government develops and operates electric power sources and provides for flood control, irrigation, and land reclamation.

U.S. Department of the Interior, Bureau of Reclamation

The government has sometimes become a producer in order that, through research and experimentation, a new product may be developed and made available to consumers. Aluminum, synthetic rubber, and synthetic gasoline are products that the government has helped to develop experimentally and to produce at least in the initial stages. In many cases private business has later bought these businesses from the government.

B. Specific aids and controls

GOVERNMENT AIDS TO BUSINESS AND AGRICULTURE

Government aids to and controls of business and agriculture are too numerous to permit discussion of all of them. Therefore, illustrations of only the major types of government aid will be given.

Aids to management. One type of service to business is the gathering, compiling, and distributing of statistics and information relative to payrolls, wages, prices, volume of production, finance, costs, and many similar aspects of businesses. These data are collected by such agencies as the Department of Commerce, the Bureau of Labor Statistics, and the Federal Reserve Board. Similar aids, such as marketing and research services of the United States Department of Agriculture, are provided for the management of agricultural production and marketing.

Protective aids to business and agriculture. The Bureau of Standards gives an invaluable service to business by testing materials and establishing standards. Many divisions of the Department of Interior and

The Weather Bureau of the U.S. Department of Commerce provides valuable service. Here a geophysicist is plotting earthquake data.

ESSA Photograph

the Department of Agriculture primarily serve producers. Additional aids to business are navigation services on rivers or lakes, weather reports, financial services through the Federal Reserve Bank, and protection of honest businessmen from dishonest competitors.

Government aids for industrial development. Following World War II, the Reconstruction Finance Corporation loaned millions of dollars to railroads, banks, insurance companies, and manufacturing companies when loans from other sources would have been almost impossible to obtain. During World War II many industries that engaged in war production were *subsidized* (financially helped) by the federal government. In some cases the government has built steamships and leased them to private owners at a price at which the owner could afford to operate them. This is a form of *subsidy*. The first synthetic rubber plants were financed by the government and operated by private industry. The rubber was urgently needed; and since private industry could not produce it at a profit, the federal government assisted. Airlines and steamship companies have in some cases been subsidized in the form of very liberal compensation for carrying mail. The aids to business paid by the federal government are often overlooked or taken for granted. The foregoing examples are only a few.

Subsidies to agriculture. The aid of the government to some phases of business is more direct and more concrete than that of providing statistical information and determining standards. For example, in an effort to guarantee a substantial income to the producer of such commodities as potatoes, eggs, butter, and cotton, the government may regulate the prices of these commodities by buying and storing or

149

otherwise disposing of sufficiently large quantities of the products to keep prices at a level satisfactory to the producer. Without government control, if potatoes or eggs are plentiful, the market price drops; consequently the consumer is able to buy at a relatively low price; however, the return to the producer is also low. Under government control of prices, the market price is maintained at a relatively high level, from which the producers of the commodity benefit by realizing a better income.

Price supports and limitations on production. The theory of subsidizing business and agriculture is that this aid is needed for the general economic welfare of the nation. For example, it is held that the safety and welfare of the whole country is benefited by protecting the farmer. However, the consumer pays for help to industry and agriculture. He pays taxes that are used for subsidies. He may pay twice— a higher price that is caused by government support of prices and taxes used by government to support prices.

When a product or service is subsidized, the consumer supports that subsidy through both higher prices and higher taxes.

In other instances, the federal government regulates the amount of a product produced or grown, as the case may be. Regulation of the number of acres of wheat planted is a typical example. By reducing the amount of wheat grown, the market price of that product is forced up by the demand for it. Consequently, the wheat farmer may have a return as great by planting 85 percent of his land in wheat as he would have had without government regulation if he planted 100 percent of his land in wheat. In order to induce the wheat farmer not to plant too much wheat, the federal government may make a direct payment to him for reducing the amount of wheat he grows. These payments are based upon the estimated net income that might have been earned if the unused acres had been planted and the crop had grown.

Price supports and subsidies for special groups of producers, whether farmers or manufacturers or distributors, are of vital interest to consumers. They are beneficial to consumers in that some of the products and services would not be available if the producers were not protected by price supports or did not benefit from subsidies. They are not beneficial to consumers if some groups of producers through political pressure are successful in obtaining the benefits of price supports or subsidies even though their products could be produced and distributed satisfactorily without government aid. A situation of this kind results in unfairness to the producers of other products for whom government aid is equally justifiable, but who do not obtain government aid. These producers help pay for the subsidies and other aids given to the business firms that receive them.

The issues of particular interest to consumers are many. Shall the producers of some kinds of products and services be subsidized or

---

Government aids to business and agriculture that affect consumer prices and taxes

1. Provides owners and managers with statistics and other facts valuable in management.
2. Protects business by offering testing services and by helping to establish commodity standards.
3. Subsidizes the producers of certain products to enable them financially to continue in operation.
4. Protects business from unfair competition and unethical practices of competitors.
5. Subsidizes and otherwise aids businesses in the development of new types of industries.
6. Controls or limits production of certain products to avoid producing a surplus and to hold prices at a particular level.

---

protected and other producers not? Shall the volume of production of some products be controlled or limited to reduce supply and thus hold prices at a certain level for those products but not for others? Is the practice of subsidizing the producers of certain products and the limiting of production of other products to keep prices up in accord with the basic principle of competition in free enterprise?

GOVERNMENT REGULATION OF BUSINESS

Laws that regulate business are designed to protect honest businessmen from unscrupulous competitors, to protect the consumer from

---

Why government regulations of business activities and practices are imposed

1. To curb monopolistic tendencies; to regulate and control prices, rates, and services of enterprises that can operate effectively only as monopolies; and to prevent practices in restraint of trade.
2. To control quality of products and services, primarily in protection of consumers.
3. To regulate prices on products and services and to prevent unfair trade practices as protection for consumers.
4. To protect business owners and managers from unfair methods of competition and unfair trade practices.
5. To protect investors by controlling the practices of financial institutions in issuing stocks, bonds, and other securities.
6. To control public utilities, which usually are monopolistic in nature, especially as to rates, services, and managerial policies.
7. To guard some aspects of the economy, such as prices of specific commodities, by curbing other aspects, such as production of these commodities.
8. To promote safety, health, and good working conditions.

---

bad business practices among competitors, and to protect the consumer directly from dishonest businessmen. Some of these laws are designed to prevent monopolies that control prices and supply, fraud through the mail, adulterated and misbranded food, false and deceptive advertising practices, unsatisfactory working conditions, fraud in selling securities, and many other undesirable conditions which will be discussed in more detail in later chapters.

Although businessmen generally regard government regulation of business as interference, they recognize that certain regulations are

The Bureau of Standards gives invaluable service to business by testing materials and establishing standards.

National Bureau of Standards

necessary and desirable. The primary concern of the businessman is that only the regulations that are absolutely necessary shall be authorized, that these regulations shall be reasonable, and that they shall be administered in a fair manner.

In previous chapters you have learned something about the economic functions of government. In later chapters you will learn more about how government aids and controls economic activities through laws relating to labor, taxes, competition, credit, money, banking, insurance, securities, prices, agriculture, natural resources, transportation, education, safety, health, and almost all aspects of our economic life.

Facts everyone should know about how government regulates business

1. Control of entry into business by requiring licenses, permits, and certificates.
2. Government ownership and operation of businesses that are difficult to finance through private sources or where business will not venture because of the enormity of the undertaking.
3. Periodic and special investigations of business practices by the officials of government agencies.
4. Detailed and summary reports of business transactions revealing business practices.
5. Control of prices and rates.
6. Regulation of advertising and selling practices.
7. Control of business activity indirectly through taxation.
8. Regulation of interest rates and credit.
9. Regulation of employer-employee relations—hours, wages, safety, and health—through labor legislation.
10. Regulation of the amount of production of industries dealing with natural resources, such as oil, coal, metals, and wood.

▪ QUESTIONS ON THE TEXT

1. Why over the years has the government increased the services it provides?
2. How are government services paid for?
3. As citizens, what are our two responsibilities regarding government provision of goods and services?
4. How may increases in services provided by the government affect the opportunities for private business?
5. What are the broad issues as to whether functions should be performed by private enterprise or government?

6. Name some groups which receive special benefits from government.
7. (a) Does the government make a profit on the goods and services that it provides?
   (b) Can it provide goods and services at less expense to the consumer than could private business?
8. Give illustrations of services and products provided by government that probably would never be provided by private business.
9. How has government aided business and agriculture?
10. Explain how consumers pay twice for price-support programs.
11. When is a price support or subsidy not justifiable?
12. Do businessmen believe that all government regulations are bad?

▪ QUESTIONS FOR DISCUSSION

1. Explain how a constantly heavier financial burden falls on taxpayers as economic functions are taken over by the government.
2. How have the responsibilities and activities of the government changed since the federal government was first established?
3. What would be the arguments against a plan for education in which public funds would not be used for education and parents would use the taxes thus saved to provide education for their children?
4. If the federal government should increase materially the kinds and extent of the services it now offers to consumers, what might be the effect upon business firms that produce services and commodities for profit?
5. What additional government services and aids for special groups or for all citizens are currently being requested from the federal government?
6. Since postal rates for the different classes of mail do not provide for sufficient income to pay for the costs of operating the postal services, the federal government must bear the remainder of the cost.
   (a) What are the arguments against eliminating postal charges entirely and permitting all mail to be carried free of charge?
   (b) What are the arguments against raising charges to cover the entire cost of this service?
7. What are some of the arguments for and against government subsidy or protection for producers of certain products and services?
8. Give some examples of government regulation of business activities from which consumers may benefit.

▪ PROBLEMS TO SOLVE

1. Prepare a report on the topic "The Evils Against Which Government Regulation Is Directed."

2. Prepare a report on how specific government agencies regulate business and the methods used to enforce such regulations.

3. Prepare a wall chart or poster (similar in design to the illustration below) showing on the one hand the specific demands of certain economic groups (e.g., farmers, bankers, railroaders, labor groups, war veterans, consumers, small businessmen) for government regulations and on the other hand the government regulations enacted to meet these demands.

GOVERNMENT REGULATIONS

Demands of economic groups	Government legislation
1. Farmers: Fair income from farm produce; protection against crop failure	1. Price parity; crop loans; acreage allotment and restriction
2.	2.

4. Using a reference such as the *World Almanac and Book of Facts* or the *Information Please Almanac,* which probably will be found in your school library, determine:

   (a) What was the per capita income for the average person in your state for the latest year for which such data are available? For the average person in the United States? For the average person in the region in which you live?

   (b) What has been the trend in income per capita in your state for the past five years? For the United States?

   (c) Compare the receipts and expenditures of the United States government for each of the last 20 years, showing the deficit or surplus for each year, and the total surplus or deficit for the 20-year period.

▪ COMMUNITY PROBLEMS AND PROJECTS

1. Make a study of your community to determine the extent to which services are provided by local government and federal government.

2. From local government officials obtain information pertaining to the city's income and expenditures. From this information prepare pie charts showing both the dollar amounts and percentage amounts for each category of income and expenditure. Compare these categories with the income and expenditure categories for the federal government.

3. From local government officials and from any other sources available to you, prepare a list of the buildings, bridges, roads, and other public works in your community that were paid for, at least in part, from federal funds. Also give on the list the names of the local, state, and federal agencies that cooperated in the construction of the project and the amounts each contributed.

Chapter 9

National income and its distribution

PURPOSE OF THE CHAPTER

Each person who contributes to the production of economic goods and services receives a share of the national income. The purpose of this chapter is to show how national income is divided among people and why some receive more than others.

You will find the answers to these questions:

1. What does gross national product include?
2. What is national income?
3. What entitles a person to a share in national income?
4. What affects the share of total income received by each of the following: (a) labor and managers, (b) lenders of money, (c) owners of land or other natural resources, (d) owners of business, and (e) government?
5. Why do some persons receive more income than others?

A. Gross national product and national income

THE NATIONAL ECONOMY

We think of economics as being concerned with how man satisfies his needs and wants for economic goods and services. We may approach the study of economics in two ways. One approach is to study production, distribution, and consumption from the standpoint of the individual or family, the business firm, or an industry. In such study we are concerned with economic problems affecting individuals and business firms, such as supply and demand, prices, savings, profits, and investments in capital.

Another approach to economics is to study economic and business activities for the nation as a whole as they affect all citizens as a group and all business firms as a group. This approach deals with the *national economy* in total rather than personal or business firm economy. It is concerned primarily with production, income, distribution, and consumption for the nation as a whole. This chapter deals primarily with the national economy.

WHAT IS GROSS NATIONAL PRODUCT?

Gross national product, sometimes referred to as GNP, is the total current market value of all final goods and services produced in the nation as a whole during a given year. By *final goods* is meant a product or a service as it is when sold to its final purchaser. If the goods and services that are produced are to be used, they must be bought and paid for by those persons who will use them. These goods and services are purchased by consumers, government, business investors, and foreigners (export minus imports).

Who uses the product? The Office of Business Economics, U. S. Department of Commerce, compiles the statistics from which the GNP is determined. These statistics are drawn from many sources, and they include all business activities. The users or purchasers of the products and services produced fall into four groups:

1. *Individual consumers.* This group uses two kinds of goods. One kind is known as *durable goods*, including items such as automobiles, household appliances, and furniture. The other kind is known as *nondurable goods*, including items such as food, clothing, and gasoline and oil for our automobiles. Individual consumers also buy many services. These include items such as rents, private education, medical care, legal advice,

GROSS NATIONAL PRODUCT

BILLIONS OF DOLLARS

SEASONALLY ADJUSTED, ANNUAL RATE

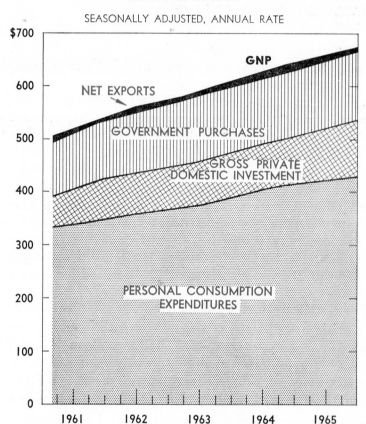

Source: *Business Outlook Charts,* National Industrial Conference Board, Inc., New York, New York, 1965, for 1961-64, and *Survey of Current Business,* March, 1966, for 1965.

shampoos, and transportation. The amount of services used by individual consumers is almost equal to the amount of non-durable goods they purchase.

2. *Business investors.* Business investors buy products such as new homes, factories, shopping centers, and public utilities. This group also buys factory machinery, tools, and equipment that are used in the production of other goods and services. Some of the purchases of this group are in the form of raw materials, semifinished and finished goods to be used in manufacturing, and inventories in wholesale and retail business firms. The level of purchases for business investments is an indication of the level of growth of our economy.

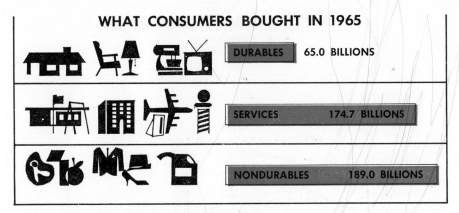

WHAT CONSUMERS BOUGHT IN 1965

DURABLES | 65.0 BILLIONS

SERVICES | 174.7 BILLIONS

NONDURABLES | 189.0 BILLIONS

Source: Survey of Current Business, March, 1966.

3. *Government.* Local, state, and federal governments purchase a wide variety of goods and services. The items included in government purchases range from items such as tanks and guns and equipment for national defense, public buildings, roads, and dams to items such as pensions for veterans, health services, education, and welfare.

Total state and local government purchases of goods and ⸱services are approximately the same in amount as the total purchases of the federal government. Approximately one fifth of the total goods and services produced in a year are used by local, state, and federal governments. Government purchases are a highly important factor in determining business conditions.

4. *Foreign purchasers.* The people and business firms of other countries buy many of our products, and we buy many of theirs. The goods we sell to other countries are called *exports*; and the goods we buy from them are *imports*. The difference in dollars between the total exports and our total imports represents our net exports, and it increases our GNP. If the value of our total imports exceeded the value of our total exports, the net difference would decrease our GNP. The importance of foreign trade in our economy will be discussed in Chapter 16.

The chart on final purchasers or users of gross national product in 1965 indicates that of the $676.3 billion of goods and services produced, local, state, and federal governments used $134.8 billion, and people as consumers used $428.7 billion. Changes in the purchase and use of the total products and services by consumers, business investors,

GOVERNMENT PURCHASES OF GOODS & SERVICES

BILLIONS OF DOLLARS
SEASONALLY ADJUSTED, ANNUAL RATE

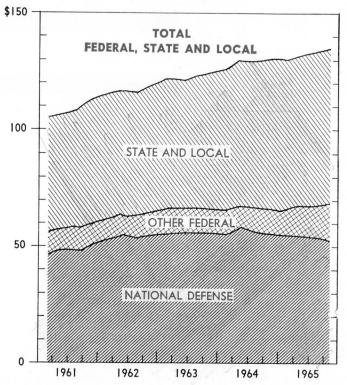

Source: *Business Outlook Charts,* National Industrial Conference Board, 1965, for 1961-64, and *Survey of Current Business,* March, 1966, for 1965.

governments, and foreign interests may indicate changes in business conditions in general.

The gross national product, we have noted, is the total market value of the final goods and services for any given period, usually a year. To those who buy these goods and services, the amount they spend is a cost or expenditure; to those who receive a payment for goods or services, the amount received is income. Now, let us learn more about income and who receives it.

WHAT IS NATIONAL INCOME?

A business firm can readily calculate its income for a given period by finding the total market value of the goods it has produced or its

FINAL PURCHASERS OR USERS OF GROSS NATIONAL PRODUCT

(1965 GNP=676.3 BILLIONS)

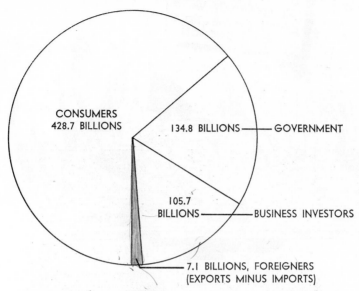

Source: "National Income and Product Table, Revised Basis," *Survey of Current Business,* March, 1966.

total sales. The income for the nation as a whole is calculated in a similar manner. The *national income* for a given period of time, usually a year, is the total income received by all who contributed to the production of goods and services. National income arises only from productive effort. This means that national income excludes such items of income as your weekly allowance if you do not work to earn it, interest received on government bonds, and pensions.

The national income of the United States for 1965 was $554.7 billion. This is the total amount earned by all individuals, such as laborers and managers, owners of plant and equipment, lenders of money, and owners who originate ideas and assume the risks of business.

The main problems in which we are interested in this chapter are: (a) who earned the income and (b) what percent of the total national income was earned by each class or group of individuals who had a part in the production of goods and services?

WHO EARNS A SHARE IN NATIONAL INCOME?

In industry the results of production are divided among those who represent the factors involved in the production of goods and services.

The economic problems: (1) Who earned a share in national income? and (2) What portion of the total national income should each group of contributors to production receive?

These factors, usually classified as natural resources, labor, capital, management, and government, were discussed in Chapter 3. The results of productive effort are divided into classes or categories known as rents, wages, interest, profit, and taxes. These are various forms of income. Rents go to the owners of land or other natural resources; wages go to the workers; interest goes to lenders of money; profits go to the owners of business or industrial enterprises; and taxes go to the government.

One may earn income by contributing to more than one of the essential aspects of production of goods and services. For instance, Mr. Hunt, the owner of a garage, has a house that he rents. In this way he earns rent. He has some money in a savings bank and gets interest on it. In this way, he earns interest. From the business that he operates, he probably draws a weekly or monthly salary. In this way he earns wages. Since he owns the business, he earns profits, if there are any after all the expenses of operating the business have been paid. If he owns some stock in a corporation, he shares also in the profits of that business.

B. Distribution of income among producers

An illustration of distribution of income. Studying the income and the expenses of a business provides a concrete picture of the ways in which those who represent the various factors of production share in the income from production. The Whirlaway Manufacturing Company, a corporation, was organized to produce electric fans. The stockholders, through their board of directors, hired a manager to operate the business. The manager rented a building and land. He borrowed money from a bank in order to buy equipment and to help pay the expenses that would be incurred in manufacturing and in selling. He also hired people to do the work in the factory and in the office, and to sell the goods.

At the end of the first year, the manager prepared the statement on page 164 for the stockholders to show the income and expenses. From the data on the statement one can readily determine how those who have contributed in some way to the production of electric fans have been rewarded by receiving earnings.

This statement briefly illustrates that rent, wages, interest, profits, and taxes claim rights to the income of the Whirlaway Manufacturing Company. After all other deductions have been made, the balance of the income, or net profit, goes to the stockholders, who own the business. If there is nothing left after the other items have been deducted, the owners do not get any share of the income. If there is a loss, the owners are the ones who lose.

RENT—INCOME EARNED BY LANDOWNERS

In an economic sense, *land* includes all natural resources. Thus, it includes farms, urban building sites, minerals, forests, and water because all are natural resources. In many instances, land has man-made improvements, such as buildings, permanent equipment, or dams. These improvements increase the usefulness of the land and hence its value.

In the ordinary use of the term, *rent* is the contract price received from a tenant for the temporary use of land including buildings and other improvements. In a more restricted sense, *economic rent* is that portion of income that is due solely to the land without buildings and other improvements. The more productive the land is, the greater the economic rent. In the usual sense, however, we speak of rent as income earned for the use of land and the buildings and other improvements on it.

WHIRLAWAY MANUFACTURING COMPANY
INCOME AND EXPENSE STATEMENT FOR THE YEAR 19—

Income from sales	945,000	00		
Cost of merchandise sold	340,000	00		
Gross profit			605,000	00
Rent of land and buildings [1]	14,600	00		
Wages of clerks and factory workers [2] ..	310,000	00		
Interest on borrowed money [3]	7,400	00		
Salary of manager [2]	18,000	00		
Taxes [4]	115,000	00		
Other expenses (supplies, insurance, etc.) [5]	45,000	00		
Total expenses			510,000	00
Net profit (to owners) [6]			95,000	00

[1] Earnings of landlords for use of land and buildings.
[2] Earnings of employees (labor and managers) for services.
[3] Earnings of lenders of money.
[4] Income to government for protection and services.
[5] Income and earnings to suppliers of materials and services.
[6] Earnings to owners who originate ideas and assume risks.

Statement showing the sharing in the fruits of production

What regulates the rent of land? Rent depends upon the usefulness, the productivity, and the desirability of the property. For example, a piece of land that will produce fifty bushels of wheat per acre is theoretically worth at least twice as much as land that will produce only twenty-five bushels per acre. Richness of the soil, mineral deposits, and location with regard to water or transportation facilities are a few of the many factors that have a bearing on the value of land.

The law of supply and demand applies to land just as it does to wages and interest. If an individual has land available for rent, he can obtain a rent only in proportion to the productivity of the land measured in comparison with that of competing land.

Rent and prices. Only a slight relationship exists between the rent that a producer pays for the use of the land in production and the price that he charges for his product.

Merchants sometimes advertise that, because their rent is lower, they can sell merchandise at a lower price than other merchants. Their statements are sometimes, but not always, true. Other factors, such as the quantity of merchandise that can be sold, affect the price at which the merchandise can be sold.

The merchant in a good shopping center of a large city pays a high rent, but he has many times as many customers as the merchant

Rent of land depends upon its productivity.

in an outlying district. He probably sells his goods faster and therefore needs less borrowed capital to finance his purchases. The person in an outlying community or a small town has fewer customers and sells his goods more slowly. His rate of profit is not any higher, and frequently is lower, than that of the city merchant.

WAGES—INCOME EARNED BY LABOR

Wages constitute that part of the income from production which belongs to those who perform either mental or physical labor. Wages are the prices paid for the labor and management factors. The price of labor in terms of money is the value of labor.

The price of labor is determined in the same manner as the price of any other economic good or service. Supply of and demand for labor are the primary factors that influence wage rates. The supply consists of the working force that is available at a given time. The demand consists of the needs of employers for workers. The principle of supply and demand of labor applies to an occupation as well as to all occupations collectively. For example, except when there are wage controls, the relative supply of shipping clerks seeking employment and the demand for shipping clerks determine the wages they receive.

The supply of labor. The *supply of labor* is indicated by the number of workers who are seeking employment in each kind of work at each of the wage rates offered in the occupation. If the wage rate for an occupation is low, it is usually because there is a large supply of workers (such as unskilled). When wages are high, it is usually because the supply of labor for those jobs is limited or scarce (such as skilled). Workers compete for the better jobs, and employers compete for workers when labor is scarce. Competition for employment and for wages is just as active among workers as it is for sales among business firms.

The fact that there are many occupations for which a large number of persons can qualify affects the supply of labor. The attractiveness and the working conditions of certain occupations also affect the supply. Many persons prefer clerical occupations, even at low wages, because they like the working conditions in such occupations better than those in occupations requiring manual labor. The desire to live in certain sections of the country or in a city affects the supply of labor. Many other factors, such as minimum age at which employment may begin, economic condition of older workers who may wish to retire, amount and cost of training, and the policies of organized labor, influence the supply of labor.

The demand for labor. The demand for labor reflects the demand for the products of labor. If, for any reason, the demand for a product or a service declines or disappears, the demand for the labor that produces that product or service will likewise decline or disappear. The worker will therefore become unemployed unless he is able to shift to a new type of work. The development of a demand for a new product or service may result in abnormally high wages for the comparatively few workers able to produce the product or provide the service. Wages will tend to decrease, however, as more persons prepare to perform the type of work that is rewarded so highly.

Factors affecting supply of and demand for labor. Wage rates, above the minimum required by law, are determined by demand and supply; but many conditions may affect either factor. Demand may fall off because of lack of consumer purchasing power. Supply, too, may be affected in many ways. One common method of regulating supply is through the unionization of workers and the closed shop. Unions often attempt to maintain in a given business a *closed shop,* which means that only members of the labor unions representing the occupations in that business may be employed by the management. Thus, nonmember workers are prevented from being employed. Other factors that may affect demand and supply are the substitution of other types of labor and the substitution of machines.

Wage differences. Why does one worker get $12 a day and another get $20 a day? Why are those who do some of the more disagreeable work of the world rather poorly paid?

Education and training are two of the most important factors causing wage differences. Natural ability is another. The supply of people who can handle the low-paying positions is greater than the supply of those who can handle the better positions. If a certain kind of work demands more training and knowledge than another, an employer is willing to pay more for someone to do this work. Essentially, however, the wages in each group are determined according to the supply of labor in that group. The supply of labor becomes smaller as the training and knowledge required for the job become greater.

From the accompanying table on income, it can be seen that there is a very close relationship between the number of years of school completed and the money income or wage an individual receives. Fewer than 2 individuals in 100 who completed less than 8 years of school have an income of $10,000 or more; however, almost 34 in 100 having completed 5 or more years of college have incomes of $10,000 or more.

Legislation affecting the wages of labor. The Fair Labor Standards Act, commonly known as the Federal Wage-Hour Law, which was passed by Congress in 1938, regulates wages and hours of work. The original act applies to employees engaged in or producing goods for interstate commerce (that is, goods produced in one state and sold or used in another state), including any closely related process or occupation directly essential to the production. In 1961 the act was amended, broadening its coverage to include employees in enterprises engaged in commerce or in the production of goods for commerce. The provisions of the act are applicable generally to business enterprises according to the dollar volume of business they do annually. The act as amended in 1961, 1963, and 1966, includes the following:

1. Minimum wage rate of $1.25 an hour.*†
2. Normal number of hours a week designated as 40.*
3. Overtime pay at one and one-half the hourly rate for the number of hours per week over 40 hours. Saturday, Sunday, or holiday work as such does not require overtime pay.*
4. Minimum age for employment of minors: 16 years for most jobs; 18 years for work designated by the Secretary of Labor as work in a hazardous occupation; between 14 and 15 years for a limited number of jobs, such as office and sales work for a limited number of hours and times of day; and under 14 years, no employment is permitted.*

---

* 1961 amendment to Fair Labor Standards Act of 1938.
† 1966 amendment increases rate to $1.40, February 1967; $1.60, February 1968.

PERSONAL INCOME BY YEARS OF EDUCATION COMPLETED

(Percent of Male Individuals 14 Years Old or Over in Each Group)

[Education data as of March 1962. Includes Alaska and Hawaii. Based on approximately 25,000 sample households of the current population; see source.]

TOTAL MONEY INCOME	Total	Elementary School		High School		College			Median School Years Completed
		Less than 8 years [1]	8 years	1 to 3 years	4 years	1 to 3 years	4 years	5 years or more	
Under $1,000	15.8	27.0	16.5	22.8	7.6	14.1	3.5	5.3	9.3
$1,000 to $1,999	11.3	21.5	14.4	9.2	7.9	8.5	4.6	3.8	8.8
$2,000 to $2,999	9.9	15.2	12.5	9.0	9.2	7.0	3.2	3.9	9.5
$3,000 to $3,999	10.6	10.9	13.4	10.3	11.9	8.7	5.0	5.4	10.8
$4,000 to $4,999	11.2	9.4	13.8	12.7	12.6	8.3	8.6	4.6	11.1
$5,000 to $5,999	12.2	7.2	11.3	12.8	15.5	13.8	12.4	9.2	12.1
$6,000 to $6,999	8.9	3.7	7.4	9.3	12.5	9.3	9.7	11.1	12.2
$7,000 to $9,999	12.5	3.6	8.4	10.2	16.2	17.5	25.7	23.0	12.5
$10,000 and over	7.5	1.6	2.6	3.6	6.7	12.7	27.2	33.7	14.5
Percent	100.0	100.0	100.0	100.0	100.0	100.0	100.0	100.0	
Thousands of Individuals	61,098	11,453	9,875	13,277	14,821	5,812	3,491	2,369	11.1
Thousands with Income	55,839	10,230	8,571	11,280	14,360	5,602	3,457	2,339	11.4
Median Income	$4,189	$2,090	$3,452	$3,865	$5,052	$5,246	$7,261	$7,691	

Source: Dept. of Commerce, Bureau of the Census; Current Population Reports, Series P-60, No. 39.

[1] Includes persons reporting no years of school completed.

Inasmuch as the supply of highly trained workers is often limited, these workers command high wages.

United Aircraft Corporation

5. Wage discrimination is prohibited on the basis of sex in establishments having employees subject to the minimum wage requirements of the Fair Labor Standards Act.*

Exemptions from some or all of the foregoing requirements are provided for employees in certain occupations and industries. The minimum wage provision is applicable at the rate of $1.25 for a 40-hour week even though an employee is paid by salary, piecework, or by any other method. Learners, apprentices, messengers, handicapped workers, and full-time students employed outside of school hours, under certain circumstances, may be paid special lower rates.

In general the Fair Labor Standards Act and its amendments apply equally to men and women, to homeworkers as well as factory and office workers, and generally regardless of the number of employees of an employer. The Fair Labor Standards Act is enforced by the U. S. Department of Labor. Many states have their own wage or hour rates to supplement the federal regulations.

The Walsh-Healey Act and the Bacon-Davis Act supplement the Wage-Hour Law by regulating the minimum wages that may be paid by a producer under contract to the federal government.

INTEREST—INCOME EARNED BY LENDERS

The amount paid for the use of borrowed funds is *interest*. Another concept of interest is that it is that portion of national income attributable to the use of capital, not including land. Usually, interest in considered payment for the use of money borrowed.

The *interest rate* is the price that one must pay in order to obtain the use of money. The rate is quoted as a percentage or so many dollars for every one hundred dollars borrowed. For example, an interest rate of six percent per year means that the price of borrowing $100 for one year is $6. The rate of interest is established by supply and demand in the same way that wages are determined by

---

* The Equal Pay Act of 1963, which amends the Fair Labor Standards Act of 1938.

supply and demand. However, government agencies, such as the Federal Reserve Board and the United States Treasury, also influence interest rates as described in Chapter 11.

Suppose that Mr. Jacobs, the owner of a department store, needs to borrow $5,000 to buy a stock of goods for the season. He goes to an individual or a bank and inquires about the rate that is being charged on loans made at that time. If the rate quoted him seems too high, he may go to another individual or bank. Frequently the rate of interest asked by one bank may be the same as that asked by another in the same community. In some cases, however, one bank may have more money on hand to lend than another, and may therefore be willing to take a lower rate of interest in order to make the loan. When large loans are being negotiated, the bargaining for rates of interest is frequently prolonged and carefully considered on a competitive basis.

When banks have available plenty of money for which there is no immediate need, they are usually anxious to lend it; and when few business firms wish to borrow money, there is a lack of demand for money loans in relation to the available supply. As a result, the rates on loans are low. When, on the other hand, banks have already lent most of their funds and there is an active demand for loans, the rates are high.

The simple laws of supply and demand, however, do not work exactly as described because of governmental controls and psychological factors. When profits and the prospects of profits are good, borrowers are willing to pay higher rates of interest if necessary, and banks are willing to lend money because they can charge good rates and because they are reasonably sure that the borrowers will have the ability to repay the loans.

Why is interest paid? If money is to be borrowed for business purposes, the amount that can be paid for its use is determined by the amount of profit that can be made from business operations. If interest rates are high, businessmen are less likely to borrow, but they will borrow if there is a sufficient chance for a profit. The borrower's willingness is dependent upon the intensity of his needs and upon alternatives open to him. For example, a restaurant owner estimated that the installation of new fixtures would increase his gross profits by $90 monthly. Yet, the interest costs on the money which he would need to borrow to pay for the fixtures would cost him $100 monthly. Therefore, he decided to postpone installation of new fixtures until interest rates declined.

Risk in lending money. The person who lends money takes a risk that the borrower may not be able to repay the loan when it becomes due. If a person lends money and it is not repaid, he suffers a loss. A person who lends money is entitled to a reasonable return for the services performed by his money and also as compensation for the risk that he is taking. If the risk is great, the rate will be high; if the risk is low, the rate will be low.

PROFIT—INCOME EARNED BY OWNERS

Profit is a portion of the income earned by owners; it is the remaining portion of income after all expenses have been paid and all claims of those who have contributed to production have been met.

Rent is paid to the owner of the land, buildings, and equipment that have been leased; wages, to laborers and employed management; interest, to the one from whom funds have been borrowed; and taxes, to local, state, and federal governments. Anything left over out of income after these claims have been paid is the property of the owner. It is his profit. If the income in a given period is not large enough to pay the claims of rent, wages, interest, taxes, and other expenses, the loss must come out of previously accumulated surplus or must be paid by the owners.

The economist and the accountant do not compute profit the same way. *Pure profit,* as computed by the economist, is the income remaining after all expenses have been deducted, including economic rent for the use of land owned by the business firm and interest for the use of capital goods, that is, equipment and buildings also owned by the business. *Net profit,* as computed by the accountant, is the income remaining after paying all expenses that require money to satisfy. These expenses do not include economic rent for land and interest on capital investment owned by the business, as no money is required to satisfy them, but they do include depreciation which is a loss in value of property due to use and age.

In order to induce men to invest in a business and to devote their time and energy to its management and operation, the business must have the possibility of profit after allowances are made for a normal return on the investment and for the wages of management.

Competition and profits. On the average, the profits of a business are limited to a fair return on the investment and a reasonable compensation for risk. Sooner or later competition retards the increase in profits. New competition always tends to develop when someone makes a success of a business.

If one businessman has a secret that will enable him to operate at a profit that is greater than the profits of competitors, he has an important advantage. If his competitors learn the secret and become as skillful as he, he will lose his advantage.

Owners' right to profits. A business must build up a surplus to take care of times when there may be no profits. In order to build a surplus, a reasonably high rate of profit must be earned when business is good. If a firm has no surplus, adverse times may cause the firm to fail. Building a surplus out of profits from income will enable the businessman to assume the risks involved in ownership and management.

If state and federal governments demand taxes that make accumulation of profits impossible or if labor demands wages that take too great a portion of the employer's income, a business may be forced to discontinue operations. This, of course, would mean not only a loss of the goods or services it produces but also the disappearance of jobs for labor. In a competitive economy not only the right of business to make a profit but also the actual making of profit over a period of time is imperative.

Many people who work for wages or a salary think that the man who owns or manages a business has an easy life and that his profits are far greater than they rightfully should be. In 1963, an average profit on net worth of 5.5 percent was made by 3,831 leading corporations. The fact is overlooked that the owner often works long hours in

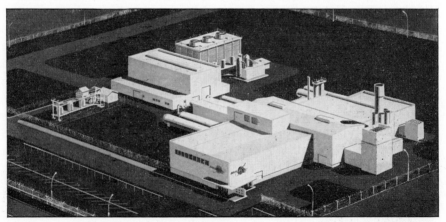

Douglas Aircraft Company

Owners of productive plant and equipment must have an opportunity to make a profit.

his place of business and sometimes takes work home with him. He risks not only his money but also his health. He is planning ahead while the employed person may be resting or enjoying recreation. He must often meet difficult competition. He searches continuously for ideas that will make his business more profitable. He must be resourceful and creative. These are some of the reasons why many men are willing to be employees and let their employers do the creating, planning, and worrying.

TAXES—CLAIM OF GOVERNMENT ON INCOME

Every business benefits in many ways from services provided by local, state, and federal governments. The costs of these services are met by taxes. Furthermore, the general welfare of the people as a whole is promoted by government through developmental and research activities and public works. Governments, in turn, claim a portion of the income or earnings of individuals and of business firms.

It will be recalled that the motive of business is to make a profit and that profits are necessary in order to provide new capital for replacement, growth, and expansion. Hence, there is a close relationship between profits and taxes. If taxes become large enough to absorb

DISTRIBUTION OF 554.7 BILLIONS OF NATIONAL INCOME IN 1965

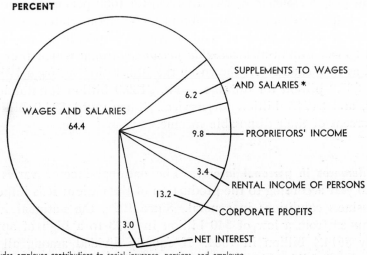

PERCENT

WAGES AND SALARIES
64.4

6.2 — SUPPLEMENTS TO WAGES AND SALARIES *

9.8 ———— PROPRIETORS' INCOME

3.4 — RENTAL INCOME OF PERSONS

13.2 — CORPORATE PROFITS

3.0 — NET INTEREST

* Includes employer contributions to social insurance, pensions, and employee welfare funds

Source: U. S. Department of Commerce, Office of Business Economics, *Survey of Current Business*, March, 1966.

most or all of the income of business after other expenses are paid, there will be no growth or expansion, hence no new jobs; and, unless a profit is earned in at least some of the years, a business will not be able to withstand losses in poor years.

PERSONAL INCOME

A person's share in national income. As individuals we are interested not only in the total income for the nation but also in the portion of national income that we receive. *Personal income* may be defined as the annual income received by persons from all sources. It includes amounts received by individuals such as wages and salaries from employers, proprietor's income from his business or farm, dividends from corporations, rental income from properties leased, and interest from savings accounts and bonds. Personal income does not include that portion of an employee's pay which the employer and employee pay to government for items such as social security and unemployment insurance. Neither does personal income include a transfer of money for which no current goods or services are produced. For example, a retired person may receive a business or government pension. These are known as transfer payments.

How people use their income. In 1965, the total personal income was $530.7 billion. From this amount personal, local, state, and federal taxes of $65.4 billion were paid, leaving the people of the United States $465.3 billion as *disposable personal income* which they could spend as they choose. As shown by the illustration on page 175, they spent $65.0 billion for durable goods, $189.0 billion for nondurable goods, and $174.7 billion for services. They saved $24.9 billion or 5.4 percent of their disposable income.

Differences in personal income. The national income varies from year to year according to the production of the nation; it is influenced by business conditions in general. Since 1929, the national income has ranged from a low of $40 billion in 1933 to a high of approximately $514.4 billion in 1964. If equally divided among all men, women, and children in the United States, this would have given each an income of approximately $2,633 (before taxes) for the year or about $50 a week ($2,633 ÷ 52 weeks).

PERSONAL INCOME
Billions of Dollars
Seasonally Adjusted, Annual Rate

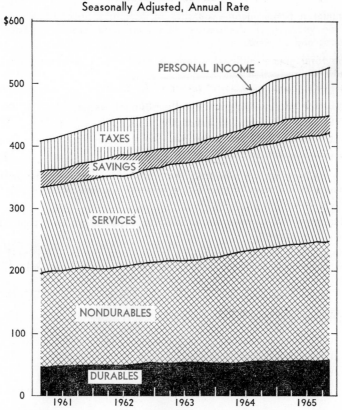

Source: *Business Outlook Charts,* National Industrial Conference Board, Inc., 1965.

Of course, many people received more than the average (per capita) income and many received less. In some sections of the country, per capita income is higher than in other sections. Although the average total income received per person in the United States in 1964 was about $2,600, in the state of Nevada it was $3,248; and in Mississippi, $1,438.

Numerous factors account for the differences in income distribution among people. Among these factors, personal traits, habits, and abilities are the most important. We are not alike in our earning ability. Such factors as general economic conditions in the geographical area in which one lives and works, education, accumulated savings, and employment opportunities also affect the amount any one person may earn.

Facts everyone needs to understand about the national income and its distribution

1. Annual national income consists of the total income received in a given year by all the people who contributed to the production of goods and services.

2. The total annual national income is received as earnings for contributions to production by:
   a. Land owners, in rent.
   b. Labor and management, in the form of wages.
   c. Lenders of money, in interest.
   d. Owners of business, in profits.
   e. Government, in taxes.

3. The primary factors affecting the share of national income earned by owners in the form of profits are general economic conditions, competition, and managerial ability.

4. Managers and owners are entitled to a just share in income for the risks they assume.

5. The primary causes of inequality in receiving shares in national income are differences among people in personal traits, habits, and abilities.

▪ QUESTIONS ON THE TEXT

1. What are two ways to approach the study of economics?
2. What is "gross national product"?
3. What is meant by "final goods"?
4. Who are the users or purchasers of the product and services included in GNP?
5. Of the four groups of users or purchasers, which group uses the most goods and services?
6. Distinguish between durable goods and nondurable goods.
7. How does the amount of services purchased by individuals compare with the amount of nondurable goods purchased? With the amount of durable goods purchased?
8. Part of our GNP is invested by private individuals in business. Give examples to illustrate the type of items in which business investments are made.
9. Goods and services purchased by the local, state, and federal governments are used for what major purposes?
10. How does the amount of purchases by the state and local governments compare with the purchases of the federal government?
11. Compare the government's use of goods and services with the total amount of goods and services produced in a year.
12. Define the terms "imports" and "exports."

13. What is national income?
14. What are the major classes or categories of national income?
15. Who receives each class or part of the national income?
16. What is rent?
17. What regulates the cost of rent?
18. What factors may affect the supply of labor?
19. How are the wages of labor determined?
20. What relationship exists between the number of years of school completed and the money income or wages an individual receives?
21. What, in addition to wages, hours, overtime pay, and the employment of minors, does the Fair Labor Standards Act now regulate?
22. Do the provisions of the Wage-Hour Law apply to all workers? What are the main provisions?
23. What is interest?
24. What factors influence the rate of interest charged borrowers at a given time?
25. What is profit?

▪ QUESTIONS FOR DISCUSSION

1. In what way does the domestic policy of the federal government affect gross national product?
2. Study the graph which is entitled "What Consumers Bought in 1964" on page 159. Note that consumers spent about one third as much for durable goods as they did for nondurable goods and about one third as much for durables as they did for services. Consumers spent about one sixth as much for durable goods as for nondurable goods and services combined. (a) What are the probable reasons that consumers spent so much less for durables in 1964 than they did for nondurables and services? (b) Is it likely that the proportionate amounts for durables, services, and nondurables will change in the future?
3. Explain how the value of goods and services may be an expenditure for some and income for others.
4. Why are such items as weekly allowances, interest received on government bonds, and pensions excluded from national income?
5. An increase in the level of purchases for business investments indicates an increase in the level of growth of our economy. Under what conditions might an increase in business investments be misleading? Would you favor a regulation or law making it compulsory for everyone who receives income to invest a certain percentage in business? Why?
6. Since the passage of the original Fair Labor Standards Act, the minimum wage has been raised several times. What are the arguments in favor of raising the minimum wage, and what are the arguments

against? Do you believe a minimum wage per hour should be established for all workers? Why?

7. A merchant in a large shopping center advertises that he sells a large volume of goods and that he therefore can sell at lower prices than competitors. Discuss the merits of this statement.

8. Does a dividend paid to a stockholder represent a share of income in the form of wages, rent, interest, or profits? Explain your answer.

9. Assume that there is only one hardware store in a city of 10,000 population. Since there is only one store, the owner charges very high prices and makes an exceptionally large profit. What natural economic controls are likely to remedy this situation?

10. Why do some companies earn a higher rate of profit than others?

11. In recent years, the federal government has used tax cuts to stimulate the economy. In what way does this action affect the economy? Why not eliminate all taxes in order to stimulate the economy?

12. Would you favor paying the same wage to all workers who are in a particular occupation, such as stenography or over-the-counter retail selling? Why?

13. Many people dream of owning their own business some day. Others are content to be employees and let others own the businesses for which they work. Do you desire to own a business some day? Why or why not?

14. Explain why the income that an owner-manager receives from the operation of a small business may not be all profit.

15. The average total income received per person will vary widely from state to state or from one geographical area to another. What accounts for this wide variation in *per capita* income?

16. The income received annually by individuals for the work they do varies from no income to hundreds of thousands of dollars. What makes it possible for some to earn high incomes? Make a list of the reasons why you believe some people earn nothing or very little. (a) To what extent is an individual responsible for the low, average, or high personal income he may receive? (b) To what extent are the factors influencing his income under his control? (c) Do you believe every person should be guaranteed a certain minimum income by the government? Why?

▪ PROBLEMS TO SOLVE

1. Your school and public libraries will have copies of the *Statistical Abstract of the United States*, which is published annually by the United States Department of Commerce. In the latest edition find the answers to the following questions:
   (a) What was the gross national product for each of the last five years for which data are given?

(b) What has been the percentage increase or decrease in GNP from one year to the next? What has been the general trend?

(c) Has there been any significant change in the percentage of purchases that any one group of users or purchasers (individual consumers, business investors, government, foreign purchasers) has made in GNP during these five years?

(d) What has been the general trend in percent of purchases made by foreign purchasers (exports minus imports) during these five years?

2. In the latest edition of *Statistical Abstract of the United States* find the answers to the following questions:

(a) What was the national income for each of the last five years for which data are given?

(b) For the latest year for which figures are given, compute the percent of the national income that represented (1) wages and salaries, (2) supplements to wages and salaries, (3) income of unincorporated businesses, (4) rental income of persons, (5) corporate profits, and (6) net interest.

(c) What percent of the national income for the latest year for which figures are available originated in (1) agriculture, forestry, and fisheries, (2) contract construction, (3) manufacturing, (4) wholesale and retail trade, (5) finance, insurance, and real estate, (6) transportation, (7) public utilities, (8) services, and (9) government enterprises?

3. In the latest edition of *Statistical Abstract of the United States,* find the answers to the following questions:

(a) What was the per capita personal income for the United States as a whole for each of the last five years for which figures are given?

(b) What was the per capita personal income for your state for each of the last five years for which figures are available?

(c) What was the average net income for each of the last five years for which figures are given for physicians, dentists, and lawyers?

4. Refer to the table on page 168 which is entitled "Personal Income by Years of Education Completed." Assume that the number of years worked in a lifetime continues to be approximately 40 and that the differences between median income for each of the groups will remain the same. Calculate how much more income would be earned by a person completing more years of school in each of the following cases:

(a) How much more income would be earned in 40 years by a person who completes high school than by one who completes eight years of school?

(b) How much more income would be earned in 40 years by a person who completes high school than by one who completes one to three years of high school?

  (c) How much more income would be earned in 40 years by a person who completes four years of college than by one who completes high school?

  (d) How much more income would be earned in 40 years by a person who completes five years of college than by one who completes four years of college?

5. Various sources (weekly business magazines, almanacs, government publications) publish the actual yearly profits in percentage of net worth for various leading corporations. Find for the latest year the percentage of profits for a variety of leading corporations (drug, food, petroleum, automobile, electrical, farm machinery manufacturing, and processing firms). Compare these various profit rates with the rate of interest you could get by investing your money in a local savings and loan association. Considering the total risks involved, how would the two compare?

▪ COMMUNITY PROBLEMS AND PROJECTS

1. The United States Employment Service has an office in most large towns and cities. Business firms seeking employees inform the office as to the kinds of jobs that are open, what the qualifications are, and what the rate of pay will be. Unemployed persons file statements of their experience and qualifications and the kind of job they seek.

   Go to or write the nearest Employment Office to obtain a list of the open jobs and inquire about the number of people who are seeking employment. Compare the supply (persons seeking employment) and the demand (jobs that are open). How does the total supply match the total demand in numbers? How well do the qualifications and experience of the unemployed people on record meet the requirements of the open jobs?

2. Investigate the hourly wage rates in your community for various classes of workers, such as carpenters, painters, lawn-care men, and typists. What is the present trend in wages? How do present wages compare with wages five years ago? Next, compare the present local rates with the national averages for such workers. The national figures can be found in the *Occupational Outlook Handbook*, which should be in your school library or guidance office. What explanation can you give for the difference in rates?

3. Investigate the prevailing interest rates in your community for (a) loans on real estate, (b) short-term personal loans from banks, and (c) loans for the purchase of automobiles. Find out how the interest rates compare with those of the year before, of five years before, and of ten years before. Give a report to indicate the reasons for the variation.

4. List as many as possible of the risks involved in operating a business.

Chapter 10

Money and credit

PURPOSE OF THE CHAPTER

Money and credit make possible the orderly exchange of goods and services among producers, distributors, and consumers. Intelligent use of money and credit is vital to the gaining by individuals of happiness and financial security. Problems always come from improper use of either money or credit. Money and credit leaks due to poor financial management are fundamentally losses of income. In studying this chapter you will learn why money and credit are important and how you can make them work for you.

You will find answers to these questions:

1. What are the functions of money and credit?
2. What are the kinds of money in the United States?
3. What is the basis of the value attached to money and credit?
4. How does credit increase the money supply?
5. What is the nature of consumer credit?
6. What is purchasing power?

A. Money

NATURE OF MONEY

Money is anything that is generally accepted in exchange for other things or in payment of debts. In America, money is valuable, it is convenient to handle, and it is in the form of amounts as large or small as necessary.

Functions of money. Authorized by the government, money serves as a medium of exchange. People are willing to take it as payment for their labor, for the goods they have for sale, or for the services they render. It is money that provides a measure of the value of labor, goods, and services. Money also serves as a means of accumulating the power to purchase goods and services, and it makes credit possible. What makes money valuable is the work it does in implementing the economic growth and development of individuals and of the nation.

Functions of money

Money serves us in four major ways:

1. *Medium of exchange.* Money enables you to exchange your services, such as mowing Mr. A's lawn or serving as a waitress at a restaurant, for goods, such as a new jacket at X Department Store.

2. *Measure of value.* Just as scales measure weight in pounds and ounces, money measures the value of a commodity in dollars and cents. The X Department Store may price a white orlon jacket at $19.95, which indicates that the store judges it to have that value to a customer. You, as a customer, may or may not agree.

3. *Store of value.* Wages or other income received may be saved or may be exchanged immediately for goods and services. Wages saved are usually in the form of money or bank deposits. The wages thus saved really are purchasing power that you have earned but not yet used. Thus, money is a store of value.

4. *Standard of future payments.* A neighbor has purchased a home on which he made a down payment and promised to pay the remainder over a 12-year period. The amount he pays each month was determined in advance rather than determining it each month by discussing price trends, the changing values of real estate, and similar factors with the mortgage holder.

Acceptability. The basic standard for judging the value of money is *acceptability.* Any money becomes acceptable when it performs the functions that are demanded of it. In economic usage, true wealth consists of goods capable of being bought, sold, or stocked for future disposition. Through the use of money it is possible to accumulate wealth without having to collect and store goods. Money, except metallic money that has some real value, is, therefore, only a right or a claim to wealth. To have value, money must therefore be acceptable to those who have things to sell. Whenever anyone has accumulated a large amount of money, he is wealthy as long as money is exchangeable for goods and services. If money ceases to be of value, he is no longer wealthy. In such a case only those who have their wealth in the form of usable goods are wealthy.

KINDS OF MONEY

Money, it will be recalled, is defined as anything that people will accept in exchange for goods or services, in the belief that they may, in turn, exchange it, now or later, for others goods or services. There are three forms of money in common use in the United States: coins, currency, and checkbook money.

Coins. Money made of metal, that is, coins, are made for convenience in paying small amounts. The U. S. Treasury has the responsibility for minting coins; they are issued by the federal reserve banks. All coins currently in circulation in the United States are made of alloys, or mixtures, of metals. Thus, the face value of a coin is more than the value of the metal of which it is made. For example, the value of the silver and metal alloys in a silver half dollar is less than 50 cents. No gold coins have been made since 1934.

Currency. The Congressional Committee on Banking and Currency has defined currency as paper, or folding, money. In the past, it has been issued by national banks, federal reserve banks, and the U. S. Treasury. About 94 percent of the currency now in circulation consists of federal reserve notes, which are issued by each of the twelve federal reserve banks. The other 6 percent of paper money in circulation consists of national bank notes, federal reserve bank notes, silver certificates, treasury notes of 1890, and U. S. notes, most of which are no longer being issued.

Silver certificates, which were secured by silver held by the U. S. Treasury, were issued in $1 and $5 denominations but are no longer issued. Federal reserve notes are now being issued in $1 and $5 denominations as well as in larger amounts.

MONEY IN THE UNITED STATES
(In millions of dollars)

Year	Coins in circulation	Paper money in circulation	Demand deposits in banks (checkbook money)
1939	$ 590	$ 7,008	$ 29,793
1945	1,274	27,241	75,851
1950	1,554	26,187	92,272
1955	1,927	29,231	109,914
1960	2,427	30,442	115,200
1965	4,027	38,029	131,200

Source: Federal Reserve Bulletin, March, 1966.

Checkbook money. Checks drawn on demand deposits in commercial banks are accepted by people in exchange for goods or services. Thus, according to the definition of money by the Committee on Banking and Currency, they are money. Demand deposits account for more than 80 percent of all money circulating in the country. It is estimated that the total number of checkbook dollars used to make payments now exceeds $2 trillion a year.

There are three ways by which a person may accumulate checkbook money in the form of demand deposits. He may deposit currency in a checking account in a commercial bank, he may similarly deposit a check that has been given to him, or he may borrow from the bank and have the amount credited to his account. To the extent that banks make loans to individuals and businesses, they actually create new money in bank deposits. As loans are repaid, the demand deposits are decreased. Since banks have the capacity to increase or decrease the amount of money available, it is said that they "create and destroy" money in response to the changing demands for it.

Most people receive their wages in the form of checks that are immediately deposited in banks. Through the use of checking accounts, people simply write checks in payment of bills and often they conveniently mail them. The canceled checks serve as receipts. For businessmen, demand deposits are even more valuable. A businessman who receives numerous checks can quickly deposit them in his bank, where they are credited to his account. In this manner most business transactions are completed with only a minimum amount of the kind of inconvenience and possible loss that is involved in the handling and possession of much currency. In Chapter 17, the use of checking accounts is discussed further as are the other important services rendered by banks.

UNITED STATES MONEY IN CIRCULATION BY DENOMINATION

(Outside Treasury and Federal Reserve Banks)

DECEMBER 31, 1965

Coin and denomination currency	Amount (in millions)
Coin	$ 4,027
$1 bills	1,908
$2 bills	127
$5 bills	2,618
$10 bills	7,794
$20 bills	13,369
$50 bills	3,540
$100 bills	8,135
$500 bills	245
$1,000 bills	288
$5,000 bills	3
$10,000 bills	4
Total	$42,058

Source: *Federal Reserve Bulletin*, March, 1966.

It is appropriate to note here the use of the term "cash" as its relates to kinds of money. In general, *cash* is any ready money that a person or business firm actually has, including money on deposit. Therefore, the total supply of money or cash available for financial transactions of business firms and individuals is the sum of the paper money and coins in circulation plus the total of the balances in checking accounts.

WHAT BACKS U.S. MONEY?

Formerly backed by silver or gold. The currency of a country is said to be on a silver standard or on a gold standard when the paper currency is backed by silver or gold dollars or by bullion.

Prior to 1873 United States currency could be converted either directly or indirectly by the bearer, upon request to the United States Treasury, into either gold dollars or silver dollars. In the period from 1873 to 1933, we had a gold standard, and currency could be converted into gold. The gold dollar contained 23.22 grains of fine gold.

Under an act of Congress in 1933, amended in 1934, the right of a bearer of United States currency to convert the currency to gold was rescinded; and the President was given authority to reduce by not more than 50 percent the standard upon which the value of the dollar was based if economic conditions warranted. Accordingly, the amount of gold upon which the value of the dollar is based was reduced from 23.22 grains to 13.71 grains of fine gold. Since 1934 the United States currency is not redeemable in gold to private citizens but is redeemable in gold to foreign banks and business firms. So the United States currency is really not on the gold standard at home, but is on the gold standard for international transactions.

Backed by credit and reserves. Federal reserve notes, which comprise about 94 percent of the currency in circulation, are backed by the credit of the United States government. American citizens holding federal reserve notes cannot demand anything for them except that they be accepted in payment for taxes and all debts, public and private. But since foreign banks may exchange United States dollars for gold, some gold must be held in reserve to meet such demands. Presently a gold reserve must be maintained equivalent to 25 percent of the amount of federal reserve notes in circulation. This reserve is available to foreign holders of our currency but not to American citizens.

Managed paper currency. Checkbook money is created on the basis of valuable assets pledged as security. When a bank makes a loan to a business firm, secured by inventories of machinery, or to a farmer, secured by farm assets, it has, in effect, created dollars backed by inventories, machinery, or farm goods.

Obviously, if more dollars were created in this way than were merited or backed by the real value of the assets, the value of those dollars would be in question. Now, what safeguard is there to prevent too many dollars being created in this way? The answer is that the Federal Reserve System consciously determines the maximum amount of money which can be created by bank lending. So indirectly, adequate backing of our checkbook money is provided by seeing that the assets securing the bank loans through which the checkbook money is created are adequate. In a sense we have a managed currency. The basic policy upon which the managed currency practice rests is that the amount of money created, that is, the supply of money, is controlled.

B. Credit

NATURE OF CREDIT

Credit in the form of a debt is involved whenever cash, goods, or services are provided on a promise to pay at a future date. Most people and business organizations use credit in one form or another. Consumer credit is the financial tool with which most Americans acquire what they want when they want it and pay for it out of future earnings. Based on the faith of one individual in another, credit, like money, represents buying power now. A person or a firm has ability to buy when a promise to pay at some time in the future is acceptable to the seller in exchange for a good or a service.

Credit increases purchasing power. As is true of money, what makes credit valuable is the work it does by providing purchasing power. If everyone, including business firms and the federal government, had to pay cash for everything purchased, business would slow down almost to a standstill. As with money, the value of credit is determined by its acceptability. When credit is used wisely, it performs vital functions just as money does.

Functions of credit

Credit serves us in four major ways:

1. *Stabilize the economy.* Credit has a stabilizing effect on the economy as it enables individuals and businesses to buy goods and services with regularity even when income is temporarily limited. Through borrowing, the government may help the economy as it spends money for roads, schools, unemployment benefits, and so forth.
2. *Promote business formation.* Many people start new businesses and thousands of others continue in business through the use of credit. This use of credit is illustrated when wholesale firms grant credit to retailers, thus permitting them to operate with relatively little money.
3. *Expand production.* Business firms may expand the production of goods and services by means of long-term loans from banks, insurance companies, and other financial institutions. By borrowing, an individual, too, may increase his productive (earning) power through obtaining additional education or through investment of the borrowed money at a rate of return that is greater than the cost of the borrowing.
4. *Raise the standard of living.* The general standard of living is raised as things such as homes, automobiles, furniture, appliances, insurance, and health service are purchased on credit. Demand is created without money, production is increased, and jobs are created through credit. Today, a young family does not wait for savings to accumulate before beginning to acquire those things that make for a stable, comfortable life.

Functions of credit. It is true that proper use of credit has a stabilizing (avoiding unusual increases and decreases in business) effect on the economy. There is, however, a major problem in that wise use of credit is necessary to avoid violent changes in business conditions.

For example, if credit is too easy to obtain and is used excessively, debts may not be paid when due. When this situation occurs widely on a national scale, many creditors suffer losses; and buying decreases, causing a weakening of business conditions and a decrease in production and jobs. For that reason, those granting credit and those using it have a basic responsibility to society and to themselves to use it wisely.

Credit may sometimes permit persons to start businesses that really should not have been started. Industrial expansion that takes place largely on the basis of consumer credit depends upon the consumer's future earning power. Should this future earning power fail to increase, these industries are likely to experience a severe reduction of their business. Because business can be expanded or reduced rapidly through the use of credit, businessmen are sometimes overconfident. Credit causes a businessman to be dependent upon others. He usually must use credit and extend credit. In order to extend credit, he must have faith in others and faith in the future.

Effect of credit. The ease and convenience with which credit may be used stimulates the flow of products to consumers. If the head of a household has a job and can expect to continue to earn money, the family can buy now with credit.

If a family uses credit properly, it can plan carefully to meet all payments and enjoy many goods without having cash at the time of purchase; but goods purchased on credit should last beyond the time the last payment is made.

If people fail to meet their legal and moral obligations of credit, they cannot pay their debts; they will get into serious legal trouble; they will lose their credit standing; and their purchasing power and level of living will decrease.

KINDS OF CREDIT

As a means of obtaining goods or services now on a promise to pay for them later, credit exists in many forms and may be classified in a variety of ways. When consideration is given to who uses credit and the purposes for which it is used, three categories quite naturally develop: government credit, business credit, and consumer credit. The *instruments of credit* most commonly used include checks, bank drafts, promissory notes, bonds, conditional sales contracts, and real estate mortgages. These are defined and discussed in Chapters 17, 19, and 31.

Government credit. Governments build highways, schools, and hospitals. They promote these and many other projects for public use. Frequently a government will pay only part of the full cost of a project from tax funds already available. Thus, governments, like individuals, borrow when they spend more than their current income. The usual procedure is to sell bonds, with the interest and the principal to be paid back out of future taxes. A local government will usually levy taxes sufficient to pay its policemen and teachers and to defray the cost of other ordinary operating expenses. It will, through the sale of bonds, utilize credit when it must build a new school, a courthouse, or a street.

Business credit. Businesses use *commercial credit* to cover the cost of producing and marketing goods. A manufacturer buys raw materials and gives his promise to pay for them in 30, 60, or 90 days. A retailer buys goods from a wholesaler on similar terms. A farmer may buy seed or fertilizer and pay for it when his crop is harvested.

Businesses also use commercial credit in acquiring productive facilities such as land, buildings, and machinery. Through borrowing, a restaurant can obtain land for a parking lot, an automobile manufacturer can acquire a new building, and an oil company can set up a new refinery. Bonds, maturing over periods of ten or more years, are commonly issued for such purposes.

Consumer credit. Use of *consumer credit* enables many people to buy the goods and services required to satisfy their immediate wants. A person may borrow money from a bank or a finance company so that he can pay cash for an automobile or for modernizing his home. He may engage in installment buying whereby he makes a down payment on a washing machine and pays the remainder in 12 or 18 months. Too, he may regularly use his credit card and charge-a-plate for purchases at service stations and at his favorite department store. Many people prefer credit buying to paying cash simply because of its convenience. Others find it easier to pay for things by means of regular installment payments than to accumulate through saving the same amount of money. Cost and other important factors in the use of consumer credit will be discussed in Chapter 18.

Another important type of credit is represented by *home mortgages*—loans that are secured by real estate. Although not ordinarily classified as consumer credit by the *Federal Reserve Bulletin,* this type of credit is used extensively by consumers and is a part of the total

CONSUMER CREDIT OUTSTANDING
SELECTED YEARS, 1939 TO 1965
(In millions of dollars)

Year	Total consumer credit outstanding
1939	$ 7,222
1945	5,665
1957	44,970
1960	56,028
1965	85,983

Source: *Federal Reserve Bulletin*, March, 1966.

outstanding consumer debt picture. An individual may pay only a small portion of the full cost of his home in cash. He then borrows the remainder from a bank or a savings and loan association. The borrowed money, plus interest, is paid back in monthly payments spread over a period of 10 to 20 or even 40 years. In the meantime, the house and lot serve as security for the loan. If the borrower cannot fulfill his payment obligation, the bank or association can sell the property and get its money back. The total amount of real estate mortgage debt outstanding at the end of 1965 was approximately $213 billion.

The total amount that consumers owed for appliances, clothing, home furnishings, automobiles, and similar items increased almost 3 times between 1950 and 1965. In a like manner, the amount of home mortgage credit increased approximately 3 times during that 15-year period. In 1965, the total amount of consumer debt outstanding, including mortgage credit, was approximately $260 billion. At the same time, the total consumer assets were estimated to be $2,090 billion. Thus, the ratio of all consumer assets to all consumer debts was about 8 to 1.

C. Effect of money and credit on purchasing power

NATURE OF PURCHASING POWER

Production is today so specialized that most people engage in the production of goods and services almost none of which they themselves consume. The exchange of the goods and services they produce for goods and services they can consume must, therefore, involve two transactions with money serving as the medium of exchange. The goods and services produced are given for money, and the money, in turn, is used to acquire other goods and services to be consumed.

The purchasing power or value of money is measured by the quantity of goods that a given amount of money will buy. Of course, the quantity of goods a dollar will buy depends upon the price of the goods. When prices are high, it takes more money to buy the same amount of goods than it did when prices were low. If prices begin to fall, we say that the purchasing power of money increases, for the dollar will buy more than it would formerly. With this in mind, it may be said that prices of commodities and services vary inversely with the purchasing power or value of money.

You will recall our consideration in Chapter 6 of how the value of a dollar affects the level of living and the problems that can arise when there is too much or too little money. Some control must be maintained over the value of money, the amount of it available, and the rate at which it is spent. Such control must influence the flow of money payments in order to help the money supply adjust to the changes in the flow of goods and services. Through increasing or decreasing the amount of money in existence, the Federal Reserve System attempts to exercise this kind of control.

The purchasing power of the dollar at one time is frequently compared with the purchasing power of a dollar at another time by a device known as a *price index number.* The United States Department of Commerce and the Bureau of Labor Statistics prepare price index numbers on many groups of commodities.

PURCHASING POWER OF THE DOLLAR
SELECTED YEARS 1940 TO 1965
(1957-1959 = 100)

Year	Monthly average as measured by	
	Wholesale prices	Consumer prices
1940	232.6	204.8
1945	172.7	159.5
1950	115.2	119.4
1955	107.3	107.1
1957 1958 1959	100.0	100.0
1962	99.4	94.9
1964	99.5	92.5
1965	97.6	91.0

Source: U.S. Department of Commerce, Office of Business Economics; monthly data for wholesale and consumer prices published in *Survey of Current Business.*

The figures in the foregoing table mean that in 1940 a dollar would have bought on an average 232.6 percent as much goods at wholesale prices as it did in the 1957-1959 period; and that in the year 1965 it would buy 97.6 percent as much goods at wholesale as it would have bought in the 1957-1959 period. Another method of interpreting the change in the purchasing power of the dollar may be illustrated by observing the figures in the consumer prices column. Roughly, a dollar in 1940 would have bought a little more than two times the amount of consumer goods that it would have bought in the 1957-1959 period; and a dollar in the year 1965 would have bought only slightly more than nine-tenths as much as it would have bought in the 1957-1959 period. It may be noted that there has been a steady, continuous decrease in the purchasing power of the dollar since 1940. This means that prices have increased as the value of the dollar has decreased. In Chapter 14, a further, more detailed, explanation of inflation will be given.

EXPANDING PURCHASING POWER WITH CREDIT

Assume that all the people of a community or city had five or ten times as much money as they now have. Their wants for goods and services would immediately increase greatly and they would buy many commodities that now they do not buy. Expansion of credit, or increasing the amount of debts that individuals or business institutions may have, has the same effect as increasing the amount of money they have. Expansion of credit is a process whereby banks increase their ability to make loans to customers.

The money that banks have available to loan to customers ordinarily is obtained from the deposits other customers have made. People who deposit money expect to be able to get it when they ask for it. Experience has shown, however, that all depositors do not ask for their money at one time; thus the bank may make loans to other customers from the deposits, making certain it maintains a certain cash reserve as required by law. Any bank cannot by itself increase its ability very greatly to make loans; but, if it can sell to another bank some of the notes from its customers, it may obtain money which in turn it can loan to other customers. Hence, bank credit can be expanded.

The process of expanding credit by a member bank discounting customers' notes at the federal reserve bank in its district is explained in Chapter 11. An illustration here will further explain the effect of

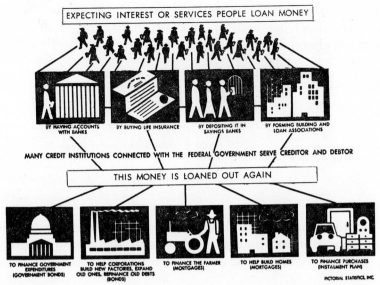

Source: Maxwell S. Stewart, *Debts—Good or Bad?* The Public Affairs Committee, Inc., New York City

Creditor and debtor relationships in expanding the use of money

rediscounting customers' notes on increasing a bank's ability to loan more money to customers, thereby creating more credit.

The following simple bank statement shows the status of the Central National Bank at a specific time:

BALANCE SHEET OF CENTRAL NATIONAL BANK

Assets:		Liabilities and ownership:	
Cash	$ 80,000	Amount due depositors	$100,000
Bonds	120,000	Capital stock	150,000
Deposits in federal reserve bank	20,000	Surplus	50,000
Equipment	20,000		
Building	60,000		
Total assets	$300,000	Total liabilities and ownership	$300,000

The American Manufacturing Company, a customer of this bank, obtains a loan of $10,000 for three months at 6 percent and gives as security its promissory note. The bank deducts (discounts) its interest in advance and gives the customer credit for $9,850 in its account. The latter may use this credit by writing checks to the extent of $9,850. The note, which is a credit instrument, has become an asset of the bank, for it represents a promise of the American Manufacturing Company to pay $10,000 at the end of three months. After the loan has been made, the statement of the bank appears as on page 194.

It is evident that there has been no increase in the amount of money, but there has been an increase in the use of money. The deposits are almost 10 percent larger than they were previously.

BALANCE SHEET OF CENTRAL NATIONAL BANK

Assets:		Liabilities and ownership:	
Cash	$ 80,000	Amount due depositors	$109,850
Bonds	120,000	Capital stock	150,000
Deposits in federal reserve bank	20,000	Surplus	50,000
Loans to customers	10,000	Undivided profits (interest)	150
Equipment	20,000		
Building	60,000		
Total assets	$310,000	Total liabilities and ownership	$310,000

Since this bank is a member of the Federal Reserve System, it can sell, or rediscount, the note of the American Manufacturing Company at a federal reserve bank. The Federal Reserve Board regulates the rediscount rate. Suppose that the note is rediscounted in this case at 3 percent. The Central National Bank accepts federal reserve notes (lawful money) for $5,000 and leaves the remainder on deposit in the federal reserve bank. The statement of the Central National Bank then is as follows:

BALANCE SHEET OF CENTRAL NATIONAL BANK

Assets:		Liabilities and ownership:	
Cash	$ 85,000	Amount due depositors	$109,850
Bonds	120,000	Capital stock	150,000
Deposits in federal reserve bank	24,925	Surplus	50,000
Equipment	20,000	Undivided profits	75
Building	60,000		
Total assets	$309,925	Total liabilities and ownership	$309,925

The Central National Bank now has $5,000 more cash that can be loaned to customers and it has $4,925 more on deposit in the federal reserve bank, which also increases its capacity to make loans to customers. This process of expanding the use of money by means of credit could continue indefinitely. Under present laws the expansion of credit can continue until the reserve in the federal reserve bank drops to a specified percentage of the bank's deposits.

OTHER ASPECTS OF CREDIT AND DEBT

For the country as a whole, the total debts owed are equal to the total credit extended. Whenever an individual, a business firm, or government contracts a debt by promising to pay at some future time, credit is expanded. Credit expansion has the same effect on the economic activities of the country as increasing the amount of money that people, businesses, and government have to spend. Debts must be repaid. Therefore, credit expansion must always be kept within reasonable bounds. During the process of expansion, prices tend to rise and the purchasing power of the dollar decreases. In other words, prices are inflated. If debts rise generally to the extent that many of the debtors are unable to pay them when they fall due, business is faced with depression, which means that production is curtailed or stopped, jobs decrease in number, wages fall, and everyone in the economy is affected adversely.

As we have already learned, credit means that someone has contracted a debt and has promised to pay at some future time. He really has borrowed money, but where does the money that he borrows come from? One may say it comes from a bank, a loan company, or some person who has great resources. But where did these agencies get the money? Money available for loans comes from the savings of people. Banks receive customers' deposits of funds saved, insurance companies receive life insurance premiums from the savings of people, and wealthy people have wealth because they or someone else did not spend all of their income. It would be impossible to borrow money if nobody had ever saved a part of his income. Credit, therefore, is based upon the savings of others.

Idle money does not stimulate business; but if money is used to buy goods or is lent for productive purposes, production is increased, more workers are needed, and business is improved. The illustration on page 193 shows how the money of individuals is lent to various institutions and is then loaned out again for various productive purposes.

In summary, it is almost impossible to exaggerate the importance of money and credit in our society. As tools of exchange, they are essential to efficient production, distribution, and consumption. They aid in the achievement of personal happiness and security. They promote economic growth and development for both the individual and the nation. Without money and credit, the present high standard of living in the United States could not have become a reality. Only by means of careful handling of the money and credit resources of individuals and prudent control of the supply of money and credit by financial institutions will the high standard of living be maintained or made even higher.

What everyone should understand about money and credit

1. Authorized by the government, money represents purchasing power in terms of prices so that values can be established in the specialized production of goods and services.
2. Money makes for ease and simplicity in bringing together the factors of production and in organizing markets through which goods may be distributed to consumers.
3. Based on faith, credit is available to individuals in almost all income categories and, therefore, tends to compensate for inequalities arising from differences in amounts of income.
4. Use of credit tends to stimulate buying and supports continued increases in the production and the use of goods and services.
5. Productive power is increased, not only for the individual but also collectively for the nation, as the use of credit promotes economic growth and a higher standard of living.
6. Individual financial integrity and a sense of business responsibility are readily recognized in the marketplace, whether a person proffers his credit card or cash.
7. Banks represent the basic set of institutions that provide the machinery for the monetary system and for control over the amount of money and credit available.
8. Money and credit require careful handling, regardless of the size of one's income, if financial goals are to be reached and satisfaction is to be gained as the result of spending.

▪ QUESTIONS ON THE TEXT

1. What is the basic standard for judging the value of money?
2. Why must money be exchangeable for goods in order to have value?
3. (a) What is true wealth?
   (b) If money ceases to be of value, who are the only persons who possess wealth?
4. What backs up or makes valuable the currency of the United States?
5. In general, money is accepted and paid out without regard to the value of the material in the coin or paper. Why?
6. What happens to the amount or supply of money when a borrower from a bank draws checks against his deposits?
7. Of what is the supply of money principally composed?
8. What is meant by "managed paper currency"?
9. (a) What is credit?
   (b) In what ways are money and credit alike?
   (c) What makes them truly valuable?
10. How widespread is the use of credit today?
11. (a) What are the three most common kinds of credit?
    (b) How do they differ?
12. How is the purchasing power of the dollar measured?

13. Why is the ability of banks to expand their credit important?
14. Whenever credit is given, a debt has been contracted that must be paid at some time in the future. This means that someone has borrowed money. Where does the money come from?

■ QUESTIONS FOR DISCUSSION

1. What would be the effects on the conduct of business affairs if everyone were required to pay in coin or paper money for everything he purchases?
2. (a) How does money serve as a store of value?
   (b) Under what conditions would a person not be wise to use money as a store of value?
3. Individual bankers must make decisions about who shall have loans. How do such decisions affect the quality and the quantity of the money supply?
4. Inasmuch as Americans cannot demand gold in exchange for their currency, would it affect Americans if the president increased the amount of gold that would be exchanged with a foreign bank for a U.S. dollar?
5. There are people who use credit in extravagant and careless ways. It has been said, however, that this does not demonstrate the use of a bad thing, but the abuse of a very good thing. What do you believe?
6. No one should incur mortgage debt or consumer debt beyond his ability to pay. What, then, determines the amount of debt that an individual or family may properly have?
7. A young family may not today have to wait for savings to accumulate before beginning to acquire those things that make for a higher level of living. What are some of the arguments that support this kind of thinking?
8. Explain why balances in checking accounts are a part of the available money supply.
9. What are the primary functions of credit? How are they related?
10. Why do you think some bankers need to keep more cash than others in order to be sure that they have enough to pay depositors on demand?
11. Explain the functions of banks in expanding purchasing power through credit.

■ PROBLEMS TO SOLVE

1. Make a study of several issues of *The Wall Street Journal, Business Week, Newsweek,* or the financial pages of a city newspaper for information relative to money and credit. Look for articles that deal with topics such as expansion of credit, control of interest rates, home financing, consumer price changes, and so forth. What are the money

and credit trends shown in these sources of information? Write an explanation of what these trends mean to individuals and to families.

2. Prepare a table showing in one column the government debt, sometimes referred to as the public or federal debt, of the United States for selected years beginning about 1940 to the present; in another column show the business debt for the same years; and in a third column show the consumer debt, including mortgage debt. The figures may be obtained from the *Statistical Abstract of the United States* or the *World Almanac and Book of Facts*. When you have the figures accumulated, study the apparent relationships that exist. Write a brief explanation to accompany the table you prepare.

3. Refer to the table on page 191. Approximately how much more consumer goods could have been purchased for $1 at retail prices in 1940 than in 1957-59? How much less in 1965 than in 1957-59?

■ COMMUNITY PROBLEMS AND PROJECTS

1. Discuss with your parents the relationship between their income and the prices of specific goods and services in 1950 to their income and prices today. Prepare a brief statement to show how the purchasing power of the dollar has affected the financial development of your family.

2. List and give explanations or examples of all the different types of credit (that is, debts to be paid in the future) that each of the following may have: (a) you or a classmate, (b) a young family, (c) a neighborhood retail store.

3. Prepare in one column a list of ten things you own that vary considerably in value (for example, football, sports jacket, bicycle, transistor radio). Then select ten additional things you own and list them in a second column so that each item is comparable in value to the item opposite it in the first column. Indicate in a brief explanation how you arrived at your decisions as to which items were of comparable value.

4. Many retail stores permit customers to open charge accounts. Prepare a list of questions you would like to ask the credit manager of a large retail store. For example, you may wish to inquire about the average size of a credit purchase, the period of time taken to pay for it, the number of people that ask for extension of time in making payments, and many similar questions. You probably will want to ask for advice from the credit manager about how you should plan for use of credit.

Your teacher may invite the credit manager of a large department store to discuss your questions or may ask you to make a report to the class.

Chapter 11

Banks and the banking system

PURPOSE OF THE CHAPTER

Banks are very important in the daily activity of a community. Most persons need bank services in order to carry on their personal or business affairs. This chapter will help you understand how banks serve us.

You will find answers to these questions:

1. What are the functions of banks?
2. What role do banks play in a community?
3. How does a bank make a profit?
4. How does a clearinghouse operate?
5. What are the primary functions of the Federal Reserve System?

A. Banking institutions

BANKS AND THEIR FUNCTIONS

A *bank* is a financial institution authorized by its *charter* (permit to do business) to perform certain functions. Some of these functions

are: to receive deposits of money subject to withdrawal by the depositor either on demand or after notice has been given, to make loans, and to pay interest. Depositors are creditors of a bank because the bank owes them money. Subject to regulations, a bank may invest or loan the money deposited in it.

Commercial bank. A *commercial bank* is a financial institution owned by its stockholders, who elect a board of directors to manage the bank's operations. A commercial bank is distinguished from other types of banks by the fact that it is authorized by its charter to receive deposits subject to withdrawal upon demand, such as by writing a check. The bank may, within regulations, make loans for relatively short periods of time ranging from 30 to 90 days. Commercial banks serve the day-to-day needs of both business firms and individuals. The charters of most commercial banks also permit them, within certain regulations, to receive savings deposits and to make loans for a year or longer.

Industrial bank. The *industrial bank* is a stock company that is owned and controlled by stockholders who invest money in the business. An industrial bank is a special type of institution which is not operated like an ordinary commercial bank. It is a special type of saving institution that is permitted to make only certain types of loans, normally small loans.

Industrial banks are also called industrial loan companies, savings banks, and finance and trust companies. The *Morris Plan* bank is a well-known type of industrial bank.

Industrial banks usually accept deposits in savings or thrift accounts. They often sell investment certificates, which are essentially the same as time deposits in a commercial bank. With these deposits obtained from individuals, loans can then be made to other individuals.

The process of obtaining a loan from an industrial bank is essentially the same as obtaining a loan from a commercial bank. Loans are usually made for the same purposes.

Savings bank. A *savings bank* is a financial institution that may accept savings deposits on which interest is paid to depositors. Savings banks may be stock companies or mutual companies. A *stock savings bank* is owned by stockholders, who, through a board of directors, manage the bank. Profits go to the stockholders. A *mutual savings bank* is owned by the depositors and is operated primarily for their benefit. Mutual savings banks are further explained in Chapter 24. Most commercial banks have savings departments, and some commercial banks are organized as savings banks.

The following customs are relatively uniform among savings banks and the savings departments of commercial banks:

1. Deposits are usually accepted for amounts as small as one dollar.
2. Checks cannot be drawn against deposits.
3. The bank reserves the right to demand several days' notice before any funds may be withdrawn.

Trust company. Some banks are chartered and authorized by states to serve in capacities of trust such as by operating trust funds, managing real estate, or serving as administrator or executor to manage or settle the estate of a deceased person. An institution having this privilege is known as a *trust company*. If a bank also serves as a trust company, both the words "bank" and "trust" are often included in the name of the institution.

The trend is toward banks becoming combination institutions that perform commercial, savings, and trust functions.

Other financial institutions. Some other financial institutions, although not technically looked upon as banks, nevertheless serve some of the same functions as banks, such as accepting deposits, paying interest on certain types of deposits, and making loans.

Various mutual savings societies are organized under certain laws and operate under special rules. For example, the *credit union,* a type of mutual savings association, also makes loans to its members.

Savings and loan associations and credit unions will be discussed in Chapter 24.

KINDS OF BANKS AS TO ORGANIZATION

Banks classified according to their authorization are (1) state banks and (2) national banks. In addition to these types of banks, there are federal reserve banks, or bankers' banks. Although federal reserve banks deal largely with individual banks that are members of the Federal Reserve System, they also have dealings with other banks.

State bank. A *state bank* is a bank that is organized as a corporation. It obtains its authority through a charter granted by the state in which it operates. A state bank may be a commercial bank, a savings bank, a trust company, or an investment bank. It may also be a member of the Federal Reserve System.

National bank. A *national bank* obtains its charter from the federal government and is subject to the regulations of the Federal Reserve System and the banking laws enacted by the federal government. A national bank is always organized as a corporation and must be a member of the Federal Reserve System.

ECONOMIC FUNCTIONS AND SERVICES OF BANKS

When a bank is organized, the owners invest money in the bank and become stockholders. Individuals, businesses, and other institutions deposit their money in banks for safekeeping. Some deposit their money for savings purposes so that they can earn interest, while others deposit money so that they may write checks to pay their bills.

The money of the stockholders and the depositors is then available for the bank to lend or to invest. The bank charges interest on loans and earns an income on its investments. From these two sources of income the bank is able to pay for its various expenses of operation, pay interest on savings deposits, and pay a profit to stockholders if there is any profit.

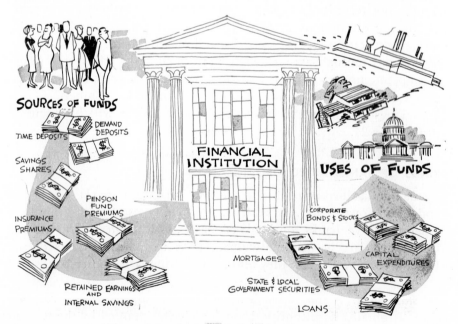

Flow of funds through financial institutions

Businesses and individuals are helped by banks through the borrowing of money. A business may borrow from a bank in order to buy merchandise to sell so that the business may make a profit on the merchandise. Individuals may borrow from a bank to buy a home or other property.

There are many other services performed by banks. Without some kind of banking services, we could not conduct our business affairs. These various services of banks and other financial institutions will be explained in Chapter 17.

CUSTOMER AND STOCKHOLDER PROTECTION

The establishment of new banks is controlled by state and federal laws. These laws are designed to protect stockholders and depositors by making certain that the bank is financially sound and that there are adequate funds available for the operating needs of the bank.

Bank operations are subject to state and federal regulations pertaining to capital stock, surplus, and reserves; policies and practices for making loans; and other regulations to safeguard both stockholders and depositors.

State and federal laws limit banks, according to their classification, in the types of loans that they can make. State banks are governed by the laws of their respective states. Members of the Federal Reserve System are governed by restrictions pertaining to the types of loans they can make and the conditions under which they may make them.

INSURANCE PROTECTION OF DEPOSITORS

Protection of depositors against loss due to bank failure has been provided through insurance on bank deposits. This insurance is administered by the Federal Deposit Insurance Corporation, which all

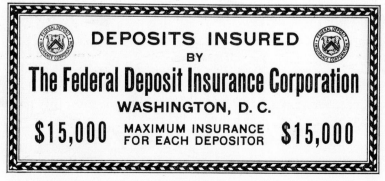

A sign announcing that a bank's deposits are insured

national banks are compelled to join and other banks may join voluntarily. The total deposits of an individual in a given bank are insured up to $15,000.

CLEARING CHECKS BETWEEN LOCAL BANKS

A problem arises when a customer of a particular bank either cashes or deposits a check that was drawn on some other bank. In order to collect the amount of the check, the customer's bank must collect from the bank on which the check was drawn. This process is called *clearing*. Banks located near each other can easily make such collections by messenger.

The clearing of checks is more complicated in large cities and among banks widely separated. In order to solve the problem of clearing checks, clearinghouses have been established in many cities. A *clearinghouse* is a voluntary association of banks that has as its purpose the solving of problems common to the member banks. One of those problems is the clearing of checks and the making of collections between banks.

A common practice in a clearinghouse is for representatives of the banks to meet at an appointed hour each morning to exchange checks

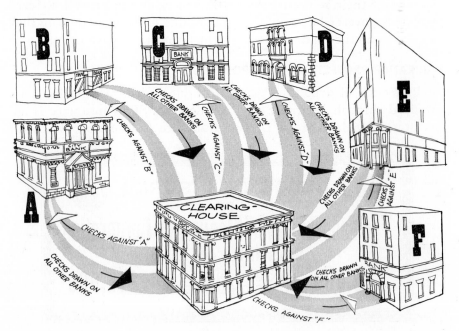

How a clearinghouse operates

drawn on other member banks. If the total amounts of the checks exchanged by two banks are not the same, the difference is settled by check from the one bank to the other. In some instances these payments are made to the clearinghouse which, in turn, settles with each bank. Checks having insufficient funds, fraudulent signatures, or that are otherwise unacceptable are returned to the banks that accepted them.

CLEARING OUT-OF-TOWN CHECKS

The Federal Reserve System also assists banks in clearing out-of-town checks. Assume that you live in Albany, New York, and that you send a check for the payment of a debt to Mr. Black in Sacramento, California. The process of clearing this check works as follows:

1. Mr. Black will deposit the check in his account in his bank in Sacramento.
2. The Sacramento bank will deposit the check for credit to its account in the federal reserve bank of its district (San Francisco).
3. The Federal Reserve Bank of San Francisco will send the check to the Federal Reserve Bank of New York for collection.
4. The Federal Reserve Bank of New York will send the check to your bank in Albany, which will deduct the amount of the check from your account.

Smaller banks often have arrangements with other larger banks whereby the larger banks clear the checks of the smaller banks.

B. The Federal Reserve System

ORGANIZATION OF THE FEDERAL RESERVE SYSTEM

The banking system that is the outgrowth of the Federal Reserve Act passed in 1913 is called the *Federal Reserve System*. Under this Act the country was divided into twelve federal reserve districts. In each district there is a federal reserve bank, which is a separate and distinct organization and is managed by a board of directors of nine persons. Six of the directors are elected by the member banks in the district and three are appointed by the Board of Governors of the Federal Reserve System. The twelve federal reserve banks are coordinated by this Board of Governors, which consists of seven members. The members of the Board of Governors are appointed by the President of the United States.

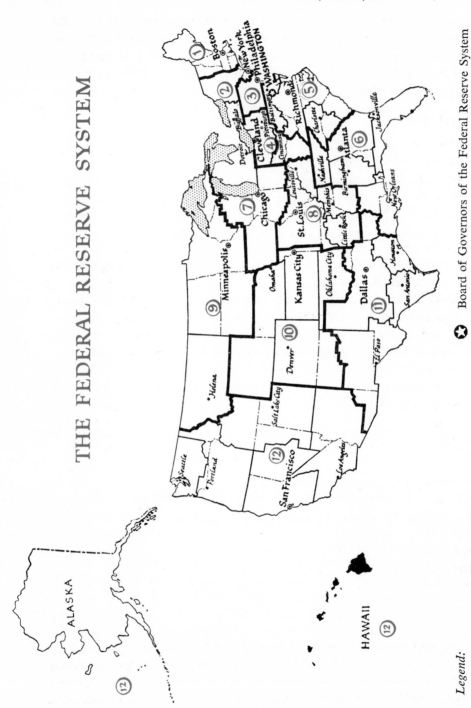

THE FEDERAL RESERVE SYSTEM

Legend:

Board of Governors of the Federal Reserve System

Federal Reserve Bank Cities

Federal Reserve Branch Cities

━━ Boundaries of Federal Reserve Districts

── Boundaries of Federal Reserve Branch Territories

Each member bank in the district in which the federal reserve bank is located must subscribe to capital stock of the federal reserve bank equal in amount to 6 percent of its paid-up capital and surplus. In the past, however, a federal reserve bank has called for payment of only a part of the stock subscribed for by a member bank.

FUNCTIONS OF THE FEDERAL RESERVE SYSTEM

In many respects a federal reserve bank is similar to any ordinary state or national bank. Both are corporations operating under a charter, both issue stock, both receive deposits, both pay checks drawn on deposits, both discount (buy) ordinary promissory notes, and both make loans according to law. However, the federal reserve banks deal largely with member banks, although under specified conditions they make certain types of loans to responsible business enterprises. The federal reserve banks may rightfully be called *bankers' banks,* for their stock is owned by the member banks. They do not accept deposits of individuals or businesses. The theory of the Federal Reserve System is that the funds of the entire United States should be organized so as to permit the rapid shifting of money and credit from one place to another to take care of supply and demand and regulated to promote economic stability and growth.

The main functions of the Federal Reserve System are: (1) issuing notes (paper currency), (2) maintaining centralized bank reserves, (3) making loans to member banks, (4) rediscounting notes, and (5) regulating business activity.

Issuing notes (paper currency). The Federal Reserve System issues one type of currency, the *federal reserve note,* which is our main type of currency. It serves as credit money and is accepted in all business channels as *legal tender,* any kind of money (coin or currency) which by law will be and must be acceptable in paying debts and taxes. The federal reserve banks act as the agent of the United States government in issuing this type of note. The federal reserve note and other types of currency were discussed in Chapter 10.

Maintaining centralized bank reserves. A member bank must maintain a deposit in the federal reserve bank equal to a fixed percentage of its own deposits. This percentage is governed by the Federal Reserve Board and may be changed from time to time. This deposit is known as a *required reserve.* Banks, of course, may and often do deposit more than the Federal Reserve Board requires. In this case these additional deposits are known as *excess reserves* or *free reserves*. It is from these excess reserves that banks can extend personal and business loans and make investments for their stockholders. The combined deposits of all member banks comprise a centralized reserve in a federal reserve bank.

Member banks, of course, must keep on hand a sufficient amount of cash to take care of the demands of their customers. The deposits in the federal reserve banks make it unnecessary, however, for member banks to keep a great amount of cash on hand, for these deposits are practically the same as cash in that they are available quickly. This system causes a federal reserve bank to act more or less as a financial reservoir for its district. Each member bank can draw upon the pool or reserves. The pooling of a portion of the funds of each member bank serves to strengthen every bank in the district.

Making loans to member banks. Member banks may obtain a loan from the federal reserve bank by turning over to the federal reserve bank government bonds, notes, or other bonds to guarantee the payment of the loan when it is due. When used for this purpose, bonds, notes, or other negotiable paper are known as *collateral*. The federal reserve bank gives the local bank credit either by increasing its reserve or by issuing to it federal reserve notes (paper money).

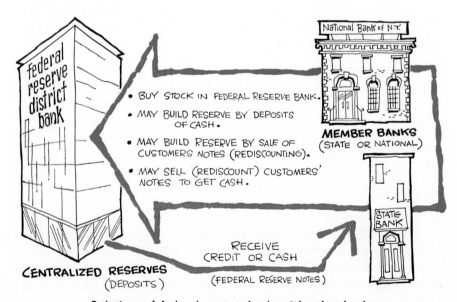

Relations of federal reserve banks with other banks

Rediscounting notes. Another way a member bank may obtain funds from its federal reserve bank is to sell to the federal bank the notes it holds. Let us say that a customer gives a business firm a $1,000 note for 60 days in payment of goods. The business firm, not wishing to wait 60 days for its money, may take the note to a bank and *discount* (sell) it. The note may be discounted any time before *maturity* (due date). If it is discounted 30 days before maturity and the rate of discount is 6 percent, the business firm will receive cash or credit amounting to $995. At maturity, the original signer of the note will pay the face of the note plus interest at the agreed rate.

The bank now holding the discounted note in the foregoing illustration may *rediscount* the note by exchanging it for cash or credit before its maturity date. The amount received is equal to the face value of the note less the interest from the date of discount to the date of maturity. Assuming that the member bank rediscounts the note on the day it is received from the business firm and that the rediscount rate is 3 percent, the bank would receive $997.50 which is $2.50 more than it gave the business firm that sold it originally. Not only did the bank make a profit of $2.50 but it also received $997.50 in reserve credit or in cash (federal reserve notes) which it may now loan to another customer. Inasmuch as the member bank purchased a note from the business firm for $995 and recovered the entire amount immediately from the federal reserve bank, credit actually was created. By this process business firms and individuals can expand business very rapidly as long as the local bank can provide funds to discount (buy) notes from customers.

Regulating business activity. One of the most important functions of the Federal Reserve System is to regulate business expansion and contraction. This regulation is achieved in part by stimulating business activity through low interest rates or by discouraging business activity through high interest rates.

Generally speaking, when it is difficult to borrow money, we say that money is scarce and interest rates are high. When money is plentiful, it is relatively easy to borrow and interest rates are low. The Federal Reserve System helps to make money scarce or plentiful by controlling credit. The controlling of credit is brought about by adjusting the rediscount rate upward or downward.

When business activity decreases rapidly, and wages and prices also decrease, there is a condition called *deflation*. In such cases it is the policy of the Federal Reserve System to stimulate the expansion of business by making money available to local banks at a low enough rate of discount that will enable local banks to lend more money to business firms. Banks can lower their interest rates and rediscount their notes with the federal reserve bank and obtain more reserves and cash to use as a basis for additional lending.

The rediscount rate of the federal reserve banks is usually lower than the discount rate of the member banks. We saw in the illustration in a preceding paragraph how the difference between the two rates created a profit of $2.50 for the member bank on one transaction. The bank not only made a profit due to the difference between the two rates but also received either a reserve deposit in the federal reserve bank or cash (federal reserve notes). If its total cash had a safe relation to its deposits, the member bank could then lend more money to its customers. Since the bank would earn interest on this money, the operation would be profitable to the member bank.

When business activity expands too rapidly, prices and wages also increase rapidly. This economic condition is known as *inflation*. Economists tell us that many of our depressions are partly caused by *overexpansion*—business firms and individuals borrowing too much money.

To prevent overexpansion and inflation, the Federal Reserve System follows a policy of raising the rediscount rate. The higher rediscount rate discourages banks from rediscounting notes, raises interest rates, and tends to discourage borrowing and business expansion.

Suppose, for instance, the Federal Reserve Board in Washington issued instructions to all federal reserve banks to raise the rediscount rate to 5 or $5\frac{1}{2}$ percent. The increased rediscount rate would mean that a member bank could not continue to make loans and to rediscount its notes profitably unless the bank could also raise its own interest rate. However, the higher rate would tend to discourage its customers from borrowing. The individual member banks would therefore probably not find it profitable to rediscount their notes. Thus, the ability of the individual banks to continue to lend more money would be restricted. Through this process, referred to as *control over bank credit*, the banks would be limited in the amount of loans they could make, and businesses would also be limited in their expansion.

Required and excess reserves. In 1935 Congress gave the Federal Reserve Board another method for regulating business expansion and contraction through the lowering or raising of the percentage or ratio for *required reserves* of member banks. If overexpansion of business and inflation occur or are about to occur, the Federal Reserve Board will raise the percentage of required reserves of member banks. This action would force member banks to transfer some or all of their *excess reserves* (from which they can extend business and personal loans and make investments) to meet the newly raised required reserve percentage. If, on the other hand, business activity is slowing down rapidly and deflation is expected, the Federal Reserve Board will lower the percentage of required reserves, thereby making it possible to transfer a percentage of the required reserves to excess reserves so that member banks will have more free funds with which to extend loans and to make investments, thus stimulating and expanding business activity.

Open-market operations. The Federal Reserve Board has a less drastic method of expanding or contracting business activity than by altering the required reserve ratios. This method is known as *open-market operation*, the purchasing or selling of short-term government securities, such as Treasury bills. For example, if the Federal Reserve Board wishes to reduce the excess reserves of member banks, thereby reducing the amount of free reserves from which loans and investments can be made, the federal reserve banks sell their short-term government securities. The purchaser of these securities pays for them with a check drawn on a member bank and made payable to the reserve bank. The reserve bank collects the check by reducing or deducting the amount of the check from the member bank's excess reserve account.

Buying short-term government securities by the federal reserve banks expands or increases the excess reserves of member banks, thus providing them with more free reserves with which to extend loans and make investments to increase business activity. For example, the federal reserve bank pays the seller of these securities with a check drawn on itself. The seller deposits this check in a member bank, which forwards the check to the federal reserve bank for collection. The federal reserve bank credits (increases) the member bank's reserve balance, thereby providing the member bank with additional excess reserves. Since the check was drawn on the federal reserve bank rather than another member bank, no other member bank's reserves are lowered by this transaction. This was not the case, however, when the reserve bank sold government securities. The net effect of buying government securities, then, is an increase to member bank reserves.

Control of speculation. The Federal Reserve Board has the power to control certain types of credit directly. For example, the Securities and Exchange Act of 1934 provided the Board with the power to limit the amount of credit one can obtain for the purpose of purchasing stocks on registered security exchanges. This means that if the Board wishes to reduce speculation and credit purchases of stocks, it can require member banks to reduce the amount of credit (bank loans) they extend to individuals and businesses who wish to borrow money to buy stocks. For example, if a stock is purchased at a market value of $1,000 and the margin requirement is 30%, the loan value is 70% or $700. Had the Board been given this power prior to 1929, the great stock market crash of 1929 and the resulting depression might not have occurred.

Facts everyone should know about banks and bank operations

1. Banks serve business firms and individuals by accepting demand and time deposits, making loans, and operating trust funds.
2. The primary objective of the Federal Reserve System is to achieve economic stability through the control of credit.
3. The Federal Reserve System issues paper currency.
4. Federal reserve banks are banker's banks.
5. Banks play an important role in the economic and business development of a community.
6. Unlike most other types of business, customers and stockholders of banks are protected by many strict regulations.

▪ QUESTIONS ON THE TEXT

1. What are the functions of a bank?
2. May a check be written on a savings account in a bank?
3. What is a trust company?
4. How are banks classified according to their authorization and organization?
5. What is the difference between a state bank and a national bank?
6. What are some of the economic functions of banks?
7. How do banks clear or exchange their local checks?
8. How is an out-of-town check collected or cleared?
9. What do we mean when we say that a federal reserve bank is a bankers' bank?

10. What are the five main functions of the Federal Reserve System?
11. What notes are issued by federal reserve banks and circulated as currency?
12. How is the currency issued by the Federal Reserve System obtained by a member bank?
13. How do member banks build up reserves in the federal reserve bank?
14. Explain how the Federal Reserve System may regulate business expansion.

▪ QUESTIONS FOR DISCUSSION

1. In what respect is a bank similar to any other business?
2. Why do you think a savings bank should require reasonable notice before funds are withdrawn?
3. Explain how loans made to business firms can serve as the basis for increasing the supply of currency.
4. The raising of the rediscount rate of the Federal Reserve Board is supposed to restrict business expansion. Can you think of any cases in which this action by the Federal Reserve Board would not be very effective? Explain your answer.
5. In order to encourage business expansion, the Federal Reserve System reduces the rediscount rate. Can you explain any situation when you think that a reduction in the rediscount rate would not be effective?
6. If every depositor in a bank wanted his money immediately and the bank attempted to furnish it, what would happen?
7. It is said that when a bank lends money to a business, the bank can get new currency to lend again. Is this true? If so, how does it happen?
8. Explain some ways in which banks make a profit.
9. What would be the effect on your community if there were no banks or any other similar institutions to take their place?

▪ PROBLEMS TO SOLVE

1. The Central National Bank made a loan of $1,000 at an interest rate of 6 percent for 60 days.
   (a) What interest is collected by the bank in advance?
   (b) The bank rediscounts this note immediately with the federal reserve bank at a rediscount rate of 3 percent. How much currency or reserve credit will the bank receive?
   (c) If the Central National Bank loaned the currency obtained by rediscounting the original note to another customer at an interest rate of 6 percent for 60 days, what interest is collected by the bank in advance?

(d) How much total profit will the bank make on these transactions?

(e) What conclusion can you reach regarding the effect of rediscounting notes on bank profits?

2. Study these figures as reported in the Federal Reserve Bulletin:

	December 1959	December 1965
	(dollars in billions)	
Treasury currency outstanding	$ 5,311	$ 5,566
Federal Reserve credit outstanding	29,435	43,853
Required reserves	18,450	22,270
Excess over required reserves	482	447
Federal Reserve rediscount rate	4%	4½%
Maximum interest rate on savings accounts	3%	4%

What has happened between 1959 and 1965 and what actions, if any, does the Federal Reserve Board appear to be taking and for what purposes?

▪ COMMUNITY PROBLEMS AND PROJECTS

1. Bankers, businessmen, and government officials are always interested in business and economic conditions, including bank clearances, which refer to the monetary volume of checks cleared through the local clearinghouse. From the financial page of your newspaper or any other source, obtain information in regard to bank clearings for a recent month. Compare these with clearings for the same month in the year previous or in some other year, and give your conclusions as to the local business activity.

2. Banks are required to publish financial statements showing their assets and liabilities. Obtain a financial statement from your local bank or one published in a newspaper and answer the following questions:

    (a) What are the different kinds of assets in which the bank has its money invested?

    (b) How much cash does the bank have on hand or on deposit with the federal reserve bank?

    (c) What are the different kinds of liabilities or amounts owed by the bank?

3. From newspaper reports or from banks secure the present rates that are being charged on commercial loans and the present rediscount rate of the federal reserve banks. On the basis of the average existing rate on commercial loans and the present rediscount rate, compute the amount of profit that a bank can make by lending money and rediscounting the note, assuming that there are no miscellaneous service charges.

Chapter 12

Price, demand, and supply

PURPOSE OF THE CHAPTER

Every person is affected by prices. The purpose of this chapter is to help you understand the significance of prices for consumers, why prices change, and some of the economic factors that affect them.

You will find answers to these questions:

1. What is the meaning of the price system?
2. How do supply and demand affect prices?
3. How do competition and monopoly affect prices?
4. How are prices controlled?

A. Nature and significance of prices

Both goods and services have value if they are capable of satisfying man's economic needs and wants. *Economic value* is the estimate of worth or usefulness that individuals and business place on goods and services because of their usefulness in satisfying wants and needs.

Goods that are free, like the air we breathe, have great value to man because he cannot live without them; but the free air we breathe does not have economic value because it ordinarily cannot be bought or sold. If ordinary air were so scarce that the only way a person could get it were to buy it in tanks, it would have economic value. *Price* is the exchange value of goods or services stated in terms of money. For example, the price of wheat is the amount of money that is required to buy a bushel of wheat.

THE PRICE SYSTEM

In the days of barter, the value of wheat as compared to that of shoes depended largely upon the supply and the degree of usefulness of each product. When wheat was plentiful and shoes were scarce and difficult to produce, a considerable amount of wheat was required in return for a pair of shoes. When people found that a great many others had wheat to trade, but very few had shoes to trade, more people began to produce shoes. As the supply of shoes increased, more shoes were required in return for a bushel of wheat. Under the barter system, therefore, the supply of products regulated to a large extent the relative values of products. When the demand for a product was great, the product could be traded easily for other products. As the demand decreased, trading became more difficult.

The barter system was inconvenient for both buyers and sellers, and it was inefficient. It gave way to the price system in which one's product or labor is exchanged for money, and the money is used to buy goods and services. All prices are stated in terms of money. Thus, money serves not only as the medium for exchanging one kind of goods or services for another, but also as a measure or standard of value by which prices are determined. Under the price system, a general rise in all prices or a general fall in all prices may occur. A general rise or fall in prices means that the purchasing power or

---

Essentials of the price system

1. The product of one's efforts or labor is exchanged for money; the money may be saved or may be exchanged for goods or services.
2. Price is the money value placed on the product resulting from one's efforts; price is also the money value placed on the goods and services one buys.
3. Thus, price is a common measure of the value both of the products of one's efforts and of goods and services one may desire.

value of money has changed. Inflation results in higher prices in general, which means that the value or purchasing power of money has decreased.

PRODUCTION, PROFITS, AND PRICES

No businessman wishes to produce unless he receives enough money to pay all his costs and make a profit. Costs include wages, raw materials, insurance, rent, interest, transportation, and many other items. Some businessmen will continue temporarily to produce goods without profit in the hope that they will eventually make enough profit to repay them for their previous losses.

Price tends to govern production. For instance, if the price of wheat goes up while the price of corn and hogs remains the same, many farmers will shift to the production of wheat. Then the production of wheat will rise, while the production of corn and hogs will decrease.

If price remains much above cost of production, new competitors will enter the field.

Production, in turn, tends to govern price. If too many farmers have shifted to the production of wheat, as indicated above, the supply of wheat will increase and the price will go down. Because of the decrease in the supply of corn and hogs, the price of corn and hogs will rise. Then there is likely to be a new shift in production. These examples serve to illustrate the fact that there is a constant interplay of price and supply, each influencing the other.

The fluctuation in price and supply, however, will generally be steadied by a basic factor: the cost of production. If price long remains much above the cost of production, new competitors will usually enter the field; supply will increase; and the price will be driven down. On the other hand, if the price falls below the cost of production and remains there long, some producers will drop out or will decrease production; supply will be curtailed; and the price will rise.

Production cannot be continued indefinitely unless the selling price is greater than the costs of production. More efficient methods of production permit the lowering of the selling price. It is for this reason that the first producers driven out of a field are those who are the least efficient. Their departure may cut the supply enough to steady prices above the production costs of the more efficient.

The federal government has influenced both the price and the quantity of production of agricultural products through subsidy and guaranteed prices. A *subsidy* is a direct payment to the producer to increase his income. There is a further discussion of government controls later in this chapter.

Production and prices

1. Prices must be high enough to make a profit possible; otherwise there will be no production.
2. Prices influence the kind of products that are produced. No one will produce a product that is too costly to be of practical use; no one will produce a product that is so valueless as to have no price.
3. High prices of a given commodity tend to stimulate the quantity of production; low prices curtail it.
4. High volume of production of a commodity tends to lower prices; low volume, to raise prices.

PRICE AND SUPPLY

The amount of goods and services offered for sale is governed considerably by the price. If the price is favorable to the producer, he will offer large quantities of his product for sale. If the price is not favorable, he will not produce. Similarly, a farmer may have harvested 10,000 bushels of wheat. If the price of wheat is $2.30 a bushel, he may sell all his wheat; but if it is only $1.50 a bushel, he may sell only enough to supply himself with sufficient cash until he can dispose of the rest at a better price. A southern cottongrower may have harvested 1,000 bales of cotton. If he can get 30 cents a pound for his cotton, he may sell all the bales; but if he can get only 12 cents a pound, he may be willing to sell only 500 bales. Price therefore tends to regulate supply.

If the price is favorable to the producer, large quantities of the product will be offered for sale.

Theoretically, *supply* represents the quantity of goods offered for sale at a given time and price. If the supply increases—in other words, if more goods are offered for sale—the price tends to be lowered. If

---

Supply and demand

1. Supply of a commodity is the amount offered for sale at a given time and price.
2. Demand for a commodity is an indication of the desire for that commodity by people who have the money to buy and who are willing to pay the price; it is the amount that will be purchased at a given price.

---

the supply continues to increase, the price will eventually reach a level that closely approximates the cost of production. When the price goes below this point, producers frequently fail and go into bankruptcy, for they cannot continue to produce without profit. The supply then tends to decrease, and the price becomes more stable. As the supply decreases, the price rises.

An opportune time to buy is when the supply is great and the demand is low. This condition is called a *buyer's market.* When the

---

Price and supply

1. An increase in the supply of a commodity tends to make its price fall; a decrease in the supply tends to make the price rise.
2. The available supply of a commodity depends upon its price and upon the prices of products that could be produced instead.
3. If the quantity supplied is greater than the quantity demanded, prices will fall; if the quantity demanded is greater than the quantity supplied, prices will rise.

demand is high and the supply is low, the condition is referred to as a *seller's market*. In the first case the buyer has the bargaining advantage; in the second, the seller has this advantage.

HOW CONSUMPTION IS INFLUENCED BY PRICES

The person who buys goods wants to pay the lowest price possible. This is because he is interested in getting all he can for his money. The businessman usually has to buy this way to make a profit.

As the price of a commodity increases, the number of people who buy that commodity at the price asked decreases. Take the example of clothing. Normally an increase in the price of clothing will reduce the amount of clothing bought unless the incomes of people are increased.

Price and quantity of commodity used

1. In general, as the price of a given commodity rises, the quantity of it used will decrease; in general, as price decreases, quantity used will increase.
2. If the quantity demanded is greater than the quantity produced, the price will rise; if the quantity demanded is less than the quantity produced, the price will decrease.

PRICE AND DEMAND

Ordinarily people think of demand as simply how much of some given commodity is wanted, but in economics the term *demand* refers to the amount of a product or service that people would buy at several different prices, assuming that their income remains the same. Ordinarily people will buy less of a product or a service at a high price than they will at a low price. For instance, people would buy fewer T-bone steaks at $3 a pound than at $1.50 a pound. Furthermore, when the demand for a product increases, the price may go up also. Using food as an example again, if the price of eggs has been approximately 60 cents a dozen for some time and the demand for eggs increases 10 percent per month for 5 consecutive months, it is probable that the price of eggs will go up also.

Three things may affect the demand for a product or a service. The amount of money people have to spend may change. If it increases, demand will increase; and if it decreases, demand will decrease. The habits and desires of people may change, affecting their willingness to buy the product or service. For instance, water sports may become increasingly popular, thus increasing the demand for boats, water skis,

YOUR PRICES ARE AFFECTED BY MANY FORCES

and similar equipment. On the other hand, the popularity of water sports may decline, thus decreasing the demand for equipment. Margarine is a substitute for butter. If the price of margarine goes up, the demand for butter may increase. Likewise, if the price of margarine goes down, the demand for butter may decrease.

ELASTICITY OF DEMAND

A commodity is said to have an *elastic demand* when a change in price will bring about considerable change in the amount of that commodity that will be purchased. The demand for a commodity is *inelastic* when a change in price will bring about little or no change in the quantity of the commodity purchased.

As an example of elastic demand, let us consider the case of automobiles. Many car manufacturers have discovered that, by reducing the price of their cars, a much larger number can be sold. The sale of a larger number will enable the manufacturer to produce cars at lower per unit cost. The reduction in price in many instances has resulted in the manufacturers making more profit than they made at the previous higher price.

A hypothetical case on the demand for automobiles will serve to illustrate the general principle of elastic demand.

Price per car	Number that can be sold	Total receipts from sales	Profits from sales
$3,600	75,000	$270,000,000	$16,200,000
3,200	125,000	400,000,000	28,000,000
2,800	175,000	490,000,000	38,400,000
2,400	250,000	600,000,000	30,000,000

The principle of elastic demand

It is evident from this analysis that the reduction in price proves profitable up to the point where the price is approximately $2,800 a car. Any further reduction in the selling price of the car results in a decrease in the total profit.

As an example of inelastic demand, a decrease in the price of bread may cause only a slight increase in the demand. The profit becomes less at the reduced price if the cost of production remains about the same. A hypothetical example will serve best to illustrate the principle of inelastic demand.

Price per loaf of bread	Number of loaves that can be sold	Total receipts from sales	Profits from sales
20¢	6,000,000	$1,200,000	$120,000
18¢	6,250,000	1,125,000	90,000
16¢	6,500,000	1,040,000	12,000
14¢	6,750,000	945,000	Loss, $30,000

The principle of inelastic demand

From these analyses we see that demand and price are interrelated and that demand has an important effect on price. Demand for a commodity tends to make the price increase when the supply of the commodity is limited.

Demand and prices

1. Demand for a product is *elastic* when a change in its price has considerable effect on the quantity used.
2. Demand for a product is *inelastic* when a change in its price has little or no effect on the quantity used.
3. In general, an increase in demand for a product having an elastic demand tends to make its price rise; a decrease in demand makes its price fall.
4. Price increases when supply in relation to demand of a commodity is limited.

Even in the case of an inelastic demand these rules do not hold strictly true when prices get too high. Although the demand for bread, regardless of price, is relatively inelastic, if the price were to go high enough relative to the price of potatoes, people with limited income would shift to the buying of potatoes as a substitute. This represents *substitution* as a principle of economics.

Principle of substitution

The amount of a commodity used becomes smaller when the price of a substitute product is reduced.

COMPETITION AND PRICES

An essential feature of the free-enterprise system is the competition among producers of economic goods for the favor of the consumer. The rivalry is of two kinds, known as price competition and nonprice competition. Through *price competition* a producer or distributor attempts to take business away from his competitors by offering his goods or services at lower prices than his competitors. In addition to competing for the business of the consumer on the basis of lower prices, some producers and distributors offer nonprice incentives, such as higher quality of goods, latest styles, inventions and innovations, and installation and maintenance services. These nonprice inducements to attract consumers are collectively referred to as *nonprice competition.*

Price competition tends to force prices down to the lowest possible level that will still permit full coverage of the costs of production plus a reasonable profit.

Competition is one means of protection for the consumer, for it helps to minimize prices, to promote efficiency, and to assure buyers that they can obtain what they want at the time they want it. Fundamentally we operate on the basis of a competitive system; but as will be discussed later, we also have some regulated monopolies and occasionally price controls, which set the maximum prices allowed on various goods.

Under free competition, no producer can persistently sell goods at prices that are much higher than those of his competitors. If producers make excessive profit—in other words, if they charge prices that are relatively high—their customers will buy from competitors that sell at lower prices. New competitors may also enter the field. As a result of this competition, the high prices that were formerly charged will be reduced.

The efficient businessman may make more profit than the inefficient. The inefficient producer who cannot succeed in keeping his costs low finds that he cannot compete with the efficient producer. When he tries to lower his prices to compete with the efficient pro-

"IT MAKES YOU FEEL CLEAN AND FRESH."

Price competition is based upon sell-ing price.

Nonprice competition is based on factors other than price.

ducer, he fails to make a profit and has to quit business. Through competition, buyers tend to get goods at the lowest prices at which the goods can be produced.

Competition and prices

1. Free competition among producers of a commodity tends to assure efficiency in production, high-quality products, and low costs of production.
2. Free competition among retailers and wholesalers of a commodity tends to cause the consumer price to fall towards the cost of production plus handling charges.

The economic principle of substitution is also an important factor in the competitive system. If prices of cotton go to a high level, there is likely to be a shift to substitutes such as rayon.

B. Economic factors related to price

Demand, supply, and competition are factors which affect price; in addition, monopoly, the value of money, credit, and taxes are factors which indirectly affect price.

MONOPOLY AFFECTS PRICES

In a few instances, a producer free from competition may have absolute power to determine the selling price by releasing for sale a supply of his goods or services that is less than the amount that would be purchased, thus keeping prices high. This is a situation known as *monopoly*. As there is no competition, the person who has the monopoly may try to charge what he pleases. He usually will limit production to keep prices artificially high. He undoubtedly will attempt to create and maintain demand so that he can get the prices he asks. In a monopoly, prices are not necessarily determined by the cost of production; rather, as has been explained, they may be determined by the monopolist.

The telegraph and the telephone companies provide interesting examples of monopolies, or at least partial monopolies. If one telephone company has a monopoly on the telephone service in a particular city, it has control over the supply of that service. In the absence of any legal control, the telephone company could set its own rates. A rise in the rates would cause some people to discontinue phone service. If the rates were to continue to rise, the telephone company might lose so many customers that it would not be able to make a profit. State governments, however, reserve the right to regulate the rates, or prices, charged by such companies.

The production of diamonds is controlled largely by monopoly. The monopoly governs the price and keeps it high. As a result of a restriction in the supply, diamonds are in constant demand. The volume of sales is limited, however, by the high price. At the high price at which diamonds are sold, a large profit is made. If the price were lowered, the rate of profit would decrease, although the demand would increase. If the price were lowered still more, it would eventually reach a point at which the total sales would not pay the producers as much profit as that which resulted from the total sales at the former high price.

Monopoly and prices

1. Government regulation, rather than supply and demand, determines price for some monopolies such as public utilities.
2. In monopolies, wherein price is not regulated by government, supply and price are manipulated in relation to demand to yield the maximum profit.

MONEY AFFECTS PRICES

Money is our medium of exchange. It also serves as the basis for establishing the relative values of goods. The value of money is determined by the amount of goods that a dollar will purchase. When the value of a dollar is low, the dollar will not buy so much as when its value is high. In other words, money is cheap if it buys little, and dear if it buys much. When money changes in value, prices in general change.

Two factors that affect the price level are (a) the quantity of money and (b) the rapidity with which money is used. The amount of money in the United States is less than the total value of goods that are being exchanged at a particular time. It is estimated that the total quantity of money in the United States changes hands from twenty to forty times a year. The quantity has been increased several times during the history of the United States by the issue of new paper money in the form of representative money or credit money. When there is an increase in the money available to buy goods and this money is used rapidly, prices tend to rise (a) because the supply of dollars is greater and (b) because the increase in rapidity with which money is used has the same effect as an increase in the amount. The general rise in prices is not always in proportion, however, to the increase in the supply of money or to the increase in turnover.

As a simple example, let us consider an island on which there is a certain amount of money and a relatively elastic demand for certain goods. The people who have money will soon establish the values of goods. If the total supply of money is suddenly doubled, however, everyone is in the same relative position. Each person has twice as much money as he formerly had, but he cannot buy twice as much goods because all the people want the goods in the same proportion as they formerly wanted them. If he attempts to buy goods with the same amount of money that he formerly used, he will find that other people are willing to pay more because they have more money. He will therefore have to pay just as much as anyone else. Prices in terms of money will rise because of the increase in the supply of money. In other words, increasing the supply of money has caused inflation of commodity prices.

CREDIT AFFECTS PRICES

Increases and decreases in credit affect prices in very much the same way as increases and decreases in the supply of money. Since credit expands the use of money, it serves to increase the rapidity with which money is used. If a person has $100 to spend and borrows $100, he has a total purchasing power of $200. If, at the same time, the supply of products and services remains unchanged, prices will increase

Amount of money available to consumers
affects both demand and price

because there is an increased amount of money and credit with which to buy products and services. When money and credit are increased, however, the supply of products and services may also increase. If the purchasing power continues to increase faster than the supply of goods and services, prices will continue to rise. When credit decreases, prices tend to decrease.

TAXES AFFECT PRICES

Generally, high taxes on producers and distributors tend to increase prices, for taxes constitute part of the cost of producing any article or rendering any service. If a high tax is levied on a building, it must be included in computing the rent of the building. If a sales tax is levied on any item, such as gasoline, clothing, or drugs, regardless of the person against whom it has been assessed, it constitutes part of the cost of the product. Part or all of the taxes are usually passed on eventually to the consumer, either directly or indirectly, so that the levying of a tax against a particular product will eventually cause a rise in the price of that product.

Such taxes as state and federal income taxes levied on the incomes of individuals reduce the purchasing power of consumers, tend to decrease the demand for goods and services, and therefore tend to lower prices.

CONTROL OF PRICES

The preceding discussion of prices has assumed that there would be no control of prices. Nevertheless, prices are controlled to a certain extent by government, by businessmen, by farmers, and by workers. Organized groups representing various aspects of production, distribution, and consumption attempt to obtain governmental protection or regulation on their behalf. Labor, professional, business, and farm groups practically all seek some kind of federal legislation primarily to give them an economic advantage. Some of the legislation is undoubtedly desirable, and some is necessary. However, from the early days of the Roman Empire to the present, attempts to control price and to regulate income have created many other problems.

As citizens, we vote in state and national elections on economic issues. It is highly important that we understand clearly the issues having to do with prices, subsidies, and government ownership of industry so that we may have a basis for intelligent voting.

Goods and services. The federal government owns and operates some industries and sometimes sets the prices of its commodities or services at less than cost and sometimes at more than cost. Among these industries owned by the federal government in which prices are controlled are the postal system, the Panama Canal, and the Tennessee Valley Authority. Some states also engage in production and distribution. States and municipalities own and operate many industrial and commercial enterprises, most of which have some characteristics of monopolies. In many government-owned enterprises, prices are arbitrarily set almost without reference to costs. Deficits are paid from funds derived from taxation.

The rates for services provided by public utilities, not government owned, are usually regulated or controlled by the state or federal government. For example, the rates for telephone service are under the control of the government. Likewise, railroad passenger rates and freight rates are controlled.

At various times, primarily since 1930, the federal government has extended its powers to control prices because of either a real or assumed economic emergency. During the depression years of 1933 to 1936, the National Industrial Recovery Act regulated minimum prices of certain commodities and determined the volume of production of some industries by restricting the quantity of raw materials available. The purpose was to aid in recovering from the economic depression. About the same time, the Secretary of Agriculture was empowered to set up a quantity restriction on the production of certain farm crops. If this quantity restriction on production was agreed upon by the growers of the crop, then the government would make subsidy payments to the farmers if the market price of the crop fell below the established figure, called *parity*. This agreement to limit production and this guarantee of a specified minimum price constitute, of course, control through price supports.

During World War II, the Emergency Price Control Act regulated maximum prices for most goods. The maximum prices allowed were called *price ceilings*. The regulations affected the producers of raw materials, manufacturers, wholesalers, and retailers but did not include farm commodities, wages of labor, or the compensation of professional workers (wages were restricted through the War Labor Board). The regulations were administered by the Office of Price Administration, commonly known as OPA.

Interest rates. For many years, the various states have had regulations as to the maximum interest rates that may be charged for borrowed money. In more recent years, the Board of Governors of the Federal Reserve System has exercised the power of control over the discount or interest rates that federal reserve banks may charge member banks. This control influences the rates of interest that banks charge.

Wage rates. With the enactment of laws regulating the minimum wages per hour and the maximum hours per week for labor, a control of the price of labor has been in effect. Not all workers are covered by the laws, but the wages of all are influenced by the legislation.

Credit. From time to time the federal government may exercise control over prices by means of credit policies designed to prevent inflation and rapidly increasing prices. For example, when automobile dealers are forbidden to sell automobiles on terms such as "36 months to pay" and are required to reduce the credit period to a time limit such as "18 months to pay," there will be fewer buyers. As a result, the volume of sales will fall and prices will tend to stop their upward climb. When government later eliminates such credit controls, demand will rise, sales increase, and prices begin their upward climb.

INDEX NUMBERS

Business managers and consumers have an interest in the trends in production, wages and salaries, prices, costs of production and dis-

PRICE INDEXES FOR COMMODITIES AND SERVICES

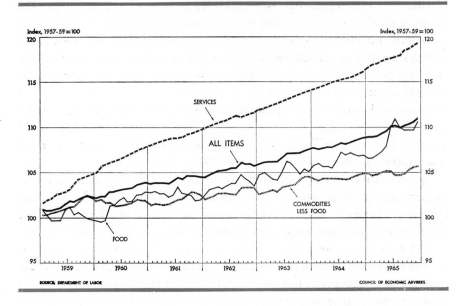

Period	All items	Commodities						Services		
		All commodities	Food	Commodities less food				All services	Rent	Services less rent
				All	Durable	Non-durable				
1955	93.3	94.6	94.0	94.9	95.3	94.4		90.5	94.8	89.4
1956	94.7	95.5	94.7	95.9	95.4	96.5		92.8	96.5	91.9
1957	98.0	98.5	97.8	98.8	98.5	99.1		96.6	98.3	96.1
1958	100.7	100.8	101.9	99.9	100.0	99.8		100.3	100.1	100.2
1959	101.5	100.9	100.3	101.2	101.5	101.0		103.2	101.6	103.6
1960	103.1	101.7	101.4	101.7	100.9	102.6		106.6	103.1	107.4
1961	104.2	102.3	102.6	102.0	100.8	103.2		108.8	104.4	110.0
1962	105.4	103.2	103.6	102.8	101.8	103.8		110.9	105.7	112.1
1963	106.7	104.1	105.1	103.5	102.1	104.8		113.0	106.8	114.5
1964 [1]	108.1	105.2	106.4	104.4	103.0	105.7		115.2	107.8	117.0
1965	109.9	106.4	108.8	105.1	102.6	107.2		117.8	108.9	120.0
1964: Nov ..	108.7	105.6	106.8	104.8	103.5	106.1		116.0	108.3	117.9
Dec ..	108.8	105.7	106.9	104.9	103.4	106.3		116.2	108.4	118.2
1965: Jan ..	108.9	105.6	106.6	104.9	103.6	106.1		116.6	108.4	118.6
Feb ..	108.9	105.5	106.6	104.7	103.3	106.1		116.9	108.5	118.9
Mar ..	109.0	105.6	106.9	104.8	103.2	106.2		117.0	108.7	119.1
Apr ..	109.3	105.9	107.3	105.0	103.0	106.8		117.3	108.8	119.3
May ..	109.6	106.2	107.9	105.2	102.9	107.2		117.5	108.8	119.5
June ..	110.1	106.9	110.1	105.1	102.6	107.3		117.6	108.8	119.7
July ..	110.2	106.9	110.9	104.7	102.3	106.9		117.8	108.9	120.0
Aug ..	110.0	106.6	110.1	104.7	101.8	107.1		117.9	109.0	120.0
Sept .	110.2	106.6	109.7	104.9	101.7	107.7		118.5	109.1	120.7
Oct ..	110.4	106.9	109.7	105.3	102.1	108.0		118.7	109.2	121.0
Nov ..	110.6	107.1	109.7	105.6	102.4	108.3		119.0	109.3	121.3
Dec ..	111.0	107.4	110.6	105.7	102.4	108.4		119.3	109.5	121.6

[1] Beginning with January 1964, new index with revised weights, coverage, and sampling procedures.

Source: Department of Labor, Council of Economic Advisors.

tribution, and similar factors that reveal economic and business conditions. A system known as index numbers has been developed to make trends more easily observed and understood.

Index numbers are percentage figures to measure such economic activity factors as industrial production, consumer prices, and wholesale prices. A *base period* is arbitrarily selected as the period with which current prices or current production is to be compared. The base period with which comparisons are to be made usually covers a period of three years. The one currently in use is the three-year period 1957-1959, representing an average for the years 1957, 1958, and 1959. The index number for this period is 100.

In December, 1965, consumer prices were 11.0 percent higher than the average of consumer prices in the base period of 1957-1959. Hence, the index number for consumer prices in December, 1965, is 111.0. If in 1965 consumer prices decreased 2 percent, the index number would have been 109.0; or if they increased 1.5 percent, the number would have been 112.5. Many trade organizations of retailers, wholesalers, manufacturers, and others prepare index numbers for their commodities and services.

What everyone should know about values and prices

1. The price system is the process by which one exchanges his labor or his products for the goods and services he needs through the medium of money.
2. High prices tend to increase production, whereas high production tends to decrease prices.
3. As the supply of goods (quantity offered for sale) increases, the price tends to be lowered.
4. The greater the demand for goods in relation to the supply, the higher prices tend to be.
5. The price of a commodity influences consumption.
6. Competition tends to force a reasonable relationship between (a) the cost to produce and (b) the price asked.
7. When money is plentiful and credit relatively easy to obtain, prices tend to be high.
8. Taxes on producers tend to increase cost of goods, hence to increase prices; taxes on consumers reduce purchasing power and, therefore, tend to decrease consumption.
9. Many prices are partially or completely controlled by state and federal governments.

▪ QUESTIONS ON THE TEXT

1. What is meant by the term "economic value"?
2. What is the meaning of price?
3. Under what conditions would water have value?
4. What determined value in the barter system?
5. What is the relationship between prices and money?
6. Under what condition would a businessman continue to produce goods without making a profit?
7. What is the relationship between price and production?
8. How does the cost of production affect the price of a product in the long run?
9. What is a subsidy?
10. What are the two characteristics of a buyer's market? Of a seller's market?
11. How is the word "demand" used in economics?
12. Under what conditions would a consumer substitute one product for another?
13. What is meant by "nonprice competition"?
14. What is the distinguishing characteristic of a monopoly?
15. What really determines the value of a dollar?
16. What effect does credit have on prices?
17. How do taxes affect prices?
18. Give an example of a government service which is operated in such a manner that the prices charged for services do not cover all expenses.
19. What government agency has the responsibility of regulating interest rates?
20. What is the purpose of an index number?

▪ QUESTIONS FOR DISCUSSION

1. State and explain the essentials of the price system.
2. If we are to have an ideal economic society, why is it absolutely necessary for the prices of goods and the prices of wages to remain relatively stationary or to fluctuate up and down together?
3. Discuss the relationship between production and price.
4. Discuss the relationship between production and profit.
5. The consumption of frozen orange juice in the United States has increased rather rapidly within the last twenty years. Why do you think the increase has taken place?
6. (a) What would be the effect on prices if the supply of a commodity (such as pencils) increases, but the demand for it remains approximately the same? Why?
   (b) Discuss the effect on prices, if the demand for a commodity increases, but the supply remains approximately the same.

7. Describe the conditions under which a buyer's market may exist for the buyer of fresh fruits and vegetables.

8. Discuss the principles of elastic and inelastic demand. Give several examples other than those in the chapter to illustrate each of the principles.

9. If you were a retailer, would you prefer to sell products with an elastic demand or to sell products with an inelastic demand?

10. The history of most newly introduced products, such as the automobile and air-conditioning equipment, shows that the products at first sold at high prices, although they were not nearly so good as they were later. How do you account for the reduction in price?

11. How can automation affect prices?

12. Discuss the need for regulation of public utility rates.

13. What logical reasons can be given for the governments of diamond-producing countries not regulating the production of diamonds?

14. What would be the effect on prices of goods if all installment sales and all charge sales were to be discontinued?

15. How do you think a sales tax affects prices?

16. How can the federal government affect prices of goods through control of wage rates?

17. Should prices of consumer goods and services be regulated by government, or should they be regulated by competition? State the reasons for your point of view.

▪ PROBLEMS TO SOLVE

1. Write a paper describing the immediate and long-range effects of a rapid rise in prices in general on: (a) farmers, (b) wage earners, (c) policemen, (d) retired persons, (e) government expenses, and (f) retail merchants.

2. In your school or public library, locate the latest copy of *Economic Indicators,* published monthly by the United States Government Printing Office. Study and analyze the tables and charts on consumer prices, wholesale prices, and prices received and paid by farmers. Prepare a report indicating such observations as general trends in prices, rapid increases and decreases in prices, and effects of prices on consumer goods.

3. Analyze the prices advertised in an edition of your local newspaper for common food items such as bread, sugar, potatoes, bananas, milk, head lettuce, bacon, and potato chips. Compare the prices advertised by the stores. Report the differences in prices that you find. Why do such differences exist? What keeps the differences from becoming greater?

4. In studying this chapter, you have learned that when the price of a commodity increases, the number of people who buy that commodity

at the price asked will ordinarily decrease. In an attempt to deal more thoroughly with this idea, prepare three lists of items: (a) things people will buy with almost no regard for price, (b) things people will tend not to buy if prices are sharply increased, and (c) things people will stop buying if substantial price increases go into effect. Study the three lists you have prepared, and in general terms describe or characterize the items in each list. What conclusions can you reach regarding the relationships between prices, demand for various commodities, and the nature of peoples' needs?

▪ COMMUNITY PROBLEMS AND PROJECTS

1. Make a study in the stores in your community and accumulate evidence that the prices for comparable products vary in numerous ways. Make a list of the stores that offer trading stamps, door prizes, coupons, credit premiums, and other "rewards" that in effect make prices different. Ask several merchants to describe their efforts to meet the price competition provided by other merchants.

2. The business sections of the Sunday issues of large city newspapers, *The Wall Street Journal, Business Week, Newsweek,* and other sources frequently contain articles about the prices consumers pay. Make a study of such materials, going back about six or eight weeks. Search out the reasons given for the price increases and/or decreases during that time. Then prepare a report to the class on the trends in consumer prices and the reported reasons for their changes or lack of change.

3. Analyze an issue of your local newspaper for prices of major home appliances such as washers, dryers, television sets, and air-conditioners. Note the advertisements which indicate a price with the provision that the buyer must offer a trade-in. Visit the stores that advertise such prices and determine what price you would have to pay if you did not have a trade-in. What conclusions can you reach about this form of price competition?

4. Ask the librarian in your public library to show you the files of newspapers. There probably will be newspapers from your local area and some from distant cities. On the financial page or in the financial section of the newspapers will be found quotations (prices) on agricultural products such as wheat, corn, beef, and eggs. Select five items for the study of prices. Look up the prices of the five selected items for the corresponding month for each of the last five years. Prepare a table of the price trends of the selected items for five years. What changes in prices did you observe? What do you believe to be the reasons for the changes in prices?

Chapter 13

Economic changes, fluctuations, and stabilization

PURPOSE OF THE CHAPTER

Income, prices, and profits are affected by the level of business activity. This chapter is intended to help you understand business fluctuations and cycles and to acquaint you with economic indicators that assist in measuring business activity.

You will find answers to these questions:

1. What is the business cycle?
2. What is the nature of inflation and deflation?
3. How does measurement of business activity help individuals, owners, and managers in planning future operations?
4. What economic indicators are available, and how are they used?

A. Fluctuations in business activities

Business conditions are almost always changing. There are periods of great activity and of less activity. The changes occur in the total

amount of goods produced, total employment, average prices, income, and other business activities. Fluctuation or change in business activities is not necessarily undesirable, for economic growth could not take place without change. Change may be anticipated, but the amount or severity of the change and when the change may come constitute problems for all who are engaged in business activity.

THE BUSINESS CYCLE

In an earlier chapter economic activity was defined as being any step or procedure or act that is concerned with satisfying man's wants and needs for goods and services through production, distribution, and consumption. It was pointed out that we speak of the combined or total production of all goods by all people and all business firms in the country as *aggregate production*. Likewise *aggregate income* refers to the combined or total income earned in the country, aggregate supply of goods to the total supply for the country, and so forth. Applying this idea, it may be said that the business cycle is a fluctuation in aggregate (total) economic activity. Ordinarily, fluctuation in one business activity, such as production, is accompanied by fluctuation or change in other basic economic activities, such as employment.

The *business cycle* may be defined as alternating periods of expansion and contraction in production, employment, income, and other economic activities. Once an expansion or contraction of economic activity gets under way it spreads from firm to firm, from area to area, and from process to process until a peak or bottom in aggregate (total) activity is reached.

PHASES OF THE BUSINESS CYCLE

The business cycle seems to be characteristic of free markets and free enterprise. If managers of business enterprise were able to forecast with certainty whether the period ahead will be one of increased business activity, planning as to how much to produce, how much to buy, what prices to be charged, and similar activities would be greatly improved. It would be helpful to know whether business is entering a period of general increase in activity or general decrease in activity.

A study of business cycles indicates that each major cycle has four phases or periods. The first is *prosperity*, which means that all economic activity is at a relatively high level. The second period of the business cycle is known as *recession* or *decline* during which time there is a marked decline in the level of economic activity. *Depression* is the third period in a business cycle. It is the time when business activity has dropped to a level as low as it will go during the cycle. The fourth and final period in the business cycle is the period of *recovery* during which the level of business activity begins to increase. The length of the business cycle is the number of months or years from the peak of one period of prosperity to the peak of the next period of prosperity.

The illustration below shows the four phases of a business cycle. The essential characteristics of each of the four phases are given in the accompanying chart.

CAUSES OF THE BUSINESS CYCLE

The average person is aware that business conditions change, but he is not always aware of the causes or of the significance of the changes. Even experts disagree on the analysis of the business cycle.

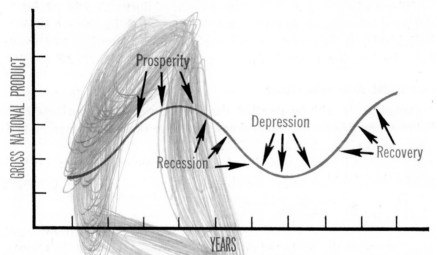

Source: Thomas J. Hailstones, *Basic Economics* (2d ed.; Cincinnati: South-Western Publishing Company, 1964), p. 281.

Phases of the business cycle

Many explanations have been given by businessmen and economists for changes in business conditions. These explanations vary widely. Some explanations credit or blame the current state of business activity on the political party in power, on labor troubles, on communism, or on conditions brought about by the weather. No completely satisfactory or reliable explanation has ever been given for the cyclical changes that occur in business activity.

Prosperity	Recession	Depression	Recovery
1. Wages increase.	1. Business stops investing and begins paying off loans.	1. Spending declines.	1. Interest rates are low.
2. High level of employment is reached.	2. Borrowing is reduced.	2. Prices become lower.	2. Most debts are paid.
3. People are overly optimistic.	3. Inventories accumulate.	3. Unemployment increases.	3. Banks are willing to lend.
4. Increased demand for consumer goods.	4. Demand for goods decreases.	4. Inventories decline.	4. Production increases.
5. Increasing demand for loans.	5. Average hours worked declines.	5. Buying is for immediate purposes only.	5. Employment increases.
6. Interest rates increase.	6. Profits decline.	6. Borrowing is low.	6. Prices begin to increase.
7. New businesses are started.	7. Prices decline.	7. Business failures increase.	7. Profits increase.
8. New construction and expansion of business nears completion.	8. Banks are unwilling to make loans.	8. Banks accumulate excess reserves.	8. Construction is begun.
9. Prices increase further.	9. People become pessimistic.	9. Interest rates fall.	9. Incomes increase.
10. Banks loan all their excess reserves.	10. Volume of business declines.	10. Operating costs decline.	10. Demand for goods increases.
11. Profits are high.	11. Business failures increase.	11. Production efficient, but low.	11. Consumer goods are produced.
12. Production is high.	12. Number of jobs decline.	12. Wage rates are low.	12. Capital goods production increases.
	13. No business expansion.		13. Installment sales increase.

Characteristics of the business cycle

There will always be a certain amount of fluctuation in profits, in the total amount of business that is done, and in the incomes of individuals. If we could prevent the extreme fluctuations, we would have the cure for depressions.

INFLATION AND DEFLATION

Inflation. It will be recalled that one stage of the business cycle is known as prosperity. Sometimes this stage of the business cycle is erroneously referred to as inflation.

The essential characteristics of a period of prosperity are: (a) high production, (b) high employment, and (c) stable prices. In a period of inflation we also have high production and high employment but highly unstable prices in general. Prices in a period of *inflation* increase not only to unreasonable heights but also at alarmingly rapid rates. In periods of inflation the purchasing power of the dollar declines rapidly.

Inflation occurs when the total demand for goods and services is greater than the supply available at a given time. This situation usually produces a shortage of goods, which ordinarily results in an increase in prices. Inflation also may occur when wage increases cause the prices of goods in general to rise.

General price increases are often followed immediately with a demand for wage increases on the grounds that the cost of living has increased. Likewise, a general increase in wages is often closely followed by increases in prices of commodities and services supported by the argument that the cost of producing goods and services has risen

During inflation some firms can adjust to rapidly rising prices and attract capital and labor from other businesses which, as a result, become lost to the economy.

because of increased wages. Thus as prices tend to increase, wages also tend to increase; and as wages increase, prices rise. This relationship between price increase and wage increase is sometimes referred to as a *wage-price spiral*.

In the long run an alternating increase in wages and in prices (that is, when a wage-price spiral has been created) causes the purchasing power of the dollar to decrease.

Rapid increases in prices and in wages and rapid decreases in the purchasing power of the dollar tend to be detrimental to our economy. Inflation can be disadvantageous to business and many groups of people unless it is kept under control. Several ways are available to halt or curb undesirable inflation.

Deflation. A rapid fall in general prices and income extending over a period of a few months results in *deflation*. This means that noticeably more goods and services may be obtained for a dollar than was true before deflation took place.

Deflation and economic depression are not the same, but they are related. If deflation is rapid and continues over several months, business activity is curtailed sharply, which means that not only do prices fall but also production of goods and services decreases and, therefore, unemployment increases.

There are advantages from deflation. Money that has been saved prior to deflation will buy much more than it did in periods of inflation. Likewise, a dollar of income from investments from savings

Ways to halt inflation

Government

   Control money and credit supply, thus avoiding overexpansion of
      business activity.
   Increase taxes, thus reducing private spending power.
   Avoid further increases in the national debt, except for grave emer-
      gencies such as war.
   Reduce nonessential government expenditures.

Business Firms

   Keep production geared to reasonable demand.
   Avoid unnecessary stockpiling of raw materials and semifinished
      products.
   Increase productivity per employee.
   Postpone construction insofar as feasible.
   Maintain present prices, increasing only as necessary.
   Be content with reasonable profit.
   Cooperate with labor and government in stabilizing prices.

Labor

   Increase productivity per man which in turn will decrease costs, hence
      prices.
   Give a full day's service for a day's wages; wages collected for work
      not done increase costs, hence prices.
   Cooperate with management in controlling the wage-price spiral.

Consumers

   Engage in productive effort of some kind; work, earn, produce.
   Increase personal savings.
   Reduce personal spending.
   Participate actively in civic and political activities with a view toward
      halting continuous rise in prices.

Government-Business-Labor-Consumers

   Before making any economic decision, weigh its ultimate effect on the
      wage-price spiral.
   Cooperatively attack with courage and fortitude the task of prevent-
      ing further inflation.

that were made under conditions of inflation will also buy more than
was true under inflation.

   Although some advantages from deflation are recognized, deflation
can reach a point that it is very harmful to business activity in general.
It is necessary that we should have some ways of controlling deflation.

THE PROBLEM OF FLUCTUATING BUSINESS CONDITIONS

   Extreme changes in business activity resulting in rapid changes in
prices may be detrimental to both business firms and individuals. The

Ways to halt deflation

Government

Encourage credit expansion which will stimulate business activity and employment.

Decrease federal taxes, leaving more money in the hands of people.

Increase federal spending on public works, relief, subsidies, national security, etc., which tends to stimulate business activity.

Business Firms

Extend credit to consumers to stimulate consumer buying.

Improve service, thus stimulating demand for goods and services.

Encourage people to spend more of their savings.

Consumers

Use personal savings for purchase of needed goods.

Within reasonable bounds, increase personal spending.

Cooperate with civic and government movements to increase business activity.

problem is to find effective means of reducing, if not eliminating, the effects of changes in business conditions on people.

In the Employment Act of 1946, provision was made for a Council of Economic Advisers, the primary purpose of which is to recommend to the President economic policies for the maintenance of employment, production, and purchasing power and to avoid the extreme fluctuations in business activity that lead to periods of inflation and depression. The Council is required to make a report to the President on the economic conditions of the nation in December each year. The

Facts everyone should know about fluctuating business conditions, changing prices, and inflation and deflation

1. Ordinarily, extreme fluctuations in general business activity are not caused by one but rather by a combination of several factors.

2. Sharply rising prices result in lowering the purchasing power of wages and income, an economic condition known as inflation.

3. In periods of decreasing prices, the purchasing power of savings and wages increases, but chances to earn wages or an income diminish. This economic condition is known as deflation.

4. Inflation has been ruinous to many nations; rapid deflation can harm both individuals and business firms. In the long run, everyone is hurt by both severe inflation and severe deflation.

5. The combined efforts of government, business firms, laborers, and all consumers are required to halt inflation and deflation.

recommendations of the President in his Economic Report to Congress are ordinarily based upon or at least substantially influenced by the report made to him by the Council of Economic Advisers. The Council thus becomes the central governmental agency for analyzing and interpreting business conditions for the guidance of Congress.

B. Measuring business activity

MAKING DECISIONS IN BUSINESS

In operating either a small individually owned business or a large corporation, managers are aware that their success is dependent upon many factors that affect the profits they make. Among these factors are such matters as demand for their product, that is, the kinds of products people want and the amount or quantity they will buy; price level, such as the cost of raw materials; wage rates for employees; rates of interest on borrowed funds; expenses, such as taxes paid; and the income that the business may expect. These are economic matters that affect the individual, the local businessman, and the corporation.

Every manager of business whether large or small has to make decisions, most of which will affect the profits in the year or years ahead. He knows that his business activities will be affected by general business conditions. If he had the answers to some questions, he probably would make wiser decisions than he would without the answers. Some of these questions are: Is it probable that expansion and growth in business activity in general will hold steady, increase, or decrease? Will the total demand for all goods and services change? Will the average level of all prices hold steady, go up, or go down? Will the total income for the country tend to remain about the same, rise, or fall?

Business inventories are affected by the level
of business activity.

The answers to the questions that are concerned with business conditions in general are found by measuring and analyzing the *aggregate* (or total) economic activities for the country as a whole. Let us see how business conditions in general may be measured and analyzed.

SOURCES OF INFORMATION ON BUSINESS ACTIVITY

Government surveys and statistics. The federal government undertakes the complex task of gathering, recording, and classifying the statistical information needed to study business conditions for the country as a whole. Among the federal agencies that prepare information on business conditions are the Bureau of the Census, Department of Commerce, Department of Labor, Department of Agriculture, Securities and Exchange Commission, Council of Economic Advisers, and Federal Reserve Board. The system and process used by the government for recording statistical information about the total economic activity of all people, business firms, and government is known as *national income accounting* or *social accounting*.

The governments of some states and a few private agencies, such as foundations, trade associations, and chambers of commerce, also gather and prepare information that is useful in measuring changes occurring in business conditions.

Types of information on business. The information pertaining to business activity includes such items as population and employment, production, personal and national income, wages, prices, finance, and foreign trade. By comparing current statistics with those of last month and previous years, the trend of general business conditions may be determined. Among the most commonly used indicators to determine business conditions are:

1. *Gross national product (GNP)*, which is the value of all goods and services produced in a period of time in the United States.
2. *National income*, which is the total income earned by those who contribute to current production. It represents the gross national product remaining after deductions are made for indirect taxes, depreciation, and the use of capital.
3. *Consumer prices*, which is the cost in dollars of nondurable goods used by consumers, such as food, clothing, and rent.
4. *Wholesale prices*, which represent the dollar cost to producers and distributors of farm products, nonfarm products, and processed foods.

5. *Consumer credit*, which is the total amount of debt owed by consumers on installment purchases and charge accounts.

6. *Industrial production*, which roughly is the quantity of durable and nondurable products manufactured and of minerals mined.

7. *Employment status and wages*, which indicate the number of persons employed and unemployed and the average hourly, weekly, and monthly wages of employees.

8. *Sales and inventories figures*, which show the dollar value of goods sold to consumers and of inventories of merchandise on hand by business.

Other figures that may indicate general business conditions are statistics dealing with such items as prices of stocks, amount of bank loans, new construction, farm income, and imports and exports.

GROSS NATIONAL PRODUCT

What does GNP measure? In earlier chapters we learned how gross national product may be useful in studying economic growth, income, and the distribution of income among those individuals who contribute to production. Our interest here in GNP is its usefulness as a measure or indicator of business conditions as a whole for the country. Let us consider what GNP really measures and how it may be used in planning business operations.

An understanding of what GNP includes is essential to using it as a measure or indicator of business conditions.

GNP is the total dollar market value for a year

1. Of all goods produced by all individuals, business firms, and government agencies at the time when the goods were transferred to their last purchaser—the person or firm who finally owned them or used them; and

2. Of all services performed directly for individuals, that is, services such as medical or dental care, legal advice, haircuts, laundry and dry cleaning, and maid service.

The total GNP for several of the past twelve years is given in the table on page 245 on gross national product for selected years. The total GNP for 1965 was $676.3 billion. This figure when compared with the total output or product of the country as a whole in previous years indicates the extent to which business conditions in general have

GROSS NATIONAL PRODUCT FOR SELECTED YEARS
(Billions)

Year	Total GNP in current prices *	Total GNP in 1958 prices
1954	364.8	407.0
1960	503.8	487.8
1961	520.1	497.3
1962	560.3	530.0
1963	589.2	550.0
1964	628.7	577.6
1965	676.3	609.6

* In terms of current dollars; that is, the 1965 GNP is valued in terms of 1965 prices.
Source: Council of Economic Advisers, *Economic Indicators,* February, 1966.

changed and whether the direction of the change is up or down. It may be observed that there has been a continuous increase in business activity as measured by total GNP in the past twelve years and that the amount of increase varies from year to year but has remained substantially high.

GNP as an indicator of business conditions. In planning their business operations for the future, individuals and managers of business firms rely upon what has happened to business conditions in the immediate past as the best indication of what conditions will be in the year ahead. Comparisons of the current GNP to previous years are useful to managers and owners in planning their operations.

Let us refer again to the GNP for recent years as given in the table above. It may be noted that GNP in 1958 prices, increased approximately $20 billion in 1963 over 1962, approximately $27 billion in 1964 over 1963, and $32 billion in 1965 over 1964. On the basis of total output or product, which is measured by GNP, business conditions were good and the following years will probably be good also. One must realize, however, that GNP is only one indicator of business conditions, and a downward swing could occur from causes not reflected in GNP. The GNP in 1958 prices showed uninterrupted growth. For 1960 through 1965, however, the amount of growth was not the same from one year to another; and although GNP increased steadily, there was no definite assurance that GNP for 1966 would be higher than it was for 1965.

In Chapter 9, we learned that the products and services produced in the United States as a whole are purchased and used by four major groups—consumers; business investors in this country; local, state, and federal governments; and foreign enterprises owned by both citizens of the United States and citizens or business firms of other nations. If an analysis of who purchased the goods and services of which GNP was comprised in 1964 were compared to a similar analysis for 1963 or earlier years, trends may be revealed that would indicate changes greatly affecting the goods and services that a business enterprise produces in 1965 and succeeding years.

An analysis of the purchases of total products and services for 1964 and 1965 is presented in the table below. Consumers spent almost $30 billion more for goods and services in 1965 than they spent in 1964. Of this increase approximately $11 billion more was spent on nondurable goods, that is, clothing, food, and similar items, and $12 billion more on services than in 1964. Approximately $13 billion more was invested in new factories, equipment, etc., in 1965 than in 1964. Other comparisons may also be made which would help business managers in planning their production for the following years.

PURCHASERS AND USERS OF THE PRODUCTS AND SERVICES PRODUCED IN THE UNITED STATES: 1964 AND 1965

(In Billions)

	1964		1965	
Individual consumers: purchases of				
Durable goods		$ 58.7		$ 65.0
Nondurable goods		177.5		189.0
Services		162.6		174.7
Total purchases		$398.8		$428.7
Business investments: purchases of new plant, equipment; additions, etc.		92.9		105.7
Government purchases of goods and services				
Federal government—				
National defense	$49.9		$49.9	
Other	15.4		16.7	
Total federal purchases	$ 65.3		$ 66.6	
State and local	63.1		68.2	
Total state and local purchases		128.4		134.8
Goods and services purchased by foreign countries (excess of exports over imports)		8.6		7.1
GNP		$628.7		$676.3

Source: *Economic Indicators,* February, 1966.

NATIONAL INCOME

Another measure or indicator of business conditions in general is national income. The Office of Business Economics defines *national income* as the annual earnings derived from the production of final goods and services. National income is closely related to GNP. It represents the sum of all the incomes received by individuals for their contributions to the production of all goods and services. The incomes received by individuals for their contributions, which are illustrated in the table below, fall in five classes:

1. *Compensation of employees.* This includes wages and salaries for private, business, military, and government employment. Seventy-one percent of the total national income in 1965 was for wages and salaries.

SHARE OF NATIONAL INCOME EARNED BY CONTRIBUTORS
TO PRODUCTION OF GOODS AND SERVICES: 1965

(Billions)

Item	Amount		Percent
Compensation of employees		$391.9	70.6
Proprietors' income			
Farm	$14.3		
Business and professional	40.3	54.6	9.8
Rental income of persons		18.6	3.4
Net interest		16.5	3.0
Corporate profits			
Before deduction of taxes	$74.7		
Less inventory adjustment	1.6	73.1	13.2
National income		$554.7	100.0

Source: *Economic Indicators,* February, 1966.

2. *Proprietors' income.* This consists of incomes to doctors, lawyers, small merchants, farmers, and others from unincorporated business, professional, and agricultural establishments. In 1965, proprietors received 9.8 percent of the national income.
3. *Rental income of persons.* Rental income includes income from royalties from patents, copyrights, rights to natural resources such as oil, and the rental value of owner-occupied residences. Rental income comprised 3.4 percent of national income in 1965.
4. *Net interest* is the net amount of interest that is earned by persons and business firms in the United States but does not include interest received from the government. Individuals and business

firms received 3.0 percent of the national income in 1965 for interest.

5. *Corporate profits* refer to earnings of privately owned corporations that are organized for profit before deductions are made for federal, state, and local taxes. The profits of corporations accounted for 13.2 percent of national income in 1965.

Comparison of the national income for 1965 to the national income in 1964 and earlier years will indicate whether income is holding steady, going up, or falling. This information is an indication of the condition of business in general and is helpful to individuals and business managers in planning operations for the next year.

EXAMPLES OF ECONOMIC INDICATORS

The records from which GNP and national income are derived are made up of many parts, each of which is a factor representing an economic activity. Each of these factors may be useful as a measure of business activity and a predictor of business conditions for the immediate future. Selection of the factors to use in prediction of future business activity depends partly on the nature of one's business.

The indicators of change in general business conditions are numerous. Each person who is interested in business conditions generally may select the indicators he wishes to use. The changes in selected indicators of business conditions in a 5-year period are shown in the table on pages 249 and 250. It is an illustration of a simple device for observing the changes that have taken place. Some other indicators of change that may be used under appropriate circumstances are changes in:

Population	Total time deposits in banks
Median family income	Total installment debt
Total employment	Total consumer credit
Rate of unemployment	Amount of new construction
Agricultural employment	Retail and wholesale sales
Manufacturing employment	New housing starts
Government employment	Exports and imports
Total bank loans	Inventories
Total demand deposits	Interest rates

The chart of selected indicators on pages 249 and 250 shows how the trend of change in any economic activity factor may be presented graphically as an aid in determining general business conditions.

MAJOR BUSINESS INDICATORS: ANNUAL SUMMARY, 1961-65

Item	1961	1962	1963	1964	1965
National Income and Product					
Gross national product, total (bil. $)	520.1	560.3	589.2	628.7	676.3
Personal consumption expenditures	335.2	355.1	373.8	398.9	428.7
Gross private domestic investment	71.7	83.0	86.9	92.9	105.7
Net exports of goods and services	5.6	5.1	5.9	8.6	7.1
Govt. purchases of goods and services	107.6	117.1	122.6	128.4	134.8
Gross natl. prod., total (bil. 1958 dol.)	497.3	530.0	550.0	577.6	609.6
National income (bil. $)	427.3	457.7	481.1	514.4	554.7
Personal Income					
Total (bil. $)	416.8	442.6	464.8	495.0	530.7
Wage and salary disbursements, total	278.1	296.1	311.2	333.5	357.4
Other labor income	12.7	13.9	14.8	16.5	18.2
Proprietors' income	48.4	50.1	50.8	51.1	54.6
Rental income of persons	16.0	16.7	17.6	18.2	18.6
Dividends	13.8	15.2	15.8	17.2	18.9
Personal interest income	25.0	27.7	31.1	34.3	37.1
Transfer payments	32.4	33.3	35.2	36.6	39.2
Less personal contributions social insur.	9.6	10.3	11.8	12.4	13.2
Total nonagricultural income (bil. $)	400.0	425.5	447.4	478.7	512.1
New Plant and Equipment Expenditures					
All industries, total (bil. $)	34.37	37.31	39.22	44.90	51.96
Manufacturing	13.68	14.68	15.69	18.58	22.45
Durable goods industries	6.27	7.03	7.85	9.43	11.40
Nondurable goods industries	7.40	7.65	7.84	9.16	11.05
Mining	.98	1.08	1.04	1.19	1.30
Railroads	.67	.85	1.10	1.41	1.73
Transportation, other than rail	1.85	2.07	1.92	2.38	2.81
Public utilities	5.52	5.48	5.65	6.22	6.94
Communication	3.22	3.63	3.79	4.30	4.94
Commercial and other	8.46	9.52	10.03	10.83	11.79
Manufacturing and Trade Sales, Inventories, and Orders					
Sales, total (bil. $)	729.0	780.9	816.0	871.8	944.8
Manufacturing, total	370.6	399.7	417.3	445.6	483.3
Durable goods industries	186.4	206.2	216.8	230.8	252.2
Nondurable goods industries	184.2	193.5	200.4	214.8	231.1
Retail trade, total	218.8	235.4	246.4	261.6	283.9
Durable goods stores	67.0	74.5	79.5	84.2	93.7
Nondurable goods stores	151.8	160.8	166.9	177.5	190.2
Merchant wholesalers, total	139.5	145.9	152.3	164.6	177.6
Durable goods establishments	56.9	60.3	62.9	69.0	76.2
Nondurable goods establishments	82.6	85.6	89.4	95.6	101.3
Inventories, book value, end of year, unadjusted, total (bil. $)	94.4	99.0	103.8	109.2	119.8
Manufacturing, total	54.8	57.4	59.7	62.6	68.0
Durable goods industries	32.2	33.9	35.6	38.0	42.3
Nondurable goods industries	22.5	23.5	24.2	24.6	25.7
Retail trade, total	25.4	27.1	28.5	30.2	33.9
Durable goods stores	10.7	11.4	12.1	12.9	14.7
Nondurable goods stores	14.7	15.7	16.4	17.3	19.1
Merchant wholesalers, total	14.2	14.5	15.5	16.4	17.8
Durable goods establishments	7.7	7.9	8.2	8.9	10.0
Nondurable goods establishments	6.5	6.6	7.3	7.5	7.8

(Continued on next page)

MAJOR BUSINESS INDICATORS: ANNUAL SUMMARY, 1961-65 (CONCLUDED)

Item	1961	1962	1963	1964	1965
Manufacturing and Trade Sales, Inventories, and Orders—Continued					
Manufacturers' orders (bil. $):					
New (net), total	372.7	398.0	420.4	452.4	492.3
Durable goods industries	188.0	205.0	219.6	237.6	260.7
Nondurable goods industries	184.8	193.0	200.8	214.7	231.5
Unfilled, end of year, unadjusted	47.9	46.2	49.1	56.0	64.9
Durable goods industries	44.8	43.7	46.2	53.0	61.5
Nondurable goods industries	3.0	2.6	3.0	2.9	3.3
Prices					
Consumer prices (1957-59 = 100)	104.2	105.4	106.7	108.1	109.9
Wholesale prices (1957-59 = 100); All					
commodities, combined index	100.3	100.6	100.3	100.5	102.5
Production					
Industrial prod., total (1957-59 = 100)	109.7	118.3	124.3	132.3	143.3
Manufacturing	109.6	118.7	124.9	133.1	144.9
Durable manufactures	107.0	117.9	124.5	133.5	148.3
Nondurable manufactures	112.9	119.8	125.3	132.6	140.6
Mining	102.6	105.0	107.9	111.3	114.5
Utilities	122.3	131.4	140.0	151.3	161.4
Construction					
New construction, total (bil. $)	55.4	59.6	62.8	66.2	71.7
Private, total	38.3	41.7	43.9	45.9	49.9
Residential (nonfarm)	21.7	24.3	25.8	26.5	26.6
Public, total	17.1	17.9	18.9	20.3	21.7
Civilian Labor Force					
Total, persons 14 years of age and over, monthly average (mil.)	71.6	71.9	73.0	74.2	75.6
Employed	66.8	67.8	68.8	70.4	72.2
Unemployed	4.8	4.0	4.2	3.9	3.5
Percent of civilian labor force	6.7	5.6	5.7	5.2	4.6
Employment, Payrolls, Hours					
Employees on payrolls (nonagricultural estab.), mo. avg., total (mil.)	54.0	55.5	56.6	58.2	60.4
Manufacturing	16.3	16.9	17.0	17.3	18.0
Prod. workers on mfg. payrolls:					
Payroll index (1957-59 = 100)	105.4	113.8	117.9	124.2	135.9
Average weekly hours per production worker	39.8	40.4	40.5	40.7	41.2
Finance					
Consumer credit (short- and intermediate-term), outstanding, end of year:					
Total (bil. $)	57.7	63.2	69.9	76.8	86.0
Installment	43.5	48.0	53.7	59.4	67.4
Federal finance (bil. $):					
Budget receipts and expenditures:					
Receipts, net	78.2	84.7	87.5	88.7	96.7
Expenditures, total	84.5	91.9	94.2	96.9	101.4
Money supply, etc. (av. of daily fig.) (bil. $):					
Money supply, total	143.2	146.2	150.6	156.3	162.6
Currency outside banks	29.1	30.1	31.5	33.5	35.2
Demand deposits	114.1	116.1	119.0	122.8	127.4
Time deposits adjusted (bil. $)	78.5	91.1	105.5	119.4	137.6
Foreign Trade					
Exports, incl. reexports (bil. $)	21.0	21.7	23.3	26.5	27.3
General imports (bil. $)	14.7	16.4	17.1	18.7	21.4

Source: Survey of Current Business, April, 1966.

CHANGES IN INDICATORS OF BUSINESS CONDITIONS IN FIVE YEARS

Item	1960	1965	Increase	
	Billions		Amount	Percent
GNP	$503.8	$676.3	$172.5	34.2
National income	414.5	554.7	140.2	25.3
Personal income	401.0	530.7	129.7	32.3
Disposable personal income	350.0	465.3	115.3	32.9
Personal consumption expenditures	325.3	428.7	103.4	31.5
Personal expenditure for durable goods ..	45.3	65.0	19.7	43.5
Personal expenditure for nondurable goods.	151.3	189.0	37.7	24.9
Personal expenditure for services	128.7	174.7	46.0	35.8
Personal savings	17.0	24.9	7.9	46.5
Compensation of employees	294.2	391.9	97.7	33.2
Corporate profits	49.9	73.1	23.2	49.9
Dividends	13.4	18.9	13.4	41.0

Source: *Economic Indicators,* February, 1966.

Facts everyone should know about measuring economic activity and predictors of business conditions

1. The federal government undertakes to gather, classify, and publish statistical information useful in studying general business conditions.
2. Many departments and agencies of the federal government participate in the complex task of recording and publishing statistics on business activities. The system used is known as national income accounting.
3. Several basic measures of total business activities have been designed. The two most commonly used are GNP and national income.
4. The GNP and national income totals and the factors of which they are comprised are useful to individuals and business owners and managers in planning their operations for the next year.
5. The goods and services that comprise the GNP are purchased and used by individual consumers, investors in business, governments, and foreign customers. Consumers use approximately 70 percent of all the goods and services produced.
6. National income represents the sum of all the incomes received by individuals for their contributions to the production of all goods and services.
7. Many economic activity indicators are available for studying general economic conditions. A selection of those to use should be made by each individual who is interested in general business conditions as a basis for planning operations.
8. The use of economic indicators singly or in combination to determine business conditions for the future is not infallible.

▪ QUESTIONS ON THE TEXT

1. What is meant by *aggregate* production and *aggregate* income?
2. (a) What is a business cycle?
   (b) How is the length of the business cycle measured?
   (c) What are the phases of the business cycle?
3. In what way will an understanding of the business cycle help the managers of business enterprise?
4. What conditions ordinarily exist when there is an upswing of business activity toward a period of prosperity?
5. Why are general price increases usually followed by a demand for wage increases?
6. Why is a general increase in wages affecting most industries and businesses usually followed closely by an increase in the price of commodities and services?
7. We all like prosperity, but we would like to avoid uncontrolled inflation. Who can help to halt inflation?
8. What business conditions usually exist when there is a period of deflation?
9. What is the primary responsibility of the President's Council of Economic Advisers?
10. Upon what factors does the making of profit in business primarily depend?
11. What items of information pertaining to general business conditions are available to business managers and the public?
12. How can such items of information about business conditions be used by business managers?
13. What are the most commonly used indicators of general business conditions?
14. What does GNP measure?
15. How can GNP serve as an indicator of business conditions?
16. How reliable is GNP when used alone as an indicator of general business conditions?
17. What does national income include?
18. In 1965 what percentage of total national income did each of the following earn: (a) wage and salary earners, (b) owners of farms, business firms, and professional offices (physicians, lawyers, etc.), (c) owners of property who receive rent, (d) lenders of money who receive interest, (e) corporations?

▪ QUESTIONS FOR DISCUSSION

1. How is it possible to determine the present level of business conditions?
2. Trace the effect of each of the four phases of the business cycle on each of the following: (a) wages, (b) prices in general, (c) business profits, (d) employment opportunities, and (e) volume of production.

3. The recession and depression phases of the business cycle usually cause some business firms to discontinue operations. What characteristics did those firms that discontinued operations probably have?

4. What are the differences between a period of prosperity and a period of inflation?

5. Explain how a wage-price spiral works.

6. Excessive installment selling is sometimes given as one of the main reasons for the beginning of a business depression. Why?

7. Why is production, in general, more efficient during recessions than during periods of prosperity?

8. Explain why a wage-price spiral causes the purchasing power of the dollar to decrease.

9. Some people yearn for the return of the days when $2 would buy plenty of food for the average family for one week. Did people live any better in those times than they do during periods of high prices?

10. Refer to the box summary on page 240, which deals with the ways to halt inflation. In your judgment, which of the five groups named in the box summary can be the most effective in halting inflation? Give reasons to support your answer.

11. Explain how deflation works to the advantage of individuals who made investments from their savings in periods of inflation.

12. Which of the various economic indicators shown on page 248 would probably be of greatest value to business managers engaged in the following businesses: (a) a wholesale food distributor, (b) a construction firm that builds houses, (c) a manufacturer of children's shoes, and (d) a bank in a small, rural community?

13. From what source or sources may a business manager get information about general business conditions that will help him in planning for the future and in managing his business?

▪ PROBLEMS TO SOLVE

1. With the help of your teacher or librarian, secure data relative to the gross national product for the past year. Prepare a pie chart that shows the makeup of the GNP for that year. Reveal in your chart: (a) the total amount of GNP, (b) the dollar amount of each part of GNP, such as government purchases, consumer expenditures, business investments, and foreign purchases, and (c) the approximate percentage for each part of GNP.

2. With the help of your teacher and librarian, search out information relative to how tax cuts, tax increases, and government spending have been used in recent years for stabilizing the economy of this country. (a) What specific devices have been used by the government to halt inflation or to halt deflation, and (b) what is the government now

doing or planning to do in the near future to stabilize the price structure or to stabilize the general economy?

3. Assume that you bought a utility bond costing $100 and kept it for 20 years. Assume also that the price level increased 16 percent over the period of 20 years. How much of the original investment of $100 would you have lost over the period of 20 years?

4. In April of a recent year, government economists were predicting that annual rate of the gross national product would grow by $5 billion to $6 billion for that year. In late June, the annual rate of growth was reported to be about $8.5 billion. The increase was attributed primarily to a boost in consumer spending for nondurable goods, a rise in business inventories, and an increase in exports. (a) Write a statement in which you explain the meaning of each of the three reasons given for the increase in growth of the GNP. (b) From reports of business trends in *Newsweek, Business Week, United States News and World Report,* or *The Wall Street Journal,* determine whether the GNP is now increasing or decreasing. (c) Write a second statement in which you explain the meaning of each of the reasons given for the current increase, decrease, or stable condition of the GNP.

▪ COMMUNITY PROBLEMS AND PROJECTS

1. After careful study of the material in this chapter about the forces affecting general business conditions and the economic indicators about which data can be obtained, arrange to talk with the owner of a business. Ask him how he makes use of various kinds of information available to him. Find out what he does to determine what and how much he should produce or what he should buy for resale to consumers. Prepare an oral report of your findings to present to the class.

2. Write a report incorporating the principles discussed in this chapter. Indicate whether the present time is the time to purchase real estate as an investment or whether one would be wiser to save money in anticipation of buying real estate later.

3. Using the latest edition of *Economic Indicators,* which should be available in your school or city library, make an analysis of present employment conditions and wages. Prepare a report indicating not only the current status of employment and wages but also pointing out trends as revealed by the various indexes that, in your judgment, will affect business conditions in the months ahead.

4. In 1965 the United States was in the 50th month of a prosperity phase of the business cycle. The economy was exhibiting all of the characteristics of prosperity that are indicated in the chart in this chapter. Using the latest edition of *Economic Indicators,* determine the current status of the economy. Then write a report that describes the changes in the business cycle that have occurred since the middle of 1965.

Chapter 14

Economic stability and government finance

PURPOSE OF THE CHAPTER

In the early days of government, its function was to protect people; to provide for national defense; to promote health and education; to construct and maintain public works, such as public buildings, roads, and dams; and to provide services that could be more efficiently and more economically performed by government than by individuals. In recent years some economists and politicians have advocated that it also is a primary function of government to promote economic growth and to maintain economic security; other economists and politicians oppose this point of view.

You will find answers to these questions:

1. How does government control economic stability?
2. Is government spending an economic stability factor?
3. How do federal budget surpluses and deficits affect business condititons?
4. What are the facts about the national debt?

255

A. Controlling business fluctuations

ROLE OF GOVERNMENT

The function of government in maintaining conditions favorable to economic growth and economic stability is an issue about which there is considerable disagreement. Some economists believe that the federal government should strongly influence, if not control, the national economy. This requires policies regarding such matters as balance between government revenue (income) and expenditures; control of government expenditures as a factor in influencing business conditions; management of federal taxation programs; reduction of unemployment through federal programs; government spending; and management of the national debt.

Other economists believe that under a free-enterprise system government should not, except in case of emergency, attempt to influence economic growth or to control economic stability through government spending, taxation, or management of the national debt. In a general way they are opposed to the establishment or adoption of government policies that are designed to control the national economy.

Government policies pertaining to economic growth and stability are determined primarily by the political party in control. The president, the cabinet members, the President's Council of Economic Advisers, and the heads of government agencies determine the policies that are adopted. The representatives in Congress, whom we elect to represent us, enact the legislation that puts government policies into action. This is as it should be in a government controlled by the citizens. The purpose of the treatment on government influence on economic growth and stability is not to argue for or against present government policies but rather to help you understand the policies that currently control the economy.

CONDITIONS FAVORABLE TO ECONOMIC STABILITY

The term *economic stability* is used ordinarily to describe a set of conditions about business and economic activity that are considered to be good for the economy as a whole and also desirable for individuals. Among the most important of these conditions are the following:

1. National income is rising slowly but steadily, meaning that business is active and economic growth is taking place.
2. There is full employment, meaning that there are steady jobs for those who want to work.

3. The general price level is relatively stable, meaning that the average price level is changing slowly if at all and that the prices of particular products rise and fall according to the supply and demand for them.

4. Business activity in general is holding relatively steady but increasing to accommodate growth and expansion.

EFFECT OF EXTREME FLUCTUATIONS

Extreme fluctuations in business activities and in prices hurt many people. Not only does extreme fluctuation result eventually in unemployment for many workers, but it also results in the loss of investments for those who have saved. Economic growth for the nation as a whole is fostered by steady income and by prices that remain firm even though they fluctuate in response to changes in supply and demand. If, therefore, economic stability is good for the nation generally, by what means may business booms and depressions be controlled?

TYPES OF GOVERNMENT CONTROL

The federal government promotes a steady rise in income and full employment through two major types of controls. The first is by control of the sources of the money supply, which is known as *monetary policy*. The second is control through government spending, taxation, and management of the national debt. This practice is known as control through fiscal policy. *Fiscal policy* governs the programs of actions that are adopted by government to deliberately achieve certain aims such as to promote economic growth, to increase consumption, to halt price increases, or to reduce unemployment.

Economic stability may be achieved or partially achieved through management of government expenditures, taxation, and national debt.

The three keys to economic stability and prosperity

Governments need goods and services, however; they must have income (from taxes and other sources) to pay the costs of government; and national debt is the result of current spending in excess of current revenue.

The discussion in this chapter includes an explanation of the present role of spending, taxation, and debt as essential features of government operations and of the possible use of these factors in the maintenance of economic stability.

B. Control through monetary policy

Money, banking, and credit were explained in Chapters 10 and 11. You learned what money is, what its function is in our economy, where it comes from, how government tries to control the money supply, and why the government tries to control the money supply. Now let us learn how money and credit may be used to control business conditions.

WHAT MONETARY POLICY IS

Monetary policy is a plan the government devises to promote economic growth and to maintain a stable economy through control of the supply of money and bank credit. The plan may be changed or modified as current conditions may indicate it is desirable or necessary to do so.

The Federal Reserve System, through changes in monetary policy, has a powerful influence on business expansion. The Federal Reserve System exercises major control over the credit-expanding activities of commercial banks. The commercial banks frequently borrow funds from the federal reserve banks to accommodate business expansion in the communities they serve or to prevent a crisis if many depositors should suddenly seek to withdraw their deposits. Both of these situations have the effect of stabilizing business in the communities served by the commercial banks, which in turn helps stabilize the economy of the nation as a whole.

The Federal Reserve System indirectly helps to maintain stable business activity and employment through the influence of recommendations it makes pertaining to loans and conditions under which banks can safely make loans. These recommendations are not mandatory on commercial banks, but they do influence the maintaining of a desirable financial balance in the community.

EFFECT OF SUPPLY OF MONEY ON TOTAL SPENDING

Economists do not always agree on the effectiveness of controlling the supply of money on the total spending of individuals and business

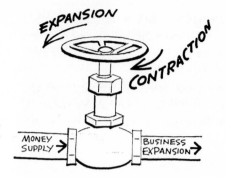

Federal reserve monetary policy may control business expansion or contraction, depending on the level of business activity.

firms. Some believe that causes other than supply of money may affect total spending. For example, the invention of a new reasonably priced product that everyone wants may cause total spending to increase very rapidly for a period of time. Monetary policy probably would have little or nothing to do with total spending in this case. The effect that a depression or a war may have on people generally through the creation of fear of immediate danger may cause people generally to curtail total spending even though the supply of money is plentiful. All economists probably would agree that the amount of money created by banks through monetary policy and total spending are related, but some would believe more than would others that control of money supply is more effective.

C. Control through fiscal policy

Economic activity consisting of production, distribution, and consumption engaged in by individuals and business firms is referred to as the *private portion* or *private sector* of the economy. The activities of government spending, taxing, and consuming goods and services are known as the *public portion* or *public sector* of the economy. The private sector, which pertains primarily to the interests of individuals and business firms in the economy, is strongly influenced by three factors that are controlled by the government. These factors are: government spending, taxing, and managing the national debt.

GOVERNMENT SPENDING

The plan of the government for the management of the foregoing three factors for the purpose of controlling business conditions in general is based upon the fiscal policy. For example, the fiscal policy of the government in periods of decreasing business activity may be to maintain a relatively high level of activity, income, and employment through increasing government spending for a given period of time. The purpose or intent of increasing government spending is to stimulate business activity, resulting in more income and better employment opportunities. As an alternative fiscal policy on the maintenance of favorable business activity, income, and employment, the government could choose to stimulate activity by reducing federal taxes. Either policy would leave more funds in the hands of people, which would tend to increase purchasing on the part of people generally. Determining fiscal policy requires economic decisions that are sometimes very difficult to make.

Effect of government spending. In 1965, the federal government purchased approximately 9 percent and local and state governments approximately 10 percent of all the goods and services produced in the United States. This means that of a total GNP of $676.3 billion in 1965, almost $135 billion were purchased by federal, state, and local governments. Government spending is a very important factor in providing both income and employment for people.

There is little attempt on the part of local and state governments to influence or affect economic conditions in general through spending. Their expenditures ordinarily are for public improvements and current operations that are considered immediate necessities and, therefore, the time for spending is not optional. The federal government also must take care of public works and current operations; but the amount of its spending at a given time may be increased or decreased, which, in turn, affects business conditions and employment in general. Our interest here is primarily in the spendings of the federal government as a factor in stimulating business activity if there are indications of slowing down, such as an increase in unemployment, or depressing business activity if it appears there may be indications that the current level of activity would lead to inflation.

Payments for pensions, subsidies, and interest. Some of the spendings by the federal government are not in payment of purchases of goods and services. Examples of such payments are pensions to veterans and others, social security payments in excess of social security receipts, subsidies to farmers and others, and interest on the national debt. These payments are known as *transfer payments*. When the government spends for food for the army, construction of a bridge or a dam or a building, or paper for use in government office operations, it is purchasing goods and services that were produced as a part of GNP.

Social security payments are from funds accumulated from employees and employers. They are known as transfer payments.

When it makes payments for pensions, interest, or subsidies, it is merely transferring to the recipients funds out of current tax collections. The individuals who receive the transfer payments may use them to buy goods and services; hence, they have the same effect on business activities in general and on employment as government payments for goods and services that were produced as a part of GNP. The total spending of federal, state, and local government in 1965 was $134.8 billion for the purchase of goods and services plus $39.2 billion for transfer payments, making a total of $174.0 billion.

Total spending. Total spending in the United States is comprised of the payments made by both the private sector and the public or government sector of the economy. Government spending, including both purchases of goods and services and transfer payments, is believed by some economists to be highly important in maintaining favorable business activity and employment. In case the spending in the private sector of the economy decreases, government spending may be increased to maintain a satisfactory level of business activity and employment. If the government decreases its spending, the effect is to force income and employment downward. In a way, government spending in a given period of time provides balance by adjusting its spending upward or downward to maintain total spending (private and public combined) on an even keel at a level that maintains favorable income and employment.

FEDERAL TAXES—A STABILIZER

Taxes take money away from consumers and business firms. The amount paid in taxes reduces the money available to spend in the private sector of the economy. During wars when the danger of inflation is great due to rising prices, governments sometimes increase taxes with the result that people and business firms will have less money to spend. The more money people have, the greater is their willingness to pay high prices; the smaller the amount of money they have, the more conservative they are in paying high prices. Thus, indirectly, raising taxes is a way of controlling prices by reducing the total spending.

In 1964 and 1965, some federal taxes were decreased, leaving more income in the hands of people. This action had a stimulating effect on business activities and on employment.

THE FEDERAL BUDGET

Each year the Bureau of the Budget prepares a budget of estimated government receipts and expenditures for the next fiscal year.

In the illustration of the federal budget below, the difference between estimated total receipts and estimated total expenditures is given. If the estimated total receipts are greater than the estimated

---

THE FEDERAL BUDGET: 1966 (Estimate)
(Billions)

Receipts

Personal taxes	$52.2	
Corporate taxes	24.7	
Indirect business taxes	16.1	
Contributions to social security	28.0	
Total		$121.0

Expenditures

Purchases of goods and services	$66.7	
Transfer payments	35.2	
Grants-in-aid to states and local governments	13.0	
Net interest paid	8.6	
Subsidies, net	3.5	
Total		127.0
Budget deficit		(—) $ 6.0

Source: *Statistical Abstract of the United States*, 1965.

When voting for taxes, one should analyze budgets in order to determine the sources of funds and to evaluate the purposes for which the funds are to be spent.

THE FEDERAL GOVERNMENT DOLLAR: 1966

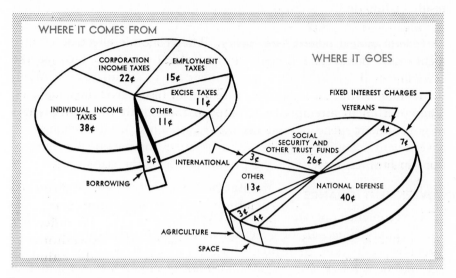

Source: Statistical Abstract of the United States, 1965.

total expenditures, there is a *budget surplus*. If estimated expenditures exceed estimated receipts, a *budget deficit* results. A budget surplus or a budget deficit may have a significant effect on the economy. The device of budget surplus or budget deficit is used effectively by government to promote economic growth and stability.

Budget surplus. A budget surplus really means that more money is taken from individuals and business firms in the form of taxes than the government is paying out to them through its spending for goods and services. A budget surplus, therefore, has the effect of reducing total spending, which may reduce business activity and may possibly also have an effect on employment opportunities.

Budget deficit. A budget deficit, it is argued by some economists, means that government is spending (making payments to individuals and business firms) in excess of the money it takes from them in the form of taxes, and, therefore, stimulates the economy. The deficit, that is, the difference between government expenditures and receipts, must come from some source. The practice is to borrow through selling government bonds, which increases the national debt. The wisdom of increasing the national debt through the sale of bonds and other securities to provide for current operating expenditures is challenged by many economists; others warn that creating credit too rapidly may result in inflation.

Federal budget reflects fiscal policy. The economic effect of government fiscal policy is reflected in the federal budget. Two of the economic goals of the federal government are to stimulate continuous economic growth at a reasonable rate and to foster economic stability. The government attempts to accomplish these goals through changes in government spending and taxing. It attempts through changes in government spending and taxing to offset or compensate for fluctuations in business activity in the private sector of the economy.

GOVERNMENT FINANCE

Governments operate at three levels—local, state, and national. The primary functions of government are to provide protection, to promote production, to regulate business and civic activities, to provide public services, and to promote both economic growth and economic stability. These functions are fulfilled in varying degrees at the local and state levels. All of them are fulfilled at the federal level; however, the major expenditures at the federal level are for past wars and national defense.

Financing the functions of government. *Public finance* is concerned with the financing of the functions of government by providing sources of revenue and income for government, controlling and making expenditures for goods and services purchased and for other necessary causes, administering the public funds, and managing the public debts. The tendency for governmental expenditures to increase continuously for several years has caused considerable concern. Although some of the increase in dollar spending is due to rising prices, it also is true that both individuals and business firms are requiring government to perform more functions than before. Individuals demand public services of various kinds, and business firms tend to insist that the federal government promote economic growth and economic stability. In a democracy the goods and services provided by government, whether they are local, state, or federal, depend upon the will of the people. Everyone, therefore, has a real interest in public finance.

Financial operations of government. The financial operations of local, state, and federal governments are affected by income and expenditures much the same as individuals. Income or revenue of governments is thought of as coming primarily from taxes of some kind. Some revenue, however, may be received from such sources as tariffs and government-owned utilities.

When expenditures exceed income, governments must borrow. Hence, we may have local, state, and federal debts. As consumers, we are interested in three phases of government financial operations. First, we want to know how much government services and protections cost; second, how much the average person must pay in taxes to support government; and finally, the amount of government indebtedness per person.

GOVERNMENT EXPENDITURES AND RECEIPTS

The total direct expenditures of federal, state, and local governments for selected years (1950 to 1963) are shown in the table below. By reference to the table, it may be noted that in 1963 of the total direct expenditures of more than $186 billion, approximately $110 billion were federal government expenditures, $27 billion were state government expenditures, and $48 billion were local expenditures. Roughly, of the total direct expenditures of government for the country as a whole, the federal government spends about 60 percent; state government, 15 percent; and local government, 25 percent.

DIRECT GENERAL GOVERNMENT EXPENDITURES
SELECTED YEARS, 1950-1963

(Millions)

Fiscal Year	Total	Federal	State	Local
1950	60,701	37,914	8,033	14,754
1955	98,029	64,305	11,190	22,534
1960	129,039	76,724	17,945	34,370
1962	148,415	88,953	20,373	39,089
1963	186,057	110,298	27,698	48,062

Source: Bureau of Census.

Federal, state, and local expenditures. Since 1950, the proportionate share of total direct government expenditures by the federal government has decreased slightly, while that expended by state and local governments has increased. This shift toward a greater percentage of total expenditures by state and local governments is due in part to increased local costs of schools, public buildings, and civic improvements. The increased state and local expenditures have, of course, made increased state and local taxes necessary.

Federal, state, and local tax revenue. The per capita revenue from taxes received by local, state, and federal governments in the United States is shown in the table below. This table shows that the per capita combined tax revenue collected by federal, state, and local governments increased more than four and one half times from 1942 to 1963, that federal tax revenue per capita increased more than five times in the same period, and that both state and local increased between two and three times. During this same period the value of the dollar decreased approximately 50 percent.

TAX REVENUE PER CAPITA FOR FEDERAL, STATE, AND
LOCAL GOVERNMENTS FOR SELECTED YEARS, 1942-1963

	1942	1950	1960	1963
Federal	$ 91	$232	$428	$460
State & Local	63	105	201	235
Total	154	337	629	695

Source: 1942 and 1950 data, Government Revenue in 1950, Department of Commerce; 1960 and 1963 data, Department of Commerce, Bureau of Census.

Budget of expenditures and revenue published. The budget of the federal government is published for the examination and study by individuals and business firms. The estimated federal expenditures classified by major purpose or function for the fiscal year 1966 are given on page 267. The kinds of items for which the federal government spends money and the increases and decreases in the items may be observed by examining the table.

D. National debt

The *national debt* is the amount of money that the federal government has borrowed from individuals and business firms (including banks). The federal government owes individuals, business firms, and others who hold government securities. In the 189 years that our government has been in operation it has spent approximately $317 billion more than it has received in revenue. As the table on page 268 shows, most of this indebtedness has been incurred in the last 50 years.

Federal Expenditures by Major Function
Fiscal Year 1966
(In Millions of Dollars)

	Fiscal '66 Estimated	—Change from— Fiscal '65 Estimated	—Change from— Fiscal '64 Actual
National Defense	$ 51,578	— 582	—2,603
International Affairs & Finance	3,984	— 59	+ 297
Total Defense	**$ 55,562**	**— 641**	**—2,306**
Space Research & Technology	5,100	+ 200	+ 929
Agriculture	3,944	— 533	—1,616
Natural Resources	2,691	— 44	+ 213
Commerce & Transportation	2,804	— 568	— 198
Housing & Community Development	10	+ 290	+ 90
Health, Labor & Welfare	8,328	+2,120	+2,853
Education	2,663	+1,154	+1,324
Veterans Benefits & Services	4,623	— 760	— 869
Interest	11,594	+ 308	+ 829
General Government	2,462	+ 45	+ 182
Total Nondefense	**$ 44,219**	**+2,212**	**+3,737**
Allowances:			
Appalachia	107	+ 104	+ 107
Contingencies	400	+ 300	+ 400
Less: Interfund Transactions	600	— 233	— 64
Total Budget Expenditures	**$ 99,687**	**+2,206**	**+2,003**
Trust Fund Expenditures (incl. Govt.-sponsored Enterprises)	32,898	+3,853	+4,013
Less: Intragovt. Trans., etc.	5,188	+ 54	—1,049
Total Cash Outlays	**$127,398**	**+6,005**	**+7,066**

Note: Details may not add to totals because of rounding.

Source: Monthly Economic Letter. First City National Bank, N. Y., February, 1965.

Growth in national debt. The growth of the public debt, as shown by the chart on page 269, has taken place particularly at five different periods since 1916. These periods coincide with certain events in history as follows:

1916–1919	World War I
1930–1939	The Great Depression
1939–1945	World War II
1950–1955	Korean War
1957–1964	Cold War

Per capita national debt. The per capita federal, state, and local debt represents an accumulated excess of expenditures over revenue received by governmental units. The table on page 269 shows the public debt per capita.

NATIONAL DEBT
SELECTED YEARS 1915-1966
(Billions of dollars)

Fiscal Year	Public Debt
1915	1.2
1925	20.5
1935	28.7
1945	258.7
1955	274.4
1960	286.3
1961	289.2
1962	298.6
1963	306.5
1964	312.5
1965*	316.9
1966*	322.5

* Estimated
Source: *Our National Debt*, U. S. Treasury, 1963, and Census Bureau.

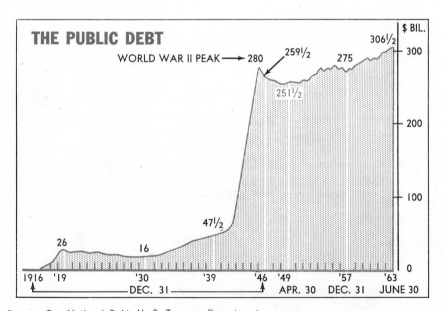

Source: *Our National Debt*, U. S. Treasury Department.

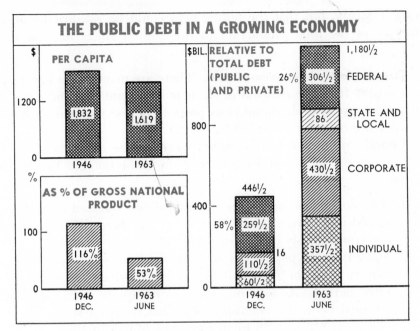

Source: *Our National Debt*, U. S. Treasury Department.

PER CAPITA FEDERAL, STATE, AND LOCAL DEBT
AT END OF SELECTED YEARS 1942-1963

	1942	1950	1960	1963
Federal	$538	$1,708	$1,607	$1,605
State	24	35	102	118
Local	122	122	262	318
Total	684	1,865	1,971	2,041

Source: 1942 and 1950 data, *Government Debt in 1950*, Department of Commerce; 1960 and 1963 data, Department of Commerce.

Concern about national debt. Some economists have expressed fear that the value of money will decline if the national debt is permitted to rise still higher. They believe that the country is facing continuously rising prices leading to more inflation. Others are concerned that the interest on the national debt is approximately $11 billion a year or roughly 9 percent of the total federal budget. Some individuals believe we can never pay off the present debt. Others believe that the size of the public debt is not a serious threat to the economic well-being of the nation. They argue that many individuals and business firms have debts that would require their total income for several years to satisfy, but that the public debt could be satisfied by about one half of the total production in the United States for one year.

Essential facts about national debt. There are many issues and problems arising from the national debt. It is important that there should be as widespread understanding as possible of the national debt and its influence on our economic life.

Consideration of a few essential aspects of the debt may help us understand the debt and its influence on the economic life of the nation.

1. The dollar amount of the national debt increased at an accelerated rate during World War II. It has increased more slowly but continuously since World War II.
2. Since 1946 the population of the United States has increased 33 percent, and the federal debt has increased 18 percent in the same period. As a result, even with rapidly increasing total national debt, the per capita debt has dropped from approximately $1,832 in 1946 to an estimated $1,625 in 1965.
3. The annual GNP, that is, the dollar value of the goods and services produced, is an indication of the ability to pay off the debt. In 1946, the national debt was 116 percent of the GNP; in 1965, the national debt had dropped to 50 percent of our GNP.
4. The growing economy adds to our ability to pay the annual interest on the national debt and to reduce the total amount by paying off the debt gradually.
5. In order to pay off the national debt, the total receipts must exceed the total expenditures of the federal government. This means that debt reduction is possible only when there is a budget surplus.
6. The interest on the national debt, estimated at $11.6 billion for the 1966 fiscal year, is approximately 12 percent of the total estimated expenditures. These interest dollars received by individuals and business firms help the economy.

Management of national debt. The national debt cannot be paid off at one time. To do so would disturb the economy very greatly. It would place an additional sum of money in the hands of individuals and business firms almost equal to one half of the total GNP for a year. Good management of the debt will require that an honest effort must be made to maintain a healthy balance between government receipts and expenditures and to retire bonds and other indebtedness when possible through budget surpluses without hampering sound economic growth.

Facts everyone should know about economic stability and government finance

1. One of the primary objectives of the federal government is to maintain economic stability.

2. Economic activity in which individual and business firms engage directly is known as the private sector of the national economy; and activity involving government spending, taxing, and consuming is known as the public or government sector.

3. An attempt is made by government to maintain economic stability through control of the supply of money and credit, known as monetary policy, and through control of total spending by adjusting upward or downward the amount of government spending, which is known as fiscal policy.

4. Variation in the amount of spending in a given period by local, state, and federal governments is one of the essential devices for stabilizing business conditions.

5. Variation in the amount of federal taxes may be used as a means of stabilizing business conditions.

6. A federal budget surplus tends to decrease the amount of money people have and thus depress business activity; a federal budget deficit is said to stimulate business activity.

7. Public or government finance is concerned with the maintenance of proper balance between government revenue and expenditures and the management of national debt.

8. The national debt has been created largely by wars and economic depression. One measure of the ability of the nation to pay its debts is the dollar value of the goods and services it produces each year. The national debt was 116 percent of GNP in 1946; 50 percent, in 1965.

9. The only way the national debt can be paid is through budget surplus—excess of federal income over federal expenditures.

■ QUESTIONS ON THE TEXT

1. What conditions are usually present when the economy is said to be stable?

2. Why do extreme fluctuations in business activities and in prices hurt many people?

3. **(a)** What are the two major areas of control by which the federal government promotes stable economic conditions?
   (b) What economic factors are included in each type of control?
4. **(a)** What agency of the federal government is primarily responsible for stimulation of economic growth and the maintenance of economic stability through monetary policies?
   (b) What does the agency do to achieve these goals?
5. **(a)** What is meant by the private sector or portion of the economy?
   (b) What is meant by the public sector or portion?
6. How can the government help control fluctuations in the private sector of the economy?
7. Approximately what portion of the total goods and services (GNP) produced in the United States are purchased and used by federal, state, and local government?
8. Why is spending by state and local governments less likely to affect general economic conditions than is federal spending?
9. What are transfer payments?
10. How will a reduction in federal income taxes affect the incomes of consumers?
11. What is meant by a budget surplus? a budget deficit?
12. Will a federal government budget surplus tend to stimulate or depress business activity? Why?
13. What two devices are used primarily by the federal government to foster economic growth at a reasonable rate and to maintain economic stability?
14. What government functions and responsibilities are included in *public finance?*
15. In what way are individuals and business firms partially responsible for the level of government spending?
16. What are the primary causes of increasing state and local government expenditures during the past ten years?
17. What is meant by the national debt?
18. To whom is our federal debt owed?
19. What relationship is there between increase in national debt and historical events?
20. Since 1950, what has been the trend in the per capita national (federal) debt? state? local?

▪ QUESTIONS FOR DISCUSSION

1. Discuss the difference between economic growth and economic stability.
2. Until recent years most economists and businessmen believed that economic stability, like good weather, is desirable, but that little or nothing could be done to control or regulate it. Discuss this statement.

3. Why are many people concerned about the increased level of spending by the federal government?
4. Should the various states attempt to influence or affect economic conditions through their level of spending?
5. Discuss the effect of transfer payments on the economy.
6. The federal, state, and local governments are currently using more than one fifth of all the goods and services produced in the United States. If these governments were to decrease sharply the amount of goods and services they use, what would be the effect on: (a) prices in general, (b) employment, (c) personal income, (d) sale of durable or nondurable goods to consumers?
7. Discuss the ways in which the government can maintain economic stability and prevent inflation during time of war when consumer goods are in short supply and personal incomes are high.
8. Why is continuous economic growth necessary?
9. Discuss the reasons why state and local government expenditures are increasing at a more rapid rate than federal.
10. Discuss a citizen's responsibility in public finance.
11. Discuss the statement "No public service is free."
12. Interest on the national debt in 1966 is estimated at more than $11.5 billion. Most of the interest is payable to individual business firms such as insurance companies, foundations, and banks. What effect does the payment of the interest on the national debt have on: (a) taxes, (b) personal income, (c) GNP, (d) consumption of goods and services, (e) employment?
13. In both 1964 and 1965, the decrease in federal income and excise taxes stimulated business activities and employment. Why could federal taxes not be eliminated entirely? Give your reasons.
14. Explain how a federal budget deficit may stimulate business activities and employment.
15. Should government during periods of war increase taxes so that an increase in the public debt would be held to a minimum?

▪ PROBLEMS TO SOLVE

1. Referring to the federal budget illustrated on page 267, (a) determine the percent of the estimated total federal expenditures for 1966 that is allocated for defense and space research and technology. (b) How do these estimated items for 1966 compare in dollar amount and percentage of the total budget to the same items for fiscal 1964? (c) What generalizations might you draw from these comparisons?
2. Comparing the interest figures for 1964 and 1966 on the national debt from this same budget, what conclusions and generalizations can you draw?

3. From current issues of *The Statistical Abstract* and *World Almanac* find data to prepare the following charts to show certain economic changes in the United States from 1900 to the present: (a) gross national product and the GNP per person, (b) national income and total disposable income, (c) employment and unemployment, and (d) consumer prices.

4. You learned in this chapter that federal taxes may be used as a stabilizer on the economy by increasing or decreasing the amount of money available for spending in the private sector of the economy. Prepare a list of other stabilizers or "cushions" and tell how they, too, can serve to prevent our economy from tumbling into a serious economic depression.

5. Discuss possible changes in fiscal policy that might have a favorable effect on employment.

▪ COMMUNITY PROBLEMS AND PROJECTS

1. Investigate the position your state takes with respect to state debt or deficit financing. What or who determines whether your state can create debts or engage in deficit financing? What has been the trend in your state with reference to the dollar amount of debt?

2. Collect the following data for the years specified and develop a chart showing trends:
   (a) National income from 1950 through the latest year for which data are available
   (b) Compensation of employees for the same years
   (c) Proprietors' income for the same years
   (d) Rental income of persons for the same years
   What are your conclusions?

3. The money supply on these dates was as follows:

	December, 1957	December, 1965
	(in billions of dollars)	
Currency	$ 28.3	$ 36.3
Demand Deposits	107.6	131.2
Total	$135.9	$167.4

The Federal Reserve discount rates on these dates were:

    December, 1957   3%
    December, 1965   4½%

What conclusions can you draw?

Chapter 15

Taxation

PURPOSE OF THE CHAPTER

Everyone benefits directly or indirectly from many of the services provided by local, state, and federal governments. The cost of these services and the costs of operating government departments must be paid for. The funds for paying these costs must come from individuals and business firms. There are no other sources. The plan used for collecting these funds is known as taxation. The funds collected are referred to as tax.

You will find answers to these questions:

1. What is taxation?
2. What are the principles of taxation?
3. What are the kinds of taxes?
4. How much tax does the average individual pay?

A. Principles of taxation

Local, state, and federal governments provide protections and services that are for the common good of all citizens, organizations,

associations, and business enterprises. It will be recalled that in Chapter 2 the characteristics of free enterprise were stated as the right of individuals to own property, the operation of free markets, profit motivation, and competition. These rights and privileges can be assured only by a government that both protects and regulates. The government, however, is subject to the same natural laws as are individuals. Expenses and costs must be paid.

The average citizen looks upon taxes as a burden and as something to be avoided if possible. If there were a better understanding of the purposes and the uses of taxation, citizens might have a different attitude toward being taxed. Every person and business firm benefits from services provided by government. Few, if any, of us benefit directly from the use of all government agencies, but each of us benefits directly from the use of some of the agencies and indirectly from the use of many, if not all.

NATURE OF TAXES

Expenses and costs are incurred by governments in providing protections and services. These expenses and costs must be paid, and a federal, state, or local government must have some device or plan for raising funds to meet those expenses. Such a device or plan is known as *taxation*.

A *tax* is a compulsory contribution of money to be made to a government to provide for services for the common good. This definition distinguishes taxation from payments to government agencies. For instance, a postage stamp pays for a service, but its use is not compulsory unless the service is desired. Citizens who violate laws have to pay fines as penalties. The fines are compulsory, but they are not taxes; they are penalties. Every person in a state may pay a tax for some general improvement in the state, but an assessment on certain property for the construction of a street or a sewer does not constitute a tax. It is a payment for the improvement of the property. In some cases assessments are voluntary in the sense that the majority of property owners who benefit from the improvement agree to the assessments.

CONTROL OVER TAXES

In a primitive civilization there is little need for taxes because few services are expected or are necessary. As civilization develops, greater demands are made for public services. Citizens rarely realize, however, what additional tax burdens these demands cause. Services, whether

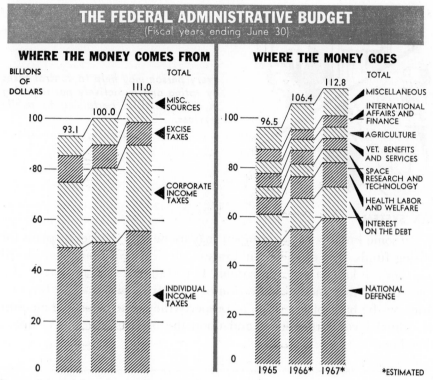

THE FEDERAL ADMINISTRATIVE BUDGET
(Fiscal years ending June 30)

WHERE THE MONEY COMES FROM

BILLINGS OF DOLLARS

TOTAL

111.0
100.0
93.1

MISC. SOURCES
EXCISE TAXES
CORPORATE INCOME TAXES
INDIVIDUAL INCOME TAXES

WHERE THE MONEY GOES

TOTAL

112.8
106.4
96.5

MISCELLANEOUS
INTERNATIONAL AFFAIRS AND FINANCE
AGRICULTURE
VET. BENEFITS AND SERVICES
SPACE RESEARCH AND TECHNOLOGY
HEALTH LABOR AND WELFARE
INTEREST ON THE DEBT
NATIONAL DEFENSE

1965   1966*   1967*   *ESTIMATED

Source: Adapted from *Finance Facts*, March, 1966.

When voting for taxes, one should analyze budgets in order to determine the sources of funds and to evaluate the purposes for which the funds are to be spent.

produced by governments or by private enterprise, cost money. Any additional service rendered by a government must be paid for by some group of citizens. The real questions to the consumer are: How can I get the service most economically and effectively? Does my tax money produce more service in the hands of government than it would in the hands of private enterprise? These questions are not answered easily. Most taxpayers consider only how much they pay in taxes. An important consideration and a more basic one is how tax money is spent.

People who vote for taxes should evaluate the advantages of each particular tax in the light of the benefit to the entire community. It should be remembered that no public service is free; someone has to pay. The person who ultimately bears the burden is the taxpayer.

Analysis of the budgets of local, state, and federal governments will reveal the sources of government funds and the kinds of services for which they are expended.

Every person may help to control taxes by voting and by actively participating in civic activities pertaining to public services.

TAX SYSTEM

In some instances a government may use several devices or plans for raising funds. All of these fund-raising devices and plans considered together are known as a *tax system*. For example, the tax system of a town or city may include collection of taxes from citizens and business firms on the basis of the value of property they own, upon the amount of annual income they have, and upon the basis of the cost of goods they buy.

Essentials of a tax system

1. The plan or system must produce sufficient income to pay the costs of government.
2. It must be relatively simple to understand and easy to administer.
3. The tax each individual should pay must be determined by a formula or rule, not arbitrarily.
4. The tax must be just, that is, based upon a plan that is considered to be fair to all taxpayers.
5. The system should make tax evasion difficult, if not impossible.

FAIRNESS IN TAXATION

Public services and public facilities such as schools, streets and roads, parks, and city halls, whether produced by private enterprise or by governments, cost money. The money must come from citizens and business enterprises. There are no other sources. The question is, how may the costs of government services and public facilities be divided among the citizens and business firms so that each pays his share? What is a fair basis for charging each citizen and business firm his share? Several different ideas on how to charge the costs of government have been developed. Let us consider two of the most popular theories.

Cost-of-service-received theory. One theory, as to apportioning the tax burden among taxpayers, is that they should be assessed according to the cost of the service or benefit received. The cost-of-service-received theory would charge taxes to citizens and business firms on the basis of the amount of service received or the benefit gained from government services and facilities. For example, a family with four children in elementary school would be assessed taxes for educational purposes at twice the rate charged to a family having two children in school. In theory, a person would pay for the upkeep of streets according to how much he uses the streets. He would be taxed for police protection on the basis of the number of persons in his family and according to the value of his property that is protected.

In one sense the cost-of-service-received plan of taxation is based upon the principle that the more property, such as real estate, one owns, the more protection and benefit of government services he receives; therefore he should pay taxes proportionate to the service he receives. This principle is followed in tax based upon a percentage of the appraised value of real estate.

The difficulty in the cost-of-service plan of assessing taxes is that it is practically impossible to determine the amount of service or benefit a person or business firm has actually received from government services.

Ability-to-pay theory. The ability-to-pay theory or plan is the most widely accepted tax plan in use. It is based upon the principle that individuals and business firms which have large amounts of property or large incomes are more able to pay taxes than are individuals and business firms that have little property or small incomes. For example, it is assumed that an individual having property worth $100,000 is more able to pay $5,000 a year in real estate tax (that is, 5 percent of the value) than an individual owning property worth $10,000 is able to pay $500 (also 5 percent). The question is whether or not the sacrifices made by the two individuals are the same. Some people argue that the individual paying $500 tax on property worth $10,000 is making a greater sacrifice (that is, he misses the money more) than the individual paying $5,000 real estate tax on property worth $100,000.

What should be the basis for determining the ability of an individual to pay for government services through taxes? Does the amount of real estate property an individual owns indicate his ability to pay? Does the amount of stocks and bonds and amount of life insurance an individual has indicate ability to pay? Or is ability to pay indicated more accurately by an individual's annual income? These are difficult questions to answer.

The federal income tax, which applies a progressively higher rate as the amount of taxable income increases, is based upon the ability-to-pay theory. For example, according to the federal income tax rates for 1965 income for a single person, the tax rate increases as taxable income increases as follows:

Taxable * income	Amount of tax	Percent of taxable income
$ 1,000	$ 70	7.0
2,000	310	15.5
10,000	2,190	21.9
20,000	6,070	30.5
100,000	55,490	55.5

*Taxable income is income after all allowances for exemptions and personal deductions have been subtracted.

DIRECT AND INDIRECT TAXES

Taxes are frequently classified as direct and indirect, although this distinction is not entirely accurate. A *direct tax* is one that is levied upon a particular group of persons or organizations and which may or may not be passed on to others. An *indirect tax* is one that is levied upon a group of individuals or organizations but which is passed on indirectly to others.

Real estate tax. A tax on real estate is usually considered to be a direct tax because it must be paid by the owner of the real estate. Nevertheless, the tax on real estate can be passed on to the renter by charging higher rent. From this point of view, it may be considered as an indirect tax.

Sales tax. Some sales taxes are direct, and others are indirect. If a sales tax is charged on the total sales of a merchant, it will probably be passed on indirectly to the individual customers through increased prices; whereas if the tax is added to each sale, it is direct because it is paid by the consumer.

Poll tax. The *poll tax* is imposed by several states on every male citizen from the time he is of legal age to vote until he reaches a certain age, usually 50 years.

Excise tax. There are many excise taxes, some of which are direct and others, indirect. An *excise tax* is one that is levied upon the commodities, facilities, privileges, or occupations within a country. Some excise taxes are supposed to be direct, but many of them become indirect. For example, a federal excise tax on cigarettes is imposed as a direct tax upon the merchant, but he includes it in his selling price. The consumer therefore pays the tax. This process is referred to as "shifting the tax burden." Whenever the cost of a product is increased to include a tax, the tax is being passed on to the buyers.

Gasoline tax. Many of the taxes on gasoline were supposed to be direct taxes on the producers or the distributors, but they have become indirect taxes by being passed on to the consumers through an increase in the retail price. These taxes thus resemble many other taxes that are supposed to be direct but which, in practice, become indirect. Legislators have discovered that the least "painful" taxes are the ones that arouse least opposition. Indirect taxes are in this class.

HIDDEN TAXES

Many of the so-called indirect taxes are referred to as *hidden taxes* because most people are not aware of the fact that they are paying those taxes. For example, one may pay a sales tax when he purchases a new radio. The purchaser is aware of paying that tax, but he is not aware of paying many other taxes that are included in the selling price. For instance, taxes have been paid on the labor that was required to produce the radio or on raw materials that were needed in manufacturing the radio. Taxes have been paid on the factory in which the radio was manufactured. Transportation costs have been included in the selling price. The transportation companies that handled the radio have included a certain amount of taxes in their charges. Many of these taxes cannot be traced definitely to their original sources, but it has been estimated that hidden taxes represent almost 20 percent of every dollar of retail sales.

B. Kinds of taxes

Taxes are levied and collected by local, state, and federal governments. The major kinds of taxes are: property; individual income;

corporation profits; sales and gross receipts; and others, including estate, inheritance and gift, licenses, and permits.

By referring to the table below, it may be observed that property taxes are levied primarily at the local level, whereas individual and corporation income taxes are, although used some at the state level, primarily federal taxes. Sales and excise taxes are used extensively by local, state, and federal governments.

PROPERTY TAXES

A *property tax* is one levied upon real estate or any personal property that has value and that can be bought and sold. This tax is based upon the assumption that the ownership of property is an indication of the owner's ability to pay tax.

Exemption of property. In some states certain property, such as real estate owned by churches, is exempted from the general property tax. In other instances a taxpayer may be exempted from paying tax on the full value of the property if there is a mortgage on it. In other cases, local governments may exempt certain individual or business property from the general property tax in order to attract new industry.

TAXES COLLECTED BY LOCAL, STATE, AND FEDERAL GOVERNMENTS—1963
(In millions of dollars)

Kind of tax	Taxes collected by			
	Local	State	Federal	Total
Property	$20,089	$ 688	—	$ 19,401
Individual income	313	2,956	$47,588	50,857
Corporation income (profits) ..	—	1,505	21,579	23,084
Sales and gross receipts	1,583	12,873	14,215	28,671
Motor vehicle and operator's licenses	120	1,780	—	1,900
Death and gift	—	595	2,167	2,762
Other taxes	747	1,720	1,248	3,715
Total	$22,852	$22,117	$86,797	$130,390

Source: Department of Commerce, Bureau of the Census, Annual Report, *Government Finances in 1963.*

Assessment of property. Inasmuch as the property tax is based upon value, it is necessary to determine the taxable value of the property. Local assessors estimate the value of the property. The assessed value (usually a percentage of the estimated market value) of the property becomes the basis for calculating the amount of tax the owner should pay.

Property tax rates. Property tax rates may be stated in terms of mills, dollars per thousand, percentages, or other units. The total tax rate on property is the sum of the separate rates on property imposed by the various units of government that are empowered to levy taxes. The following is an example of the total tax rate on property, comprised of the sum of the separate rates levied by different units.

Taxing unit	Tax rate percentage on assessed value
State	1.5
City	1.7
County	.9
School district	2.8
Total tax rate	6.9

This tax rate means that the taxpayer will be assessed property taxes at the rate of 6.9 percent of the assessed value of his property.

A	REAL ESTATE TAX STATEMENT		MONROE COUNTY	APPROVED FOR MONROE COUNTY BY STATE BOARD OF ACCOUNTS-1960.
			BLOOMINGTON, INDIANA	
1964 PAYABLE 1965	THIS IS A VALID RECEIPT WHEN STAMPED PAID BY TREASURER			
	MAKE ALL CHECKS PAYABLE TO TREASURER OF MONROE COUNTY.			

For the FIRST Installment of State, County, Township and Corporation Tax for the year 1964 on the following property

B47120X ROYAL MCBEE, ATHENS, O. & INDIANAPOLIS

	TAX VALUE	EXEMPTION	NET TAX VALUE	HALF POLL	DUPLICATE NO.	
PLEASE CORRECT ANY ERROR IN ADDRESS	12,500	1,000	11,500	3	12051	

EXAMINE RECEIPTS. SEE THAT DESCRIPTIONS ARE CORRECT.

TAX RATE 9.58

SEE THAT PERSONAL AND POLL TAX IS PAID.

DESCRIPTION
Hoosier Acres 1st Addition, Lot 1 — TWP. OR CORP. Perry Twp.

NAME Bloom, Nicholas A. and
Elizabeth
R. R. 3
Bloomington, Indiana

EXEMPTION	NET TAX VALUE	HALF POLL	FIRST INSTALLMENT
1,000	11,500	3	553.85
DELINQUENT TAX AND PENALTY			
TOTAL			

TO PAY FULL YEAR TAX BEFORE FIRST MONDAY IN MAY. DOUBLE FIRST INSTALLMENT · ENCLOSE SELF-ADDRESSED STAMPED ENVELOPE WHEN PAYING BY MAIL.
FIRST INSTALLMENT DELINQUENT AFTER 1ST MONDAY IN MAY.
SECOND INSTALLMENT DELINQUENT AFTER 1ST MONDAY IN NOV. RETURN ALL COPIES TO COUNTY TREASURER
MAIL OR BRING THIS STATEMENT WHEN PAYING TAXES

TREASURER, MONROE COUNTY

A real-estate tax statement payable in installments

Advantages and disadvantages of property taxes. One of the most important arguments for a property tax is that, since property receives protection such as police and fire from the government, the owners should be required to pay for the protection. In the early days when our tax system was established, the ownership of real estate was a reasonably good index of the ability to pay taxes. Now, however, there are many persons who do not own real property but who have much greater incomes than some other people who own real estate. The ownership of real estate, therefore, should not be the only criterion of one's ability to pay taxes.

Property valuations or assessments are not always computed fairly, for they are based on judgment. Judgment is sure to vary. If one person's piece of property is valued low and another person's property is valued high, the latter person pays a greater tax in proportion to the actual value of his property.

INDIVIDUAL AND CORPORATION INCOME TAXES

The principal source of revenue of the United States government is the income tax. In 1965 approximately 40 percent of the revenue of the federal government came from the individual income tax, approximately 20 percent from corporate income and profits tax, 14 percent from employment taxes such as social security taxes, and the remainder from miscellaneous sources.

Who must file a federal tax return? The federal income tax applies to both business firms and individuals. Therefore, both must file federal income tax returns.

Every citizen or resident of the United States who has $600 or more of gross income for the calendar year must file a federal tax return. An exception to this regulation is that the minimum amount of gross income for persons 65 years old or older is $1,200. The United States Treasury Department furnishes complete instructions yearly as a guide to taxpayers.

Withholding wages for federal income tax. An employer must withhold on each payday from the wages or salaries of employees an amount for federal income tax. The amount withheld depends upon the number of dependents the employee has and upon the amount of his earnings.

At the end of each year, a withholding tax statement, known as Form W-2, is prepared by the employer. This form shows the total wages paid the employee and the amounts withheld for federal income tax and social security tax. The employer sends one copy to the District

Director of Internal Revenue and gives two copies to the employee, who files one copy with his tax return and retains the second copy as part of his own records. If the amount of income tax withheld by the employer is more than the actual amount of the tax, the excess will be refunded; if it is less, the employee will be required to pay the difference to the Director of Internal Revenue.

Having the federal taxes withheld and paid by one's employer does not relieve a person from filing an income tax return.

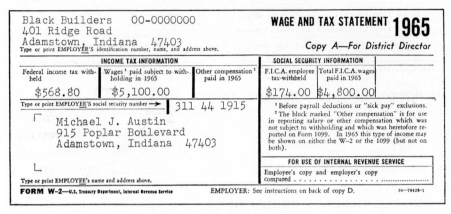

Black Builders 00-0000000	WAGE AND TAX STATEMENT 1965
401 Ridge Road	
Adamstown, Indiana 47403	
Type or print EMPLOYER'S identification number, name, and address above.	Copy A—For District Director

INCOME TAX INFORMATION			SOCIAL SECURITY INFORMATION	
Federal income tax withheld	Wages [1] paid subject to withholding in 1965	Other compensation [2] paid in 1965	F.I.C.A. employee tax withheld	Total F.I.C.A. wages paid in 1965
$568.80	$5,100.00		$174.00	$4,800.00

Type or print EMPLOYEE'S social security number → 311 44 1915

Michael J. Austin
915 Poplar Boulevard
Adamstown, Indiana 47403

[1] Before payroll deductions or "sick pay" exclusions.
[2] The block marked "Other compensation" is for use in reporting salary or other compensation which was not subject to withholding and which was heretofore reported on Form 1099. In 1965 this type of income may be shown on either the W-2 or the 1099 (but not on both).

FOR USE OF INTERNAL REVENUE SERVICE
Employee's copy and employer's copy compared . . . .

Type or print EMPLOYEE's name and address above.

FORM W-2—U.S. Treasury Department, Internal Revenue Service   EMPLOYER: See instructions on back of copy D.   16—78428-1

A withholding tax statement

Individual tax returns. Taxpayers now have two tax forms from which to choose—Form 1040A and Form 1040—for preparing their individual tax returns. However, there are limitations on the use of Form 1040A. In order to decide which form you should use, you should consult the local agent of the Internal Revenue Service or obtain a copy of *Your Federal Income Tax,* which is published annually by the Government Printing Office. Many employed individuals must also file a declaration of estimated income tax. The responsibility falls on each individual to determine whether or not a federal tax return and a declaration of estimated income tax should be filed.

Corporation and partnership income tax returns. Corporations must file federal income tax returns in a manner similar to that of individuals. Although the corporation federal income tax is similar in nature to the individual income tax, the regulations and rates are not the same as for individuals.

A partnership does not pay federal income tax. It merely files a tax information return (Form 1065) to inform the Internal Revenue

1040 A U.S. Individual Income Tax Return (Less than $10,000 total income)   **1965**

Please print →

1. Name (If a joint return of husband and wife, use first names and middle initials of both)

Michael J. and Alice M. Austin

Home address (Number and street or rural route)

915 Poplar Boulevard

City, town or post office, State and Postal ZIP code.

Adamstown, Indiana   47403

2. Your social security number (Husband's if joint return)   311 :44: 1915

3. Wife's number, if joint return   315 :21: 1451

4. Check one:
- ☐ a. Single;
- ☒ b. Married filing joint return (even if only one had income);
- ☐ c. Married filing separately—If your husband or wife is also filing a return give his or her first name and social security number.

If Item 7 is $10,000 or more, or if interest, dividends and non-withheld wages are over $200, use Form 1040.

Enter the name & address used on your return for 1964 (If the same as above, write "Same.") If none filed, give reason. If changing from separate to joint or joint to separate returns, enter 1964 names and addresses.

Same

5. Enter total wages, salaries, tips, etc. Enclose Forms W-2, Copy B. If not shown on enclosed Forms W-2 attach explanation. Yours ▶	5,100 :00
Wife's ▶	
6. Interest and dividends Yours ▶	29 :90
Wife's ▶	
7. Total income (add Items 5 and 6)	5,129 :90
8. Tax from Tax Table or tax computation schedule ▶	563 :38
9. Total Federal income tax withheld (from Forms W-2) ▶	568 :80

If your income was $5,000 or more, you must compute your tax. However, if your income was less than $5,000, you may have the Internal Revenue Service compute your tax by omitting Items 8, 10, and 11. If you compute your own tax, pay balance (item 10) in full with return to your District Director.

10. If Item 8 is larger than Item 9, enter balance due ▶	
11. If Item 9 is larger than Item 8, enter refund ▶	5 :42

Apply refund to: ☐ U.S. Savings Bonds, & excess refunded; or ☒ Refund only.

U.S. TREASURY DEPARTMENT ● INTERNAL REVENUE SERVICE   (OVER)   LIST YOUR EXEMPTIONS AND SIGN ON OTHER SIDE.

---

12. EXEMPTIONS FOR YOURSELF—AND WIFE (only if all her income is included in this return, or she had no income) Check boxes which apply

	Regular	65 or over	Blind	
Yourself	☒	☐	☐	Enter number of exemptions checked ▶▶▶ 2
Wife	☒	☐	☐	

13. First names of your dependent children who lived with you   Jane

Enter number ▶   1

14. DEPENDENTS OTHER THAN THOSE CLAIMED IN ITEM 13.

(a) NAME ▶ Enter figure 1 in the last column to right for each name listed (if more space is needed, attach schedule)	(b) Relationship	(c) Months lived in your home. If born or died during year also write "B" or "D"	(d) Did dependent have income of $600 or more?	(e) Amount YOU furnished for dependent's support. If 100% write "ALL"	(f) Amount furnished by OTHERS including dependent. See instruction 14
				$	$

15. TOTAL EXEMPTIONS FROM ITEMS 12, 13, AND 14 ABOVE .... ▶   3

Your present employer   Black Builders   Wife's present employer

City and State where employed   Adamstown, Indiana   City and State where employed

If you had an expense allowance or charged expenses to your employer, see instructions for "Reimbursed Expenses" and check here ☐ if appropriate.

Sign here ▶ Michael J. Austin   Alice M. Austin   1/15/66

If joint return, BOTH HUSBAND AND WIFE MUST SIGN even if only one had income.   Date

Form 1040A may be used to make federal income tax returns if the income is less than $10,000 and is primarily from wages or salary.

Service of the share of profits which each partner has earned. Each partner reports his share of profits when he files his individual return.

SALES OR COMMODITY TAXES

There are two principal forms of the sales tax (sometimes called excise tax): (a) general and (b) selective.

General sales taxes are of several different kinds, among the most common of which are: the retail sales tax; the wholesale tax; the gross income tax, usually levied on all income from sales both of commodities and of services; the gross sales tax, which is applicable to all sales including those of manufacturers; and the gross profit tax, levied on gross profit. Taxes on luxuries, amusements, and gasoline are good examples of *selective* taxes.

An argument in favor of the sales tax is that many who do not pay other taxes are thus required to contribute to the support of government. Many people argue also that this tax meets one of the basic requirements of taxation not only by charging those who have the ability to pay, but also by charging them in proportion to the ability to pay. The general sales tax is obviously open to many criticisms. For instance, it places a heavy burden especially upon those who scarcely can earn a living. Some of these objections are overcome, however, by the selective sales tax.

BUSINESS OR SERVICE TAXES

Business or service taxes are direct taxes based upon the idea that a business should pay for the privilege of existing and operating. It is argued that a business benefits from the services of government and, therefore, should pay its share of the costs of government. Among the common business or service taxes are *licenses, permits,* and *franchises* which give the business a right to operate; others are based upon the quantity of natural resources sold, such as a *severance tax*; upon the amount of capital stock of a corporation; or upon some aspect of its operations, such as payroll. A tax on gasoline is sometimes classified as a *benefit tax*. This is based upon the thought that those individuals who use the roads should be taxed to build and maintain them.

INHERITANCE AND GIFT TAXES

During the twentieth century the growth of inheritance, estate, and gift taxes has been very rapid. Such taxes, commonly referred to as *death taxes*, are now levied under federal and state laws.

Two general types of inheritance taxes are: (a) the estate tax and (b) the inheritance, or share, tax. The federal government largely employs the estate tax, whereas most states employ the inheritance tax.

Estate tax. The *estate tax* is calculated on the entire amount of the net estate, regardless of the interests of the beneficiaries.

Inheritance tax. The *inheritance tax* or *share tax* may be taken out of each share of the will provided the will so specifies. In the absence of specification, the tax is taken out of the part of the estate remaining after specific bequests have been distributed. The rate of this tax may vary according to the individuals who share in the estate. Under some state laws, the portions of an estate that go to distant relatives are subjected to higher taxes than the portions going to close relatives.

Gift tax. A *gift tax* is levied upon a gift from one person to another. Ordinarily, gift taxes are levied to prevent avoidance of estate and inheritance taxes.

SOCIAL SECURITY TAXES

The federal government collects payroll taxes to provide partial financial support for three social security insurance programs that are commonly known as: (a) unemployment insurance; (b) old-age benefits, including disability, death, support of children and widow, and monthly pension; and (c) health and medical assistance insurance for the aged.

Taxes for unemployment insurance. An employer who has four or more employees must pay a federal unemployment tax on the first $3,000 of wages paid each employee in each calendar year. In states that have a compulsory unemployment tax, the employer is allowed a credit against the federal unemployment tax for the amount of payments he has made to the unemployment insurance funds of his state. An employee does not pay unemployment tax to the federal government, but he may in some states be subject to a state unemployment tax on wages.

Employer-employee tax. In businesses in which employees are covered by social security regulations, an employee and his employer each pay social security tax on the first $6,600 of wages paid to the employee in each calendar year. According to the regulations, the employer must deduct from a paycheck the employee's social security tax for the period covered by the check and send the amount deducted with an additional amount equal to the deduction to the government. The rate per employee and per employer varies from 4.2 percent on the first $6,600 of wages in 1966 to 5.65 percent in 1987 and thereafter. This tax covers both the old-age assistance provided under social security and medicare. A table giving tax rates for social security is given on page 568 in Chapter 29.

Self-employment tax. Self-employed owners of businesses that are covered by social security and medicare regulations pay a self-employment tax on the first $6,600 of income from the business in a calendar year. The self-employment tax rate increases from 6.15 percent in 1966 to 7.80 percent in 1987 and thereafter.

SPECIAL TAXES

Various special taxes are levied by the federal government, state governments, and local governments. Many of these, such as the tax on legal papers (deeds, notes, and mortgages), are *stamp taxes*; that is, they are collected through the use of revenue stamps. Some are customs taxes on imports; others, excise taxes in the form of automobile, dog, and hunting and fishing licenses; and still others, special licenses for conducting certain types of businesses.

Facts everyone should know about principles of taxation and taxes

1. Taxation is a device or plan by which funds are raised to pay the costs of operating local, state, and federal governments.
2. The more services and benefits people want from government, the more government costs, and the higher taxes become.
3. In order to make taxes fair to all, the tax each individual and each business firm should pay must be determined by a formula or rule, not arbitrarily.
4. The only agency that has the power and right to tax is government.
5. Taxation plans are based upon ideas such as fairness to the taxpayer, cost of service given, benefit from the service, and ability to pay.
6. The federal government collects about 66 percent and the local and state governments about 17 percent each of all taxes.
7. Tax payments require approximately one third of the income of the typical individual. Every individual has a vital stake in taxes.

▪ QUESTIONS ON THE TEXT

1. In what ways do individual citizens benefit from taxes?
2. What is a tax?
3. How is a tax distinguished from a payment to a government agency?
4. Who ultimately bears the burden of paying for public services?
5. What is a tax system?
6. What are the essentials of a tax system?
7. Why is it often impracticable to apportion the tax burden according to the cost of the service or benefit received?
8. What is the most widely accepted theory for apportioning the tax burden?
9. Upon what theory of taxation is the federal income tax based?
10. What is (a) a direct tax? (b) an indirect tax?
11. Under what conditions are the following taxes direct and indirect: (a) real estate, (b) sales, (c) poll, (d) excise, (e) gasoline?
12. What is meant by "shifting the tax burden"?

13. What is meant by the term "hidden taxes"?
14. Describe the process by which the amount of a property tax is determined.
15. What plan of payment of federal income tax for individuals is in operation?
16. Who must file a federal income tax return?
17. Does a corporation have to file an income tax return and pay income taxes?
18. Explain the features of the two principal forms of the sales tax.
19. Explain business or service taxes.
20. What are the two general types of inheritance taxes?
21. What kinds of benefits are provided by the Social Security Act?
22. Who must pay the federal unemployment insurance tax?
23. What are the most common special taxes?

▪ QUESTIONS FOR DISCUSSION

1. Discuss why it is important to a taxpayer how the tax money is spent by the government.
2. (a) Two major plans for apportioning or charging taxes to individuals and business firms are the cost-of-service-received plan and the ability-to-pay plan. Explain the principle upon which each plan works.
   (b) Discuss the major problems encountered in using each of these plans.
3. (a) Distinguish between a tax on gasoline to pay for roads in all parts of the state and an assessment on adjoining property for a new sewer.
   (b) What are the benefits derived in each case?
   (c) Why is one a tax and the other not a tax?
4. A new expressway and an overpass are constructed from the center of a city into an outlying district. Part of the cost is paid from a general tax fund, and part is obtained through the assessment of adjoining property owners. Some taxpayers believe that the entire cost should be paid by the adjoining property owners. Would this plan be fair or unfair?
5. Explain how the people have control over taxes.
6. Discuss the property tax as a source of government income.
7. Is it fair or not fair to charge a single person who has a taxable income of $2,000 a year, $310 in federal taxes and a single person who has a taxable income of $20,000 a year, $6,070 in federal taxes?
8. A single person pays a considerably higher rate of federal income tax than a married person. Discuss the fairness of this practice.
9. Explain why partnerships are not required to pay federal income taxes.
10. Is the gasoline tax a fair tax?

11. Suppose a sales tax of 2 percent were levied by a state on all commodities and services. If this tax were the only state tax, why would it be fair or unfair?

12. What are the arguments for and against a sales tax?

13. What are the advantages and disadvantages to the individual of the withholding tax on wages and salaries?

14. What is the theory or purpose of inheritance taxes?

15. Why are local schools financed largely through property tax?

16. Discuss the practice of exempting from the general property tax: (a) real estate owned by churches, (b) a sum such as $1,000 if the property is mortgaged, and (c) real estate owned by new business and industrial firms.

17. Discuss the advantages and disadvantages if your town or city should discontinue the collection of all present taxes and adopt as a simple tax to provide the income needed the following: (a) tax on real estate, (b) tax on income, (c) sales tax on groceries and foods, (d) tax on merchants who sell goods and services to consumers, and (e) tax on manufacturers and producers on the value of goods and services.

■ PROBLEMS TO SOLVE

1. The assessed valuation of the real estate in a certain city is approximately 25 percent of the market value and the tax rate is $6.50 per $100 assessed valuation. A mortgage exemption of $1,000 on the assessed valuation is allowed if there is an indebtedness of $1,000 or more on the property. Mr. Allison builds a house that costs $18,500 on a lot valued at $2,500. He has a mortgage of $16,000 on the house and lot. What is a reasonable estimate of the taxes on this property that he will have to pay each year?

2. Prepare a list of all the different kinds of direct taxes that might be paid during a year by a typical family.

3. Some countries raise supplemental funds (in addition to taxes) to provide government services by conducting national lotteries. Some states in this country have thought this would be a good plan to acquire additional revenue without raising tax rates or imposing new taxes upon the people. Prepare a report stating the pros and cons for a state or national lottery as a means of raising government funds.

4. Prepare a report on the early history of taxation in this country. In your report make references to such items as the Constitution and the limitations it imposed on the federal government with respect to taxation; the purpose for imposing excise taxes on certain items (tobacco, liquor, cosmetics) as opposed to other consumer items in the early history of our country; when the graduated income tax came into existence and who proposed it; and the first attempt to tax personal incomes, why it was dropped and then resumed.

5. From data found in the current issue of *The Statistical Abstract,* prepare a series of charts showing (a) the total amount and sources of revenues for your state, (b) the expenditures for various functions (education, highways, public welfare, natural resources, etc.) by your state, (c) kinds of taxes and amount received from such taxes in your state, and (d) the amount and purpose of the state debt (if any) for your state.

6. Prepare a wall chart showing the number and kinds of taxes imposed upon the people (including businesses) of your community by the federal, state, and local city governments.

▪ COMMUNITY PROBLEMS AND PROJECTS

1. A tax calendar giving the dates on which the various local, state, and federal tax payments and reports are due for your state usually can be obtained from the local or state chamber of commerce. Your instructor will give you a tax calendar or will instruct you in how to prepare or obtain one.

   Using the tax calendar for your state, prepare a list of tax reports and payments that need to be made each year by:
   (a) An individual who is employed as a toolmaker by a manufacturer.
   (b) A retail grocer who owns his own store building; the equipment, including delivery trucks; merchandise; and who employs six full-time and four part-time people.
   (c) A local manufacturing firm that owns its plant, all equipment and necessary trucks, and that employs 500 people.

2. Make a study of one of the local or state taxes that is used in your county, city, or state. The tax you select may be a property tax, a sales or receipts tax, or an individual income tax. In your study find: (a) the rates of taxation, (b) the basis on which the taxes are levied or assessed, (c) how the taxes are collected, and (d) the purposes for which the money collected is used.

3. Determine how much it costs your community each year to provide education for each high school pupil.

4. Obtain a copy of the budget for your city, county, or parish. From the budget, prepare two financial statements. One should show the total estimated expenditures classified under such topics as schools, police protection, city or county administration, and payments on indebtedness. The other statement should show the sources of income and the estimated amount of income from each source.

   Based upon the statements of estimated expenditures and estimated income, what recommendations would you make regarding: (a) the expenditures? (b) the sources of income and the kinds of taxes used to obtain the income?

Chapter 16

International trade, balance of payments, and tariffs

PURPOSE OF THE CHAPTER

International trade is growing continuously in volume. It is of great significance culturally, politically, and economically to the nations of the world. The major problem relative to international trade confronting a nation is the maintaining of approximately the same total value of goods exported and imported.

You will find answers to these questions:

1. Why is international trade important to a country?
2. What is the effect on a country if its total payments to foreign countries substantially exceed its total receipts from foreign countries for a given year? for several years in succession?
3. What is the significance of international trade agreements?
4. What are the arguments for and against tariffs?

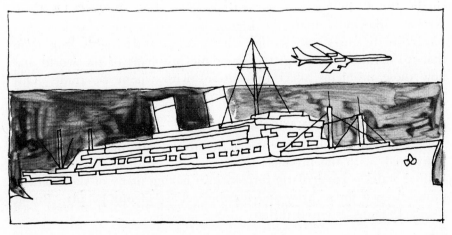

A. International trade

WHAT INTERNATIONAL TRADE INCLUDES

International trade, or *foreign trade* as it is sometimes referred to, is the buying, selling, and exchanging of goods and services by individuals and business firms in one nation with the business firms of other nations. Many American citizens and business firms transact a great volume of trade with other nations. Their international trade consists of imports, exports, private investments abroad, and the establishment of manufacturing and distribution branches abroad. Foreign nations and their citizens carry on similar activities in the United States. Our government gives direct and indirect economic aid to underdeveloped nations. The direct aid consists of dollars and materials. The indirect aid is comprised of technical assistance and other means of helping those nations to help themselves.

INTERNATIONAL TRADE AFFECTS RELATIONSHIPS AMONG NATIONS

International trade has an important bearing on the relationships among nations. On the positive side, trade among nations promotes the sharing of cultural traditions, particularly in literature, the arts, and inventions; it helps the people of the participating nations understand each other; it provides the basis for both individual and international friendships; and, through trade, the peoples of the participating nations are enabled to enjoy the benefits of many commodities and services that otherwise would not be possible for them. From another view, international trade gives rise to economic problems between nations that in some instances lead to wars, revolutions, and political crises. International trade is probably the most important single factor in promoting lasting friendships between nations. Nations, like individuals, are highly sensitive to the treatment they receive in business transactions with others. It is highly important that we should understand the economic problems of the world and how those problems affect the nations with whom we trade. Our welfare, security, and our prosperity are affected by those problems.

IMPORTANCE OF INTERNATIONAL TRADE

No nation is self-sufficient. Many things are needed to supply individuals with the products they need for satisfactory living. The United States is particularly fortunate in having many of the essential things needed for security and for the welfare of our people. But it also lacks many essential things.

STRATEGIC IMPORTS ARE ESSENTIAL TO OUR INDUSTRY

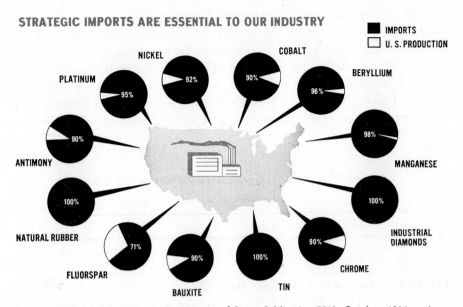

■ IMPORTS
☐ U. S. PRODUCTION

NICKEL — 92%
COBALT — 90%
PLATINUM — 95%
BERYLLIUM — 96%
ANTIMONY — 90%
MANGANESE — 98%
NATURAL RUBBER — 100%
INDUSTRIAL DIAMONDS — 100%
FLUORSPAR — 71%
BAUXITE — 90%
TIN — 100%
CHROME — 90%

Source: *ABC's of Foreign Trade*, Department of State, Publication 7713, October, 1964, p. 6.

The United States produces only a small portion of many products that are essential to our industry.

The United States imports many essential commodities. We find it necessary to import many products either because we do not have them at all or because we do not have enough to supply our needs. For example, we must import such products as coffee, tea, spices, industrial diamonds, ore from which aluminum is made, chrome, cobalt, copper, tin, wool, and zinc. Some of the products we import are for the use of individuals or are used in the manufacture of goods for individuals. Others are particularly important in national defense, especially metals and minerals used in the manufacture of weapons of many kinds.

Foreign nations need our exports. The nations from which we import products have need for our wheat, automobiles, and many other products that we extract from the earth or that we manufacture. They buy some of our products and we buy some of theirs. Many groups of items of merchandise may be both imported and exported by the same country. For instance, the United States imports small compact automobiles largely from western European countries and at the same time exports both small and large automobiles to the countries of South America. Another illustration of importing and exporting the same class of product is food. The United States exports wheat and at the same time imports rice. Precision instruments, manufactured in western Europe and Japan, are imported by the United States, and at the same time machinery and transportation equipment manufactured in the United States are exported to the free countries of Asia and Africa. The table below on U.S. import and export values by merchandise group indicates the major kinds of merchandise involved in our international trade.

U.S. IMPORT AND EXPORT VALUES BY MERCHANDISE GROUPS

(In millions of dollars)

Merchandise Group	Imports	Exports
Food and live animals	$ 3,487	$ 3,983
Beverages and tobacco	536	554
Crude materials, inedible, except fuels	2,815	2,950
Mineral fuels, lubricants, and related materials	2,030	912
Animal and vegetable oils and fats	119	435
Chemicals	714	2,390
Manufactured goods classified chiefly by material	4,538	3,224
Machinery and transport equipment	2,216	9,337
Miscellaneous manufactured articles	1,640	1,448
Commodities and transactions not classified according to kind	590	865
Special category commodities *		965
Total	$18,684@#	$26,136#

* For security reasons these classified materials are not specifically itemized in records of the Census Bureau.

@ Since each figure has been independently rounded, the details do not add to the total given.

This total is not identical with that of The Office of Business Economics because the recording pattern of the Census Bureau differs slightly from that of OBE.

Source: U.S. Foreign Trade, U.S. Department of Commerce, 1965.

International trade is essential to the U.S. economy. International trade for the United States represented between 5 and 6 percent of all business activity. The amount paid to foreign countries was approximately 5.8 percent, and the amounts received from foreign countries approximately 5.4 percent of our GNP. This ratio of foreign trade to domestic trade may seem relatively small when compared to amounts as high as 40 to 50 percent in some countries. However, the volume is highly important from the standpoint of the employment of our people and prosperity in general. It is even more significant in our relations with the nations of the world, for they need our products.

BASIS FOR INTERNATIONAL TRADE

Every nation wants the opportunity to export its goods and services to other countries. A foreign outlet for sales enables a manufacturer or a distributor to increase the volume of his business activity, thus increasing his chance to make a profit and increasing employment opportunities. Every nation also wants the opportunity and privilege of buying from foreign countries products and services that are scarce or unavailable at home that would be useful and beneficial to its people. In short, every nation wants foreign trade as a means of raising the level of living for its people.

Most nations would find it impracticable to import goods and services unless they can export their goods and services to others. Without exports it would be difficult in the long run to pay for goods and services that it would like to import. This means that the factors which enable a nation to build a volume of export trade are important.

Factors in export competition. Manufacturers and merchants within a country such as the United States compete for business on the basis of price asked, quality of merchandise or service offered, and usefulness and serviceability of the product or service to consumers. Business firms and individuals within a country compete with business firms and individuals in other countries in the world for exporting their products and services to nations needing them. The business firms and individuals in some nations have more favorable conditions than others to meet the competition of international trade. The essential factors in determining the ability to meet export competition are stated in summary form on page 298.

The factors that determine ability to compete with other nations for export trade must be considered collectively in making decisions about entering the international trade market. Rarely will there be a situation in which all of the factors are favorable. Even though some factors are only partially favorable to engaging in export trade, collectively the factors may merit entering the international trade market.

Low cost, a competitive advantage. A basis for engaging in international trade may be illustrated by the following situation. Assume a situation in which (a) free trade (no duties or tariffs) exists between the nations, (b) products produced by one country are equal in quality to the products produced in the other country, and (c) there

Factors that determine a nation's ability to compete for export opportunities

1. Raw materials from which consumer goods are made for export trade are readily available at a reasonable cost.
2. The production and distribution operations of business firms are efficiently managed.
3. Management is imaginative, creative, and resourceful in inventing, innovating, and designing products that are useful and have strong appeal to consumers.
4. The competencies and skills of available labor are adequate for and compatible with the work to be performed in the production and distribution of the goods to be produced for export trade.
5. Labor is available at a cost which is fair to employees and at the same time that enables a producer or distributor to compete in the export market.
6. Transportation of the finished goods from the exporting country to the importing country is available at costs that enable the exporter to compete in the international trade market.
7. Through technology the production process is continually improved, resulting in high-quality products at low production costs.
8. The quality of the product is compatible with the quality needed for the use to be made of it.
9. The product in total is acceptable to the people of the importing country from the viewpoint of total cost, quality, usefulness, and service.
10. The trade regulations and restrictions of the exporting country are favorable.

is no national prejudice between the nations involved. Further assume that costs to produce are as follows:

Product	Nation A Cost to produce	Nation B Cost to produce
Bicycle	$20.00	$19.00
Roller skates	2.00	2.50

The manufacturer of the bicycle in Nation *B* can compete favorably for export business with Nation *A*. Manufacturers of bicycles in Nation *A* will either find a way of reducing cost to produce a bicycle or they may be forced to shift to another product if they wish to engage in international trade.

The situation is just reversed in the case of roller skates. Manufacturers in Nation *A* can compete favorably with manufacturers of roller skates in Nation *B*. Manufacturers of roller skates in Nation *B* will have to find a way to reduce cost to produce roller skates or shift to some other product.

FOREIGN EXCHANGE

In domestic trade in the United States a merchant expects to be paid in dollars for goods he sells. He can use these dollars to buy more materials, to pay labor, or to meet other expenses. When a merchant in the United States exports merchandise to a merchant in London, the London merchant pays not in dollars but in British pounds.[1] But the U.S. merchant cannot use British pounds to pay his bills; he must have dollars. Unless the U.S. merchant can find a way of converting the pounds he receives to dollars, he cannot continue to export. The dollar amount of the invoice for the goods sold by a U.S. merchant to a merchant in London is eventually received by the U.S. merchant through a process known as foreign exchange. The process is rather complex. We are concerned here only with the basic principle upon which it operates.

The basic principle upon which foreign exchange operates is that the debts of merchants in Country *A* payable to the merchants in Country *B* are offset against the amounts owed by the merchants of Country *B* to the merchants of Country *A*. Perhaps a better understanding of how foreign exchange operates may be gained by studying an illustration.

A simple illustration in foreign exchange. Let us refer to the diagram on page 300 and assume the following facts. First, the exchange rate for the British pound is $2.80. This means that the pound is worth $2.80 in U.S. currency. Next, let us assume that in April of last year U.S. merchant *A* exported goods worth $2,800 to merchant *C* in Britain, and that at approximately the same time British merchant *D* exported to American merchant *B* goods worth £1,000 in Britain. There is really no relationship between the two transactions except that they happened to occur at about the same time and that the merchants involved were in America and in Britain.

Now how can merchant *C* pay merchant *A*, and how can merchant *B* pay merchant *D*? Merchant *C* does not have U.S. dollars, he has only British pounds; and merchant *A* cannot use those British pounds

---

[1] The pound (£) is the unit of money in Britain as the dollar is in the United States. At the current rate of exchange, the British pound is equivalent to $2.80 in the United States.

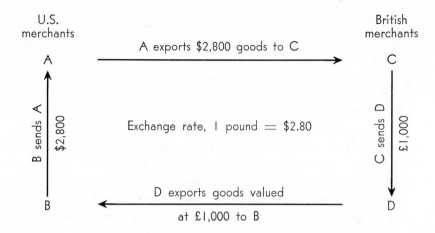

An illustration of a simple foreign exchange situation

Result of the transactions: *A* in the United States is paid in full in U.S. dollars for the merchandise he exported to *C* in Britain; *D* in Britain is paid in full in British pounds for the merchandise he exported to *B* in the United States; no currency was transferred from the United States to Britain or from Britain to the United States.

In actual practice, *B* transfers his payment of $2,800 to a New York bank, and *C* transfers his payment of £1,000 to a London bank. The banks then pay *A* and *D* respectively.

to pay wages, taxes, invoices for materials, and similar items of expense. Likewise, merchant *B* has only U.S. dollars and merchant *D* cannot use them to pay his bills.

Through a New York exchange bank arrangements were made for U.S. merchant *B* to pay $2,800 to the New York bank, which in turn transferred the $2,800 to U.S. merchant *A*. Also, a London exchange bank received £1,000 from British merchant *C* and then transferred the £1,000 to British merchant *D*. Thus, no currency was actually transferred between the two countries and yet both the U.S. merchant who exported to England and the British merchant who exported to America have been paid in full. The exchange banks make a small charge for their services in making such exchanges.

In our illustration the value of the goods from England to the United States and from the United States to England was stated to be the same. In actual practice these amounts would rarely be the same, so a balance would remain in the bank of the country having made the largest export shipments.

Foreign exchange involving several exporters and importers. This illustration of foreign exchange is more complicated than the simple illustration that involved only two U.S. and two British merchants.

In this illustration there are several exporters and several importers in both countries involved in the exchange of goods; also the total amount imported in dollars by the United States is greater in dollars than the total amount of goods exported.

In this illustration it is assumed again that the exchange rate is £ = $2.80. First, let us trace the flow of goods:

1. U.S. exporters designated as "A" on the chart sold $112,000 (equivalent of £40,000) of merchandise to several British importers who are designated as "C" on the chart.

2. At approximately the same time British exporters (designated as "D") sold merchandise valued at £50,000 (equivalent of $140,000) to several U.S. importers designated as "B" on the chart.

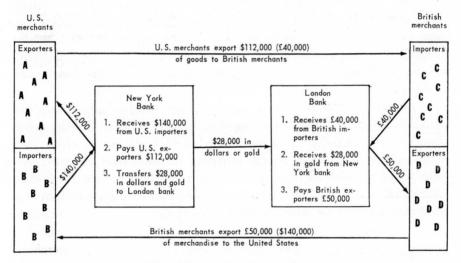

Illustration of Foreign Exchange

Now, let us trace the flow of money from British importers "C" and British exporters "D" through the London bank.

1. British importers "C" paid the London bank £40,000 (equivalent of $112,000) for the merchandise received from U.S. exporters "A."

2. The London bank paid British exporters "D" £50,000 (equivalent of $140,000).

3. The London bank has received £40,000 (equivalent of $112,000) and paid out £50,000 (equivalent of $140,000), leaving a deficit of £10,000 (equivalent of $28,000).

Now, let us trace the flow of money from U.S. importers and exporters through the New York bank:

1. U.S. importers "B" paid the New York bank $140,000 (£50,000) for the merchandise received from British exporters "D."
2. The New York bank paid U.S. importers "A" $112,000 (equivalent of £40,000).
3. The New York bank has received $140,000 and paid out $112,000, leaving a balance of $28,000.

The New York bank now has a surplus of $28,000, and the London bank has a deficit of the same amount resulting from the transactions. How can the difference of $28,000, which represents the excess of the value of U.S. imports over U.S. exports to England, be settled? The answer is that the London bank may demand from the New York bank the payment of the £10,000 (equivalent of $28,000) in gold, or it may accept U.S. dollars in payment. The London bank, if it accepts dollars, may later demand gold for the dollars if it wishes to do so.

Through the use of foreign exchange, merchandise valued at more than $252,000 (£90,000) was imported and exported by the merchants of two nations. The merchants in each nation received payment for goods exported in the currency of their own country. No money was transferred from one nation to another except the difference in value of the goods exchanged by the two nations, which at any time may be paid in either gold or U.S. dollars.

BALANCE OF TRADE

The term *balance of trade* refers to the balance between a nation's exports and its imports of goods. The balance of trade is said to be favorable if the value of exports exceeds the value of imports. This means that the nation receives more in payment for goods sold to foreign countries than it paid for goods imported from foreign countries. An unfavorable balance of trade means that a nation has imported more than it exported. The balance of trade for the United States was favorable in each of the years from 1962 to 1965, inclusive. The table on balance of trade on the next page indicates that the excess of exports over imports for 1965 was $5,201 million. In that year the United States exported about $1.25 of goods for every dollar of goods it imported.

U.S. BALANCE OF TRADE
EXCESS OF MERCHANDISE EXPORTS OVER IMPORTS
(In millions of dollars)

	1962	1963	1964	1965
Exports	$20,576	$21,989	$25,671	$26,567
Imports	16,134	16,996	18,684	21,366
Excess of imports (favorable) ..	$ 4,442	$ 4,993	$ 6,987	$ 5,201

Source: Statistical Abstract of the United States.

We should be aware that the favorable balance of trade (excess of exports over imports) does not tell us how well we as a nation fared financially in *all* of our transactions with foreign countries. In our study of balance of payments in the next section of this chapter we shall learn about other foreign transactions that affect our international financial status.

B. U.S. balance of payments

The meanings of "balance of trade" and "balance of payments" are sometimes confused. "Balance of trade," as we learned in the preceding section of this chapter, is concerned only with the import and export of goods. If the value of exported goods exceeds the value of imported goods for a nation, that nation is said to have a favorable balance of trade. On the other hand, "balance of payments" includes all financial transactions that take place between the United States and the rest of the world during a given year. It includes both receipts and payments for export and import of goods, foreign tourist spending in the United States and American tourist spending abroad, amounts received and spent on shipping services involving other nations, and amounts received and paid on interest and dividends. Other financial transactions with foreign nations that are included in our balance of international payments are support of troops and military bases overseas; transfer of gold in foreign exchange; and gifts, loans, and assistance to foreign countries.

DEFINITION OF BALANCE OF PAYMENTS

The U.S. *balance of payments* is the difference between total payments to other nations and the total receipts from foreign nations. The U.S. balance of international payments for 1960 to 1964, inclusive, are shown in the table on the next page.

U.S. BALANCE OF PAYMENTS
(In millions of dollars)

	1961	1962	1963	1964 *
Payments	$32,789	$34,597	$36,329	$40,674
Receipts	30,419	32,394	33,685	37,913
	$ 2,370	$ 2,203	$ 2,644	$ 2,761

* Preliminary.

Source: *Statistical Abstract of the United States,* 1965.

In each of the four years for which U.S. payments and receipts for international transactions are given in the table, there was a substantial excess of payments over receipts. This indicates an unfavorable net balance of payments. The deficit in 1964 was approximately $2.8 billion. It may be recalled that the balance of trade (excess of exports over imports) for the same periods of time was favorable.

BALANCE-OF-PAYMENTS DEFICITS AND GOLD OUTFLOW

What does the excess of payments over receipts mean? In 1964 it means that $2.8 billion of gold and money have been transferred to foreign owners. Since 1934 it has been the policy of the U.S. government to settle international balances in gold at $35 an ounce if the foreign country holding U.S. dollars (excess payments over receipts) so demands. Some foreign governments have demanded the gold payments. Inasmuch as U.S. dollars held abroad are redeemable in gold and therefore secure, some of the foreign governments holding them have not demanded gold payments. Since 1958, over $7 billion in gold has been paid to foreign governments because of balance-of-payments deficits.

In Chapter 11 mention was made that under present law 25 percent of the federal reserve notes and deposits must be backed by gold. The amount of "free" gold reserve has diminished rapidly in recent years. To stop the drain on our diminishing gold reserve, efforts must be made to balance our international payments.

DEFICITS AND LIQUID LIABILITIES

The deficit created by an excess of payments over receipts cannot be measured alone by the outflow of gold. It is indicated also by our liquid liabilities held by the peoples of foreign nations. A *liquid liability* is a financial obligation on which payment may be requested at any time. The U.S. liquid liabilities held by foreign nations consist primarily of U.S. dollars that we have paid for goods we have imported. These dollars are held in banks by the foreigners or are invested in U.S. assets that can be converted into cash on short notice. The U.S. dollars held by foreigners may be exchanged for our gold or used to buy goods. The problem created by this situation is that our reserve of gold is being decreased; and if it is reduced too much, our ability to back our dollars with gold may be in danger.

U.S. PAYMENTS TO AND RECEIPTS FROM FOREIGN COUNTRIES

The U.S. balance of payments for any given period of time, such as the year of 1964, is the net result of many financial transactions with foreign countries. The question arises as to what were these transactions. The financial transactions resulting in payments to and receipts from foreign countries are given by classes or kinds in the table below on U.S. payments to and receipts from foreign countries for 1964.

U.S. PAYMENTS TO AND RECEIPTS FROM FOREIGN COUNTRIES FOR 1964

(In millions of dollars)

Payments or credits		Receipts or debits	
Expenditures for goods and services and payments of income on foreign investments in the U.S.	$28,314	Receipts for goods and services and income from U.S. investments abroad	$36,523
Net outflows of U.S. private capital	6,360	Foreign capital other than liquid funds (net)	696
Remittances and pensions ...	549	Repayments on U.S. government loans	694
Government grants and capital outflows	4,558	Total	$37,913
Plus unrecorded transactions	893	Deficit	2,761
Total	$40,674	Total	$40,674

Source: *Statistical Abstract of the United States*, 1965.

An examination of each of the transactions for which each kind of payments was made and from which receipts were received will help us to understand the nature of international trade and balance of payments.

Expenditures for goods and services and income on foreign investments in the United States. This item is comprised of three kinds of transactions: expenditures for merchandise (imports); expenditures within foreign countries for the support of U.S. military establishments; and expenditures for other services abroad, such as travel and transportation expenditures in foreign countries; and payments on the investments of foreign countries in the United States.

Net outflows of U.S. private capital. Foreign individuals and business firms make investments in the United States in stocks, bonds, and other items of value. Likewise citizens and business firms of the United States make investments in foreign countries in factories, land, business firms, and stocks and bonds. In 1964, American citizens and business firms invested approximately $4 billion more abroad than foreigners invested in the United States.

Remittances and pensions. Remittances by individuals, organizations such as CARE, and religious bodies are made to the people of foreign countries. Pension payments are made by the U.S. government and by some business firms to individuals living in foreign countries.

U.S. government grants and capital outflows. This item includes our expenditures for economic aid to foreign countries. In 1964, the total expenditure for this purpose was more than $4.5 billion. It includes the U.S. Department of State programs to aid underdeveloped nations, gifts of farm surplus products, loans, the operations of the Peace Corps, and other goods and services to help the people of other nations. A small part of the financial aid—gifts and loans of money—to other nations is used to buy goods and services in the United States. Thus, a small portion of the total helps business in the United States.

Unrecorded transactions. The Office of Business Economics, whose responsibility it is to keep records of international trade and international payments, does not receive complete figures on all foreign payments made by United States citizens and business firms. For example, an American tourist in Europe may not report accurately all the money he spent; hence the Office of Business Economics finds it necessary to estimate certain payments. The Office lists these estimates as "unrecorded transactions."

Receipts for goods and services and income from U.S. investments abroad. This item includes the sale of exported goods and services by

American citizens and business firms. Services include intangible items such as transportation costs, insurance premiums and payments, hotel accommodations, foods consumed abroad, and interest and dividend income received on foreign securities owned by them.

Foreign capital. This item refers primarily to the payments made by foreigners for the purchase of investments in the United States.

Repayments on U.S. government loans. In 1964, foreign countries repaid $694 million on loans made to them by the United States government.

Deficit. Our receipts from financial transactions in foreign countries in 1964 were $37.9 billion; and our payments were $39.7 billion, creating a deficit balance of payments of approximately $1.8 billion.

Solving the deficit problem. Although it has a favorable balance of trade (excess of merchandise exports over imports), the United States has been plagued for several years with deficits in balance of payments of substantial amounts. The unfavorable U.S. balance of payments is a problem of major concern to our government and to us as individuals. It must be solved, but time will be required. The United States government is studying each item of the balance-of-payments account (see table of balance of payments on page 304) to scale down the outward flow of international payments and to increase the inward flow of receipts from foreign financial transactions.

Some of the steps that may be taken to reduce or eliminate the deficit balance-of-payments are:

1. Under the leadership of industry and government, expand our exports.
2. Encourage our military establishments abroad to buy U.S. goods rather than foreign goods; promote the selling of military equipment to our allies rather than lending the equipment to them; and encourage other industrial nations to assume a greater share of the cost of "keeping of world peace."
3. Attract foreigners to visit the United States as tourists; encourage American citizens to travel at home first and abroad second, which probably would reduce the volume of American tourist traffic abroad.
4. Adjust interest rates to compete with those of foreign countries to encourage American investors to invest at home.

5. Stimulate the sale of U.S. goods abroad by making it a provision in agreements for U.S. foreign aid grants and loans to buy U.S. goods and services.
6. Reduce U.S. aid to foreign countries.
7. Reduce our military operations in foreign countries.

C. International trade agreements

Practically all nations want foreign trade for two reasons. First, they are dependent upon imports for some goods that are essential to the well-being and lives of their citizens; and, second, through exports of their goods and products, the opportunity for employment is increased, and exports provide additional income. These same nations are also interested in maintaining a control over trade to provide a favorable balance between exports and imports. Ordinarily, a greater volume of exports than imports is considered favorable to economic growth and stability of business activities.

HOW NATIONS CONTROL TRADE

Numerous controls are used by governments to limit imports or to increase exports. Among the most commonly used controls are: (1) place high tariffs (a tariff is an import tax) on imports; (2) require import licenses which limit the volume and values of goods that each merchant may import; (3) set national limits or quotas on the total value or volume of a product that may be imported in a year: (4) require licenses for obtaining foreign currencies (money) by people who want to use foreign currencies to buy goods from abroad—thus limiting the amount of foreign goods they may buy for import purposes; and (5) subsidize selected export products by making payments to the producers, thus enabling them to sell at lower prices abroad and hence encourage foreign sales.

Nations often attempt to control foreign trade to avoid a balance-of-payments deficit or to protect industries at home against the competition of foreign goods.

THE POSITION OF THE UNITED STATES ON FOREIGN TRADE

Nations of the free world exchange about $135 billion worth of goods each year. America exports about one sixth of that total. The United States is the largest seller and also the largest buyer of goods on the world market.

The economic welfare of not only the United States but also of the other countries of the free world is affected by the volume of world trade in which the United States engages annually. The United States and its citizens, therefore, have a great interest in trade agreements designed to control or to stimulate trade among the nations participating in the agreements.

TRADE AGREEMENTS

Numerous agreements by nations have been made for the purpose of removing trade barriers and promoting trade among the participating members of the agreement. Only a few will be mentioned here. Most of the trade agreements are among the free nations of Western Europe.

General Agreement on Tariffs and Trade. The *General Agreement on Tariffs and Trade* (GATT) was entered into by 23 nations (including the United States) in 1947. Its purpose is to lower tariffs and expand world trade. There now are 37 members.

European Coal and Steel Community. The *European Coal and Steel Community* (ECSC) was formed in 1952 by six European nations to abolish all controls on the free movement of coal, steel, and iron among the members of the organization. The organization has proven to be effective.

European Common Market. In January, 1958, a treaty established the European Economic Community, commonly referred to as the *European Common Market.* The six countries signing the treaty were France, Germany, Italy, Belgium, the Netherlands, and Luxembourg. The purpose of the treaty is to abolish all barriers to the free movement of goods and of people among the six nations signing the treaty. All tariffs among the six countries will be eliminated by 1970 and a common external tariff toward all other countries will be established. By 1963 trade among the member states had more than doubled since 1958, and imports from other countries had increased by 52 percent. It appears that the European Common Market is becoming one of the world's dynamic markets.

European Free Trade Association. In 1960, the *European Free Trade Association* (EFTA) was formed by Austria, Denmark, Norway, Sweden, Switzerland, and the United Kingdom. The purpose of this association is to abolish gradually all barriers to trade among the member countries. It did not provide for the creation of a common external tariff as was established by the European Common Market.

European Atomic Energy Community. The *European Atomic Energy Community* was established in 1958. Its purpose was to create within member countries a strong industry and uniform policies for the peaceful uses of atomic energy.

TARIFFS

Tariffs, sometimes known as *customs duties,* are taxes levied on exports or imports, usually the latter. Tariffs are levied on two bases, *ad valorem* and *specific.* The former is a percentage of the value of a commodity; the latter is a given payment on a unit of the commodity, as per bushel or per ton.

Purposes of tariffs. Tariffs may be levied for purposes of (a) revenue, (b) protection of an industry or of labor, or (c) both. While tariffs produce a revenue, the amount of revenue from tariffs is relatively insignificant in relation to the total revenue that is necessary to run the federal government. Most of our tariffs are intended to protect business interests and labor. They are sometimes used to protect industries that are vital in our national defense. Tariffs are also used to protect infant industries and certain other industries that might be destroyed by competition of foreign goods.

Tariffs affect markets. The common practice of placing tariffs on foreign products is the result of the desire of domestic producers to have the national market to themselves. While a tariff on an import gives the domestic producers some control over the market, it also tends to limit their foreign markets because foreign countries tend to retaliate and place tariffs on products produced in a country with high tariffs like the United States. Of course, a high tariff policy affects various producers differently. From the viewpoint of a manufacturer whose entire market is in this country, a high tariff is desirable; from that of a manufacturer whose main market is abroad, a high tariff may be unfortunate.

Tariffs affect prices. From the consumer's point of view, a tariff on a foreign product is simply a tax. Tariffs, although they protect certain manufacturers or other producers, necessarily result in higher price levels. Most consumers are quite unaware of the fact that they daily have to pay high prices for certain commodities or have to accept similar inferior products simply because of the existence of tariffs.

A tariff is a hidden tax. For example, woolen blankets are manufactured in certain foreign countries and sold at prices much lower than the prices prevailing in the United States. If a person in this country wishes to purchase a woolen blanket that was produced abroad, he must pay the foreign price of the blanket plus the tariff. He may, however, purchase a similar blanket produced in this country, but he will have to pay a price that is approximately the price of the foreign-produced blanket plus the tariff. Or the consumer has the alternative of purchasing a lower-grade, domestic blanket at a price approximately the same as the price of the foreign blanket without the tariff.

Tariffs affect labor. One of the most frequent statements favoring a high tariff is that such tariffs protect workers from the competition of foreign countries where labor is cheap and standards of living are low. Whether or not this argument has a basis of fact depends upon (a) the purchasing power of the worker's dollar and (b) whether or not the benefits of the tariff accrue to the worker or to the manufacturer. If a general high tariff results in a high price level, obviously the worker's wages will not purchase so much as they would if the price level were lower.

Tariffs affect agriculture. Tariffs affect farmers in two ways. They affect the manufactured products the farmers must buy; and they affect, in some cases, the products the farmers sell. In the United States the major farm crops have been protected by high tariffs, although the tariffs on some agricultural products have been reduced. There have also been tariffs on clothing, machinery, and other products that a farmer must have. Thus, the advantages that a farmer might gain from higher prices on his crops are offset by higher prices he must pay for the products he buys.

Tariffs affect manufacturing. Very early in the history of the United States, certain manufacturers, notably in the textile field in New England, sought government protection by the encouragement of high tariffs. They argued that infant industries would be protected and encouraged and that in case of war, certain industries were necessary; they also defended the idea that high tariffs brought about high standards of living. Manufacturers whose market is largely domestic are the chief gainers from tariffs. Other manufacturers may actually be injured and their foreign market destroyed when foreign nations react against our tariff policies.

Tariffs affect the consumer. Although an individual as a producer may gain from tariffs, as a consumer he suffers because high tariffs are generally injurious. From the consumer's point of view solely, tariffs result in (a) high prices and (b) a narrower range of choice. In some few instances tariffs may protect a consumer from cheap and shoddy goods. In general, however, the competition of foreign products would necessarily make domestic manufacturers more efficient so that they could compete with foreigners or have to withdraw from the market. As productive efficiency is always to the consumer's advantage, tariffs indirectly serve to discourage efficiency and therefore penalize the consumer. In general, it may be said that high tariffs decrease the consumer's purchasing power.

Conflicting theories. The tariff problem has long been a source of political and economic debate. Economists have generally agreed that low tariffs or no tariffs are desirable from a national and a consumer point of view, but political representatives have usually been powerful enough to overcome the opposition to tariffs. There are many pros and cons with respect to tariffs. The tariff advocates point out that tariffs keep out cheap foreign products made by low-paid labor; that they maintain industries necessary in case of war; that they promote young and weak industries; and that they help to make the nation self-sufficient. Economists and others point out that tariffs reduce productivity by limiting specialization and markets; that they penalize the consumer; that they help, not labor, but only particular groups; and that they create international ill will.

The dominant point of view seems to be that tariffs are undesirable; but in a world in which national rivalries are increasing, it is difficult to reduce tariffs. If tariffs are reduced, certain industries, especially those in which foreign competition is strong, will be affected adversely.

The Trade Expansion Act of 1962. In 1962, the Congress enacted the Trade Expansion Act that confers on the President broad new authority to enter into trade agreements. The purposes of the act are, through trade agreements: (1) to stimulate economic growth of the United States and maintain and enlarge foreign markets for American products; (2) to strengthen economic relations with foreign countries; and (3) to prevent communist economic penetration.

Essentially the act provides the President with authority to reduce tariffs, and thus stimulate economic growth and strengthen economic relations with other countries.

Facts everyone should know about international trade, balance of payments, and tariffs

1. International trade has an important bearing on the relationship between nations.

2. International trade has cultural and political as well as economic implications; the goal of a nation in entering into international trade is to provide a higher and more satisfactory level of living for its citizens.

3. The value of exports and the value of imports of goods and services for any country must be approximately the same; otherwise an unfavorable balance of trade is created.

4. Nations compete for export sales just as merchants at home compete through producing a better product at a lower price.

5. Foreign exchange is essential for international trade. Through it exporters of any country receive pay for their goods in the currency of their own country.

6. The balance of international payments for a nation is the difference in the total amount received from and the total amount paid to foreign nations for all purposes including export and import of goods and services.

7. The balance of trade of a given nation may be favorable and the balance of payments unfavorable.

8. When the United States makes greater total payments to foreign countries than the total revenue it receives in a given year, the deficit is paid to foreign countries in gold or liquid liabilities that may be converted to gold at will.

9. An unfavorable balance of payments for a given country may be corrected in the future by encouraging its citizens to buy domestic products, reducing purchasing and spending abroad, and promoting more export business.

10. Many countries enter into trade agreements with other countries to promote the free flow of goods and services among the countries. The European Common Market is an outstanding example of such an arrangement.

11. Tariffs and other trade barriers tend to retard international trade; at the same time they may protect new business, employment opportunities, high wage scales, and the development of defense industries.

▪ QUESTIONS ON THE TEXT

1. What is international trade?
2. What specific items of goods does the United States import?
3. What major kinds of merchandise does the United States import more than it exports? export more than import?
4. From the table on U.S. Import and Export Values on page 296, does the United States import more or less merchandise than it exports, and how much?

5. Approximately what percentage of the total goods and services produced in the United States (GNP) is exported?
6. How is it possible for a nation to import annually 40 percent or more
   of the goods and services used in that country?
7. If nation *A* produces a bicycle at $20 and nation *B* produces a com-
   parable bicycle at $19, which nation will be the more likely to export
   bicycles?
8. What is meant by "balance of trade"?
9. What has been the trend in the balance of trade for the period from
   1960 to 1965?
10. What is meant by the term "balance of payments"?
11. What does "balance-of-payments deficit" mean?
12. Assuming that the United States has spent more money in foreign
    countries than foreign countries have spent in the United States, how
    can the United States pay the deficit?
13. What is the purpose of the gold reserve in the United States?
14. What is a liquid liability?
15. How do U.S. liquid liabilities affect the gold reserve?
16. What steps could the United States take to reduce or eliminate the
    balance-of-payments deficit?
17. Why do nations want foreign trade?
18. Why do nations who want foreign trade also want to maintain control
    over it?
19. What are the ways by which nations attempt to limit imports and
    increase exports?
20. What is a tariff?
21. What are the main purposes of the Trade Expansion Act of 1962?

□ QUESTIONS FOR DISCUSSION

1. Discuss the importance of international trade.
2. What would be the effect on the United States if all imports were
   discontinued?
3. Which is more important to a nation—the ratio of its domestic trade
   to its foreign trade or the ratio of its exports to its imports? Why?
4. Assume that two nations are both highly productive in producing
   goods and services, but one of them is able to sell great volumes of its
   products to foreign nations and the other one is able to make very
   few sales abroad. What conditions make foreign trade opportunities
   more favorable to the one nation than to the other?
5. Discuss how payments for merchandise sold in a foreign nation are
   made through foreign exchange.
6. Discuss the meaning of "favorable" and "unfavorable" balance of trade.
7. In 1965, the United States exported about $1.25 of goods for every
   dollar of goods it imported. What would have been the effect on

business conditions in the United States if the United States had imported $1.25 of goods for every dollar that it exported?

8. In 1964, the U.S. balance of trade was an approximately $6.5 billion surplus (i.e., exports of goods exceeded imports) and in the same year the balance of payments resulted in an approximate $2.8 billion deficit. Explain how this is possible.

9. What would be the effect if the United States were to refuse to pay its balance-of-payments in gold?

10. What kinds of business transactions do foreign countries conduct with the United States that would result in those nations making payments to the United States?

11. Many United States business firms are making substantial investments in foreign branches or in the establishment of separate foreign firms. These investments result in the outflow of U.S. payments to foreign nations. Would it be possible for the United States government to prohibit such investments? What would be the effect of making such a regulation?

12. American tourists spend money abroad each year. Discuss the possibility of limiting the amount an American tourist could take with him to spend.

13. Assume that a tariff would be placed on all apparel and foods entering the United States from foreign countries. What effect would such tariffs probably have on consumers?

14. Several arguments have been advanced for and against tariffs. State and defend your position on the tariff question.

▪ PROBLEMS TO SOLVE

1. Select ten foreign countries, identify the currency which they use, and determine the official exchange rate in terms of U.S. dollars. Assume that you wish to purchase a $10 pair of shoes with foreign currency. How much would the shoes cost in terms of each of the ten foreign currencies?

2. If the official exchange rate is one British pound for $2.80 American, how many ounces of gold would have to be transferred to Great Britain in settlement of a balance of international payments amounting to 116,000 British pounds?

3. Prepare a report on one of the following topics: (a) The Export-Import Bank, (b) The European Common Market, and (c) The World Bank—International Bank for Reconstruction and Development. Include in your report a complete description of these agreements or institutions, when they were established, the countries or agencies involved, and the purposes for such agreements or institutions. Your school librarian will assist you in locating the information you need.

4. From recent issues of publications such as the *World Almanac, Information Please Almanac,* and the *Statistical Abstract of the United States,* all of which are probably in your school library, prepare charts showing the top ten exports and imports of the United States, the leading countries receiving the exports, and the total dollar values of each of the imports and exports.

5. Compile a list of minerals the United States imports annually, and prepare a report on the uses of these minerals.

▪ COMMUNITY PROBLEMS AND PROJECTS

1. Visit a local department store and make a list of some of the foreign-made products offered for sale. Some stores have import gift departments. Compare the prices of these products with similar products made in the United States.

2. Identify someone in your community who has recently made a trip to a foreign country. Discuss with him the difference between the official exchange rate and the unofficial exchange rate. Determine whether or not U.S. citizens can make purchases when they are in foreign countries with dollars.

3. Investigate local manufacturing industries in your city to find out what, if any, goods are being exported to other countries. Try to find out specifically what is being exported, to what countries, and the approximate percent of production that exports represent for the business.

4. From information provided by your state's Department of Commerce and from recent issues of various almanacs, prepare a chart or graph showing the role your state plays in world trade (goods exported and imported and the dollar value).

5. Investigate the source of various goods sold in the stores in your city (clothing stores, gift shops, grocery stores, drugstores, department stores, appliance stores, etc.). Prepare a list of the various articles (and the countries from which they were imported) which are sold in your community but which were not manufactured in the United States.

Chapter 17

Bank services and loans

PURPOSE OF THE CHAPTER

Almost every individual and family at some time need to utilize many banking services and find it necessary to obtain a loan to pay debts. This chapter will explain how you may use the services of your banks effectively and the sources and problems of obtaining a loan.

You will find answers to these questions:

1. What are the major bank services of interest to individuals?
2. How is a checking account used?
3. How should you endorse a check or other commercial paper?
4. What are the most desirable sources of loans?
5. What interest rates should one expect to pay?

A. Bank services

The organization and economic functions of banks were discussed in Chapter 11. In that chapter reference was made to the many services banks provide in order for us to conduct our business affairs. Many of these services will now be described and explained.

CHECKING ACCOUNTS

Banks accept money deposits from businesses and individuals and pay out this money when the depositors write checks on the deposits. This service is called a *checking account service,* and the deposits in a checking account are called *demand deposits.* These deposits are so called because the bank must pay out the money whenever the depositor demands or orders it to do so. This demand is in the form of a *check,* which is a written order by which the depositor directs a bank to pay a certain amount of money to another person. The depositor who writes the check is known as the *drawer.* The person to whom the check is payable is called the *payee.* The bank on which the check is drawn is called the *drawee.*

The checking account service is perhaps one of the most important services provided by banks. Nearly 90 percent of all money transactions (payments for goods and services and debts) are made by checks. Money on deposit in a checking account is safe from loss or theft. Payments by checks are convenient because people do not have to carry large sums of money with them at all times, and checks can be mailed more easily and cheaply in most instances than having to walk or ride to all the places where payments have to be made.

Economic service. Equally important to the safety and convenience of the checking account service is the economic service provided by checking account deposits. From experience banks realize that a percentage of demand deposits is always on hand. Rather than to allow this money to lie idle in vaults or on deposit with a reserve bank, banks are permitted by the Federal Reserve System to make personal and business loans out of this percentage of unused deposits. Therefore, not only do checking account customers enjoy a safe, convenient service for conducting their business affairs, but they also help to expand business activity by making it possible for banks to make additional loans from the percentage of unused demand deposits.

Joint accounts. Often two persons will want to use the same bank checking account or savings account. Such an account, which is called a *joint* or *survivorship account,* is usually opened by a man and his wife. Each must fill out a signature card, and either person has authority to withdraw funds during the life of both parties. In most states when one of the parties operating a joint account dies, the bank is forbidden by law to honor any further checks until all tax

---

Advantages of using checks

1. A personal check is a convenient way to pay bills.
2. Usually it is more economical to pay bills by check through the mails than to make a trip to the places where accounts are to be paid.
3. The check stubs and canceled checks provide a record of expenditures, deposits, and bank balances.
4. Money in a checking account is safe from theft or loss.
5. A canceled check is proof of payment; therefore, it serves as a receipt.
6. A checking account helps to enhance one's personal business standing; it also serves as a reference.

---

claims of the state and federal government and all other claims against the estate are paid.

Reconciliation of bank statement. At regular intervals, usually monthly, a bank makes available to a depositor with a checking account a report of deposits and checks called a *bank statement.* It is a good business practice to compare this statement with the entries on the checkbook stubs to be sure that there are no mistakes. This process is called *reconciling* the bank statement or *reconciliation.* The purpose of reconciliation is to see whether the checkbook balance is correct on the date on which the reconciliation is made and to detect errors, if any, in the bank statement. It is the depositor's responsibility to reconcile the bank balance and to report any mistakes to the bank immediately.

Reconciliation of bank statement

Cash balance (on statement) ...$225.42	Checkbook balance $278.03
Deposit not on statement $100.00	
$325.42	
Less checks outstanding:	
No. 152 ....$15.50	
No. 153 ....$33.24	
Total checks outstanding 48.74	Less service charge 1.35
Balance $276.68	Correct checkbook balance $276.68

Stopping payment on a check. The bank should be requested to stop payment if a check is lost or stolen or if for some other reason (such as fraud) you do not want the check honored. The request may be given orally or in writing; but if it is given orally, it should be followed by a written notice on a special form provided by the bank.

Although banks will attempt to stop the payment, they may not assume responsibility for damage or loss if the check is paid inadvertently.

Postdating checks. *Postdating* a check (using a date later than the current date) is legal and sometimes convenient, but the privilege should not be abused. Let us assume, for example, that one has a debt of $100 due on June 20, and he wishes to pay it on June 15 before going on his vacation. If he does not want the check cashed until June 20, he can postdate it. The bank will not cash it before that date, although some banks will accept it for deposit if the difference in dates is not more than one or two days. Bankers ordinarily discourage the practice of postdating checks.

Service charges on a checking account. When deposits are made in an account and checks are written, a bank incurs expenses in operating that account. Unless the account balance is large enough for the bank to earn a profit by lending the money, a service charge will be made. This service charge may be determined by each bank, or all banks in one city may follow the same plan.

A common plan is one in which the bank charges a flat fee plus a charge for each deposit and each check that is written. The customer is given a credit based upon the smallest balance of the account during the month. Here is an example of how the plan works:

Maintenance charge, 50¢ plus 21 items at 5¢ $1.55
Less credit for minimum balance during month, $1,059. 1.06
Net service charges . . . .$ .49

As a checking account customer, it is the depositor's responsibility to take every precaution to see that he uses this service carefully, wisely, and accurately. Banks are ready and willing to provide demonstrations and instructional materials to their customers to aid them in making deposits, writing checks, reconciling bank statements, and to understand special checking account services, such as "Checkmaster," "Thrifti-checks," and "Pay-as-you-go Check Way."

BANK DRAFTS AND SPECIAL CHECKS

Sometimes you may wish to make a payment to someone who will not accept your personal check. It could be an important payment in a distant city; it might be a deposit for the buying of a house; or it could be any one of several other situations. In such cases you may

---

Your obligations as a depositor

1. Keep an accurate record of each check on the check stub.
2. Keep a sufficient balance in your account; do not overdraw. (To overdraw an account is a criminal offense in most states.)
3. Reconcile your checkbook and bankbook balances promptly upon receipt of the bank statement.
4. Keep all canceled checks for at least a year; keep important canceled checks indefinitely.

---

go to a bank and obtain a bank draft, a certified check, a cashier's check, a bank money order, or a traveler's check, any one of which may serve your purpose. A small fee is charged by the bank for issuing any of these.

Bank draft. A *bank draft* is a check of one bank drawn upon funds deposited to its credit with some other bank. A bank draft is a convenient means of transferring money when the individual who is making payment is not known in the place to which the money is to be sent.

Certified check. A *certified check* is an ordinary check drawn by a depositor in the usual way but presented to the bank for certification by the drawer. The bank stamps or writes a certification on the check. The amount of the check is deducted immediately from the depositor's account balance, and the check becomes an obligation of the bank rather than of the depositor. The bank thus guarantees its payment. A certified check has practically the same status as a bank draft, provided the bank is known and has a good reputation.

One disadvantage of a certified check to the depositor is that it will not be returned with his canceled checks; hence, he will not have available the endorsed check to serve as a receipt. If for any reason a certified check is returned to the maker, it should not be destroyed but redeposited in the maker's checking account at the bank. Otherwise, the balance of the checking account will be short, for the amount of the check was deducted when it was certified.

Cashier's check. A *cashier's check* or *treasurer's check* is one that a bank draws on itself. It is used to pay bills owed by the bank. Also, one may buy a cashier's check to transmit money to another person in much the same way as a person buys a bank draft.

Liberty Bank & Trust Company 10-15 / 220

No. *5699*

Buffalo _____ *April 24* 19--

PAY TO THE
ORDER OF *Richard Kirkhart* _____ $ *159.87*

The sum of $159 and 87 cts _____ DOLLARS

CASHIER'S CHECK   *Michael Sauner*
                                          AUTHORIZED SIGNATURE

A cashier's check

Bank money order. A *bank money order,* also called a *register check* or a *personal money order,* serves essentially the same function in transmitting money for a customer as the cashier's check. In many banks, the bank money order is replacing the cashier's check as a means of transmitting a customer's money to another person. The name of the remitter is on the bank money order; however, the name of the remitter ordinarily is not on a cashier's check and never appears on a bank draft.

BANK MONEY ORDER
N⁰ 04897

Thomas Egan REMITTER   Selby, North Carolina *August 9* 19-- 66-14 / 512

PAY TO THE
ORDER OF *Duncan-Culman, Inc.* ● $ *40.15*

The sum of $40 and 15 cts _____ DOLLARS
18

To The First National Bank of Selby
Selby, North Carolina   *Charles Powell*
                                          AUTHORIZED SIGNATURE

A bank money order

Traveler's checks. People who travel do not like to carry large amounts of cash, and they find it difficult to cash personal checks. Although a few large banks issue and sell their own *traveler's checks,* the best known are the American Express Company traveler's checks. These may be purchased from the American Express Company or from almost any bank. A fee is charged for each check. Traveler's checks can be purchased in amounts of $10, $20, $50, $100, or more. At the time it is purchased, each check is signed by the buyer in the presence of the bank agent. The check can then be cashed anywhere in the world. When it is cashed, it must be signed again in the presence of the person cashing it with a signature that matches the original signature.

A traveler's check

OTHER BANK SERVICES

Savings accounts. Savings accounts may be maintained in what are commonly known as savings banks or in the savings departments of other banks. Interest is usually paid on savings accounts in banks, ranging from 3½ to 4 percent. There is some difference in the interest earned, depending upon the rate and the number of times a year the interest is calculated. Obviously, the income from a savings account is greater when interest is compounded semiannually than when it is compounded annually at the same rate. Savings by depositing money in a bank is a conservative means of investing, but it is usually a safe means compared with investments in many types of securities. Checks ordinarily cannot be written on savings deposits.

Many banks also accept a *time deposit* or *certificate of deposit,* a negotiable receipt for funds left with a bank as a special interest-bearing deposit on which a slightly higher rate of interest (from 4 to 4½ percent) may be paid. These special deposits, however, may not be withdrawn until the time specified, usually 3 months, 6 months, or a year.

Trust functions of banks. The trust functions of banks have proved especially useful to people who wish to preserve their wealth to be managed for the benefit of others. Many wills include clauses that appoint certain trust companies or trust departments of banks to administer the property left to wives and children. *Administering* an estate (property) means managing it for the benefit of the persons entitled to it or dividing it among these people according to law.

The trust officer of a bank serves, in a sense, as the business manager of an estate left in his care. He may also serve as a trustee for a fund that has been created to serve some special purpose, such as to provide an income for a charitable organization or to spend money for the care of a park.

Safe-deposit boxes. Safe-deposit boxes in the vaults of banks are provided on a rental basis. Such a box provides protection against burglary and fire and should be used for storing valuables that cannot safely be kept in the home or in the business office. Each customer has a key to the box that he rents, and the bank has a master key. Both keys are necessary to unlock the box; neither one alone will unlock it. A bank cannot open a private safe-deposit box except upon the order of a court. In case of a customer's lost key, the bank may in the presence of witnesses and legal representatives of the renter of the box have a locksmith drill the lock to open it.

In most states, if a safe-deposit box is registered in the names of a man and his wife, the bank is legally required to seal the box upon notice of the death of either person. When it is opened, a list is made of taxable items in the box by a legal tax representative. When the estate is settled according to law, the property in the safe-deposit box is then turned over to the rightful owner.

Financial and tax advice. Most bankers have the problem of advising those who apply for credit. This advice must be given to individuals as well as to business owners. A wise banker will not make a loan to an individual if he believes that the loan cannot be repaid or that to repay the loan would place an undesirable hardship upon the borrower. Bankers also provide other financial advice, such as how to invest money.

Some banks maintain tax departments with a staff of lawyers and accountants who give advice on tax problems to the customers of the bank. These tax specialists, in some cases, will prepare income tax returns.

Travel service. Certain banks operate travel departments and sell tickets. They also help travelers obtain foreign money and credit for use in foreign countries. For example, if a person is traveling to Europe, the bank may arrange in advance to obtain for the traveler foreign money that he will need in the countries in which he will be traveling, or the bank may arrange for deposits to be made in foreign banks, along with a letter of identification, so that the traveler can go to those banks and withdraw the money as he needs it.

Charge account services. In many cities one or more banks may offer a *charge account service.* A customer is given a charge account credit card which is accepted in all stores that participate with the bank in the charge account plan. Under this plan, purchases are made at stores and charged the same as on any other charge account. The cooperating stores send the charges they have made to customers' accounts to the bank offering the charge account service. The bank pays the bills sent to it. The bank in turn sends the customer a monthly bill accompanied by the original sales slips from each of the stores at which purchases were made. Ordinarily, the monthly bill from the bank is due in 30 days.

Instant credit. Some banks have established a system of issuing credit cards to individuals permitting those persons to come to the bank and to borrow money instantly up to an agreed amount. This same bank credit card can be used in a manner similar to the bank charge account service. In other words, the person carrying the card can present it to a store when buying merchandise, and the bill will be sent to the bank for payment.

Revolving credit. Banks have a system of making loans (extending credit) that is commonly known as *revolving credit.* It is also called *ready-credit, write-a-check, line-o-credit,* and other similar names. The bank's plan of revolving credit is similar to that of retail stores.

Under a plan of revolving credit, the bank agrees with the customer as to the amount of money that can be borrowed and how it must be repaid in regular installments. The customer may write checks against this amount, but will be charged interest only on the amount used. The customer can continue to write checks and to make repayments as long as the amount owed the bank does not exceed the amount agreed upon.

Sale of government bonds. All banks sell United States government bonds. Banks will also cash these bonds at maturity and will serve as an agent to cash a bond before maturity. Banks also serve as brokers for purchase and sale of stocks and bonds.

NEGOTIABLE INSTRUMENTS

Borrowing, lending, and transfer of money center largely around a negotiable instrument. A *negotiable instrument* is a written evidence of some contractual obligation and is ordinarily transferable from one person to another by indorsement. The instrument is frequently referred to as "negotiable paper" or "commercial paper." The most common forms of negotiable instruments are checks, drafts, certificates of deposit, and promissory notes. Checks, drafts, and certificates of deposit have already been discussed.

A *promissory note* is an unconditional written promise to pay a certain sum in money at a certain time or on demand to the bearer or the order of one who has obtained the note through legal means. The one who executes a promissory note—the one who promises to pay the amount specified in the note under the terms indicated—is the *maker*. The person to whom the note is payable is known as the *payee*.

The maker of a note or the drawer of a check is unconditionally required to pay the amount specified. This obligation assumes, of course, that the transaction relating to the use of the instrument is proper and legal. The drawer of a check is required to pay the amount of the check if the drawee (the bank) does not pay it, but there are certain limitations on this rule in many states.

The person who indorses a negotiable instrument and transfers it to someone else is known as the *indorser*. The person to whom he transfers the negotiable instrument is referred to as the *indorsee*.

Transfer of negotiable instruments. Much of our money consists of Federal Reserve notes that circulate as money without indorsement. The promissory notes issued by individuals and businesses may also circulate, although they usually require an indorsement.

A person who signs a negotiable instrument as an indorser is liable under varying conditions. For instance, if he indorses a note to help a friend obtain a loan from a bank, he must pay the amount of the note to the bank or to a subsequent indorser if his friend fails to pay it when it is due. The principal kinds of indorsements used in transferring negotiable instruments are explained and illustrated below.

Indorsement in full. An *indorsement in full* is frequently referred to as a *special indorsement*. It mentions the name of the indorsee who must, in turn, indorse the instrument in order to transfer or cash it. This type of indorsement should be used when checks are sent by mail or by messenger.

Blank indorsement. A *blank indorsement* consists in merely the name of the indorser. It makes a check or note payable to the bearer; consequently, anyone might be able to cash it. Checks to be deposited should never be indorsed in this manner until after the owner is in the bank because if the check is lost, anyone finding it can cash it.

Qualified indorsement. A *qualified indorsement* is, as its name implies, one that limits the obligation of the indorser. Assume, for instance, that a person has a check that he wishes to transfer to another. He does not wish to assume responsibility for the payment of the check if the drawer cannot or will not pay it. He may therefore use a qualified indorsement with words such as "without recourse," which means that he will not be responsible for payment if the signer fails to pay. The qualified indorsement is infrequently used mainly because both people and banks are reluctant to accept negotiable paper for which the payee or another indorser is unwilling to assume responsibility for its payment.

Restrictive indorsement. The *restrictive indorsement* is very common. It is one which specifies that the person to whom the instrument is indorsed (the indorsee) may dispose of it only in the manner indicated by the indorser. For instance, a restrictive indorsement on checks to be deposited frequently includes the phrase "for deposit only" or "for deposit only to the account of. . . ."

Pay to the order of
W. P. Lucas
A. L. Nieman

Indorsement in full

Without recourse
A. L. Nieman

Qualified indorsement

A. L. Nieman

Blank indorsement

Pay to
William Weber
for deposit only
A. L. Nieman

Restrictive indorsement

Forms of indorsement

B. Obtaining personal loans

Both individuals and families occasionally need to borrow money for periods of time ranging from a few days up to five years. Loans to meet personal and family needs are relatively small in amount, the average being about $200. They are known as *short-term* and *intermediate-term loans,* whereas loans for the purchase of real estate are usually classified as *long-term* loans. Money may be needed for emergencies such as unexpected medical and hospital bills. In many instances, small loans or personal loans enable families to buy necessary household equipment, make permanent additions and improvements to the home, and to do other things that cannot wait until the money could be saved. Borrowing money to go to school in many instances falls in the personal loan class.

In order for you to be able to borrow money, you must establish a good credit rating in ordinary buying. If you have a good credit reputation, you can borrow the money you need when you need it.

Before borrowing, one should always consider how great his need really is for the goods or services he intends to buy with the money. Under some circumstances one may be exercising very good judgment to borrow money, and under other conditions it may be very unwise to borrow. The advantages and disadvantages of borrowing for a specific purpose should be carefully determined and analyzed as a basis for making one's decision.

WHERE SHOULD YOU BORROW THE MONEY?

Once it has been decided that a small loan is needed, you should shop for a loan with the same care that you would use in shopping for furniture or appliances for the home. The primary factors to be considered in shopping for a loan are: (a) the reliability of the lender; (b) the real cost of the loan to the borrower; and (c) the special terms or conditions of the loan that affect the borrower, such as the provisions for security of the loan, payments, and claims that may arise against wages or other property in case of inability to make payments when they fall due.

TYPES OF LOANS

There are two types of loans as to the methods of repayment. One type of loan permits you to repay in a lump sum (single-payment loan). The other type of loan permits you to repay in regular installments (installment loan).

There are also two types of loans as to security. One type is an *unsecured loan.* In other words, you merely sign a contract, binding yourself to the terms of the contract. Your character and honor are sufficient to enable you to obtain a loan. If you fail to abide by the contract, you can be sued, of course, for the amount due. The other type is a secured loan. A *secured loan* means that you have to pledge or turn over to the lender some kind of property called *collateral,* (bonds, stocks, rights to proceeds from an insurance policy, or other personal property, such as an automobile, furniture, or livestock) which serves as security for the loan. The lender has a claim against this property until you repay the loan. If you fail to repay the loan, he can keep the property or sell it to satisfy his claim against you.

Another type of protection that a lender sometimes requires is the signature of an additional person who becomes jointly responsible with you and promises to pay if you fail to do so. This person is called a *cosigner* or a *comaker.* The illustration below shows a loan agreement signed by comakers.

15-1

$ 150.00 PERSONAL LOAN DEPARTMENT No.

The FIFTH THIRD UNION TRUST Co.
CINCINNATI, OHIO

CINCINNATI, OHIO January 5, 19

FOR VALUE RECEIVED, WE, THE UNDERSIGNED, JOINTLY AND SEVERALLY, PROMISE TO PAY TO THE ORDER OF THE FIFTH THIRD UNION TRUST COMPANY OF CINCINNATI, OHIO, THE SUM OF One Hundred and Fifty DOLLARS AT ITS OFFICE IN CINCINNATI, OHIO, WITH INTEREST AT THE RATE OF EIGHT PER CENT PER ANNUM AFTER MATURITY UNTIL PAID, WAIVING PRESENTMENT, DEMAND FOR PAYMENT, PROTEST, NOTICE OF PROTEST AND NOTICE OF NON-PAYMENT OF THIS NOTE. THE FIRST OF THE UNDERSIGNED (NAMELY, THE BORROWER) HEREBY AGREEING TO PAY PROMPTLY $ 12.50 ON March 6, 19 AND AT REGULAR monthly INTERVALS THEREAFTER FOR 11 INSTALLMENTS AND $ 14.50 AS THE LAST INSTALLMENT.
(SEMI-MONTHLY OR MONTHLY)
AND THE OTHERS OF THE UNDERSIGNED JOINTLY AND SEVERALLY AGREEING TO MAKE EACH OF THE SAID PAYMENTS PROMPTLY IF THE SAID BORROWER SHOULD DEFAULT IN MAKING THE SAME. AS OFTEN AS THE MAKING OF ANY SUCH PAYMENT MAY BE DELAYED BEYOND THE DAY AS HEREIN AGREED TO BE MADE, THE UNDERSIGNED JOINTLY AND SEVERALLY PROMISE TO PAY TO THE HOLDER HEREOF AT OR BEFORE THE MATURITY OF THIS NOTE, A SUM CALCULATED AT THE RATE OF FIVE CENTS FOR EACH ONE DOLLAR OF SUCH DELAYED PAYMENT, BUT IN NO EVENT SHALL THE TOTAL CHARGE IN CONNECTION WITH ANY ONE DELAYED PAYMENT BE IN EXCESS OF FIVE DOLLARS ($5.00), AND TO MAKE SUCH PAYMENTS AS COMPENSATION FOR THE DAMAGE OCCASIONED BY SUCH DELAY.

UPON FAILURE TO MAKE ANY PAYMENT AS HEREIN AGREED, OR IN THE EVENT OF THE DEATH OF THE SAID BORROWER, OR IN CASE OF INSOLVENCY, BANKRUPTCY, OR FAILURE IN BUSINESS OF ANY OF THE UNDERSIGNED, THIS NOTE SHALL, AT THE OPTION OF ITS HOLDER, BECOME IMMEDIATELY DUE AND PAYABLE, WITHOUT DEMAND OR NOTICE. UPON THIS NOTE MATURING UNDER ANY OF ITS TERMS AND PROVISIONS, AND NOT BEING FULLY PAID AND SATISFIED ON THE DAY OF ITS MATURITY, THE TOTAL SUM THEN DUE HEREUNDER MAY FORTHWITH BE DEBITED TO ANY ACCOUNT OR ACCOUNTS MAINTAINED BY ANY OF THE UNDERSIGNED WITH THE HOLDER HEREOF, WITHOUT NOTICE TO OR FURTHER CONSENT FROM ANY OF THE UNDERSIGNED, THEY HEREBY AGREEING TO BE AND REMAIN JOINTLY AND SEVERALLY LIABLE FOR ALL INDEBTEDNESS REPRESENTED BY THIS NOTE IN EXCESS OF THE AMOUNT THEN TO THE CREDIT OF SUCH ACCOUNT OR ACCOUNTS.

EACH OF THE UNDERSIGNED HEREBY AUTHORIZES SAID TRUST COMPANY TO (1) PAY THE PROCEEDS OF THIS NOTE TO Mr. J. C. Murphy (2) DATE THIS NOTE AS OF THE DAY WHEN THE LOAN EVIDENCED HEREBY IS MADE; (3) COMPLETE ANY BLANK SPACES IN THIS NOTE ACCORDING TO THE TERMS UPON WHICH IT GRANTS SAID LOAN; AND (4) CAUSE THE SIGNATURE OF ONE OR MORE CO-MAKERS IN ADDITION TO THE ORIGINAL NUMBER, TO BE ADDED AT ANY TIME OR TIMES HERETO, AND TO DO SO WITH OR WITHOUT NOTICE TO ANY OF THE UNDERSIGNED, WHO HEREBY CONSENT THERETO AND ACKNOWLEDGE THAT SUCH MAY BE DONE WITH OUT AFFECTING THE JOINT AND SEVERAL OBLIGATION OF EACH OF THE UNDERSIGNED, AS HEREINBEFORE SET FORTH.

UNDERSIGNED, JOINTLY AND SEVERALLY, HEREBY IRREVOCABLY AUTHORIZE ANY ATTORNEY AT LAW, CLERK OF COURT OR PROTHONOTARY TO APPEAR FOR UNDERSIGNED, JOINTLY OR SEVERALLY, BEFORE ANY JUSTICE OF THE PEACE, OR IN ANY COURT OF RECORD, STATE OR FEDERAL, IN THE UNITED STATES OF AMERICA, IN TERM TIME OR VACATION, AND TO WAIVE ISSUE AND SERVICE OF PROCESS AND CONFESS JUDGMENT AGAINST THE UNDERSIGNED, JOINTLY OR SEVERALLY, IN FAVOR OF THE HOLDER HEREOF, FOR SUCH AMOUNT AS MAY APPEAR TO BE UNPAID HEREON, AFTER MATURITY, TOGETHER WITH INTEREST, AND TO RELEASE ALL ERRORS AND WAIVE ALL RIGHT OF APPEAL.

ADDRESSES (GIVE COMPLETE ADDRESS)	SIGNATURES (WRITE IN FULL AND IN INK)
528 Wakefield Drive, Cincinnati, Ohio	1. J. C. Murphy — BORROWER
528 Wakefield Drive, Cincinnati, Ohio	2. Catherine Murphy — CO-MAKER—WIFE OR HUSBAND OF BORROWER
2564 Williams Street, Norwood, Ohio	3. Carl A. Frederick — CO-MAKER
3151 Reading Road, Cincinnati, Ohio	4. Clifford Edwards — CO-MAKER

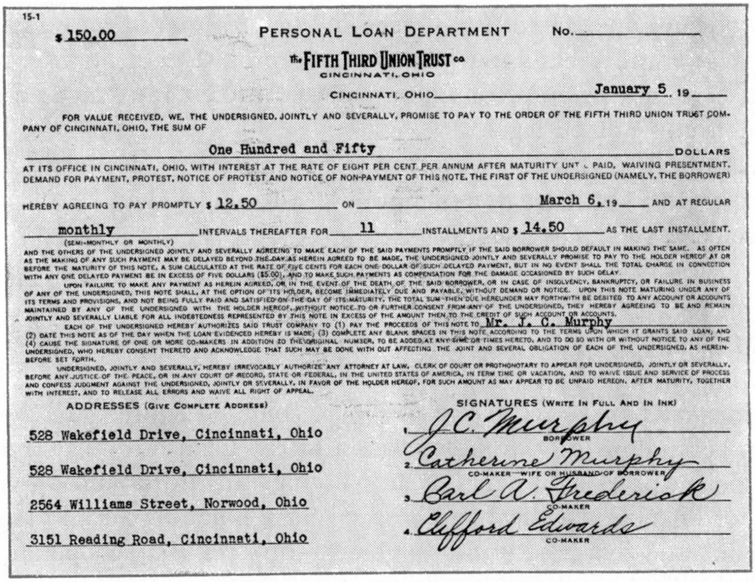

A personal loan agreement

INTEREST RATES

Interest rates vary according to the states and the types of lending institutions. Laws in most states govern the interest rates of such institutions as pawnshops and consumer finance companies. The state banking laws and the rules of the Federal Reserve System govern largely the interest rates of banks, although the demand for and the supply of money have important influences on interest rates on bank loans.

In nearly all of the states, there are two interest rates recognized by law: (1) the legal rate and (2) the maximum interest rate.

Legal rate. The *legal rate* is applicable if no rate is specified in a contract. For example, let us assume that a man purchased a used car for $1,200 on which he was to pay $200 down and $1,000 in six months with no interest. If he did not pay the $1,000 until nine months after the purchase was made, he could be charged interest at the legal rate by law in his state for the three months the $1,000 was past due.

Maximum interest rate. The other interest rate is known as the *maximum interest rate,* sometimes referred to as the *contract rate.* It is the maximum rate that it would be possible to charge by law for the use of money. For example, assume that Smith needs money desperately and that he would be willing to pay Jones $125 in 30 days if Jones would loan him $100 today. This would be $25 interest for one month, or on an annual basis it would be $300 or 300 percent interest. In most states having a maximum or contract interest rate, such an agreement would not be legal.

A typical legal rate is 6 percent per year and a typical contract rate is 8 percent. In some states, however, the range may be from 6 to 30 percent.

BORROWING FROM BANKS

Most of the small loans made to consumers are made by commercial, industrial, and savings banks (discussed in Chapter 11). In fact, commercial banks are among the most common sources for personal loans because of the favorable interest rates. Loans are made for such specific purposes as buying an automobile, furniture, and appliances and for financing medical and hospital bills, home repair and modernization, and charge-account purchases at stores that cooperate in a credit-bank plan.

Many commercial banks have established a somewhat permanent borrowing plan called a *revolving loan.* The plan works essentially like this: You apply to the bank for a revolving loan. If you have a steady income and a good credit rating, you will be granted a revolving loan of a certain amount. A checking account will be opened for you.

Modern full-service banks provide a number of services in addition to checking and savings accounts.

First National Bank of Cincinnati

You will not be charged any interest on the loan until you write checks on the account. Interest is usually charged at one percent a month on the outstanding average account balance plus a charge for each check. You will be required to repay the loan, including the interest and check service charge, in monthly installments.

Commercial and industrial banks handle personal loans on stated discount rates ranging from 3.3 to 12 percent. Since the installment method of payment of personal loans makes the annual true rate of interest roughly double the stated discount rate, the true cost of interest on commercial and industrial bank loans is approximately 6 to 24 percent.

BORROWING FROM SAVINGS AND LOAN ASSOCIATIONS

A *savings and loan* association is a term generally applied to an institution organized for the purpose of accepting deposits from individuals. These institutions are sometimes called *building and loan associations, cooperative banks, building associations, homestead associations,* and *savings associations.* In most states, savings and loan associations make loans only on homes. Most of them make only first-mortgage loans. The purpose of savings and loan associations is to promote savings, thus encouraging home ownership.

Where state laws and local policy permit, savings and loan associations make small personal loans at rates from 1 to 2 percent above the rate that is being paid depositors. For example, if the savings and loan association is paying depositors 4 percent, it will charge 5 or 6 percent on personal loans.

BORROWING FROM LIFE INSURANCE COMPANIES

Life insurance policies, except term insurance, accumulate a cash value as premiums are paid year after year. A policyholder may borrow from his insurance company up to the cash or loan value of his policy. A table of loan values at the end of each year is shown in most

CHARACTERISTICS OF PERSONAL LOANS COMPARED BY SOURCES

Source of loan	True annual interest rate for $100 loan repayable in one year	Security required	Range of amount of loans
Commercial banks, (Personal loan departments)	6-24%; 12% common	Cosigner; chattel mortgage on acceptable property	$50-$3,500
Industrial banks	6-24%; 16% common	Cosigner; chattel mortgage on acceptable property	$50-$5,000
Savings banks	6-24%; 12% common	Cosigner; chattel mortgage on acceptable property	$50-$5,000
Savings and loan associations	5-12%; 6% common	Usually first mortgages only; in a few states secured by personal property	60-80% of value of real estate. Local policy on small loans.
Life insurance companies	4-6%	Loan value of policy	95-100% of cash value of policy
Consumer finance companies	16-42%; usually 2½ to 3% a month on unpaid balance of loans of less than $300	Cosigner; chattel mortgage; frequently on signature only	$25-$1,000 in most states, higher in several
Credit unions (For members only)	6-12%; 1% a month on un- paid balance, common	Depends upon credit commit- tee action	$1 up, depending upon rules of credit union; $750 maxi- mum for federally char- tered unless secured
Pawnbrokers	24-120%; 36% common	Pledged or pawned personal property at arbitrary per- cent of current value	$1-$500; depends upon state laws
Unlicensed lenders	50-1,500%; 250 to 300% common	No pattern; varies	$5-$1,000; some higher

policies. In some states insurance companies may require 90 to 180 days' advance notice before making a loan on a policy.

The rate of interest that one will pay on an insurance loan will be from 4 to 6 percent. There is no credit investigation; therefore, no fee. The insurance company has no control over how the money is used by the borrower. The loan may be for a short or long period, and one does not need to repay the loan at all if he does not choose to do so. If interest is not paid, it will be added to the amount of the loan. In case of death before the loan is repaid, the amount of the loan plus accumulated interest will be deducted from the death benefits of the policy.

When one borrows on life insurance, the insurance protection is reduced by the amount of the loan because the loan is deducted before the amount of the insurance is paid. Since it is relatively easy to borrow on life insurance and the insurance companies usually do not try to seek repayment of the loan, one may be slow to make repayments and, therefore, not have adequate insurance when needed.

SECURED FHA LOANS

The Federal Housing Administration has provided a system of partially guaranteeing small loans made through commercial banks for purposes of home repair and modernization. Ordinary real-estate loans are made for a period of ten to thirty years, but the FHA loans for home repair and modernization are granted for a maximum period of five years, 32 days, and may not exceed $3,500. Because of the FHA guaranty, these loans are available at quite reasonable rates.

BORROWING FROM CONSUMER FINANCE COMPANIES

Small loan companies, now commonly known as *consumer finance companies,* have been established in all states except Arkansas. These companies lend primarily to wage earners and others of moderate means who may not have established a credit rating and who may not have security to be used as collateral for loans from other sources. Consumer finance companies rank next to commercial banks in the total amounts lent annually to consumers. It is estimated that one out of every five families borrows from consumer finance companies every year. These companies are legitimate institutions and fill an important place in our economic system. The licensed consumer finance company should not be confused with "loan sharks."

About 70 percent of the loans made by consumer finance companies are covered by a security agreement, which usually is a mortgage on household furniture or some other item of property or by comaker, and the remainder are made on the borrower's signature only. Loans are usually made for a period of 10 to 20 months. Consumer finance companies frequently make a smaller loan than a bank, and they frequently accept applications which banks might refuse.

Most states have laws governing the operation of consumer finance companies. Some states permit maximum loans of only $300, but other states permit loans up to $5,000. Consumer finance companies must have a license if they operate in states where there are laws governing this kind of institution. In most of the states the laws are modeled after the Uniform Small-Loan Law and the Model Consumer Finance Act, and in all states (except Arkansas) there are laws that reflect many provisions of the Model Act.

Model laws. In general, the state laws modeled after the Uniform Small-Loan Law and the Model Consumer Finance Act provide that: (a) the lender must be licensed by the state; (b) state supervision of small-loan companies is required; (c) maximum monthly rates of charge and maximum amount of loans are prescribed; (d) amount of the loan, security, payment schedule, and monthly rate of charge must be disclosed in the loan agreement, a copy of which is given to the borrower; (e) borrower must be granted privilege of prepaying the loan and receiving credit for the interest on the unused time; (f) lenders are prohibited from obtaining judgment against a borrower before notifying the borrower; and (g) concealed and unauthorized charges and false and misleading advertising are prohibited. No borrower should deal with any consumer finance company that is not licensed by the state and is not under state supervision. If there is any question about a consumer finance company, information can be obtained from such organizations as the better business bureau, the chamber of commerce, and the local welfare organization.

Interest rates. Consumer finance companies usually quote interest rates on a monthly basis on unpaid balances. The small-loan laws in most states require that the stated rate must be calculated on the decreasing periodic balance rather than on the entire original amount of the loan. A typical rate of charge for consumer finance companies is 3 to $3\frac{1}{2}$ percent a month on unpaid balances up to $100, and 2 or $2\frac{1}{2}$ percent on balances from $100 to $300. This means that the true annual rates range from 16 to 42 percent. One should consult the regulations in the small-loan law in his state before borrowing to learn what the maximum rate of charge and amount of the loan may be.

Month	Amount paid on loan	Monthly interest charges	Total payment
1	$ 8.33	$ 3.00	$ 11.33
2	8.33	2.75	11.08
3	8.33	2.50	10.83
4	8.34	2.25	10.59
5	8.33	2.00	10.33
6	8.33	1.75	10.08
7	8.34	1.50	9.84
8	8.33	1.25	9.58
9	8.34	1.00	9.34
10	8.33	.75	9.08
11	8.33	.50	8.83
12	8.34	.25	8.59
Totals	$100.00	$19.50	$119.50

Repaying a small loan

Some loan companies permit and even suggest level total payments (interest and principal combined). The table above illustrates how a loan of $100 at the rate of 3 percent a month is repaid in one year on the level-principal payment plan.

Reasons for charges. Many borrowers wonder why obtaining small loans costs more than the flat 6 percent or less that is charged on larger loans. Let us take the case of a loan of $50 to a stranger who applies to the lending agency for the first time. Let us also assume that the interest on a loan of this size, to be paid in ten monthly installments, would be $2.75. The agency lending the money has to investigate the applicant, close the loan, keep bookkeeping records, collect the money, allow for a certain percentage of loss on bad loans, and earn something on the investment. When one takes these expenses into consideration, it can be seen why rates are higher on small loans than on large loans. With the same amount of effort, the lending agency could handle a $5,000 loan.

BORROWING FROM CREDIT UNIONS

A *credit union* is a cooperative organization of people who agree to pool their savings and to make loans available only to members at a low interest rate. The members of a credit union are comprised of people who work for the same employer; who are members of the same church, labor union, or fraternal order; or who live in the same community. There are now more than 21,500 credit unions and 15 million members in the United States. They are chartered either under federal or state laws.

Membership and operation. Membership is obtained by paying a small entrance fee and by buying one or more shares, which usually sell for $5 each. Dividends are paid to savers (shareholders); and in many credit unions partial interest rebates, sometimes amounting to 5 percent, are being paid to borrowers. The members manage and operate the credit unions, each having one vote regardless of the number of shares he owns.

Loans are made to members out of accumulated capital. Loans as small as $5 are sometimes made; the maximum amount for loans may be determined by the board of directors provided it does not exceed $750 for unsecured loans for credit unions organized under federal law. Although more than half of the loans are not secured, comakers sometimes sign the notes with the borrower; and occasionally a chattel mortgage is signed by the borrower to secure the loan. Loans may not be made for periods of time longer than five years.

Interest rates. The interest rates charged by credit unions range from $\frac{1}{2}$ to 1 percent a month on unpaid balances. On a loan of $100 to be repaid in twelve equal monthly installments with interest at 1 percent a month on the unpaid balance due at the end of the previous month, the interest would be $6.50. At first this appears to be at a rate of 6½ percent per year. But the borrower did not have the entire $100 for a whole year. At the end of each month he reduced the amount he owed by $8.33; consequently, the true annual interest rate is 13 percent. Nevertheless, this is considerably less than the true annual interest rate of 39 percent for the $100 loan described in the chart on page 335. Borrowing from credit unions usually results in a saving in interest of $3 to $15 over most loan departments of commercial banks and consumer finance companies.

Interest rates in credit unions can be low because expenses of operation are low. Most credit unions have little or no expense for rent, salaries, credit investigations, or collections. They are exempt from federal income taxes. A credit committee makes all credit investigations, and losses from bad debts are negligible.

Guides in borrowing

1. Be sure you borrow from a company that is under state supervision.
2. Borrow no more than is necessary.
3. Borrow no more than you can repay according to your agreement.
4. Be sure that you understand your obligations and the obligations of the lender.
5. Be sure that you understand the amount of the loan, the cost of the loan, and the specific details with regard to repayment.
6. Read the contract carefully before you sign it.
7. Be sure that you get credit for every payment and receive a canceled contract when you have completed the payments.

BORROWING FROM PAWNBROKERS

The rate of interest charged on loans obtained from pawnbrokers usually is extremely high, ranking from 24 to 120 percent and higher on an annual basis.

To obtain a loan from a pawnbroker, one must turn over personal property, such as jewelry or tools, as a pledge or *pawn*. The maximum amount of the loan is usually extremely low in proportion to the value of the property; it is seldom more than 50 percent of the appraised value. Loans from pawnbrokers must be paid in full before pledged property will be returned.

In some states, if the loan is not paid by a specified time or within the length of time provided by state law, the property pawned may be sold. If there is a surplus from the sale, it is supposed to be given to the borrower. In other states, if the property pawned is not redeemed before the expiration of a specified period, title passes to the pawnbroker.

BORROWING FROM UNLICENSED LENDERS

There are still some states that do not have any small-loan laws. In these states the unlicensed lenders, commonly known as *loan sharks*, are sometimes sources of loans for many persons with low incomes who need an occasional loan. Unlicensed lenders also operate in states that do have regulatory laws. The person who patronizes an unlicensed lender is the one who needs credit the worst and who needs the most protection. Studies have shown that the lowest rate commonly charged by these illegal lenders is 120 percent a year. It is common for the rate to be 240 percent a year, and examples have been found of rates as high as 1,200 percent a year.

The rates alone are not the only evils. Some of these unscrupulous lenders never allow their clients to get out of debt. The borrower is sometimes required to pay the whole loan at one time or no payment will be accepted. He is constantly in debt because he can never get enough money together to pay the whole loan.

Facts everyone should know about banking services and loans

1. A checking account provides a convenient and economical way to handle money transactions.
2. Money in a savings account is not only safe, but it also earns interest.
3. A depositor has an obligation to follow the accepted practices and routines in using bank services.
4. Banks provide several means of transmitting money.
5. Negotiable instruments are the means by which many banking services are performed.
6. One's real need should be determined before borrowing money to purchase goods or services.
7. One should shop for a loan as carefully as he would for the purchase of an expensive commodity.
8. Most loans require security of some kind.
9. The range of costs for small loans is very great.
10. True interest rates on an installment payment plan are approximately double the stated discount rates.

■ QUESTIONS ON THE TEXT

1. What are some of the advantages of using checks instead of cash for paying bills?
2. Ordinarily what happens to a joint checking account when one of the parties operating the account dies?
3. If you discover that you have been cheated after writing a check to pay someone, what can you do to prevent him from cashing the check?
4. Assume that you are going on vacation on July 1 and wish to write a check to pay a bill that is due July 15, but you do not want the person to cash the check until July 15. How can you write the check in this manner?
5. What is a certified check?
6. What is a bank draft?
7. What is a cashier's check?
8. What is the major difference between a cashier's check and a bank money order?
9. Why is it not desirable for a man and his wife to have their safe-deposit box registered in both names?
10. Explain revolving bank credit.

11. In the case of negotiable instruments, identify the following persons: (a) the maker, (b) the payee, (c) the drawer, (d) the drawee, (e) the indorser, (f) the indorsee.

12. When it is necessary to obtain a small loan, what are the factors that one should consider in selecting a place to borrow money?

13. (a) What is meant by security or collateral for a loan?
    (b) Are loans ever made without security?

14. Who is a comaker or cosigner?

15. Do all lenders of money follow the same practices in collecting interest on loans? Explain.

16. A borrower agreed to repay a non-interest-bearing loan in six months. He could not make payment in the specified time but paid the loan in nine months. Was the lender entitled to any interest?

17. If an insured person borrows money on an insurance policy but dies before the loan is repaid, how do these circumstances affect the proceeds of the insurance?

18. In what way does the Federal Housing Administration participate in the obtaining of small loans?

19. Why do many small loans cost more than the flat 6 percent or less that is charged on large loans?

20. What is a credit union?

21. How can a credit union afford to charge lower rates of interest than can some of the other lending agencies?

22. Why should one avoid patronizing an unlicensed lender?

▪ QUESTIONS FOR DISCUSSION

1. In many states there are laws against overdrawing bank accounts. Do you believe these laws are justified?

2. Do you recommend keeping canceled checks indefinitely? State your reason.

3. If the interest rate on savings deposits in banks drops from 3 percent to 2 percent, what do you think such a decrease indicates as to the condition of banks?

4. Why are funds frequently left in trust with a bank instead of in the care of the widow or the children?

5. Would you recommend putting cash in a safe-deposit box? Why or why not? Discuss.

6. Dr. Mason, a highly respected citizen, felt insulted when he applied for a loan at a bank and was asked for considerable information on his assets, debts, and income. He believed that the bank had no right to this confidential information. What is your opinion? Discuss the situation.

7. Your friend asks you to indorse a note for him so that he can obtain a loan at a bank. You do so. What is your obligation?

8. What kind of indorsement would you recommend using if you were away from home and were mailing a check to your bank for deposit? Why?
9. Name at least one disadvantage of borrowing money on a life insurance policy.
10. What are some of the good features of borrowing on insurance?
11. Explain the difference between a character (unsecured) loan and a chattel mortgage loan.
12. Why is the interest rate on a small bank loan of $100 to an individual higher than the rate on a bank loan of $50,000 to a businessman?
13. Explain how borrowing is related to budgeting.
14. Why would you recommend that one avoid borrowing from a pawn-broker?

▪ PROBLEMS TO SOLVE

1. On the basis of the following information from the checkbook stubs and from the bank statement for Mr. J. J. Osborn, prepare a reconciliation of the bank statement.

   (a) From checkbook stubs:

   January 1—Balance on check stub, $446.53. January 2—Deposited $74.33. January 3—Paid (Check #1) $150 to L. M. James, rent for January. January 4—Paid (Check #2) $45 to Superior Cars, car payment for January. January 5—Paid (Check #3) $17.85 to Dr. Taylor, dental work. January 9—Deposited $74.33. January 14 —Paid (Check #4) $8.45 to M. L. Wheeler, life insurance for January. January 16—Deposited $74.33. January 18—Paid (Check #5) $32.24 to Figg Grocery, grocery bill to date. January 19—Paid (Check #6) $3.60 to Bell Telephone, telephone bill to date. January 23—Deposited $74.33. January 24—Paid (Check #7) $48.34 to Gross Income Tax Division. January 30—Paid (Check #8) $12.50 to License Bureau, car license. January 31—Deposited $61.27. January 31—checkbook balance, $487.14.

   (b) From bank statement at top of page 341:

   Draw a reconciliation form like the one shown on the bank statement, which appears on the back of Mr. Osborn's statement.

   (1) Compare checkbook stubs with bank statement and record in columns 1 and 2 each check written but not yet paid by the bank as indicated by bank statement. Add column 2.

   (2) Compare the deposits as shown on checkbook stubs with those shown on the bank statement and record in columns 3 and 4 of the reconciliation statement the dates and amounts of any deposits not shown on the bank statement. Add column 4.

BANK STATEMENT for month of January, 19—

Checks	Deposits	Date	Balance
			446.53
150.00	74.33	Jan. 4	370.86
45.00		Jan. 6	325.86
17.85		Jan. 7	308.01
	74.33	Jan. 10	382.34
8.45	74.33	Jan. 17	448.22
32.24		Jan. 20	415.98
3.60		Jan. 21	412.38
	74.33	Jan. 24	486.71
1.00SC *		Jan. 31	485.71

* This is a service charge deducted by the bank.

(3) Your reconciliation is correct if the total of column 4 subtracted from the total of column 2 is the same as the service charge. (This amount should be deducted from the balance on the checkbook stub.)

CHECKS OUTSTANDING		DEPOSITS NOT RECORDED BY BANK	
COLUMN 1	COLUMN 2	COLUMN 3	COLUMN 4
NUMBER	AMOUNT	DATE	AMOUNT
Total of checks outstanding ...			
Balance as on checkbook stub		Balance shown on bank statement	
Total		Total	

2. Using your own signature, write models of three different types of indorsements that you might use on a check or a note. Then explain how you would use each one of them.

3. Mr. D. H. Collins borrowed from the Merchants' National Bank $500 on a 90-day note. The bank gave him cash for the face of the note less interest at 5 percent for 90 days.
   (a) How much cash did he receive?
   (b) How much cash did he pay at maturity?

▪ COMMUNITY PROBLEMS AND PROJECTS

1. From your own bank or one of your choosing, obtain information in regard to the various types of services offered by the bank, including those mentioned in this chapter and any other services that may be offered. Describe each service and indicate whether there is a charge for it.

2. Select a committee to go to a local bank and obtain the following: (a) All forms necessary for opening a checking account. (b) A list of the regulations governing a checking account. (c) Samples of all the forms used by depositors, such as a bank statement, a bankbook, a regular check, a counter check, and a deposit slip. Make a report on the method of opening a checking account and on the activities of depositors using such an account. Next, prepare a bulletin board display showing the steps (with actual forms) a depositor goes through in establishing a checking account.

3. Find out whether there are small-loan laws in your state or your community and make a study of the nominal and the actual interest rates charged by small-loan agencies. Write a report that summarizes your findings.

Chapter 18

Understanding and using credit

PURPOSE OF THE CHAPTER

Credit is used by business and industry in the production of goods and services and in their distribution. Credit is used by consumers in the acquisition of those goods and services provided by business firms. The American family uses numerous forms of credit primarily to improve its level of living. The development of a variety of good sources of credit, combined with the improved judgment of consumers, has led to the current widespread use of consumer credit. The purpose of this chapter is to help you understand credit, its importance to you, and how to use it most wisely.

You will find answers to these questions:

1. What are the common forms of consumer credit?
2. What qualifies one to use credit?
3. What is one's responsibility for debts?
4. How may credit help to shape a family's growth and financial security?

A. Essentials of credit

IMPORTANCE OF CREDIT

Credit is a vital force in our economy. It is of economic and social importance to every family and business organization. Credit was first used in business transactions to make barter (the exchange of goods for goods) more flexible. Credit was used before the existence of money. The custom of charging interest began early, and the cost of credit is something that has been reckoned with in all of recorded history.

In Chapter 10 we learned that *credit* means either an advance (or loan) of money with which to purchase goods and services or an advance of goods and services in exchange for a promise to pay at a later date. The use of credit by consumers is similar to its use by governmental units and by private business organizations. Whenever an immediate need for cash, goods, or services is met through the proper use of credit, the economy of the nation is strengthened and the standard of living is raised. The immediate need is actually met because of the faith one person has in the integrity and responsibility of another—faith that the debt will be repaid at maturity or that each installment payment on the debt will be paid as it becomes due.

Credit first became important in America when people developed need for cash to help them meet financial emergencies for which they were unprepared. More recently, its importance has increased as people have used the installment plan as a means of adjusting the high and low points that develop in their spending patterns. This is illustrated in the purchase of an automobile at a relatively high price that is paid over a period of many months in relatively small payments. Similarly, the installment plan is used in the purchase of insurance when an individual pays monthly, semiannual, or annual premiums throughout a lifetime so that he may have a large amount of protection from the very beginning of the life of his policy. Insurance premiums are based on the past experience of large groups who have shared risks. Thus, it is possible to determine accurately the amount of the installment payments or premiums that an individual must pay to maintain his financial protection. Since the late 1940's, the widespread use of long-term credit by families in buying homes has been very important to the national economy. Throughout this nation, concern is felt whenever consumer resistance to the use of credit tends to slow down the buying of automobiles, homes, and other major items.

FORMS OF CREDIT

The term "credit" is often used to refer to one's potential ability to borrow money or to buy goods on time. In other words, it means credit standing or ability to use credit. A debt is incurred whenever an individual makes use of his credit standing. Each exchange of economic goods or services that is based on credit remains incomplete until such time as full payment of the debt is made. Many consumers buy on credit (go into debt temporarily) because it is more convenient to pay for several purchases at one time at a later date than it is to pay for each purchase separately. Consumers also frequently buy on credit because it is a convenient way to buy or because they do not have cash available to pay for a purchase immediately. In either case a debt is incurred. Consumers often borrow cash with which to pay current bills, to buy goods and services, to meet emergencies, or to consolidate existing debts. Thus, they demonstrate another form and additional uses of credit.

Classification of credit. In general, *consumer credit* is debt that is incurred by a consumer for a home, goods, or services for personal and family use and consumption. For certain purposes, however, consumer credit is considered to be comprised of debts for goods and services for personal and family use having a maturity of less than five years. The Federal Reserve Board classifies such debts as *short-term credit* and *intermediate-term credit*. A debt on an owner-occupied home that is financed by a long-term loan secured by a real estate mortgage is not always considered to be consumer credit. Debt incurred for repair or modernization of an owner-occupied home ordinarily matures within a few months and, therefore, is generally classified as consumer credit.

It is interesting to note that many consumer transactions that seemingly involve cash rather than credit actually are forms of "credit-in-reverse." For example, when one travels on a bus, he buys a ticket prior to beginning the ride. The bus company must thereafter provide him with transportation, and considerable time may elapse before the trip and the credit transactions are finally completed. Similarly, when consumers pay in advance for school tuition, house rent, vacation tours, and lay-away purchases, they become parties in the use of reverse forms of credit, that is, credit which is extended by the purchaser rather than the seller.

Obviously, the extensive credit needs of salary and wage earners in this country are met through the use of numerous forms of credit. Involved with consumers in using the different forms of credit are retail merchants, commercial and industrial banks, consumer finance companies, sales finance companies, credit unions, pawnbrokers, and others. With its many aspects and in its many forms, credit is truly one of the important tools of money management used by consumers.

Installment debt. Debts on which payments are to be made at periodic intervals are considered *installment debts,* or more commonly known as *installment credit.* Such consumer debts may arise from purchases of goods and services for personal and family consumption or from obtaining loans for the payment of such purchases. The arrangement for repaying this kind of debt ordinarily includes finance charges, stipulated regular payments, and the use of a negotiable instrument that provides for legal action when there is default in payment.

Much installment credit involves arrangements between consumers and retail merchants for purchases of automobiles and other consumer goods. An even larger portion of the volume of installment credit consists of cash loans from commercial banks, credit unions, sales finance companies, and consumer finance companies. The money borrowed is used to buy goods, to meet emergencies, and to consolidate debts.

Noninstallment debt. Debts for which the full payment is to be made in a single payment at a specified maturity date are known as *noninstallment debts* or *noninstallment credit.* A cash loan to be repaid in a single payment may be made to a consumer by a commercial bank, pawnbroker, savings and loan association, or miscellaneous lender for any one of many goods reasons. Also, noninstallment credit is used by a consumer whenever he arranges to make a single payment for goods that are charged at a retail store; for gas, electric, or telephone service; or for a hospital, medical, or other similar debt.

The study of consumer credit or debt outstanding in the following table shows that approximately 75 percent of all consumer debt is to be paid by installments and 25 percent by single payments. It is interesting to observe that over 40 percent of all installment debts owed by consumers is for automobiles and that over 30 percent of all debts incurred by consumers is for automobiles.

We shall study credit particularly in reference to charge and service accounts in the remainder of this chapter. Information about personal loans was presented in Chapter 17, and the problems of installment buying will be presented in Chapter 19.

Consumer debt in the United States
(including Alaska and Hawaii)
December 31, 1965
(Millions of dollars)

NONINSTALLMENT DEBTS
(Debts to be paid in single payments)

Charge accounts (for goods purchased)	$ 6,940	
Service accounts (for such as medical or legal service)	6,746	
Personal loans	4,891	
Total noninstallment consumer debts		$18,577

INSTALLMENT DEBTS
(Debts to be paid by periodic payments)

Debts on automobiles	$28,201	
Debt on other consumer goods	17,414	
Loans for repair and modernization of owner-occupied homes	3,625	
Personal loans to consumers	18,166	
Total installment debt		67,406
Total consumer credit (consumer debt outstanding)		$85,983

Source: *Federal Reserve Statistical Release G. 19*, February 8, 1966.

THE CHARGE ACCOUNT

Many stores and business firms sell merchandise on *open account* or on *charge account*. This means that at the time of the sale, the title to the merchandise passes to the purchaser and that the store accepts the customer's promise to pay for it later, usually within 30 days. The customer is required to sign the sales slip as evidence that he received the merchandise.

A *service account* is similar to a charge account except that the charges made to it are for services rendered, such as legal or medical service.

The privilege of charging purchases may be withdrawn by a business firm at any time the customer fails to pay the amount he owes in accordance with the terms of the account. A brief summary of the advantages of a charge account to a customer appears on page 348.

A charge account may be a disadvantage for a person who has a tendency to spend without regard to his income or ability to pay.

CREDIT TERMS

No down payment is required for purchases through a charge or open account. The time allowed between the date of purchase on a charge account and the date the payment is due is the length of the

---

Advantages of charge account to customers

1. A charge account represents a very convenient and simple way to buy.
2. Payment for purchases may be delayed until a future specified time.
3. A record of purchases is made automatically.
4. Money is not needed at the time of purchase; therefore the danger of loss while shopping is minimized.
5. Charge accounts make it easy to order merchandise by mail or telephone.
6. Salespeople and owners learning to know a charge customer may result in better service.
7. The privilege of charging purchases adds to one's prestige.
8. Payment for several purchases may be made at one time.

---

credit term. The usual credit term for charge accounts is 30 days; however, it may be for a different period of time. A charge account ordinarily carries no service charge. The customer is expected to pay the full amount he has charged at the end of each credit term. In many stores, if this part of the bargain is not fulfilled, a service charge is made on the past-due balance and added on at the next billing. Usually the charge is 1 percent for each 30 days that the debt is past due. Thus, when the consumer postpones payment of his debt, the cost of that credit is at the rate of 12 percent a year.

Under a plan known as *cycle billing,* the balance owed by a certain customer falls due regularly on a certain day of the month regardless of the date of the last purchase. This means that a bill for a purchase made late in a customer's credit month becomes due in much less than 30 days. The reason some stores use cycle billing on charge accounts is to spread the work of preparing monthly statements over the entire month for the accounting department.

DISCOUNTS

Sometimes discounts are allowed to individuals for prompt payment. Common terms in such a case are "2% ten days, net 30 days." These terms mean that, if the purchaser pays the amount within ten days after date of the invoice, he may deduct a discount of 2 percent from the amount of the bill; but if he does not desire to take advantage of the 2 percent discount, he may pay the net amount at the end of 30 days. The person who sells on this basis is willing to forego 2 percent of the sale value in order to obtain his money promptly. If the purchaser chooses not to take the 2 percent discount, he is paying 2 percent for the use of the money for 20 days. In other words, if he buys on these terms goods amounting to $100, he may take a discount of $2 at the end of 10 days and therefore pay only $98. Suppose, however, that he has enough money to pay the bill but believes that he can use the money better in some other way. He therefore prefers to wait until the end of 30 days before paying the bill. By doing so, he pays $2 for using $98 for 20 days. If interest is figured on the basis of 360 days, he is paying interest at the rate of 36 percent a year to use this money.

TYPES OF CHARGE ACCOUNTS

Revolving charge account. The *revolving charge account* is in common use in some cities. Under this plan, payment for purchases may be extended to four, five, or six months. The consumer and the store representative determine at the time the account is opened the maximum amount that may be owed to the store at any one time. To illustrate the revolving charge account, let us assume that the maximum amount that may be owed is set at $240 and that the store will allow the consumer a maximum of six months to pay for purchases. Equal monthly payments of $40 (240 ÷ 6 months) are to be made whenever there is an unpaid balance in the account at the end of a month. New purchases to be charged to the account may be made at any time so long as the total amount owed by the consumer does not exceed the established maximum of $240. Usually a service charge of $1/2$ to $1\frac{1}{2}$ percent of the unpaid balance is charged each month for this type of account.

Budget charge account. A *budget charge account* is a system of credit under which regular purchases can be made. Payments must be made in monthly installments based upon the size of the account balance (examples: $10 monthly on a $40 account balance; $20 monthly on an $80 account balance). Interest is charged on the monthly balance.

Divided charge account. One charge account plan permits a consumer to charge a large item like a refrigerator or a living room suite and then pay one third of the cost in each of the succeeding three months. This plan is known as a *divided charge account*.

Credit-bank plan. In the previous chapter a type of charge account was described in which the bank pays the customer's bills when they are submitted to it. This charge account service is available only in those retail stores that agree to participate in the *credit-bank plan*.

Depositor's account. Another type of charge account is the *depositor's account*. Under this plan a customer may deposit an amount of money with the store against which future purchases may be charged.

Coupon or scrip account. A variation of the depositor's account is the *coupon* or *scrip account* plan in which coupons or scrip are issued the customer, who may then use them instead of money to pay for purchases in the store.

CREDIT CARDS

A *credit card* is issued by some business firms, such as oil companies, restaurants, hotels, airlines, railroads, and telephone and telegraph companies. The card identifies a customer particularly when he is traveling, thus enabling him to charge purchases of goods and services even though he is not known in the city where the purchase is made. There is no charge for most of these credit cards.

Other organizations issue the more general-use type of credit card. For example, the Diners' Club, organized in 1950, issues a credit card which permits a person carrying this card to charge meals, hotel rooms, flowers, gifts, auto rentals, and other services. The bills are sent to the Diners' Club, which sends a monthly bill for all purchases to the person holding the credit card. For combining the charges, collecting from the consumer and transmitting payments to those providing services, and for absorbing losses from the few nonpayers, the Diners' Club takes a discount from the business organizations. The card-holding consumer pays a relatively small annual fee. A similar plan is operated by the American Express Company and by the Hilton Hotels which, through the Hilton Credit Corporation, offer a credit card called *Carte Blanche*.

Credit cards constitute convenient substitutes for cumbersome cash.

COST OF CHARGE ACCOUNTS

Selling on credit adds extra costs to every sale. The principal extra costs result from: (a) the clerical work necessary for recording sales and collecting accounts, (b) interest on the money that is invested in accounts receivable from customers, (c) losses due to bad debts, and (d) the greater tendency of charge customers to return goods for exchange.

Merchants who sell on open account may be classified as follows: (a) those who have uniform prices for credit and for cash sales; (b) those who charge more for credit than for cash sales.

Some stores set their sales prices high enough to cover the cost of charge accounts; others use a two-price system, one for cash sales and one for sales on account. Let us assume that a television set is priced at $159.95 cash or $164.95 if charged, payable in 30 days. The actual cost of charging the purchase to the customer's account is $5.00. This means that he is paying $5.00 for the use of $159.95 for 30 days. This is an annual rate of interest of $37\frac{1}{2}$ percent.

In stores that do not carefully investigate a customer's ability to pay before charging sales to his account, the losses from failure to collect debts are likely to be great. One may well expect to find high prices in stores that recklessly advertise generous credit terms to everyone. Stores that have sound credit policies have practically no losses from bad debts. We need not assume, therefore, that a merchant who sells on credit must necessarily sell at higher prices than a merchant who sells for cash. If selling on credit increases sales, the total overhead cost of each sale may actually be decreased. The costs of selling on credit, however, are reported by some stores to be as much as 6 to 8 percent higher than costs of selling for cash. On the other hand, stores that regularly sell on credit often also offer delivery services and other conveniences. These services, combined with possible higher costs due to charge accounts, may cause the store to sell at higher prices than a cash-and-carry store.

B. Using credit

ESTABLISHING A CREDIT STANDING

Our *credit standing* or *credit worthiness* is an indication of our ability to secure goods, services, and money in return for a promise to pay. It represents our ability to incur debts because some lender trusts us. A favorable credit standing does not come automatically.

It comes as the result of slow growth. It must be nurtured, fostered, strengthened, and improved. It is an asset of tremendous value to those who develop it over a long period of years. It can be destroyed easily; it is sensitive to abuse; and it usually continues only as long as it is justified. A favorable credit standing over a period of time is enjoyed only by persons who deserve it and who have wisdom to protect it.

A commonly recognized formula for determining the credit of a person or a business consists of the "three C's"—character, capacity, and capital.

Character. *Character* is revealed in one's conduct, attitudes, and achievements. It does not necessarily have any relation to one's wealth. It represents the sum total of the principles for which one stands. One's reputation is the result of how other people evaluate his character traits. We would not be able to borrow money or buy goods and services with the promise to pay later if others judge our character to be questionable.

Capacity. *Capacity* is merely another term for earning power. It represents one's ability to earn and to pay obligations when they become due. An individual may have an honorable character and perfectly good intentions of paying an obligation; but unless he has the ability or capacity to pay, he cannot pay satisfactorily. It is often more difficult to judge character than it is to judge capacity. Capacity, or earning power, can be measured reasonably accurately, but character is an intangible quality.

Your credit record is concrete evidence of your character, capacity, and capital.

H. Armstrong Roberts

Capital. The third measuring standard, *capital,* applies only to people who have property. Naturally our net worth or capital affects our ability to pay debts when they become due and, consequently, affects our credit standing. A person with a temporary lack of earning power but having a substantial net worth may still have a favorable credit standing; that is, others will be willing to make loans to him or to sell to him based on his promise to pay.

Capacity and capital without character will affect our credit standing adversely, making it impossible to borrow money or buy goods and services on time.

ESTABLISHING A LINE OF CREDIT

Credit standing or credit worthiness refers to the chances or the probability that one will pay a debt when it becomes due. We have just learned that it depends upon the trust or confidence others have in our intention to pay. *Line of credit* means the maximum amount a lender or creditor will permit a customer to owe him at any one time.

Name *Martha Thomas*	Date *May 25, 1966*
Home Address *313 Maple Street*	How Long *8 yrs.*
Town *Freeport, Ohio*	Phone *381-4763*
Previous Address *Somerset, Ohio*	How Long *20 yrs.*
Employed by *Grunhill Pottery Co.*	How Long *8 yrs.*
Position *Secretary*	Married ☒ Single ☐
Business Address *5101 Vine St.*	Phone *261-3877*
Previous Employer *Rutger's Department Store*	
Previous Employer's Address *12 Front St. — Somerset, Ohio*	
Bank *First National Bank*	Checking ☒ Savings ☒
Real Estate Owned *none*	Equity Clear —
Other Accounts *Borton Dept. Store*	Reference *S. L. Barr*

Answers to the above questions have been made by me for the purpose of securing credit and I declare them to be true and correct. In consideration of your extending credit on the above account, I agree to pay promptly, as bills are rendered any sums that may become due on this account.

NATIONAL CLOTHIER SERVICE, CHICAGO F.AP-2   Signed *Martha Thomas*

An application for credit

Every responsible family should establish its line of credit with a good retail store or retail credit association regardless of whether it is used extensively or not. By so doing you also will take your first step in establishing your line of credit with a bank.

To establish your credit standing and your line of credit, the usual procedure is to go to your favorite store and discuss the matter frankly with the credit manager or the owner, who will request information of a personal nature about your character, capacity, and capital. Such information should be provided accurately and completely. The credit manager must have such information as a basis for determining how much credit to extend to you.

The illustration on page 353 shows a typical application for credit for customers of a department store. In some cases the forms are more complicated, but in general they require the same information.

CREDIT RATING AGENCIES

In general there are two types of credit agencies: (a) agencies that provide credit rating information on businesses, and (b) agencies that provide credit ratings on individuals.

Banks sometimes give confidential credit information on individuals and businesses. It is therefore important to maintain satisfactory relations with a bank if a good credit rating is desired.

Private credit agencies collect information and issue confidential reports for the benefit of their subscribers who are retailers. Each subscriber contributes information about customers to the agency. Additional information is gathered from local newspapers, notices of change in address, death notices, and court records. Such information is valuable to the retailer in protecting himself from loss on accounts. If one of his customers moves, he will want to know of the change in address. If a customer dies, he will want to be sure that his claim is presented. If someone is taking court action against one of his customers, he will want to protect his own claim.

The Associated Credit Bureaus of America has more than 3,000 credit bureau members serving over 600,000 business firms. Any of these local credit bureaus can develop a report on any individual in North America and in many foreign countries within a short period of time. Through the interchange of information, the credit records of an estimated 100 million consumers are already compiled and are readily available to all members of the Associated Credit Bureaus of America. The services of this nation-wide credit reporting system are an advantage to you if you have safeguarded your credit. You can move from one community to another, and your credit record will follow you or it can be checked upon very easily. However, a bad credit reputation also will follow you wherever you go.

Dun and Bradstreet, Incorporated, issues a book of credit ratings on commercial houses and manufacturers. The service, which is available on a subscription basis, covers the entire United States. In addition, a subscriber can obtain a special report on any businessman or professional man in any part of the country. The reliability of this agency has been established through many years of effective service to all types of businessmen.

RESPONSIBILITY FOR DEBTS

Responsibility for the payment of one's debts is one of the oldest moral and ethical principles recognized by man. In addition to this principle, laws have been enacted specifying man's legal responsibility for debts. Furthermore, his relationship to creditors in case he does not pay or cannot pay has been fixed by law.

A husband is responsible for debts incurred by his wife unless he gives legal written notice that from the date of the notice forward he will not be responsible for them. A merchant, therefore, may sell on account to a man's wife with confidence that the husband is responsible for payment.

Parents are generally legally responsible for debts incurred by their children when permission has been given to the children to make purchases and to charge them to the parent's account. For instance, if it has been customary for a child to use a charge account of the parents, the parents are responsible for the debts. But there are exceptions to this rule as indicated in the next paragraph.

Awareness of responsibility for debts is vital to the young consumer who wants to create and preserve a good credit rating.

Children are often referred to as minors. A *minor* is a person who is not yet considered to be an adult under the laws of the state in which he lives; that is, the person has not yet reached the age of majority. In most states the age of majority is 21; in a few states the age of majority for girls is as low as 18. Minors or their parents are legally responsible for debts incurred for necessities such as medical care, clothing, and food. However, necessities purchased by a minor must be suitable and appropriate if he or his parents are to be responsible for any debts incurred. For example, even though the son of a family with a moderate income has had the privilege of using the charge account regularly, the boy or the parents could not be held responsible for an expensive watch sold by the store to the child. Of course, the store can insist upon having the watch returned.

Garnishment. If a debtor refuses to pay a debt, a creditor may succeed in having an order issued by a court requiring the employer of the debtor to pay the creditor a certain percentage of the debtor's wages until the full amount or an amount specified by the court has been paid. This procedure is called the *garnishment* or the *garnisheeing of wages*. Those states that permit the garnisheeing of wages have widely varying practices.

Attachment. If you owe a debt and refuse to pay or cannot pay as agreed, you may be sued in court to force you to pay it. A common procedure in such a case is to ask the court for an attachment on some of your property until the case is settled. An *attachment* is simply a legal process whereby the property attached comes under the control of the court until the case is settled. Property upon which an attachment order has been placed may not be sold and may not be moved except by court approval. The court can order the property sold to pay the debt.

Statutes of limitations. The *statutes of limitations* in most states set a time limit after which a creditor cannot enforce a legal claim. For instance, in one state if an account is not collected within five years, the creditor cannot sue for the amount. If the debtor, however, makes a payment or a promise to pay during the five years or at any time thereafter, the account is revived or reinstated.

Bankruptcy. If a person is unable to pay his debts when they become due, he is said to be *insolvent*. If his debts are greater than the total fair value of his assets, a federal court may declare him to be *bankrupt*. Recognizing the impossibility of paying his debts, a man may ask the court to be declared bankrupt. This process is known as *voluntary bankruptcy*.

Any one of a person's creditors who holds a past-due debt against him may also petition or ask the court that he should be declared bankrupt. This process is known as *involuntary bankruptcy*.

The circumstances under which one may petition for voluntary bankruptcy are regulated by law. If the court declares a person to be bankrupt, a *receiver* is appointed as an agent of the court. The receiver then takes charge of the bankrupt's affairs, sells the property, and pays off the debts on a proportional basis among the creditors. The latest federal bankruptcy laws, under certain circumstances, provide that a debtor against whom bankruptcy suits have been filed may request the court to extend the time, or to rearrange his payment plan, or to otherwise alter or modify his relation with creditors. If such a request seems possible and is granted, the debtor may be able to pay his debts in due time.

Bankruptcy discharges all of a debtor's former debts and enables him to start to acquire property for himself again. Property acquired after bankruptcy proceedings have been completed is not subject to claims for prior debts. The great advantage of bankruptcy to creditors is that they all fare proportionately to their claims in the net proceeds resulting from the sale of the bankrupt's property.

ECONOMIC PROBLEMS OF CREDIT

The use of credit tends to increase purchases and to stimulate business. Government officials, bankers, businessmen, and many others constantly watch the figures that are collected to show the amount and the nature of debt that is owed by individuals. If consumer debt increases too fast and is not being paid off, this situation indicates that buyers on credit are not able to pay their debts. Such a condition would, therefore, be an indication that we might be entering a period of bad business conditions.

The delicate economic problem is to keep purchases and payments in balance. When an individual cannot pay his debts, the business that sold to him may suffer a loss. Therefore, when great numbers of people buy more on credit than they can repay, we experience an overexpansion of consumer credit. The result may be that many businesses lose money because they cannot collect for goods sold on credit. You will recall that in Chapter 14 you learned how we are all affected by bad business conditions that arise when great numbers of people cannot pay their debts.

Facts everyone should understand about credit

1. Consumer credit is debt that is incurred for a home, goods, or services for personal and family use and consumption.
2. In its many forms, credit is a useful tool if one stays in command of it, does not use it unnecessarily, and gets it at low cost.
3. Because it is convenient and often is a means of adjusting high and low points in spending, credit is used by people in all income categories.
4. Each credit transaction remains incomplete until such time as all legal responsibilities and repayment obligations of the debt are fulfilled.
5. A good credit rating must be earned and maintained if one wants to obtain credit when it is needed and to get it at little or no cost.
6. If it becomes impossible for an individual to pay his debts, prompt action should be taken to notify creditors and to establish an adjusted payment schedule that can be met.
7. When credit is used as a substitute for good money management, there is usually a tendency to make excessive use of it.
8. When overextension of credit forces a person to declare bankruptcy, there is a weakening of the economic and social structure.

▪ QUESTIONS ON THE TEXT

1. What does the term "credit" mean?
2. On what is the extension of credit by a seller to a purchaser based?
3. What is involved in the adjustment of high and low points in spending through the use of consumer credit?
4. What is the principal item purchased by installment credit?
5. From the point of view of the customer, what are some of the advantages of a charge account?
6. How does a revolving charge account work in a retail store?
7. What extra costs are incurred by business in making charge sales?
8. What are the "three C's" for determining credit? Explain each.
9. What are some of the agencies through which credit information can be obtained?
10. Is a wife personally responsible for the debts she incurs, or is her husband responsible? Explain your answer.
11. In most states at what age does a person cease to be a minor?
12. What is meant by the garnishment of wages?
13. What is meant by an attachment?
14. What is the purpose of the statutes of limitations?

15. What relief may an individual debtor obtain under the bankruptcy laws?

16. Why are governmental officials, bankers, and businessmen sometimes concerned about the amount of debt owed by individuals?

▪ QUESTIONS FOR DISCUSSION

1. Many credit managers feel that the character of the individual is more important than his wealth in establishing credit. Do you believe this is true? Why?

2. What are some of the kinds of goods and services that consumers most frequently buy on credit? What are the advantages and disadvantages of buying them on credit?

3. How may the use of credit affect the individual consumer, the community, and jobs in industry?

4. How can a good credit reputation at your present place of residence help you if you move to another city?

5. Describe your point of view toward the use of charge accounts.

6. (a) Do you think you can open a charge account in the name of your parents and use the charge account?

   (b) Can you use the charge account of your parents if it has been established by them?

7. Why is it that many retailers seem to be more considerate of credit customers than of cash customers?

8. What is cycle billing? Why have some stores adopted it?

9. Millions of people now buy on credit terms. How does this affect the prices we pay for important durable goods?

10. Assume that you are selling electrical appliances. Would you want to sell a refrigerator on credit to a person who has become a voluntary bankrupt?

▪ PROBLEMS TO SOLVE

1. A retail store doing a cash business of $500,000 a year made a net profit of 2 percent. It decided to change from a policy of cash sales only to a policy of selling for either cash or credit. As a result of this change in policy, the sales increased 25 percent; uncollectible accounts amounted to 1 percent of total sales; and the net profit decreased to a rate of 1.75 percent.

   (a) What was the net profit in dollars when the business operated on a cash basis?

   (b) What was the dollar amount of the uncollectible accounts after the business changed to a policy of selling on cash and credit?

   (c) What was the net profit in dollars after the business changed to a policy of selling on cash and credit?

   (d) What are your conclusions?

2. Assume that you needed a lawn mower that was priced at $75. Becoming aware that you were undecided about the purchase, the store owner offered the mower to you at a 5 percent discount if you paid for it within 10 days. You took the mower home; but, because of unexpected demands for cash, you could not pay for it until 30 days later. At that time you paid the full price of $75.

   (a) How much would the mower have cost you if you had paid for it within 10 days?

   (b) How much would you have saved?

   (c) If you consider the discount offered as interest for using the money for 20 more days, what annual rate of interest did you actually pay?

▪ COMMUNITY PROBLEMS AND PROJECTS

1. The form for opening a charge account, such as the one illustrated in this chapter, may cover such information as:

   (a) Customer's name, wife's or husband's name, size of family.

   (b) Customer's address, how long he has lived there, does he rent or own his home.

   (c) Customer's occupation, length of time worked for present employer.

   (d) Stores where the customer has previously bought on credit, name of bank where he has a checking or savings account.

From a local merchant who sells on credit, obtain an explanation of why each item of information is needed. Write a report on the information you gain from the merchant.

2. Under the direction of your teacher, investigate the policies of local retail stores in selling for cash and on credit. Learn (a) which ones have variations in price, (b) how much the difference is, and (c) what additional carrying charges are added in the case of credit sales.

3. From local merchants, your local credit bureau, or your state credit association, obtain information with regard to (a) the percentage of merchandise sold on credit in your community or state, (b) the average amount of credit losses, (c) the reasons for the credit losses, and (d) policies with regard to uniformity in granting credit.

Chapter 19

Using installment credit

PURPOSE OF THE CHAPTER

Using installment credit means buying and then making regular payments over a period of months or borrowing money to make a purchase and making payments on the loan in the same manner. In this chapter you will learn how installment credit is used to advantage and how it may cause serious trouble.

You will find answers to these questions:

1. What are the different types of installment contracts?
2. Under what conditions should one buy on the installment plan?
3. What items may be included in finance or carrying charges?
4. How can the cost of installment credit be figured?

A. The nature of installment credit

WHAT IS INSTALLMENT BUYING?

Buying on an installment plan differs from buying on charge or open account in four ways: (1) a down payment is usually required,

(2) a finance or carrying charge is added to the price, (3) payments usually of equal amounts are spread over a period of time, and (4) security for the amount of the unpaid balance is taken by the seller in the form of a security agreement.

The importance of installment buying. Estimates indicate that more than 60 percent of our yearly retail sales are credit transactions. About three fourths of these credit sales are made on the installment plan. More than half of the automobiles, furniture, and household appliances are purchased on the installment plan.

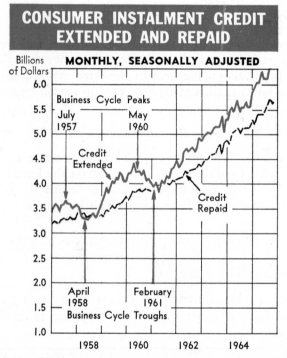

Source: Federal Reserve Board.

Some economic problems of installment buying. We have learned how mass production helps us to get the goods and services we want at a price we can afford to pay. But mass production is not possible except when people buy freely. Many families cannot pay cash for major items such as automobiles, furniture, and appliances. Under the installment plan, however, these families are able to purchase without cash. The opportunity for consumers to buy now and to pay later has increased mass consumption of goods and services. If charge-account privileges and other time-payment plans of purchasing were to be withdrawn and purchases were to be made wholly on a cash basis, sales would decrease rapidly, and business activity would slow down. Consumer credit, mass distribution, and mass production are closely interrelated.

Some economists believe that selling goods and services to consumers on a time-payment plan is one of the major factors in making our high standard of living possible. They reason that installment selling increases the consumption of goods, which in turn increases production and thus tends to lower costs, and that the greater production is, the more jobs there are at good wage rates.

There are some people who argue that many families would never save enough to make major purchases, but when they purchase on the installment plan, they are obligated to pay the installments when they come due.

Of course, government officials, bankers, and businessmen express concern about excessive purchasing on the installment plan. If the incomes of many people who owe money on installment contracts would be reduced or if they lost their jobs, these people would probably not be able to make their payments. If great numbers of people are not able to pay their installment debts, there is a possibility that businessmen cannot collect their debts and will therefore lose money. If businesses lose enough money or fail to make a satisfactory profit, the possibilities of having a depression are increased. There is a more complete discussion of this problem in Chapter 13.

TYPES OF INSTALLMENT CONTRACTS

Every installment contract sets forth the specific terms of the purchase, including the amount of the down payment, dates and amounts of future payments, finance charges, and the protections to the seller in case payments are not made as scheduled. The seller may be protected by either of two types of installment contracts (called a security agreement under the Uniform Commercial Code)—a chattel mortgage or a conditional sales contract. Each of these contracts provides a legal claim upon the merchandise until the obligation has been paid.

Chattel mortgage contract. A *chattel mortgage contract* is essentially the same as any other mortgage contract except that it applies to goods that are ordinarily movable, such as a piano or an automobile. It is a claim against the goods mentioned in the contract. The laws in the states are not uniform in regard to the use of a chattel mortgage.

Essentially, a seller gives title of the goods to the buyer; but the chattel mortgage permits the seller to retain a claim against the goods until the debt is paid. If the buyer fails to perform his part of the contract, the seller either automatically has a right to repossess (take back) the goods or he may take legal action to repossess the goods. An example of a chattel mortgage is shown below.

TAYLOR APPLIANCES
LOUISVILLE, KENTUCKY

County__Jefferson__ State__Kentucky__ City__Louisville__ Date__June 14, 19--__

CONSIDERATION ACKNOWLEDGED. — I do hereby grant, bargain, sell, convey and confirm unto TAYLOR·APPLIANCES (mortgagee) or assigns, the following described merchandise, to have and to hold said merchandise forever, provided, however, that I shall pay to the mortgagee or its assigns the full purchase price in installments on the day of each month that the installment becomes due, then this mortgage to be void.

DESCRIPTION AND TERMS

Item__Major Washer__ Serial No.__4974206KM__ Cash Purchase Price $____179.95____

__Ajax Dryer·__ __M01-A263__ $____129.00____

$_____

Less Down Payment Received by __Wm. L. Keel__ $____50.00____
(Signature)

Balance to be paid as follows: Principal $__21.47__   BALANCE $____258.95____

Carrying Charges $__1.73__

Total $__23.20__ each and every month.

If I fail to make any monthly payment then all remaining installments may be declared due and payable, and upon failure to make any monthly payment, or all, if all declared due, I agree to deliver said Merchandise as described, upon demand to the Company, or its assigns, and all payments made and the used Merchandise applied on purchase as described shall be retained by said Company, or its assigns, as stipulated damages. I Further Agree to take good care of said Merchandise and to be responsible for its loss by theft, fire or other casualty, and not to remove it from

__4876 Austin Drive__   __Louisville__   __Kentucky__   __JA 1-9021__
Name of Street   City   State   Tel. No.

unless I first obtain the written consent of said Company, or its assigns.

It is Understood and Agreed that no other agreement or guaranty, verbal or written, expressed or implied, shall limit or qualify the terms of this contract.

Not valid unless accepted by Dealer.

Accepted _Michael Jonas, Treasurer_ Signed _Gil E. Murray_

Date____June 14____ 19 -- __ Salesman _Wm. L. Keel_
                                                Salesman sign here

A chattel mortgage

Conditional sales contract. A *conditional sales contract* is the most common type of agreement used to provide security for the seller. Under this plan the title to the goods remains with the seller until payments for the goods and interest and finance charges have been made in full. The title to the property is transferred to the buyer upon the completion of all payments. In the event that the buyer does not make his payments when due, the goods may be repossessed by the seller. A conditional sales contract is illustrated on page 365.

Security agreement. Under the Uniform Commercial Code the recommended installment contract is called a *security agreement*. It is essentially the same as a chattel mortgage contract. The seller (secured party) may take back the property _____ contract is not fulfilled.

CONDITIONAL SALES CONTRACT

<u>   4580   </u>
Account No.

The undersigned seller hereby sells, and the undersigned purchaser hereby purchases, subject to the terms and conditions hereinafter set forth, the following property, delivery and acceptance of which in good order is hereby acknowledged by purchaser, viz.:

DESCRIPTION	SERIAL NO.	PURCHASE PRICE
1 Norstad Radio	T-10006-31	$ 95.00
	Tax	2.85
Salesman Raymond Ellis	Total	$ 97.85

Purchaser's Down Payment .... $ 20.00

Unpaid Balance of Purchase Price .... $ 77.85

Time Price Differential .... $ 6.40

Deferred Balance of .... $ 84.25

Payable at the office of The Philip Stern Company in ___11___ installments of $___7.02___

each and in one final installment of $___7.03___, on the ___15th___ day of each month,

commencing _____June 15_____ 19 -- , making a total time sale price of $ 84.25

Interest is due on installments after maturity at the highest lawful contract rate, and if this contract be placed with any attorney for collection, 15% of the amount due hereunder shall be paid by purchaser as attorney's fees, or if prohibited, the amount permitted by law.

The title in the property above described shall remain in the seller until the terms of this contract have been fully complied with. In case of any default in the performance of the terms and conditions hereof, the seller shall have the right to declare the full unpaid amount immediately due and payable and/or retake all the property. Buyer agrees not to move, sell, mortgage, encumber, pledge, or otherwise dispose of the property until paid for in full. Upon the performance by the buyer of all the conditions of this contract, title to the property is to vest in the buyer. It is mutually agreed that this instrument sets forth the entire contract.

Executed this_____23rd_____day of_____May_____19--

William Sayler	466 Elm	Canton	Michigan
(Purchaser's Signature)	(Street)	(Town)	(State)

Raymond Ellis	105 East First	Canton	Michigan
(Seller's Signature)	(Street)	(Town)	(State)

Edward Burnet	_Lawrence Davis_
(Witness)	(Witness)

A conditional sales contract

Uniform Conditional Sales Act. The Uniform Conditional Sales Act, which is a law in several states, provides that if the buyer has paid a substantial portion of the purchase price at the time the goods are repossessed, he is entitled to get back that sum less service charges, interest, and depreciation on the goods caused by wear and tear.

In most states that do not have the Uniform Conditional Sales Act, the buyer recovers no portion of his payments in case of repossession; and if the subsequent sale price of the repossessed goods is less than the amount he still owes for them, he may be called upon to pay the difference between the two amounts. The difference is called a *deficiency*.

Later in this chapter there is further discussion of what happens when goods are repossessed.

CHARACTERISTICS OF INSTALLMENT CONTRACTS

Installment contracts are usually written in triplicate. One copy is kept by the purchaser; another copy is filed in some local recording office; and the third copy is kept by the seller. The purpose of recording an installment contract is to make the record public so that anyone can determine whether a claim has been made against the property listed as security.

Installment contracts differ as to their wording and content, but a similarity is found in all types. In each case the purchaser must agree to do certain things. For example, he must agree to make the payments as specified; he may not remove the property from the state without permission; he may not sell the property to someone else without permission; the balance of the contract may be due if one payment is missed; there may be a claim against the salary or wages of the purchaser if payments are not made; and he has to keep taxes paid and the property insured for damage or loss and free from other claims.

FINANCE COMPANIES

Most stores and business firms do not have sufficient money to finance their business if they sell on an installment plan. They need their money to reinvest in replacement merchandise so they can have a rapid turnover. Therefore, these business firms use the services of a finance company.

Sales finance company. A finance company that deals only in installment notes arising from sales by business firms is sometimes known

---

Checkpoints on installment contracts

The following checkpoints may serve as guides for the protection of installment buyers before signing a contract:

1. What is the cash price of the article?
2. How much money is actually advanced?
3. What are the total finance or carrying charges?
4. What are the insurance, investigation, legal, recording, and other charges in addition to the purchase price and carrying charges?
5. How do the installment costs compare with costs on other plans such as a personal loan at a bank?
6. Are all the facts about the contract known and fully understood?
7. Are all figures in the contract correct? Are all blank spaces filled in?
8. Specifically what security has been given? Does it include merchandise previously bought or to be bought in the future?
9. May wages be assigned in case of delinquent payments?
10. Does the buyer have the privilege of paying the total amount due and settling the contract at a reduction in cost?
11. Will a fair notice be given before repossession?
12. What rights in the property does the buyer have in case of repossession?

---

as a *sales finance company*. In effect, the sales finance company purchases the installment notes from the business firm at the time of the sale, thus immediately replenishing the merchant's cash. In some instances the customer's payments are made to the merchant but more often directly to the finance company.

The following illustrates how a sales finance company operates: Mr. Baker buys a refrigerator from Ace Appliance Company and owes Ace Appliance Company $200, which, under the terms of the installment contract, is to be paid off monthly over a period of two years. Ace Appliance Company sells the installment contract to Top Finance Company for $180. Top Finance Company makes the collections of $200 from Mr. Baker.

There are several thousand finance companies in the United States who deal in installment credit. Each of the large automobile manufacturers owns a finance company or has an agreement with one to handle the installment notes on cars sold by their dealers. Some finance companies confine their transactions to the purchase of one kind of installment note, such as notes from the sale of automobiles.

Consumer finance company. A finance company that makes loans directly to consumers not arising from a sale of merchandise by a

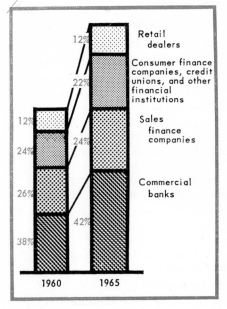

12% Retail dealers

22% Consumer finance companies, credit unions, and other financial institutions

12% Sales finance companies

24%

24%

26% Commercial banks

38%

42%

1960   1965

About two thirds of all consumer installment debt is owed to commercial banks and sales finance companies.

Source: Federal Reserve System.

business firm is sometimes referred to as a *consumer finance company.* Some finance companies serve consumers directly and also purchase installment notes from business firms. Others make installment loans which may be used to purchase various kinds of durable goods, to pay debts, to pay emergency expenses, or for home repairs.

Banks and other lending agencies. Well-established business firms frequently sell directly to commercial banks installment notes that arise from the sale of merchandise to their customers. In the following chapter, there will be a discussion of the roles played in financing by banks, credit unions, finance companies, and other lending agencies.

B. Buying on the installment plan

BUYING ON THE INSTALLMENT PLAN

Installment buying is a poor practice for the buyer and for the seller if it is abused. Installment buying may be harmful to the consumer if he buys luxuries or other commodities not actually needed. For example, no wise home manager would purchase expensive clothing or elaborate jewelry on the installment plan.

On the other hand, buying on an installment plan may be both economical and wise. It can be used frequently as a means of enforced saving. It should, however, be used carefully and with common sense. For example, if one is furnishing a home, the purchase of furniture on the installment plan would be justifiable if the payments could be made within the budget. Using the installment plan would be better than spending all available funds to buy cheap furnishings, which would soon wear out and then have to be replaced. A railroad engineer, however, would be justified in buying a good watch on the installment plan if it were needed in his work. If a radio is needed to entertain a sick person or an automobile is required for business, installment buying is usually justified. Another example of using the installment buying privilege wisely is that of a young doctor, starting his profession, who may finance the purchase of equipment through the installment plan.

Often the income of a family is planned in advance to such an extent that additional periodic payments on installment purchases are neither feasible nor wise. For example, let us assume that the monthly income of a family is $600, and that the family's monthly expenses are $350, not including housing. Further, assume that payments on a mortgage, taxes, and insurance on the house in which the family lives are $165 a month; on an automobile, $50 a month; and on a refrigerator, $25 a month; making a total of $590 of each month's income that is committed. Under these conditions, to purchase a television set on installment would be very unwise. The seller and the buyer of merchandise should consider together the advisability of the buyer contracting an installment debt.

Before buying on the installment plan. Before one buys an article on the installment plan and accepts the financing plan suggested by the seller, it is well to consider the following other alternatives: (a) buying

"Should I wait two years to get it?"

Sometimes an installment purchase permits labor saving and time saving in household tasks to start two or three years sooner.

Source: Using Commercial Credit, Commercial Credit Company.

from another seller who offers better terms; (b) paying cash from accumulated savings or waiting until one has saved enough money; (c) borrowing from a bank or another lending agency and paying cash; (d) borrowing on a life insurance policy and paying cash.

Policies to follow in making an installment purchase

1. Make a substantial down payment.
2. Pay the balance as quickly as possible.
3. Buy only durable goods that will be of value long after the final payment.
4. Don't use the full extent of your installment credit.
5. Budget your income and your expenditures to be sure that you can pay all obligations.
6. Leave a safety margin for unforeseen expenses and possible reductions in income.
7. Consider before you buy whether it is more profitable and more desirable to save your money and wait until you can pay cash.
8. Check other ways to get what you want that may be cheaper.

Advantages of installment buying. The following are some of the recognized advantages of installment buying:

1. Necessities may be enjoyed before the full price is available for payment.
2. Better and more substantial merchandise can sometimes be obtained by utilizing the installment plan instead of paying cash for cheap merchandise.
3. Without the aid of installment buying, many young married people would be unable to furnish a home and start housekeeping.

Disadvantages of installment buying. The disadvantages of installment buying arise, not necessarily out of the faults of the system, but often out of its abuses. The following are some of the disadvantages of installment buying:

1. Some people buy assets because of false pride. They are encouraged to buy more expensive assets than they can afford.
2. When the number of dealers allowing installment purchases is limited, the person who wishes to make an installment purchase may have to accept an inferior product because the grade of goods he wants is not sold where he can make purchases on the installment plan.

3. The person who buys on the installment plan usually pays interest at a rate of from 6 to 25 percent on the unpaid balance. He therefore pays more than he would have paid if he had purchased the merchandise for cash. If one uses installment buying extensively, he will reduce his total purchasing power substantially.

4. Some people may overbuy because installment buying seems easy.

5. "Credit competition" sometimes leads businesses to put customers under pressure in the hope of selling goods on "easy terms."

6. Some merchants and dealers encourage buyers to use the installment plan because the finance charges produce additional income.

7. Some users of the installment plan lower their standards of food, clothing, education, and environment in order to meet obligations on installment purchases.

8. One of the greatest disadvantages is in committing oneself to future obligations. By promising to pay future income, one limits his freedom of action and reduces his margin of safety in financial emergencies.

It is evident that installment purchases should be made only on the basis of necessity and convenience after a careful study of needs and ability to pay. In general, installment buying is recommended only for accumulating worthwhile assets that will outlast the debt.

Terms of payment. The percentage of down payment and the amount of time in which the debtor may pay vary according to the product and the policy of the finance company. The table on page 372 provides a summary of the usual percentages of down payment and the usual time periods for making payment for particular types of merchandise.

Finance charges for installment service. When goods are sold on an installment plan, the seller or the one financing the sale incurs costs that would not arise with cash or charge sales. The expenses of investigating the credit standing of the purchaser, making the loan, collecting, bookkeeping, insurance, repossessing in case of delinquent payments, reselling, bad debts, and general office expenses must be covered either by increasing the sales price or by adding separate charges.

Product	Usual percentage of down payment	Usual time allowed to pay (months)
New automobiles	10 - Up	12 - 36
Used automobiles	10 - Up	12 - 33
Used automobiles (not late models)	20 - Up	12 - 24
Mobile homes (new)	10 - 25	36 - 120
Mobile homes (used)	10 - 25	12 - 36
Furniture	10 - 25	12 - 24
Refrigerators	5 - 10	18 - 36
Television sets	10 - 25	18 - 36
Jewelry	10 - 25	6 - 18
Men's clothing	10 - 25	3 - 9

Usual down payments and time allowed on installment sales

The *time balance* on an installment sale is the total due and to be paid in regular installments over a period of time. The finance charge or carrying charge is generally included as a part of the time balance. In some instances the charges are listed separately, such as "charge for investigation," "insurance," "service charge," and "interest." The total *finance charge* is often confused with interest, but it is legally very different. Although the finance charge includes use of the money loaned to the consumer, it also includes other costs such as those already mentioned. Interest is regulated by state law. In some states maximum finance charges are also regulated; but in many states finance or carrying charges are not regulated. The charges vary not only for different kinds of goods but also among the firms that sell on an installment plan.

Although a nominal rate (called add-on) of 5 to 8 percent per year may be quoted for all charges on an installment plan, it must be borne in mind that this rate is not comparable to straight interest rates as we ordinarily think of them.

In some cases the finance or carrying charges may seem to be unduly high; and yet in most instances they are reasonable when the extra costs of making and collecting installment loans are considered. When dealing with a reputable business firm, finance company, or bank, it is not so much a question of whether the cost of buying on an installment plan is fair or unfair; it is a question of whether the merchandise is needed sufficiently to justify paying the amount of the finance or carrying charges.

The following table shows typical finance charges for purchasing new automobiles on the installment plan.

Amount financed *	Length of contract	Total finance charges	Total amount of loan	Monthly payment
$ 500	12 months	$33.64	$ 533.64	$ 44.47
800	12 months	53.80	853.80	71.15
1,000	12 months	67.28	1,067.28	88.94
1,200	12 months	80.64	1,280.64	106.72

* Amount the borrower gets.

Credit life insurance. In Chapter 26 there is a discussion of *consumer-credit insurance,* which is also called *credit life insurance.* Credit life insurance will be discussed briefly at this point because of its connection with installment buying. This kind of insurance is short-term insurance on the life of the purchaser. Under the terms of the purchase contract and the life insurance policy, in case of the purchaser's death, the money from the insurance will be used to pay off the remaining debt under the installment plan. Usually the amount of the insurance decreases as the debt is paid.

Credit life insurance is inexpensive. Any reliable insurance agent can tell you what you should pay for this kind of insurance. Sometimes the cost of the insurance is included in the total cost of the installment purchase. If it is not shown as a separate item, it is sometimes difficult to determine how much is being charged. Any purchaser on an installment contract has a right to know the cost of the merchandise, the carrying charge, and all other charges that are being made.

COMPUTING FINANCE CHARGES

Although there are many ways to calculate the finance charges on installment transactions, they are commonly computed on either the add-on basis or on the percent-per-month basis.

Add-on basis. On the *add-on basis,* a flat percentage or sometimes a flat sum is charged for making the loan. Usually the amount of the charge is proportionately higher for small than for large balances. (The percentage is not an interest rate, but a rate that includes all costs.) The add-on basis is used for most installment sales and for a large share of installment loans.

The following tables show the typical finance charges on an add-on basis on installment contracts for new automobiles and household appliances. In the case of automobiles, the finance charge may include premiums on life insurance on the buyer of the car. Insurance on the car itself is usually included in the overall cost of a car purchased on an installment plan.

EXAMPLES OF CARRYING CHARGES ON NEW AUTOMOBILES, INCLUDING LIFE INSURANCE ON THE BUYER (BUT OFTEN ARE HIGHER)

Unpaid balance due	12 Months	18 Months	24 Months
	Carrying charges		
$ 200	$13.96	$ 17.26	$ 22.72
300	17.16	25.26	33.36
400	22.64	33.44	44.24
500	28.00	41.44	54.88
600	33.36	49.44	65.76
700	38.72	57.62	76.40
800	44.08	65.62	87.26
900	49.44	73.62	97.92
1,000	54.80	81.80	108.80
1,500	81.72	122.16	162.48

CARRYING CHARGES ON HOUSEHOLD APPLIANCES

100	10.76	xx	xx
150	14.52	21.72	29.04
200	17.68	28.96	36.40
250	22.76	34.22	45.68
300	29.23	38.58	51.36

NOTE: The carrying charge is added to the unpaid balance due to determine the total amount to be paid.

Carrying charges added to the unpaid balance

The following example shows how the add-on basis of financing is applied to an automobile installment sale transaction.

Unpaid balance on car $300.00
Number of monthly payments 18
Finance charges, including premium for life insurance
   on buyer for 18 months (add-on) 25.26
Total amount of note signed by buyer 325.26
Monthly payment (325.26 ÷ 18 months) 18.07

It will be noted that the amount of the note signed by the buyer is the sum of the amount needed to pay for the car plus finance charges.

Percent-per-month basis. The *percent-per-month plan,* frequently used by small-loan companies and credit unions, is illustrated by the following transaction:

Purchase price of furniture	$600.00
Down payment	200.00
Unpaid balance	$400.00
Finance charge	20.00
Amount advanced (total loan)	$420.00

Interest is to be charged at the rate of 6 percent per year or one-half percent each month on the unpaid balance at the beginning of the month. There are to be eight monthly payments of $52.50 plus interest. The schedule of payments on principal, charges, and interest is given below:

Monthly installment	Payments				Outstanding	
	Principal	Charges	Interest	Total	On note	On advance
1	$50.00	$2.50	$2.10	$54.60	$420.00	$400.00
2	50.00	2.50	1.84	54.34	367.50	350.00
3	50.00	2.50	1.57	54.07	315.00	300.00
4	50.00	2.50	1.31	53.81	267.50	250.00
5	50.00	2.50	1.05	53.55	210.00	200.00
6	50.00	2.50	.79	53.29	157.50	150.00
7	50.00	2.50	.53	53.03	105.00	100.00
8	50.00	2.50	.26	52.76	52.50	50.00
Total	$400.00	$20.00	$9.45	$429.45		

In the foregoing illustration, the finance charges were equally distributed among the eight months and the monthly interest charges were based upon the unpaid balance. In many instances the finance charges are also based on the unpaid balance and at the same percentage rate each month.

TYPICAL NEW-CAR FINANCING PLAN

The following calculations represent an actual transaction in which an old car worth $950 is traded for a new car. Since there is still a debt of $412.60 on the old car, this debt must be paid off at the time the new car is purchased. The dealer usually requires a down payment of approximately one fourth of the total cost of the new car less the insurance. Therefore, the purchaser must pay $157.75 in cash besides the net value of his old car. Out of the money received by the dealer he will pay off the debt of $412.60 on the old car.

Example of new-car financing

Net price of new car	$2,692.45
State sales tax (3%)	80.78
State title fee and transfer of tag costs	7.35
Total cost less insurance	$2,780.58

Value of used car traded	$950.00	
Amount owed on used car	412.60	
Net value in used car	$537.40	

Amount needed for 1/4 down payment	$695.15	
Value in used car	537.40	
Cash required with order	$157.75	

Old car, $537.40, and cash, $157.75 down payment	695.15
Balance to finance	$2,085.43
Amount of cash deposit made at time order was written	42.43
Subtotal to finance	$2,043.00
Plus auto insurance	47.00
Total amount to finance	$2,090.00

Payments: $184.72 each month for 12 months, including credit life insurance on purchaser, $2,216.64. Payments of $2,216.64 less $2,090.00 = $126.64 carrying charges, including insurance on life to pay off debt in case of death.

FIGURING THE COST OF AN INSTALLMENT PURCHASE

There are numerous installment plans. Some of these reveal the true cost by making a charge, in the form of interest, on the unpaid balance. In such a case the actual cost of the merchandise to the purchaser is easy to figure. On the other hand, some plans involve discounts, fees, and carrying charges which may conceal the real interest rate.

There are many ways of stating the installment costs, some of which are confusing. Therefore, in order to shop wisely for the best installment plan, one must be able to compare costs. The precise calculation of installment rates involves mathematical procedures that are too complex for most people to use. However, a simple process by which a close approximation of the true interest rate may be secured will give a reliable basis for comparison of costs.

The cost of financing installment purchases may be shown in the following illustration. Let us assume an item selling for $100 is sold on the basis of 25 percent down, the balance to be paid in eight

---

Typical Credit Charges

If charges are based on the **beginning amount owed** and are included in the 12 equal monthly installments:

If Charged:	Simple Annual Rate Is:
$4 per $100 or 4% per year	7.4%
$6 per $100 or 6% per year	11.1%
$8 per $100 or 8% per year	14.8%
$10 per $100 or 10% per year	18.5%
1% per month	22.2%

If charged only on **unpaid amount owed:**

If Charged:	Simple Annual Rate Is:
3/4 of 1% per month on unpaid balance	9%
5/6 of 1% per month on unpaid balance	10%
1% per month on unpaid balance	12%
1¼% per month on unpaid balance	15%
1½% per month on unpaid balance	18%
2½% per month on unpaid balance	30%

---

monthly payments and that the finance charge is quoted as 6 percent of the balance, or $4.50. How much does the buyer actually borrow in this case and what interest rate on an annual basis does he pay?

Each monthly payment will reduce the principal by $9.375 ($75 ÷ 8 months). Thus, the buyer had the use of:

$75.00 for the first month	$37.500 for the fifth month
$65.625 for the second month	$28.125 for the sixth month
$56.250 for the third month	$18.750 for the seventh month
$46.875 for the fourth month	$ 9.375 for the eighth month

Or, the buyer had the use of $337.50 for one month, which is the equivalent of $28.125 for a year ($337.50 ÷ 12 months). [1] The total finance charge was $4.50; therefore, instead of the nominal rate of 6 percent, the rate of interest actually paid by the buyer was

$$\frac{\$4.50}{\$28.125} \times 100 = 16.00 \text{ percent per year}$$

The same result may also be obtained by the use of the constant-ratio formula (for the person who wishes to use an algebraic formula):

---

[1] The average amount that the buyer had to use for one year was $28.125.

$$r = \frac{2 \times m \times i}{P \ (n + 1)}$$

In the formula, r equals the annual rate charged; m, the number of payments in a year; i, the total finance charge; P, the net amount to be paid; and n, the number of installments.

Applying the formula to the installment transaction previously described:

$$r = \frac{2 \times 12 \times 4.50}{75 \times (8 + 1)} = \frac{108}{675} = 16.00 \text{ percent}$$

Regardless of how the terms of an installment sale plan are stated, comparisons of the actual cost of financing can be made in this manner. In order to make this calculation, the finance charges and the sale price of the article, not including finance charges, must be known.

In some instances, goods such as jewelry and clothing are offered for sale on monthly payments with "no charge for credit." However, a purchaser who offers cash usually will be able to buy the article for less than the stated price. The difference between the cash price he would pay and the stated price on installment with "no charge for credit" is the finance charge. Thus, the rate for financing can be calculated the same as for other installment plans.

Low rates because: (1) amount of transaction is very large; (2) risk is very small

Higher rates because amount of transaction is small

Still higher rates because: (1) amount of transaction is small; (2) risk is higher

Source: *Using Installment Credit*, Commercial Credit Company.

Interest rates also depend on risks.

When making comparisons of costs of financing contemplated installment purchases, it will be well for the buyer to remember that legitimate lenders of small sums find it necessary to charge from 10 to 36 percent per year to cover their actual costs of operation and to give them a fair profit.

Warnings on installment buying

1. Do not allow yourself to be rushed into signing a contract until you know all the facts.
2. Refuse to sign any contract if you are not given an exact duplicate copy.
3. Do not sign any contract before all the blank spaces are filled in.
4. Do not pledge any security besides the article being purchased.

REPLEVIN OR REPOSSESSION

When an article is sold under an installment contract and the buyer later fails to live up to his part of the contract, the seller, in order to protect himself from loss, sometimes has the right to repossess the article. The legal action necessary is usually referred to as *repossession* or *replevin*. The law of replevin differs widely in various states. In some states the law permits the seller to repossess the property, and, regardless of the amount that has been paid, he need not compensate the buyer for anything that the latter has already paid. Under the laws of many states, however, the person who repossesses an article must, according to a definite plan prescribed in the law, compensate the buyer for any interest that the latter may have had in the article.

ECONOMICS OF INSTALLMENT CREDIT

In Chapter 10 there was a discussion of money and credit, but at this point let us take another brief look at what installment credit does for us.

When people who do not have money buy on the installment plan, they are using the money of someone else. They are borrowing, in a sense, from the merchant or from someone, such as a bank, who loans the money for buying the goods. Money used in this manner has been saved by someone. It is put to work. It earns interest for the lender; it causes purchases to be made; and it creates demand for goods. It also increases the money supply. It is easy to see that it stimulates business, but the worry of businessmen and government officials is that people may buy more than they can pay for on the installment plan. In a later chapter you will learn what happens when many people cannot pay their debts.

Principles of installment buying everyone should know

1. Installment buying stimulates mass production and thus is an important factor in our economy.
2. Installment buying really means that one is borrowing money.
3. A chattel mortgage, a conditional sales contract, or other form of security agreement commonly provides security for the seller.
4. Installment selling involves many extra costs that must be borne by the buyer.
5. The finance or carrying charge is the difference between the cash price and the total cost paid under an installment contract.
6. Finance charges vary widely both in amount and in method of calculation.
7. Buying on an installment plan costs much more than buying on a regular charge account or for cash.
8. An installment buyer should fully understand the provisions of the contract before buying.

▪ QUESTIONS ON THE TEXT

1. What do we mean by the term installment buying?
2. How does installment buying affect the buyer and affect business?
3. Two general types of contracts are used in selling merchandise on the installment plan.
   (a) What are they?
   (b) When does the title pass in each case?
4. How is the seller protected under each type of installment contract?
5. What are the common elements in all installment contracts?
6. What is the major difference between a sales finance company and a consumer finance company?
7. Name at least three things you should check when entering into an installment contract.
8. Explain a situation in which buying furniture on the installment plan might result in a saving to a family.
9. Name the policies that should be followed if you are going to buy on the installment plan.
10. Before you buy on the installment plan, what are some other alternatives to consider?
11. What are some of the advantages of installment buying?
12. What are some of the disadvantages of installment buying?

13. What costs other than interest costs are included in finance charges?
14. When a new automobile is purchased on the installment plan, what is usually (a) the down payment required? (b) the time allowed for payment?
15. What is meant by credit life insurance, and how is it used?
16. According to the tables in this chapter, what is a typical carrying charge added to the price of a refrigerator costing $300 if the payments are to be made over a period of 18 months?
17. Study the typical new-car financing plan that is described in this chapter and explain what happens on the purchase of a new car when an old car is traded in on which there is still an unpaid balance.
18. Explain briefly the regulations in regard to replevin.

▪ QUESTIONS FOR DISCUSSION

1. Explain how purchases on the installment plan should be worked into budget planning.
2. (a) What do you think would happen to automobile sales if automobiles could no longer be purchased on the installment plan?
   (b) What do you think would happen to automobile sales if dealers did not require any down payment?
3. Why do you think it might be advisable for a certain family to borrow money in order to buy a washing machine instead of buying it on an installment plan?
4. What do you think of the advisability of buying jewelry on the installment plan?
5. Some retail advertisements do not state the prices of household appliances but merely indicate the down payments and the daily or weekly costs of payments. As a buyer, what do you think of advertisements of this type?
6. A business advertises that it sells on the installment plan at no extra charge.
   (a) Is this practice fair to all customers of the business?
   (b) What should a cash customer expect?
7. If the law in your state or the contract that you sign requires the seller to compensate you for the financial interest that you have in an article when it is repossessed by the seller, how much would you expect to get back if you had paid $100 on a refrigerator and had used it two years?
8. Assume that you have made a purchase on the installment plan at a time when the store is very busy. The manager suggests that you merely sign the contract, a copy of which he will mail you. Is this a good practice if you are well known by the store manager?

▪ PROBLEMS TO SOLVE

1. Harley Bryant borrowed $800 and agreed to pay it back in monthly installments over a period of 18 months. Keeping in mind the constant ratio formula given in this chapter, what was the annual interest rate if:
    (a) He borrowed from a credit union charging 1 percent per month?
    (b) He borrowed from a bank charging 6 percent under the add-on method?
2. Assume that you are buying a new automobile on which the unpaid balance will be $1,500, which you agree to pay over a period of 18 months. According to the tables in this chapter,
    (a) What will be the carrying charges?
    (b) What will be the monthly payments?
3. Mr. Jamison is undecided about whether to purchase a color TV set for $490 cash or to pay $50 down and $50 a month for 10 months. What annual rate of interest would he pay if he purchased the set on the installment plan? (Remember that, regardless of the number of months involved, the average for one year is determined on the basis of 12 months.)

▪ COMMUNITY PROBLEMS AND PROJECTS

1. Visit the showroom of an automobile dealer and select a car you would like to own. Obtain the following information in regard to the purchase of that car: (a) the price f.o.b. the factory, (b) the delivered price, (c) the particular items and the amounts of the items that add to the cost in delivering the automobile, (d) the guarantee, (e) the service agreement, (f) the type of bill of sale used, (g) the carrying charge on the unpaid balance, and (h) the plan of paying the balance. Write a report summarizing the information that you have obtained.
2. Obtain a copy of either a chattel mortgage or a conditional sales contract (whichever is most commonly used and is legally permitted in your state) and analyze the contract by submitting your answers to the following questions:
    (a) When does the title pass?
    (b) How may the title be transferred?
    (c) What happens if there is a default of any payment?
    (d) Are there any warranties?
    (e) What other rights, privileges, or limitations of use are extended the buyer?

Chapter 20

Advertising and the consumer

PURPOSE OF THE CHAPTER

Advertising is a part of our marketing distribution system and is, therefore, an important part of our free-market production system. The function of advertising is to sell goods and services and by so doing to create jobs for those who produce them. A study of this chapter will help you to understand the functions and practices of advertising.

You will find answers to these questions:

1. What is the economic function of advertising?
2. How does advertising help the consumer?
3. What is the cost of advertising?
4. Who pays the cost of advertising?

A. Nature and functions of advertising

ECONOMIC FUNCTIONS OF ADVERTISING

In Chapter 4 we learned that marketing distribution is a part of the production process. Advertising is a part of the marketing distri-

bution process and is a great economic force in the free marketing system.

If wants are simple and few, there is very little demand for production of goods and services. Until a want or need is changed to a demand (buying), there is no need for production.

Producers know (or guess) that certain wants and needs will become a demand. They create certain products or services and offer them for sale. Unless they are sold, the business will fail and there will be no jobs for those who want to produce. To reduce the risk of failure, a business uses advertising to create demand. The producer tells the consumer what he has to sell, what it will do for him, why he should buy it, how much it will cost, and where he can get it. By appealing to certain human desires, the advertiser changes wants into demand.

Demand causes production, and production creates jobs and wages. Wages make it possible for workers to buy, so advertising stimulates business.

Competition causes the development of more and better products and services, more jobs, more advertising, and a constantly expanding demand for goods and services that raise the level of economic living.

Stimulation of demand. Stimulation of consumer demand for goods is done primarily through (1) personal selling and sales promotion methods and (2) advertising. The ultimate objective of both personal selling and advertising is to sell goods. The methods employed, however, are different. A salesman or clerk directs his efforts toward persuading an individual or a business firm to buy goods through a person-to-person approach. The *objective of advertising,* however, is to sell goods and services by stimulating demand through advertising statements or messages directed toward groups of people, individuals,

ADVERTISING
\ HELPS TO CREATE DEMAND /

PRODUCTION   SALES

NEW FACTORIES

NEW MACHINES

NEW JOBS · MORE WAGES

Advertising helps to create demand and adds to sales, consumption, investment, production, jobs, mass production, and profits.

or to the public at large. Advertising messages vary in nature from those that are wholly informative and factual to those that stir the emotions. Likewise, the media range from a handbill placed under the windshield wiper of a parked car to elaborate displays and television programs.

How demand is stimulated. People have certain natural wants, such as food to satisfy hunger, clothes for warmth, and a home for shelter; but even with these wants, the demands to satisfy them may be very simple unless stimulated to buy something new or different. For example, think of the many new foods developed and sold, the many new styles of clothes, or the modern home as compared with the old.

Besides the common natural wants, there are other wants that are created by advertising and converted into demand. Many of these are based upon emotions, but they are very real and give happiness when the wants are satisfied. Some of these emotions to which the advertiser appeals are the desire to be beautiful, to gain attention, to be the first to follow the leader, to do as others do, to be different, and many others. Wants are created and changed into demand by appeals to fear, greed, love, comfort, pride, economy, style, and prestige.

Advertising and mass production. When our country was young, production and distribution were very simple. Most consumers produced the goods they consumed, or they traded with nearby acquaintances. Stores often traded goods across the counter, and very little money changed hands. The first common form of advertising was the sign of the doctor, the merchant, the blacksmith, the wigmaker, or other professional men. In those days mass production was not known; therefore, there was no need for mass distribution.

Now we have mass production with producers and consumers widely separated. A complicated system of transportation and communication is needed to help producers reach the consumer and to tell the consumer in distant places what the producer has to sell.

Under our economic system advertising is essential to the development of mass production facilities.

General Motors

Under our present economic system, advertising is essential. Advertising helps both agriculture and business, and it creates jobs both directly in advertising occupations and indirectly by creating demand for many products.

Of course, in the completely controlled societies, such as a communistic society, advertising is not so useful because producers are told what to produce and consumers can buy only those goods placed at their disposal. In such countries, few kinds of goods are available from which to make a selection. Imagine how different life would be in the United States if many of the things now offered for sale were withdrawn and if we had no choice among those commodities that were made available to us.

Specific functions of advertising. The ultimate purpose of all advertising is to sell goods. Manufacturers, wholesalers, and retailers seek to achieve this objective through the several functions of advertising, which are listed on page 387. Many functions of advertising are beneficial to consumers as well as to producers and distributors.

CRITICAL VIEWS OF ADVERTISING

Although large-scale distribution and, therefore, mass production would not be possible without advertising, there are critics who believe that advertising is both unnecessary and wasteful.

The fact that critics argue against advertising does not make their arguments necessarily valid. It is very easy for us to look at a disadvantage or an undesirable outcome of advertising without considering at the same time the advantages and benefits that come from adver-

From the standpoint of the seller, one of the major functions of advertising is to establish a trade name, slogan, or product image.

Union Pacific Railroad

Major functions of advertising from the standpoint of the seller

1. Stimulate consumer demand through obtaining:
    a. Wider acceptance and greater use of products not yet universally used, such as wash-and-wear apparel.
    b. Greater use of products already widely used, such as potatoes or citrus fruits.
    c. Wider acceptance of a commodity by consumers who have not used it.
2. Educate prospective consumers regarding:
    a. The personal benefits and satisfactions to be derived from using a particular product.
    b. Various uses of a product.
    c. Merits of a particular brand or make.
3. Inform consumers about new products, developments in present products, and changes in fashions and customs.
4. Maintain contact with consumers who, without advertising, may never know a product is available.
5. Stress exclusive features and important advantages of a product.
6. Build consumer preference for a particular brand of product, thus making it possible to price thep roduct above competitive brands.
7. Develop large-scale distribution, thus making possible low-cost mass production.
8. Establish a trade name slogan or product image.
9. Create goodwill and develop consumer respect for the firm.
10. Obtain a list of prospective customers and prepare the way for salesmen.
11. Obtain a larger share of the business available.
12. Promote the use of one class of product, such as margarine as opposed to butter.

---

tising. Undoubtedly, there is some basis for each of the criticisms; but before accepting the criticisms, the benefits of advertising to both the business of the nation and to consumers should also be considered. Let us briefly examine some of the criticisms.

Creates discontent. Seeing an advertisement for a $6,000 luxury automobile or a $50,000 house should not make a person discontented or unhappy just because he cannot afford to buy them. Each of us has a certain income which determines the limits of his expenditures. Each person decides for himself whether he spends $6,000 for an automobile or whether he would get more real pleasure and satisfaction from spending half that amount for an automobile and the other half for the living costs of food, clothing, and shelter.

Major critical views of advertising

Among the major criticisms of advertising are the following:

1. Makes consumers discontented, dissatisfied, and unhappy with conditions under which they live.
2. Fosters the buying of commodities that some consumers cannot afford.
3. Builds consumer preferences for particular goods without consideration of the merits of the products.
4. Stimulates buying on emotional rather than on rational appeal.
5. The cost of advertising per unit of product is unreasonably high for many products.
6. The cost of advertising increases the price of products and reduces the total quantity of goods consumers can buy.
7. Fails to focus consumer interest on improvements in social and cultural interests.
8. The language of advertising—multiple adjectives, informality, violations of rules of good English usage—is detrimental and confusing, especially to impressionable young people.
9. Many advertising messages are absurd, meaningless, misleading, and easily misconstrued.

In America each person is considered to have both the ability to reason and the right to make decisions for himself. That is one of the foundation pillars of our liberty. Just because an article that is out of our price range is advertised is no reason for our buying it. If we do act unwisely and buy it, the blame is not to be placed on the advertising but on us.

Promotes unwise choices. Undoubtedly, many of us develop preferences for particular brands without comparing the quality and price with competing brands. Also, we are motivated by emotional appeal to buy many things. Here, again, we are a free people and freedom means that if we prefer a brand of peaches in a can with a red label to a brand with a blue label, we may choose the brand we prefer to purchase.

Increases consumer prices. Although the cost of advertising may increase the price of goods, there is no assurance that if there were no advertising, prices to consumers would be less. For example, two manufacturers offer mattresses for sale. The quality of their respective lines of mattresses is comparable. One manufacturer advertises widely, the other very little. Yet, the price for mattresses of comparable quality is little different between the manufacturer that does not advertise and the one that does. The additional cost of advertising for the one who advertises heavily may be offset by lower production costs due to greater volume of sales.

KINDS OF ADVERTISING

Most of the advertising with which we are concerned is directed toward the ultimate consumer, that is, the person who buys for personal or household use, not for a business or a profession. Advertising addressed to or intended for the ultimate consumer is known as *consumer advertising.*

Advertising may be classified also as to "approach," that is, as to its intention. If the advertising is intended to stress the benefits of a certain class or type of product rather than particular brands of that product, it is known as *primary advertising.* An example is the dairy industry stimulating the demand for cheese through advertising.

DAIRY PRODUCTS, AMERICA'S MOST ECONOMICAL FOOD

The primary approach in advertising focuses attention on a type or a class of product, rather than on a particular brand.

Another classification of advertising as to approach or intention is known as *selective advertising,* which attempts to persuade consumers generally to buy one brand rather than another. This is the kind of advertising that is most frequently addressed to consumers.

B. The control, costs, and use of advertising

CONTROL OF ADVERTISING FOR CONSUMER PROTECTION

Every buyer must recognize the fact that, although the majority of advertisers are honest, some are unscrupulous. Substantial and well-established business concerns recognize the fact that honesty, in other relationships with consumers as well as in advertising, must be the basis for permanent success.

Of the thousands of advertisements that are printed and broadcast over the air annually, only a very small percentage are dishonest or misleading. In a recent year the Federal Trade Commission examined more than a half million advertisements and made complaints to the advertisers in only seventy-two cases. The best safeguard of advertising integrity is the sense of responsibility that advertisers have.

There are two effective types of regulation and control over advertisements. One type is self-imposed standards. These standards are adopted by individual business firms, advertisers' associations, and often by the businesses providing advertising media, such as newspapers, magazines, and radio and television. The publishers of magazines and newspapers recognize the fact that dishonest advertising reacts unfavorably against their publications as well as against the products advertised. A second type of regulation and control of advertising exists in state and federal laws and regulations. The regulation and control of advertising to protect consumers through state and federal legislation are explained in Chapter 21.

THE COST OF ADVERTISING

Advertising costs are reflected in the selling price of a product or service. Therefore, the consumer ultimately pays for advertising. It may seem unreasonable to spend $40,000 for a full-page advertisement in one issue of a national magazine or $250,000 for one television program. But, these advertising media respectively reach thousands and millions of people; hence the advertising cost per unit of product sold is very small. Consumers should be interested in knowing how much of the dollar cost of their purchases represents advertising cost.

Expenditures for advertising. Approximately $9 billion a year is spent in advertising. This amount is less than 1.1 percent of the total value of all goods and services produced in the United States. About three fifths of the total expenditure is for national advertising and about two fifths for local advertising. Approximately one third of the expenditures for advertising is for newspaper advertisements, about one seventh for direct mail, and an equal amount for television.

Advertising cost per dollar of sales. Advertising expenditures per dollar of sales for selected types of industries indicate that the smallest expenditure per dollar of sales or income is in the insurance business, which spends about 3/10 of a cent per dollar. The largest expenditure by type of industry is 5 2/10 cents by tobacco manufacturers. Manu-

Of $100 spent for food, an average of $1.10 is for advertising.

facturers of beverages rank second in cost of advertising per dollar of sales. It is interesting to note that in general about 1 1/10 cents per dollar of sales is spent for advertising foods. These facts are given in the table below.

Typical advertising expenditures per dollar of sales for selected types of businesses	
Types of business	*Advertising expenditures per dollar of sales*
Tobacco manufacturers	5.2 cents
Beverage manufacturers	5.0 "
Apparel and accessories (retail)	2.8 "
General merchandise	2.5 "
Banks	1.4 "
Furniture manufacturers	1.3 "
Food (retail)	1.1 "
Motor car manufacturers	.9 "
Insurance	.3 "

Source: Treasury Department, Internal Revenue Service; *Statistics of Income.*

Large-scale distribution possible through advertising. Without advertising it would be impossible to have mass distribution. Without mass distribution it would be impossible to have mass production. Without mass production it would be impossible to have manufacturing processes improved to the high degree to which we are now accustomed. Without improved manufacturing processes it would be impossible to have many of our commonly accepted necessities produced at a low cost. For instance, in 1922 a few thousand people with radio sets costing from $100 to $500 were the envy of most people. There are now approximately 57 million homes equipped with radios which have cost in some cases as little as $20. Advertising has made mass production of radios possible and through mass production, prices have decreased.

Net effect of advertising on consumer prices. Advertising has two effects on the prices paid by consumers for many of the products that are widely used. First, the cost of advertising adds to the price of the goods that the consumer buys. Second, advertising makes large-scale distribution possible, which in turn makes mass production at a low unit cost possible. The lower production cost in a competitive market such as we have in the United States decreases prices to consumers. Thus, the net effect of advertising on the price a consumer pays for a product depends upon the two factors—first, the amount of the added cost per unit due to advertising and, second, the decreased consumer price per unit because of the benefits of mass production.

The fact should not be overlooked that were it not for the greater demand for products stimulated by advertising, we would not enjoy many of the products we use today because it would not be economical to make them. Certainly, it cannot be said that the cost of advertising that is ultimately borne by the consumer is without a net benefit to him.

Hidden benefits of advertising. In Great Britain there is no commercial advertising on radio or television. The government owns the broadcasting stations, and they are paid for from taxes collected from the people. The government decides what programs will be broadcast. In the United States the cost of operating radio and television stations is paid for through advertising. Therefore, the cost that is indicated for advertising also includes the services furnished the consumer through radio and television programs.

Advertising also pays most of the cost of newspapers and magazines. These would cost much more than they do if it were not for advertising. In other words the price that you pay for the hidden cost of advertising also includes other services.

CONSUMER ANALYSIS OF ADVERTISING

As consumers, we are exposed daily to literally hundreds of advertising messages—in newspapers and magazines, on billboards and show cards, and by radio and television. Without doubt, these advertisements develop in us desires for products and services that otherwise we would not want. This, in many respects, is good for us, for it acquaints us with commodities and services that may make living more pleasant. It is important, however, that as consumers we not only understand the motives, methods, and practices of advertisers but also that we know how to use advertising wisely in satisfying our wants. In order to use advertising wisely we must be able to analyze advertising. In Chapter 23, you will learn how advertising may be used in buying wisely. Here we shall merely list some general guides for consumers to use in analyzing advertisements.

Guides for consumers in analyzing advertisements

1. Study advertisements continually to learn about new products and services, improvements, and developments; learn to recognize trademarks, brand names, and both the manufacturers and retailers of the commodities you want. Use advertisements as a source of information.
2. Discover the kind of appeal used in an advertisement—emotional or reason-why. This knowledge will help you in using the advertisements wisely in making consumer choices.
3. Look for statements indicating the quality of the product advertised; if the advertisement is not adequate, seek more information from manufacturer or retailer.
4. Do not be influenced by absurd and meaningless statements and implications in advertisements. Many of them are not complimentary to your intelligence if you permit them to influence you.
5. Evaluate with great care testimonials used in advertisements; ordinarily an advertising testimonial is of little value to you.
6. Search for informative statements that explain the essential features of a product—specifications, standards, and performance.
7. Develop a pattern to follow in analyzing advertisements; you will be a more efficient and wiser consumer if analytical habits for evaluating advertisements are formed.

ADVERTISING BENEFITS YOU

Advertising has a tremendous influence on the development of our standard of living by improving our diet, our health, our living conditions, and our comforts and conveniences. This lifting of our standards has been brought about through constructive education and by increasing our wants for things that now seem necessary although at one time they may have seemed unnecessary. It may be true that advertising has caused us to want things that we really do not need, but after all, we are free to decide what we need. It is therefore necessary for the consumer to be well enough informed so that he may intelligently decide what he needs.

Educational value of advertising. The history of food consumption is a good illustration of the educational influence of advertising on our diets and general health. For example, authorities on diet long have advocated the use of orange juice, tomato juice, fresh vegetables,

Advertising may have educational value.

and fresh fruits in our everyday diet. Very little progress was made in establishing these foods as a part of our basic diet until producers began to use advertising as a means of educating the people as to the desirability of the daily use of these foods.

The story of popularizing desirable foods is somewhat parallel to the story of popularizing the telephone, sanitary plumbing, ventilation, lighting, refrigeration, radio, television, and many types of labor-saving devices that are now considered essential in the home. We can live without these conveniences, but how greatly our standard of living would decrease if we did not have them.

Product information. Another benefit of advertising is that it acquaints consumers with the uses of certain products, particularly new ones. In many instances, consumers must be familiarized with the uses of a product before they are willing to buy. A typical example of such a product is a portable room air purifier. People will not be interested in it if they do not know that it is used to remove pollen and dust to which some are allergic, to remove unpleasant odors, and to introduce oxygen.

Social and cultural goals. Finally, because advertising arouses mass desire and penetrates so deeply into American life, it potentially can be a powerful influence in formulating the health, social, and cultural goals of the people. For example, as our wants increase we may demand better food, better housing, better education, and better recreation.

Economic benefits. No less important than the educational benefits of advertising are the benefits of an economic nature. As stated earlier in the chapter, advertising makes large-scale distribution possible, which in turn provides an outlet for the products of mass-production methods. Thus, many products are available to consumers at reasonable prices that without advertising would not be available at all or if they were available, the prices would be prohibitive. Many of the products we enjoy we could not have if it were not for advertising to stimulate a demand for them, thus lowering the cost of production.

Another economic benefit of advertising is that both directly in the advertising business and indirectly in manufacturing firms, advertising creates many jobs for many people.

Facts about advertising everybody should know

1. The objective of advertising is to sell goods and services through stimulating demand and influencing consumers in their choices.
2. Advertising is an essential factor in distribution; it makes mass production possible, which in turn means many more products are made available at costs consumers can afford to pay.
3. There is disagreement among economists and consumers as to the value of advertising to consumers; the criticisms of advertising are focused primarily on its usefulness.
4. Various kinds of advertising are intended to serve specific purposes, such as informing and educating consumers about certain products; promoting sales for an entire industry, such as the growing of citrus fruits; and persuading consumers to select and buy a particular product.
5. Advertising is controlled by (a) self-imposed standards by individual advertisers and by advertising associations, and (b) state and federal legislation. For the most part, the integrity of advertisers is commendable, and advertising in general maintains high standards.
6. Advertising costs consumers from a fraction of one cent to a maximum of four or five cents per dollar paid for goods. The cost of advertising paid by consumers is offset in part or wholly by the benefit of lower prices which advertising indirectly makes possible through mass production.
7. An analysis of the motives, methods, and contents of advertisements may provide the basis for wise consumer decisions.
8. Advertising provides valuable consumer benefits, some of which are educational and others economic in nature.

■ QUESTIONS ON THE TEXT

1. What methods are used to stimulate demand for goods?
2. How does advertising make possible low-cost mass production?
3. What is the ultimate purpose of advertising?
4. List the major functions of advertising.
5. Explain why some people argue that advertising creates discontent.
6. How may advertising promote unwise choice-making?
7. What are the types of regulation and control over advertising?
8. Who ultimately pays for advertising?
9. Approximately how much is spent each year for advertising?
10. What industry spends the most per dollar of sales for advertising?
11. Advertising adds to the price of goods and at the same time tends to reduce the consumer prices of goods. How is this possible?
12. Give your views of the relative merits of the British and United States systems of paying for radio and television programs.
13. What suggestions do you offer as a guide to analyzing advertisements?
14. Give some examples of the educational value of advertising.

■ QUESTIONS FOR DISCUSSION

1. Why is advertising necessary for mass production and mass consumption?
2. Why is advertising of products almost useless in completely state-controlled countries, such as in a country under communistic rule?
3. Explain the ways by which advertising stimulates consumer demand.
4. Select a specific advertisement that illustrates the education of the consumer and explain how it is educational.
5. Are the major criticisms of advertising justifiable? Discuss, from the standpoint of the possible effect upon you and other members of the class, each of the nine criticisms listed on page 388.
6. How does the consumer advertising usually differ from business advertising?
7. To what extent do you think advertisements are misleading or dishonest?
8. Explain the probability that pressure advertising may lead people to act unwisely.
9. Assume that you buy a new suit costing $49.95 of which 75 cents is advertising cost. Explain how you have benefited by that 75 cents additional cost.
10. How has advertising affected our diets?
11. What would happen to consumption if all consumer advertising were limited to a factual statement of the characteristics of the product?
12. Why should consumers analyze advertisements?
13. Of what social value is advertising?

▪ PROBLEMS TO SOLVE

1. In magazines or newspapers in your home find advertisements that contain appeals to (a) health, (b) beauty, (c) economy. Paste these on a sheet of paper, and opposite each one, write a brief notation indicating how the appeal is emphasized.

2. The customers of a suburban drugstore bought an average of $1,000 worth of drugs and other items each of 300 days during a particular year. The store owner spent $3,500 for newspaper advertisements; $1,200 for direct mail messages; $2,800 for radio commercials; $1,000 for printed advertisements left on doorsteps; and $1,800 for displays within his store.

   (a) What percent of his gross income did he spend for advertising?

   (b) Approximately what percent of his total expenditure for advertising was spent on each type of advertising?

   (c) How much of each customer's dollar was involved in the total advertising cost?

3. (a) From five magazines or newspapers make a list of all the high-sounding titles and terms used in advertising products. This list should include meaningless, but attractive, slogans and terms.

   (b) After listing these terms, analyze their truthfulness, their intent, and their usefulness from the point of view of the buyer.

▪ COMMUNITY PROBLEMS AND PROJECTS

1. Watch your local newspapers for what you consider false advertising and state why you feel it is false. If your community has a better business bureau, find out exactly what functions it performs in regard to maintaining the ethics of local advertising. Write a report of your findings.

2. Develop both affirmative and negative arguments on the debate question: "Resolved, That Most Advertising Is Economically Valuable and Helps to Reduce the Cost of Living." If possible, arrange to have an informal debate on this question in class or as a part of an assembly program.

3. On a large cardboard or on a bulletin board prepare a display of advertisements properly captioned and labeled to illustrate each of the following contrasting features: (a) emotional and rational appeal; (b) business and consumer advertisements; and (c) primary and selective advertising.

   Prepare another display of properly captioned and labeled advertisements to illustrate each of the following characteristics: (a) quality emphasis, (b) essential features emphasis, such as specifications, standards, and performance, (c) absurd and meaningless statements, and (d) information of an educational nature.

Chapter 21

Aids and protection
for consumers

PURPOSE OF THE CHAPTER

If a consumer is to be a wise buyer and get the most from his income, he needs information to guide him in buying, and he needs protection. In this chapter we shall learn about many of the private and government sources of aid and protection.

You will find answers to these questions:

1. What are the types of information from private and business sources?
2. How may labels be used as guides?
3. What kind of protection do cities and states provide?
4. What protection is provided by the federal government?

A. Private sources of consumer protection

CONSUMER NEED FOR INFORMATION

In attempting to spend his money wisely for goods and services, a consumer encounters three problems. First, is the product or service

of such a nature that it adequately meets his needs? Second, how can he know the quality of the product or service? And, third, how can he be certain that the price is fair and reasonable? To solve these problems, the consumer needs a great deal of information about the product or service he is considering in order to protect himself from making poor choices and also from questionable and unethical practices on the part of sellers.

The consumer can help himself to make good choices and can avoid being influenced by misleading labeling, deceptive advertising, or questionable business practices by seeking information about the product or service he wants and then by using that information as a basis for making his decision. A wise consumer searches for information that will guide him in choosing the products he buys.

The consumer needs to be able to determine enough about the product to protect himself from unethical practice and from poor choice.

CONSUMER-SPONSORED SERVICES

Information about consumer products is sometimes difficult, if not impossible, for an individual to obtain. In some cases he does not have access to the information, and in other instances, obtaining the needed information requires investigating and testing which he usually cannot do. Because of this difficulty, agencies and organizations have been established whose primary purposes are to obtain and distribute product information to consumers.

Consumers' Research, Inc. Consumers' Research, Inc., is the outgrowth of what was originally a small club for the study of consumer goods. It is now a national organization, organized as a nonprofit corporation, with extensive laboratory and testing facilities. Subscribers are not members, but rather purchasers of periodical literature.

Sewing machines are tested at Consumers' Research to determine quality and value in performance so that ratings may be developed for the guidance of buyers.

The organization maintains a large staff of professional research and technical personnel who test and rate the efficiency of consumer products through scientific test methods; develop testing methods and procedures; advise educators in the economics of consumption; and provide consulting service on technical problems of consumers, government agencies, and others. One of the significant contributions of Consumers' Research has been the development of methods for testing costly consumer goods, such as washing machines, dryers, refrigerators, mowers, and mattresses. To guide buyers, Consumers' Research publishes monthly and annual reports on products.

Consumers Union of United States, Inc. Consumers Union is a nonprofit organization. Its purposes are: (1) to provide consumers with information and counsel relating to consumer goods and services, (2) to give information and assistance on all matters relating to the expenditure of family income, and (3) to initiate and to cooperate with individual and group efforts that seek to create and maintain acceptable living standards.

In addition to a large technical research staff employed in the laboratories of Consumers Union, part-time shoppers distributed widely over the country buy sample products which are sent to the laboratory for testing. Ratings of consumer products are based on laboratory tests, controlled use-tests, expert opinion or experience, or a combination of these factors. To guide buyers, Consumers Union publishes monthly and annual reports on tests of products.

The Council on Consumer Information. The Council on Consumer Information is a nonpartisan, nonprofit organization serving consumers primarily through the publication of a series of booklets dealing with issues that are vital to consumers. Typical titles are *Consumers*

Look at Fair Trade, What You Should Know About the Law of Estates, and *Consumers Look at Antitrust Laws.* In addition to the publication of pamphlets, the Council's activities include publishing a newsletter, serving as a clearinghouse for consumer information materials, and conducting an annual conference devoted to consumer problems.

CONSUMER PROTECTION BY PROFESSIONAL ASSOCIATIONS

Some of the associations comprised of professional people have as an objective the welfare of consumers. In some instances the activities to achieve this objective are legislative in nature; in other cases informational and educational materials are prepared and distributed.

American Home Economics Association. For more than 50 years the American Home Economics Association has been one of the most effective influences in the United States in promoting the education, welfare, and protection of consumers.

The Association supports legislation designed to protect the interests of consumers through the establishment of standards of quality and identity; provisions for informative labeling and informative advertising; prohibition of fraudulent practices and sale of harmful goods and services; and prohibition of restraints on trade which increase consumer prices.

Through the Consumer Interests Committee, the American Home Economics Association makes available a series of buying guides that are valuable to consumers.

American Medical Association. One aspect of the program of the American Medical Association of particular value to consumers is the improvement of the quality of medical products. The responsibility for testing medical products and apparatus is assigned to special committees and councils. The Association makes useful information available to medical societies and the general public through a monthly periodical known as *Today's Health.*

American Dental Association. The function of the Council on Dental Therapeutics, which was established by the American Dental Association, is to protect and inform the public in respect to dental products. The Council studies products that are claimed to have healing or curative qualities, which are referred to medically as *therapeutic* values.

Most of the products studied by the Council are used directly by the dentist or are prescribed by him in the treatment of diseases of the mouth. Upon investigation, a product may be accepted by the Council, which means that it meets certain standards with respect both to its composition and to the manner in which the product is advertised. A seal of acceptance may be used by the manufacturer of a product if it has been accepted by the Council.

Legal aid societies. Under the belief that getting justice should not depend upon one's ability to pay fees and hire a lawyer, organizations that are generally called *legal aid societies* or *legal aid organizations* have been formed throughout the country. These organizations are found principally in the larger cities. Sponsored by lawyers, they provide an organized method of handling cases for persons who cannot afford to obtain legal assistance.

People without money can get legal aid.

TESTING AND LABELING FOR CONSUMER PROTECTION

There are many business firms, stores, associations of business firms, and independent testing and certifying agencies that provide information for the guidance and protection of consumers. In many cases the products that are tested as to safety, quality, use, content, strength, or other characteristics may carry a label of approval or in some cases a guarantee as advertised.

Besides these well-recognized labels, many manufacturers and retail stores attach their private labels to merchandise to indicate the content, quality, care required in use, and warnings. By state and federal law these labels must be truthful. As will be learned later in this chapter, federal law requires certain specific labeling of such products as furs, fabric, drugs, cosmetics, and foods when sold across state lines.

SEALS AND LABELS FOR YOUR PROTECTION
(Look for these and other labels when buying)

LABELS OF INDEPENDENT OR ASSOCIATION LABORATORIES

American Institute of Laundering

May be found on fabrics, clothing, draperies, or bedding. The product must pass tests for shrinkage, color fastness, strength, and other requirements.

American Gas Association

May be found on gas appliances, such as stoves, ranges, heaters, dryers. The label certifies that the product meets standards.

Underwriters Laboratories, Inc.

May be found on any product where safety is involved, such as electrical, gas, or chemical. The product must meet standards of safety and performance.

United States Testing Company

May be found on any product and must pass tests of quality, construction, safety, and use.

LABELS OF CONSUMER MAGAZINES

Good Housekeeping—Parents' Magazine—McCall's

May be found on any product tested and approved by the magazine. The product must meet the standards set up by the magazine and may be guaranteed, commended, or accepted as indicated on the seal.

American Standards Association. The American Standards Association is a federation of more than 110 technical societies and trade associations and 2,300 companies. Its function is not to write standards but rather to provide a systematic means among its members for the development of American standards. Since 1918, when the Association was formed, more than 1,650 national standards have been developed. An example of standards from which consumers have benefited is the reduction of many different styles of bases for household electric bulbs to two or three. Similar standards apply to other items, many of which we use every day. Standards of quality as well as of size and type have also been developed.

National Canners Association. The National Canners Association has been responsible for setting up certain minimum standards for can sizes, fill, quality, and description of the product. Association members are encouraged to pack their products in accordance with these standards.

Better business bureaus. The better business bureaus were originally organized to improve advertising by the elimination of misleading advertising and unethical promotional schemes. The activities have expanded now to include investigations of unfair competition among distributors and unfair treatment of consumers.

Functions of better business bureaus

1. Elimination of causes of customer complaints against business by—
   a. Preventing unfair treatment.
   b. Promoting fair advertising and selling practices.
   c. Promoting informative advertising.
   d. Prosecuting for fraud.
2. Cooperation with educators and business to provide students with sound knowledge of the functions of our economic system.
3. Provision for adult education in matters pertaining to management of personal business affairs and understanding of the free-enterprise system.

Consumers can protect themselves from unfair business practices and from fraudulent schemes by consulting the local better business bureau. Consumers who have become the victims of unfair practices should report such incidents to the bureau so that other citizens may be protected. Many local better business bureaus publish booklets providing information for consumers.

Fact booklets of better business bureaus

National Consumer-Retailer Council, Inc. The National Consumer-Retailer Council is a nonprofit organization of consumer and retail organizations. The Council promotes adequate standards for consumer goods and encourages informative labeling and advertising.

Facts that everyone should know about consumer protection by private agencies

1. Several consumer-sponsored organizations provide informative and protective services, such as testing and rating of widely used consumer goods, and publishing newsletters and pamphlets on issues of vital interest to consumers.

2. Consumers derive benefits from the activities of professional organizations in the sponsorship of legislation, preparation of informative materials, and encouragement of informative labeling and advertising.

3. Many large retail stores and mail-order houses do research and testing of consumer goods. The results usually are made available to buyers through labels on the merchandise and special consumer reports.

4. Some trade associations have set up institutes for testing consumer items and for establishing standards to assure acceptable quality. Seals of approval and seals of acceptance are issued by a few of the trade associations for products meeting specified minimum standards.

5. Some business firms and business associations that provide services, such as dry cleaning, laundering, and lending money, assist consumers through the publication of consumer information.

B. Government sources of consumer protection

CITY AND STATE PROTECTION

The city and state governments provide information, services, inspections, and other forms of protection for consumers. Many cities have passed ordinances and states have passed laws to protect the health, safety, and rights of citizens. Common among these are regu· lations pertaining to sanitation, food handling, weights and measures, quality standards, safety, advertising, and trade practices.

The laws for consumer protection vary so widely among the states that it is possible to give here only illustrations of the subjects covered by the laws.

Illustrative subjects of state laws for consumer aid and protection

Many states have consumer laws and are considering additional ones on subjects such as:

1. Consumer loans and credit, savings and investments.
2. Solicitations for contributions to foundations and associations purporting to make significant contributions to society.
3. Wholesomeness, sanitation, and quality standards of foods both for consumption at home and in public eating places.
4. Health and personal welfare through licensing of medical personnel, licensing and inspection of private and public hospitals and nursing homes, use of drugs, and licensing and control of funeral homes and cemeteries.
5. Standards for and regulation of the sale of household goods, such as bedding, upholstery, and fabrics.
6. Sanitation—water supply, sewage disposal, etc.
7. Real estate zoning and restrictions.
8. Insurance—life, liability, and casualty.
9. Private and public education.
10. Recreation—movies, pools and beaches, travel, motels, etc.
11. Standards—weights and measures, quality grades.
12. Personal care—licensing and control of barber and beauty shops.

UNITED STATES DEPARTMENT OF COMMERCE

The primary purpose of the United States Department of Commerce is to serve business; however, in serving business, the Department also serves consumer interests. The setting of standards for business and the testing of products indirectly aid consumers. Encouraging the use of self-certifying labels makes useful information available to the consumer. These services to business and others that also help consumers are presented here.

National Bureau of Standards. Although the National Bureau of Standards is not a consumer service agency, it indirectly has a great influence on our lives daily. The Bureau does not test products nor recommend or endorse products, but it does provide a system of measurement standards for scientific and technological use. The Bureau has in its custody the standards of length, weight, and volume by which instruments for measurement of the inch, ounce, and pint may be calibrated. Radio wavelengths, the length of a second of time, and a degree of temperature are all measured by standards maintained by the Bureau.

The Bureau evaluates products for the United States government but not for the public. It performs tests upon instruments for scientific and research laboratories by which the accuracy of their measuring devices may be determined. The Bureau is the ultimate source for the accuracy and reliability of the thousands of standards used in the mass production of interchangeable parts, in the development of new products and devices, in the commercial exchange of goods, and in the measurement of scientific quantities. For example, the manufacturer of automotive engines depends upon standard measurements in producing cylinders and pistons of accurate sizes.

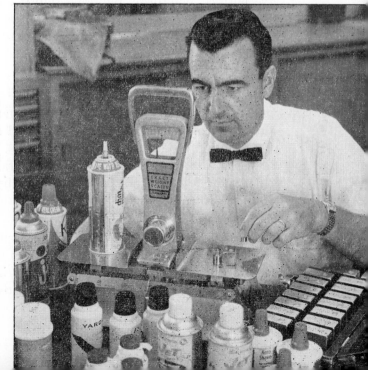

One of the many research projects conducted by the National Bureau of Standards involves the weighing of aerosol cans to establish effective test procedures for determining the net content of aerosol products.

National Bureau of Standards

Office of Technical Services. The Commodity Standards Division of the Office of Technical Services issues bulletins on current simplified practices pertaining to commodities ranging all the way from flashlight batteries to shoelaces. *Simplified practice* means reduction of excessive variety of manufactured products or of methods. Simplified practice is of great value to consumers because it not only reduces the number of sizes and designs of a commodity, such as lawn hose or tin cans for foods, but it also reduces the consumer price inasmuch as a manufacturer makes and a distributor stocks fewer sizes.

Another function of the Commodity Standards Division is the establishment of *Commercial Standards Recommendations*—standard quality requirements, methods of testing, rating, certification, and labeling of commodities. Manufacturers are encouraged to use self-certifying labels on their products. On these *self-certifying labels* the manufacturer states that his goods conform to commercial standards.

Other indirect consumer services. The Patent Office administers the laws pertaining both to patents and to trademarks. By protecting the rights of inventors, this office encourages the development of new products and processes. Trademarks are registered for the protection of business firms that have established a symbol by which a product is easily recognized by consumers.

The Office of Business Economics, although created primarily to serve business enterprise, publishes statistics useful to individuals on wages, costs, income, and debts. The Weather Bureau's forecasts and warnings are protections to consumers against loss due to extreme variations in temperature, rainfall, and wind.

UNITED STATES DEPARTMENT OF AGRICULTURE

The primary functions of the United States Department of Agriculture are concerned with the research and experimentation dealing with scientific production of farm products, farm management, and the agricultural education of people in rural areas. Services of particular value to all consumers are provided by two agencies, the Agricultural Marketing Service and the Agricultural Research Service.

Agricultural Marketing Service. The inspection program of the Agricultural Marketing Service, which is carried on continuously at many food-processing and manufacturing plants, has two purposes. First, federal inspection is provided to assure that the food is wholesome and

The Agricultural Marketing Service grades meats for quality and inspects for wholesomeness.

Swift & Company

sanitary, not contaminated by foreign materials, and is handled by disease-free workers. The second purpose of inspection is to assure that foods are of the quality indicated on the packages or containers. Quality is designated by a *grade,* such as A, B, or C.

Foods approved by the federal inspectors for wholesomeness and grade are so designated on the container or package.

Agricultural Research Service. The Agricultural Research Service makes studies and issues reports to aid in the improvement of farm products, to improve marketing of farm products, to suggest the best use of farm products, to improve cooking of foods, to improve storing of foods, and many other subjects of value to the farmer and the consumer.

The Agricultural Research Service is responsible for the enforcement of the federal meat inspection laws which assure not only the wholesomeness of meat and meat products but also the quality of meats as indicated by federal grades. The inspection begins with the animals before slaughter and continues through all stages in the meat-processing and packing plants. Meats and meat products sold or transferred for consumption across state lines must be federally inspected. Fish and seafood products are inspected by the Department of Interior.

DEPARTMENT OF HEALTH, EDUCATION, AND WELFARE

Several programs are administered by the Department of Health, Education, and Welfare that are of vital importance to consumers.

Public Health Service. The principal activity of the Public Health Service is the prevention of disease and the protection of health. The

409

major activities of the Public Health Service are to: (1) conduct research in medicine and in public health methods, (2) aid in development of hospitals, and (3) assist the states in the use of new knowledge for the control and prevention of disease.

Although the Public Health Service works primarily with organized groups of individuals and with state and local health authorities, its services indirectly are of great benefit to all people.

The Federal Food and Drug Administration. The primary function of the Federal Food and Drug Administration is to develop and enforce food and drug standards. Its activities are directed mainly toward promoting purity, standard strength, and truthful and informative labeling of essential commodities. The laws enforced by the Administration are among the most important of all federal laws for the protection of consumers.

Enforcement is carried out by inspection of factories for sanitary conditions and raw materials used, and through controls in processing, packaging, and labeling products for shipment. Imported foods and drugs are analyzed and examined after arrival in this country. Retail drugstores are kept under observation to prevent the selling of dangerous drugs without a doctor's prescription.

Federal Food, Drug, and Cosmetic Act. The purpose of the Federal Food, Drug, and Cosmetic Act is to insure that foods are safe, pure,

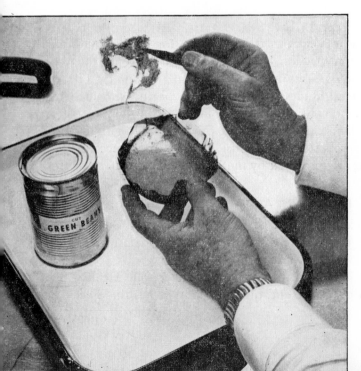

A Food and Drug scientist checks "stringless" green beans against requirements of the legal standards set by law "to promote honesty and fair dealing in the interest of consumers."

Food and Drug Administration

and wholesome, and made under sanitary conditions; that drugs and therapeutic devices are safe and effective for their intended uses; that cosmetics are safe and prepared from appropriate ingredients; and that all of these products are honestly and informatively labeled and packaged. The Act protects consumers by making it illegal to move or sell in interstate commerce goods that do not meet acceptable standards.

Food standards. Any food that is injurious to health is barred from interstate commerce. Unsafe amounts of harmful ingredients may not be added to any food product. The Act makes it mandatory that harmful pesticides used as sprays or dusts on edible fruits and vegetables shall be removed by washing before the food is marketed. The traces of the spray or pesticide remaining after washing may not exceed a specified amount. A recent amendment to the Food, Drug, and Cosmetic Act regulates the use of food additives that retard spoilage or modify flavor.

The Act permits the Food and Drug Administration to write a definition specifying the minimum standards for commonly named foods. Only foods meeting these standards can be marketed under that name. Foods that do not meet the standards, but that are clean and wholesome, may be marketed but must be labeled "substandard." Even these must meet all standards of sanitation and nutrition.

Drug standards. Proper use of drugs may be of great value to individuals; improper use may be highly dangerous. Except for standard home remedies as recommended for the home medicine cabinet by the Food and Drug Administration, an individual who is not medically trained should not be permitted to obtain drugs for indiscriminate use. Thus, the Food and Drug Administration has set up certain controls over drugs in regard to their sale.

For the protection of consumers, the sale of adulterated drugs is prohibited in interstate commerce. Drugs are considered to be adulterated when contaminated, impure, unsanitary, if the strength or quality differs from established standards, or if color has been added that has not been approved.

Drugs must carry labels giving in terms ordinarily understood such information as the name of the manufacturer or distributor; quantity in terms of weight, measure, or count; adequate directions for use and warnings against misuse; and complete description and amounts of ingredients. The label of drugs containing a habit-forming ingredient must carry the name of the ingredient and the statement, "Warning—may be habit forming."

Cosmetic standards. The term *cosmetic* applies to articles intended to be rubbed, poured, sprinkled, sprayed on, introduced into, or otherwise applied to the human body for cleansing (except soap), beautifying, or altering appearance.

Consumers are protected from contaminated, impure, or unsanitary cosmetics since the sale of such items is considered illegal in interstate commerce. Cosmetics are also considered adulterated and injurious to health if they or the containers in which they are packed contain a substance that is poisonous or injurious to users under ordinary conditions of use or if they contain coloring that has not been certified.

The label on cosmetics must not be false or misleading. It must identify the manufacturer and distributor; must contain an accurate statement of the quantity in terms of weight, measure, or count; and must contain easily understood statements pertaining to directions for use and cautions regarding possible injury from misuse.

Household products labeling. Some common household products, such as furniture polish, cleaning fluids, rust removers, and metal polishes, contain substances which, if improperly used, may cause illness or death. The Federal Hazardous Substances Labeling Act, passed in 1960, provides that labels must warn of the hazards of using products containing toxic substances, must contain directions for precautionary measures, and must describe antidotes or first-aid treatment in case of accident.

Other Food and Drug Acts. The Tea Importation, Import Milk, and Filled Milk Acts are concerned with the fitness of imported foods for human use. The Caustic Poison Act regulates the labeling, packaging, and handling of caustic and corrosive substances that are dangerous to life and health.

FEDERAL TRADE COMMISSION

The basic objective of the Federal Trade Commission, which was established in 1915, is the maintenance of free competitive business. The purpose of the Commission is to prevent the free-enterprise system from being injured by monopoly or by unfair or deceptive trade practices. The principal functions of the Commission relate to the consumer as well as to business.

Principal functions of Federal Trade Commission

1. Promote free and fair competition through prevention of price-fixing agreements, unfair methods of competition, and unfair or deceptive practices. (Sherman Antitrust Act, 1890; Clayton Act, 1914; and Federal Trade Commission Act, 1914.)

2. Prevent price discrimination among buyers and arrangements among business firms that result in lessening competition. (Robinson-Patman Act, 1936; Miller-Tydings Act, 1937; McGuire Act, 1952.)

3. Safeguard consuming public by preventing use of false and deceptive advertisements. (Federal Trade Commission Act, 1914; Wheeler-Lea Act, 1938.)

4. Enforce truthful labeling of wool and fur products. (Wool Products Labeling Act, 1939; Fur Products Labeling Act, 1951.)

5. Protect consumers by requiring that textile fiber products bear truthful labels that identify and disclose the fiber content. (The Textile Fiber Products Identification Act, 1960.)

6. Protect consumers from dangerously flammable wearing apparel or fabrics by preventing its sale. (Flammable Fabrics Act, 1953.)

7. Protect buyers from misrepresentation of real value and price of automobiles. (Automobile Information Disclosure Act, 1959.)

8. Protect consumers by preventing monopolies, mergers, and combinations of firms that lessen competition.

Promotion of free and fair competition. One of the principles upon which free enterprise is based is that there shall be unrestricted but fair competition among manufacturers who make commodities, among wholesalers and among retailers whose function is to get commodities to the people who want and need them, and among individuals in their occupational or professional pursuits. Unrestricted but fair competition forces us to strive continuously to improve our product or service, to develop better and more effective methods and procedures of doing our work, and to expect only a reasonable financial return for our efforts. Consumers benefit from competition by way of better products and services and lower prices.

Prevention of exclusive deals and price discrimination. Another principle upon which the concept of free enterprise is based is that goods or services should be offered to all purchasers at the same price, allowances being made for differences in costs due to quantity, method and place of delivery, and specifications. Selling goods on the condition that the buyer promises not to make purchases from the seller's competitors or that he will purchase all future requirements of similar commodities from the seller, substantially lessens competition. Such agreements would restrain trade, and in the long run, be detrimental to the consumer.

The Robinson-Patman Act was passed in 1936 to prevent such agreements in restraint of trade. One of the purposes of this law is to prevent the seller from giving unusual discounts to one customer while requiring another to pay the standard price.

Fair-trade laws. Under the provisions of the antitrust laws, agreements between a manufacturer and a wholesaler or retailer to fix retail prices were held to be in restraint of trade and considered to be acts signifying unfair competition. In 1931, however, California passed a law that made it possible for manufacturers to establish the retail prices of their products. Many other states passed similar laws, all of which were clearly in contradiction to the purposes of the Sherman Antitrust Act. Recognizing the conflict between the state laws and the Sherman Act, Congress passed the Miller-Tydings Act in 1937 which in effect made the state fair-trade laws valid.

Provisions of fair-trade laws. The state laws permitting a manufacturer to set the retail price of his product are popularly known as the *fair-trade laws.* Most of them contained a provision whereby if a manufacturer and one retailer had an agreement as to the retail price of an article, the agreement was binding on all other retailers in the state even though they had not entered into a price agreement with the manufacturer. In practice this meant that if an appliance manufacturer entered into agreement with one retailer in a state to sell a coffee maker for $29.95, all other retailers would be obligated to sell at the same price. Thus, competition among retailers on the prices of articles for which there were fair-trade agreements virtually disappeared.

The fair-trade laws are clearly not compatible with a free market system. Discount stores and others have ignored fair-trade laws, and there have been many lawsuits, both to maintain prices and to cut prices established under fair-trade agreements and laws. The effect of and the future of fair-trade laws is in doubt.

Arguments pro and con on fair-trade laws. Many arguments prevail in favor of and against price-fixing agreements. Some of the principal arguments are listed on page 415.

The fair-trade issue is of vital importance to consumers. A solution agreeable to all interested parties has not been reached.

Control of advertising. The first regulations pertaining to advertising were concerned with "unfair methods of competition" that would be damaging to an advertiser's competitors. In response to public opinion that the interests of consumers should also be protected in

---

Arguments in favor of a fair-trade law

1. Eliminates unethical and ruthless price cutting to force a competitor out of business.
2. Protects consumers from monopoly practices by giving small retailers a chance to compete with the large distributors.
3. May reduce retail prices of some articles.
4. Protects consumers from misleading and hidden merchandising practices, such as that of discount houses, who sometimes, in pricing an article, do not include delivery and installation costs.
5. Results in better quality merchandise at lower costs because "cutthroat competition" is eliminated.
6. Protects the trademarks and goodwill of a manufacturer.

Arguments against a fair-trade law

1. Contradicts the basic principles of antitrust laws.
2. Violates free enterprise principles of open competition.
3. Protects the inefficient merchant by keeping his prices up.
4. Denies consumers the benefits of lower prices resulting from price competition among retailers.
5. Encourages monopolistic trend.
6. Reduces freedom of retailers in determining their own price policies.
7. Encourages discount houses and other retailers to eliminate or greatly reduce services, such as delivery, instruction as to use and operation, and installation.

---

advertising, the Wheeler-Lea Act, an amendment to the Federal Trade Commission Act, was passed in 1938. The following provisions of the amendment are significant to the consumer:

1. In general, all unfair methods of competition in commerce, as well as unfair or deceptive acts or practices, are declared unlawful.

2. It is unlawful to publish or distribute false advertising in order to induce purchases of foods, drugs, devices, or cosmetics.

3. Publishers, radio broadcasters, advertising agencies, and other advertising media are relieved from liability for advertising

statements, unless they refuse to furnish the Commission with the name and address of the manufacturer, packer, distributor, seller, or advertising agency that caused the distribution of the advertisements.

4. False advertising is defined as advertising that is "misleading in a material respect," including the failure to reveal facts as to consequences that may result from the use of the advertised commodities.

An illustration of deceptive or false advertising would be to state or imply that a pain-killing drug, such as aspirin, will cure a decayed tooth when it really does nothing more than relieve the pain which is a symptom. Another case of deception in advertising is to state or imply that a fabric, such as cotton, will not shrink. Statements that cotton will not shrink more than a certain percentage are permissible. In examining thousands of advertisements annually, the Federal Trade Commission finds relatively few that are actually deceptive or false.

To supplement the federal laws, there are state laws that represent barriers against deceptive and fraudulent advertising. Many years ago *Printers' Ink* magazine prepared a model statute for state control of advertising, the latest revision of which was made in 1945. This model statute, which has been adopted in 43 of the 50 states in either complete or modified form, has had a good influence in reducing deceptive and misleading advertising.

Wool and fur products labeling. Proper, informative labeling of wool and fur products has been made compulsory for the protection of consumers. The Federal Trade Commission was given jurisdiction over the Wool Products Labeling Act of 1939 and the Fur Products Labeling Act passed in 1951. Under these laws, each product made of wool or of fur must be identified with a stamp, tag, or label giving specific information as to the kind, name, and grade of the wool or fur used in the product.

A *wool product* is any product made wholly or in part of new, unused wool, reprocessed wool, or reused wool. The label for such a product must indicate the class of wool used (such as kind and whether reused or reprocessed), the percentage of the fibers that are actual wool, and whether it is loaded or weighted in any way. The name of the manufacturer, distributor, or retailer must also be on the label.

A *fur product* is any article made in whole or in part of new or used fur. *Used fur* is a term applied to fur in any form which has been worn or used by an ultimate consumer. *Waste fur* refers to mats or plates made from ears, throats, or scrap pieces which have been severed from the animal pelt.

Protection from flammable fabrics. Some synthetic fabrics are highly flammable and burn with an intense heat. They are highly dangerous when used in wearing apparel. The Flammable Fabrics Act, passed in 1953, prohibits the manufacture for sale and the sale of any article of wearing apparel made of fabric that does not meet the Commercial Standard for Flammability of Clothing Textiles prepared by the Commercial Standards Division of the Department of Commerce. The enforcement of the Flammable Fabrics Act is under the Federal Trade Commission.

Automobile Information Disclosure Act. The Disclosure Act of 1959 is intended to prevent misrepresentation by dealers of the value of the cars they are selling and the trade-in allowances they are giving.

Complaints against padded prices and exaggerated trade-in allowances led to passage of the Automobile Information Disclosure Act of 1959.

Padded prices and exaggerated trade-in allowances have been common complaints against some automobile dealers in recent years. With full knowledge of the suggested retail price in his possession, the consumer can now make a more accurate appraisal of the deal he is getting.

Identification of content of textile fiber products. The Textile Fiber Products Identification Act, which became effective in 1960, protects consumers by requiring that textile fiber products bear a label identifying each fiber by the name for it that was approved by the Federal Trade Commission. The identification label must also give the percentage of the fiber, by weight, in the piece of textile fabric. This act was made necessary because of the use of many synthetic fibers

Federal Government Aids and Protection to the Consumer

Agency	Areas of Aid or Protection
Council of Economic Advisers	All economic problems
Department of Agriculture	Nutrition studies Home management Food inspection Food standards
Department of Commerce	Testing Standards
Department of Health, Education, Welfare	Child health Food, drug, cosmetic control Public health
Department of Interior	Fish standards Fish inspection
Department of Justice	Enforces federal laws
Department of Labor	Price information
Department of the Treasury	Alcohol and tobacco
Federal Aviation Agency	Safety standards
Federal Communications Commission	Licenses and rates
Federal Power Commission	Services and rates
Federal Trade Commission	False advertising Deceptive practices Fraud Labeling
Federal Housing Administration	Insures loans
Interstate Commerce Commission	Rates, services, safety on railroads, buses, trucks, boats
Post Office Department	Fraud, postal savings
Securities and Exchange Commission	Fraud and trading regulations
Veterans Administration	Insured loans
President's Committee on Consumer Interests	To consider any consumer problem

State Aids and Protection to the Consumer

The following states have specific agencies for the protection of the consumer: California, Connecticut, Illinois, Kansas, Maryland, Massachusetts, Michigan, Missouri, Minnesota, New Jersey, New York, Ohio, Washington, Wisconsin.

to which manufacturers have given technical names which have little meaning to consumers.

OTHER PUBLIC AGENCIES

United States Department of Labor. The Department of Labor has responsibility for the promotion of the welfare of wage earners, improvement of their working conditions, and advancement of their opportunities for profitable employment, all of which are of interest to consumers. The Bureau of Labor Statistics collects and publishes regularly data in regard to retail prices, wholesale prices, employment, wages, hours of work, and cost of living.

United States Post Office Department. For the protection of individuals and business firms, postal laws declare it illegal to use the mails for the promotion of lotteries and for sending materials pertaining to schemes to defraud. Explosives, poisons, firearms, intoxicants, and certain narcotics also are not mailable. It is a criminal offense to place in the mails letters of extortion containing threats to injure the reputation of any person or to accuse him of a crime. It is illegal to send through the mails indecent, obscene, defamatory (false or damaging statements about a person) or subversive (damaging to the security of the United States) matter. Violations of postal laws carry heavy penalties.

Federal and state regulation of securities. Federal legislation administered by the Securities and Exchange Commission protects investors against malpractice in the issuance and sale of stocks and bonds in interstate commerce. These securities laws require public disclosure of information that will enable prospective investors to make a realistic appraisal of the securities and the possible risks in their purchase. Registration of issues of stocks and bonds is required before sales may be made.

Many states also have laws commonly known as *blue-sky laws* that apply to the issuance and sale of securities.

President's Committee. The President's Committee on Consumer Interests consists of representatives of ten governmental agencies and private citizens appointed by the President of the United States. The duty of this committee is to advise the President and governmental agencies about methods of aiding and protecting the consumer and to suggest any new laws that are desirable.

Facts everyone should know about consumer aids and protection provided by government agencies

1. Informative and protective services for consumers are provided by three levels of government agencies—local, state, and federal.

2. Through the federal government, business and consumer statistics, weather reports, and other information are made available to consumers, producers, and distributors.

3. Several agencies of the federal government conduct extensive research to discover new truths and procedures that will assist consumers.

4. Enforcement of standards and regulations insuring purity, potency, and truthful and informative labeling of drugs and cosmetics protects consumers.

5. The federal government promotes free and fair competition among business firms and among individuals, thus assuring better products and reasonable prices.

6. The consuming public receives protection from false and deceptive advertising.

■ QUESTIONS ON THE TEXT

1. What kind of information does a consumer need about the product or service he is considering?

2. How can a consumer avail himself of the services of Consumers' Research, Inc., and of the Consumers Union of the United States, Inc.?

3. How does the Council on Consumer Information assist consumers?

4. How has the American Home Economics Association protected the welfare and improved the status of the consumer?

5. What does "acceptance" of a dental product by the Council on Dental Therapeutics mean?

6. In most large cities how can a person without money obtain legal advice or assistance?

7. (a) Name some labels of independent testing organizations or associations that are guides to quality.

   (b) Name some labels of magazines that are guides to quality.

8. In what way is the work of the American Standards Association of benefit to consumers?

9. How do the better business bureaus help protect consumers?

10. Give examples of state and local protection of consumers.

11. How does the Department of Commerce serve the consumer?

12. How do consumers benefit from the work of the National Bureau of Standards?

13. Explain the direct and indirect benefits to consumers from the activities of the Commodity Standards Division of the Office of Technical Services.

14. Which agency of the federal government is responsible for the prevention of disease and the protection of health?
15. How does the Federal Food, Drug, and Cosmetic Act protect the consumer?
16. What is the purpose of the Federal Trade Commission?
17. What is meant by a fair-trade agreement and how does it operate?
18. How is the buyer of (a) a wool product and (b) a fur product protected from misleading information?
19. What is the intent of the Automobile Information Disclosure Act?
20. What protection for businesses and individuals does the United States Post Office Department provide?

▪ QUESTIONS FOR DISCUSSION

1 Give an example of how you need information to help you buy.
2. Some manufacturers oppose such organizations as Consumers' Research, Inc., and Consumers Union, Inc., whereas others approve them. How do you account for the differences in attitude?
3. Why do you think that some manufacturers organize an association and use a seal indicating that products of the members of that association meet certain requirements?
4. Some people assert that the scientific laboratories maintained by publishers of periodicals are operated for the benefit of manufacturers and therefore render little service to buyers. Do you think this assertion is true? Why?
5. Suppose a door-to-door salesman calls on you. You would like to obtain information as to his reliability and that of his company. From what source might you be able to obtain help or advice?
6. How do the laboratories of the National Board of Fire Underwriters save money for all of us?
7. In what way does the standardization program of the National Bureau of Standards help you as a buyer?
8. (a) How do the grading and inspection services of the Department of Agriculture aid the consumer?
   (b) How do you as an individual benefit from these services?
9. Discuss the arguments for and against fair-trade laws from the viewpoint of (a) the consumer, (b) the retail merchant, and (c) the manufacturer.
10. Why is it necessary to have state laws that control deceptive and fraudulent advertising?
11. Assume that you buy a product sold in interstate commerce on the basis of an advertisement in a magazine and find that the article does not conform to the quality or the description in the advertisement. What means of protection have you?

▪ PROBLEMS TO SOLVE

1. Prepare a complete list of the products that are advertised in a current issue of some popular magazine. Opposite the name of each product indicate whether there is any seal, label, certified test, or testimonial used to indicate the standard of quality of the product. Indicate the specific proof that is given.

2. Make a list of food products and drugs that you find bearing seals or labels of approval. Indicate the particular seal or label for each product. If you find any seal or label with which you are not acquainted, inquire about the conditions under which it is awarded.

3. Analyze a recent copy of *Consumer Bulletin* and one of *Consumer Reports*. What special contributions do these publications make to the consumer? Prepare a one-page paper on the nature of the contents of these publications and their value to consumers.

4. In compliance with the terms of the Automobile Information Disclosure Act, a model of a new "compact" car carries a suggested retail price of $2,300. (a) A dealer offers to sell this car for $2,200 and will allow $1,200 for the trade-in. (b) Another dealer offers to sell this car for $2,300 and will allow $1,250 for the trade-in. (c) A third dealer offers to sell the car for $2,250 and will allow $1,225 for the trade-in. Which is the best deal for the consumer?

▪ COMMUNITY PROBLEMS AND PROJECTS

1. Read a daily newspaper for one week; clip the advertisements of the "special bargains" that appear. What kind of aid would be available to help you determine whether or not each of these "specials" is an outstanding bargain? Analyze one or two of the offers to determine the factors one would need to consider before purchasing the product.

2. Invite a representative from one of your local daily or weekly newspapers to discuss with the class the policies of the paper regarding (a) accepting advertising, and (b) publication of articles relative to product information of value to consumers.

3. Prepare a list of laws and regulations in your state that in some way protect consumers. Examples to help start the list are: laws governing small loans and credit, sanitation laws, and laws for the licensing and control of barbers.

4. (a) Go to a hardware, drugstore, or the small appliance department of a large department store, and make a list of ten items that are sold under the fair-trade laws, and ten items that are not sold under the fair-trade laws; be sure to list the selling price for each item.

   (b) Go to another similar store and check the prices for the same items.

   (c) Compare the lists and explain why some prices are the same and some are different.

Chapter 22

Legal relations important to consumers

PURPOSE OF THE CHAPTER

Many of our economic problems involve dealings with other people, and many of these dealings involve legal relations. There are laws that guide and protect us in our everyday dealings. In this chapter you will learn about the common legal problems of consumers.

You will find answers to these questions:

1. Why do you need legal advice?
2. What are the essential elements of a contract?
3. Can a child be held responsible for debts?
4. Must a contract be in writing?

A. The contract

WHEN TO USE LEGAL ADVICE

In this world of specialization it is sound practice for one to go to a doctor when he is ill. Likewise, it is sound business procedure to

obtain competent legal advice on important problems. Some of the problems on which an individual should consult a lawyer are the writing of an important contract, the writing of a will, protecting or gaining one's rights, and obtaining protection against lawsuits. In selecting a lawyer, one should be careful to avoid the so-called shyster who is often too eager to take a case or who solicits a case. It is a practice among reputable lawyers to wait for the client to request legal counsel. Only lawyers who are members of the local or state bar association should be considered. Select your lawyer with the same care that you would select your physician or dentist.

If you ask a lawyer a question, his answer will be given to you in what he calls an *opinion*. Most lawyers will never state definitely what the answer is because it depends upon many circumstances. What appears to be true may not be true when all the facts are known. For example, two judges in different courts, giving decisions on what may appear to be identical sets of circumstances, may give completely opposite decisions. Sometimes these decisions are reversed by higher courts.

Although many things in law appear to be definite, it must be borne in mind that any statement in the field of law cannot be com-

---

Common legal questions

Here are some common legal questions.

THE ANSWER TO EACH OF THESE QUESTIONS IS "NO":

1. Is a contract binding if it is entered into under pressure or a threat?
2. Is a contract binding if it involves breaking the law?
3. Is an agreement of a boy fourteen years of age to buy a bicycle binding?
4. Is it necessary to sign a written order for the purchase of a suit of clothes in order for the contract to be binding?
5. Are you obligated to return or pay for merchandise sent to you that has not been ordered?

THE ANSWER TO EACH OF THESE QUESTIONS IS "YES":

1. Is a contract binding if it is signed without being read?
2. Is a contract binding if you sign it just to get rid of a persistent salesman?
3. Is a contract binding if you misunderstand part of it?
4. Is an installment sale agreement a contract?
5. Must a contract to purchase real estate be in writing?

pletely definite without knowing all the circumstances. Therefore, the statements in this chapter are general statements of law and represent additional reasons why in many cases you should consult a lawyer.

WHAT IS A CONTRACT?

A *contract* is an agreement between two or more competent parties that creates an obligation enforceable by law. If one of the parties does not carry out his part of the agreement, the other party may resort to court action.

When you buy goods on account in a store, you make a contract with the store to pay the cost of the merchandise. If you leave shoes in a repair shop to be repaired, a contract is made on the part of the repairman to repair the shoes and on your part to pay the prescribed charges. When you rent a house, you enter into a contract to pay the rent; and the owner obligates himself to let you have possession of the property. Many other situations that involve contracts exist in everyday life. Buying life insurance, buying fire insurance, shipping merchandise, or accepting a position, all involve contracts.

When the repairman accepts the shoes, he implies that he will repair them; the customer implies that payment will be made.

The basis of a contract is an agreement between the parties. But not all agreements are contracts because some agreements do not have all the essentials of contracts. Ashworth agrees to go hunting with Stillwell; but if Stillwell changes his mind and decides not to go, he is not breaking a contract. On the other hand, if Ashworth and Stillwell make arrangements to go on a hunting trip together and arrange for a professional guide to provide them with hunting equipment, food, and lodging, they have entered into a contract with the guide. They are both responsible to the guide for carrying out the contract or for settling it in some satisfactory manner if they change their minds. It is also quite possible that a court would decide that there was a contract if both or either had made certain preparations and spent any money for mutual benefit.

Elements of a contract

1. There must be offer and acceptance.
2. The parties must be competent.
3. The purpose or subject of the agreement must be legal.
4. There must be a consideration.
5. The agreement must be in proper legal form.

UNIFORM COMMERCIAL CODE

Our laws are not exactly the same in all states; but under the Uniform Commercial Code (law), which has been adopted by most of the states, the laws relating to sales contracts are essentially the same. The discussions in this chapter follow the new code.

ELEMENT NO. 1: OFFER AND ACCEPTANCE (MUTUAL ASSENT)

Mrs. Burton bought a stove and had it sent out to her home. She used it for two weeks; and when the store asked for payment, she insisted on returning the stove although she had no complaint as to its performance. She insisted that she had never accepted it because she had not paid for it. Courts would undoubtedly hold that there was an offer and an acceptance. On the other hand, if she had ordered it sent out on approval, an acceptance would not have been indicated until she had signified her approval or had kept the stove an unreasonable length of time without expressing dissatisfaction or a willingness to return it.

In every contract there is an *offer* and an *acceptance*. For example, one person offers a one-acre tract of land for sale at a price of $1,000; another person accepts the offer, therefore promising to pay the price asked. There was *mutual assent* between the two parties; one made the offer, the other accepted the offer.

Under the principles of law, it is not considered that there is mutual assent unless both parties have freely, intentionally, and apparently assented to the same thing.

The essential characteristics of an offer are: (a) the proposal must be definite; (b) the proposal must be made with the intention that the

THIS AGREEMENT is made on May 10, 1966, between James A. Wiley, 3144 Beechwood Drive, Columbus, Ohio, the party of the first part, and Harry L. Segal, 5967 Rosetree Lane, Columbus, Ohio, the party of the second part.

The party of the first part agrees to install aluminum triple-track storm windows in the home of the party of the second part at 5967 Rosetree Lane, Columbus, Ohio, by June 10, 1966, in accordance with the specifications attached hereto. In consideration of which the party of the second part agrees to pay the party of the first part $385.75 upon the satisfactory completion of the work.

James A. Wiley

Harry L. Segal

A contract

offeror (person making the offer) be bound by it; (c) the proposal must be communicated by words or actions to the *offeree* (the one to whom it is made). If you were to offer to work for an employer for "all that you are worth," the offer would be too indefinite to be the basis of an enforceable agreement. If an offer is made in obvious or apparent jest, or in disgust or anger, it is not a real offer. If someone in jest says that he would give a thousand dollars to see the expression on a friend's face when he opens a comic birthday greeting, the offer is not real. Or, if the motor in your new automobile will not start, it would not be a real offer if in disgust you say, "I would take $5 for it." Most advertisements are not offers. They usually merely invite the prospective customer to buy or to make an offer to buy. If you walk into a store and find goods on display with a price marked on them, you might think the goods are offered for sale at that price; but the law holds that price tags on merchandise merely indicate a willingness to consider an offer made by a buyer on those terms.

An offer for the purchase of goods may be accepted in any way that is reasonable. For example, the seller may ship the goods or promise to do so promptly.

As in the case of an offer, the acceptance must be indicated by some word or act. For instance, you cannot be bound against your will by an offeror who states in his offer, "If I do not hear from you by ten o'clock, October 10, I shall consider that you have accepted this offer." The acceptance must also be made by the party to whom the offer was made. If someone has made an offer to you and you tell a friend about it, the person who made the offer does not have to recognize an acceptance by your friend. The acceptance may be in the form of a definite promise that completes the mutual agreement, or it may be made in the form of some act.

When an offer is made by mail, the contract is formed when the acceptance is mailed.

A definite and reasonable expression of acceptance is legal and binding if it is within a reasonable time. It may also include additional conditions not in the original offer.

As a general rule, when offers are made by letter with the acceptance to be made by mail, the offer is considered to be accepted when the acceptance is deposited in the mail. Likewise, if the acceptance is to be made by telegram, the agreement is considered to be completed when the message is given to the telegraph company.

Acceptance is indicated by:
1. Specific indication that the buyer accepts the goods, or
2. Use of the goods, or
3. Retention of the goods for an unreasonable length of time.

Terminating an offer. An offer can be terminated in many ways. It may be terminated at a definite time stated in the offer. If no definite time is stated, the offer will be terminated in a reasonable amount of time, which often has to be determined by the court if a dispute arises. Definite refusal of the offer or a *counteroffer* (a new offer by the person to whom the original offer was made) will terminate the original offer. Unless it is specified that an offer must be accepted just as made, it may be accepted and at the same time propose new or additional terms without bing considered a rejection if the offeror assents to the changes. The withdrawal or revocation of the offer before it is accepted is a clear termination. Other unusual circumstances that terminate offers are death or insanity of the offeror.

Ordinarily, if an offer is made for a specified length of time, it may still be revoked before the expiration of that time if proper notice is given of the withdrawal. However, if a general offer is made to the public, such as a reward published in a newspaper, it is in effect until it is withdrawn in the same way that it was offered.

Keeping an offer open. Offers are sometimes kept open for specified periods of time by a special contract that is known as an *option*. If the offeror receives cash or something of value as an inducement to keep an offer open for a certain specified time, the offer cannot be withdrawn for the period of time covered by the option. This is an important type of offer that is used in large transactions. For example, a person considering buying a home or a company considering buying a new factory would want time to consider the matter with the assurance that if a decision were made to buy the property, the original price quotation would be accepted.

Options are very useful in many types of negotiations leading up to a sale. It is important, however, that an option be in writing and signed by the person granting it.

An offer in writing by a merchant to sell goods and to keep the offer open for a reasonable time (not to exceed three months) cannot be revoked and does not require a consideration.

ELEMENT NO. 2: COMPETENT PARTIES

The question of competence of parties determines who is legally qualified to make contracts. Anyone who is not otherwise prevented by law from making enforceable agreements may make a contract. Intoxicated persons and insane persons are not competent to contract. The reason for making voidable the contracts entered into by these persons is obvious: it is considered that they are not capable of exercising their own judgment. In certain states there are special laws applying to contracts that may be made by convicts, foreigners, or married women, but there is a wide variation in these laws. In many cases *minors* (those who are not of legal age) are not competent to contract and may not be required by law to carry out agreements. There are, however, some exceptions to this rule, such as contracting for necessaries. When a minor makes an agreement with an adult, the adult is required to fulfill the contract if it is legal; but if the minor chooses to *rescind* (cancel) the contract, he can, in most cases, escape his responsibility. When a minor reaches the minimum age at which he may make a contract, he is said to have attained the *age of majority*.

Usually contracts made by a minor are *voidable* (that is, they may be broken) by the minor. He may break them while he is still a minor or within a reasonable time after he becomes of age. If he reaffirms the agreement after he becomes of age, it becomes a binding contract. The voidability of a contract applies generally whether it has been fully performed or only partially performed.

The Ridge Hardware Store accepted a properly signed order for a bicycle for $40 from Bob Hansen, age 12. When the bicycle arrived from the factory, the price had risen and the dealer insisted on getting $50 for the bicycle or canceling the contract. He argued that the original agreement was not binding because Bob Hansen was a minor and was, therefore, incompetent to contract. This agreement is binding, however, on the dealer. Because he is a minor, Bob could cancel

Although minors may void contracts to buy, they are, however, held responsible when they contract for necessaries.

Ewing Galloway

the contract if he wished. A situation such as this and many others are involved in contracts with minors and certain other types of people.

Age of majority (becoming of age)
(Minimum legal age to make a contract)

18 years for women and 21 years for men in Arkansas, Idaho, Illinois, Montana, Nevada, North Dakota, Oklahoma, South Dakota, and Utah
18 years for men and women in Kentucky
19 years for men and women in Alaska
20 years for men and women in Hawaii
21 years for men and women in all other states

A minor who acquires reasonable necessaries is obligated to pay the reasonable value of his purchases. A merchant who furnishes jewelry, tobacco, or sporting equipment to an ordinary minor usually cannot collect payment, but one who furnishes necessary clothes or food can collect if the amounts charged are reasonable and the goods are needed and are actually delivered. On the other hand, if all these necessaries of life are provided by the parents, any contract made by the child to obtain them is voidable. A contract by a poor child to buy expensive clothing beyond his means would be voidable also.

Because contracts made by minors for some things are voidable, some merchants ask the parents of the minor to *countersign* the contract, thus confirming it. A practice that is increasing is for department stores to open charge accounts for minors, permitting the minors to buy on account in a manner similar to adults. In many of these instances, the store asks the parents of the minors to countersign the agreement between the store and the minors.

Howard Martin, age 20, signed a contract for the purchase of an automobile. The dealer questioned him as to his age, and he assured the dealer that he was 21 years old on his last birthday. When the dealer notified him that he was ready to deliver the car, Howard refused to accept it, asserting that he misrepresented his age at the time of making the contract and, therefore, he could not be held responsible. In some states a minor is held responsible for his agreement if he deliberately misrepresents his age; but if a child, age 12, were to misrepresent his age, the dealer might find it difficult to hold the child responsible because of his obvious young age. The reason for this principle of law is that a minor who misrepresents his age places the other party in an unfair position, particularly if the minor is close to the age of majority. However, it is assumed that if a much younger child misrepresents his age, the other party would enter into the agreement knowing that the person is a minor.

Some other examples in regard to competent persons

1. A person who cannot read is bound by a contract if it has been read to him and is understood by him before signing.
2. A person who cannot read or write, but who signs a contract with an "X" or other symbol is bound by the contract if it has been read to him and if he understands it.
3. Generally, a person who has made a contract while a minor may repudiate or affirm the contract when he becomes of age, but failure to repudiate it generally makes the contract binding.

ELEMENT NO. 3: LEGAL PURPOSE

The purpose for which a contract is formed must not be contrary to law or to the interests of society. In other words, the subject of the bargain must be legal. This is referred to as *legal bargain*. In fact, in most cases, when the purpose of the contract is not legal, there is not even a contract. Neither party can be held under the agreement.

Examples of illegal bargains are those involving agreements to steal or to accept stolen goods. Anyone buying stolen goods does not get a valid title to the goods. They must be returned to the rightful owner if the ownership can be proved. All agreements to wager or gamble are illegal except in the cases of certain states in which betting on horse and dog racing has been legalized. For instance, if you make a bet with somebody, you have not made a legal contract; but in a state where betting on horse races is legal, your placing of a bet is a legal contract.

In all states there are so-called *usury laws* that establish the highest contract rate of interest that may be charged. If a contract is made and interest is charged at a higher rate than that stated by law, the contract is an illegal contract. Exceptions to these laws are the small loan regulations that permit licensed small loan organizations to charge higher rates.

It is always illegal to enter into any contract to obstruct justice, such as an agreement to give false testimony or to avoid giving testimony.

Generally speaking, when a certain type of business or professional man is subject to licensing, any contract made with one who is unlicensed may be void. For instance, in most cities electricians and plumbers are licensed. If you make an agreement with an unlicensed electrician or plumber, the agreement may not be a legal contract.

In almost all cases, agreements that unreasonably restrain trade are void. Examples of such agreements that are void are those involving control of prices, limiting production, creating a monopoly, creating an artificial scarcity, or causing unreasonable injury to competitors or to consumers.

ELEMENT NO. 4: CONSIDERATION

A contract usually is an agreement whereby one person agrees to do something and another person agrees to do something else in return. What either party agrees to do in return for that which was promised by the other is known as *consideration*. For example, an automobile dealer and you may enter into a contract for you to buy an automobile in which you promise to pay for it and the dealer promises to transfer ownership of it to you in return. Every legal contract must have consideration.

In the case of a sale of goods, a change agreeable to both parties can be made in the contract without additional consideration being required.

J. R. Jackson, a wealthy member of Summit Hills Country Club, offered to give his old set of golf clubs to a caddy at the end of the golf season. He changed his mind and did not give them to the caddy. The caddy insisted that a contract had been made. Mr. Jackson insisted that there was no consideration on the part of the caddy in the nature of goods, money, services, or promises. If the caddy can prove that the clubs were promised him for caddy service or any other favor to Mr. Jackson, he probably can consider that there is a contract; but in the absence of such proof, there is no contract. It is simply in the nature of a promise to make a gift. A gift without a consideration is not regarded as a contract.

Ordinarily the promise made in an agreement is not enforceable unless something of value is received for the promise. The value may consist of goods, money, services, refraining from doing something that one has a right to do, or giving up a privilege. A common example of a consideration is the down payment made to a merchant when an agreement has been reached for the delivery of a piece of furniture. When one takes a job, the employer promises to pay for the services and the employee promises to perform the duties required in the job. A landlord may pay a tenant a certain sum of money to give up his lease and vacate the property. The amount paid is the consideration for the giving up of a legal right on the part of the tenant if the lease has not expired.

ELEMENT NO. 5: PROPER LEGAL FORM

To qualify as legal contracts certain agreements must be made in the form specified by law. Most contracts, however, are informal and very simple. Every day you enter into informal contracts. It may be as simple as placing on your tray in the school cafeteria the food you have selected from the variety that was offered and accepting the offer by paying the amount the cashier requests. Other contracts, such as the purchase of real estate, must be formal.

Oral and written contracts. Generally, there are two main types of contracts: (a) *oral* and (b) *written*. Ordinarily, oral evidence of a sale is sufficient when the price is less than $500. If the requirements are not met, the oral agreement to sell goods is legal, but is voidable by either party. It may be carried out by mutual agreement. If it is clear and evident that the parties reached an agreement, the contract is binding, even if some elements are missing, such as the date, the exact method of fulfilling the contract, or a price to be determined later.

The essentials of a written contract are:

1. The date and place of the agreement.
2. The names and the identifications of the parties entering into the agreement.
3. A statement of the purposes of the contract.
4. A statement of the money, the services, or the goods given in consideration of the agreement (an act to be performed, refraining from any act, or the relinquishing of a privilege by a party, also consideration).
5. The signatures of *both* parties or the signature of legal agents.
6. In the case of some contracts witnesses are required, and in such cases the witnesses must sign in accordance with the provisions of the law.

Contracts for labor and materials generally need not be in writing. Contracts for medical or dental services need not be in writing regardless of the amount involved. A contract for the painting of a house

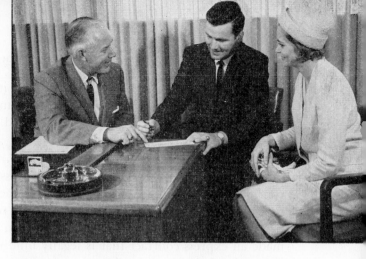

When a written contract is required by law, the contract signed by both parties constitutes evidence of their agreement.

Underwood Reserve Illustrations, Inc.

need not be in writing, although it should be to avoid any misunderstanding.

Mr. and Mrs. Waltham bought a house from the Oval Realty Company for $10,000 on an oral agreement. This is not a regular contract because the law requires that agreements of this type must be in writing.

A great many contracts do not have to be in writing because the offer, acceptance, payment, and delivery of goods often occur within a short space of a few seconds or a few minutes. In general, a contract should be written instead of oral when there is any chance for misunderstanding or disagreement between the parties and when a written contract is required by law. When a written contract is required by law, evidence of an agreement signed by one party binds that party to the agreement, but not the other until he signs.

A *bill of sale* is a written contract with which many consumers are acquainted. It is required in most states for the transfer of ownership of such items as automobiles or refrigerators. Even in states where a bill of sale is not required for these items, it is often desirable to obtain one because it provides evidence of ownership.

These contracts must be in writing

1. An agreement to be responsible for the debt, default, or obligation of another person.
2. An agreement that is not to be executed or performed within a period of one year after it is made.
3. An agreement to buy or sell real estate, including land, buildings, minerals, or trees.
4. An agreement to sell goods in excess of $500. (Exceptions are when there has been a part payment or part of the goods have been delivered.)
5. An installment contract.

435

In states where the bill of sale is used, it is usually necessary to register the bill of sale with the proper county authority so that the ownership of the property can be established.

Express and implied contracts. Contracts may be classified in another way. They are said to be either express or implied. An *express contract* is one that arises out of an agreement expressed by oral or written words. If you orally agree to buy a refrigerator at a specified price and the dealer agrees to sell it to you at that price, you have made an express contract that is legally binding. An *implied contract* is one that is made through an agreement implied by the acts or the conduct of the parties involved. If you pick up an article in the store and hand the required amount of money to the clerk, who wraps the article and hands it to you, you have made an implied contract.

For your protection

1. Read the entire contract *before* you sign.
2. Ask for explanation of parts you do not understand.
3. Make sure the contract states all conditions and promises as you understand them.
4. Do not accept your copy without the signature of the other party.
5. Keep your copy of the contract in a safe place.

DEFECTIVE AGREEMENTS

An agreement may not be enforceable because it is found to be defective. Misrepresentation, use of undue influence, concealment of vital facts, or use of threats or force in obtaining agreement may make an agreement *defective*.

Agreements that are not enforceable may be classified as void or voidable. When an agreement is *void,* it has no legal force or effect. In other words neither party can enforce the agreement. A *voidable contract* is one that may be broken (rescinded or voided) by one or both of the parties. Such an agreement is enforceable if the party or parties having the option to reject it choose not to do so.

Ordinarily a mistake made by one party, such as quoting the wrong price, does not make the contract void or voidable. Mistakes that make a contract void include mutual mistakes as to the existence of the subject matter or a mistake as to the identity of the parties. For instance, a man agreed to sell a certain dog at a definite price, but

---

Examples of voidable agreements

1. If there is fraud in the form of misrepresentation.
2. If a person makes an agreement as a result of threat or the use of violence.
3. If there has been undue and unfair influence and pressure to the extent that one person has not reached the agreement through the free exercise of his own judgment.

---

later it was found that the dog had died before the agreement was made. The agreement was void because of a mistake as to the existence of the subject matter.

B. Carrying out the contract

PREVENTING FRAUD AND MISUNDERSTANDING

Never sign a contract in blank or with part of the figures or conditions left to be filled in. If someone hurries you or suggests that you sign the contract with the rest of the information to be filled in later, your suspicion should be aroused.

Do not sign a contract with the understanding that supplementary agreements will be made later. Be sure that all agreements are in the contract. In the absence of substantial proof with regard to oral agreements or supplementary written agreements, only the agreements stipulated in the contract are enforceable.

WARRANTIES

When a seller makes promises before or after the sale that an article will operate in a specific way or that it has a certain specific quality, he makes statements on which the buyer has a legal right to rely. These promises or representations are called *warranties*.

There are two types of warranties: (a) *express* and (b) *implied*. For example, if a merchant states definitely that cloth is pure virgin

---

A WARRANTY

GUARANTEE. Upon receipt of the guarantee registration card packed with this appliance, your Suntrol Automatic Toaster is guaranteed for one (1) year against electrical and mechanical defects in material and workmanship, which will be repaired or parts replaced free of charge during this period. The guarantee does not cover damage caused by misuse, negligence, or use on current or voltage other than that stamped on the appliance. This guarantee is in lieu of any other warranty either expressed or implied. If service is required, send the appliance prepaid to the nearest Suntrol Appliance Service Company branch or authorized service station. Please include a letter explaining the nature of your difficulty.

wool, that is an express warranty. A written guarantee is also an express warranty. An example of an implied warranty is one in which the buyer has a right to expect that the article purchased will serve the purpose for which it is sold, although there is no definite statement in regard to it. For instance, if you buy an air-conditioner, you have a right to expect that it will operate; if it does not operate, you have a legal recourse. If you go into a restaurant and order food, there is an implied warranty that the food is fit to eat. If you become poisoned, the restaurant owner is liable. If it can be proved that the manufacturer or processor of the food was responsible because of improper processing or handling of the food, that person may also be liable for any damages resulting from the sickness.

Generally speaking, when a buyer has an opportunity to inspect the goods, there is no implied warranty that the goods are of a particular quality; but there is an implied warranty that they will serve the purpose for which they are intended. If the buyer does not inspect the goods but relies largely on the judgment and honesty of the seller, there is an implied warranty that the goods will be satisfactory. When a sample is used to indicate the kind and quality of the goods, the seller impliedly warrants the goods to correspond in kind and in quality with the sample shown. When merchandise is purchased by description, such as by specifications, the seller impliedly warrants the goods to correspond to the description.

"Trade puffs" or "trade talk" are not warranties and should not be relied upon by the buyer. A *trade puff* is a general claim, such as "This is the best merchandise you can buy," "This is the most popular item on the market," or "This suit is very becoming to you."

REMEDIES FOR BREACH OF WARRANTY

In the case of misrepresentation or if goods do not fulfill the reasonable expectations of a warranty, there has been a *breach of warranty*. Several different remedies are available in case of a breach of warranty. The following general recourses are open to the buyer: (1) to keep the goods and to deduct from the price the amount of the damages; (2) to keep the goods and to bring an action against the seller for damages; (3) to refuse to accept the goods and to bring an action against the seller to recover damages; (4) to rescind (break, void, or refuse) the contract and to refuse to receive the goods or, if the goods have been accepted, to return them to the vendor and to recover the price that has been paid.

PASSING THE TITLE

When a cash sale is made, the title passes immediately. This means that the seller ceases to own the goods and the buyer becomes the owner. When a sale on credit is made, the title also passes immediately; the buyer merely has an agreement as to the time when he will pay for the goods. Ordinarily C.O.D. sales result in a transfer of the title at the time the goods are shipped; the seller merely does not give possession of the goods until the charge has been paid.

The buyer need not accept delivery if the seller violates his contract.

When one buys something on approval, the title does not pass to him until the article has been approved and an acknowledgment of its acceptance has either been given or implied. The buyer has the right to return all the goods or any whole units. For example, the buyer could use one can out of a case of twelve and return eleven cans.

In the case of installment sales in which the conditional contract is used, the seller has a right to reclaim the goods if payments are not regularly made. The buyer may in that case lose what he has paid and may even have to pay something extra if he does not fulfill the provisions of the contract. When the provisions of the contract are fulfilled, the title then passes to the buyer.

In a sale subject to return, the title passes at the time of the sale; but if the goods are returned, the title reverts to the seller.

REMEDIES OF SELLER WHEN BUYER FAILS TO PERFORM

If the buyer of merchandise fails to perform his part of the contract, the seller may select any of these remedies:

When a buyer does not fulfill his part of a installment sales contract, the seller may reclaim the item.

1. The seller may sue for payment (if the title has passed). When the buyer refuses or neglects to pay, the seller may sue for the price of the goods.
2. The seller may sue for damages (if the title has not passed). When the buyer wrongfully refuses or neglects to accept and pay for the goods, the seller may sue for damages. The amount of damages will usually be the difference between the contract price and the market price.
3. The seller may rescind the contract. When the buyer repudiates the contract, or when he cannot perform the contract or fails to perform it, the seller is allowed, under most laws, to rescind the contract.

REMEDIES OF BUYER WHEN SELLER FAILS TO PERFORM

If the seller fails to perform his obligations, the buyer has the choice of one of the following remedies:

1. The buyer may obtain possession of the goods (if the title has passed and payment has been made). When the seller wrongfully refuses or neglects to deliver the goods, the buyer may sue for the possession of the goods, for the recovery of the value that has been paid, or for damages.
2. The buyer may sue for damages (if the title has not passed). If the seller wrongfully refuses or neglects to deliver the goods, the buyer is entitled to damages for nondelivery. The amount of the damages is ordinarily the difference between the contract price and the market price at the time and the place of delivery. The amount may also include any other damages for loss resulting from the failure to fulfill the contract.

3. The buyer may insist upon the fulfillment of the contract. The buyer has the right to sue for specific performance if damages will not be adequate compensation or if they cannot be computed. When the buyer sues for specific performance and wins the case, the seller is ordered by the court to carry out the original contract.

4. The buyer may cancel the contract and refuse to accept the goods. If the seller has broken his part of the contract or in any way has failed to carry out his part of the contract, the buyer may refuse to accept delivery of the goods or may return them if delivered. If damages have resulted, he may also sue for damages.

GOODS NOT ORDERED

You do not have to accept goods that you have not ordered. Some firms and other organizations follow a practice of sending unsolicited merchandise in the hope that persons receiving them will send a remittance. If you receive such a package, you may refuse to accept it, you may return it, or you may hold it subject to whatever the sender wishes to do with it. However, you must not use the merchandise or in any way indicate an acceptance of it unless you intend to pay for it. On the other hand, if you are in the habit of receiving and accepting such merchandise, you may be responsible unless you return it or notify the sender that you do not accept it.

GOODS ENTRUSTED TO OTHERS

Let us say that you entrust your automobile to a garage or a parking lot for safekeeping. The garage or parking lot is responsible for its safekeeping. This is especially true if you are given a parking ticket that is a receipt for your car and if you are required to leave the keys in the car so that it can be moved. However, if you regularly place your own car in a lot and take the keys with you, the operator of the parking lot is generally not liable.

If you rent or borrow an article, such as a lawn mower, you are responsible for taking reasonable care of it to prevent damage or theft. Likewise, if you take a lawn mower to a repairman and he damages it in the process of repairing it, he is liable because he is expected to exercise reasonable care and skill. He is assumed to have the skill to do the job for which he is paid.

Generally speaking, people who accept the property of others are responsible for it. On the other hand, if a neighbor brings you some jewelry and asks you to keep it while he is gone on a vacation, you are not responsible for its loss or theft if you exercise reasonable care over it.

MECHANIC'S LIEN

In most states a person who sells the materials and who may also provide the labor for a new building or for other improvements to land has a claim against the property until the bill is paid. This claim is known as a *mechanic's lien*. If the bill for the supplies and labor is not paid, the supplier may foreclose on the lien by filing suit, which means that the property on which the lien was filed may be sold to satisfy the debt. The right to file a mechanic's lien is given by law; the debtor's consent is not required. In practice, any bill for material or labor used in the building, repairing, or maintenance of buildings, or on the improvement of land, if not paid in accordance with its terms, may result in a mechanic's lien on the property.

Legal information and principles that everyone needs to understand

1. Consult a lawyer for legal advice; do not attempt to serve as your own lawyer.
2. A contract involves the elements of offer and acceptance, the competency of the parties, a legal purpose, consideration, and required legal form.
3. Some contracts must be in writing.
4. Some contracts are expressed or implied.
5. Some contracts are voidable.
6. There are specific remedies if a warranty is broken.
7. The seller has certain choices of remedies if the buyer fails to perform.
8. The buyer has choices of certain remedies if the seller fails to perform.
9. Generally, when property is entrusted to another party, that party is responsible for reasonable care in safekeeping.

■ QUESTIONS ON THE TEXT

1. What are some of the problems on which an individual should consult a lawyer?
2. How should you select a lawyer and what factors should you consider in selecting him?
3. What is a legal opinion?
4. What are some of the situations in everyday life that involve contracts?
5. Why aren't all agreements contracts?

6. What is meant by mutual assent?
7. What are the three essential characteristics of an offer?
8. What evidence may there be that a buyer has accepted the goods offered him?
9. How and when can an offer be terminated?
10. What is an option?
11. (a) What is meant by "age of majority"?
    (b) Why is an adult dealer in merchandise held to a contract he made with someone who has not reached the age of majority?
12. Under what conditions may a minor be held to a contract?
13. Name the kinds of bargains for which a contract is not legal.
14. What is meant by a consideration?
15. Why is the promise of a gift by a competent person not enforceable as a contract?
16. Under what conditions may a contract for a sale be oral?
17. What is a bill of sale?
18. Distinguish between an express and an implied contract.
19. Under what circumstances is a contract voidable?
20. Why should you never sign a blank contract or a contract containing blank spaces?
21. What is an express warranty?
22. In case of a breach of warranty, what possible recourses are open to the buyer?
23. (a) When the buyer of merchandise fails to perform his part of a contract, how may the seller protect himself?
    (b) What recourse does the buyer have if the seller fails to perform his obligations?
24. How may you indicate a refusal (rather than an acceptance) of merchandise you did not order?
25. (a) What responsibility do you have for property you have rented or borrowed?
    (b) What responsibility do you have for property entrusted to you by a neighbor for safekeeping?
26. What is a mechanic's lien?

▪ QUESTIONS FOR DISCUSSION

1. Why are quite different decisions given by courts in apparently similar or identical cases?
2. Mr. Martin insists that he will not fulfill a contract because he did not know all the terms of the contract when he signed it. His reason for not having read the contract carefully is that he finds it difficult to read fine print. He admits, however, that the signature on the contract is genuine. Is there anything he can do to avoid fulfilling the contract?

3. Assume that Brown offers a car for sale at $2,000 and Jones submits a written reply stating, "I accept your offer with the understanding that the snow tires will be included." Is the offer terminated?

4. Explain why each of the following is or is not an offer: (a) an advertisement; (b) an application letter; (c) goods on display with the price marked.

5. When making a contract, what facts should you know about competence of the other party in order to assure enforceability of the contract?

6. What would be the effect on business (a) if all contracts had to be in writing? (b) if implied contracts were prohibited?

7. You are given a sales demonstration in a store. During the demonstration the salesman tells you many ways in which his product is better than some other product. Later you find that what he has told you is not true.
   (a) Do his statements constitute fraud?
   (b) Have you any legal basis for returning the merchandise and demanding your money?

8. Several days after you purchased a raincoat, you had occasion to use it. It was found that the buttons had been omitted and that in stitching, certain seams had been missed. What recourse do you have?

▪ PROBLEMS TO SOLVE

1. Jim Wade, age 14, bought an electric road racing kit from the Ace Model Toy Shop and asked the proprietor to bill his father (whom the proprietor knew) for the $25 cost of the kit. Upon receipt of the bill two weeks later, Jim's father refused payment and returned the racing kit. The proprietor claimed that since Jim had played with the model racing kit, the proprietor could not resell the kit as new and that Jim's father should at least pay the difference between what the kit cost new and what it would bring as a used kit. Does the proprietor have a legal claim against Jim's father or Jim?

2. Williams agreed to sell his outboard motorboat and 75 h.p. motor to his neighbor, Barnes, for $495. Barnes said he would need a few weeks to get the money but that he would pay Williams $75 down and the balance in five weeks at which time he, Barnes, would take possession and title to the motor and boat. Three weeks later Williams was offered $700 for the boat and motor from Mr. Petty. Williams tried to get Barnes to take back the $75, claiming that there was no legal contract since the agreement was not in writing. Can Barnes hold Williams to the original agreement?

3. On March 1, Mr. Warren, proprietor of Warren's House of Cameras, sold a camera to Mr. Reedy for $100. The following day Mr. Reedy came storming into Warren's House of Cameras, slammed down a

newspaper advertisement, dated February 28, which advertised a camera like the one Reedy purchased for only $85, and demanded a refund of $15. Mr. Warren claimed the contract entered into between Mr. Reedy and himself was legal and that Mr. Reedy was not entitled to the refund. Does Reedy have a legal claim against Warren?

4. Arthur Knight arranged with the Ace Building Company to build a home for him. He did some of the work himself and went to a furnace company and selected a furnace, which the heating company said would heat satisfactorily. After the house was completed, Mr. Knight could not get his furnace to heat the house to a warm enough temperature to suit him in cold weather. Was there any warranty, and does Mr. Knight have any claim against the contractor or the heating company?

5. Both Smith and Brown live in New York State. Smith owned a hunting lodge in Colorado. On July 15, Brown entered into a written agreement to purchase the lodge for $50,000, possession to be given on the date of the contract. Smith accepted Brown's check for $50,000 and transferred the title to Brown. On July 16, Smith was notified that the lodge had been destroyed by fire on July 14. Discuss Smith's rights and obligations in this case. Discuss Brown's rights and obligations.

▪ COMMUNITY PROBLEMS AND PROJECTS

1. Obtain copies of five written contracts. Probably some of these may be obtained from members of your family; others may be obtained from friends and businessmen. Your class officers may have entered into contract with a dance band for the junior or senior dance. Examine each of the five contracts to identify: (a) each of the five elements of a contract and (b) each of the six parts of a written contract. Prepare a report in which you list your findings.

2. Give examples of three different kinds of contracts that you, a member of your family, or a friend made within the last week and show how all five essential elements of a contract were present in each. For each contract, explain when and how the offer was made; how it was accepted; and if it could have been accepted in any other way. When would each offer have been terminated if it had not been accepted?

3. Court cases involving contracts are reported in local newspapers. Search the papers to locate three cases involving contracts. Try to discover from the newspaper reports the real question of controversy in each case. Then, analyze the case in light of each of the five elements of a contract and also in light of the six parts of a written contract. Which, if any, of the essential elements of the various contracts were involved in each case? What, if any, parts of the written contract were involved in each case?

Chapter 23

Buying and spending wisely

PURPOSE OF THE CHAPTER

Earning money is important, but how you spend it can be more important. Some people with large incomes spend more than they earn; others with smaller incomes save money. The difference is in spending. This chapter will give you a few guides in buying and spending.

You will find answers to these questions:

1. What choices must you make?
2. Are you buying to fill a real need?
3. How does advertising help?
4. What kind of sale is a bargain?
5. What do standards, brands, and labels mean?

A. General guides in spending

BUYING IS CHOICE MAKING

Buying is always a matter of making choices. Choices must be made (a) between wants and needs, (b) between luxuries and necessi-

446

ties, (c) between one product and another of the same kind, (d) between two entirely different kinds of products, or (e) between spending your money now or saving it for another purpose.

No product is worth buying unless it is worth more to the buyer than the money he spends for it. If you will think carefully about every purchase that you make, there is less chance that unneeded and unwanted luxuries will be purchased under high-pressure advertising and selling in preference to filling the real needs of the family.

Before you buy, ask yourself these or similar questions:

1. Do I really need it? If so, why?
2. Is it worth the cost in terms of my effort to earn the money?
3. Is there a better use for the money?
4. Am I buying it—
   —to do as others do?
   —to show off?
   —to make someone envious?
   —to make myself feel important?

The real needs of the average family are relatively limited, but wants can be increased almost without limit. As a result of high-pressure advertising and selling and our rising standards of living, there is a tendency on the part of every person to want to "keep up with the Joneses" and to justify in his own mind that what really is a luxury is actually an urgent need.

The vast majority of families do not earn enough money to enjoy unlimited purchases of luxuries. In fact, many families cannot purchase all their real needs without very strict self-restraint in making their purchases. In the average family the tendency is to follow individual selfish urges in filling emotional wants rather than practicing individual self-restraint for the benefit of the whole family. If mother wants something, she may buy it on an emotional urge; if father wants something, he buys it without consulting the family; if children want something, they spend their own money without much thought or they put pressure on mother and father to obtain the things they want. If family purchasing is considered from the point of view of unselfish group needs, most families can get the most out of their income.

Even in the case of small purchases, a great amount of money can slip through the fingers of every member of the family in buying little things that merchants call *impulse items*. They are the little things in the nature of luxuries that sit by the cash register and are easy to pick up for 5 to 25 cents or even more, just on an impulse because the buyer has a little money in his pocket.

A PLAN FOR SPENDING

Very few people earn so much money that they can buy all they want without considering whether they have enough money to pay for their purchases. Therefore, a plan of buying is necessary. Although budgeting is presented in Chapter 24, it is desirable to emphasize it at this point because of its relationship to buying. A budget is a plan of spending and saving. The plan will help a person to determine how much to spend and how much to save. When the spending program is broken down into months and weeks, it should be checked periodically with the original plan to be sure that over-spending is not taking place. The budget often must be revised and adjusted to take care of unforeseen problems as they arise.

Advantages of a budget spending plan

1. It will help you to live within your income.
2. It will help you to save.
3. It will help you to determine what you can and must have so that you will not recklessly spend your money for foolish things and deprive yourself of things you really need.

SPECIAL SALES AND BARGAINS

All retail stores have special sales during which prices are lower than at any other time. Some sales include standard items that are kept in stock regularly. Other sales are clearance sales to close out styles, models, or items at the end of the season. Some are sales of special goods brought in for the sale.

In almost every community a pattern is followed yearly by most stores, such as sales of housewares in March, school clothes in August, furniture in August, toys after Christmas. Bargains can be found and money saved by waiting for sales.

WHEN TO BUY

The previous discussion indicates some types of sales in which one can often purchase bargains. This is especially true when merchants

---

Examples of bargain sales

1. Remnant sales of merchandise of odd lengths, sizes, and assortments.
2. Sales of soiled goods that may be returned goods, shopworn goods, or sample merchandise.
3. Preseason sales in advance of the regular season.
4. Preinventory sales to reduce stock of merchandise on hand.
5. Out-of-season sales of merchandise left over at the close of a season.
6. Odd-lot sales of merchandise, such as irregulars or seconds.
7. Surplus stock sales resulting from overbuying of a merchant or overproduction of a mill.
8. Anniversary sales as a special event to stimulate business.
9. Special seasonal sales that offer bargains in season.

---

sell their regular merchandise at reduced prices. However, some merchants bring in special merchandise for special sales and do not reduce the price on their regular merchandise. Some of the special merchandise may be good, but it should be compared with the regular merchandise normally sold by the store.

At the beginning of a season, style goods sell at their highest prices. As the season progresses, the prices are gradually lowered, for merchants hope to dispose of their goods before the end of the season.

There are important price cycles for many other products. For instance, in cities in which coal is used for heating purposes, it is usually sold at its lowest price in April and May and at its maximum price during the winter months. If fuel oil tanks are filled in the summer, the price is usually lower than in the fall.

Fresh fruits and vegetables usually sell at their cheapest prices during the summer. As one might suspect, products that are most

Odd-lot sales of merchandise, such as irregulars or seconds, represent one kind of bargain sale.

Harold M. Lambert

difficult to store have wide fluctuations in price. The prices of canned goods are lowest soon after the canning season.

During periods of generally high prices the wise consumer will avoid buying anything that he does not really need. He will save his money and wait until prices are lower. Of course, families have to eat regularly. Purchases of food cannot be deferred until prices fall. However, one can watch prices and buy the kinds of foods that are currently being sold at the most attractive prices.

QUALITY, ECONOMY, AND VALUE

There are two extremes of thinking in regard to prices. One is that the highest priced item is the best; the other is that the lowest priced item is the best bargain. Neither viewpoint is correct. The price of an item must be related to its quality, its economy, and how it satisfies your needs and wants.

Many things determine quality for different people. For some people, beauty is what they want; for others, long-wearing economy is sought; still others want special features, such as a timer on a stove.

What is quality? It may be many things to many people, but in general it is a combination of design, color, workmanship, beauty, wearing quality, and economy. On the other hand, the best bargain may be the product that is the best buy for the money. It could be the cheapest, but it might be the highest priced.

SERVICES MAY BE IMPORTANT

Price may not be the most important consideration in buying, even when buying the same product or brand of product. In all cases of buying mechanical or electrical equipment, as well as many other products, the main consideration is to obtain a product that will operate without trouble, but when trouble occurs, you can get good repair service.

Be sure you get a product that will wear well, and above all, one that you can get repaired when this service is needed.

Other services that may be important

1. Delivering
2. Parking
3. Credit
4. Phone orders
5. Lunchroom
6. Nursery

TRADING STAMPS AND PREMIUMS

Nothing is free in this world. Somebody pays. If you receive premiums or trading stamps, the cost of these is included in the prices you pay. Buying where premiums and stamps are offered is a poor guide. You should check to see if you are paying fair prices on all items you purchase, and decide whether this plan of buying may limit your shopping when you might do better elsewhere.

QUANTITY BUYING

People who buy in the smallest units pay more than those who buy in larger units. For example, an 8-ounce can might sell for 30 cents, but a 16-ounce can may sell for 50 cents. Besides buying in larger units, if they are needed, it is often possible to buy more units at a reduced price. For example, one unit might sell for $1; two for $1.80; three for $2.50. But buying more than needed or a larger size than can be consumed without waste is not economical.

BUYING FROM DISCOUNT HOUSES

In almost every community there are establishments commonly called *discount houses* that attempt to sell merchandise at prices lower than those of anyone else. Generally, discount houses operate in the fields of household equipment and appliances, but they may

The cost of trading stamps or premiums is included in the prices the consumer pays.

Ewing Galloway

also operate in clothing and other fields. Sometimes these firms sell standard merchandise like that sold in other stores, but very often they sell unknown brands. Some of the brands may be good, but others may be of questionable quality. A discount house attempts to sell a great deal of merchandise at a low margin of profit in the hope that there will be a large total profit on the operations.

Some discount houses provide delivery service and repair service on equipment, but often they do not. Many times there is an extra charge for such services. If you buy a piece of equipment from a discount house, you may find it necessary to obtain service from an independent repairman. However, if you buy a piece of equipment made by a nationally known company with a local service organization, you can obtain service and repair parts from the local service agency of the manufacturer. On some products you may be able to obtain the same guarantee from a discount house as from any other store; but in buying from a discount house, you should assure yourself that you are getting good merchandise.

B. Specific guides in buying

DISCOVERING THE VALUE OF ADVERTISING IN GENERAL

Have you ever analyzed advertising in general to discover whether it is really of value to you? If it is of no value to you, then it is wasteful. If advertising is of value, you should learn how to use it wisely.

Wise use of advertising in making consumer decisions. Advertisements should be analyzed from two points of view: (a) for information about

Could you buy as confidently if no goods were branded and advertised?

The value of advertising in general

A study of the following questions should indicate how useful advertising is to consumers.

1. If you were a farmer, could you get all the information you want about the latest farm equipment without referring to advertisements?
2. What facts and other information about the latest developments in home appliances and equipment have you obtained through advertising?
3. What can be learned about foods from newspaper advertisements?
4. What new products have you learned about through advertising in the past two years?
5. What information of an educational nature about health, recreation, or sanitation have you received through advertising?
6. If all home appliances were sold without trade names and trademarks, how would you select them?
7. If canned foods did not carry labels and trademarks, how could you select canned goods wisely?
8. How do you benefit by reading the advertisements of local stores?
9. How is attendance at your school events, such as plays, athletic contests, and operettas promoted? Is advertising involved?

---

the product, and (b) for deceptive or misleading statements. Some advertisements are neither informative nor deceptive. They are simply evasive or general, or they merely appeal to the emotions. The intelligent consumer will look for helpful information. Learn to distinguish between emotional appeals and rational appeals. Learn to evaluate testimonials and to discern the facts that are included.

From a consumer's point of view, an advertisement may be considered primarily good if it provides facts in regard to quality, standards, specifications, and performance. It cannot be considered good if it fails to provide this information and instead appeals only to the emotions.

BRAND NAMES

A *brand name* or *trademark* is used for one purpose only: to encourage people to ask for the product again after using it the first time. In the absence of information that would permit comparison, the recognized brands of reputable producers are usually more reliable than other brands. If other information is available, however, the brand on a product should not be used as the only means of comparison.

Follow these guides in analyzing advertisements

1. Do I need the item advertised?
2. What does the product contain and how is it made?
3. Is the product beneficial?
4. How economical is the product?
5. How long will the product last?
6. How does its price compare with the prices of similar products?
7. Does the item carry any seals identifying its quality or any evidence of authoritative scientific tests?
8. What proof is used to back up the statements?
9. Are there any service or maintenance problems?
10. Are any of the advertising statements evasive or misleading?
11. Does the advertisement appeal to your intelligence?
12. Does the advertisement make you feel confident that, if you buy, you will be a satisfied customer?

Brand names or trademarks, however, are important guides for a consumer, because after a person has tried a certain product, he can ask for the same brand again with reasonable assurance that he will get the same quality that he has used before. Reputable manufac-

By means of brand names, the consumer is able to purchase the same brand again and again and be reasonably certain that each time he will receive the same quality as before.

Ewing Galloway

turers attempt to maintain standards of products carrying their brand names. Nearly all products carry a brand name now, but some branded products are not reliable; the manufacturers make no attempt to maintain standards. Quality may vary considerably from time to time, but the manufacturer that advertises his product intensively with the idea of building a reputation for the brand usually attempts to maintain a satisfactory standard.

Trial use is an important means of buying any product, whether it is trial use from a sample, trial of merchandise bought by a friend, or trial use from a small purchase before making a large purchase.

WHAT IS A STANDARD?

Imagine trying to get along without standards. A *standard* is a unit of measure. A pound is a measure of weight; a foot, a measure of distance or length; and a gallon, a measure of liquids. How would we buy coffee, or fabric, or milk without these standards of quantity? How could prices be set? How could you indicate how much of a commodity you want?

There are other standards too. We designate the size of a shirt by neckband size and sleeve length; shoes, by length and width; and some articles, such as hats and sometimes dresses, by arbitrary numbers. Other kinds of standards pertain to performance, such as the octane rating of gasoline or the heat units, known as British Thermal Units, in coal.

A standard ordinarily is thought of as a measure of quantity, weight, or extent, and sometimes of quality. A standard for consumer goods is usually a definition that states fully what the measuring stick is.

USING GRADES AS GUIDES

With the exception of foods, standards usually define a single level of quality of a commodity that is considered satisfactory. A drug, for example, either complies with the formulae of the official United States Pharmacopeia, which is known as the U.S.P. standard, or it does not. There are no degrees of conformance to the drug standard. But when applied to foods, standards often are established to define several levels of quality, each of which is known as a grade. For example, there are four grades of butter, each of which is defined by a standard. A *grade,* then, is a term applied to standards of quality when more than one quality of a particular food is defined. The federal government agencies sometimes refer to the definitions as *standards of identity,* because the definition describes or identifies the standard or grade so it is recognizable.

USING LABELS AS GUIDES

Back in the days when practically all food, clothing, and other necessities were prepared and made in the home, there was little need for standards and grades. Consumers purchased raw materials from which to make the things they needed. Processed goods and ready-made clothes were practically unknown. Purchasers could see what they were buying and in some instances they even tasted the food before they bought it. There were few choices to make, for usually the merchant had available for sale only one kind of coffee, shoes, or furniture.

Study the labels and identify standards and grades. A label must be truthful, and a standard requires the contents to be as labeled.

Now that most of the food, drugs, clothing, and other things we buy are finished products and ready to be used, merchants keep in stock a variety of each kind of commodity from which we choose the one that appeals to us. Many commodities, such as food and drugs, are in cans or otherwise packaged so that we do not actually see them until we use them. Standards and grades thus are very important to modern consumers. Standards indicate to us what the commodity really is, what it is made of, and what its characteristics are. If there are several qualities of a commodity, such as there are in foods, grades indicate the level of the quality.

A *label* is a written statement attached to an article or a commodity describing its essential characteristics. Standards and grades, as well as other information of importance to consumers, may be indicated on the label. A consumer should familiarize himself with standards and grades; he should carefully read the labels on merchandise to learn the characteristics of the goods that he is contemplating buying.

Informative labeling. Good informative labels can provide the kind of information one wants and needs for the selection of commodities he wishes to buy. Good labeling gives not only quality standards and grades but also important facts that you, as a consumer, may want.

Informative labeling applies to many products, including appliances, clothing, and fabrics. In the case of fabrics, there are various terms used to indicate shrinkage, such as "preshrunk." If this term is used, the fabric should not shrink more than 2 percent. Other information on fabrics and clothing may indicate the type of fiber used, the weave, the water repellency, the finish, the crease resistance, and other special features.

Industry standards for informative labeling. Some canners and distributors have developed a more descriptive type of labeling that they believe is better for the consumer than the A, B, C, or other grade labeling. It is often referred to as *descriptive labeling*. Descriptive labels for foods, for instance, would contain such information as: (a) style of the pack; (b) degree of maturity of the food; (c) number of units in the can, such as the number of slices or halves of peaches; (d) the quantity in terms of cups if the units are small, such as cherries; (e) the quantity in terms of servings; (f) the size of the can; (g) the description of the raw product and the method of processing; (h) the suggested methods or ways of serving.

Trade names and terms. There are many trade names and terms used in connection with the labeling of various products. Most of these names and terms are not intended to be deceptive or misleading, but they are confusing unless a person knows what they mean and knows something about the differences in quality. For instance, stainless steel is a general term used to identify a steel alloy that will not tarnish so easily as ordinary steel; but there are many qualities of stainless steel.

Let us consider a few other common examples. Wool cloth may be made from all virgin wool, reprocessed wool, reused wool, or a mixture of these with some other fibers. Parchment paper and parchment lamp shades are very seldom made of sheepskin; they are usually made of paper. Chinaware usually does not come from China; the word designates a type of clay from which the pottery is made. The product may or may not be better than a similar product made in China. Silverware is not sterling silver, but usually plated ware. Sterling silver is solid silver.

When buying woolen products, read the labels.

How to read the label. The buyer should read labels carefully to obtain information with regard to (a) the weight or the volume, (b) the grade or the quality, and (c) an analysis or a description of the contents. The labels of some private agencies have been discussed previously.

Until uniform grade standards have been established and are used for a particular product, it is impossible to rely upon the existing grade designations without knowing what those grades mean. Much of the terminology in use means one thing to the seller, but a different thing to the buyer. If the buyer takes the words at their face value, he is sometimes misled into believing the goods to be of a grade higher than they actually are. Furthermore, the terminology is made confusing by the wide variation in its use. In other words, buyers and sellers do not speak the same language. When this situation exists, grade designations are of very little value.

For instance, one would suppose that the "first" grade of butter is the best grade, but as a matter of fact it is the third grade when compared with government standards. To get the best grade of butter, one has to buy the "AA" grade. Similar confusing grades are used for other products.

The partial label shown on page 459 illustrates the type of information that a consumer may find on a good label. If one learns to use such labels in buying, he will find that they not only serve as helpful guides but also encourage other producers and distributors to use equally informative labels.

Many products, including food products, sold in stores today do not carry information in regard to standards or grades; but many labels, particularly on foods, do contain certain helpful information. This information can be relied upon to be generally truthful and accurate.

The contents indicated on labels are also important, for the size of the container is frequently misleading. Deceptive containers are now illegal if the products are sold in interstate commerce. In examining a label, one should look for the following information:

1. Specific descriptive statements.
2. Facts regarding quality.
3. Facts regarding quantity.
4. Grades or other similar designations.
5. Certificate or other mark of approval or guarantee.
6. How to use and care for it.
7. Warnings.

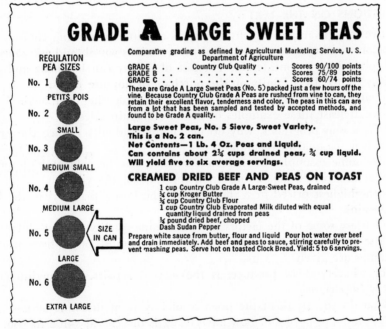

An example of specifications and information on a food label

CASH AND CREDIT BUYING

In Chapter 19 there is a discussion of installment buying. Buying on the installment plan may allow you to have what you want earlier than if you pay cash, but installment buying costs more than cash buying. If you can save and wait to pay cash, you can get more for your money.

Facts everyone should know about buying and spending

1. Buying is a matter of making many kinds of choices.
2. Buying should be based on budgeting.
3. Determine your needs and go shopping to fill those needs rather than make impulse purchases.
4. Some advertising is misleading, some is helpful and informative, and some is meaningless.
5. Advertising should be studied carefully as a guide in buying.
6. Some standards are measures of size, weight, and distance; others are used to measure quality.
7. Informative labels give information about standards, grade, content, and other characteristics of goods.
8. Consumers should learn what standards and grades mean.

▪ **QUESTIONS ON THE TEXT**

1. Give some examples of why buying is a matter of making choices.
2. Before you buy, what are some of the questions you should ask yourself?
3. Explain how a considerable amount of money can be spent and possibly wasted by a family on the purchase of impulse items.
4. What should be the relationship between budgeting and buying?
5. Give at least three examples of genuine bargain sales.
6. As a season progresses, why do merchants gradually reduce the prices of their seasonal merchandise?
7. Give some examples of merchandise that may be sold at high prices or at low prices, depending upon the time of the year.
8. Is the highest priced item the best and the lowest priced item the best bargain?
9. What are some of the factors that determine quality in a product?
10. How should you determine whether you should buy where trading stamps are given?
11. For what types of products is the service, repairs, and maintenance very important?
12. What do you think of the practice of buying at discount houses?
13. Give some examples of how advertising is of general value to you.
14. What suggestions do you offer as a guide in helping you to analyze advertisements?
15. Are brand names of any value in buying merchandise?
16. What is a standard?
17. What is a grade as applied to a product?
18. Indicate the type of information that one should expect to obtain from a good informative label.
19. In examining a label for information, indicate some information that you should attempt to find, depending upon the product.

▪ QUESTIONS FOR DISCUSSION

1. Explain how you can help yourself stay within your budget and become a more careful buyer if you make a careful decision as to whether the item you are buying is worth more to you than the money you are spending for it.
2. What are some of the limitations to the benefits derived from buying in order to take advantage of low prices during price cycles?
3. Give an example of how the highest priced item can be the best bargain.
4. Mrs. Hart prides herself on buying only nationally advertised goods.
   (a) What do you think of her practice?
   (b) Is she following good judgment? Why?
5. Let us say that you went into a strange grocery store for the purpose of buying peas, and found on the shelf two brands of peas, one of which was well known to you and the other was not known. What procedure would you follow in buying? Why?
6. Give an example of how you could save money by quantity buying if you have the money or the credit to do so.
7. From the viewpoint of the buyer, discuss some of the advantages and the disadvantages of brands or trade names.
8. Some people argue that discount houses should not be allowed to operate because they provide unfair competition. What do you think of this argument?
9. Try to recall and describe a recent advertisement that you feel was informative. Give your reasons.
10. Name some grades and descriptions of products that you have seen which have meant nothing to you.
11. Give some of the arguments for and against informative or descriptive labeling without fixed standards for grades.

▪ PROBLEMS TO SOLVE

1. Make a list of the trade names or brand names of products that you have learned are reliable. Give the name of the product with each trade or brand name. Indicate why these names have proved to be reliable guides to you in buying.
2. From your local newspaper, over a period of a week, make a list of the different kinds of special sales that, in your opinion, come under the classification of legitimate bargain sales as described in this chapter.
3. Make a list of at least six items (not more than four foods) and state the time when you think each item is at its lowest seasonal price.
4. Analyze the reasons why you and your family buy the following items from the places where you are accustomed to buy: (a) groceries, (b) drugs, and (c) clothing. Prepare a list of reasons for each classification. If you buy in more than one place, give the reasons.

5. Prepare a bulletin board display using labels from foods and clothing in which you point out the important information consumers need to know about the products. The display should be constructed in two parts, one display depicting good labels which give the consumer considerable information, the other depicting poor labels which provide the consumer with insufficient information.

6. Make a careful study of a number of different advertisements from newspapers and magazines as to the kinds and amount of information given, the specific and implied claims made, and the conclusions the advertisements make the consumer draw (whether valid or not). Report your findings and show at least one of the advertisements you studied.

▪ COMMUNITY PROBLEMS AND PROJECTS

1. Make a comparison of purchasing through discount houses as compared with purchasing through other regular stores. In order to do this, go to a discount house and obtain the prices of well-known branded merchandise and obtain complete information as to guarantees, delivery service, and repair service. Then go to regular stores and obtain prices on exactly the same merchandise if it is available and check all the service and guarantees available through the regular store. Be sure that you compare the same merchandise. Write a report on your findings.

2. Make a study of some of the special sales of clothing or dry goods and report whether the store is selling its regular merchandise at reduced prices, or whether special merchandise has been brought in for the sale.

3. There are some instances where quantity buying (particularly large units as opposed to small units of the same product) result in inconsequential or no savings even though the consumer would be led to believe otherwise. Compare prices with quantities of a number of items at a local supermarket to find out what products provide the consumer with little or no savings on large-unit purchases. What marketing practices make it difficult for consumers to know whether or not large-unit purchasing will result in real savings?

4. Compare as to price and service a number of identical supermarket, drugstore, and service station products at stores and service centers which offer trading stamps with those that do not. Next, compare the value of the many different trading stamps as to their redemption value for premiums. What general conclusions can you draw from this investigation? What are some things a wise consumer will consider as to buying products from stores that give trading stamps as opposed to those that do not?

Chapter 24

Managing our finances

PURPOSE OF THE CHAPTER

Any successful person, regardless of his income, must do some financial planning. Financial planning includes budgeting, keeping certain records, and providing for savings. Financial planning can be difficult or simple. This chapter provides some simple guidelines.

You will find answers to these questions:

1. What is the first step in financial planning?
2. How can income and expenditures be estimated?
3. What records should be kept?
4. Where can savings be placed?

A. Budgeting and keeping records

BUDGETING IS THE FIRST STEP

Operating without some kind of budget is like trying to drive a car without a steering wheel. A *budget* is a systematic plan for using available money to obtain as many as possible of the things we want.

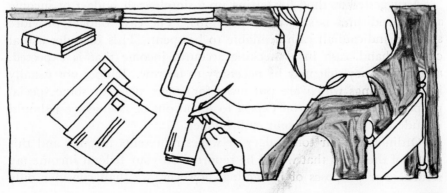

A budget involves (a) estimating how much cash will be available that can be spent or saved, and (b) planning the expenditures.

Income includes not only what we receive in wages or salaries, but also any net profits from business, interest on savings, dividends on stock, or earnings from any other sources. Income from wages or salary is greater than the cash actually received because there are deductions from income for tax purposes. To determine how much cash one will have available, it is necessary to include the cash that one has at the beginning of the period plus the estimated income plus any money that is borrowed.

Expenditures, for the purposes of a budget, include not only actual expenses (money spent for items that will be used up and never recovered), but also the spending of cash for items that will last a long time, and the placing of money into savings and investments. The expenditures also include payments on homes and repayments of loans.

All members of a family should plan the budget.

ESTIMATING CASH AVAILABLE

A suggested method for setting up a simple cash budget of income and expenditures is shown on page 465. The cash budget provides space to indicate all cash available to be spent. This includes actual cash on hand, cash in a checking account, income that is expected, and any money that may be necessary to borrow. It does not usually include savings which are put away for emergencies or some special purpose. However, if you expect to spend out of savings, you should include this amount in your cash budget.

Ordinarily, your total salary or wages represents income, and this is one of the items that would be reported on your federal income tax return. For purposes of budgeting, however, we shall consider only

CASH BUDGET OF INCOME AND EXPENDITURES
(Shown for two months only)

Cash received and paid	January			February		
	Last year	Estimate this year	Actual this year	Last year	Estimate this year	Actual this year
Cash available						
Cash at beginning	$160.00	$180.00	$175.00	$295.30	$300.00	$333.40
Net wages (Take-home pay)	460.00	460.00	480.00	460.00	460.00	480.00
Dividends and interest	6.00	8.00	8.00	6.00	8.00	8.00
Borrowed						
Other:						
Bonus	100.00	100.00	120.00			
Total cash available	726.00	748.00	783.00	761.30	768.00	821.40
Fixed payments (Expenditures)						
Rent or payment on mortgage	80.00	80.00	80.00	80.00	80.00	80.00
Life insurance	50.00	50.00	50.00			
Fire insurance				20.00	20.00	20.00
Auto insurance				55.00	55.00	55.00
Real estate taxes				100.00	100.00	105.00
Payments on debts		25.00	25.00		25.00	25.00
Other insurance (not taken out of pay)	18.00	18.00	18.00			
Contributions to church	10.00	12.00	12.00	10.00	12.00	12.00
Savings	10.00	20.00	20.00	10.00	20.00	50.00
Other:						
Total fixed payments	168.00	205.00	205.00	275.00	312.00	347.00
Variable payments (Expenditures)						
Water				8.00	8.00	10.00
Heat	18.00	17.00	18.00	22.00	22.00	25.00
Telephone	6.50	6.50	6.50	6.50	6.50	6.50
Gas and electricity	6.20	6.50	6.00	16.50	16.50	17.00
Medical	25.00	20.00	28.00	20.00	20.00	18.00
Food	104.00	108.00	105.40	106.00	110.00	112.00
Clothing	31.00	21.00	37.40	71.00	51.00	66.00
Car operations and repair	35.00	30.00	29.30	25.00	22.00	22.00
Other purchases				25.00		20.00
Other contributions						
Recreation and education	23.00	20.00	2.00	20.00	20.00	21.00
Personal	14.00	14.00	12.00	10.00	14.00	15.00
Other taxes						
Other:						
Total variable payments	262.70	243.00	244.60	330.00	290.00	332.50
Summary						
Total cash available	726.00	748.00	783.00	761.30	768.00	821.40
Total payments (fixed and variable)	430.70	448.00	449.60	605.00	602.00	679.50
Cash balance at end	$295.30	$300.00	$333.40	$156.30	$166.00	$141.90

the net wages, or the *take-home pay*. There is no reason to complicate the budgeting or record keeping by including the total wages and then deducting those items that are withheld by the employer. For purposes of expenditures, we will then consider only those items that are spent out of the take-home pay. Wages and salary may be estimated fairly well for a year in advance by considering the wages or salary received in the past year and by making any adjustment that you may anticipate because of wage increases or decreases or because of any expected overtime or unemployment.

Probably the best way to estimate the amount of dividends, interest, bonus, or any other income is to assume that it will be the same as the past year. Sometimes it is necessary to borrow money. If so, this will be part of the cash available and should, therefore, be included in the money that is available to spend. When borrowed money is repaid, it is an expenditure.

ESTIMATING EXPENDITURES

Notice in the cash budget on page 465 that there are two classifications of expenditures: (a) fixed payments and (b) variable payments.

In estimating your expenditures, record first those payments that you know have to be made. These are the *fixed payments,* many of which represent large expenditures. For example, you know that you have to pay the rent or make a payment on your home. You will have certain insurance policies and will know in advance when the payments are due and how much they are. Note that savings are included in this group of fixed payments. If you do not plan your savings in advance, before you allow money for the many optional items, you will probably never save any money. Savings should, therefore, be taken out of each paycheck and put away before the money is spent for other things.

The fixed expenditures should also include payments on money borrowed, interest on money borrowed, church contributions, and installment payments that come due.

The *variable payments,* those that are smaller in amount or more subject to change, may be estimated on the basis of past experience but adjusted to fit anticipated needs. Water, heat, telephone, gas, and electricity are included in the variable payments group because many of these payments are small. The time of payment is known, but payments may vary. In most cases, in setting up your budget, you must decide whether you spent too much last year or whether you will have to spend more. Making this decision is a matter of judgment. You may decide that food prices have gone up and you will have to spend more, that the children are becoming older and you will have to spend more, or that more must be budgeted for personal expenses and school allowances. If you anticipate any major repairs on the automobile, this amount should also be included in your budget.

DAILY CASH RECORD NEEDED

The cash record on page 467 provides a column for the actual cash available and one for the actual expenditures for each month. However, there is only one line for each item in these columns. Several times during the month you may receive wages or salary and purchase

DATE	EXPLANATION	CASH AVAILABLE	RENT	LIFE INSURANCE	FIRE INSURANCE	AUTO INSURANCE	REAL ESTATE TAXES	PAYMENTS ON DEBTS	OTHER INSURANCE	CHURCH	SAVINGS	OTHER PAYMENTS	WATER	HEAT	TELEPHONE	GAS AND ELECTRICITY
Jan. 1	Cash Available	17500														
2	Life Insurance			5000												
4	Groceries															
6	Gasoline															
7	Dental Bill															
7	Dress for Mary															
9	Interest	800														
10	Accident Insurance								1800							
11	Groceries															
15	Personal Allowances															
15	Magazines															
16	Salary	24000														
15	Bonus	12000														
18	Groceries															
19	Theater Tickets															
20	Gasoline															
21	Church									600						
22	Insurance for John															
23	Gift Dr. Smith															
24	Rent		10000													
25	Groceries															
26	Installment Payment							2500								
30	Salary	24000														
31	Church									600						
31	Heating Bill													1800		
31	Savings Account										2000					
31	Gas and Electric Bill															600
31	Groceries															
31	Telephone														250	
	(Cash) Totals	17300	10000	5000				2500	1800	1200	2000			1800	250	600
Feb. 1	Cash Available	33340														
3	Fire Insurance				2000											
4	Rent		10000													
5	Groceries															
6	Auto Insurance					5500										

A partial illustration of a daily cash record for January and February, 19—

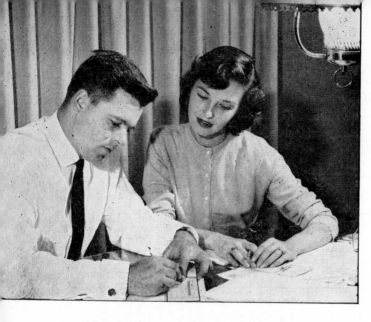

Careful, systematic record keeping is important to the proper maintenance of the budget.

groceries and other items. Therefore, it is necessary to keep a continuous daily record in a cashbook of all types of cash income and expenditures so that these amounts can be summarized at the end of the month and then recorded in the proper columns in the budget. One form of cashbook record is illustrated on page 467.

The entries in your cashbook should be made regularly at the time money is received and paid. If you use a checkbook, some of this information can be recorded from the checkbook stubs.

Another method of keeping the daily records is to use a notebook in which one page is devoted to each kind of income and expenditure. From this notebook you can determine the totals and insert them in the proper columns in your budget.

Check your budget regularly. At the end of each month when the actual expenditures are transferred to the proper column in the cash budget, you can then make a comparison to see how well you are following your budget. If you are spending too much money, you may find it necessary to reduce your budgeted expenditures in the future.

STATEMENT OF ASSETS AND LIABILITIES

Occasionally, it is desirable for a family or an individual to determine how much is owned (*assets*) and how much is owed (*liabilities*). A *statement of assets and liabilities* will show what the real net worth or ownership is.

On the opposite page is a statement of assets and liabilities for a family. Of course, the family had to estimate the value of the household equipment and the automobile. By looking at their life insurance policies, they were able to determine the cash value of their

468

policies. The value of the United States savings bonds was determined by examining the table on the bonds.

W. A. JAMES FAMILY
STATEMENT OF ASSETS AND LIABILITIES
DECEMBER 31, 19—

Assets owned by the family		Debts owed by the family	
Cash in checking account	$ 232.00	City Savings Bank	$ 100.00
Cash in savings account	305.70	(due on refrigerator)	
U. S. savings bonds	250.00	Owed to Central Store	25.00
Life insurance (cash		Total debts	125.00
value)	391.33		
Household equipment	950.00		
Automobile	1,000.00		
Vacant lot	800.00	Net worth (ownership)	3,804.03
Total assets	$3,929.03	Total debts and net worth	$3,929.03

(Total assets, $3,929.03 — Total debts, $125.00, = Net worth, $3,804.03)

RECORDS NEEDED FOR INCOME TAXES

Besides the records required for the cash budget and the statement of assets and liabilities, one will also need to accumulate during the year some information that will help him fill out an income-tax return in case he plans to itemize certain deductions.

At the end of the year, an employer is required to furnish each of his employees a statement (Form W-2) indicating the amount of income tax withheld. If a person's income is less than $10,000 he may fill out a short form, Form 1040A, which does not require him to list all his deductions. However, if it is to his advantage to do so, he may fill out the long Form 1040 and itemize deductions.

For federal income-tax purposes, one is required to list *all* income before deductions from wages. Other types of income must be included, but not money obtained from borrowing or from gifts. If one of the long forms of income tax return is submitted, the taxpayer is entitled to itemize deductions for: (a) state and local taxes and licenses, (b) contributions to church and charity, but not personal gifts, (c) a certain proportion of medical expenses if they are great enough, and (d) certain losses and thefts which are not covered by insurance.

OTHER FINANCIAL RECORDS NEEDED

A record of items having value, such as furniture, appliances, books, jewelry, and silverware, should be kept to provide an inventory in case of loss by fire or theft. Dates of purchase, from whom purchased, and cost should be shown on the record.

Though deeds to property, stock certificates, bonds, and insurance policies should be kept in a safe-deposit box, a record of these items should always be kept.

B. A savings plan

SAVINGS AND FINANCIAL MANAGEMENT

In the discussion of budgeting, it was emphasized that a budget should include regular amounts for savings. Unless savings are planned, there usually will be no savings. Unless there are savings, an individual or a family can never look forward to having the really important things they want.

As was explained in Chapter 6, the savings of millions of people, when used for financing business, create new capital, new jobs, and greater production for the benefit of all. Therefore, as each person saves and puts his money to work where it will draw interest, he is helping his country.

Some decisions that must be made

For immediate or short-range pleasure		For permanent value or longer-lasting happiness
1. Shall I spend 50 cents a day on little pleasures?	or	Should I save 30 cents a day and have $100 for a summer vacation?
2. Shall I wear the latest styles?	or	Should I wear good clothes longer?
3. Shall I be satisfied with a limited education?	or	Should I save and go to college?
4. Shall I spend foolishly on dates now?	or	Should I save to have money to furnish a home after marriage?
5. Do I really need a car now?	or	Should I buy life insurance or invest the money?
6. Shall I drive or take a bus?	or	Shall I walk and save for new clothes?
7. Should I buy lots of new clothes now?	or	Shall I save for a down payment on a home after marriage?
8. Should the family spend all and live lavishly now?	or	Should the family plan to educate the children and prepare for old age?
9. Should we "keep up with the Joneses"?	or	Should we live our own lives and save for the future?
10. Should we rent a home and spend the rest?	or	Should we buy a home and invest all we can?
11. Shall we buy now on the installment plan and pay more?	or	Shall we save and pay cash?
12. Shall we let the future take care of itself?	or	Shall we build a savings, investment, and insurance program?

SAVING CAN BE REWARDING

Setting aside a part of income regularly is known as *saving*. A regular plan of saving is evidence of good money management. Saving can be fun if you will look forward to some greater future pleasures by giving up some of your present spending for foolish or unnecessary things. The question before you is whether you are willing to make a plan that will enable you to reach a desirable and pleasant goal. Some of the decisions that you have made in planning a savings program are discussed in the following sections.

SETTING GOALS FOR SAVINGS

Most people have some definite goals in life, some things toward which they are striving. Some of these goals are really ideals and ambitions, and some are desires for material things that will add to the comfort and pleasantness of living. Regardless of the kind of goals we may have for ourselves, money is usually a factor in achieving them. Most of us have to set aside a little at a time from our income in order to accumulate enough to realize our goals.

Worthwhile goals of saving

1. Further education.
2. Marriage and furnishing a home.
3. Buying a home.
4. Starting a business.
5. Buying insurance for protection and future income.
6. Investments in securities for future income.
7. Buying major comforts and luxuries for better living.
8. Providing for emergencies, such as unemployment and hospital bills.
9. Paying cash to save on the purchase of important items instead of buying on the installment plan.
10. Retirement.
11. Vacation.

MAKING MONEY WORK FOR YOU

Very few people realize the cumulative power of compound interest. Interest is a very faithful worker, but it will work for you only if you have savings. This fact explains why many people live comfortably after retirement. Although they cease to work, their money continues to work for them by earning interest.

One of the most important goals of a savings program is the provision for an education for a chosen occupation.

Ewing Galloway

Let us see how a savings program will grow. The following table shows how much will be accumulated if $10 is deposited each month in a savings account at various rates of interest. In this table the interest is computed semiannually. For example, if a young man starts saving $10 a month in the second grade and if the interest is computed semiannually at 3 percent a year, he would have $1,399.56 at the usual age of graduation from high school.

Amount of savings at end of	Annual rate of interest		
	3%	3½%	4%
7 years	$ 935.13	$ 952.19	$ 969.62
10 years	1,399.56	1,436.61	1,474.85
12 years	1,733.04	1,788.74	1,846.61
15 years	2,272.03	2,364.93	2,462.48
20 years	3,284.56	3,469.10	3,666.40

Growth of regular savings

WHERE TO PUT SAVINGS

The average individual saves only a few dollars a month. Hence, he needs a place to put his monthly savings until a sufficient amount accumulates to invest in bonds, stocks, real estate, or in some other form of permanent investment. In deciding upon a place to put savings where they will earn income, consider these questions:

1. Will the savings be safe?
2. Will the savings earn a reasonable rate of interest?
3. Will the savings be available at any time?
4. How often is interest compounded?

Commercial banks. As mentioned in Chapter 11, most commercial banks have savings departments. These banks generally pay a fixed rate of interest.

472

Watch your savings grow.

Banks usually are conveniently located, making it easy to deposit savings at the time of cashing a paycheck. The interest on savings may be credited quarterly, semiannually, or annually. Some banks require thirty days' notice before withdrawing a savings deposit. This right is not always exercised, but it may be if necessary. The savings departments of commercial banks will usually accept time deposits at a slightly higher rate of interest than is paid on regular savings accounts. A *time deposit* is usually made for six months, one year, or longer; and a certificate is issued to the depositor indicating that the deposit, plus interest at the agreed rate, may be withdrawn at the end of the specified time.

Each deposit account in all national and in many other banks is insured by the Federal Deposit Insurance Corporation to the extent of $15,000.

Savings banks. Some savings banks are organized as stock companies in which the owners invest money and also accept deposits in savings accounts. Interest is paid on these deposits and usually these banks make loans only to consumers. Some savings banks, however, operate as trust companies and in other ways are similar to commercial banks since both institutions lend to businesses. Besides accepting money for regular savings accounts, savings banks also accept time deposits in the same manner as commercial banks.

Mutual savings banks. A *mutual savings bank* is a slightly different type of bank because it is owned by the depositors. The depositors are not promised a fixed rate of interest. If there is a profit, each depositor is paid a dividend instead of interest. But, if there is no profit earned on the operations of the bank, the depositors do not get a dividend. In most other respects, however, a mutual savings bank is operated the same as the savings department of any other bank.

Mutual savings banks permit a depositor to withdraw his funds on demand or after giving notice. The laws of most states require notice of 30 to 90 days, but usually withdrawals may be made instantly on demand. Mutual banks do not ordinarily accept checking accounts, but in a few states they do.

The accounts in most mutual savings banks are insured by the Federal Deposit Insurance Corporation up to $15,000, and in a few states all deposits are insured under the state banking laws.

Industrial banks. As explained in Chapter 11, industrial banks are owned and controlled by stockholders who invest their money. Most industrial banks accept regular deposits and time deposits in the same manner as commercial banks, and they pay interest on these deposits.

Savings and loan associations. The savings and loan association is organized for the purpose of lending money to people who do not have enough money to buy or to build a home. The money that the association lends is accumulated from depositors. In many states, when a person makes deposits in a savings and loan association, he really buys shares and becomes a part owner. These shares earn income generally at a slightly higher rate of interest than that on a savings account in a bank.

Many savings and loans associations will also accept time deposits at a slightly higher rate of interest or dividend than is generally paid on demand deposits. In this respect, the practice is similar to that of savings departments of commercial banks.

Most savings and loan associations are mutual associations and in this respect are similar to mutual savings banks. Those who have money deposited in the savings and loans association receive dividends, which are the earnings. There usually is no guaranteed dividend rate, but the expected rate is announced from time to time. A few savings and loan associations are organized as stock companies in which the owners invest money and accept deposits in a manner similar to that of a stock savings bank. Interest is paid on these deposits.

All federal savings and loan associations are members of the Federal Home Loan Bank and operate under regulations established by the federal government. The accounts of these associations are insured with the Federal Savings and Loan Insurance Corporation. All state-chartered savings and loan associations may have their accounts insured with the Federal Savings and Loan Insurance Corporation if they are members of the Federal Home Loan Bank and if they pass rigid insurability tests.

Under normal conditions, withdrawals may be made from savings and loan associations on demand. However, under most state laws the institution is allowed thirty days in which to fill a request for a withdrawal. In times of economic stress, state laws impose additional restrictions on withdrawals for the protection of the institution and the depositor.

United States savings bonds, Series E. United States post offices sell United States savings bonds. Banks and some savings and loan associations sell United States savings bonds without any charge or commission for this service. Several types of government bonds may be purchased by investors; however, the most popular among people who are saving small amounts regularly are the Series E bonds. Series E bonds may be purchased in denominations of $25, $50, $75, $100, $200, $500, $1,000, and $10,000. The purchase price of a $25 bond is $18.75 and will be redeemed at maturity at $25. A $50 bond costs $37.50, a $75 bond costs $56.25, a $100 bond costs $75, a $200 bond costs $150, a $500 bond costs $375, a $1,000 bond costs $750, and a $10,000 bond costs $7,500.

While the rate of interest earned on United States savings bonds is not high, it is reasonable in comparison with the rate of earnings on some other savings. If a bond is held until maturity (seven years), it has a yield of 4.15 percent interest, compounded semiannually.

THRIFTY Sez—

THRIFTY Sez—

The promotion of interest in U.S. savings bonds by the Treasury Department and by various private agencies helps to stimulate investment in bonds as a form of savings.

Treasury Department

United States savings bonds, Series H. Another type of United States savings bonds is known as the Series H bond, which is sold in denominations of $500, $1,000, $5,000, and $10,000. Series H bonds may be purchased at the prices indicated from federal reserve banks and most other banks and financial institutions. The difference between the Series H bond and the Series E bond is in the method of paying the interest. In the case of the Series E bond, for example, one pays $18.75 for a $25 bond and gets $25 when it is redeemed at maturity. If it is held longer, the interest will continue to accumulate. In the case of the Series H bond, one pays $500 for a bond and receives checks from the United States Treasury each year for the interest at an average rate of approximately 4.15 percent.

Credit unions. *Credit unions* are cooperative associations operating both as savings and as lending institutions for the benefit of their members. In most states, credit unions have operated and are authorized to operate under state laws. With the passage of the Federal Credit Union Act of 1934, federal credit unions may be organized and operated under a federal charter.

Credit unions are usually formed by large groups of people with common interests. For instance, they may be formed by such groups as teachers in a large school system, workers in a large factory, store employees, and members of a church.

While the credit unions established under the laws of the various states are by no means uniform, there is uniformity in the organization of federal credit unions. A member of a federal credit union must buy at least one $5 share. He may subscribe for a larger number of shares if he desires.

When a member has paid for one share, he is eligible for his proportionate share of the annual dividends that may be declared by the members. These dividends represent interest earned on the money deposited with the credit union and loaned to others.

Endowment insurance. In Chapter 27 you will learn more about life insurance. Most life insurance policies provide not only protection but also savings. *Endowment insurance* policies combine life insurance with a high degree of savings. An endowment policy is purchased over a stated number of years, such as ten, twenty, or thirty. The cash value of such policies builds up rather rapidly. Many people use endowment policies as a combination of protection for the family while saving for some specific purpose. For example, a young man in high school may buy a $2,000 endowment policy at age 16 with the idea that when he is 26 years of age and married, the face value of the policy will become due, and he will have $2,000 to make a down payment on a home.

Annuities. Although life insurance annuities will be discussed in detail in Chapter 27, they are mentioned at this point as another means of saving. If one has a certain sum of money, such as $3,000, he can purchase a life insurance *annuity,* which at a stipulated age will be paid back to him in monthly payments with interest. Annuities can also be purchased on the installment plan, which is a method of saving that will build up an income for retirement, at which time the amount of the policy will be paid back in monthly installments with interest.

ECONOMIC PROBLEMS OF SAVINGS PROGRAMS

There is always some risk in any savings or investment program. That is why it is important to put savings in a safe place.

Interest rates may change from time to time; and the amount of dividends declared may vary, depending upon economic conditions. For example, if banks have more money than they can invest at a profit, they will reduce the interest rates they pay on deposits.

There is another economic problem involved in saving. Let us assume that you have $5,000 in a savings account on which you are drawing interest or dividends. If prices and the cost of living rise over a period of ten years to the extent of 20 percent, the original amount that you had in the savings account will purchase approximately 20 percent less than it would have purchased at the time it was deposited. In the chapters on investments you will learn how some people invest their savings to try to protect themselves against this situation, which is called inflation.

Facts everyone should know about a savings program

1. Choices must be made between immediate spending or saving for later substantial spending.
2. A budget is desirable in any savings program.
3. Goals for saving should be established.
4. There are several safe places in which to put savings where interest will be earned.
5. Savings of a small amount each week are worthwhile and will grow at compound interest.

▪ QUESTIONS ON THE TEXT

1. What is a budget?
2. For purposes of budgeting in this chapter, what is meant by income?
3. For purposes of budgeting, why should you consider only take-home pay?
4. Give examples of (a) fixed payments or expenditures; (b) variable payments or expenditures in a family budget.
5. How can you keep records so that your daily expenditures can be compared with your budget?
6. In addition to the regular budget, why is it necessary to keep a daily record of income and expenditures?
7. In the preparation of a statement of assets and liabilities, name at least two items that are usually placed in the assets column.
8. From a statement of assets and liabilities, how can one determine his net worth or ownership?
9. Besides the information shown in the budget in this chapter, what information will be needed for income-tax purposes?
10. From the point of view of economics in our society, why are the savings of people so important?
11. Indicate some decisions that you must make daily to determine whether to spend for immediate pleasure or to save and spend for greater values and longer-lasting happiness.
12. Name at least three important goals of saving.
13. From the proper table in this chapter determine the amount of savings that will be accumulated if $10 a month is deposited in a savings account at 4 percent interest for a period of twenty years, if the interest is computed semiannually.
14. What facts should be considered in selecting a place to open a savings account?
15. What is a time deposit?
16. What kind of savings institution often has the privilege of requiring a depositor to wait before withdrawing his money?
17. What are the primary purposes for which savings and loan associations are organized?
18. (a) What rate of interest is paid on a United States savings bond if it is held to maturity?
    (b) How long must a bond be owned until maturity?
19. Explain the difference between United States savings bonds, Series E, and United States savings bonds, Series H.
20. Why is endowment insurance considered a method of saving?

▪ QUESTIONS FOR DISCUSSION

1. Why does information gathered from past experience help in establishing a budget?

2. If Mr. Murphy finds that, according to his budget, he is not going to have enough cash in his checking account to take care of expenses, what can he do to avoid this situation?
3. Why is it recommended that savings be classified under fixed payments in the cash budget?
4. Can you explain why savings and purchases in a cash budget are considered to be expenditures?
5. According to the cash budget in this chapter, how would the receipt of a Christmas gift of $50 be recorded, and how would it be handled if it were placed in savings?
6. If a person keeping the family budget discovers by monthly comparisons that expenditures for food are exceeding the budget, what would you recommend be done?
7. According to the classifications in the budget, how would you record the cost of a hunting license?
8. If income proves to be less than was originally expected, what must be done with the budget?
9. Indicate some choices that you can make in your present spending to save for additional education.
10. Why is it necessary to correlate budgeting, saving, and buying a home?
11. Suppose a young man finds that he is able to save $50 a month. After ten months he has accumulated $500 and decides to use this amount as a down payment on an automobile. It will cost him $50 a month to complete paying on an automobile. Is he justified in buying the automobile?
12. Many people like to keep up with the Joneses; therefore, they borrow money and buy many things on the installment account in order to live like their neighbors and friends who may have larger incomes. What advice would you give to a person of this kind?
13. If prices and the cost of living increase and we have inflation, how does this affect savings in a savings account or United States savings bonds?

■ **PROBLEMS TO SOLVE**

1. Make a rough estimate of what you think is the dollar value of your personal ownership. Check the accuracy of your estimate by actually preparing a personal statement of assets and liabilities similar to the illustration in this chapter. You may have to get some assistance from your parents in finding the cash value of life insurance that they may have purchased for you and in estimating the value of some of your personal possessions. Be sure to include in your statement those personal possessions that would have a dollar value to someone else, such as a bicycle, record player, or a stamp or coin collection. How close were you to your first estimate of your net worth?

2. Suppose you wish to finance the purchase of a used car priced at $600. After financing charges have been added to the cost of the car, you find that you must make 12 monthly payments of $54. If, on the other hand, you would have invested the $54 monthly for 12 months at 4 percent, compounded semiannually, how much would you have saved at the end of the year?

3. Make an investigation by polling the students in your school (or limit your investigation to just the junior and senior classes) to find out (a) how many students have some sort of savings program, (b) for what are they saving, (c) whether a larger percentage of boys establish and maintain a savings program than girls—or vice versa, and (d) how different are the objectives or purposes for maintaining a savings program between teenage boys and girls.

▪ COMMUNITY PROBLEMS AND PROJECTS

1. Using the cash budget and the cashbook in this chapter as models, prepare a budget of your own, basing it on your past experience. Also prepare a cashbook with columns that will meet your own needs. Keep a record of your income and expenditures for at least two months.

2. From time to time various household magazines print articles and budgets prepared and followed by actual families with varying yearly incomes. Select one of these budgets and with your parents analyze the budget in terms of whether (a) any important items have been omitted or unimportant items included, (b) the amounts allotted for the various items are realistic for your geographic area. Be ready to discuss in class why it might not be wise or possible for a family to try to follow a budget prepared by another family.

3. Under the guidance of your teacher, make a study of your local savings institutions, such as banks, saving and loan associations, and credit unions. Make a detailed analysis of the procedures for depositing and withdrawing savings. In such cases as the savings and loan associations, find out whether, when you deposit savings, you become a purchaser of shares or whether you are a depositor as in a bank.

4. Select a particular college that you prefer and make a study of the cost of attending that college. From the college obtain information with regard to tuition, laboratory fees, room rents, and cost of meals and laundry. Add to these amounts the cost of clothing, amusement, transportation, and any other items that you believe should be included in the cost of a college education. Make an estimate of the total cost for each of the four years of a college education. Prepare a report showing how you believe it will be possible to finance this education through (a) income from parents or relatives, (b) loans, (c) scholarships, (d) personal savings, (e) earnings made while you are in school.

Chapter 25

Principles and procedures of investing

PURPOSE OF THE CHAPTER

In this chapter you will learn about the various choices of investing savings and about the ways in which decisions must be made in investing.

You will find answers to these questions:

1. What are the differences between stocks and bonds?
2. What are the different kinds of bonds?
3. What is a mutual fund?
4. How can you obtain information on investments?
5. How are securities bought and sold?

A. Kinds and choices of investments

GOVERNMENT BONDS

U.S. government bonds. In addition to United States government savings bonds, discussed in Chapter 24, there are other types of federal

government bonds that can be purchased as an investment. Remember that a bond represents a promise to pay the face value of the bond at some time in the future, with yearly interest at a specified rate. A bond is as good as the government that issues it.

Generally, federal government bonds rank at the top as to quality. However, there are many other good governmental bonds. Any broker or dealer selling bonds can provide information as to the reputation of the governmental unit in paying interest and in paying bonds when due.

Municipal bonds. Besides federal government bonds, there are bonds issued by states, countries, cities, school districts, villages, townships, and other governmental agencies. These are called *municipal bonds*.

Any governmental unit that issues a bond is required by law to make provision to pay the interest and to pay the debt when it becomes due. The money for interest payments and debt retirement usually comes from taxation. The tax receipts of a governmental unit are comparable to the earnings of a business. The economic conditions within such a unit are comparable to the competitive conditions within an industry. Such factors have a definite effect upon the ability of the issuer of the bonds to pay interest and to repay the principal on the maturity date. State and national legislation also have a definite bearing upon the value of governmental bonds. For instance, state legislation allowing a governmental unit to postpone interest payments on bonds would have the effect of reducing the value of the bonds.

Interest earned on municipal bonds is exempt from federal income taxes. For that reason, many people like to buy municipal bonds even though they may not be quite so safe as federal or state bonds.

Because most governmental bonds are considered safe investments, the rates of interest paid on these bonds are relatively low. However, the rates are often higher than can be earned on deposits in a savings account.

Foreign bonds. Some investors are tempted to purchase foreign governmental bonds. For the average investor these are not good investments even though the interest rates may be high. In the past, some foreign governments have failed to pay their bonds when they have become due and have not made their interest payments regularly.

COMMON STOCK

Owners of *common stock* of a corporation are ordinarily entitled to participate in the earnings and in the election of a board of

A stock certificate

directors. Common stock is issued in what are called *shares*. In other words, when you buy stock in a corporation, you are buying a share in the ownership. The extent of your ownership depends on the number of shares that you own in relation to the number of shares that have been issued and sold. For example, if 1,000 shares of common stock of a corporation have been issued and sold, and you own 100 shares, you own a 10 percent interest in the corporation.

A corporation makes no promise or guarantee that a dividend will be paid. Since a dividend is a share of profits, there may be none; and the dividend may be greater or less than the dividend on preferred stock, which will be discussed later.

Some corporations issue more than one kind of common stock, such as Class A and Class B. There is such a great variety in each class of stock that it is difficult to distinguish between the different grades. The provisions governing a stock should be read carefully to determine one's rights and obligations. The holders of one grade of common stock may have voting power, whereas the holders of another grade may not. When there are various grades or classes of a common stock, the public is usually urged to buy the least desirable class. The better classes are often reserved for those who are promoting the sale of the stock.

Par-value and no-par-value stocks. Stocks are also designated as *par-value stocks* or *no-par-value stocks*. Par value means very little to the average investor or even to the expert, for the par value of a stock has no specific relation to the actual value. A stock may bear a par value of $100, but it may be sold for $65 or $110. The use of a definite par value for a stock was probably intended originally to indicate the worth of the stock, but the practice of assigning par values to stocks has resulted in many abuses. For instance, there have been cases in which promoters have sold stock to unsuspecting investors on the assumption of the latter that the stock was worth approximately the par value assigned to it.

The use of no-par-value stock is intended as a means of avoiding the inference that the stock is worth a certain amount. A no-par-value stock bears no designated value. Its value, like the value of par-value stock, is regulated by what the investing public believes the stock is worth.

Stock splits. Common stocks sometimes increase in value. For example, a stock that is selling for $40 a share may eventually sell for $140 a share. For some reason, investors do not like to buy stocks that sell at such high prices. Therefore, the corporation may *split* the stocks. Let us assume that there were 100,000 shares of a corporation whose stock was selling for $40 a share, and that the price of this stock eventually increased to $140 a share. The corporation may then decide to issue two new shares of stock for each share outstanding, which would make 300,000 shares outstanding. If you owned 100 shares of stock before the split, you would have owned 1/1,000 share of the corporation. After the stock split, you would still have the same proportionate share in the ownership, but you would have 300 shares of stock.

It is difficult to predict what will happen to the price of stock after a stock split. In the case above, one share of stock was worth $140 before the split. The three shares of stock after the split should still be worth $140. However, there might be an increased demand for the stock at the lower price. Therefore, the three new shares together might sell for $150, or $50 a share.

Stock rights. The shares of some common stocks sometimes carry with them certain special *rights* that may have some value. For example, when a corporation is formed and stock is sold, the stock certificates might carry a promise that if any additional stock is issued by the corporation, the original stockholders may purchase the new stock in some proportion to the shares they own and at a stipulated price. If the value of the stock has gone up, there may be some advantage in exercising these rights. Usually the rights can be sold to someone else. Let us say that you own ten shares of stock selling at $50 a share and that you have the right to buy one new share at a price of $30 a share for each five that you own. You can either buy these two shares for $30 each or sell your rights to someone else.

PREFERRED STOCK

The owners of *preferred stock* have a share in the ownership of a corporation, but usually they do not have a right to vote in the election of corporate directors. They do, however, have certain preferred claims, and that is the way in which this stock gets its name. Preferred stock usually has a preference as to dividends; that is, the owners of preferred stock receive their stipulated and fixed share of the profits before the common stockholders are paid their dividends. Sometimes the stock is preferred as to assets in case the corporation discontinues business. In other words, if the assets of the business are sold, the preferred stockholders will be paid before the common stockholders.

Cumulative preferred stock. There is one type of preferred stock that is issued under the agreement that back dividends will be paid to the holders of the stock at the regular rate if the dividends are ever discontinued temporarily. This type of preferred stock is called *cumulative*. For example, if the dividends on cumulative preferred stock are discontinued for one year, the cumulative preferred stockholders will receive those dividends as soon as the company earns enough profits to pay them. These back dividends must be paid before any other dividends are paid.

Noncumulative preferred stock. Preferred stock may also be *noncumulative*. If the stock is noncumulative, the preferred stockholders are not guaranteed their income in case the corporation ceases temporarily to pay dividends. If the corporation does not earn a profit, dividends may not be declared. When profits are earned again, the preferred stockholders begin to receive dividends again, but they do not receive dividends for the period of time during which no profits were earned.

Participating preferred stock. Some preferred stocks are classified as *participating*. In the case of such stocks, if there are excess earnings after the regular dividend on preferred stock and a specified dividend on common stock have been distributed, the preferred stockholders will participate with the common stockholders in the surplus earnings. For example, the regular dividend rate on a preferred stock may be 6 percent of the par value of the stock. If the earnings of the company, however, become large enough to pay a dividend at a specified rate on the common stock, in addition to the 6 percent dividend on the preferred stock, the preferred stockholders will share with the common stockholders in the surplus earnings.

Convertible preferred stock. If a preferred stock is *convertible*, it may be converted into or traded for other securities of the same corporation, usually common stock, at a specified price, or one share of preferred stock is convertible into a certain specific number of shares of common stock. For example, the owner of one share of convertible preferred stock might have a right to trade one share for two shares of common stock under certain conditions or at a certain time. This privilege may have an advantage if the common stock increases in value.

CLOSE AND OPEN CORPORATIONS

Close corporation. A *close corporation* (often called *closely held*) is one in which the stock is owned usually by a small group of people and sometimes by only one or two families. Those who own the greater share of the stock are generally the managers. Those who own the minority share of the stock have practically nothing to say with regard to the management but take what dividends are allotted to them on the basis of their holdings. Those who operate the business may pay themselves large salaries and thus leave very little for dividends.

There is considerable risk in buying stock in a close corporation because of the difficulty in selling the stock if one should try to do so. There are not many people who will want to buy stock in a corporation of this type.

Open corporation. The most common type of corporation is an open corporation. An *open corporation* (often called *public corporation* or *publicly held corporation*) is one whose stock is available for public sale. The securities (bonds and stocks) of these corporations will be discussed in detail in this chapter. The securities of open corporations may be either listed on stock exchanges or unlisted; but even in the case of an unlisted security of an open corporation, there is still a better market for these securities than those of a close corporation because it is not listed on a stock exchange, the corporation need not publish financial statements, and it might be difficult to sell.

CORPORATION BONDS

Bonds are evidence of a debt owed by the enterprise; they do not represent a share in the ownership of an enterprise. When a business issues bonds, it acknowledges that it owes the holders a certain sum of money and agrees to repay the sum on a certain date and under certain conditions. It also agrees to pay interest at a specified rate and at specified intervals.

Coupon bonds. Anyone who owns a *coupon bond* can tear off each coupon as it becomes due and present it to his bank for the collection of interest.

Registered bonds. A *registered bond* is a bond that is recorded by the issuer in the name of the person to whom it has been sold. The

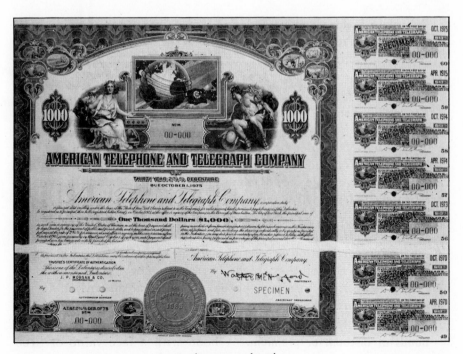

A coupon bond

interest on the bond will be paid only to the registered owner. From the point of view of theft, a registered bond is therefore safer than a coupon bond.

Mortgage bonds. When a bond is issued, the issuing corporation usually pledges some security, such as specific property or the right to certain earnings. A railroad may pledge some of its equipment or its real estate. When some property is pledged to the buyers of the bonds, these bonds are known as *mortgage bonds*.

Although certain property or rights are pledged to insure the safety of the principal of a mortgage bond, various difficulties are encountered if the bondholders are forced to take over the property or the rights in case the interest is not paid. It is therefore desirable to investigate bonds from the following points of view:

1. Record of past earnings of the company and likelihood of future earnings.
2. Record of past market prices of the bonds.
3. Competitive and general business conditions.
4. Marketability of the bonds.

Debenture bonds. Some bonds are issued by corporations without any specific pledge of property. The bonds are backed by the general credit, reputation, and assets of the corporation. Bonds of this type are called *debenture bonds*.

Convertible bonds. Some bonds are designated as convertible. A *convertible bond* is one in which there is an agreement that permits or forces the bondholder under certain conditions to accept stock in exchange for his bond. There are so many possible stipulations in relation to convertible bonds that any particular bond should be investigated and studied carefully.

Callable bonds. A *callable bond* is one that may be repaid or retired by the issuing corporation before the date on which the bond matures. For example, a corporation might borrow money by selling bonds and reserve the right to repay the bond owners at an earlier date if the corporation is able to do so.

Bonds at discount or premium. A bond with a face value of $100 may be issued at $2\frac{1}{2}$ percent interest. If the buyers of bonds at that time feel that the interest rate is not high enough, they might pay only $90 for the bond. Paying less than the stated value of the bond is called buying at a *discount*. The bond will not only increase in value from $90 to $100 by the time it is redeemed, but it will also earn interest at a rate of $2.50 a year on a $90 investment.

On the other hand, a bond may be issued at a face value of $100 at 3½ percent interest. If it is a good bond and buyers feel that this is a high rate of interest, the bond might be sold for $105. Paying more than the stated value of the bond is referred to as buying at a *premium*.

The selling of bonds below or above par, or face value, is not necessarily an indication of their value. The selling of bonds below par may result from (a) unsatisfactory security that has been pledged by the issuer of the bonds, (b) an interest rate that is low in comparison with interest rates on other similar securities, or (c) unfavorable economic conditions that result in a lack of demand for bonds.

Prior claims on earnings. Under the laws of most states, dividends cannot be paid on either preferred stock or common stock unless all interest has been paid on outstanding bonds. It is also a general rule that dividends cannot be paid on common stock unless those on preferred stock have been paid.

In other words, bondholders have first claim on earnings, before preferred stockholders; preferred stockholders have second claim on earnings, before common stockholders; and common stockholders receive dividends only to the extent that there are sufficient earnings to pay them. Dividends are never promised or guaranteed. In poor years the preferred stockholders are therefore more likely than common stockholders to get their dividends; in good years, however, common stockholders have the possibility of getting much more than is paid to preferred stockholders.

COMPARISONS OF CORPORATION BONDS AND STOCKS

In order to illustrate different types of bonds and stocks, let us consider a corporation with $100,000 of 3 percent first-mortgage bonds outstanding; $100,000 of 4 percent debenture bonds; $200,000 of noncumulative 6 percent preferred stock (2,000 shares at $100 par); and 20,000 shares of common stock. If the corporation makes a profit of $47,000 after $7,000 has been paid to bondholders and after taxes have been paid, the preferred stockholders will get $12,000 in dividends, leaving a remainder of $35,000 available for the common stockholders. At the discretion of the board of directors, all or part of the amount available may be declared as a dividend to common stockholders. If a dividend of $1 a share is declared, the common stockholders will get $20,000, leaving $15,000 to be added to the surplus of the corporation.

Let us assume, however, that in another year the corporation makes only $9,000 net profit after paying taxes but has some money in the bank. The mortgage bondholders are entitled to their interest at 3 percent, amounting to $3,000. The debenture bondholders have a first claim on whatever earnings remain. They are therefore paid $4,000, leaving $2,000 to be divided among the preferred stockholders. The common stockholders get nothing.

MUTUAL FUNDS

One of the principles of investment is not to place "all your eggs in one basket." Many small investors, however, are not able to buy a variety of stocks or bonds. Therefore, these investors may prefer to buy shares of stock in investment companies or mutual funds. The money received from the sale of shares in an investment company or a mutual fund is invested in a great variety of securities. The owner of a share in one of these companies is a part owner of a company that owns several different types of securities. These companies are called *investment companies, investment trusts,* or *mutual funds.*

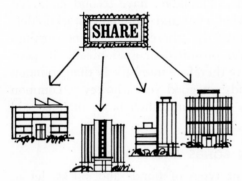

One share in a mutual fund is part ownership in shares of many corporations.

They vary widely as to their method of organization, their management, the type of securities they buy, and the methods by which ownership shares are sold. In all cases, however, the purpose is to obtain money from investors which is then reinvested in a variety of securities so that the investor in the investment fund owns a share in a wide list of securities. For example, instead of investing $1,000 in one particular corporation, it is possible for an investor to buy

$1,000 worth of shares in an investment company and thereby have an interest in perhaps 100 or more different securities.

The purpose of an investment company is therefore to provide a wide diversification of investment that is managed by experts, so that an individual who has only a small investment to make and who is not an expert may have these advantages. However, in selecting an investment company in which to invest funds, it is desirable to study the purposes and organization by consulting a reliable broker. Each investment trust follows certain policies. One investment company may invest its funds principally in conservative securities that do not pay especially high dividends, but another may invest its funds in speculative securities that may have greater opportunity for growth in value.

Open-end investment company. Some investment companies follow a policy that requires the company to purchase back the shares of stock owned by investors if requested to do so and continue to sell new shares and invest the money. They are called *open-end companies*.

Closed-end investment company. Another type of investment company is called a *closed-end company*. This type of company does not continue to sell new shares and does not agree to buy back shares. In the case of the open-end company, there is an assured market; but in the case of the closed-end company, the investor has to take his chance on selling his shares to any investor who might want them.

INVESTING IN A SMALL BUSINESS

For some people, owning and operating a small business is one of the most important dreams and objectives in their lives. These people may be able to save their money until they have enough to go in business for themselves. Before anyone decides to invest his life savings by buying or starting a business, however, he should make a very careful study of all the problems involved. To own and operate a small business is not easy, and one should have some experience in the business before attempting to operate it alone.

People with money are frequently tempted to buy an interest in a partnership, or stock in a small corporation in which a friend is interested, or to lend money to a friend or a relative in business. Such investments should be made with the utmost care.

Investing in a partnership involves complicated legal responsibilities in most states. Even though one of the partners may not be actively engaged in the business, under the laws of many states he is equally responsible with the other partners for debts of the firm. For instance, suppose that you become a part owner of a business and allow your partner to operate it. The business fails to make a profit, and the creditors demand payment. If your partner cannot pay, the creditors can demand payment from you.

Many people with experience will advocate not investing in the enterprise of a friend or a relative. The friend or the relative usually feels that he has the right to operate the business as he sees fit. He may legally have the right, but sooner or later trouble may arise.

INVESTING IN REAL ESTATE

When one is planning the purchase of real estate as an investment, the following seven points should be considered carefully after the desirability of the location and the quality of the property have been determined:

1. Can the property be rented?
2. At what price can the property be rented?
3. What will be the annual cost of repairs?
4. What will be the taxes and assessments?
5. What will be the yearly loss from depreciation?
6. During what percentage of time will the property be vacant?
7. What will be the approximate net earnings?

Real estate is subject to fluctuations in price. The current cost of a piece of property is therefore no indication of its future value. The community may change rapidly with a resulting decrease or

A person well acquainted with managing property may find real estate to be a suitable type of investment.

Ewing Galloway

increase in the value of the property. Because of a change in business conditions, the value of the property may be raised or lowered.

The purchase of unimproved real estate (with no buildings) is usually a speculative investment made in the hope that it can be resold at a profit. A person well acquainted with managing property may find real estate more suitable than any other type of investment; but if one is not in a position to manage real estate with buildings on it, it may not prove to be a desirable investment.

REAL ESTATE MORTGAGE BONDS

The illustration below shows a *mortgage note,* which is a written promise to pay with interest the specified sum that is secured by the specific property described in the mortgage. A mortgage makes it impossible for one to sell property on which the mortgage is given

---

$*14,000*   Cincinnati, Ohio *June 15*, 19*66*

On or before *June 15*, 19*76*, for value received, I promise to pay to the order of

THE FIRST NATIONAL BANK OF CINCINNATI

Cincinnati, Ohio, the sum of *Fourteen thousand*————————Dollars,

($*14,000*) with interest on the unpaid balance at the rate of *6* per cent per annum, payable monthly

on the *15th* day of each month beginning *July 15, 1966* until the principal and interest called for shall be paid in full; the principal being payable in monthly payments payable on the *15th* day of each month hereafter until maturity, each such payment, except the final payment, to be in an amount not less than the difference between $*118.14* and the monthly interest payable hereon at the time of such payment, and the final payment at maturity to be in the amount of the entire balance then unpaid hereon. Any instalment of interest or principal not paid when due shall bear interest at the rate of *6½*% per annum after its due date until paid.

This note is secured by mortgage on real estate in *Cincinnati, Hamilton Co., Ohio* In the event of default in the payment of any instalment of principal or interest on this note when due, or in the event of default in the performance of any of the covenants contained in said mortgage to be performed by mortgagor therein, the holder of this note may at its option, without notice, declare the principal of this note and the interest accrued thereon to be immediately due and payable and may proceed to enforce the collection thereof by suit at law or in equity or proceedings to foreclose said mortgage. Waiver of any default shall not be deemed a waiver of any other default or impair the holder's rights arising out of any default.

Kevin McCartny

Lynn McCartny

Due *June 15, 1981*   Address *2416 Beech Street*

No. *349*   *Cincinnati, Ohio*

A mortgage note

without payment of the loan that it secures. In some states *mortgage bonds* are used instead of mortgage notes.

When a person borrows money on real estate, he usually signs (a) a mortgage and (b) a note or series of notes. He gives both the mortgage and the note or notes to the one from whom he is borrowing the money. The *mortgage* is a written contract giving the lender permission to acquire ownership of or to dispose of the property to satisfy the debt in case the debt is not paid.

There are first-mortgage notes, second-mortgage notes, and third-mortgage notes. The first-mortgage note is the most common. The loan that it represents should not exceed 50 or 60 percent of the appraised value of the property.

A first mortgage has first claim against the assets. The holder of the second mortgage cannot be paid until the claim of the first mortgage is settled. Interest rates are lower on first mortgages because these mortgages have first claim. Interest rates on second and third mortgages are higher because greater risk is involved.

Mortgage bonds are usually issued by a *mortgage company* who loans the money to the mortgagee and who in turn sells mortgage bonds to investors. Most mortgage bonds are issued in one of three ways:

1. The mortgage company acquires the mortgage on a particular piece of property, issues a bond, and sells it to an investor.
2. The mortgage company acquires a large mortgage; issues bonds in denominations of $50, $100, or $1,000; and sells these to investors.
3. The mortgages on several pieces of property are pooled. One large bond or a number of bonds in smaller denominations are issued against these mortgages and sold to investors.

The value of mortgage bonds is measured by the value of the property behind them and the ability of this property to provide funds for the payment of the interest and the principal on the due dates.

B. Investment procedure

INVESTING AND SPECULATING

Investing is buying assets, such as securities, with the expectation of receiving a certain, though maybe small, income over a long period of time. *Speculating* is buying securities or other assets with the hope that the value of those securities or assets will increase in a relatively short period of time. In both cases there are risks, but the risks increase as the possibilities of large gains or losses increase.

When we speak of investing, we ordinarily think of securities although there are many investments in real estate and other property. It is rather difficult to define securities. We have already used the term security in another sense as being the property pledged to a lender. For purposes of investments, however, we use the term security in a slightly different way. A *security*, for investment purposes, refers to stocks, bonds, notes, and mortgages, which indicate either ownership or indebtedness. These examples of securities represent some kind of pledge, promise, agreement, or right. They can be bought and sold if they have any value.

GROWTH, INCOME, AND SAFETY

We must assume that the average investor will not gamble, but that he will be interested in the income and safety of his investment. He may also be interested in a security that will grow in value. If one were interested in the safest investment at a low income, he would probably buy high-grade bonds. If he were interested in investments that will probably increase in value (with some risk), he would probably buy good stocks. Because of the peculiarities of people buying on the stock market, there are some stocks that pay a good rate of dividend based on the price of the stock. These are excellent stocks, but buyers do not expect them to increase in value to any great extent in the future. Therefore, they are not popular with many buyers who want stocks that they think will increase in value.

Generally, government bonds of various types are considered among the most conservative investments. Therefore, let us look at corporation securities in order to determine their merits in regard to growth, income, and income safety. Their relative merits are indicated in a general way in the following table.

SECURITY	GROWTH	INCOME	SAFETY
Preferred Stock	steady	steady	good
Common Stock	best	variable	least
Bonds	generally none	very steady	best

SOURCES OF INVESTMENT INFORMATION

There are two main sources of professional help to which any investor can turn without obligation. One is an investment broker and the other is a bank. The broker and the bank receive their compensation as a commission on any purchase or sale of securities.

An *investment broker* is a person or firm specializing in the study of securities, advising investors, and arranging for the purchase or the sale of securities. A *stockbroker* provides some of the same services as an investment broker. In fact, a stockbroker and an investment broker are often the same.

There are specialists in some banks who devote their time to serving as investment advisers. The selection of a broker or a bank may be difficult for a new investor. The best procedure is probably to talk to friends and get their advice based upon their past experience.

The price of a share of stock does not necessarily indicate whether it is a good or a bad investment. For example, two equally good corporations of exactly the same size may have common stocks that are selling for widely different prices. A share of stock of one corporation might be selling for $20 a share with 2 million shares outstanding. One share of stock of the other corporation may be selling at $40 a share with 1 million shares of stock outstanding.

If one prefers to do so, he can make a study of his own in regard to various kinds of securities. For the average investor, this is too great a task because there are many thousands of kinds of stocks, bonds, and other securities for sale. However, there are excellent monthly financial services available to which one can subscribe to obtain current investment information. There is also good current financial information available in some newspapers. If a person is going to do his own studying and investigating, it will be necessary for him to confine his attention to a few securities in order to make a thorough analysis.

If one is in doubt about whether a security is legally offered for sale or whether the person promoting its sale is using honest and legal methods, it is possible to investigate the sale of the stock by contacting the Securities and Exchange Commission, the state securities commission, the local better business bureau, a reliable broker, a banker, or the local stock exchange.

SAFETY OF PRINCIPAL

The safety of the principal invested in a bond of a corporation, whether it is a mortgage bond or a debenture bond, is really only as good as the corporation itself. The safety of the principal in a common stock or in a preferred stock is likewise only as good as the corporation issuing it. We have already learned that common stocks may increase or decrease in value in terms of dollars. The face value of bonds, however, will not increase in value in terms of dollars. Preferred stocks have preferred claims on earnings or assets or both, but they may decrease in value if the corporation has financial trouble.

The safety of the principal is also involved in any other kind of investment, such as in a government bond or in real estate. One's investment in a government bond is only as safe as the government itself. Cities, counties, and states have credit and financial ratings just the same as businesses.

There are three main factors to be considered as to the safety of the principal when one invests in real estate. First is the question of whether the investor receives a good legal title to the property, second is the question of location, and third is the question of economic conditions. Checking on the title involves legal assistance, and in checking on the location one should make sure that it is in a location that will not decrease in value. For instance, some residential neighborhoods are gradually depreciating in value while others are increasing in value principally because of the location. Economic conditions affect the value of real estate just as they affect the value of all other investments.

THE DOLLAR-AVERAGING PRINCIPLE

When stocks are purchased as an investment (as contrasted with the speculator or trader who buys and sells with the idea of making a profit by buying and selling), they are usually held for a long period of time. Prices of stocks may change considerably. The buyer may, for example, pay $85 a share for stock and may want to keep it because he thinks it is good. The price may go up or down. For example, it may go down to $80 a share, at which time he may buy more stock. If he owns 100 shares at $85 and buys 100 shares at $80, his average cost is $82.50 a share. This process is called *dollar averaging*.

In some cases a buyer may decide to purchase a certain stock and may want 100 shares. Assume he buys 10 shares a month for 10 months at prices of $85, $90, $92, $90, $84, $83, $82, $80, $80, and $81. His average cost is $84.70. If he had bought all on the first day of purchase, the cost would have been $85 per share.

GROWTH POSSIBILITIES

In the previous discussions we have already mentioned the growth possibilities of securities. If growth in value is important to the investor, he will not purchase bonds (unless they are purchased at a discount), and he will not purchase preferred stocks (unless these are purchased at a discount). The greatest growth possibilities are in good real estate and good common stocks, but there is also the risk that they will decrease in value.

SATISFACTORY INCOME FROM THE INVESTMENT

The safety of the principal is more important than a satisfactory income. If the principal is lost, there will be no income.

Rate of return. A sound investment does not have a yield that is higher than the average rate of interest used to attract investors. A conservative rate of interest on a good bond will be determined by the conditions that exist at the time the bond is offered for sale. A high-grade bond sometimes pays no more than 2 or 3 percent interest on the face value, but these rates change. Remember, however, that even though the stated interest on a bond may be only 3 percent, the bond may be sold at a discount so that the rate of return on the investment is actually higher than the stated amount. On the other hand, if one has to pay a premium for the bond, the rate of return on the investment will be lower than the stated amount. When the rate of return offered on a bond is much above the rate of interest on high-grade government bonds, special care should be taken in investigating the quality of the security.

Regularity of income. A corporation makes no promises as to the amount of dividends, if any, that will be paid on common stock. There will not be any dividends paid unless there are sufficient earnings from which to pay them. Bondholders must receive their interest first, and the preferred stockholders must be paid their dividends before common stockholders receive anything.

Most investors are interested in having a steady and reliable income. The continuous payment of interest or dividends is therefore one of the first considerations in evaluating a security.

The past history of a corporation in earnings and dividends can be determined from the records of any stock listed on an exchange, but expert advice is needed to determine the possible future earnings.

Margin of safety. For investment purposes, a good corporation should earn considerably more money than is paid out as bond interest and stock dividends. Unless the corporation is regularly earning more than is needed for these purposes, there is not an adequate margin of safety.

MARKETABILITY OF SECURITIES

Although an investor, in the true sense of the word, is not interested in buying a security with the thought of selling it immediately, he must give consideration to this possibility.

For most investors, the most desirable securities are those that are listed for public sale on stock exchanges or at least those securities that are sold directly through brokers. The least desirable securities for the small investor would be the stock in a close corporation unless he is closely associated with that business. Real estate would be a poor investment for a person who might suddenly need the money and then find it difficult to sell the real estate at a satisfactory price.

BUYING AND SELLING SECURITIES

Stock exchanges. There are two main types of markets through which stocks and bonds are easily bought and sold. These are the local stock exchanges in various cities and the national exchanges located in New York City. The two national exchanges are the New York Stock Exchange and the American Stock Exchange. Local stock exchanges in the various cities have connections with the national exchanges.

Buying and selling stocks on a security exchange is carried on by means of the *auction method*. A stock may be offered for sale at a certain price, or someone may bid for the same stock at a different price. A sale is made when someone buys the stock at the price offered. These offers and bids are going on regularly so that anyone owning a stock has a pretty good idea of the price at which the stock can be sold.

Listed securities are regularly sold through stock exchanges by means of the auction method.

New York Stock Exchange

Brokers deal on stock exchanges. They represent buyers and sellers of securities. Banks will also handle these transactions through a broker. In order for a broker to deal on an exchange, he must be a member of the exchange. If he is not a member, he can deal through another broker who is a member.

Listed and unlisted securities. A security that is said to be *listed* on a stock exchange is one on which there are regular quoted prices on either local or national exchanges. It may be listed and traded on both national and local exchanges. *Unlisted securities* are not listed on stock exchanges but may be bought and sold through individual brokers or may be bought and sold on exchanges without being listed. When unlisted securities are sold through brokers, the transactions are called *over-the-counter transactions.* Unlisted securities are usually stocks in which there are not regular transactions. The market for these stocks is therefore not quite so dependable as it is for listed securities. An unlisted stock may be equally as good as a listed stock, but it is generally not considered so conservative an investment as a listed stock because it is not so easily sold. Unless a security can be sold easily by some satisfactory means, it may have to be sold at a sacrifice in an emergency, or perhaps it cannot be sold at any price.

Buying on margin. Most investors pay cash for securities. However, some regular dealers on the stock market buy on margin. When *buying on margin,* the buyer will authorize the broker to purchase stock for him and the buyer will pay part of the price at once. The broker will lend the remaining amount of the purchase price and, of course, charge interest on it. Federal government regulations determine what proportion of any security sale may be made on margin in order to control speculation on credit.

Installment purchases. Brokers who are members of many of the stock exchanges have established an installment method of selling securities for the benefit of small investors or those who want to make regular purchases. This plan is sometimes called the *pay-as-you-go method* of purchasing securities. Installment purchase plans usually require the investor to invest at least $40 monthly or quarterly. The regular payments are made to the broker who buys the stock that has been selected by the investor. Installment purchase plans may also be used for buying stock in mutual funds.

Investment clubs. There are many *investment clubs* among men and women for the purpose of studying investments and of making regular investments as a group.

The usual procedure for investment clubs is to meet weekly or monthly and to study various investments regularly and often have an expert as an adviser. At each meeting decisions are made as to the security in which a new investment should be made or whether any of the old investments should be sold and the money reinvested in another security. Membership in an investment club is a good means of learning about investments.

Information everyone should know about investments

1. Government bonds are a conservative type of investment.
2. A real estate investment is not suitable for all persons.
3. Stocks, bonds, and mortgage notes represent the various securities of a corporation available for investment purposes.
4. Speculative securities are primarily for the persons who can afford to take a chance on the growth in value of securities.
5. Most people should invest, but not speculate or gamble.
6. The important factors to consider in selecting investments are:
   a. Safety of the principal.
   b. Growth possibilities.
   c. Satisfactory and certain income.
   d. Marketability of securities.
7. Do not listen to tipsters, but consult only reliable sources of investment information.
8. Beware of the typical methods of deception practiced by unscrupulous promoters.

▪ QUESTIONS ON THE TEXT

1. From the viewpoint of safety and the rate of income on the investment, how are government securities classified?
2. What is a municipal bond?
3. What are the two general types of stocks?
4. Do all stocks have the same voting power?
5. What is meant by a stock split?
6. What is meant by stock rights?
7. Distinguish between cumulative preferred stock and noncumulative preferred stock.
8. (a) What is meant by participating stock?
   (b) To what general type of stock does the term apply?
9. What is meant by convertible preferred stock?

10. (a) What is a close corporation?

   (b) What is an open corporation?

11. Why is it sometimes inadvisable to buy stock in a close corporation?

12. Distinguish between a coupon bond and a registered bond.

13. (a) If a $100 bond is selling for $90, is it selling at a premium or a discount?

   (b) What are some of the reasons why bonds sell below their par value?

14. In what ways does a bond differ from a stock?

15. Distinguish between an open-end investment company and a closed-end investment company.

16. What words of caution would you give to a person who is considering investing his life savings in a business which he will own and operate?

17. Why do some people advise against investing in an enterprise that is managed by a friend?

18. Before investing in real estate, what are some of the factors that should be investigated to determine its desirability?

19. Why is real estate not a good investment for a person who does not have time to take care of it and manage it?

20. Express briefly the difference between a mortgage note and a mortgage bond.

21. Distinguish between investing and speculating.

22. Among preferred stocks, common stocks, and bonds which has (a) the greatest growth possibilities, (b) the least growth possibilities, (c) the steadiest income, and (d) the greatest safety or principal?

23. What are the main sources of investment information available to an investor?

24. What are some of the factors that determine the safety of the principal of an investment?

25. What is the dollar-averaging principle of investing?

26. Considering all types of investment, which have the greatest growth possibilities?

27. How are stocks sold on a stock exchange?

▪ QUESTIONS FOR DISCUSSION

1. If a definite income is desired with maximum safety, what investment would you recommend?

2. Assume that you are offered some stock to buy in a small corporation owned by three people. What might be some of the problems if you bought it and later wanted to sell it?

3. Some people believe that, if a person is going to buy stock, he should buy common stock instead of preferred stock. Why do you think that they are of this opinion?

4. What do you think are the merits of investing in convertible preferred stock as a protection against inflation?
5. What are the merits of investing in participating preferred stock?
6. Assume that you are contemplating the purchase of some common stock in either of two outstanding corporations of approximately equal size. Both corporations have good reputations and good records of past earnings. They have issued approximately the same number of shares of stock. One has cumulative preferred stock and one grade of common stock; the other has noncumulative preferred stock and one grade of common stock. From your point of view, which purchase of common stock would be more desirable? Why?
7. Why are shares in investment trusts or mutual funds recommended for many investors who do not know much about stocks and bonds?
8. Quite often corporations split their stock. For example, each stockholder may be given two new shares for one old share.
   (a) Under this plan is there any change in ownership?
   (b) Why do you think that the price of a particular stock sometimes rises after a stock split? (For example, one share may be selling for $100; and if two new shares are traded for one old share, the value of each share would be assumed to be $50; but the market price might quickly rise to $51 or $52 each.)
9. Would you suggest that an elderly woman invest her money in real estate?
10. Assume that you have $3,000 to invest and wish to continue working at your present job. What do you think of the idea of investing this money in a partnership with two other men in a neighboring town?
11. "A bond is an investment; a stock is a speculation." Discuss this statement. Is it true or false?
12. A person who is earning 3 percent interest on a savings account considers buying bonds that pay interest at a net rate of 4 percent. Discuss the merits and the demerits of this plan.
13. (a) What is your opinion of the securities of mining corporations?
    (b) Is the average person justified in buying such securities?
    (c) Who should buy these securities?
14. Do you think a mutual fund would be good for you? Why?
15. Why is a listed security usually a better investment than an unlisted security for an investor who may want to sell quickly?

■ **PROBLEMS TO SOLVE**

1. From your library or some other source obtain a book on investments that discusses stocks and bonds. Write a report of at least 500 words in which you present additional information about stocks and bonds that is not included in this chapter.

2. Mr. Walsh has ten shares of each of ten different preferred stocks. The total value amounts to $6,323. He also has ten different bonds valued at a total of $1,116. Ten shares of stock valued at $46 a share become worthless. Mr. Holt has fifty shares of stock in three different corporations, the total value of which is $5,200, and ten bonds, the total value of which is $1,046. Fifty shares of Mr. Holt's stock are the same kind as the ten shares of Mr. Walsh's stock that became worthless.

   (a) Figure Mr. Walsh's percentage of loss on his total investment.

   (b) Figure Mr. Holt's percentage of loss on his total investment.

   (c) Can you draw any conclusions?

3. Your school building was probably financed by bonds and the public school district where you live undoubtedly is now issuing bonds or plans to do so soon. Check with the superintendent of schools or some other local school official for information about this type of investment. When and why were the bonds issued? Under what kind of arrangement were they issued? What is the interest rate on them? Is money being set aside to pay the bonds and interest? Where does that money come from? On the basis of the responses to these and other questions, prepare an oral report to your class.

▪ COMMUNITY PROBLEMS AND PROJECTS

1. Under the direction of your teacher assume that you have $1,000 to invest in stocks. Obtain as much information as you can about the stocks of various corporations and then select the stocks in which you would want to invest your money. Assume that you buy the stocks and set up a record of your imaginary purchases. In this record show the cost of each stock and the fees charged by the stockbroker. Keep a record of dividends and after a period of time (determined by your teacher) compute the value of the stock that is owned and the amount of dividends received. Make a report on your income or loss and evaluate the worth of the stock as compared with that at the time it was purchased.

2. From the financial page of a newspaper obtain the names of at least three of the following types of securities on which prices are quoted: (a) securities listed on a national stock exchange, (b) securities listed on a local stock exchange, (c) mutual funds, (d) municipal bonds, and (e) unlisted securities.

3. Investigate through a stock exchange, an investment broker, or a local bank to find out the current rate of margin required when securities are purchased on margin.

Chapter 26

Protection through property and liability insurance

PURPOSE OF THE CHAPTER

Many risks make family economic planning uncertain. Property owned by the family may be destroyed or damaged by any one of a number of hazards. Actions by members of the family may cause damage to the property of others or perhaps injury or even death. And guests of the family may suffer injury or death while on the property of the family. These are only a few of the risks that each family must consider in making its plans. The purpose of this chapter is to analyze the ways by which the family may be protected against these risks through property and liability insurance.

You will find answers to these questions.

1. What is the nature of property and liability insurance?
2. How are property and liability insurance companies organized, operated, and regulated?

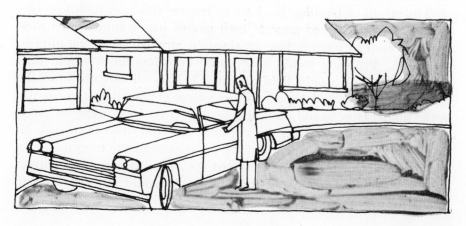

3. What factors should be considered in insuring against the hazards involved in home ownership?
4. What factors should be considered in insuring against the hazards involved in automobile ownership?

A. The nature of property and liability insurance

THE NEED FOR INSURANCE

The fact that large numbers of property and liability insurance companies are successfully operated in the United States and that most families purchase some form of property and liability insurance is ample evidence that there is a broad need for such insurance. Family life has become complicated, particularly as it relates to home ownership and automobile ownership. Family investment in a home built up over a period of years may be destroyed in a matter of minutes by fire or tornado. Or family resources may be completely wiped out by a judgment resulting from a lawsuit involving an automobile accident. The possibility that such an event might occur in a family normally would make financial or economic planning quite uncertain.

SHARING LOSSES

There are various ways by which a small but certain cost can be substituted for the uncertain and quite possibly large cost of a major loss. For example, groups of families could band together and agree that they would share equally in any loss sustained by one of the group. In this case, however, the families within the group would not know when they might be called upon to share in a loss until the loss occurred. Thus, there still would be uncertainty.

The group of families, in order to remove this uncertainty, might agree to pay a specified amount each month into a fund which then could be used to pay the loss sustained by any one of the families in the group. Problems would arise, however. How much would each family pay? Who would hold the funds? How should the funds be invested? What would happen if losses were greater than the balance in the fund? How would the funds be used if no losses were sustained in a given period? An additional problem would arise from such an arrangement. Suppose that all of the families lived in one community and that a fire or a tornado destroyed the entire community. Under such conditions, it is obvious that the funds would not be adequate to pay for all of the losses.

INSURANCE COMPANIES BEAR THE RISK

Property and liability insurance companies are organized in such a way that they can satisfactorily handle all of the problems listed above. These insurance companies receive relatively small payments from large numbers of families in many different communities, invest these funds, and pay for losses sustained by the member families. The amount of the small payment required of each family is based on the experience of the company. For example, let us assume that the Midland Insurance Company carries fire insurance on 100,000 homes, each having an average value of $10,000; each homeowner pays an average of $25 a year for insurance. The company would collect $2,500,000 from the owners of the property with which to pay its operating expenses and losses due to fires. The rates charged are based on past experiences so that the insurance company should take in enough money to pay losses when they occur. The insurance company takes a calculated risk, while each property owner pays a certain amount each year so that if his home is burned, he will be paid for his loss by the insurance company. Most property owners can afford to pay $25 a year, but they cannot afford a $10,000 fire loss. In a sense, therefore, the 100,000 homeowners are pooling or sharing their risks, and the insurance company is the agent that handles the financial matters.

It may seem strange at first that a property insurance company, for instance, can assume the risk of paying all losses and yet charge each policyholder only a small fee. Frequently the total yearly fee is as low as one tenth of one percent of the possible loss. The reason insurance companies can follow this practice is that they know from experience what losses can be expected. They can therefore keep in a reserve fund a sufficient amount to pay each loss as it occurs. It is true that unusual circumstances, such as an exceptionally large fire, may cause unforeseen losses; but over a long period of time, losses are predictable. The reserve fund of an insurance company is used as a protection against unusual losses.

THE INSURANCE CONTRACT

Definitions. An insurance agreement is a form of contract. An insurance contract is called a *policy*. The person who buys an insurance policy pays periodically what is called a *premium*. He is known as the *policyholder, insured,* or *assured.* The party from whom he buys the insurance and who agrees to pay the loss is called the *insurer* or *underwriter. Risk* is the possibility of loss. *Face value* is the amount of insurance stated in the contract; *cash value* is the actual market value of the property destroyed. Cash value may be greater or less than the face value of the contract.

Insurable interest. When property is insured against loss due to fire or other causes, the purpose of the insurance is considered to be the protection of the interest of the person who buys the insurance. The policyholder must have an insurable interest in the property. A person is considered to have an *insurable interest in property* if there is a reasonable expectation that he will derive a financial benefit from the existence of the property or will suffer a loss from the damage or the destruction of the property. For instance, both the owner of a home and the person who holds a mortgage on the home have an insurable interest. If the property is not insured and is later destroyed, the owner will lose the money he has invested in it, and the person who owns the mortgage may lose the money that is due him on the mortgage.

Most mortgages contain a clause that requires the owner of the property to carry enough insurance to protect the mortgagee, the person lending the money.

In the case of property, the insurable interest ordinarily must exist at the time of the loss; otherwise, the contract is not enforceable. For example, a person might carry some insurance on property that he rents and occupies. If he moves out of the property without canceling the insurance, he could not collect for a fire loss in case the building burns after he moves.

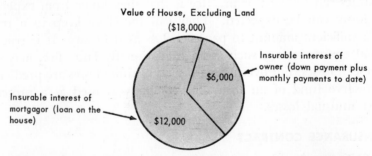

There are two parties with insurable interests in the case of a home with a mortgage on it.

Transfer of policy. If you carry an insurance policy on property that you later sell, you cannot transfer the insurance policy to the new owner without the approval of the insurance company. If there is any change in the title to insured property, the protection under the policy usually becomes void. The insurance company need not contract with the new owner, but with the approval of the insurance company, the policy can be assigned or transferred to the new owner. This transfer is called an *assignment*. An exception to the rule concerning a change in title arises in case of the death of the person who has purchased insurance, such as fire insurance on a home. If such person dies, his heirs are protected under the insurance.

TYPES OF INSURANCE COMPANIES

All property and liability insurance companies set rates based on past experience and anticipated claims from their policyholders. Policyholders make periodic (usually semiannual or annual) premium payments to the insurance company. These premium payments are used by the insurance companies in somewhat the same manner as deposits are used by banks. In other words, insurance companies use the funds paid by policyholders in making investments that will earn an income. The insurance companies must, of course, keep a reasonable amount of cash available to pay the claims of policyholders.

There are two types of property and liability insurance companies: stock and mutual.

Stock company. A *stock company* is a corporation that is formed according to the laws of the particular state. The stockholders own the company and elect directors, who in turn hire executives to run the business. The stockholders may or may not be policyholders. A stock insurance company gets funds with which to begin operation from the sale of stock. Additional operating and reserve funds come from premiums and from income earned on investments. Profits of the stock insurance company may be paid to the stockholders in the form of dividends.

Stock insurance companies may issue *participating* or *nonparticipating* policies. Holders of participating policies may receive dividends that reduce the cost of insurance to the policyholder. Holders of nonparticipating policies do not receive dividends; their premium payments are fixed.

Mutual company. The policyholders of a *mutual* insurance company are the owners of the company; there are no stockholders in a mutual insurance company. Each person that is insured in a mutual insurance company becomes a member of the company and is entitled to a share in the ownership and control of the company.

Mutual insurance companies sell only participating policies. Generally, mutual insurance companies set premium rates high enough to cover anticipated losses. If losses are not as high as expected, the excess of premium payments over loss payments can be returned to the policyholders in the form of dividends or lower premium rates, or the excess can be retained as a reserve for future losses.

STATE REGULATION OF INSURANCE COMPANIES

The operations of insurance companies within a particular state are regulated by the state, usually through a department of insurance and/or an insurance commission. One of the important functions of the insurance commissioner is to make sure that the insurance companies keep sufficient reserves to pay all claims as they are presented by policyholders.

State regulation also protects insurance buyers from fraud. Most states require reports from insurance companies, as well as inspection of the securities, accounting records, and business methods of the companies. In most states, insurance companies are regulated as to the ways in which they can invest the money collected from policyholders. These investments are usually confined to high-grade bonds of the federal and state governments, utilities, and cities, and high-grade real-estate mortgages and mortgage bonds. Although special bureaus provide information for establishing fire and casualty rates, the state governments retain the right to regulate these rates.

B. Insurance for the home

The greatest risks of loss to a family or individual usually are associated with the ownership and operation of a home and an automobile. Therefore, we shall consider the different types of property and liability insurance as they relate to the home and the automobile. This section of the chapter deals with property and liability insurance for the home. Insurance for the automobile will be treated separately in the next section of the chapter.

The homeowner must consider the many risks that he faces and the possible losses which he may incur. He must consider the possible loss of his home, its contents, and other personal property. He must consider possible losses arising from lawsuits resulting from personal injury to guests. While each of these risks can be insured against

A homeowner can insure against the costs of rebuilding a fire-ruined home by seeing that he has adequate insurance coverage.

separately, insurance companies have developed insurance policies that insure against groups of perils. These are called *homeowners policies*. Homeowners policies are also referred to as "all-risk" policies.

The homeowners policy is available to owner-occupants of one- and two-family private residences. Although the policy insures against many perils, there is only one policy and only one premium payment with which to be concerned. In addition, the package of insurance ordinarily costs 20 to 30 percent less than that of separately purchased coverages.

An example of a homeowners policy covering all risks would have the following coverages and limits:

Coverage A—Dwelling building, $15,000 (as an example).

Coverage B—Appurtenant private structures, 10% of coverage A.

Coverage C—Personal property, 40% of coverage A.

Coverage D—Additional living expense, 20% of coverage A.

Coverage E—Comprehensive personal liability, $25,000 per occurrence.

Coverage F—Medical payments, $5,000 per person.

Coverage G—Physical damage to property, $250 per occurrence. (This coverage provides payment of losses to property of another caused by the insured regardless of legal liability.)

Coverages A, B, C, and D are explained in the section under "Property Insurance Under the Homeowners Policy," starting on this page. Coverages E, F, and G are explained under "Liability Insurance Under the Homeowners Policy" on page 514. Costs of different coverages are discussed on page 515.

PROPERTY INSURANCE UNDER THE HOMEOWNERS POLICY

The chart on the next page shows the three basic policy coverages that may be purchased to protect against certain perils to the house and appurtenant private structures.

What perils are covered? Under a homeowners policy, the house or dwelling is covered. Guesthouses, sheds, garages, and other structures used in connection with and belonging to the home are known as *appurtenant private structures.* They usually are covered up to 10 percent of the amount of coverage carried on the house. Notice that the illustration below shows eleven perils covered under the standard form; nineteen perils under the broad form; and all risks covered under the comprehensive form.

Personal property is covered along with the house. *Personal property* includes household contents and other personal belongings used, owned, worn, or carried by the family. The protection applies both at home and away from home. Pets are not included as personal property. Automobiles and the property of roomers or boarders not related to the family are not covered.

The family is insured for additional living expense in the event of major damage to the home that requires the family to live else-

HOMEOWNERS POLICY—PROPERTY INSURANCE

SUMMARY OF COVERAGE—STANDARD, BROAD, AND COMPREHENSIVE FORMS

Policy Form	Perils Covered
STANDARD	1. fire and lightning 2. loss or damage to property removed from premises endangered by fire 3. windstorm or hail 4. explosion 5. riot, riot attending a strike, and civil commotion 6. aircraft 7. vehicles, if not owned or operated by occupant of premises 8. smoke or smudge caused by sudden, unusual, or faulty operations of a cooking or heating unit 9. vandalism and malicious mischief 10. theft 11. breaking of glass constituting a part of the building
BROAD	12. falling objects 13. weight of ice, snow, or sleet 14. collapse of building or any part thereof 15. accidental discharge, leakage or overflow of water or steam from within a plumbing, heating, or air-conditioning system 16. sudden and accidental tearing asunder, cracking, burning, or bulging of a steam or hot water heating system 17. sudden and accidental tearing asunder, cracking, burning, or bulging of appliances for heating water for domestic consumption 18. freezing of plumbing, heating and air-conditioning systems and domestic appliances 19. sudden and accidental injury to electrical appliances, devices, fixtures, and wiring, (TV picture tube not included)
COMPREHENSIVE	All perils except: earthquake, landslide, flood, surface water, waves, tidal water or tidal wave, the backing up of sewers, seepage, war, and nuclear radiation

Source: A Family Guide to Property and Liability Insurance, Insurance Information Institute.

where. These expenses must actually be incurred and are limited to the period of time it takes with due diligence and dispatch to repair the damage property.

What perils are not covered? Under the standard and broad forms of coverage, certain perils are not covered if they are caused initially by earthquake, landslide, or other earth movements (but are covered under the comprehensive form). Shrubs, trees, plants, and lawn are not covered against windstorm and hail in the homeowners policy. Damage from perils other than fire and lightning are usually subject to a deductible clause; that is, under a $50 deductible clause, the insurance company would pay the homeowner only $75 of the $125 loss, the homeowner being required to assume the first $50 of the loss.

Amount of coverage. The homeowner should carry enough property insurance, but not too much. The amount of insurance that should be purchased is determined by the replacement cost of the home. Replacement costs usually are determined through an *appraisal* by a competent appraiser.

Assume that the appraisal indicates that $15,000 of insurance should be carried on the house. This amount then determines the amount of other property coverages included in the homeowners policy. These coverages would be as follows:

Dwelling $15,000
Appurtenant private structures
    (10 percent of dwelling) 1,500
Personal property (not otherwise covered)
    (40 per cent of dwelling) 6,000
Additional living expense
    (20 percent of dwelling) 3,000

Need for inventory. An inventory of personal property is desirable and necessary in the event of loss. This inventory serves as the basis for making claims and eliminates the need for depending on memory. Some homeowners keep accurate listings of their personal property; others photograph each room in the home. Of course, the inventory or photographs must be kept in a safe, fireproof place. Although the insurance company will frequently accept a sworn statement as to the loss of personal property, the safest practice is to keep some type of inventory record of the insured property. An illustration of a portion of a household inventory record is shown on the next page.

KITCHEN, UTILITY ROOM				
NO.	ARTICLE	YEAR PURCHASED	ORIGINAL COST	PRESENT CASH VALUE
	Chairs, Tables, Stools			
	Draperies, Rugs			
	Dishes, Glassware			
	Refrigerator			
	Range			
	Dishwasher			
	Washing Machine			
	Dryer			
	Waste Disposer			
	Electrical Appliances (Vacuum Cleaner, Toaster, Coffeemaker, Fry-Skillet, etc.)			
	Kitchen Equipment (Foodstuffs, Supplies, Cutlery, Utensils, etc.)			
	Kitchen Cabinets			

A portion of a household inventory record

LIABILITY INSURANCE UNDER THE HOMEOWNERS POLICY

People may injure themselves or may suffer damage to their property while on the premises of a homeowner. In addition, the actions of the family may result in injury to other persons or damage to their property either on the premises of the homeowner or away. The members of the family may become personally liable for claims arising as a result of these situations.

The liability insurance portion of a homeowners policy protects the family against claims in three areas: (1) comprehensive personal liability, (2) medical payments, and (3) physical damage to the property of others.

Comprehensive personal liability. Coverage under a comprehensive-personal-liability policy protects the homeowner against claims arising from bodily injury to others or damage to their property. No claim is paid by the insurance company under this provision unless it has been established that the insured is legally liable. A guest in the home might fall down a basement stairway, break a leg, and then file suit for damages. Under this provision, the insurance company would represent the homeowner in court, pay the cost of defending the homeowner, and pay the damages, if any, up to the limits of the policy. Usually, the basic coverage of this provision is $25,000 for each occurrence.

Medical payments. Coverage under a medical-payments provision in a homeowners policy protects the homeowner from accidental injury claims arising from actions of the homeowner, members of his family, or family pets either on or off the homeowner's property. The insurance company pays the claims of the injured party, regardless of who is at fault, for the cost of medical and surgical services incurred within one year of the accident. The amount of coverage for each person usually is $5,000. This coverage does not apply to members of the homeowner's family or the homeowner.

Physical damage to the property of others. A clause providing coverage for physical damage to the property of others protects the homeowner and his family when any member of the family damages someone's property. For example, the homeowner's lawn mower might throw a stone through a neighbor's window. Such damages are paid up to the limit of the policy, usually $250 for each occurrence. Coverage is provided whether the act is committed on the property of the homeowner or off and whether the homeowner is at fault or not.

FACTORS AFFECTING THE COST OF PROPERTY AND LIABILITY INSURANCE

As is shown in the chart on page 512, three types of homeowners policies are available: the standard form, the broad form, and the comprehensive form. Specimen comparative costs of these policies based on the replacement value of a home worth $20,000 are:

Coverage	*Cost for 3 years*
Standard form (11 perils)	$136 *
Broad form (19 perils)	174 *
Comprehensive form (all risks)	371 **

  * $50 deductible on wind and hail only.
 ** $100 deductible on all perils except fire and lightning; if the
     loss is $500 or more, the deductible provision does not apply.

Cost of coverage varies according to geographical location, water supply available for fire fighting, efficiency of the local fire department, type of construction of the home, and other factors.

C. Insurance for the automobile

No automobile owner or driver should be without automobile insurance. In fact, some states require that automobile owners and drivers have certain types of insurance to protect others from loss. Other states may require in the event of an accident that the automobile owner or driver show evidence of having insurance or post a bond; if he is unable to do either, he must go to jail.

Family economic security is very uncertain unless the perils arising from automobile ownership are insured. The owner or operator of an automobile should consider the following types of coverage:

1. Bodily injury liability 20-30
2. Property damage liability
3. Medical payments
4. Comprehensive physical damage — what it's worth
5. Collision
6. Protection against uninsured motorists

These six coverages may be purchased separately; but, as in the case of the homeowners policy, it is more common to purchase the six coverages as a package. Each of the coverages will be discussed separately in the following pages.

BODILY INJURY LIABILITY

All members of the family are protected by this insurance as well as those who drive the insured's car with his permission. In addition, members of the insured's family are covered while driving another person's car if the owner has given his permission. This insurance protects the insured against claims or suits of people injured or killed by the insured's automobile. State financial responsibility laws indicate the minimum amount of this coverage that must be carried. The minimum amount of coverage issued is $5,000 for one person or $10,000 in total for more than one person who is injured. Some automobile owners carry as much as $100,000 for one person or $300,000 in total for more than one person who is injured.

PROPERTY DAMAGE LIABILITY

All members of the family and all those driving the family car with permission are covered by this policy provision. And members of the family are covered even while driving someone else's car as long as they have permission from the owner. This coverage protects

The owner or driver of a wrecked car may need insurance for bodily injury, property damage, medical payments, and collision.

the insured whenever his automobile damages the property of others. It does not cover damage to the insured's automobile, however. Property damage liability is available in amounts ranging from $5,000 to $100,000.

Both bodily injury and property damage coverage are absolutely essential for the automobile owner. The perils that face the automobile owner are too great to risk without adequate insurance coverage. In purchasing this coverage, it should be remembered that large amounts of coverage cost relatively less than smaller amounts. For example, if coverage of 25/50/5 ($25,000 bodily injury for one person; $50,000 bodily injury for more than one person; and $5,000 property damage) cost $100 a year, 50/100/10 might cost only $111; thus, the insured may double his coverage with an increase of only 11 percent in his premium cost.

MEDICAL PAYMENTS COVERAGE

This coverage is similar to that discussed under the homeowners policy. However, this coverage applies only to the operation of an automobile, and it covers all members of the family and any guests while riding in the insured car. Under the provisions of this coverage, the insurance company agrees to pay all reasonable expenses incurred within one year of the date of the accident for necessary medical, surgical, X-ray, and dental services, up to the limits set in the policy. It may also include ambulance services, hospital services, nursing services, and funeral services. The insurance company pays regardless of who was at fault. The limits of coverage for each individual may range from $500 to $5,000.

Medical payments coverage is particularly important for families with children and for families who transport other children as in a school car pool.

COMPREHENSIVE PHYSICAL DAMAGE INSURANCE

This insurance coverage protects the insured against possible loss due to damage to the car or if it is stolen. However, damage due to collision is not covered. Causes of damage covered include fire, lightning, flood, and windstorm. Glass breakage is covered under this insurance. Since this type of insurance is relatively inexpensive, most automobile owners include it in their coverage. The cost of replacing one windshield very probably would be greater than total premium payments on comprehensive insurance for a number of years.

COLLISION INSURANCE

Collision insurance coverage protects the insured against loss arising from damage to his own car as the result of collision. This is the most expensive insurance coverage among those discussed, primarily because of the many minor accidents that require expensive body and paint work. The car owner can reduce the cost of this type of insurance by purchasing a deductible policy, usually either $50 or $100 deductible. In the event of damage, the insurance company would pay only the amount of the loss in excess of $50 or $100. Since the car owner has a large investment in a new car, he should purchase collision insurance on a new car. As the car gets older and its value decreases, the owner should weigh the cost of this insurance coverage against the potential loss. For example, there would be little reason to carry $100 deductible collision insurance on a car with a value of $250.

Costs for collision insurance vary widely from one geographic area to another. They also vary within an area according to driver classification. Unmarried male drivers under 25 pay the highest rate. If the car owner finances the purchase of the automobile, he will be required to purchase collision insurance as well as other coverages.

PROTECTION AGAINST UNINSURED MOTORISTS

This insurance coverage is designed to protect the family against risks due to injury by hit-and-run drivers and uninsured drivers. It covers the insured to the extent that he would have been covered if the uninsured driver had been insured or if the hit-and-run driver had been identified. Therefore, the insured cannot collect from the insurance company unless the uninsured motorist was legally liable. The coverage is limited to the amount of liability required under the financial responsibility laws of the various states. The cost of this coverage is very low.

FACTORS AFFECTING THE COST OF AUTOMOBILE INSURANCE

Accidents involving automobiles are frequent, and the cost of repairs is quite high. Automobile insurance rates must reflect these costs. The insurance rates charged by automobile insurance companies are based for the most part on what the companies have had to pay out in claims over the last three-year period. State insurance departments or commissions regulate the insurance rates; however, this does not mean that all automobile insurance companies have the same rates. One company, by being very selective in choosing the owners and drivers that they will insure, can have lower costs and lower premium rates. Thus, insurance rates are affected by the practices of the companies in accepting risks.

A second factor affecting the cost of automobile insurance again relates to the experience of the company. More accidents occur in urban areas than in rural areas. More occur in some urban areas than in others. Therefore, comparable coverage in one city may cost more or less than in another.

A third factor affecting the cost of automobile insurance is the cost of automobile repairs. Some cars are more expensive and more difficult to repair than others.

A fourth factor affecting automobile insurance rates is the driver himself. Statistics prove that drivers of a certain age and sex have more or fewer accidents than others. Drivers are classified as to risk. These different driver classifications are shown at the top of the next page.

The chart indicates that the driver classification with the lowest rate is a family with no male driver under 25 years of age with the car not used for business and not driven to work. Note that the highest rate classification (2C) would be the unmarried male driver under 25 who is the owner or principal driver of the car. Experience has shown that the insurance companies have paid out more than three times as much in claims per insured person for the 2C class as for the 1A.

We as automobile drivers should remember that automobile insurance rates are based on the experience of the insurance companies. The more automobile accidents drivers have and the more claims they file, the higher rates will be.

A COMPARISON OF LIABILITY RATES BY DRIVER CLASSIFICATIONS IN LARGE CITIES

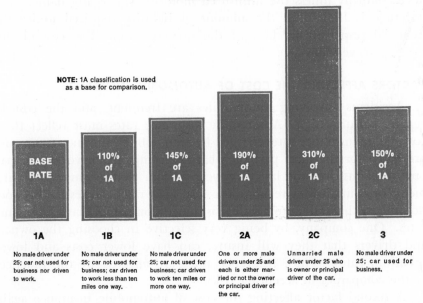

NOTE: 1A classification is used as a base for comparison.

BASE RATE	110% of 1A	145% of 1A	190% of 1A	310% of 1A	150% of 1A
1A	**1B**	**1C**	**2A**	**2C**	**3**
No male driver under 25; car not used for business nor driven to work.	No male driver under 25; car not used for business; car driven to work less than ten miles one way.	No male driver under 25; car not used for business; car driven to work ten miles or more one way.	One or more male drivers under 25 and each is either married or not the owner or principal driver of the car.	Unmarried male driver under 25 who is owner or principal driver of the car.	No male driver under 25; car used for business.

Source: A Family Guide to Property and Liability Insurance, Insurance Information Institute.

Your automobile insurance may be void

Under certain circumstances insurance companies reserve the right, either by clauses in the insurance policy or by state law, to void a policy. The following are some cases in which your insurance policy may become void, and you will be without protection in case of an accident:

1. If the car is taken into Mexico or other places outside the limits of the United States.
2. If explosives are carried.
3. If the car pulls a trailer not covered by provisions of the insurance policy. (This is not always true.)
4. If you fail to report an accident promptly and honestly in writing to the company.
5. If you agree or authorize someone to agree for you to assume liability for injuries to any person or damages to other property. (The best thing to do is to tell the other person that you are covered by insurance and will report it to your insurance company.)
6. If you or an authorized user of the car do not protect the car and prevent it from further damage after an accident.
7. If you fail to assist and cooperate with the insurance company in settling any claim.
8. If you fail to turn over to your insurance company every demand notice or legal summons received in connection with any accident.

D. Selecting a property and liability insurance company

There are many good insurance companies. Since most of us are not expert enough to determine what is a good insurance company, we have to rely upon the reputations of companies.

The rates of some companies may be slightly lower than those of others, but rates are not the only basis for selecting an insurance company. Above all else, you want an insurance company that will protect you and settle claims in a reasonable manner. An insurance company that will not pay honest claims promptly and without lawsuits is not one with which you would want to insure. One of the best ways to select a company is, therefore, to inquire among your friends in order to discover the reputation of the company as to its methods of doing business and settling claims.

Many families rely on their insurance agents rather than on their knowledge of insurance companies. By selecting an agent in whom they have complete confidence, they are in effect depending on his judgment for the selection of the insurance company. A good agent will always act in behalf of the policyholder and will render many extra services.

Facts everyone should know about property and liability insurance

1. Property and liability insurance is possible through small payments collected from many people to pay unexpected losses that may occur to any one of the policyholders.
2. Property and liability insurance rates are determined primarily from past experience.
3. The homeowners policy is the most economical way of insuring the homeowner against the perils of home ownership.
4. It is absolutely essential for the family to carry adequate automobile insurance.
5. The family should purchase its property and liability insurance from a company they know to be reputable and fair or from an agent in whom the family has complete confidence.

- **QUESTIONS ON THE TEXT**

1. How can individuals protect themselves against possible large losses by paying small amounts periodically to an insurance company?
2. (a) What is an insurance contract called?
   (b) Who is the insured or the assured?

3. In what way do insurance companies protect individuals from property and liability loss?

4. What is meant by the term "insurable interest"?

5. How does a stock insurance company differ from a mutual insurance company?

6. From the standpoint of the policyholder, is it better to have a participating policy or a nonparticipating policy?

7. How are insurance companies regulated? Why?

8. What steps should the policyholder take in order to make sure that he can substantiate his claim in case of loss?

9. What is the outstanding feature of a homeowners policy?

10. What are the names of each of the three forms of homeowners policies? Which form gives the greatest protection? the least protection?

11. What is meant by liability insurance?

12. What are the types of insurance coverage for loss and for liability that are available to owners and drivers of automobiles?

13. How does bodily-injury insurance protect the owner of an automobile insurance policy?

14. How does property damage insurance protect the owner of an automobile insurance policy?

15. How does automobile collision insurance protect the policyholder? What is deductible collision insurance?

16. What insurance is necessary to protect the driver and his family against losses due to injury to himself or his family as a result of an automobile accident?

17. Under what conditions might an automobile insurance company refuse to pay a claim by one of their policyholders?

▪ QUESTIONS FOR DISCUSSION

1. Are the following statements contradictory? Why or why not?
   (a) Total losses for a given period of time in a given state due to fire can be predicted with reasonable accuracy.
   (b) The locations and amounts of individual losses due to fire for a given period of time in a given state cannot be predicted with any degree of accuracy.

2. Insurance can be purchased for protection against almost any type of anticipated loss. Some insurance companies, for example, will insure the promoters of a baseball game or an outdoor play against possible financial loss due to rain.
   (a) How could an insurance company determine rates for insurance against possible loss due to rain?
   (b) Do you think that such rates would be high or low as compared with rates for fire insurance? Why?

3. Over a lifetime the amount of premiums on household insurance would amount to several hundred dollars. Why is it not advisable for a home-owner to save the money he pays in insurance premiums for the purpose of replacing or repairing his house if it should be damaged by fire?

4. Why may you not transfer an insurance policy on a house to a new owner of the house without the consent of the insurance company?

5. How would fire insurance rates in a city with strict building ordinances and strict inspection practices compare with rates in a city with weak ordinances and lax inspection practices?

6. Give some illustrations of the kinds of liability claims to which a home-owner might be subject.

7. What, in your opinion, represents the more serious risk of an auto-mobile owner (a) the risk of property damage, or (b) the risk of injury to a person? Why?

8. If your automobile insurance policy provides $25,000 protection against bodily injury and the court awards damages of $30,000 to an injured person, how will the claim be settled?

9. Explain a situation in which one may have an insurable interest in property at the time the insurance is bought, but may not have an insurable interest in the property at the time it is destroyed.

10. What do you think of an accident policy that provides protection against such risks as loss of one leg, loss of both arms, loss of one eye, and other similar hazards?

11. Explain why you do or do not have an insurable interest in (a) your neighbor's house, and (b) a house on which you are holding a mortgage.

12. Do the various automobile insurance companies follow the same prac-tices in paying claims?

■ **PROBLEMS TO SOLVE**

1. Assume that you have a home worth $20,000 on a lot worth $2,000 and that the fire insurance rate on the home is $5 a thousand.

As a result of improving the fire protection in the city, the fire insur-ance rate on homes is reduced to $4 a thousand.

The tax rates have been $25 a thousand. Because of the improvement in fire protection, the tax rates have been increased to $26 a thousand. For tax purposes the home is valued at $12,000 and the lot is valued at $1,000, making a total of $13,000 valuation for tax purposes.

(a) Assuming that insurance is carried on the entire value of the house, how much is saved on fire insurance as a result of the new fire protection?

(b) After the increased taxes are considered, is there any saving to the property owner? If so, how much?

2. A $50 deductible collision insurance policy on an automobile has cost Mr. Arden an average of $42 a year for ten years. At the end of the tenth year he had a wreck costing $650 to repair his car. How much has he saved or lost by carrying the insurance as compared with assuming his own risk and paying all his own damages?

Assume that he would have saved by carrying his own insurance. Is it wise for him to do so?

3. With ever-increasing auto accident rates, particularly among young drivers, state legislatures will be expected by their constituents to vote on proposed laws requiring an individual to be 18 years of age before he or she can receive a license to drive an automobile. Prepare a written report either supporting or rejecting such proposed laws.

4. Prepare charts showing (a) the number of automobile accidents in the United States for the last ten years and (b) the total dollar value of losses resulting from auto accidents for the same years. What are the trends?

5. Prepare an essay on the economic waste and the resultant effects on living standards caused by automobile accidents in the United States.

▪ COMMUNITY PROBLEMS AND PROJECTS

1. From the daily newspapers in your community, keep a tally of the number of automobile accidents reported and the number of people by ages involved in these accidents for a 10-day period. If causes of accidents and/or responsibility for accidents are given, tally this information likewise. From this very limited survey, what conclusions can you draw?

2. From a local insurance agent or driver education instructor, find out the reasons why:
   (a) male drivers under age 25 who have completed an approved driver education course often receive more favorable insurance rates than those who have not had such a course, and
   (b) female drivers under age 25 are not charged the same high insurance rates as male drivers of the same age group.

3. From a local insurance agent, collect information regarding unusual or unexpected insurance claims involving personal liability in connection with homes, pets, and places of business. In addition find out the approximate cost of liability insurance for a homeowners policy. What conclusions can you draw from this investigation?

Chapter 27

Protection through life and health insurance

PURPOSE OF THE CHAPTER

Almost everyone needs to understand financial problems that result from a death in the family, accident, or a disabling illness. This chapter is concerned with how life and health insurance may help to solve those problems.

You will find answers to these questions:

1. What are the different types of life insurance?
2. What are the features of life insurance policies?
3. How may life insurance be used as a part of a savings program?
4. How can health insurance assist in family financial planning?

A. Life insurance

PURPOSE OF LIFE INSURANCE

Life insurance serves several purposes. First, it may provide a cash reserve or a continuous monthly income in case of the death of a

member of a family, especially the death of the primary wage earner. Second, life insurance may provide funds for future use, such as financing a college education, meeting financial emergencies, or providing either income or a cash reserve for use in retirement years. And finally, many people make regular premium payments on life insurance as a means of saving. Thus, life insurance has many uses both if the primary wage earner dies and if he lives.

HOW FAMILIES USE LIFE INSURANCE

IF FATHER DIES

Cash	To pay last expenses. To pay taxes, debts, and other costs. To pay off the family mortgage.
Readjustment income	Continuing father's income while family makes necessary adjustments in living.
Family income	Monthly income for mother while children are small.
Life income for mother	Regular monthly income for life after children are grown.
Cash reserves	For use in meeting unexpected cash needs.

IF FATHER LIVES

Income for retirement	Monthly income for life for mother and father.
Money for emergencies	Cash to meet unexpected expenses.
Money for special purposes	Gifts and systematic saving for family goals.

LIFE INSURANCE TERMS

Life insurance is a voluntary financial plan whereby an individual makes periodic payments to an insurance company. The company in turn repays the individual or the one whom he designates as his *beneficiary* at a specified future time or upon the occurrence of certain events such as death, accident, or disability. The person whose life is insured is called the *insured*. Life insurance involves a specific contract (the *policy*) between the insured and an insurance company in which the company promises to pay a sum of money to the person (the beneficiary) named in the policy at the time of the insured's death. If the insured is alive at a future date specified in the policy, a certain sum or periodic sums of money are usually paid to him, except in the case of term insurance. The promise on the part of the insurance company is given in return for the payment of a sum of money (the *premium*) to the insurance company.

Insurance may be secured only by persons having what is known as an *insurable interest*. Everyone has an insurable interest in his own life. Whether a person has an insurable interest in the life of another depends upon whether he will be deprived of some benefit by the death of the other. One need not be a relative of a person in order to insure that person's life. A creditor, under some circumstances, may insure the life of a debtor. Close kinship is often, but not necessarily, sufficient to constitute an insurable interest.

Since insurance is a cooperative plan through which individuals pay the same rates under similar conditions, most general forms of insurance require a physical examination to determine the condition of health. This is done so that the cost of the insurance and the protection of all members of the insured group will be fair. For instance, if there were no physical examinations required, a person in poor health and likely to die soon would not pay any higher rate than one in good health; or a person 25 years of age would have to pay as high a rate as one 50 years of age. A physical examination determines eligibility, therefore; and the age and other conditions determine the rate. Many persons with less than perfect health or in extra-dangerous occupations can obtain insurance but at higher rates than normal.

Life insurance premium rates are based on the experience of the life insurance company and on anticipated claims. Accurate estimates of anticipated claims are developed from *mortality tables,* which indicate the percentage of a specific age group that will die from all causes each year. Many life insurance policies call for the same payment of premium each year. This is known as *level-premium* insurance inasmuch as it equalizes yearly or monthly payments even though the probability of death increases as the age of the insured increases. If it were not for the practice of level-premium, the amount of premium would increase each year.

Many states require insurance companies to maintain a continuous cash balance known as a *legal reserve*. This reserve is to make certain that funds will be available to pay the insured or his beneficiary when the policy becomes due.

If an individual wants to discontinue his insurance, his share of the reserve funds is called the *cash value*. The cash value of a policy increases until the policy matures, either as an endowment or at the end of the span of life on which the rates were calculated. The cash value is also the basis for a policy loan that will enable the policyholder to meet an emergency, to pay a future premium that is due, or to take advantage of an opportunity for which cash is needed. The reserves built up by these advance or excess payments in early years are invested by the insurance company; the income received on these investments helps to reduce the cost of life insurance protection. Thus, it is interesting to note that an insurance company may get a portion of the funds that it lends to a family to help purchase a home from insurance premiums paid by that family.

Time period	Straight life	20-Payment life	20-Year endowment
Premiums (net) paid, 10 years	$185.19	$302.51	$ 464.75
Cash value, 10 years	138.00	261.00	439.00
Premiums (net) paid, 20 years	$342.49	$566.56	$ 875.69
Cash value, 20 years	293.00	583.00	1,000.00

The table shows the cost and cash value of $1,000 of life insurance bought at age 25 in one mutual company, assuming that the dividends are used to reduce the premium cost each year.

Cost and cash value of insurance

TYPES OF ORDINARY LIFE INSURANCE

There are many types of life insurance contracts, usually referred to as policies. Some of them are simple; others involve a combination of elements that cannot be explained without considerable detail. The following are the basic types of ordinary life insurance: term, straight life, limited-payment life, endowment, combination, and annuity. These types of policies are explained in the following pages.

Term insurance. *Term insurance* covers a specified period of time and is usually obtained to cover a specific need. For example, if a man has a debt that he expects to repay in ten years, provided he lives, he can buy a ten-year term policy for the amount of the indebtedness. This insurance will pay the debt in case he dies. Consumer-credit insurance or credit life insurance, referred to in Chapter 19, is one form of term insurance.

Term insurance is often referred to as "pure insurance" because it provides protection only. It does not have a cash-surrender or a loan value. One of the major advantages of term insurance is its initial low cost for a young person compared with that of other types. Term insurance makes it possible for a young person to acquire more insurance coverage at the time protection is needed but when income is too low to buy permanent protection.

The most common periods covered by term insurance are five years and ten years, but it may cover any period of years. Term insurance policies may be purchased which are convertible into other types of contracts that provide protection over longer periods of years and that involve the accumulation of reserves. For instance, a man may wish a large amount of protection at a low cost while his children are of school or college age. After they have been educated, he may then convert the term insurance into some other type of insurance at a higher cost without another physical examination.

Straight life insurance. The basic life insurance policy that provides protection over a long period of years is called *straight life insurance*. It is occasionally called ordinary life insurance; but in our discussions we shall use the term *ordinary life insurance* to mean all forms of standard life insurance policies except those classified as industrial, group, or savings-bank insurance, which will be discussed later in this chapter.

If one has dependents and is anxious to provide primarily for their protection in the event of his death, the straight life plan is ideal. The premium rate is lower than that for any other type of permanent insurance. The policyholder has a loan or a cash-surrender value in the policy. The insured person may continue paying premiums for the entire length of his life or to age 100, at which time he is paid the face value of the insurance policy.

A straight-life insurance plan is ideal for a man who wishes to provide for the protection of his dependents in event of his death.

Most policyholders of straight life contracts actually do not pay premiums until the end of the mortality table (which may be 96 or 100). A very few do. Many people stop paying premiums and take a reduced paid-up policy, which at age 65 amounts to from 60 to 70 percent of the face value.

Limited-payment life insurance. A *limited-payment life insurance* contract is the same as a straight life contract except that premiums are paid for a limited time, such as 10, 20, or 30 years, instead of for life. Because premiums are paid only for a limited time, the rates are somewhat higher than for straight life insurance. When these premiums have been paid, the insurance policy is said to be fully paid. If the face value of the policy is, for example, $10,000, the insurance company will pay this amount whenever death occurs.

Endowment insurance. The company that issues an *endowment policy* agrees to pay a definite sum of money at a specified time to the insured, or, in the event of death, to the beneficiary of the insured. An endowment policy costs more than a limited-payment policy for an equivalent number of years. The face amount is available, however, as cash at the time of death or at the end of the period; whereas, in the case of the limited-payment policy, it is available only in the event of death, or at age 100, or a later specified age.

An endowment policy is an excellent means of accumulating a definite amount for a future need. Short-term endowments for periods of from 10 to 20 years are ideal to create sums of money that will be needed to educate children, to start a child in some particular profession or business, to purchase a home, or to repay a debt.

530

Frequently, and particularly in the case of young people, the short-term endowment policy should not be used. In such a case the amount of insurance that can be purchased may be limited by the comparatively high premium rates. For example, with one particular insurance company, a young man at age 20 could purchase straight life insurance at an annual rate of $10.65 a thousand, twenty-payment life insurance for $19.02 a thousand, twenty-year endowment insurance for $42.71 a thousand, or endowment at age 65 for $14.33 a thousand. If one is seeking the maximum permanent protection at the lowest price, the straight life policy is the cheapest.

It is usually most desirable to obtain a long-term endowment policy so that the money will become available at about the age of 60 or later. At this stage in life the insured may have little or no earning power, having reached retirement or a period of reduced income. If the policy matures at that time, its face value will be available to provide comfort during the later years of life.

Combination life insurance. Many contracts involve combinations of various types of life insurance. For example, one particular type of *combination* policy provides a low rate for the first four or five years and a higher rate in later years. The same insurance plan would be carried out if an individual purchased a term insurance policy and then, at the end of four or five years, converted it into a straight life, a limited-payment life, or an endowment policy.

Annuity contracts. An *annuity* is a sum of money payable yearly. Many people purchase an annuity by turning over to an insurance company a specified sum of money as a single premium or in regular payments. In return for this sum of money, the insurance company agrees to pay a specified monthly or yearly income over a definite period of years or until the death of the insured. The cash value that has accumulated in a permanent type of life insurance policy can be taken as income over a period of years by the insured. This, in effect, is an annuity. In this way a specified income is assured to the insured or to his beneficiary after his death.

The purchase of annuities is not limited to wealthy people. Annuities can be purchased for as little as $1,000. An annuity contract can be purchased over a period of years by annual payments of as little as $25. Under the terms of the contract, the insurance company will start annuity payments at the age selected by the purchaser and continue them as long as he lives. Some annuity contracts also guarantee a minimum number of payments. Any guaranteed payments not made before death will be continued to the beneficiary.

There are numerous types of annuity contracts. However, the principal feature of an annuity is guaranteed income starting at a certain age. Therefore, through an annuity one may, during his earning years, provide for an income after his retirement.

OTHER KINDS OF LIFE INSURANCE CONTRACTS

The types of life insurance discussed up to this point are called ordinary insurance. There are some other types—industrial, group, and savings bank—that may have some of the features of ordinary insurance but also have other characteristics.

Industrial insurance. *Industrial insurance* is the type of insurance that requires small weekly, twice a month, or sometimes monthly, payments. It is commonly sold to the industrial or wage-earning group. The payment each week is usually five cents or some multiple thereof.

Industrial insurance serves essentially the following useful purposes: it reaches many people who would otherwise not buy any insurance; it teaches these people to save and to guard against unfavorable events or circumstances; it enables many people who are not insurable under other plans to obtain insurance. Unfortunately, most of the persons who buy industrial insurance policies do not continue them until they mature or until benefits might be received at the time of death.

Some large insurance companies no longer offer industrial insurance policies; the current trend of insurance firms is not to offer new industrial policies to policyholders but only to service those already started.

Group insurance. Group insurance is usually used to protect the workers of a common employer. Under this plan many employees can be insured through one policy and without medical examination. The cost is determined by an analysis of the group and is based on the losses indicated by the ages, environment, occupation, and general health of the members. The rates may be increased or decreased, but they are usually low. Employers pay part or all of the premiums. Group insurance is also sold to members of labor unions or other associations.

There are two types of group insurance: one is *group term insurance* that does not build up any cash value; the other is *group permanent life insurance* that does accumulate a cash value.

When an employee covered under a group policy leaves the employment through which he has been insured, his protection stops. He sometimes may convert his term insurance to a regular policy (within thirty days) and will then pay annual premiums determined by his age at that time. If the employee was covered under a group permanent policy, he is usually entitled to the fully paid-up protection which has been purchased to date. Sometimes under group permanent insurance plans, individual certificates are issued which resemble individual life policies. In the case of permanent insurance, these policies may be converted to regular individual policies and continued by the former employee.

One disadvantage of group term insurance is that the premium rates for a person of retirement age increases sharply or the amount of the term insurance available to the retired employee is reduced sharply.

Savings-bank insurance. Massachusetts was the first state to institute a plan for selling *savings-bank insurance.* Under that plan, savings banks accept payments for insurance policies in the same way as they accept deposits in savings accounts. Premiums are not collected by

KINDS OF INSURANCE CONTRACTS

KINDS	AMOUNT	PAYMENTS	TYPE OF PAYMENTS	PHYSICAL EXAM	COST
ORDINARY	$500—UP	MONTHLY QUARTERLY SEMI-YEARLY YEARLY	MAIL	YES	MEDIUM
INDUSTRIAL	$100—UP	WEEKLY	COLLECTED BY AGENT	NO	HIGH
GROUP	$500—UP	DEDUCTION FROM WAGE	COLLECTED BY EMPLOYER	NO	LOW
SAVINGS BANK	$250—UP	MONTHLY QUARTERLY YEARLY	MAIL OR AT BANK	YES	LOW

solicitors. Savings-bank insurance was intended to supplant industrial insurance sold largely to wage earners.

New York and Connecticut also permit the sale of savings-bank insurance. In all cases there are certain restrictions on the amount that a person can buy. For instance, in the state of Connecticut no person can buy more than a total of $5,000; in New York, $10,000; and in Massachusetts, $38,000.

FEATURES OF LIFE INSURANCE POLICIES

There are many kinds of insurance contracts as can be seen from the table on page 533. There are some features common to all; others are peculiar to a specific contract. These features should be understood by anyone considering a life insurance policy.

Insurance as a form of saving. In considering insurance as a form of saving, one must compare it with at least two other forms of saving: (a) the deposit of savings in a bank and (b) the purchase of U. S. government bonds. There are advantages to each of the three forms. Certain types of insurance policies, such as the endowment policy, are in reality insurance plus the savings element. Of course, insurance savings do not accumulate so rapidly as bank savings because, in the case of insurance, a part of each payment is used to provide for the protection involved.

Bank savings offer no financial protection beyond the amount of the deposits and the accumulated interest. These savings can, however, be readily withdrawn. The cash value of an insurance policy can also be withdrawn. If funds are borrowed on an insurance policy, interest must be paid. U. S. government bonds offer an excellent medium of savings because they can be bought in small denominations, pay a fair rate of interest, and can easily be converted to cash.

Incontestable clause. The purchaser of life insurance should understand the meaning of the *incontestable clause* in this policy. The essence of such a clause is that, if the insurance company and its agents have not discovered within a specified time (usually one or two years) that the insured intentionally or unintentionally made misstatements of fact with regard to diseases or other information required in the application, the insurance company cannot contest the validity of the policy. In other words, if any error has been made, it is the responsibility of the insurance company to discover such a fact within the time limit specified in the incontestable clause.

The use of dividends. Life insurance companies sell participating or nonparticipating policies as described in the previous chapter. Dividends paid to participating policyholders can be used in the following ways:

1. They may be obtained in cash.
2. They may be used to reduce the amount of the next premium payment.
3. They may be used to purchase additional insurance.
4. They may be left with the company to accumulate at an interest rate determined by the company. This accumulated amount may be used later for any purpose, or it may be withdrawn in cash. If the insured dies before using the accumulated dividends, the beneficiary will be paid the face amount of the policy, plus the amount of the accumulated dividends and interest. When dividends accumulate, straight life policies may be paid up eventually, and other policies may be paid up faster than normal.

Nonforfeiture values. All life insurance companies provide a choice of *nonforfeiture values* to a policyholder who stops paying premiums on any policy except term insurance. These choices are cash value, extended term insurance, and paid-up insurance. The following is an explanation of these nonforfeiture values:

1. Each policy states the *cash value,* which is the amount of money that will be paid to the insured if the policy is canceled. The cash value is stated in his contract as required by law.
2. If the insured wishes to continue the maximum amount of insurance protection without paying premiums, he may accept *extended term insurance.* This continues the face value of the policy for as long as the accumulated cash value will pay the premium.
3. Under the *paid-up insurance* plan, the cash value is used to buy a reduced amount of fully paid insurance.

Paying premiums. Premiums are due on the date mentioned in the policy. They must be paid to the home office or to an authorized representative. Most companies do not give a receipt unless requested. A canceled check serves as a receipt.

Life insurance policies generally allow what is called a *grace period.* This is a period ranging from 28 to 31 days after the date the premium

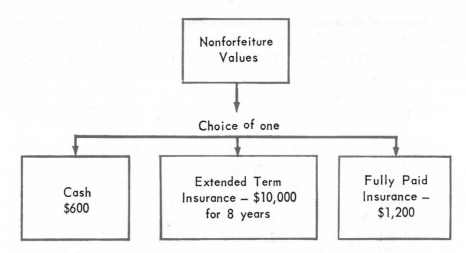

Choices of nonforfeiture values available to policyholders *

* Based on $10,000 straight life insurance, age 40, end of fourth year.

is due. If the premium is paid during this grace period, there is no penalty to the policyholder. If the premium is not paid during the grace period, the policy lapses. This means the termination of the contract and the loss of protection unless the policy has a value that will automatically continue part or all of the insurance for a time. However, if you stop payments of premiums, you may reinstate your insurance policy provided you have not surrendered your policy for a cash settlement. In order to reinstate it, you must meet all requirements of any person buying a new policy. You will be required to take a new physical examination and pay all the overdue premiums with interest or the increase in cash value. Some policies also have other requirements for reinstatement.

Changing the beneficiary. When anyone buys a life insurance policy, he names a beneficiary, or his policy becomes payable to the estate upon his death. The *estate* is the term used to describe the money and other property left by a deceased person to be distributed according to a will or the laws of the state. If you decide to change your beneficiary, you may do so at any time by filling out forms furnished by the insurance company. This may be done provided you have reserved this right in your policy. If you have not reserved the right to change your beneficiary, you must get the written consent of the original beneficiary before naming a new one.

Assigning the policy. If you have reserved the right to change the beneficiary of your life insurance policy, it can be assigned as security for a loan. Banks will lend money on some life insurance policies provided the policy is assigned to the bank as security for the loan.

Policy limitations. Some life insurance contracts limit coverage on travel in certain foreign countries that are engaged in hostilities. Almost all policies do provide protection in case of death due to war, but there are still a few exceptions. Policies now provide protection for travel on a scheduled commercial airline or on a nonscheduled private plane with a licensed commercial pilot. Premiums are higher for test pilots, however.

It is well to study the special clauses that provide such limitations. These special clauses usually are placed at the end of the policies and are called *riders*.

Death by suicide is usually not covered by an insurance policy if the suicide occurs during the first year or two of the contract. However, if suicide does occur during that time, the insurance company usually will return the premiums previously paid.

Extra benefits. Some insurance policies have provisions whereby it is not necessary to pay the premiums if the insured becomes permanently disabled. This provision is called a *premium waiver*.

Other policies provide twice the amount of death benefit if the insured dies as the result of an accident instead of from natural causes. This provision in an insurance policy is generally called the *double indemnity clause*.

Each company sets its own standard practices, provided these practices are according to law. The clauses in policies of the same type issued by one company in different states may not always be alike, however, for the various clauses must conform to the laws of the states in which the company operates and in which policies are issued.

ECONOMICS OF LIFE INSURANCE

Life insurance, except term insurance, is both an investment and a protection. Obviously, a person should not attempt to use life insurance for his entire savings or investing program. The saving element in life insurance is safe, but it has little possibility of growing in value as in the case of common stocks or real estate.

Through the accumulation of small sums of money from many policyholders, insurance companies secure huge sums of money to invest. This money is loaned for building homes, churches, offices, and factories and is invested in government bonds, corporation bonds, and corporation stocks. Therefore, individuals save money and protect themselves through life insurance and contribute to the economic needs of the entire nation.

Facts everyone should know about life insurance

1. A life insurance policy is a contract.
2. Nearly all life insurance premiums are paid at a constant rate.
3. Term insurance is the cheapest form of life insurance, but it does not accumulate a cash value.
4. Straight life insurance is the cheapest form of permanent insurance.
5. Endowment or variations of endowment insurance build the greatest cash values.
6. Several features may be combined in one policy.
7. Group insurance and industrial insurance generally do not require a physical examination.

B. Health insurance

PURPOSE OF HEALTH INSURANCE

The primary purpose of health insurance is to protect the family against the financial problems that might arise as the result of illness of any member of the family or an accident to any member of the family. In regular life insurance policies, special clauses are sometimes included to protect against financial loss due to accidents and sickness.

Health insurance may provide for one or all of the following five coverages: hospital expense, surgical expense, general medical expense, major medical expense, and loss of income.

HOSPITAL EXPENSE INSURANCE

This insurance coverage provides benefits equal to all or part of the cost of a hospital room and board. A provision of the policy usually limits the number of days that are covered by the policy. The family's choice of a room, of course, determines whether the hospital expense insurance is adequate.

Other benefits may be provided for, such as medications, X-ray services, and operating room services. Hospital expense insurance is the most widely used form of health insurance.

SURGICAL EXPENSE INSURANCE

Surgical expense insurance provides for payment of surgical costs according to a schedule of fees payable for each type of operation. The schedule of fees is based on the nature of the operation. For example, the surgeon's fee for a tonsillectomy may be $80 and his fee for an appendectomy may be $200. Surgical expense insurance is the second most widely used form of health insurance.

GENERAL MEDICAL EXPENSE INSURANCE

This type of insurance provides benefits payable toward the expenses of calls made by doctors at the hospital or at home, or for visits by the patient to the doctor's office. Benefits of $3 usually are allowed for hospital or office visits and $5 for home visits by the doctor. The number of calls of each type which the insurance company will pay for is specified in the policy.

MAJOR MEDICAL EXPENSE INSURANCE

This type of insurance is designed to cover the major portion of the costs incurred as the result of major illness or serious accident. Major illness and serious accidents may result in expenses amounting to $5,000, $10,000, or perhaps even $15,000 or more.

Basically, major medical insurance is designed to begin where hospital, surgical, and general medical insurance leave off. For this reason, most major medical policies have a deductible clause. Thus the insured person may have to pay the first $100 of any cost not covered by the basic policies. In addition, he may be required to pay 20 to 25 percent of any amount above the first $100. This is known as

The basic purpose of major medical expense insurance is to cover the major portion of costs incurred as the result of major illness or a serious accident.

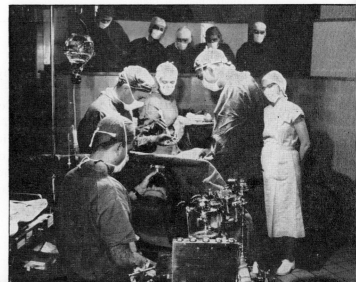

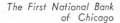

The First National Bank
of Chicago

coinsurance. It helps keep down the costs of the insurance by discouraging the insured from incurring charges for unnecessary services during his illness and recuperation.

LOSS-OF-INCOME INSURANCE

Illness or accident may mean that a wage earner loses his income. Loss-of-income insurance is designed to replace all or part of that lost income. Premiums are based on the amount of income that is to be replaced and the length of time for which payments will be made. Usually, there is a waiting period of some days or weeks before benefits are payable. Families carrying loss-of-income insurance, therefore, are assured that they will have income in the event of prolonged illness but will meet the expenses of a short illness out of current income or savings. Whether the family should carry loss-of-income insurance depends on the sick leave provisions of the wage earner's job, workmen's compensation provisions, and other factors.

Facts everyone should know about health insurance

1. Health insurance protects a family or individual against financial loss due to accident or illness.
2. The most common types of health insurance are hospital expense, surgical expense, and general medical expense.
3. Every family in moderate financial circumstances should consider hospital and surgical expense insurance coverage.
4. Major medical insurance insures against the major portion of the cost of major illness or accident.
5. The family should insure against only the most serious losses; minor medical expenses should be taken care of as part of the regular family financial plan.

▪ QUESTIONS ON THE TEXT

1. Why is life insurance an essential part of any plan providing for family financial security?
2. What is meant by the term "life insurance premium"?
3. What is meant by the term "level-premium insurance"?
4. What is the major advantage of level-premium insurance?
5. What type of insurance requires the least dollar outlay?
6. What type of insurance is used by lending agencies, such as credit unions, to guarantee that a loan to a borrower will be paid in full in the event of his death?

7. Should straight life insurance be purchased to provide temporary protection?
8. In what ways does a limited-payment life insurance policy differ from a straight life insurance policy?
9. What is the difference between endowment insurance and limited-payment life insurance?
10. How do policyholders use endowment insurance policies in their life insurance programs?
11. Which has the lower premium rate—straight life insurance or endowment insurance? Why?
12. What is an annuity?
13. Do group insurance policies require a medical examination?
14. What type of permanent insurance should a person buy to provide the maximum amount of protection for his dependents for the least possible cash outlay?
15. Explain why all types of ordinary life insurance with the exception of term insurance include an element of savings.
16. What options regarding the use of policy dividends does a policyholder have?
17. What is meant by nonforfeiture values? Explain.
18. What is meant by "the grace period" for premium payments?
19. What must one do to change the beneficiary of his life insurance?
20. May a life insurance policy be used in obtaining a bank loan?
21. Why is a "waiver of premium" provision important in a life insurance contract?
22. What is the primary purpose of health insurance?
23. What expenses are covered by hospital expense insurance?
24. Why do most major medical insurance policies include a deductible clause?

▪ QUESTIONS FOR DISCUSSION

1. If a person is borrowing money with which to buy a home, what type of insurance should he buy if he wants the lowest dollar outlay for insurance premiums until the loan is paid?
2. A widowed mother with limited funds is financing most of the college education for her son, although he is paying part of the cost from his own part-time work earnings. Should she buy a life insurance policy on his life? If so, what kind of policy should she buy? Should he buy a policy? Why?
3. Should a person whose income is to decrease sharply at some time in the future buy limited-payment life insurance?
4. Mr. Brown has no dependents but he wants to purchase a home ten years from now. What type of insurance would allow him to build up the

largest cash value and yet provide an estate for his heirs in the event of his death?

5. What kind of policy should one buy in order to provide permanent protection yet pay premiums for only a stated number of years and have a loan or cash-surrender value?

6. What type of insurance provides the greatest element of savings but the least amount of protection for each dollar spent on premiums?

7. If a policyholder has a limited-payment participating life insurance policy, what may he do with the dividends?

8. What should a policyholder do if he discovers that he is sixty days delinquent in paying a premium?

9. Under what conditions can the beneficiary of a life insurance policy prevent the policyholder from changing the beneficiary?

10. Should a person with a well-planned life insurance program buy "trip flight insurance" when making trips by airplane?

11. What options do policyholders have in the event that they wish to discontinue payments on an insurance contract?

12. Discuss the ways in which the insurance industry affects the national economy.

13. Should the head of the family carry more than one health insurance policy?

14. Should all families carry loss-of-income insurance?

▪ PROBLEMS TO SOLVE

1. Mr. Jackson bought a life insurance contract which states that if he dies, the insurance company will pay the widow for each $1,000 of insurance a monthly income of the following amounts for ten years certain, for twenty years certain, and for as long thereafter as the widow lives. (A contract for ten years certain means that the widow will be paid for her entire life, but if she should die at the end of eight years, the insurance company will pay for two more years to someone else designated by the widow. A contract for twenty years certain operates in a similar manner.)

Age of Widow	10 years certain and for life	20 years certain and for life
35	$3.22	$3.18
40	3.43	3.37
45	3.70	3.59
50	4.02	3.84
55	4.42	4.12
60	4.90	4.41

On a $10,000 policy: (a) how much will the widow at age 40 receive each month on a ten-year certain basis? (a) How much will the widow at age 55 receive each month on a twenty-year certain basis?

2. The following chart shows the premium rates charged on a straight life policy by a certain company for $1,000 of protection for a person aged 20:

Age	Straight Life			
	Annual	Semiannually	Quarterly	Monthly
20	$13.44	$6.86	$3.50	$1.19

(a) How much money does a 20-year-old person save by paying his premium annually rather than monthly? quarterly? semiannually?

(b) What percent savings does an annual premium payment represent over twelve monthly payments? four quarterly payments? two semi-annual payments?

(c) If one considered that it costs him a minimum of 5 cents for every check he writes and 5 cents postage for every check he mails, what would one annual premium payment represent to him in total cash savings over twelve monthly payments? What percent savings does this represent?

3. The following chart shows life insurance rates issued by a certain company for two types of policies. The rates are for $1,000 of protection.

Age	10-Year term		Straight life	
	Annual	Monthly	Annual	Monthly
20	$4.90	$ .44	$13.44	$1.19
25	5.17	.46	15.41	1.37
30	5.37	.48	17.88	1.58

(a) What will be the annual premium for a $15,000 10-year term policy issued to a 20-year-old man? Assume he elects to pay the premium annually.

(b) What will be the annual cost for a $10,000 straight life policy issued to a man who is 30 years old? Assume he elects to pay the premium monthly.

(c) A 20-year-old man is trying to decide whether to pay his 10-year term policy monthly or annually. (1) On a $10,000 policy, how much will he save each year if he pays the premium annually? (2) How much would he save over the 10-year period?

(Assume that it costs him 5 cents for every check written and 5 cents postage for every premium payment mailed.)

▪ COMMUNITY PROBLEMS AND PROJECTS

1. From a local life insurance agent find out (a) the procedure for borrowing on one's life insurance policy, (b) how much can be borrowed, (c) the advantages and disadvantages of borrowing on a life insurance policy.

2. Obtain a life insurance policy at home or from an insurance agent. Study it carefully as to the nonforfeiture value, the cash-surrender value, restrictions on flying, and any other special provisions which are new to you. Make a list of the facts that you learn from the examination of this policy and write a report on these.

3. Consult a local insurance agent and ask for information about "Decreasing Life" policies. Prepare a report in which you present answers to questions such as the following:

   (a) For whom is this type of policy designed?

   (b) How do the rates compare with (1) straight life policies? (2) term insurance policies?

   (c) At what age does the coverage start to decrease?

   (d) At what age does the coverage stop decreasing? What is the face value of the policy at that time?

Chapter 28

Buying life insurance

PURPOSE OF THE CHAPTER

Life insurance is important to all members of the family. Developing an insurance program that includes the father, the mother, and the children is not only desirable but also necessary. Proper coverage of family risks makes it necessary to select a sound insurance company, a good agent, and appropriate policies. The problems that the family must solve in developing a good insurance program are discussed and analyzed in this chapter.

You will find answers to these questions:

1. On what basis should an insurance company be selected?
2. How can the rates of different insurance companies be compared?
3. What factors should be considered in selecting an insurance agent?
4. What factors should be considered in planning an insurance program?

A. Selecting an insurance company and agent

BASES FOR SELECTING AN INSURANCE COMPANY

Reputation, operating success, and financial soundness should be carefully studied when selecting a company from which to purchase

a life insurance policy. Much of this information needed is readily available from your state insurance commission since an insurance company must be licensed in each state in which it operates. Also you can get a copy of the company's latest annual report from the agent or by writing to the home office of the company. Information on a company's reputation and financial standing may be obtained from the people in your community—bankers, lawyers, businessmen, or friends who may have done business with the company. You can get details about a company's operations by consulting published reports available in many libraries.

As is true with everything that we purchase, we should plan to buy insurance from the company that offers the best value. This means, therefore, that costs as well as provisions of policies should be thoroughly studied and considered.

COMPARING COSTS OF POLICIES

In comparing the cost of a policy of one company with that of another, only equivalent contracts should be considered. Caution is necessary since policies that may appear to be identical often differ significantly in nonforfeiture benefits, in settlement values, or in other policy provisions.

Some life insurance companies may pay dividends to policyholders out of profits. Policies issued by these companies are known as participating policies. Other life insurance companies do not pay dividends to policyholders and, therefore, their policies are not participating. Under a participating policy, a policyholder may receive an annual dividend based upon the amount of premium he paid. The amount of the premium less the dividend received is the net cost of the premium on his policy. Under a nonparticipating policy, the amount of premium paid is the net cost of the policy per year.

The table appearing on page 547 shows the rates on various policies of two typical companies. After deducting the average dividends of Company B, the rates of that company may or may not be lower than those of Company A. Some participating companies set their original rates higher than do other participating companies.

As an example of how the payment of dividends affects rates, assume that Company B in the table has paid out an average dividend of $2.45 a year on each $1,000 of insurance on straight life insurance policies ranging from $5,000 to $15,000 at the rates for persons of age 40. Since the stated rate for the person at age 40 is $30.95, the net rate after deducting the average dividend of $2.45 is $28.50. Of course,

ANNUAL PREMIUM RATES PER $1,000				
Age of insured at issuance of policy	Straight life ($1,000)	20-payment life ($1,000)	20-year endowment ($1,000)	5-year term convertible ($1,000)
20 .... Company A, nonparticipating	$14.65	$23.02	$46.71	$ 8.06
25	16.45	25.29	46.81	8.21
30	18.83	28.12	47.04	8.51
35	21.99	31.61	47.66	9.65
40	25.97	35.65	48.76	11.48
45	30.94	40.47	50.47	14.05
50	37.06	45.88	52.90	18.43
55	44.93	52.46	56.67	25.19
20 .... Company B, participating	$18.31	$29.81	$51.06	$ 8.96
25	22.43	32.39	51.26	9.16
30	23.10	35.39	51.68	9.54
35	26.52	38.94	52.50	10.37
40	30.95	43.22	53.96	12.33
45	36.68	48.39	56.34	15.54
50	44.19	54.84	60.15	20.79
55	51.91	63.27	66.21	28.25

the dividend is not guaranteed; in this case, the net rate for the participating company would be more than the rate of the nonparticipating company, even considering the dividend.

The cost of an insurance policy differs among companies, but competition tends to restrict these differences. The difference in cost between insurance bought on the participating as compared with nonparticipating basis can be measured accurately only over a long period of time.

FACTORS IN SELECTING AN AGENT

As a general rule, insurance salesmen are honorable and consider seriously the insurance needs of clients. The buyer of insurance should bear in mind, however, that some insurance salesmen may be so eager to sell that they may make recommendations sometimes just

---

Facts to be considered in selecting an insurance company

1. Compare rates, including dividends, among companies.
2. Select only a company that has a good reputation and that is sound financially.
3. Deal only with a reputable agent.
4. In comparing the same or similar policies of different companies, do not compare cost alone, but be sure that the policies are identical in every respect. For example, some policies have a disability clause that relieves you from the responsibility of paying premiums in case of illness or other disability.
5. The dividend rate or other factors will not necessarily remain the same in the future for any company.
6. Buy life insurance only from a company licensed in your state.

---

to please the person who is buying the insurance, even though it may not be the best possible recommendation. The buyer of insurance must therefore learn the basic principles of insurance so that he may judge the merits of an insurance salesman's recommendations.

When selecting an insurance agent, you are really selecting both a company and an agent. This may present problems. However, you can compare rates. You should then inquire among your friends for their recommendations of agents and companies with whom they have dealt. This is probably one of the best ways to find an agent who can serve you well.

Many agents study life insurance through correspondence and by taking courses in schools. This study often covers several years. The purpose is to help the agent learn the fundamental principles of life insurance, the nature of the various contracts and policies, and the principles of insurance program planning for an individual or family.

Before deciding to purchase a particular insurance policy, be sure that you have compared agents, companies, rates, and policies.

Harold M. Lambert

Upon the completion of the course of study the agent takes an examination. If he passes the examination, he is awarded the *Certified Life Underwriter* certificate. He is thus entitled to use the letters C.L.U. after his name, which means that he is well informed about insurance and is capable of giving sound advice about insurance planning.

USING THE AGENT

A reliable agent who is working for a reliable company will give sound advice to prospective purchasers of insurance. In making application for an insurance policy, the applicant is usually required to indicate the amount of insurance he already owns. This information gives the insurance company an opportunity to determine whether the applicant is justified in purchasing additional insurance. If additional insurance is needed and if its purchase will fit into the budget, the insurance agent can help the applicant select the proper kind.

A good life insurance agent is one who not only has an adequate knowledge of life insurance but who also has learned how to help people determine their insurance needs and to fit an insurance program to those needs. If a person wants to obtain the best use of his insurance dollars, he must find such an agent and put his trust in him as he would in his doctor or lawyer. Only then can the agent help him:

1. Plan insurance protection to fit his needs and those of his dependents.
2. Build an insurance program that will include the savings he wants for his retirement and for specific purposes such as the college education of his children.
3. Fit the purchasing of policies to his present and probable future income.
4. Revise his program periodically and help the insured build onto it, as the first three factors change.

B. Developing a life insurance program

PLANNING THE INITIAL PROGRAM

Every family should consider an insurance program at the time of marriage when the family is formed and then modify the program as changing conditions warrant. Three major problems are involved in insurance planning. First, how much life insurance does the family need; second, what kind of financial protection through insurance is needed; and third, how much insurance can the family afford?

The insurance needs of the family should be considered in relation to the family income. The insurance agent should be consulted at this point to recommend policies that are suitable to meet the needs of the family. The insurance plan should make provision for possible events which may affect both the income and the expenses of the family. For example, if there should be a death in the family, money should be readily available for such an emergency.

There should also be a fund of cash available so that the family can operate until certain readjustments are made in the family budget. There may be a debt on the house. One insurance policy may be needed to pay off that debt in case of death. Some insurance policies are purchased for the specific purpose of providing funds to send children to college in case of the death of the father.

Then the big question arises as to the need for providing income for living expenses for the family. Insurance for this purpose should be arranged so that payments are made monthly for a certain period of years or for an indefinite period of years.

Three key objectives for planning an insurance program
1. Adequate protection for specific needs.
2. Adequate savings through insurance.
3. Fitting the premium payments to the income available in your budget.

Life insurance programs should be designed primarily to replace income lost to a family when the husband and father dies. Except for certain sums that may be needed at the time of death, the proceeds of the insurance should be looked upon as an income that will be paid regularly under some prescribed plan to the family of the deceased husband and father. A total of $10,000 may sound like a large sum of money, and it really is, as you will find when you try to save that sum. But at 4 percent interest, $10,000 will provide only $400 a year of income from interest. Life insurance policies can be arranged to provide monthly checks consisting of both principal and interest instead of a lump-sum payment or instead of just interest.

For example, the proceeds of a $10,000 insurance policy will pay $100 a month for nine years and six months. The proceeds of a $20,000 policy will pay $100 a month for twenty-two years and ten months. Other methods of payment may enable a person to work out almost any desired program of income for his family after his death. His life insurance agent should be quite helpful in arranging the details of adequate protection and proper payments.

PLANNING FOR THE READJUSTMENT PERIOD

Emergencies come to many families through accident, death, or disability of one of the chief wage earners of the family. The reduction or complete discontinuance of a weekly or monthly wage presents a critical problem, especially where one or more small children are involved.

Many families are entitled to social security benefits, but these are seldom sufficient to take care of all the needs; however, they do supplement the insurance program and should be taken into consideration. Unless an insurance program is planned, the family will have to depend upon its own earning power or upon the income from other property already accumulated.

At the time of death there are certain unusual expenses involved. Then comes the readjustment period when the family may have to move into a smaller house and prepare for living on a smaller income. In many families there is a problem of educating the children until they are self-supporting, and then providing an income for the widow.

EXAMPLES OF INSURANCE PROGRAMS

The Wilson family. Let us take an example of an insurance program that was planned for the family of Richard Wilson, who is 31 years of age. The family consists of Richard and his wife, Mary, who is 28 years of age; and three children, ages 7, 4, and 1. Richard earns $100 a week.

Mr. and Mrs. Wilson have planned an insurance program which they believe provides the maximum financial protection that the family can afford. Beginning at the time they were married, the Wilsons have continually increased their insurance to provide family income during the period while their children were too young to earn their living. They also have provided in the insurance program for an expense fund, an emergency fund, and a means of income for Mrs. Wilson after the children have reached a wage-earning age. The policies on Mr. Wilson shown in the table on page 552 have been purchased.

The chart on page 552 shows the monthly income available to the family in the event of Mr. Wilson's death. The total monthly income available is composed of insurance income and social security payments. Mary would receive a monthly income of $352.20 until the

Policy	Age at purchase	Amount and type	Annual premium
A	22	$ 1,000 Straight life	$ 14.85
B	23	1,000 Straight life	15.25
C	25	3,000 Straight life	48.30
D	27	5,000 Group life	36.00
E	29	5,000 Ten-year term	40.00
		$15,000 Total	$154.40

7-year old child became 18. She would also continue to receive the same monthly income until the 4-year old child became 18. At that time the monthly income would be reduced to $247. Mary would receive this amount until the 1-year-old child became 18, at which time the social security payments would cease. (A further discussion of social security benefits is presented in the following chapter.)

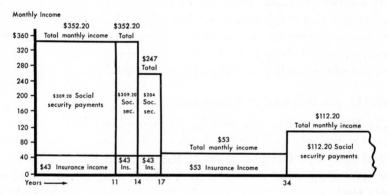

Plus: $1,000 expense fund from Policy A; $1,000 emergency fund from Policy D; $255 death benefits from social security.

Under the Wilsons' insurance program, it is planned to leave $9,000 of the insurance (Policies B, C, and E) with the insurance companies, which will pay Mary $19 each month for the first seventeen years after Mr. Wilson's death. In addition, Mary will receive $24 each month from $4,000 of the group life Policy D. The remainder of the group life policy, $1,000, will be set aside in a savings account as an emergency fund.

When the youngest child is 18 and Mrs. Wilson is 45, the $9,000 (Policies B, C, and E) will be paid out to Mrs. Wilson for the next seventeen years at the rate of $53 a month. At age 62, all life insurance benefits will have been exhausted, but social security payments will begin for Mrs. Wilson and she will receive $112.20 each month.

At the time of Mr. Wilson's death, Mary will need cash for various purposes. The Wilsons' insurance program is so planned that Mary will receive $1,000 from Policy A, which will be used for funeral and other expenses. From the group life Policy D, $1,000 will be set aside as an emergency fund in a savings account. Mrs. Wilson will also receive a lump-sum payment of $255 from social security for funeral expenses.

The Cassel family. Let us see how another family with different problems worked out its insurance problems with the aid of an insurance agent. Robert Cassel is 29; his wife, Jane, is 26; and they have a boy 4 years old. Robert earns $7,800 a year and is covered by social security. He owns his own house on which there is a mortgage of $10,000. The house cost $18,000 but is worth more now. He also has $825 in a savings account and $650 in government bonds. His insurance program is as follows:

Policy	Age at purchase	Amount and type	Annual premium
A	18	$ 1,500 Straight life	$ 23.25
B	23	5,000 Straight life	76.25
C	24	10,000 Family income (20 years)	220.00
D	28	8,000 Life-paid-up-at-65	188.00
E	24	10,000 Group life	50.00
		$34,500 Total	$557.50

In planning their insurance program Mr. and Mrs. Cassel made certain that the plan would provide income to meet certain emergencies if they should arise. The essential features of their insurance program are given here to give you an opportunity to analyze and study them.

If Robert were to die now, there would be $1,500 available from insurance policy A and $255 in a lump-sum payment from social security. The amount of $1,475 in the savings account and government bonds would be used as an emergency fund.

The chart on page 554 shows the amount that Jane and her son would have for their support. Jane would receive $383 each month until the son is 18. For the next two years until the son became 20 years of age, she would receive $179 each month. From that time until Jane became 62, she would receive $90 a month from Policies B, C, and D. Policy E would be used to pay off the mortgage. At age 62, Jane would again receive social security payments amounting to

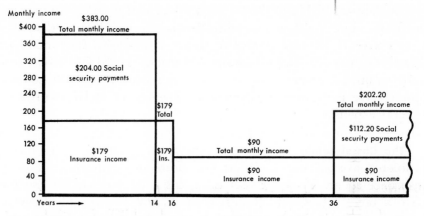

Plus: $1,500 emergency fund from Policy A; $255 death benefits from social security; $1,475 from savings and bonds.

$112.20. These payments, added to the insurance payments, would provide a monthly income of $202.20 for the rest of her life.

RELATIONSHIP OF LIFE INSURANCE EXPENDITURES AND PERSONAL INCOME

When a married person's income is small, he needs insurance because he must have some protection for his dependents. The amount that is set aside for insurance should be budgeted in the same manner as his other expenditures. As a person's salary increases, the amount spent for insurance should also increase. The only people who do not need life insurance for protection purposes are those who have investments that provide income sufficient to support their dependents.

The amount of insurance that should be bought is a special problem in the case of each individual. It must be determined by considering the income, the necessary expenditures, the accumulation of a cash savings fund, and the care of dependents. There are, however, reasonable percentages that have proved to be satisfactory. The table on page 555 shows the recommended percentage of income to be expended on insurance premiums.

Obviously the percentage expended in any particular case will depend upon (a) one's standard of living, (b) one's sense of responsibility, (c) the cost of living, (d) the number of dependents, and (e) the type of insurance that is bought.

Of course, a person with no particular family responsibilities may feel that he does not need much insurance. He may prefer to invest his money in other ways.

Annual income	Percentage	Annual outlay
$ 5,000	7½—10	$ 375 to $ 500
6,000	8½—11	510 to 660
7,000	9½—12	665 to 840
8,000	10½—13	840 to 1,040
9,000	12—14	1,080 to 1,260
10,000	12—14	1,200 to 1,400

Guide to a reasonable outlay for life insurance

INSURANCE AS A SOURCE OF FUTURE INCOME

The amount of future income that one needs may be provided in any one of three ways:

1. By creating a cash estate, which will be invested to provide an income.
2. By buying sufficient insurance to yield a fixed amount of income for life after a certain age.
3. By arranging with the insurance company to use the proceeds of the insurance policy for paying a fixed income to dependents after the death of the insured.

Creating a cash estate for investment. Under the first plan, the person can consider his insurance and his other savings in computing the amount of income that will be available. Suppose, for example, that a person has planned his insurance program so that the cash proceeds available at his contemplated retirement age of 60 will amount to $25,000. If this amount is invested at 4 percent, it will pay an annual income of $1,000. This income, plus the income from other savings, investments, and social security will represent the sum that the person may expect for use after he retires, provided he does not spend part of the principal.

Buying sufficient insurance to yield income. Under the second plan, it is possible for a person to make a contract with an insurance company whereby the proceeds of insurance are to provide: (a) a guaranteed income for life or (b) a guaranteed income for life with a cash settlement if death occurs within a certain period. The table on page 556 shows the monthly income guaranteed by one insurance company for each $1,000 of the proceeds from insurance. The payments given in this table are guaranteed for life. Tables such as this vary, of course, according to the companies with which the contracts of life insurance have been made.

Beginning at age	Guaranteed monthly income for life for each $1,000 in insurance fund
50	$4.51
55	5.07
60	5.80
65	6.75
70	8.02

Monthly income for life (no refund)

For example, if a person has, under this plan, a $10,000 matured endowment policy at the age of 50, he will receive from the insurance company $45.10 each month for the rest of his life. Some settlement options guarantee such payments for a certain number of years, such as fifteen or twenty years, and for life thereafter if the person lives longer. If he does not live beyond the fixed number of years, his beneficiary will receive a specified cash settlement.

Using proceeds to provide fixed income for dependents. Under the third plan, the person who is insured can provide for the proceeds of his insurance to be left with the insurance company after his death so that his dependents can be paid a fixed income for a specified number of years. The table on page 557 shows the proceeds that must be left with one company to provide fixed monthly payments of $50 to $150 for a period of five to fifteen years.

From this table it is apparent that, when a person dies, the proceeds from his insurance policy must amount to $5,201 to guarantee a payment of $50 each month to his dependents for a period of ten years. The values vary, of course, according to the companies.

The buying of insurance should be just one part of the plan of building up savings and providing for the protection of dependents. In deciding how much insurance to buy, a person should consider his entire financial program.

INSURANCE AS A FACTOR IN A PERSON'S ESTATE

The proceeds from a life insurance policy may become due and payable either because the policy has matured or because the insured has died. If a beneficiary was named in the policy, the life insurance

Number of monthly pay-ments	Monthly payments from cash values indicated below							Number of years pay-able
	$50	$70	$75	$90	$100	$125	$150	
60	$2,792	$ 3,909	$ 4,188	$ 5,026	$ 5,585	$ 6,981	$ 8,377	5
72	3,303	4,624	4,954	5,945	6,606	8,277	9,909	6
84	3,799	5,318	5,698	6,838	7,598	9,497	11,396	7
96	4,280	5,992	6,420	7,704	8,560	10,700	12,840	8
108	4,748	6,646	7,121	8,546	9,495	11,869	14,242	9
120	5,201	7,281	7,801	9,362	10,402	13,002	15,603	10
132	5,642	7,898	8,462	10,155	11,283	14,104	16,924	11
144	6,069	8,497	9,104	10,924	12,138	15,173	18,207	12
156	6,484	9,078	9,727	11,672	12,969	16,211	19,454	13
168	6,888	9,642	10,331	12,398	13,775	17,219	20,662	14
180	7,279	10,190	10,918	13,102	14,557	18,197	21,836	15

Cash value needed to provide a fixed monthly income for dependents for a certain number of years if 3 percent interest is paid. (The interest rate may be lower or higher than 3 percent.)

proceeds are paid directly to that person upon proof of the death of the insured. If no beneficiary was named in the policy, the proceeds are paid to the estate of the deceased. The *estate* of a deceased person includes all property of value, both real and personal; and claims, such as debts, taxes, and court and legal costs of concluding the business of the deceased, are filed against the estate for payment.

An individual may prefer to have his life insurance proceeds payable to his estate, and then through his will designate the persons who are to share in the distribution of his property after all expenses and claims have been paid. A *will* consists of legal instructions for the distribution of a person's property after his death.

A will may be changed or revoked at any time during the maker's life. Even though there is a will, creditors must be paid; and a will may not deprive the wife or husband from his rightful share in property according to the laws of the state.

When one makes a will, he should select and name in the will an *executor,* whose function is to prepare tax returns, pay the taxes, investigate claims against the estate, pay the debts that are due, determine the value of the property, distribute the property as instructed in the will, and make a report to the probate court. If a valid will is not left by the deceased person or if an executor has not been named, the court will appoint an *administrator* to settle the estate and distribute the property according to the laws of the state. The duties of the administrator are the same as those of the executor.

Many people in moderate circumstances do not feel that it is necessary to make a will, especially if most of their savings are in life insurance which is payable to some member of the family. They feel that wills are only for rich people. However, if you own only a moderate amount of property, your heirs will have less trouble and less expense if you make a will; and you are more likely to have your wishes carried out with a will than you are without it.

Even when a small amount of money or property is involved, there are dangers in assuming that it is not necessary to make a will. The situation is different in every state, but many things can happen that may not be according to the plans or wishes of the person who died. For example, a husband may assume that all of his property will automatically go to his wife; but in the absence of a will in some states, where there is a wife and one child, the wife would get one third and the child would get two thirds of the estate. In some states if there are no children, the wife would get part of the property and the rest would go to the mother, brother, sister, or other relatives.

A close relationship exists between the provisions in a person's life insurance policies and his estate. Both are comprised of the person's property. The instructions for payment of the proceeds of life insurance are given in the policy, and instructions for the distribution of other property are given in the person's will. Thus the provisions set up in life insurance policies should be considered when a will is drawn up. A competent, experienced insurance agent, preferably one who holds the C.L.U. degree, should be consulted for recommendations regarding the planning and developing of your life insurance program. Likewise, the services of a competent attorney should be secured for the planning of a person's estate and for the writing of a will.

By means of a will, an entire estate may be left to the wife. Thus, it is possible to avoid the expense and annoyance of frequent reports showing how amounts available for the children have been used.

Underwood & Underwood

Facts everyone should know about buying life insurance

1. The reputation, success, and financial resources of insurance companies are important factors in selecting a company.
2. Select an insurance agent who represents a sound, acceptable company and who is competent through experience and training to advise you about your insurance program.
3. The integrity of the insurance agent who advises you is as important as the soundness of the company from whom you buy insurance.
4. An insurance program is highly important to a family; many factors must be considered in the developing of such a program.
5. Total expenditures for insurance should be in keeping with a person's total income. Ordinarily, expenditures for insurance should increase as income increases.
6. A life insurance program may be so planned as to provide income to meet emergencies and income after the earning period of life has passed.
7. The plan of a person's life insurance program and the plan for the distribution of his estate after death should be coordinated.

■ QUESTIONS ON THE TEXT

1. Explain how you obtain information so that you can judge the standing and reputation of a life insurance company.
2. How can you determine the actual net rate that is charged for an insurance policy in a participating company?
3. In the table in this chapter that compares a nonparticipating with a participating company, what amount of dividend would be necessary on a straight life policy at age 20 in order for the net rate of Company B to be the same as the net rate of Company A?
4. Why can the cost of insurance on a participating policy be measured accurately only over a long period of time?
5. Name some guides in selecting a life insurance company.
6. What does *Certified Life Underwriter* mean?
7. Do participating insurance companies guarantee that they will pay dividends?
8. What are the three key objectives to be considered in planning a life insurance program?
9. When in a person's life should he begin his life insurance program?
10. What relation should there be between the annual cost (premiums) of an individual's life insurance program and his annual income?
11. In the case of the Wilson family illustrated in this chapter, how much monthly income will the widow and children have for the first eleven years after the death of Mr. Wilson?

12. In the case of the Cassel family in the example in this chapter, how much monthly income will the widow and children have for the first fourteen years after the death of Mr. Cassel?

13. What would be a reasonable percentage of annual income for a person to invest in life insurance if his income is $6,000? $7,000? $8,000?

14. From the table in this chapter showing the cash value needed to provide a fixed monthly income, what is the cash value needed to provide an income of $100 a month for fifteen years?

15. Explain the meaning of (a) estate, (b) will, (c) executor, and (d) administrator.

▪ QUESTIONS FOR DISCUSSION

1. Why is it desirable for a man with a family to include several kinds of life insurance policies in his insurance plan?

2. If you start buying life insurance at age 30 and there is inflation (a general increase in prices and the cost of living), what happens to the value of the money that is paid to you in your old age or to a beneficiary on your death? In other words, explain the effects of inflation on insurance.

3. If the situation in the previous question is reversed and there is deflation (if prices go down), what is the effect on insurance?

4. Give some reasons why you think it is very important to buy life insurance from a good agent and a good company.

5. (a) When a person applies for an insurance policy, why does the insurance agent ask how much insurance the person already owns?
   (b) Why is it desirable for the person to tell how much he owns?

6. Bill Brown, age 45, knows that in the position in which he works he must retire at age 65. He would like to buy a straight life insurance policy, but he wants all premium payments to cease by the time he retires. What choice does he have?

7. What kind of insurance program would you recommend for a young unmarried man of 17 years of age who expects to secure a college education and go into business for himself?

8. In the insurance program of the Richard Wilson family in this chapter, what would you recommend as a possible improvement if Mr. Wilson had sufficient income to provide additional insurance?

9. (a) Why is it undesirable for a person to carry too much insurance?
   (b) What is *too much* insurance?

10. Explain why one should avoid borrowing money to pay the first premium on a life insurance policy.

11. Many people feel that they do not have enough wealth to require the writing of a will. What do you think about this idea?

12. How may an individual's life insurance program affect his estate?

▪ PROBLEMS TO SOLVE

1. R. D. Carson, 35 years of age, has two children, aged 4 and 8. He has a good position and has almost paid for his home. He has $500 in a savings account, an endowment policy of $2,000, and a straight life policy of $10,000. His budget provides for a yearly saving of approximately $200. He decides that he wants to spend approximately $100 of this amount for insurance that will provide the maximum amount of protection, but which will become paid up before he is 60 years of age. Refer to the table of annual premium rates for Company A, nonparticipating, which is shown in this chapter. What kind of policy and how much insurance can he buy?

2. George Swenson, age 20, who is planning to marry, has $400 a year available for life insurance. He wants to be sure that he has $4,000 to use as a down payment on a home by the time he is 40 years of age. In the meantime he would like to have the maximum amount of permanent protection from life insurance. Outline a plan of life insurance for him based upon the rates of Company A, nonparticipating, shown in the table in this chapter.

3. Joy Ann Ripley is a college graduate employed as a secretary. She is 30 years old. She works in the office of an oil refinery and earns $108 a week. She is concerned about the payment of final expenses and small debts in the event of her death. She investigates the advantages and disadvantages of the various types of insurance and decides to purchase a $5,000 20-year endowment policy.

   (a) Using the premium rates for nonparticipating Company A given in this chapter, determine the amount of the annual premium she will pay.

   (b) How much more expensive is the annual premium than if she had bought a term insurance policy?

   (c) What, in your opinion, was her primary reason for buying the endowment policy?

   (d) If for any reason she can no longer afford the endowment premiums, what are some of her options?

4. With two other students in your class, select your specific roles and then plan to act out the situation involved in the following material:

   Jim and Joan Webster are both 25 years old and have been married for three years. Jim works in the business office of the local newspaper, where he earns $425 a month. Joan remains at home to care for their one-year-old son. Because they plan to borrow $10,000 to buy a house, they are concerned about the financial risks in that transaction and in other aspects of their living. Jim participates in the newspaper's group health insurance plan and he has two life insurance policies; one is a $2,000 straight life policy, the other is a $5,000 family income policy. Joan has no insurance and doubts the advisability of a wife being insured. Jim arranges for Bill Stevenson, his life insurance agent, to come to the Webster home to discuss their insurance program.

Utilize 15 to 20 minutes in acting out this sociodrama. Bring into the discussion as many different elements of insurance as you can. Following your presentation the whole class will evaluate the presentation in terms of the life insurance content you covered. They will not be critical of your acting.

▪ COMMUNITY PROBLEMS AND PROJECTS

1. If your parents are paying life insurance premiums monthly, quarterly, or semiannually, find out what the premiums would be if they were paid on an annual basis. Then compute how much savings would be involved, depending upon the way the premiums are now being paid.

2. Consult an insurance agent and ask him to give you the figures in regard to the types of policies, amounts, first-year premiums, and recommended uses of the proceeds for an insurance program for your family. The program should be based upon a stipulated yearly premium that can be afforded in the family budget.

3. From a local insurance agent or the library obtain a copy of *Life Insurance Fact Book,* which is published by the Institute of Life Insurance. Answer the following questions.

   (a) In the most recent year shown, how much life insurance was in force in the United States? Is this an increase or a decrease over the amount shown the previous year?

   (b) What is the average size ordinary life policy in force in the most recent year shown?

   (c) What is the relationship of the family income to the amount of life insurance carried? What percent of families own life insurance coverage?

   (d) According to the Commissioners 1941 Standard Ordinary Mortality Table, what is the expectation of life-years of a person 20 years old? What is the expectation of life-years of the same person according to the Commissioners 1958 Standard Ordinary Mortality Table?

   (e) What percent of applications was accepted as insurance risks by life insurance companies in the most recent year? What is the chief reason for refusing applications? What percent of applications was declined because of occupational reasons?

Chapter 29

Individual and family security through social insurance

PURPOSE OF THE CHAPTER

In addition to the private insurance protection described in previous chapters, almost all of the families in the United States also have economic security protection through various state and federal social insurance programs. In this chapter, we shall study the protection provided to the family by the federal Social Security Act and workmen's compensation laws.

You will find answers to these questions:

1. Why do we need federal and state insurance programs?
2. What are the major provisions of the federal Social Security Act?
3. Who is protected by unemployment insurance? by old-age insurance?
4. What benefits may be received under the federal old-age insurance program?
5. How is the worker and his family protected by state workmen's compensation laws?

A. The need for social insurance

THE AMERICAN'S DESIRE FOR ECONOMIC INDEPENDENCE

A characteristic of the pioneer American was his strong determination to be independent and economically self-supporting throughout his lifetime, beginning with his first gainful employment. He carved out his own destiny by working for others as an employee or by acquiring and developing land, mills, factories, stores, and other enterprises. If he became disabled, he lived from his savings or his family took care of him. In some instances he may have continued to receive some income for a short period of time from the enterprise he had developed.

Gradually, the American began to move to urban areas where he became employed in factories, stores, and other enterprises, which were owned primarily by others. Work was not always available, wage rates varied according to the demand for and the supply of labor, and the opportunity to draw income from an enterprise by which he was employed diminished greatly if he became disabled or old. The desire to be independent and economically secure throughout his lifetime was not always fulfilled for increasing numbers of persons who were disabled, who because of age became unproductive, or whose survivors were dependent upon his income. Consequently, in 1935, the United States government established the social security system that provides protection from economic insecurity, a risk that is common to all individuals.

The social security system provides a minimum foundation upon which individuals may build additional protection for themselves through their own savings. Essentially, the social security system is economic or social security insurance that is compulsory for most individuals, and for which the cost is borne jointly by the individual and his employer during the worker's years of productive employment.

Legislation that is enacted to protect and aid those who cannot help themselves is often called *social legislation*. Some of the first social legislation provided for compensation of workmen for loss due to accidents and illness. These laws, which now are common in all states, are known as *workmen's compensation laws*. Next, the concern for old people without wealth or income was reflected in old-age pension laws. Arizona was the first state to enact such laws. From these beginnings social legislation has been extended to include a wide range of benefits.

PRIVATE INSURANCE AND SOCIAL INSURANCE

In order to know the nature and extent of the economic security possessed by a family, it is necessary to consider not only the forms of private insurance that are bought through premium payments but also the forms of social insurance which the state and federal governments administer.

It should be noted, however, that social insurance, whether private or federal, is not free insurance. Someone must pay for it. The employee, employer, and in some instances the self-employed individual pay social security taxes to the federal government, which, in turn, places the taxes in a reserve fund from which social security benefits are paid to persons who qualify. The assumption is that the fund eventually will be sufficiently large in amount that social security payments can be met without drawing upon the general revenue funds of the U.S. government.

Privately sponsored and operated social insurance programs are established by some labor unions, employees of a particular business enterprise, or some other group or agency. Similar to the federal social security program, those that are privately sponsored and operated are financed by contributions by employers, and in some instances by both employees and employers, to a reserve fund from which claims are to be paid.

Social insurance programs do not provide complete economic security. For this reason, most families buy private insurance protection to supplement the social insurance provided by state and federal governments.

It is possible to determine reasonably accurately what benefits to expect from social security if one is covered by that protection. If one is covered by a retirement plan sponsored by an employer or a union, the benefits from such a plan can be determined easily. All these benefits, plus the life and health insurance program of the family, will determine the total retirement income or the benefits that may be obtained due to sickness or accident. In addition, many people will receive benefits from state workmen's compensation in case of accident.

B. The federal Social Security Act

The federal Social Security Act involves two phases: (a) benefits for unemployment, and (b) benefits for old age, death, the needy aged, dependent children, and the blind. The first phase of this program is handled primarily through state agencies with federal assistance.

The second phase is administered directly by the federal government, and the taxes for it are collected by the federal government.

UNEMPLOYMENT INSURANCE

Within the framework of the Social Security Act, each state has set up its own law providing for an unemployment insurance system. This plan is operated in cooperation with the federal government. In most cases the tax is levied directly upon the employer, but in a few states the employee also is required to pay a tax for disability or unemployment contributions.

Who is covered? The federal and state unemployment insurance that is operated under the social security laws applies to workers in factories, offices, stores, mines, shops, mills, and other places of business and industry. However, these laws do not cover farmers, domestic help, federal employees, teachers, and other professional workers, and several other groups.

Unemployment compensation. An unemployed person is entitled to compensation if he has been engaged in a specified occupation (covered by the law) for a certain length of time prior to his unemployment.

In order to obtain unemployment benefits, the worker must meet the following qualifications, besides those previously specified.

1. He must be unemployed through no fault of his own.
2. He must register at a public employment office for a job.
3. He must make a claim for benefits.
4. He must be able and available for work.
5. He must be totally unemployed for the amount of time specified in his state.

Causes for denying or forfeiting unemployment benefits

1. Participating in a strike. (Some states have exceptions to this rule.)
2. Voluntarily quitting work without a good cause. (The waiting period is usually longer, and the number of weeks of benefits is usually less.)
3. Being discharged for misconduct. (The waiting period is usually longer, and the number of weeks of benefits is usually less.)
4. Refusing to apply for or to accept suitable work. (Usually the waiting period is longer, and the benefits may be cut off entirely.)
5. Intentionally misrepresenting facts. (Payments are usually forfeited for the remainder of the current year.)
6. Being discharged for theft and found guilty.

NATURE OF OLD-AGE INSURANCE

Under the Social Security Act, a reserve fund is accumulated as in the case of life insurance. The employer and the employee must contribute regularly to the federal government a certain percentage of the employee's wages.

Wages and taxes. Since the first federal social security laws were enacted, the laws have been changed several times and probably will be changed again. Major changes were made in social security laws in July, 1965. Therefore, any published information cannot be assumed to be up to date and accurate. However, the principles of providing social security will probably not be changed. For up-to-date information on benefits and tax rates, one should consult his local social security office.

Based upon the 1965 law which took effect in 1966, the employee's contribution to the old-age insurance fund is computed on the first $6,600 of income paid him during any calendar year. The part contributed by the employee is deducted by the employer from the employee's wages. The percentage is subject to change by law; but, regardless of the rate in effect in any particular year, the employer pays a certain percentage as a payroll tax, and the employee pays the

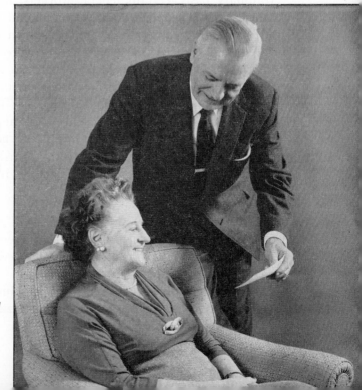

Many people, often living many years after their retirement from regular work, receive social security benefits each month.

Underwood & Underwood

same percentage as a portion of his wages that is laid aside for old-age benefits.

Under the present plan and until further changes, the tax rates are effective as shown below.

SCHEDULE OF SOCIAL SECURITY
TAXES INCLUDING MEDICARE

| Calendar Year | Social Security Tax Paid on First $6,600 of Wages or Salaries by | | | |
| | Employee and Employer (each) | | Self-employed Worker | |
	Tax Rate	Maximum Tax	Tax Rate	Maximum Tax
1966	4.2 %	$277.20	6.15%	$405.90
1967-68	4.4 %	290.40	6.40%	422.40
1969-72	4.9 %	323.40	7.10%	468.60
1973-75	5.4 %	356.40	7.55%	498.30
1976-79	5.45%	359.70	7.60%	501.60
1980-86	5.55%	366.30	7.70%	508.20
1987 and thereafter	5.65%	372.90	7.80%	514.80

Who is covered? Generally speaking, old-age benefits have applied to workers in factories, offices, stores, mines, shops, mills, farm workers, some state employees, household workers, members of the clergy on a voluntary basis, certain federal workers, fishermen, members of the armed forces, people who take work home, certain railroad workers, and workers in nonprofit organizations on a voluntary basis.

Self-employed workers are also covered. Self-employed workers include independent contractors, such as carpenters, electricians, and plumbers; independent businessmen; partners in business; independent commission salesmen and agents; life insurance agents; commission truck drivers; newspaper and magazine distributors over 18 years of age; architects; professional engineers; accountants; funeral directors; farmers; lawyers; dentists; osteopaths; chiropractors; veterinarians; naturopaths; optometrists; doctors, interns; and other similar workers.

Who is not covered? Some workers still are not covered by federal laws that apply to old-age benefits and unemployment benefits. However, these classifications may be changed from time to time by changes in the federal law.

Some types of workers specifically excluded are employees of foreign governments or international organizations; newspaper workers under 18; members of the clergy, except on a voluntary basis; student workers employed by schools; student nurses; a child under 21 working for a parent; a parent working for a child; a wife working for a husband; or a husband working for a wife.

OLD-AGE INSURANCE BENEFITS

It was pointed out previously that major changes in the federal social security program were made in 1965. Since other changes undoubtedly will be made in the future, it is impossible to predict exactly what benefits a person may expect when he attains retirement age. Nevertheless, the following illustration shows old-age and survivor benefits effective in 1965.

EXAMPLES OF MONTHLY CASH BENEFIT PAYMENTS [1]

Average yearly earnings after 1950	$800 or less	$1800	$3000	$3600	$4200	$4800	$5400	$6600
Retirement at 65 Disability benefits	$ 44.00	$ 78.20	$101.70	$112.40	$124.20	$135.90	$146.00	$168.00
Retirement at 64	41.10	73.00	95.00	105.00	116.00	126.90	136.30	156.80
Retirement at 63	38.20	67.80	88.20	97.50	107.70	117.80	126.60	145.60
Retirement at 62	35.20	62.60	81.40	90.00	99.40	108.80	116.80	134.40
Wife's benefit at 65 or with child in her care	22.00	39.10	50.90	56.20	62.10	68.00	73.00	84.00
Wife's benefit at 64	20.20	35.90	46.70	51.60	57.00	62.40	67.00	77.00
Wife's benefit at 63	18.40	32.60	42.50	46.90	51.80	56.70	60.90	70.00
Wife's benefit at 62	16.50	29.40	38.20	42.20	46.60	51.00	54.80	63.00
One child of retired or disabled worker	22.00	39.10	50.90	56.20	62.10	68.00	73.00	84.00
Widow age 62 or over	44.00	64.60	83.90	92.80	102.50	112.20	120.50	138.60
Widow at 60, no child	38.20	56.00	72.80	80.50	88.90	97.30	104.50	120.20
Widow under 62 and 1 child	66.00	117.40	152.60	168.60	186.40	204.00	219.00	252.00
Widow under 62 and 2 children	66.00	120.00	202.40	240.00	279.60	306.00	328.00	368.00
One surviving child	44.00	58.70	76.30	84.30	93.20	102.00	109.50	126.00
Two surviving children	66.00	117.40	152.60	168.60	186.40	204.00	219.00	252.00
Maximum family payment	66.00	120.00	202.40	240.00	280.80	309.20	328.00	368.00
Lump-sum death payment	132.00	234.60	255.00	255.00	255.00	255.00	255.00	255.00

[1] Generally, in figuring average yearly earnings after 1950, 5 years of low earnings or no earnings can be excluded. The maximum earnings creditable for social security are $3600 for 1951-1954; $4200 for 1955-1958; $4800 for 1959-1965; and $6600 starting in 1966. Because of this, the benefits shown in the last two columns on the right will not generally be payable for some years to come. When a person is entitled to more than one benefit, the amount actually payable is limited to the largest of the benefits.

Meaning of full coverage. After being employed in a covered occupation for 10 years or 40 quarters, a worker becomes *fully insured* or *fully covered* for life for the purposes of old-age insurance. It is not necessary that the worker be employed full time in any quarter for it to count. Under certain other conditions, one may become fully insured in a shorter length of time.

For example, under present regulations if a person is to obtain old-age benefits, he must have earned 20 quarters of wages if he retires in 1971; but a person retiring in 1968 would be fully covered and would obtain benefits with 17 quarters of earned wages.

Benefits for a wife. From the previous table it may be seen that when a husband covered by social security retires, his wife is entitled to some benefits based upon those of the husband. The maximum benefits of the wife begin at age 65. However, she may begin to take benefits at age 62, but at a lower rate.

In some families both the husband and the wife work in occupations covered by social security. If the wife is entitled to her own benefits because of previous employment, she may use her own benefits or the benefits allowed as the wife of a dependent worker, whichever of the two is larger. However, there is a maximum that any family is allowed.

If a wife does not have her own social security compensation, her old-age benefits are based upon those of the husband. Under the 1965 law, the widow may choose to receive reduced monthly payments at age 60 or full payments at age 62. However, a widow, regardless of her own age, will receive benefits if she has one or more children or if there is a dependent parent.

As each child reaches 18 years of age or marries, the benefit of the child will cease unless the child is attending school full time; in which case, the benefits will be paid until the child is age 22. If the widow is not at least 60 years of age, her benefits will cease if there are no children under 18 years of age. Any widow will lose part of her benefits if she remarries or works in a covered occupation for more than $125 a month.

Benefits for other survivors. If the wage earner leaves no widow or unmarried children under 18 years of age but does leave parents wholly dependent upon him, these parents will receive monthly payments if they are 65 years of age or older. A dependent widower may be entitled to monthly benefits if his wife has met the requirements for insurability. To qualify for benefits, a widower must be at least 65 years of age and have been receiving at least one half of his support from his wife.

Single lump-sum death benefit. The survivor of a fully covered or of a currently covered worker, or the person paying the funeral expenses, is entitled to a lump-sum death benefit. This benefit will be paid regardless of other benefits that may go to survivors. It usually amounts to $255. For example, if an insured worker were to die at age 65 or later, his widow, children, or other heirs would receive a lump-sum payment of $255. Application for this payment must be filed within two years after the death of the insured individual.

Summary of benefits to survivors

After death of a worker at any age, if the worker has the necessary "quarters of coverage," benefits go to:

—his widow, if she is 62 or over, or when she reaches 62 (she may choose reduced benefits at age 60);

—his children until they are 18 (until they are 22 if they are in school full time);

—his widow of any age if she has such children in her care;

—his dependent parents if they are 65 or when they reach 65, provided he leaves no widow or child under 18;

—her dependent widower when he reaches 65, if he has been receiving at least one half of his support from his wife.

Lump-sum benefit may be paid to anyone who pays the funeral expenses.

Special provision for disabled workers. Since the average monthly income is used to determine monthly benefits on retirement, a person who loses his income because of disability or is placed on reduced pay because of disability would have a reduction in his old-age benefits unless there were some special provision.

Under the present law and until further change, a disabled worker may qualify for disability benefits without regard to his age. If he has worked long enough under social security and if his disability is severe enough to meet the definition in the law, he may draw the benefits. As indicated in the table on page 569, the disability benefit paid is equal to the retirement benefit at age 65 or later.

The dependents of a disabled worker are also entitled to the normal benefits that they would ordinarily receive under the regular retirement of the worker at age 65 or later.

Rules for benefits after age 65. Under the 1965 amendment to the social security law, a retired worker can continue to receive the regular benefits, and the family will receive the usual benefits provided the worker does not earn more than $1,500 a year. If he earns $1,500 or more a year, his benefits and the benefits of the family will be reduced according to a scale established by law. After age 72, the retired worker may earn any amount without reducing his old-age benefits or the benefits of his family.

HEALTH INSURANCE AND MEDICAL CARE FOR THE AGED

Major changes in the social security system were made by Congress in July, 1965. A major addition to the system was provision for health and medical care for the aged. The popular term applied to this program is "Medicare." Under the program for health and medical care for the aged, two plans were provided for persons age 65 or over:

1. A basic plan providing protection against the costs of hospital and related care.
2. A voluntary supplementary plan providing protection against the costs of physicians' services and other medical and health services to cover certain areas not covered in the basic plan.

The basic plan. The basic plan is financed through a separate payroll tax and separate trust fund. This tax is included in the total social security tax rates as shown on page 568. This basic plan insures against the costs of inpatient hospital services, posthospital extended-care services, posthospital home health services, and outpatient hospital diagnostic services for all persons age 65 or over. Benefits for persons currently over 65 who were not insured under either the social security system or the Railroad Retirement Act at the time the law was changed are financed out of federal general revenues. Benefits under this coverage are effective July 1, 1966, except for services in extended-care facilities, which are effective January 1, 1967. With the exception of the provision for posthospital home health service, the benefits under the basic plan are payable for a specified period of time; the patient pays a specified deductible amount.

Who is covered? All persons entitled to monthly social security benefits or to annuities under the Railroad Retirement Act are covered. In addition, any person reaching age 65 before 1968 is covered.

Who is not covered? Any person under 65 years of age is not covered. Persons reaching age 65 after 1967 are not covered unless they have a specified number of quarters of coverage under Old Age, Survivors, and Disability Insurance.

In general, the basic plan provides the following benefits:

1. Sixty days of hospitalization, the patient paying the first $40 of the hospital costs. For each day above 60 and up to a limit of 90 days, the patient would pay $10.
2. One hundred days of posthospital care in a nursing home with the patient paying $5 for each day above 20.
3. One hundred visits after hospitalization by nurses or technicians.
4. Outpatient hospital diagnostic services, with the patient paying the first $20 of each service in each 20-day period, plus an additional 20 percent of the cost above $20.
5. Psychiatric hospital care up to a 190-day lifetime limit.

The voluntary supplementary plan. The voluntary supplementary plan is financed by a monthly premium of $3 paid by the person covered; the federal government supplies an equal amount out of general revenues. Premiums paid by persons receiving social security benefits or railroad retirement benefits are deducted from their monthly checks. Other persons make premium payments directly to the federal government. Benefits under this plan are effective July 1, 1966. As is the case with the basic plan, the supplementary plan is on a deductible basis; the insured must pay the first $50 of medical expense that he incurs in a calendar year. In addition, the insured must pay 20 percent of any cost incurred beyond $50.

Who is covered? Any person age 65 or over who is a resident of the United States and is either a citizen or an alien admitted for permanent residence and who has five years of continuous residence is eligible and may enroll within a specified time period.

Who is not covered? Persons under 65 years of age and persons who do not enroll within the specified time period.

What benefits are provided? This plan covers physicians' services, home health services, and numerous other medical and health services in and out of medical institutions. There is an annual deductible of $50; then the plan covers 80 percent of the patient's bill above the deductible for the following services:

1. Physicians' and surgeons' services, whether furnished in a hospital, clinic, office, in the home, or elsewhere.
2. Home health service (with no requirement of prior hospitalization) for up to 100 visits during each calendar year.
3. Diagnostic X-ray, diagnostic laboratory tests, and other diagnostic tests.
4. X-ray, radium, and radioactive isotope therapy.
5. Ambulance services.
6. Surgical dressings and splints, casts, and other devices for reduction of fractures and dislocations; rental of durable medical equipment, such as iron lungs, oxygen tents, hospital beds, and wheelchairs used in the patient's home; prosthetic devices (other than dental) which replace all or part of an internal body organ; braces and artificial legs, arms, eyes, etc.

Precaution!

The regulations pertaining to Medicare are complex. The Social Security Administration is the final authority, and the local office should be consulted on any question regarding eligibility or benefits.

OTHER SOCIAL SECURITY PROGRAMS

The preceding discussion on social security has dealt with the benefits that are paid as a result of deductions from wages and on the basis of previous earnings. Under the Social Security Act, however, the federal government has made provisions for assistance to other needy groups. In general, the plan provides for funds to be furnished for: (a) needy aged, (b) needy dependent children, (c) needy blind, (d) maternal welfare of infants and mothers, (e) crippled children, (f) child welfare, (g) vocational rehabilitation, and (h) public health. If a state has a plan satisfactory to the federal government, that state may obtain from the federal government a contribution up to 50 percent of the state expenditures.

APPLYING FOR SOCIAL SECURITY COVERAGE

When one accepts his first job in an occupation covered by the Social Security Act, he should fill out Form SS-5, "Application for Social Security Account Number." This form can be obtained from the employer or the nearest social security office. He will then be issued a social security card with his account number on it. The

	APPLICATION FOR SOCIAL SECURITY ACCOUNT NUMBER (Or Replacement of Lost Card)		

Information Furnished On This Form Is CONFIDENTIAL
Read Instructions on Back Before Filling in Form.   Print in Dark Ink or Use Typewriter.
— DO NOT WRITE IN THE ABOVE SPACE —

1 Print FULL NAME YOU USE IN WORK OR BUSINESS (First Name) **Judith** (Middle Name or Initial —if none, draw line——) **Ann** (Last name) **Smith**

2 Print FULL NAME GIVEN YOU AT BIRTH **Judith Ann Smith**   3 DATE OF BIRTH (Month) **10** (Day) **3** (Year) **49**

4 PLACE OF BIRTH (City) **Columbus** (County) **Franklin** (State) **Ohio**   5 AGE ON LAST BIRTHDAY **16**   6 SEX: MALE ☐ FEMALE ☒   7 COLOR OR RACE WHITE ☒ NEGRO ☐ OTHER ☐

8 MOTHER'S FULL NAME AT HER BIRTH **Jane Ann Wray**   9 FATHER'S FULL NAME (Regardless of whether living or dead) **Harry Leroy Smith**

10 HAVE YOU EVER BEFORE APPLIED FOR OR HAD A SOCIAL SECURITY OR RAILROAD RETIREMENT NUMBER? YES ☐ NO ☒ DON'T KNOW ☐ | IF ANSWER IS "YES" PRINT THE STATE IN WHICH YOU FIRST APPLIED AND WHEN (State) (Date)

PRINT YOUR ACCOUNT NUMBER IF YOU KNOW IT (Account Number)   11 ARE YOU NOW— EMPLOYED ☐ SELF-EMPLOYED ☐ UNEMPLOYED ☒

12 MAILING ADDRESS (Number and Street) **6080 Broadway** (City) **Mabana** (Zone) **98110** (State) **Washington**

13 TODAY'S DATE **May 17, 1966**   14 Write YOUR NAME AS YOU USUALLY WRITE IT. (Do Not Print or Type—Use Dark Ink) **Judith Ann Smith**

TREASURY DEPARTMENT Internal Revenue Service   Return completed application to nearest SOCIAL SECURITY ADMINISTRATION DISTRICT OFFICE
Form SS-5 (Revised 3/59)

Application for social security number

federal government keeps a separate account for each individual listed under the account number shown on the card. This account is credited for all payments made by the employer into the fund and for all deductions made for this purpose from the employee's wages.

Keeping a record of deductions. Every individual who is subject to social security taxes should keep a record of his wages and the amount of social security paid. The employer is required by law to furnish regularly to each employee a written statement or statements showing the wages paid to the employee during the year. Each statement must be suitable for permanent retention. It may cover one, two, three, or four quarters of the year.

Whenever an employee changes employment, he should see that his new employer has his correct social security number so that he will receive credit for any wages that are earned. It is the responsibility of the employee to be sure he uses the right number.

Verify your social security account. Mistakes may be made in one's social security account. The regulations provide that any insured

Social security card

person may check his account for accuracy, but any mistake more than five years old will not be corrected. Therefore, any person with a social security account should check it for accuracy and compare it with his own records at least once every five years. A convenient card usually obtainable at the post office is provided for this purpose.

REQUEST FOR STATEMENT OF EARNINGS

ACCOUNT NUMBER	400	56	5532
DATE OF BIRTH	MONTH	DAY	YEAR
	1	21	1940

Please send me a statement of the amount of earnings recorded in my social security account.

NAME { MISS MRS. MR. } *Eva May Kelly*

STREET & NUMBER *6789 Kildare Drive*

CITY, P.O., ZONE & STATE *Cincinnati, Ohio 45238*

Print Name and Address In Ink Or Use Typewriter

SIGN YOUR NAME AS YOU USUALLY WRITE IT *Eva May Kelly*

Sign your own name only. Under the law, information in your social security record is confidential and anyone who signs someone else's name can be prosecuted.

If your name has been changed from that shown on your social security account number card, please copy your name below exactly as it appears on that card.

Card for checking the accuracy of social security contributions

C. Workmen's compensation

As was mentioned in the first part of this chapter, workmen's compensation sponsored by various states is another form of social security. The laws providing protection against accidents and sickness are quite variable. For an interpretation of these laws, one should become familiar with the plan in operation in his particular state. These laws have no connection with the federal Social Security Act.

Workmen's compensation provides protection against injury arising out of employment and sometimes against diseases due to the nature of the work, but the worker is not covered for any injury that occurs away from his normal place of employment. Under most of these laws, the employee receives compensation for an accident whether the employer or the employee is at fault, except in the case of intoxication or recklessness in ignoring danger.

All states have workmen's compensation laws. In some states employers are required to pay into a fund for the protection of the workers. In other states these payments are optional; but if the employer is not insured, an employee can sue for compensation as a result of an accident and can receive compensation unless he was intoxicated on the job or has been reckless in ignoring danger.

The laws of all states provide that all medical and hospital bills will be paid regardless of the amount.

If the worker is injured, he will also receive compensation each week while disabled, and in most states this compensation will be paid for life if the worker is permanently disabled.

In the case of death of the worker resulting from an injury at work, the wife and children will receive weekly compensation. There is a limit on these payments in most states.

D. Economics of social insurance

The problems of old age and disability are both social and economic problems. They are problems of the individual and of society in general. Some people can save money and plan for the future; others either cannot or will not. If they cannot or will not provide for themselves, they will be burdens on society at some time.

Many of the social security programs compel individuals and employers to contribute part of their wages and profits which are paid into funds. In past years, as prices and the cost of living have increased, the payments for old age and disability have not been considered adequate. Therefore, the laws have been changed to increase the deductions from wages and from employers, and benefits have increased to attempt to keep pace with the rising cost of living.

Facts everyone should know about social security insurance

1. Most workers are covered by old-age and unemployment insurance benefits.
2. Old-age benefits are generally determined by the average monthly income during the time of employment.
3. Wives, widows, widowers, children, parents, and survivors of insured workers are entitled to certain benefits under old-age insurance provisions.
4. The amount of income earned by a retired worker may affect the amount of old-age insurance he can collect.
5. Social security does not replace the need for life insurance and other retirement income.
6. Workmen's compensation is a form of social security.

- **QUESTIONS ON THE TEXT**

1. Is social security compulsory or voluntary for most participants in the program?
2. How are social security benefits financed?
3. Does social security provide complete economic security?
4. Why was the federal social security plan developed?
5. What are the two phases of the Social Security Act?
6. How is the unemployment insurance system operated?
7. Who is not covered by the unemployment insurance program?
8. Are all unemployed workers in covered occupations eligible for unemployment insurance?
9. How is the old-age insurance program financed?
10. Are life insurance agents covered under the social security program?
11. Are newspaper workers under 18 covered under the social security program?
12. Can one determine now exactly what social security benefits he will receive on retirement?
13. How many quarters of coverage must an employee have to be fully covered?
14. At what age can the widow of an insured worker receive social security benefits if she has no children?
15. What is meant by the term "single lump-sum death benefit"?
16. What benefits is a disabled worker entitled to?
17. How does one apply for social security coverage? When?
18. Does the federal government maintain a separate account for each person covered under social security? May one check the accuracy of his account?
19. What is the purpose of workmen's compensation?
20. What do the state workmen's compensation laws provide regarding medical and hospital bills?
21. What would be the effect upon local, state, and federal government spending if social security insurance programs were discontinued?

- **QUESTIONS FOR DISCUSSION**

1. Explain some of the reasons why you think that changes which have taken place in the last hundred years have caused social security laws to become necessary.
2. How do the provisions for old-age benefits under social security eliminate certain economic risks?
3. Why should railroad and governmental employees not be allowed to participate in social security benefits?
4. Why are the unemployment insurance programs of the various states different?

5. What should be the relationship of one's life insurance program and the benefits he may be entitled to under social security?
6. Why do you think that widows under 60 years of age are not entitled to benefits under social security if they have no children under 18?
7. Why must one provide proof of age in order to receive old-age benefits?
8. In your opinion, are the requirements for obtaining unemployment compensation in your state reasonable requirements?
9. Under workmen's compensation, can you collect benefits if you slip on the ice at home and break an arm? Why?
10. If a worker received lead poisoning from materials that he handles and becomes ill, do you think he can obtain benefits under workmen's compensation? Explain your answer.
11. Should social security benefits be increased as the cost of living increases?

▪ PROBLEMS TO SOLVE

1. Assume that there is a 4.2 percent deduction from the first $6,600 of wages for old-age benefits and hospital insurance and a deduction of 1 percent for unemployment benefits.
   (a) How much will be withheld from the wages in 1966 for a man earning $400 a month if the withholdings for unemployment benefits are based on the first $3,000 a year earned?
   (b) How much will be withheld for a man earning $600 a month?

2. Assume that a worker is fully insured for old-age social security benefits with an average annual earning of $4,200.
   (a) How much disability income will he receive?
   (b) How much will he receive at age 65 if his wife retires at age 62?
   (c) How much will he receive at age 65 if his wife is age 55?
   (d) How much will his widow receive if she is age 50 and has two children under 18 years of age?

3. During the month of March, 1966, the Hammond Construction Company paid taxable wages to 35 employees in the amount of $16,800.
   (a) Using the Schedule of Social Security Taxes provided in this chapter, compute the amount of the FICA tax paid by the company.
   (b) What is the amount the company would pay on the same taxable wages in March, 1970?
   (c) What is the approximate percent of increase?

4. Jim Johnson was fully covered by social security when he died at age 61. His average annual earnings computed under the Act were $4,800. His widow, aged 58, decides to wait until she is 62 (42 months later) before beginning to collect survivors' benefits. How much will she be entitled to receive each month at age 62?

5. Under the basic plan of medicare, a man, 67 years old, is hospitalized for a total of 75 days. The hospital charges that are properly within the medicare plan amount to $1,267.50.

   (a) What is the amount that the man must pay?

   (b) What is the amount that will be paid through the medicare program?

■ COMMUNITY PROBLEMS AND PROJECTS

1. Obtain information from the local federal offices for each of the following programs:

   (a) Old-age, survivors, and disability insurance program.

   (b) Unemployment compensation program.

   (c) Welfare or public assistance program.

   Then compare the statistics for each program and show how much money is paid each month to people in your community, city, or county. You may want to obtain national figures for comparison. With these data available, enter into a class discussion of whether your community would be able to meet the needs of the people receiving the various benefits if the program did not exist.

2. Visit your local social security office. Obtain an assortment of materials about the social security program and in particular about medicare. Using the resource materials you obtained and information given you by people in the local office, prepare a written report in which you describe: (a) the highlights of medicare, (b) the need for supplemental health insurance, and (c) free benefits for needy aged people.

3. Make an investigation of the laws in your state affecting workmen's compensation. These laws usually cover industrial accidents and sometimes sickness and death benefits. Prepare a written report on the important features of this law and list the occupations covered.

4. Investigate the laws in your state pertaining to assistance for the blind. Write a report explaining the aid that is available to the blind.

Chapter 30

Providing housing for the family

PURPOSE OF THE CHAPTER

Every family must have housing. Several choices are open—buy a house or apartment, rent a house, rent an apartment, or build a house. The problem faced by the family, then, is which of the alternatives to choose. The purpose of the chapter is to analyze the factors that should be considered by a family in making its decisions regarding housing.

You will find answers to these questions:

1. What are the advantages and disadvantages of owning a home?
2. How much can a family afford to spend for housing?
3. What factors determine whether a family should build or buy a home?
4. How do the annual costs of owning and renting a home compare?

A. Family housing problems

Providing housing is one of the most important economic problems faced by a family. In many instances housing is one of the largest personal expenditures made by an individual or family group. The

comfort and satisfaction derived from housing also is important. It is highly important that wise decisions about housing should be made. Such decisions are based upon facts.

ADVANTAGES AND DISADVANTAGES OF OWNING A HOME

A family should consider buying a house if (1) it can finance ownership out of savings or by monthly payments out of current wages, (2) it expects to continue to live in the same area, and (3) it will derive more pleasure and satisfaction from owning than from renting. Home ownership places certain responsibilities upon the members of the family. Usually these responsibilities for financing, care and maintenance, and improving physical conditions and appearance are good for the individual and family. Assuming such responsibilities helps individual members of the family to have a sense of pride and of participation in family affairs.

Regardless of the advantages that are claimed for owning a home, one should consider the problem carefully. Even though owning a

---

Advantages of owning a home

1. Home ownership gives a sense of security, and it practically assures a home in old age.
2. Home ownership forces the establishment of a plan of saving. Payments beyond the cost of maintenance and ownership constitute savings.
3. Home ownership adds to individual and family prestige and improves credit rating, provided payments are made when they are due.
4. Home ownership is a source of enjoyment, satisfaction, and pride.

Disadvantages of home ownership

1. The owner's equity or investment in the house is not readily available for use in making other expenditures.
2. The homeowner must assume responsibility for financing, maintenance, and improvements; renters pay their rent and leave the other responsibilities to the landlord.
3. Home ownership makes moving from one community or city to another difficult.
4. In the period of making payments, home ownership may require larger monthly expenditures than renting.
5. Owning a home places upon the owner responsibilities for maintenance and repairs, such as painting, appearance of lawn, and snow and ice removal.

home may appear desirable, it may be economically unwise to buy or to build a house. For instance, if one expects to move soon to another town, if property values are declining, if insufficient capital is available to make the down payment, or if there is any likelihood that pay-. ments on the home cannot be made, buying a home would be unwise. All the costs of owning a home should be carefully computed and these should then be considered in the family budget.

NEW HOUSE, OLD HOUSE, OR BUILD YOUR OWN HOME?

Most families do not have an unlimited source of money with which to purchase the ideal home that they would like to buy. It is necessary, therefore, to make certain choices to get the most satisfactory home for the money that is available. Very often an entirely new home will cost more than an old home for the same housing facilities. However, a newly built home will probably cost less for repairs for many years. On the other hand, some old homes that are in excellent condition may be better buys than new homes. A new home may hold its value better than an old home, but in either case, it is well to consult a reliable friend who can help you judge the value. Appraisals that are made in attempting to obtain a loan will usually help to determine values. The appraisal will be discussed in the next chapter.

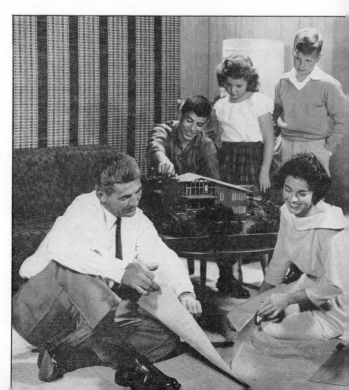

When building a new home, the plans should be carefully studied to make sure that the finished home will meet the needs of the entire family.

Underwood & Underwood

Cautions in building

1. The plans should be well designed so that the finished house will be satisfactory to the entire family.
2. The plans should meet the requirements of building codes and local restrictions.
3. The specifications should be complete, and there should be no extra charge for additional work.
4. The contractor should have a reputation for good work, financial responsibility, and fair dealing.
5. The contract should specify clearly the amount of the payments and the conditions under which the payments are to be made.
6. The contractor should be responsible for loss due to fire or to personal injury during the construction period.
7. The property should be subject to final inspection before acceptance and final payment.
8. All agreements should be in writing and have been approved by a lawyer.
9. A plan of financing the home should be worked out.
10. Economic conditions should be favorable for building.

If you intend to build a home, consideration should be given the five choices listed below, which are recommended by the National Better Business Bureau.

Five choices of ways to build a home

1. Engage the complete services of an architect.
2. Engage the limited services of an architect, furnishing him with stock plans.
3. Engage a contractor or builder, using stock plans.
4. Buy stock plans and arrange with several contractors for different parts of construction.
5. Buy a prefabricated house and engage a builder to erect it.

In some cases it is possible to engage the limited services of an architect by submitting to him stock or ready-made plans and asking him to make certain alterations. If you wish, he will arrange for the proper placement of the house on the lot and for the awarding of contracts and supervision of the building.

Buying a prefabricated home sometimes saves some of the cost of building. If you have the ability, you can do some of the construc-

In deciding to build a home, the buyer should engage the services of a contractor who has a reputation for good work, financial responsibility, and fair dealing.

H. Armstrong Roberts

tion yourself; but generally it is desirable to engage a competent builder to do at least the main part of the work.

Selecting a home. Let us say that you have decided that you want to buy a home. You will find that there are two main problems in buying the home. The first problem is to select the right place to live. The second is to select the right house. The checklist on page 586 can be used as a guide in making a selection.

Some communities are improving; some are well established and their nature is evident; some communities that are new are difficult to judge as to their future development; some are declining because property is deteriorating, factories are moving in, and people are moving out into better areas. These factors should be studied carefully if you want to protect your investment and live in a good community.

WHEN TO BUY A HOME

Ordinarily, the best time to buy a home is not when prices of real estate are high; but, on the other hand, this is usually the time when the family has its greatest income and is able to save enough money to make a substantial down payment. Therefore, the answer to when a family should buy is determined largely by the following factors:

1. Does the family have enough money saved to make a substantial down payment?
2. Is the future income reasonably assured so that the monthly payments can be continued with a margin of safety?
3. Can an adequate home in a satisfactory location be purchased or built with the down payment that can be made and with monthly payments that will fit the budget?

585

Checklist for buying a home

Location

1. Is there public transportation?
2. Is there fire protection?
3. What are the insurance rates?
4. What are the taxes and assessments?
5. What are the rates for water, electricity, gas?
6. Is there police protection?
7. Are there any protective building and zoning restrictions?
8. Is the land solid or filled and with proper drainage?
9. Are there improvements—sidewalks, streets, sewer, gas, electricity, and water?
10. Is the neighborhood good: schools? churches? parks? shopping areas?
11. Are there any undesirable characteristics: factories? railroads? dumps? heavy traffic?

Exterior

1. Is the style of the dwelling: attractive? in keeping with others in the area?
2. Is exterior construction in good condition: walls, roof, and gutters? porches, including railings? steps?
3. Are major views pleasant?
4. If there is a yard, is it large enough for: a play area? a garden?
5. Are the dwellings far enough apart?
6. Is yard landscaped and in good condition?
7. If there is a well instead of a public water system, are the following adequate: quantity of water? dependable flow of water?
8. If there is a septic tank instead of a sewer system, is it: adequate in size for your family? properly installed?
9. Are there parking facilities, such as: a garage or carport? 24-hour parking on street?

Interior

1. Are the following in good condition: windows and doors? floors, walls, and ceilings?
2. Is insulation adequate?
3. Are electric outlets where you will need them for: lamps? radio and television? large appliances? small appliances?
4. Is the wiring adequate for all purposes?
5. If there is a basement, is it: well ventilated and dry? well lighted? without hazards, such as low beams, exposed pipes, and wires?
6. Is there evidence of termite damage?
7. Are rooms adequate and wall spaces large enough for your furniture?
8. Is work space in kitchen satisfactory?
9. Is there space for laundry purposes?
10. Is the bathroom convenient?
11. Are closets, cabinets, shelves, and all other storage spaces adequate?
12. Are windows satisfactory for ventilation in all rooms?
13. Is remodeling needed?

Equipment

1. Are the following provided for all windows: shades or blinds? storm windows? screens?
2. Are the following adequate and in good condition: plumbing? heating unit? kitchen appliances? laundry appliances? water heater?
3. If needed, is there a place for storing: screens? storm windows and doors? outdoor furniture? garden and yard tools?
4. Are there facilities for disposal of garbage, such as: an incinerator? disposal in kitchen sink? garbage collection?
5. Is telephone service available?

B. Obtaining family housing

Obtaining housing for a family involves the making of major decisions. If it is the family's decision to buy or to build, problems arise as to how much the family can afford to spend for housing and how the cost may be paid. If the decision is to rent a house or an apartment, several factors must be considered, such as the amount that may wisely be spent for rent, the terms of the rental agreement, and the economic aspects of providing housing through the rental plan.

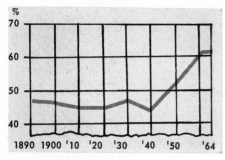

PERCENTAGE OF FAMILIES
OWNING THEIR HOMES,
1890-1964

Home ownership in 1900 was about 46%, declining to about 45% in 1920. During the 1940's and 1950's owner-ship rose steadily to about 62% in 1964.

Courtesy: 1965 Savings and Loan Fact Book.

PAYING FOR THE HOME

All authorities in home management, financing, and home build-ing insist that no family should buy a home until a very careful budget plan has been worked out. After shopping in a desirable loca-tion for a satisfactory home that will take care of the family for a reasonable time in the future, a budget should then be prepared that will take into consideration the down payment and all the carry-ing and operating charges, including the payment on principal. Ways of figuring these estimates will be discussed in greater detail later in this chapter.

Buying for cash. If a person buys a house for cash, he should not invest so much that he must use all the funds that he has laid aside for use in an emergency. For instance, if he uses all his cash to purchase a house, he may not have any reserve in case of a serious illness or some other emergency. A person who acquires a house by means of borrowed money makes a serious mistake if he buys beyond his capacity to pay the interest charge and to repay the loan. When one borrows money to buy a home, the loan must be repaid in installments. These include payments on the principal and interest on the unpaid balance.

If the loan is too great, he may become discouraged because of the necessity of cutting down the level of living and thus depriving his family of necessities that are required to maintain health. He may even lose the house through foreclosure proceedings (see Chapter 32).

In buying a house, many young people gamble to the extent of assuming that their earnings will increase. They therefore undertake a greater obligation than they should. If future earnings do not become greater, or if they become less, discouragement inevitably results. One of the first questions that should arise in the mind of a prospective purchaser is the percentage of earnings to be expended in providing the home.

Cost of home and annual income. The amount that a person may spend as the interest and the principal on a loan on a home is always a question. Studies have been made to determine reasonable amounts that should be spent in acquiring a home. Builders, realtors, and lenders of money estimate that between 20 and 25 percent of the assured income of a family may safely be spent in buying a home. This should include interest, amount of principal, taxes, and insurance.

If a person who has been renting a house decides to buy it, he may be required to make greater expenditures than those required formerly in renting. If it has not been possible for him to save money regularly in the past, it will probably not be possible to finance the purchase of the home. Some people do, however, undertake such a purchase because they are then forced to follow some definite plan of saving. The purchase of a home may result in systematic saving in order to pay for the investment.

The down payment. As will be explained in Chapter 31, there are many ways of financing the purchase of a home, but usually a person must pay part of the original price in cash.

The lender, of course, specifies the amount of down payment that he considers necessary as partial protection for his loan. The plans developed by the Federal Housing Administration permit minimum down payments of from 3 to 20 percent. Conservative financial advisers, however, recommend that a person who buys a home on contract or installment should make a cash down payment of 20 to 25 percent of the purchase price. In many cities, commercial banks and other lenders of money require a down payment of 50 to 60 percent of the appraised value of a house as a requisite for taking a first mortgage.

Veterans are entitled to obtain loans under favorable conditions that involve very small down payments and low interest rates. However, they must qualify for these loans under special regulations and there must be adequate evidence provided that the veteran will have enough income to make the regular payments on the loan. These loans are discussed in Chapter 31.

The monthly payment. Most loans on houses today are made on the basis of monthly payments. Some of the critical factors that a family must consider in purchasing a home, therefore, are the amount of the monthly payments and the conditions of payment, such as paying off the loan before it is due or missing some monthly payments due to emergencies. The monthly payment ordinarily includes an amount to reduce the principal, the interest, the insurance, and the taxes. The reason for including all of these items in the monthly payment is to protect the lender of the money from having claims accumulate against the property that would be paid before his loan is paid in case the purchaser is unable to complete his payments on the house. The financial aspects of buying a home are discussed in Chapter 31.

The initial occupancy costs. Ordinarily when moving into a new house or into one recently purchased, there are many expenses to be met that do not recur in succeeding years, such as curtains, draperies, floor coverings, and, in some instances, shrubbery and the establishment of a lawn. Although a family may be able to make the necessary down payment and the required monthly payments, its resources may not be adequate to meet all first-year costs. For this reason, careful consideration of first-year costs is a critical factor in considering the purchase of a house.

ANALYSIS OF FINANCING COSTS

The table on page 591 shows the first-year cost of financing a home. The figures given are a modification of information collected for prospective homeowners by the Bureau of Standards of the United States Department of Commerce. The various income groups are listed according to the approximate cost of the home that a person in each income group can afford. This table assumes that an initial cash payment of 20 percent of the total value will be made when the home is purchased.

The fact is recognized that families having the same annual income may not be able to devote the same amount toward purchasing a home. For example, a family having four or five children and living in a city may not be able to put much aside for buying a home; but another family with only one or two children and located possibly in a small village can afford to spend a larger portion of its income for a home.

The following is an explanation of the items in the table:

Item 1. Value of house and lot. The value of the house and the lot is the basis upon which the expenses in this table have been computed. The value of the lot will usually be from 8 to 20 percent of the total amount.

Item 2. Annual income. Because of the wide variation, the incomes have been grouped. No rule can be set that will apply to all classes. It is assumed in this table, however, that the value of the house and the lot will be between 1⅔ and 2½ times the annual income. For example, a family with an income of $7,500 could safely plan to pay from $12,500 to $18,750 for a home. The average amount to pay for a home will be about double the annual income, but usually not more than 2½ times the annual income. As the income of the family becomes larger, a higher percentage of the income can be spent for a home.

Item 3. First cash payment. The cash payment should not be below 20 percent of the value of the house and the lot. It should be much higher if possible. The greater the down payment, the better, for the financing is then simpler and the cost is less. Occasionally a home can be purchased with a down payment of less than 20 percent, but even under normal conditions a down payment of 20 percent is dangerously low for many people. When there is a shortage of money for lending purposes, the loan is difficult to obtain if only a small down payment can be made. Furthermore, the interest charge at such a time is high.

Item 4. Amount of loan. After the amount of the initial cash payment has been deducted from the value of the house and the lot, the difference represents the amount of the loan.

Item 5. Amount of yearly payments. Item 5-A represents the amount of each payment that is applicable as interest; and item 5-B, the amount that is applicable as amortization (reduction) of the principal. With a small down payment, the interest rate is usually higher than with a large down payment.

The interest rate will depend upon local conditions at the time the loan is made. It is generally considered best to pay off a loan on a home within fifteen years or less. If interest rates are unfavorable at the time the loan is to be made, the loan can be obtained for a short time in the hope that it can be renewed later at a lower rate.

Various plans of financing require weekly payments, semimonthly payments, monthly payments, semiannual payments, or annual pay-

	$14,000	$16,000	$18,000	$20,000	$22,000
1. Value of house and lot	$14,000	$16,000	$18,000	$20,000	$22,000
2. Annual income	5,600 to 8,400	6,400 to 9,600	7,200 to 10,800	8,000 to 12,000	8,800 to 13,200
3. Cash down payment (20% of value)	2,800	3,200	3,600	4,000	4,400
4. Amount of loan (80% of value)	11,200	12,800	14,400	16,000	17,600
5. Amounts of yearly payments (10% of total value)	1,400	1,600	1,800	2,000	2,200
5-A. Interest (5%)	560	640	720	800	880
5-B. Payment of principal	840	960	1,080	1,200	1,320
6. Taxes and assessments (2%)	280	320	360	400	440
7. Insurance (.5%)	70	80	90	100	110
8. Upkeep (1.5%)	210	240	270	300	330
9. Total first-year cost (5 plus 6, 7, 8)	1,960	2,240	2,520	2,800	3,080
9-A. Expense (5-A plus 6, 7, 8)	1,120	1,280	1,440	1,600	1,760
*9-B. Saving (9 minus 9-A)	840	960	1,080	1,200	1,320

*Although this amount represents the apparent monetary saving, there is a hidden expense called depreciation because of the wearing out due to the increase in age of the house. A 2 percent allowance for depreciation on the value of the house itself would be a fair estimate of the loss from this cause. In this case the amount shown is the equity or investment that the owner has in the home as contrasted to the expense or cost of living in the home.

The first-year cost of financing a home

ments. The plan of payment should be fully understood before any contract is signed.

Item 6. Taxes and assessments. Local taxes on real estate usually range from 2 to 3 percent of the market value of the property. Occasionally there are assessments against the property for a sidewalk, a street, lights, or other facilities; but ordinarily the assessments on residential property are not high. In this table 2 percent has been allowed for taxes and assessments.

Item 7. Insurance. Fire insurance rates rarely amount to more than ½ percent of the value of the house. The allowance made in this table is liberal because it has been figured on the basis of the value of the house and the lot.

Item 8. Upkeep. The cost of maintaining a house will vary considerably, depending upon the condition of the property, the age of the house, and the type of construction. The yearly cost of maintenance may, however, be estimated reasonably at 1½ percent of the total value.

Item 9. Total first-year cost. The total first-year cost of the home includes the total annual payment plus taxes, assessments, insurance, and upkeep. Item 9-A represents the yearly expense, or the cost of living in the home. The difference between the total cost for the year and the total expense is the saving (item 9-B). In other words, this is the amount of investment that the buyer has accumulated during the first year. The rest of his money has been used for interest and expenses of maintaining the house.

Of course, all these figures are estimates. By using this table as a guide, it is possible to determine at any time or place the exact amount of interest that will be charged, the taxes and assessments, and insurance. With the exact figures substituted in this table, it is then possible to make a more accurate estimate of the annual costs and savings.

RENTING OR LEASING A HOUSE OR APARTMENT

One of the largest and most important items in a family budget is the cost of housing. It likewise is an important factor in determining the pleasure and satisfaction of living. These factors of cost and satisfaction are as important in renting as in owning a home. Several points merit very careful consideration.

Renting with or without a written lease. The first consideration in renting a home, whether a house or an apartment, is to determine the advisability of renting for a shorter, indefinite period or for a longer, definite period. Renting a home from month to month gives a person greater freedom to move and to take advantage of decreases in rentals as conditions change. A person who may find it necessary to move at an uncertain future date because of a change in his work should try to avoid signing a lease, particularly one covering a long period.

In some communities it is very difficult under normal circumstances to obtain a home without a written lease. Property owners naturally do not want to run the risk of the property being vacant frequently. They therefore prefer the protection of a written lease for a specified length of time.

A person who rents for an indefinite period is subject to the necessity of moving if the owner wants the property for some other purpose. In most states, however, the custom or law requires the property owner to give at least thirty days' notice. If legal action is necessary to force the renter to move, still more time will be required before the property must be vacated.

Length and expiration of lease. A period in which monthly rental rates are falling is a poor time to obtain a long lease. A period when rentals have reached a low level or have started to rise is a good time to obtain a long lease.

Points to investigate in renting

1. Is the location suitable?
2. Is the external appearance good?
3. Is the internal appearance good?
4. Are the number of rooms and their size and arrangement satisfactory?
5. Are the lighting and heating adequate and in good condition?
6. Are the laundry, plumbing, and sanitary facilities satisfactory?
7. Does the building have shades, awnings, or other similar equipment?
8. Will the landlord paint and redecorate where necessary?
9. Will the landlord take care of the necessary repairs?
10. Is the character of the neighborhood satisfactory?
11. In the case of an apartment, are yard privileges granted?
12. If you are renting an apartment, who pays for the heat, water, electricity, and other services?
13. Can you get a written lease?
14. Will the landlord permit children or pets?

In some communities most leases expire at the same time, usually at the end of April or May. If your lease expires when other leases are expiring, you will have a better opportunity to obtain another home.

Many families find that it pays them to select a home carefully with the intention of occupying it for several years. By leasing for a long period, they can reduce moving costs and become better established in the community. By staying in one place a long time, a family has an opportunity to develop a garden and to improve the property. Landlords are usually willing to keep property in good repair if the tenants indicate a desire to stay a reasonable length of time. People who lease property will therefore usually find it advantageous to obtain a lease for one year with the privilege of extending the lease one or more years.

COMPARISON OF HOME OWNERSHIP AND RENTING

Many young families have no alternative except to rent a house or apartment until enough savings have accumulated to make a substantial down payment. Other families that are living in a geographic area only temporarily likewise will find renting more satisfactory than buying. Whether to buy or rent a home is a problem for each family to consider.

When you should rent, not buy

1. When you expect to move soon to another town.
2. When prices are declining.
3. When you do not have enough money for a substantial down payment.
4. When your budget will not allow for the payments and other expenses.

When you should own, not rent

1. When you expect to stay in the community.
2. When prices of real estate are stable or increasing.
3. When you have enough money to make a substantial down payment.
4. When your budget will allow for necessary payments and other expenses.

The provision of a place to live is usually quite closely related to the occupation and work location of the chief wage earner of the family. For this reason he often takes the lead in decisions about buying or renting. Some of the reasons why he may decide to rent are: (a) he desires freedom of movement, (b) he is unable to arrange a plan of financing a home, (c) he believes that it is cheaper to rent, (d) he doubts the investment value of owning a home, or (e) he does not care to assume the obligation for the cost and responsibility for maintaining a home as a suitable investment.

If a person needs a permanent home, he can compare the cost of renting and the cost of buying by using a procedure as illustrated in the following table:

	$14,000	$16,000	$18,000	$20,000	$22,000
1. Value of house and lot					
2. Annual income	5,600 to 8,400	6,400 to 9,600	7,200 to 10,800	8,000 to 12,000	8,800 to 13,200
3. First-year cost of buying a house ..	1,960	2,240	2,520	2,800	3,080
Expense	1,120	1,280	1,440	1,600	1,760
Saving	840	960	1,080	1,200	1,320
4. Annual cost of renting a house					
A Example of annual rent	1,440	1,500	1,560	1,620	1,680
B Example of annual rent	1,500	1,560	1,620	1,680	1,740
C Example of annual rent	1,560	1,620	1,680	1,740	1,800
D Example of annual rent	1,620	1,680	1,740	1,800	1,860

For instance, if one is considering an $18,000 house and is paying $1,680 a year rent (Example C), there would be a cash expense saving of $240 a year by owning a house ($1,680 — $1,440 = $240.)

Comparison of cost of buying with cost of renting

First-year cost compared with renting. The table above does not tell the whole story because it does not take into consideration the matter of depreciation. *Depreciation* is the term used to describe the wearing out of property or the loss in value of property because of age and use. Sometimes buildings will increase in value, that is, *appreciate*. However, properties ordinarily decrease in value as they become older.

The following tables show how one may compare the cost of renting with that of owning a home. Let us assume that a family is paying rent of $125 a month and that it would cost $14,000 to buy a home of equal quality. Using the table on page 591 as a basis for determining the first-year cost of owning a home, it will be observed that in this particular case it costs $52 a year less to own a home than to rent. In this example it is assumed that there is a down payment of $2,800 and that interest is paid at the rate of 5 percent on the unpaid balance. Since the family has an investment of $2,800 in the home, it is assumed that they are losing interest at the annual rate of 3½ percent, which could be earned on the investment if it were placed in a savings account. In a sense this loss of interest is the same as a cash outlay of $98.

Cost of renting	First-year cost of owning	
Rent at $125 a month $1,500	Interest at 5%	$ 560
	Taxes and assessments	280
	Repairs and upkeep	210
	Depreciation	230
	Insurance	70
	Interest lost on investment in down payment ($2,800 at 3½%)	98
Total cost $1,500	Total cost	$1,448

Cost of renting compared with the first-year cost of owning a home

Not all the costs of owning a home are cash expenditures, however. In this case we must take into consideration the matter of depreciation. It is assumed in this example that the house is worth $11,500, the lot is worth $2,500, and the depreciation rate on the house is 2 percent a year. This amounts to a loss of $230 in depreciation for one year.

Fitting the cash outlay into the budget. For budgeting purposes the family needs to compare the total cash outlay, including $840 a year to apply on the principal, with the cost of renting to determine whether or not the family can afford to buy the home. This comparison may be calculated as follows:

Cash outlay for renting	Cash outlay for owning	
Rent $1,500	Interest	$ 560
	Taxes and assessments	280
	Repairs and upkeep	210
	Insurance	70
	Interest lost on investment (down payment)	98
	Payment on principal	840
Total cash outlay $1,500	Total cash outlay	$2,058

Cash outlay for renting compared with the first-year outlay for owning a home

Thus, the first-year cash outlay for owning a $14,000 home is $558 greater than the outlay for renting. This illustrates the fact that even though a person is able to pay rent, an additional sum may be needed each year to buy a home.

In buying an old home there is another factor that is important. Very often it is necessary to repair or remodel the house before moving in. It may need a new roof, a new furnace, or other types of repairs. Sometimes an additional room must be added. These costs must all be taken into consideration in fitting the cash outlay into the budget.

As a family grows in size and moves from an apartment into a house or from a smaller house into a larger house, there usually are additional costs involved because of the necessity of buying new rugs or furniture for the larger home. These costs must also be included in the budget.

BUYING A COOPERATIVE APARTMENT

In many cities it is now possible to purchase an apartment in a building that is shared by other families. For example, a building may contain six apartments. Each family will own one apartment, and the whole apartment house is owned jointly or cooperatively by the six families. As each family buys an apartment, it is necessary to sign a contract covering all the agreements in regard to repairs, taxes, heating, and other matters. Usually the agreement provides that when one family wishes to sell its apartment, it cannot be sold to anyone without the approval of the majority of the other owners.

Cooperative apartments are attractive to many people who wish to own their own property, but do not want to live in a single-family house.

SAFETY FACTOR IN BUYING

If the decision to buy or to rent is to be based purely on the basis of costs or savings, these amounts can be estimated pretty accurately as

The main problems in buying a home are to select the right location and to select the right house at the right price.

H. Armstrong Roberts

you have seen in this chapter. However, it is difficult to determine if property values will go up or down or whether the earnings of the family will increase or decrease. To be safe in buying, you should make a substantial down payment and be sure there is a safe "cushion" in your budget so you will not fail to make your payments on the home and meet all other expenses.

Facts everyone should know about renting or buying

1. Some people should rent, but others should own a home.
2. There are important factors to check in renting a home.
3. A budget will determine whether you can afford to buy a home.
4. Financial advisers recommend a down payment of 20 to 25 percent on the purchase of a home.
5. A new home is not always the best buy.
6. The location is important whether buying or renting a home.

■ QUESTIONS ON THE TEXT

1. Name some of the advantages of owning a home.
2. Indicate at least three of the most important cautions in building a home.
3. Indicate the five choices of ways to build a home.
4. In this chapter there is a checklist for buying a home. Under the classification of equipment, which are the items that are most expensive to repair or replace if they are defective?
5. Name at least three factors that are important in selecting a homesite.
6. List some of the factors or conditions that will help to determine when a family should buy a home.
7. What percentage of income is considered the maximum amount that one may safely spend each year in buying a home?
8. What is the minimum down payment that conservative financial advisers recommend for a person who buys his home?
9. What is a reasonable estimate of the cost of upkeep based on the total value of a home?
10. What is a reasonable estimate of the cost of fire insurance based on the cost of a house?
11. When is it desirable to make (a) a short-term lease? (b) a long-term lease?
12. What are some of the advantages of a long-term lease?
13. Name some circumstances under which it is better to rent than to own a home.
14. Name some circumstances under which it is better to own a home instead of renting one.

15. Explain why depreciation needs to be taken into consideration in figuring the cost of owning a home.

16. If one invests $1,000 in the purchase of a home, explain why the loss of interest on this investment is part of the cost of owning the home.

17. From the viewpoint of a cash outlay, why does owning a home and making regular monthly payments require more expenditure than renting?

18. What is meant by a cooperative apartment?

19. In terms of budgeting, what is recommended as a safe practice in buying a home?

▪ QUESTIONS FOR DISCUSSION

1. In each of the following cases, give your opinion as to whether each person should rent or own a home, assuming that each can afford to buy if he should wish to do so: (a) a traveling salesman, (b) the owner of a retail store, (c) the sales manager of a district office, (d) the office manager in a local manufacturing plant. Give reasons for your answers.

2. (a) Why is location an important factor in selecting a house to rent or to buy?

   (b) Are the considerations the same in both cases?

3. Mr. Walsh, who is considering the purchase of a house, finds in an old community a house that is better constructed and otherwise more desirable than a newer one in a recently developed community. The two houses are offered at the same price. What do you think are some of the factors that he should consider in determining which house to select?

4. Jack Settle is married and has one child. He has a new job and seems to be doing well. He and his wife have selected a house which they want to buy. They have made a study of the cost of owning a home as outlined in this chapter and find that they can just barely afford the purchase of the home if they assume that he will have an increase in salary by the time the house needs painting or repairing. Do you think they should buy the home?

5. In this chapter there are two tables, one of which compares the actual first-year cost of owning a $14,000 home with the cost of renting, and the other, which compares the cash outlay for owning a $14,000 home with the cash outlay for renting. Explain why the two costs of owning are different.

6. Explain how one's budget should be the controlling guide in buying a home.

7. Under what circumstances do you think a person would be justified in making a down payment of only 5 or 10 percent of the purchase price of a home?

8. If one has been renting a home and has been taking care of the repairs, painting, and papering of the house under the rental agreement, how should these expenditures be taken into consideration in making a comparison of the cost of renting and the cost of owning a home?

9. Compare some of the advantages and disadvantages of either buying an old house or buying a new house.

10. Can you think of any difficulties that may be involved if a person tries to handle all the details of building his own home by arranging for contracts with individual workers and contractors on various parts of the work?

11. Name some of the kinds of changes in neighborhoods that cause property to decrease in value and to become less desirable for residential purposes.

▪ PROBLEMS TO SOLVE

1. On page 591 there is a table showing the first-year cost of financing a home based upon house and lot values and annual family incomes. Using this table as a guide, compute the first-year cost of financing a home under the following conditions: the value of the house and the lot is $15,000; the cash down payment is $3,000; a first mortgage is obtained on the balance of the indebtedness at 5½ percent interest, to be charged annually in advance; the yearly payments of the principal and the interest are $1,500; the taxes and assessments are 2 percent of the value of the house and lot; the insurance is .5 percent of the value of the house ($13,500); and the upkeep is 1.5 percent of the value of the house.

Indicate the first-year expense and the first-year savings. Note that the principal is adjusted at the end of the year.

2. Mr. Fred Walker owns a house and a lot that cost $17,000. The lot is valued at $3,000. Assume that over a period of 20 years the valuation of the property for the purpose of assessing taxes will remain at $17,000; the tax rate will stay at 2 percent; the yearly cost of insurance on the house will be .5 percent of the cost of the house; the annual cost of upkeep will be 1.5 percent of the cost of the house; the house and the lot will be worth $13,000 at the end of the twenty years (the loss in value to be distributed equally over the twenty years); the money invested in the home would have earned a yearly income of 4 percent if it had been invested in a federal savings and loan institution. Determine whether it is more economical for Mr. Walker to own his home than it would have been for him to pay a monthly rental of $130. Assume that all other costs of owning the home or of renting are negligible and that the rental rate would have remained the same.

3. Mr. Holmes is paying $100 a month for rent for a house valued at $12,500. He has $3,000 that he can use for a down payment on a house valued at $12,500; and he can borrow the balance of $9,500 at 5.5 percent interest, computed annually on the unpaid balance. His monthly payments on this new house would be $95, including principal and interest. Taxes would amount to $225 a year. There are no assessments; repairs and upkeep are estimated at $165 a year; depreciation is estimated at 2 percent of the value of the house ($11,000). Insurance would cost $55 a year. He would lose the interest on the $3,000 down payment because this amount is now in a savings account earning 3.5 percent, compounded annually.

   (a) Construct a table like the one in this chapter showing the cost of renting compared with the first-year cost of owning a home.

   (b) Construct a table similar to the one in this chapter showing the cash outlay for renting compared with the first-year outlay for owning a home.

▪ COMMUNITY PROBLEMS AND PROJECTS

1. Using the checklist for buying a home which you will find in this chapter, select a site in your community as a location for building or for buying a home. Make an evaluation of this location and give your conclusions as to the desirability of the site, including the costs.

2. Using the table in this chapter which shows the first-year cost of financing a home, prepare a similar table for the purchase of a home for your own family, assuming that you can make a down payment of $2,000. Obtain the latest and most accurate information that you can in regard to interest rates, taxes, insurance, and estimated repair costs. Figure depreciation on the value of the building at 2 percent a year. Set a reasonable value on the house according to prevailing real estate values. If your family is the owner of the house, construct the same table and estimate the amount of rental that could be obtained from it in order to make the same comparison.

3. Based upon the table in this chapter showing how to estimate the cash outlay for owning a home during the first year as compared with the cash outlay for renting, make a study of only the cash outlay necessary for the purchasing of a home that you select. From a newspaper advertisement or through a real estate person find out the cost of the home and the down payment that is necessary. Then obtain all the other information that is needed and prepare a report showing only the information pertaining to the cash outlay for owning the home during the first year.

Chapter 31

Financing the purchase
of a home

PURPOSE OF THE CHAPTER

Financing the purchase of a home presents the prospective homeowner with many problems that require decisions. These decisions can be made wisely only when they are based upon facts and an understanding of these facts. In order to make these decisions, which are of great importance to the family, the prospective homeowner needs to understand mortgages; sources of loans; practices regarding security, payments, and rates; refinancing procedures; land contracts; and government insurance of FHA loans and guarantee of VA loans.

You will find answers to these questions:

1. What are the sources from which money can be borrowed?
2. How much will a loan cost?
3. What are the obligations under a mortgage?
4. What special charges may there be in connection with a loan?
5. What is meant by FHA and VA loans?

A. Mortgages and mortgage loans

In 1964, the total public and private debt in the United States was approximately $1,171 billion of which approximately $292.7 billion, or 25 percent, was mortgage indebtedness on nonfarm residences. In 1964, applications were filed for loans on more than 1.5 million new nonfarm homes and 27,000 new farm homes that were started. Most of these homes were financed through mortgage loans.

MORTGAGES

A *real estate mortgage* is a contract between the borrower and the lender for purposes of buying property. It stipulates the conditions under which the money is lent and must be repaid. It serves as security for the loan and grants certain privileges to the lender if the loan is not repaid according to agreement. In addition to the mortgage contract, the borrower may also be required to sign a series of notes coming due periodically.

An old type of mortgage (but seldom used now) is one which runs for a period of time such as five to ten years. In the meantime, the borrower is required to pay interest on the debt at specified intervals. At the end of the term of the mortgage, the entire amount must be repaid or a new mortgage must be obtained to take its place. The features of a mortgage are discussed in the next chapter.

Partial-payment mortgage. Most mortgages on homes provide for periodic payments of a part of the principal and the accumulated interest. This is sometimes called a *partial-payment mortgage*. Payments are arranged so that at the end of the term specified in the mortgage the entire loan will be repaid. There are several different types of this mortgage.

Package deals. Some mortgage contracts are called *package deals*. The payments not only include interest and principal, but also include insurance on the building, taxes, and sometimes even life insurance on the borrower.

Open-end mortgage. There is also a type of mortgage that is sometimes called an *open-end mortgage*. This kind of mortgage permits a borrower, after having made substantial repayments on the loan, to borrow additional sums under the same mortgage contract without arranging for an additional loan. This extra money may be needed from time to time for making repairs.

APPRAISALS

When one applies for a loan from any lending agency, it is necessary to fill out an application. The lender will then insist upon having experts make an *appraisal,* which is an examination of the property and the setting of its value. This is done to determine its value and condition. The appraisal is important to the lender and to the borrower because it should help to disclose any defects and should help to determine a fair value of the property. There is usually a special fee charged when application is made for a mortgage loan. In many cases, the borrower is required to pay for the appraisal fee.

SOURCES OF LOANS

There are several different sources from which money can be borrowed to finance the purchase of a home. Generally, these include savings and loan associations, life insurance companies, banks, trust companies, mortgage companies, and private investors. There are other special types of lenders in some cities. Certain types of institutions, such as savings and loan associations, make a specialty of lending money for the purchase of homes. The illustration on page 605 shows the proportion of total debts on homes financed by the more important types of lenders.

Savings and loan associations. As discussed in Chapters 17 and 24, a savings and loan association is an organization created for the promotion of thrift and home ownership. The money obtained by a savings and loan association from its subscribers and depositors is used for the purpose of making loans to persons buying or building homes.

Savings and loan associations are relatively liberal in their lending. They extend loans for reasonably long periods, usually ten to twenty years. They frequently appraise property at a value equal to the full market price. First-mortgage loans are sometimes made on property to the extent of from 70 to 90 percent of the valuation. The liberality in lending depends largely on local and general business conditions and on the availability of funds.

As a guide to families interested in borrowing money, the following table was prepared by the United States Savings and Loan League, which is an organization of savings and loan associations. The first two columns show the income available by families for housing purposes, and the remaining columns show the usual amount that can be borrowed and paid off under different plans at different rates through a savings and loan association.

Income available for housing		Amount of loan which income for housing will finance								
		At 5 percent			At 5½ percent			At 6 percent		
Monthly	Annual	10 Yrs.	15 Yrs.	20 Yrs.	10 Yrs.	15 Yrs.	20 Yrs.	10 Yrs.	15 Yrs.	20 Yrs.
$ 15	$ 180	$ 1,070	$ 1,320	$ 1,500	$ 1,050	$ 1,280	$ 1,440	$ 1,030	$ 1,240	$ 1,395
20	240	1,430	1,760	2,000	1,400	1,700	1,920	1,635	1,645	1,845
25	300	1,790	2,210	2,500	1,750	2,140	2,400	1,720	2,110	2,360
30	360	2,140	2,650	3,000	2,090	2,570	2,880	2,070	2,540	2,830
35	420	2,500	3,090	3,500	2,440	2,990	3,360	2,410	2,960	3,310
40	480	2,860	3,530	4,000	2,800	3,420	3,840	2,760	3,380	3,780
50	600	3,570	4,410	5,000	3,490	4,270	4,800	3,450	4,230	4,720
60	720	4,290	5,290	6,000	4,200	5,120	5,760	4,140	5,070	5,670
80	960	5,710	7,060	8,000	5,580	6,840	7,670	5,520	6,760	7,560
100	1,200	7,140	8,820	10,000	6,980	8,540	9,590	6,700	8,450	9,450
125	1,500	8,930	11,030	12,500	8,730	10,680	11,990	8,620	10,560	11,810
150	1,800	10,620	13,200	14,970	10,380	12,780	14,360	10,230	12,590	14,150
175	2,100	12,390	15,400	17,460	12,110	14,910	16,760	11,940	14,690	16,510
200	2,400	14,160	17,600	19,960	13,850	17,050	19,150	13,650	16,790	18,870
225	2,700	15,930	19,800	22,450	15,580	19,180	21,540	15,350	18,890	21,230
250	3,000	17,700	22,000	24,950	17,310	21,300	23,940	17,060	20,980	23,590

Life insurance companies. In recent years life insurance companies have invested considerable money in loans on real estate. The loans of such a company are commonly placed through local agents, such as banks, trust companies, mortgage companies, and individuals. The applicant for a loan is required to supply the agent with detailed information about his financial standing and about the property that he wishes to purchase.

Many insurance companies will lend two thirds to three fourths of the appraised value of a house. Since their appraisals usually are very conservative, however, the available loan may be considerably less than two thirds or three fourths of the purchase price. Some insurance companies are willing to make mortgage loans on a twenty- or even thirty-year basis. Interest is charged at the rate prevailing when the loan is made. Some allow interest and principal to be paid monthly; in other cases, payments are made semiannually. Provision usually is made for the borrower to pay off the loan after the third year without penalty.

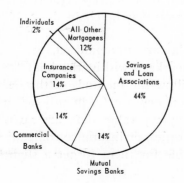

Proportion of total home-mortgage loans by type of lender, 1964

Courtesy: 1965 Savings and Loan Fact Book.

Banks. An important source of borrowing on homes is a bank, especially a savings bank. When application is made for a loan, an officer of the bank or a committee usually visits the property and makes an appraisal. The size of the loan that such a bank can make is generally restricted by state law (or federal regulations in the case of national banks) to a certain percentage of the value of the property. In some states this is 50 percent, but in others it is as high as 60 percent. State laws do not, however, restrict the banks with respect to making liberal or conservative appraisals. Thus, a liberal bank in a state that limits loans to 50 percent of the property value might lend more than a conservative bank in a state that limits loans to 60 percent of the property value.

Some banks extend loans for only short periods, such as three, five, or ten years. Short-term loans can usually be renewed, but a charge may be made for the privilege of extension. Unless the property has been taken care of satisfactorily, it is difficult to renew the loan.

Trust companies. Trust companies and the trust departments of banks usually have funds available for real-estate loans. The lending policies and methods of trust companies are similar to those of savings banks.

Mortgage companies. In many large communities mortgage companies are an important factor in home financing. There are two classes of these companies. One class lends on first, or senior, mortgages; and the other lends on second, or junior, mortgages. There is a great lack of uniformity in the policies and the methods of these companies. They are usually not placed under such legal restrictions as are savings and loan associations, banks, trust companies, and insurance companies. On a first mortgage they ordinarily do not lend in excess of 50 percent of the valuation of the property. When a greater amount is lent, an extra commission may be charged.

Private lenders. Private lenders, who are unorganized, are free to operate as they please so long as they keep within the bounds of state laws on lending. They usually follow the methods of the lending institutions in their communities. They are frequently willing to lend a higher percentage of the property value than are savings and loan associations, banks, trust companies, or insurance companies. They do so especially when it is possible for them to get a slightly higher rate of interest.

The person who borrows from a lending institution can usually depend on being able to renew his mortgage if he has been prompt with his payments. When he borrows from an individual, however, there is nothing but personal assurance that the loan can be renewed. Such unforeseen circumstances as the death of the lender may cause an embarrassing situation for the borrower.

B. Factors about real estate loans

The prospective homeowner comes in contact with many practices that may affect his decisions as to the nature of the loan he seeks, the source of the loan, and the manner in which he repays the loan. The decisions he makes on these matters frequently affect the amount that borrowing to finance a home may eventually cost him.

SECOND-MORTGAGE BORROWING

In communities where lending agencies are unwilling to make loans equal to from 60 to 75 percent of the value of the home, some borrowers find it necessary to use two loans, a first mortgage and a second mortgage.

The following example shows the relationship between a first and a second mortgage: A person purchases a house valued at $12,000. He pays $3,000 in cash and is successful in obtaining a first-mortgage loan of $6,000. He obtains the loan by signing a series of notes that will become due at specified intervals. The interest on the notes is 5 percent. To protect the lender, he gives a real-estate mortgage.

A second-mortgage loan is negotiated for the remainder of the purchase price, $3,000. The borrower signs a series of notes and a second-mortgage contract. The interest on the second mortgage is at a higher rate (6 percent) than the interest on the first mortgage because the holder of the second mortgage has a greater risk of loss. The lender holds the second-mortgage contract. If the payments are not made when they become due, the first-mortgage holder or the second-mortgage holder, or both, depending upon the laws of the particular state, have the option of suing for the disposal of the property to satisfy the claims against it. The first-mortgage holder has first claim on the proceeds from the sale; the second-mortgage holder has second claim.

Using a second mortgage is usually a dangerous practice for many home buyers because it is necessary to repay the first-mortgage loan

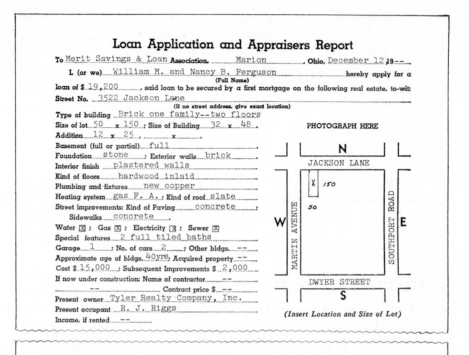

Loan Application and Appraisers Report

To Merit Savings & Loan Association, ...Marion............., Ohio, December 12 19--

I. (or we) William M. and Nancy B. Ferguson.............................hereby apply for a

(Full Name)

loan of $ 19,200......., said loan to be secured by a first mortgage on the following real estate, to-wit:

Street No. 3522 Jackson Lane

(If no street address, give exact location)

Type of building Brick one family--two floors

Size of lot 50 x 150 ; Size of Building 32 x 48 .

Addition 12 x 25 , x .

Basement (full or partial) full .

Foundation stone ; Exterior walls brick .

Interior finish plastered walls

Kind of floors hardwood inlaid

Plumbing and fixtures new copper

Heating system gas F. A.; Kind of roof slate

Street improvements: Kind of Paving concrete ;

Sidewalks concrete .

Water ☒ ; Gas ☒ ; Electricity ☒ ; Sewer ☒

Special features 2 full tiled baths

Garage 1 ; No. of cars 2 ; Other bldgs. --

Approximate age of bldgs. 40yrs; Acquired property --

Cost $ 15,000 ; Subsequent Improvements $ 2,000

If now under construction: Name of contractor --

-- Contract price $ --

Present owner Tyler Realty Company, Inc.

Present occupant R. J. Riggs

Income, if rented --

PHOTOGRAPH HERE

N

JACKSON LANE

X 150

50

W | MARTIN AVENUE · SOUTHPORT ROAD | **E**

DWYER STREET

S

(Insert Location and Size of Lot)

APPRAISAL

Legal Description of Property.

Situate in the City of Marion, County of Hardin, and State of Ohio, and being Lot No. 209 on Jackson Lane of the Lake Park Subdivision as the same appears of record in Plot Book No. 14, page 63, of the records of Hardin County, Ohio.

Appraised value of Land - - - - - - - - - - - - - - - $ 3,000.00

Appraisal value of Dwelling - - - - - - - - - - - - - $ 21,000.00

Garage - - - - - - - - - - - - - $ 300.00

Other buildings - - - - - - - - - - - $ --

Total Appraisal - - - - - - - - - - - - - - - - - - $ 24,300.00

Rights of occupants Occupancy to be given 30 days after closing.

Portions of a loan application and appraiser's report

and the second-mortgage loan at the same time. In other words, regular payments will have to be made on both loans. Under some arrangements, regular payments are made on the first-mortgage loan and at the end of a specified time, the entire second-mortgage loan must be repaid.

LAND CONTRACTS

A common form of financing used by home buyers who can make a down payment of only 5 to 15 percent involves a land contract. This plan is popular in the central part of the United States. A *land contract* is an agreement between the buyer and the seller of the property, under the terms of which the buyer usually makes a small down payment and agrees to pay the full purchase price in installments. The seller does not give the buyer legal ownership of the

This agreement, made and concluded at Dayton, Ohio, this second day of January, 1966, by and between R. D. Lawson, hereinafter called the seller, and R. O. Knapp, hereinafter called the purchaser, witnesseth:

That the seller, in consideration of the sum of eight thousand dollars ($8,000), to be paid by the purchaser, and of the promises and agreements of the purchaser hereinafter contained, does, for himself, his heirs and assigns, hereby agree to sell to the purchaser, his heirs and assigns, the following-described premises, situated in the city of Dayton, county of Montgomery, and state of Ohio, and 1022 Blair Avenue (Monroe Subdivision, R1-T4-S31 S.E. 40 x 110) together with all the appurtenances thereunto belonging.

The seller further agrees to give possession of said premises to the purchaser on February 1, 1966, and that, upon the payment by the purchaser of the full sum of four thousand dollars ($4,000) in installments, and upon the execution of a note and mortgage securing the balance of $4,000 as hereinafter provided, the seller will convey said premises to the purchaser by good and sufficient deed of general warranty and free and clear from all incumbrances whatsoever.

In consideration thereof, the purchaser hereby agrees to purchase said property and to pay the same the sum of eight thousand dollars ($8,000) as follows:

Two hundred dollars ($200) in cash upon the execution of this agreement; thirty-eight hundred dollars ($3,800) in monthly installments of fifty dollars ($50) each on the first day of each and every month hereafter, all deferred payments to bear interest at the rate of six percent per annum, payable semiannually.

The balance of four thousand dollars ($4,000) to be secured by a note and first mortgage on said property, bearing interest at six percent per annum and due on year after its date, to be executed and delivered by the purchaser when the sum of $4,000 above provided for has been paid in full.

The purchaser further agrees to pay all taxes and assessments that may for any purpose whatever be levied or assessed on said property, beginning with the taxes and assessments due January 1, 1966. The purchaser further agrees to insure the building on said property for not less than six thousand dollars ($6,000) and to keep the same insured during the continuance of this agreement, and if he fail or neglect to do so, the seller may insure the same at the expense of the purchaser.

It is mutually agreed by and between the parties hereto that if the purchaser shall fail or neglect to pay any one of said installments of purchase money or interest when the same become due, or within five days thereafter, or shall fail to execute said note and mortgage, when and as above specified, or shall fail to pay any of said taxes or assessments when the same are due and payable, or shall fail to insure said building or to keep the same insured, then all of the installments and amounts remaining unpaid shall immediately become due and payable, and the seller may, at his option, terminate this agreement by giving thirty days' written notice by mail to the purchaser, time being of the essence of this agreement; and in the event of such termination all payments made by the purchaser hereunder may be retained by the seller as fixed and liquidated damages for nonperformance by the purchaser of this agreement.

At the time of delivery of said deed to the purchaser, the seller shall furnish to the purchaser an abstract of title showing good title to said premises, free from incumbrances except such as may be caused by the act or default of the purchaser.

In witness thereof, the parties hereto have set their hands to duplicates hereof the day and year first above written.

In presence of

Alice Brown

Carol A. Cantwell

R. D. Lawson

R. O. Knapp

A land contract

property, but agrees to convey the title to him when a certain percentage of the purchase price (usually approximately 50 percent) has been paid. When the title is transferred, the seller usually accepts a first-mortgage note, or the buyer either takes care of the unpaid balance or obtains a loan from someone else to pay the balance due the original seller.

This type of agreement makes it possible for the individual who does not have enough savings to satisfy down-payment requirements to occupy the property and to make payments similar to those on a lease. When his payments are equivalent to a required down payment, the title is transferred to him, and he mortgages the property for the unpaid balance. A land contract has the effect of leasing with the privilege of purchasing.

The land contract is advantageous to real-estate brokers because it enables the seller to hold the title of the property until the buyer has invested a sufficient amount in the home to indicate that he can satisfactorily complete payment and assume the obligation of ownership. In case the buyer fails to live up to his agreement, the seller has a better opportunity to take possession of the property than if the title had been transferred.

RENEWING A MORTGAGE

In obtaining a loan on a home, the borrower should take into consideration what will happen to the mortgage obligation at the time it matures. Sometimes difficulty arises because the loan cannot be paid at maturity. Some mortgages require regular payments of the principal and interest, whereas other mortgages require payment of the interest regularly and payment of the entire principal at a specified date.

A mortgage that extends for a long period is safest. If a mortgage extends for only three, four, or five years, the person who borrows the money should obtain some assurance that the mortgage can be renewed or that a new loan can be obtained from some source. Suppose, for example, that a person will require ten years to pay for a home, but that he obtains a loan that will be due in three years. During the three years he will not be able to repay much of the principal. At the end of that period he must either have the loan renewed or obtain a new loan. He otherwise will run the risk of foreclosure on his property. The cost of the renewal of the loan should be predetermined, for this expense must be considered as part of the total cost of financing the home.

PAYMENTS AND RATES

The final decision in choosing an agency to finance the purchase or the building of a home should be based upon the reputation of the agency and the economy with which the home can be financed. The method of calculating the interest charges and the expenses involved in obtaining the loan should be investigated.

Different types of financial institutions have considerable variation in their plans of charging interest. Some loan companies calculate interest annually; others calculate it semiannually or quarterly.

The table on page 612 shows how a loan of $1,000 at an interest rate of 6 percent is paid off monthly over a period of twenty years. If this were a $10,000 loan, the monthly payment would be $71.70. In this kind of loan, known as a *direct-reduction loan*, the principal is reduced with each monthly payment; and each month a greater amount is applied toward repaying the principal. The table shows each of the first twelve monthly payments and thereafter shows only one of the payments for each year.

Loans may be obtained for ten, fifteen, twenty, or twenty-five years. Of course, each borrower will have to arrange a loan to fit his own budget. The faster the borrower repays a loan, however, the less interest he will pay. The following table, based on 5 percent interest, shows the monthly payments required for each $1,000 of a loan and the total interest charges that will be paid over the period of the loan. Notice, for example, that the monthly payments on the loan for twenty-five years are only about one half as much as the monthly payments on a ten-year loan. However, on a twenty-five-year loan, the amount of interest that is paid is approximately three times the amount that is paid on a ten-year loan.

Years of monthly payments	Monthly payment required to repay $1,000 at 5%	Total interest charges for each $1,000 borrowed at 5%
10 years	$10.61	$272.79
15 years	7.91	423.43
20 years	6.60	583.89
25 years	5.85	753.77

EXTRA CHARGES

When loans are obtained, special care should be used to detect any extra charges. Premiums, commissions, and bonuses on loans result in higher interest rates for the borrowers. When a loan is

SCHEDULE OF DIRECT-REDUCTION LOAN

Rate 6%	Monthly payment $7.17	Loan $1,000	Term: Years 20	Months 240

Payment number	Payment on		Balance of loan
	Interest	Principal	
1	$5.00	$2.17	$997.83
2	4.99	2.18	995.65
3	4.98	2.19	993.46
4	4.97	2.20	991.26
5	4.96	2.21	989.05
6	4.95	2.22	986.83
7	4.93	2.24	984.59
8	4.92	2.25	982.34
9	4.91	2.26	980.08
10	4.90	2.27	977.81
11	4.89	2.28	975.53
12	4.88	2.29	973.24
24	4.74	2.43	944.82
36	4.59	2.58	914.64
48	4.43	2.74	882.60
60	4.26	2.91	848.60
72	4.08	3.09	812.48
84	3.89	3.28	774.15
96	3.68	3.49	733.44
108	3.47	3.70	690.23
120	3.24	3.93	644.36
132	3.00	4.17	595.64
144	2.74	4.43	543.94
156	2.47	4.70	489.05
168	2.18	4.99	430.77
180	1.87	5.30	368.89
192	1.54	5.63	303.19
204	1.20	5.97	233.46
216	.83	6.34	159.43
228	.44	6.73	80.82
240	.02	4.50	4.52 *

* Final payment

obtained from some sources, the lender charges a commission for granting it. If, for example, a $40 commission is charged on a $1,000 loan that will extend for ten years, the actual amount of cash available from the loan is $960. The interest, however, must be paid on the $1,000. The actual rate of interest is therefore greater than the nominal rate.

There are other additional charges that must be considered in obtaining a loan. In some states a tax is levied. In practically every state there is a fee for having the deed recorded. The cost of having the title examined is usually from $25 to $80. The cost of an appraisal should not exceed $25 to $50. Some lenders require title insurance, which is also charged to the borrower. Ordinarily these costs are borne by the person who obtains the loan, but occasionally they are paid by the company granting the loan. Some of these charges are often called *closing costs*.

OTHER FACTORS TO CONSIDER IN OBTAINING A LOAN

After studying your budget, you will not want to agree to any financing plan that is going to involve monthly payments greater than your budget will allow. Even though you expect the family income to increase at a later date, it is better to obtain a loan with monthly payments that you can afford but with a prepayment without penalty clause in the agreement. Under the *prepayment without penalty clause*, you may pay off the loan faster than you have agreed, without any penalty. Thus, you may cut your interest costs and protect yourself against loss of income in the future.

For convenience in budgeting and managing your financial affairs, you may also wish to consider what is called a *package mortgage*. With this kind of mortgage you may be able to include the purchase of a stove, refrigerator, dishwasher, and perhaps some other items. Your payments may also include taxes, insurance, and possibly life insurance on the head of the family.

The open-end mortgage, which has already been discussed, has some advantages. For example, after you have repaid a substantial amount of the loan, you may borrow additional money for repairs if necessary and then continue paying the amount required on the loan.

PROTECTION ON REAL ESTATE LOANS THROUGH LIFE INSURANCE

When one borrows money to buy a home for his family, he likes to feel sure that the loan will be repaid and that his family will have a home even though he dies. A buyer of real estate may purchase term life insurance sufficient to repay the amount of the loan on the real estate if he should die. Then if the buyer dies, proceeds from his life insurance will repay the loan.

The lender also likes to have some assurance that the loan will be repaid even though the buyer dies. Although the lender will have a mortgage claim against the property, he probably will not like to take the property away from a family if the head of the family dies. Some lenders require the head of the family to obtain either life insurance or mortgage redemption insurance for this purpose. This protects the lender completely; and, in the event of the death of the head of the family, the family is assured of a home without any debt on it. Therefore, life insurance serves an important function in the field of real estate.

C. Government-secured real estate loans

In order to promote home ownership, the federal government has stimulated both the purchase and the building of houses by insuring loans on houses on which the prospective owners make small down payments. Under certain conditions, one program insures a lending institution against loss if an owner is unable to pay and the other guarantees the payments on houses.

Banks, savings and loan associations, and other lenders protect themselves by adequate down payments, careful screening of applicants for mortgage loans, and relatively strict regulations governing the granting of credit on a mortgage loan. Insurance companies and many other lenders making mortgage loans sometimes protect themselves by requiring that the borrowers purchase *mortgage redemption insurance,* which insures the payment of the loan in case of death or disability of the borrower.

FEDERAL HOUSING ADMINISTRATION

The Federal Housing Administration is commonly known as the FHA. The FHA provides federal insurance on loans that are obtained through an approved lending agency, such as a bank. If the FHA approves the loan, the money can be borrowed from the regular lending agency. The lending agency is protected because the FHA insures the loan, thus guaranteeing its payment. Money may be borrowed for repairing or improving a home, buying or building a new home, buying an existing home, or buying a multiple-family dwelling, such as an apartment building.

From the viewpoint of an individual seeking a loan, an FHA loan is usually no better than many other types of loans, except that a qualified person who can make only a small down payment can sometimes obtain an FHA loan, when he might not be able to make a sufficient down payment to obtain some other kind of loan. FHA regulations will not permit a loan to be made if it requires monthly payments exceeding a certain amount of the take-home pay of the principal wage earner of the family.

Where and how to apply for FHA loans. Any regular lending agency, such as a building and loan association, life insurance company, bank, trust company, mortgage company, or private investor, can help an individual apply for an FHA loan. A contractor, an architect, or a real-estate agent can also help a home buyer to apply for an FHA loan. If a loan is desired for repairing or improving a home, assistance can be obtained through a contractor or a dealer in building supplies.

FHA regulations. A loan obtained under the FHA may be repaid over periods of 10, 15, 20, 25, or 30 years, or in a lump sum at any time. The minimum down payment required on the purchase of a new home is less than that required for buying an old home. Down payments under FHA are usually lower than under other plans of borrowing.

A charge is added to the interest rate to cover mortgage insurance. This charge is based upon the decreasing balance of the loan. The interest rates permitted on FHA insured loans are regulated by law, and these rates change from time to time as the law is changed. However, FHA loan rates are usually lower than those ordinarily charged for real estate loans because the FHA loans are insured by the federal government.

VETERANS ADMINISTRATION LOANS

For persons with service in the Armed Forces during World War II, the Korean conflict and the cold war, special loan privileges are granted. These privileges are similar to those obtainable under FHA loans. The loan must be obtained through a regular lending agency. It is then guaranteed by the federal government. This privilege enables veterans to obtain real estate and borrow money for business or agricultural purposes on very favorable terms.

VA (GI) loans are insured by the Veterans Administration in essentially the same way that FHA loans are insured. If a veteran fails to repay his loan, the Veterans Administration has a claim against the borrower and has the privilege of deducting this amount from any pension, insurance dividend, or any other compensation due him.

Interest rates on VA insured loans are generally lower than those on other real-estate loans. However, these rates are changed from time to time through changes in the federal law. In addition to the interest rate, the borrower on a VA loan must also pay a small monthly charge for insurance. A down payment is urged and recommended, but the VA loan law permits the Veterans Administration to guarantee loans with no down payment if the lender is willing to make the loan for the full amount of the purchase price. A VA loan is not permitted if the monthly payments exceed a certain amount of the take-home pay of the principal wage earner in the family.

PROTECTION FOR LENDERS

FHA and VA do not lend money to purchase a home. Under FHA, lenders are insured against loss; and under VA, lenders are guaranteed that payments will be made. If payments are not made according to the contract to purchase, the bank or other lending institution must foreclose on the mortgage just the same as though FHA had not insured the lender against loss or the VA had not guaranteed payments. By *mortgage foreclosures* is meant that the lending agency files a complaint in court against the owner for nonpayment of amounts as due and takes possession of the property. The number of foreclosures per year has increased significantly since 1960. Many realtors believe the primary reasons for the failure of owners to make regular payments are that initial or down payments are too low, that credit requirements are too liberal, and that many houses, on which loans are secured by FHA and VA, are poorly constructed and hence deteriorate rapidly. The argument is put forth that many families living in these homes owe more for their homes than those homes are worth on the market.

D. Economics of buying real estate

In the previous discussion you have discovered that prices of real estate rise and fall depending upon economic conditions. If economic conditions are good, real estate values in terms of dollars will remain about the same, but the property will lose some value because of depreciation.

If the income of a family continues as expected and if the payments have been arranged to fit the budget, there probably will be no serious problems. If the family income decreases, however, it may become difficult to make payments on the home. The home may also decrease in dollar value because all property decreases in value when business conditions become bad.

During periods of rising prices and rising wages, it is not only easier to repay a loan, but the property may also actually increase in dollar value so that it will be worth more than when it was bought.

The economy of the United States is affected greatly by the building, purchasing, and financing of homes. In 1964, approximately 130,000 new nonfarm houses were started each month. The building of these homes required vast amounts of building supplies and equipment, which in turn meant jobs for many people.

But the construction of new homes is only a part of the total economic significance of home building and home owning. Many home builders and owners borrow money to finance the building or buying of a home. These loans on homes provide a good place for people who have surplus money to invest it safely and profitably. The total amount of mortgage debt outstanding on residential property is more than $292 billion. The interest on this indebtedness constitutes a good source of income for investors.

Facts everyone should know about financing the purchase of a home

1. A mortgage is a contract between the borrower and the lender.
2. An appraisal is necessary and desirable.
3. There are several sources of loans with different rates and arrangements for repayments.
4. A land contract helps a buyer to purchase a home by allowing him to pay for it in installments.
5. The extra charges should be studied in obtaining any loan.
6. The FHA and VA insure certain types of loans obtained through regular lenders.

▪ QUESTIONS ON THE TEXT

1. What is a real estate mortgage?
2. What is an open-end mortgage?
3. How can a real estate loan be obtained from a life insurance company?
4. What proportion of the value of a home will a bank ordinarily lend?
5. Explain the typical policies of mortgage companies in lending on real estate.
6. Why is it possible sometimes to obtain a loan from a private individual when it is not possible to obtain a loan from a financial institution?
7. What is meant by an appraisal?
8. Explain how a second mortgage is used in financing a home.
9. What are the principal features of a land contract?
10. Explain what happens when a mortgage matures or if regular payments are not made as agreed.
11. What is meant by a direct-reduction loan?

12. What are some of the extra charges that must be paid by the borrower of money?
13. For what purposes may FHA loans be obtained?
14. Who can assist a person in obtaining an FHA loan?
15. Explain some of the principal advantages of a VA loan.
16. Since FHA and VA do not lend money to purchase a home, how do they help the prospective home buyer?
17. What are some of the possible reasons that many FHA and VA insured real estate loans are not paid by the home purchasers?
18. What is mortgage redemption insurance?
19. How is life insurance sometimes used in connection with borrowing to buy a home so that the family will be protected if the husband and father dies?
20. Under what kind of economic condition does it become easier to repay a loan?

▪ QUESTIONS FOR DISCUSSION

1. What would be the effect on national income (see Chapter 9) if all prospective homeowners were required to pay cash?
2. Assuming that you have all sources of loans available to you, from what source do you think you could obtain the greatest loan in proportion to the value of the property? Give your reasons.
3. What do you think of the kind of loan agreement whereby the repayment of the loan includes interest, principal, taxes, and insurance?
4. Give the advantages and disadvantages of second mortgages from the viewpoint of (a) the borrower and (b) the lender.
5. Which do you consider the safer type of mortgage from the viewpoint of the borrower (a) a mortgage that extends for a short term of three or four years, or (b) one that extends for a long term of ten to fifteen years? Why?
6. Explain some of the reasons why an FHA loan may be desirable or necessary for some people.
7. When borrowing from some insurance companies, the borrower sometimes is required to pay for life insurance covering the period during which the loan will be repaid. Each payment on the loan includes a payment on the life insurance. Can you see any advantage or disadvantage in this plan? Explain.
8. Under what circumstances would a land contract be desirable or necessary for a family buying a home?
9. Can you see any advantage in the package mortgage? Explain your answer.
10. Although a house gradually gets older and therefore gradually wears out, why does a house sometimes increase in dollar value? Does it ever decrease in dollar value faster than the ordinary wearing out? Why?

11. Why do savings and loan associations lend more than twice as much money on home mortgage loans as do commercial banks?

12. Discuss why interest rates on second mortgages are higher than on first mortgages.

▪ PROBLEMS TO SOLVE

1. Mr. and Mrs. Jackson have $3,000 in a savings account which has been earning 4 percent interest, calculated annually. They buy an $18,000 home, using the $3,000 as a down payment. They succeed in obtaining a first mortgage for $10,000 at 6 percent interest and a second mortgage loan for the remainder of the purchase price at 7½ percent interest. Considering the loss of the interest on their savings as a part of the cost, figure the total interest cost during the first year if the interest on the loans is computed annually.

2. Mr. Miller buys a house costing $16,000. He makes a down payment of $4,000. A 5 percent mortgage is secured for the balance of $12,000 over a 20-year period.
   (a) Using the table on page 611, determine the amount he will be required to pay each month.
   (b) What will the actual total cost of the house be at the end of the 20-year period?

3. Ten years ago, a family obtained a 20-year mortgage loan for $10,000 at 6 percent. Use the table in this chapter showing the schedule of a direct-reduction loan to answer the following questions:
   (a) What is the balance of the loan now? (Assume that payment number 120 has just been made.)
   (b) What is the total amount that the family has paid on the mortgage (interest plus principal)?
   (c) How much has been paid in interest?

4. Already having obtained a suitable building site, Mr. and Mrs. George Johnson arranged with a builder for the construction of a house at a cost of $15,000.
   (a) Assume that Mr. and Mrs. Johnson borrow the $15,000 by means of a 5 percent, 20-year loan. Using the table on page 611, determine the amount of interest they will pay. What will be the total cost of the house?
   (b) Assume that they borrow the $15,000 by means of a 5 percent, 25-year loan. What will be the amount of the interest? What will be the total cost of the house?
   (c) Assume that they make a down payment on the construction cost of $5,000 and borrow the remaining $10,000 by means of a 5 percent, 20-year loan. What will be the amount of the interest? What will be the total cost of the house?
   (d) What conclusions can you draw on the basis of your computations?

5. Raymond Whitney bought a house costing $16,000. He made a down payment of 25 percent of the cash price. He is now making equal monthly payments over a 20-year period, with interest at 5 percent on the unpaid balance. In addition, he pays the mortgage company each month an allowance of $18.50 for property insurance and $15.30 for real estate tax. Using the information in the table on page 611, determine the amount of the check that Mr. Whitney writes each month for the payment on his house.

▪ COMMUNITY PROBLEMS AND PROJECTS

1. From your nearest office of the Veterans Administration or from the Veterans Administration in Washington, D. C., obtain the latest information in regard to regulations, procedures, and rates pertaining to loans for veterans. Ask also for information relative to the "generous terms, low-interest mortgages, and very low closing costs" which may be available when one buys a home from the Veterans Administration on which there has been a foreclosure because the first owner could not meet his financial obligation. Make a report of the important information that you obtain.

2. Study the advertisements of real estate for sale in your local newspaper or in the newspaper from a nearby larger city. Make a list of the prices asked for houses so that you can compare those prices for houses of different sizes, in different locations, and so forth. Note information in the advertisements about the possibilities of VA, FHA, and conventional types of financing. Make a report of your findings to the class.

3. Visit one or more mobile home sales lots. Note the construction of such homes and the various floor plans. Obtain information about the prices of mobile homes, and ask the dealer about methods by which they are financed. Then discuss with other members of your class the advantages and disadvantages of mobile home living, the cost of such homes, financial arrangements for buying them, and other elements of interest to you.

4. Investigate the various local sources of loans on real estate. For each type of source find out: (a) the percentage of the appraised value of property that will be lent, (b) the rate of interest, (c) the length of time during which a loan may extend, (d) the method of payment, (e) the dates on which interest is computed, and (f) any additional charges in obtaining a loan.

5. Obtain a sample form required by a bank, a building and loan association, or an insurance company for making an application for a loan. Fill out the blank, basing your figures on some particular piece of property, preferably your own home.

Chapter 32

Legal problems of obtaining a home

PURPOSE OF THE CHAPTER

The legal problems encountered in obtaining a home range from simple to complex. The laws pertaining to the leasing and purchasing of real estate vary from state to state, and practices vary within states. Because of the value of the property involved and the possible losses that could occur through improper procedures in leasing or purchasing, ordinarily it is an act of good judgment to seek the services of a lawyer to take care of the legal aspects of obtaining a home for you. The purpose of the chapter is to help you to recognize legal problems.

You will find answers to these questions:

1. What are the important points that should be included in a lease?
2. What are the rights and duties of both the landlord and the tenant?
3. How can you be sure of obtaining a clear title to real estate?
4. What are the characteristics of different kinds of deeds?
5. What is a mortgage, and how is a mortgage foreclosed?

A. Legal aspects of leasing or renting a home

Renting or leasing involves the legal rights, duties, and responsibilities of the landlord and the tenant. It is desirable and necessary that both should fully understand the relationship that exists between them.

RELATIONS OF LANDLORD AND TENANT

If you are the owner of a house and, by agreement, allow the property to be occupied and controlled by another, you are a *landlord*. The one who occupies the property is the *tenant*. The tenant has the right of possession and use of the property although he must respect the rights of the landlord. After the expiration of the agreement, the landlord has the right to regain possession of the property.

LEASING

The agreement between the landlord and the tenant is known as a *lease*. The landlord is the *lessor*, and the tenant is the *lessee*. The lease may be oral or written, the form depending upon the laws of the state governing the form. A written lease is desirable in many cases because it clearly defines the rights of the landlord and the tenant. In some states the lessor and the lessee must sign their names before a witness, such as a notary public.

The lessor grants the lessee the privilege of using the property without interference, provided the terms of the contract are carried out. The lease may state specifically the rights of each party, but some other legal rights of the lessee and the lessor may not be mentioned in the lease.

Usual content of a written lease

I. The date.

2. The names of the landlord and the tenant.

3. A description and an identification of the property.

4. The length of the tenancy period.

5. The amount of the payment.

6. The manner of payment.

7. A statement of the conditions and the agreements.

8. The signatures of the tenant and the landlord.

Agreement of Lease

THAT   Roger Gates does
HEREBY LEASE TO   Jerome F. Peterson
the premises situate in the   City   *of* Rochester   *in the County of*
Monroe   *and State of*   New York   *described as follows:*

Dwelling house, No. 4522 Monroe Court, Rochester, New York

with the appurtenances thereto, for the term of   one year   *commencing*
June 1,   *19 --, at a rental of* one hundred twenty-five
dollars per month   *, payable* monthly

SAID LESSEE AGREES *to pay said rent, unless said premises shall be destroyed or rendered untenantable by fire or other unavoidable accident; to not commit or suffer waste; to not use said premises for any unlawful purpose; to not assign this lease, or under-let said premises, or any part thereof, or permit the sale of* his   *interest herein by legal process, without the written consent of said lessor ; to not use said premises or any part thereof in violation of any law relating to intoxicating liquors; and at the expiration of this lease,. to surrender said premises in as good condition as they now are, or may be put by said lessor   reasonable wear and unavoidable casualties, condemnation or appropriation excepted. Upon non-payment of any of said rent for* ten   *days, after it shall become due, and without demand made therefore; or if said lessee or any assignee of this lease shall make an assignment for the benefit of his creditors; or if proceedings in bankruptcy shall be instituted by or against lessee or any assignee; or if a receiver or trustee be appointed for the property of lessee or any assignee; or if this lease by operation of law pass to any person or persons; or if said lessee or any assignee shall fail to keep any of the other covenants of this lease, it shall be lawful for said lessor ,* his   *heirs or assigns, into said premises to re-enter, and the same to have again, re-possess and enjoy, as in* his   *first and former estate; and thereupon this lease and everything herein contained on the said lessor   behalf to be done and performed, shall cease, determine, and be utterly void.*

SAID LESSOR AGREE s *(said lessee having performed* his   *obligations under this lease) that said lessee   shall quietly hold and occupy said premises during said term without any hindrance or molestation by said lessor ,* his   *heirs or any person lawfully claiming under them.*

Signed this first   *day of*   April   A. D. 19 --

Signed and acknowledged in presence of us:

Margaret Jensen   Roger Gates
Harold M. Terrell   Jerome F. Peterson

A lease

DISTINCTION BETWEEN LEASING AND RENTING

Generally speaking, leasing and renting mean the same thing, but some people think of renting as occupying property without a written agreement and of leasing as occupying property with a written agreement. The term renting, however, is properly applied to the occupation of property both with and without a written agreement.

A person may occupy property under an agreement covering an indefinite period; he may occupy property for an indefinite period, either party having the right to terminate the agreement when he wishes; or he may occupy property under an agreement covering a definite period. Any of these agreements may be written or oral, but the first two are more likely to be oral agreements.

RIGHTS AND DUTIES OF THE TENANT

The tenant of a piece of property is entitled to peaceful possession of it. If he is deprived of that, he may sue for damages. The tenant is also entitled to use the property for any purpose for which it is adapted, unless he is forbidden certain uses by the agreement. The property may not be used for unlawful purposes.

The tenant is under obligation to make repairs, but not improvements. For example, if the child of a tenant breaks a window, it ordinarily is the responsibility of the tenant to replace the window. He must pay his rent when it is due. Unless the lease states otherwise, the rent is not due until the end of each month.

If the lease is for a definite period of time, the tenant is not obligated to give notice when he vacates the property. The lease may be terminated, however, before the expiration of the period if an agreement is reached with the landlord. If the lease is for an indefinite period of time, the tenant must notify the landlord of his intention to give up the lease. The form and the time of notice are regulated by the customs or the laws of the community.

The tenant has the right to the undisturbed use of the property. The landlord has no right to enter the property to show it to a prospective buyer.

Bedford, Virginia, June 1, 19—

Mr. George Adams:

I hereby give you notice that I will quit and deliver possession, July 1, 19—, of the premises at No. 417 Reading Road, in the city of Bedford, Virginia, which I now hold as tenant under you.

Alice McGowan

A tenant's notice of intention to terminate a lease

The tenant should inspect carefully the property that he rents or leases. In the absence of any agreement with the landlord, he accepts the property with the risk of defects, except those hidden, being present. For example, if a tenant accepts a house with an obviously defective screen door, the landlord may not be responsible for fixing it except by agreement. However, if the tenant accepts the property in the summer and finds that the furnace will not function in the fall, the landlord is probably responsible because this is a hidden defect that could not easily be determined in the summer. In most states the tenant is liable for injuries to guests resulting from defects that he should have known and remedied.

RIGHTS AND DUTIES OF THE LANDLORD

A landlord does not have the right to enter the premises of a tenant except to do what is necessary to protect the property. He must not interfere with the tenant's right of possession. If the tenant moves from the property, however, the landlord may take possession.

At the expiration of the lease, the landlord is entitled to take possession of the property. If the tenant refuses possession, the landlord may force him to give possession through legal proceedings.

Unless there are specific laws or agreements to the contrary, the tenant is responsible for injuries arising from defective conditions of the property.

The landlord is entitled to receive the rent as specified in the lease. In some states, through legal proceedings, he may seize personal property of the tenant and have it sold to pay the rent that is due. Unless the lease specifies otherwise, taxes and assessments must be paid by the landlord.

In some states the landlord is under no obligation to make repairs or to pay for improvements on the property unless such an agreement has been made with the tenant. In most states, however, he is obligated to keep the house in habitable condition.

When the landlord retains control over a part of the property—as in the case of a landlord who leases part of a building to a tenant—he is liable for certain injuries caused by the defective condition of the part of the property over which he has control. For instance, Mr. Adams owns a two-story building. He lives on the first floor and retains control over the porch and the yard, but he rents the second floor to Mr. Brown. If Mr. Brown or a member of his family is injured as a result of the defective condition of the porch or the sidewalk, Mr. Adams is liable for the injuries. The landlord is also liable, in most cases, for injuries to any friend or guest of the tenant who may have been injured because of defects in the property which the landlord controls and therefore is obligated to maintain.

When a tenant occupies property for an indefinite period of time, the landlord may obtain possession of it by giving notice. The form and the time of the notice are regulated by local customs or laws.

Cincinnati, Ohio, April 30, 19—

Mr. Richard Dawson:

I hereby notify you to surrender possession of the premises at 5942 Ridge Avenue, Cincinnati, Ohio, on or before June 1, 19—. Your lease of the said premises expires on June 1, and I shall take possession of the property on that date.

George Carson

A landlord's notice requesting a tenant to vacate property

IMPROVEMENTS AND FIXTURES

In the absence of an agreement to the contrary, the improvements that are attached to the property become a part of the property and therefore belong to the owner. For instance, if a tenant builds a shed or a garage upon the lot belonging to his landlord, he cannot tear it down or take it away without permission. If a tenant constructs shelves or cupboards in the house that he has rented or leased, he ordinarily cannot take them away when he leaves. In some cases, however, courts have held that such fixtures attached with nails become a part of the property, whereas fixtures attached with screws may be removed.

B. Legal aspects of purchasing a home

Legal ownership of real estate is considered to be one of the treasured privileges and rights of free people. Every civilized country has laws to protect those privileges and rights. The laws are concerned with the public record and title of ownership, the transfer of title from one person to another, and the regulations pertaining to payment. The services of a lawyer should always be obtained when real estate is being purchased or sold.

REAL ESTATE AGREEMENTS MUST BE IN WRITING

State laws require that most agreements relating to the purchase and sale of real estate be in writing in order to be effective or legally binding on the parties involved. Therefore, in buying or selling real estate, the safest practice is to have all agreements in writing and properly signed.

TITLE TO REAL ESTATE

The *title* to real estate is the ownership of the property. If a person has a clear title to a piece of real estate, there are no other claims against that property. To establish evidence of a clear title involves an investigation that will prove the true ownership of the property by tracing the history and the legality of the previous transfers of the title. Usually a loan on a piece of property cannot be obtained until the lender is certain that the title is satisfactory. The charge for examining the title is usually added to the loan or is paid as a special charge.

Title examination. Each legal transfer of the title to a piece of property is recorded in a register of deeds, usually kept in the county or parish courthouse. It is advisable to have a competent lawyer examine the records and determine whether there is a clear title to the property and whether there are any back taxes due, assessments against the property, or any other claims against it.

In some states, individuals and companies specialize in the practice of making examinations of the titles to property. A report of the

information taken from the recorded history of the property is referred to as an *abstract of title*. The report of the individual or the
company making the abstract is called an *opinion of the title*. It is
also possible to obtain a *title-guarantee policy* from such a company.
This insurance policy guarantees that the title is clear and that no
claims are against it.

In order to eliminate uncertainties and to reduce the expense of
transferring the titles to property, some states have established a special system of registering titles. This is known as the *Torrens System*.
For instance, the owner of land applies for a registration of the title
to his land. An officer then examines the records, and, if the title is
good, he issues a *certificate of title*. Each time the title is transferred
thereafter, a new certificate is issued. Under this system an abstract
is usually not necessary.

Deeds, the written evidence of title. A *deed* is written evidence of
the ownership of a piece of real property and serves as a means of
conveying the title from one person to another. The one who transfers the title to the property to another is called the *grantor* of the
deed, and the one to whom the title is transferred is called the *grantee*
of the deed. There àre two general types of deeds: (a) the warranty
deed and (b) the quitclaim deed. In a few states there is also a *grant
deed*, which is a limited warranty deed.

A *warranty deed* not only conveys the interest of the grantor to the
grantee, but also involves statements that certain facts relating to the
title are true. A warranty deed is illustrated on page 629. The warranty deed is more commonly used than the quitclaim deed.

A *quitclaim deed* merely relinquishes the interest that the grantor
may have in the property. The grantee assumes the risk that the title
may not be good. In some communities a quitclaim deed is used
instead of a warranty deed.

Consider this example: Mr. Allis desires to transfer real estate to
Mr. Bush. He grants a warranty deed as evidence of the transfer of
the title. In investigating the title, Mr. Bush discovers that a former
owner, Mr. Carter, at one time had a claim against the property. Mr.
Bush is therefore not quite sure that the claim has been settled fully.
To protect his rights that are granted in the warranty deed, Mr. Bush
gets Mr. Carter to grant a quitclaim deed relinquishing any rights
that the latter may have had in the property.

The important elements in a deed are the description of the property, signature, seal, witnesses, acknowledgment, delivery, and accept-

WARRANTY DEED

Know All Men by These Presents:

That Scott Travis and Dorothy Travis, his wife

of Campbell   County,

in consideration of Five thousand dollars ($5,000)

to them *in hand paid by* Gerald H. Freeman

do *hereby* **Grant, Bargain, Sell and Convey**

to the said Gerald H. Freeman,

his heirs

and assigns forever, the following described **Real Estate** *situate in the* Inverness Subdivision
of Oakley   *in the County of* Hamilton   *and State of* Ohio

Lot sixteen (16), block three (3)

and all the **Estate, Right, Title and Interest** *of the said grantors in and to said premises;* **To have and to hold** *the same, with all the privileges and appurtenances thereunto belonging, to said grantee* , his *heirs and assigns forever. And the said* Scott Travis and Dorothy Travis

do *hereby* **Covenant and Warrant** *that the title so conveyed is* **Clear, Free and Unincumbered,** *and that* they *will* **Defend** *the same against all lawful claims of all persons whomsoever,*

In Witness Whereof, *the said grantor* s *have hereunto set* their *hands* , *this* twentieth *day of* November   *in the year A. D. nineteen hundred and* -- .

Signed and acknowledged in presence of us:

.....P. M. Shock..... | .....Scott Travis.....

.....Anton Hall..... | .....Dorothy Travis.....

State of Ohio   **County, ss.** Hamilton

On this twentieth *day of* November   *A. D. 19* -- , *before me, a* Notary Public
in and for said County, personally came

Scott Travis and Dorothy Travis *the grantor* s *in the foregoing deed, and*
acknowledged the signing thereof to be their *voluntary act and deed.*

Witness *my official signature and seal on the day last above mentioned.*

.....L. H. Cusick.....

A warranty deed

QUITCLAIM DEED

GEORGIA, Lowndes _____**County.**

THIS INDENTURE, Made ___seventh___ day of _____February_____ 19 -- , between
_____John W. Moore_____

of the County of_____Lowndes_____ , and
_____Richard M. Hamilton_____

of the County of_____Lowndes_____

WITNESSETH, That the said ___John W. Moore_____ ,

in consideration of __Ten and no/100 - - - -__ Dollars, receipt of which is hereby acknowledged, ha_S_ bar-

gained and sold, and by these presents doth remise, release and forever quit claim to the said_____

_____Richard M. Hamilton_____

heirs and assigns, all the right, title, interest, claim or demand the said___John W. Moore_____

_____has or may have had in and

to the following described property, to-wit:_____

_____Situate in the City of Valdosta, County of Lowndes, and_____

_____State of Georgia, and being Lot No. 85 on Moss Oak Drive._____

with all the rights, members and appurtenances to said bargained property in anywise appertaining or belonging;

To have and to hold the said property to the said_____Richard M. Hamilton_____

_____his___heirs and assigns so that

neither the said_____John W. Moore_____

nor___his_____heirs nor any other person or persons claiming under___dower_____shall at any time

hereafter, by any way or means, have claim or demand any right, title or interest in or to the aforesaid property or

its appurtenances or any part thereof.

In Witness Whereof, said_____James T. Ebert, Notary Public_____

_____ha_S_ hereto set___his_____hand___, affixed

___his_____seal and delivered these presents, the date first above written.

James T. Ebert   _John W. Moore_

Paul B. Cramer

A quitclaim deed

ance. The laws in different states vary in some respects. To assure a clear title, the person executing the deed should become familiar with local laws. For instance, the laws in various states differ with regard to the ownership of property by man and wife. Some states require the signatures of both, whereas others require only one signature. In some states the witnesses must sign in the presence of one another, whereas in others they must sign only in the presence of an authorized public officer. Because of the many technicalities, the average person should obtain legal advice in granting a deed or in taking title to real estate. It is best to let a lawyer write all the legal papers.

Warranty deed

Essential provisions of a warranty deed:

1. Conveys (transfers) title to buyers.
2. Asserts that title is clear and free from all claims and debts.
3. Guarantees that the title will be defended against all lawful claims if they should arise.

SALES CONTRACT

Often before the actual transfer of the title to real estate, an agreement is reached between the buyer and the seller. This agreement, which should not be confused with a deed, is referred to as a *contract of sale,* a *contract to convey,* or a *land contract.* It is a contract in which the seller agrees to sell under certain conditions and the buyer agrees to buy under certain conditions.

THE MEANING OF ESCROW

In bringing the sale of real estate to a conclusion, the seller sometimes will prepare a deed transferring ownership of the property to the buyer. He will then place this deed in the hands of a third party who is authorized to deliver the deed to the new owner when certain conditions have been fulfilled. This process is called placing the deed in *escrow.* For example, a deed may be placed in escrow until the buyer submits a certified check or bank draft in complete payment. Then the deed is turned over to the buyer. Money may also be placed in escrow to be paid when a deed is delivered.

Legal steps in buying real property

1. Writing and signing a contract of sale.
2. Making a survey of the property to determine its exact size, location, and shape to be sure that the property is exactly as described.
3. Making a title search to determine whether the seller has a clear title to the property.
4. Signing a mortgage if money is borrowed.
5. Obtaining a clearly drawn and legally accurate deed from the seller.
6. Recording the deed in the proper place of registration in the county or the parish in which the land is located.

JOINT OWNERSHIP

In most states a husband and a wife may own real estate together. When property is owned under such a condition, the husband and the wife are considered to own it jointly, neither being the owner of any particular part. Joint ownership by husband and wife is called *tenancy by entirety.* Our law in this respect is fashioned after the English law.

Under the laws of *joint ownership,* when either dies the survivor becomes sole owner of the property. In some states, however, the manner in which the title will pass to the survivor must be indicated in the deed.

There are laws in most states that grant what is called a *dower right* or *dower interest.* This right is conferred upon the wife, who has a legal right to share in the property of her husband. A similar right is granted to the husband, who shares in the property of his wife. This right is known as *curtesy.* Some of these rights have been abolished in certain states, and the laws are not uniform. The laws of many states, however, prohibit either the husband or the wife from selling property unless the signatures of both appear on the deed. This rule holds good even though the property may be recorded in the name of only one.

In some states when property that has been owned jointly by a husband and a wife becomes the sole property of the survivor, it is not subject to an inheritance tax or a state tax, for the survivor is not considered to inherit the property.

MORTGAGE, A CONTRACT BETWEEN LENDER AND BORROWER

If you borrow money to buy or to build a home, you will be required to sign a mortgage, which is given to the person from whom

Closing a deal to buy a home

you borrow the money. A *mortgage* is a contract between the lender and the borrower which states the rights and the obligations of each person. The mortgage states, among other things, how the interest and the principal must be paid and the rights of the lender in case the payments are not made as agreed.

Mortgages are not the same in all states, although they have similar characteristics. Every mortgage should be in writing, and usually the signatures should be witnessed.

In some states a *mortgage bond* is commonly used instead of a mortgage. In other states the instrument is referred to as a *mortgage contract*. Regardless of its title, the legal instrument that is used specifies the amount of the indebtedness and the method of payment. The mortgage is given as security for the payment of the debt. In some transactions in which a mortgage is issued, the borrower must also sign a note or a series of notes that will become due on certain dates.

In most states the laws require that a mortgage, in order to be effective protection against subsequent buyers or mortgagees, must be recorded in the courthouse of the county or parish in which the property is located. This procedure enables other interested people to discover any claims against the property.

DEED OF TRUST

In some states (California, Colorado, Illinois, Mississippi, Missouri, New Mexico, Tennessee, Virginia, and West Virginia), a *deed of trust* is used for the same purposes as a mortgage. It is also called a *trust deed* or a *trust indenture*.

While serving the same purpose as a mortgage, a deed of trust operates in a slightly different way. The mortgage involves the lender and the borrower. The deed of trust involves three persons: the lender, the borrower, and a trustee. The borrower executes a deed of trust to the property, conveying the property in trust to the lender. The trustee holds the deed of trust in favor of the lender. The borrower signs a series of notes and gives these to the lender. If the

Know All Men by These Presents:

That   James D. Graham   of   Montgomery   County, Ohio,
in consideration of the sum of Three Thousand ($3,000) Dollars
to   him   *in hand paid by*   Raymond E. Kelly
                    does hereby **Grant, Bargain, Sell and Convey**
to the said   Raymond E. Kelly   *his* *heirs*
and assigns forever, the following described **Real Estate**, *situate in the*   City
of   Miamisburg   *in the County of*   Montgomery   *and State of Ohio.*
    Lot No. 103 on Blanchard Road of the Far Hills subdivision.
and all the **Estate, Right, Title and Interest** *of the said grantor in and to said prem-*
ises; **To have and to hold** *the same, with all the privileges and appurtenances there-*
unto belonging, to said grantee,   his   *heirs and assigns forever. And the said*
                    James D. Graham   *does hereby*
Covenant and Warrant *that the title so conveyed is* **Clear, Free and Unincumbered,**
and that   he   *will* **Defend** *the same against all lawful claims of all persons*
whomsoever.

    Provided Nevertheless, *That* if the said James D. Graham shall well
and truly pay or cause to be paid, his certain promissory note of
even date herewith, for Three Thousand ($3,000) Dollars drawn to
the order of Raymond E. Kelly and payable in three years from
date, with interest at six (6) per cent per annum

then these presents shall be void.

In Witness Whereof, *the said*   James D. Graham
            who   *hereby releases*   his   *right and expectancy of dower in said*
premises, has   *hereunto set* his   *hand , this*   seventh *day of* November
in the year of our Lord one thousand nine hundred and -------

Signed and acknowledged in presence of us: *James D. Graham*

        Dennis Gray

        Howard Wright

The State of   Ohio   **County of**   Montgomery   **ss.**
    Be It Remembered, *That on the*   seventh   *day of*
        November   *in the year of our Lord one thousand nine*
hundred and ------   *before me, the subscriber, a*
            Notary Public   *in and for said county, personally came*
            James D. Graham
the grantor   in the foregoing Mortgage, and acknowledged the signing thereof to
be   his   *voluntary act, for the uses and purposes therein mentioned.*
                In Testimony Whereof, *I have hereunto subscribed*
                    my name, and affixed my   official   *seal,*
                    on the day and year last aforesaid.

                    Warren J. Lasure

A mortgage

notes are not paid, the trustee, after proper legal proceedings, will convey the property to the lender.

RIGHTS AND DUTIES OF THE MORTGAGOR AND THE MORTGAGEE

Any person who owns an interest in land, buildings, or even crops raised on land may mortgage that interest. The person who owns the land and borrows the money through a mortgage is called the *mortgagor*. The person who lends the money and holds the mortgage as evidence of his claim is called the *mortgagee*.

In the eyes of the law, the mortgagor is the legal owner of the property. The property is merely pledged as security for the payment of a debt, and the mortgage is the written contract acknowledging the debt. A mortgage on real estate includes equipment that has become so permanently attached to the real estate that it is considered a part of it. If a piece of land is mortgaged, and a house is later built on the land, the house will be included in the mortgage, for it has become a part of the land.

The mortgagor is under duty to refrain from destroying or damaging the property. The mortgagee must not interfere with the occupancy of the property except through agreement with the mortgagor or through legal procedure. If a mortgagee sells a mortgage to a third person, he should give the mortgagor a notice of transfer.

When the indebtedness is paid, the mortgage is automatically canceled. It is wise, however, for the mortgagor to obtain the mortgage, the mortgage note, and a statement acknowledging the discharge of the obligation. The notice acknowledging the discharge of the obligation should be recorded in the proper place of registration, usually the county or parish courthouse.

MORTGAGE FORECLOSURE

If a mortgagor fails to fulfill his obligation, the mortgagee has the right of *foreclosure*, that is, of bringing a lawsuit to obtain possession of the property and title to it. Foreclosure may consist of (a) a court order that transfers the title to the property from the mortgagor to the mortgagee, or (b) a court order that requires the property to be sold to pay the mortgagee.

Although a mortgage contract usually specifies that the mortgagor loses all rights to the mortgaged property if the obligation is not performed at a specified time, the laws in most states permit the mortgagor to regain his interest in the property by fulfilling his contract at any time before the foreclosure of the mortgage.

If the proceeds from the sale of the property exceed the total of the indebtedness and the expenses incident to the sale, the mortgagor gets the difference. If the proceeds are less than the amount of the indebtedness, the mortgagee has a right, in most states, to obtain a judgment against the mortgagor for the difference. This judgment is referred to as a *deficiency judgment.*

Points to investigate in buying real estate

1. What unsettled claims are there against the property?
2. Are any assessments or taxes due?
3. Are any street, sidewalk, or sewer improvements likely for which there will be future additional assessments?
4. Do any unfavorable zoning laws affect the property?
5. Is the property mortgaged? If so, can the mortgage be transferred to the new owner?
6. Have arrangements been made for the proper insurance on the property at the time of purchase?
7. Have the fees to be charged by the lawyer been checked?
8. Are all agreements in writing, including the settlement of old claims against the property?

Because of the possibilities of a deficiency judgment, the mortgagor does not release himself, under the laws of some states, from his obligation merely by giving up his property. For example, Mr. and Mrs. Charles purchased a home. They paid $2,000 in cash and borrowed $8,000 on a mortgage to pay for the home. They failed to repay the money as agreed. The person who loaned the money and held the mortgage foreclosed through the proper legal proceedings. The property was sold to settle the claim, which at the time of the foreclosure amounted to $7,500. The property was sold for $7,000, which was paid to the holder of the mortgage (mortgagee), leaving a deficiency of $500. The court granted a deficiency judgment of $500 against Mr. and Mrs. Charles, which they are required to pay to the mortgagee.

One piece of property may have as many as three mortgages. If it is sold through foreclosure proceedings, the mortgagees must be protected according to the preference given to their respective mortgages.

In many states a mortgagor who has lost his property through foreclosure is given a certain time (usually one year) in which he may redeem or recover his property after the foreclosure. The property may be redeemed by paying the amount due plus interest at a stipulated rate.

CLAIMS AGAINST REAL ESTATE

Any claim on real estate that arises from a debt is referred to as a *lien*. A mortgage is one type of lien. A *mechanic's lien* is another. For instance, a contractor who has constructed a building may hold a lien against the property for the payment of the amount due him. A judgment rendered by a court as the result of a lawsuit is still another kind of lien.

Facts everyone should know about the legal aspects of obtaining a home

1. Renting and leasing are legally the same and agreements may be written or oral.
2. A tenant has a right to peaceful and uninterrupted possession of the property.
3. A tenant is generally obligated to make normal repairs, but not improvements.
4. Agreements in regard to purchasing or selling real estate must be in writing.
5. A deed is a written evidence of title or ownership of real estate.
6. A man and a wife may jointly own property, but the laws of joint ownership are not the same in different states.
7. A mortgage is a contract between lender and borrower and involves many different rights and obligations.

▪ QUESTIONS ON THE TEXT

1. (a) What is the difference between a landlord and a lessor?
   (b) Between a tenant and a lessee?
2. What is a real estate lease?
3. Why is a written lease desirable?
4. What information is usually embodied in a written lease?
5. What is the distinction between renting and leasing?
6. Are there any restrictions on the use of rented property?
7. In the absence of any agreement, when is rent usually due?
8. (a) Under what circumstances must the tenant notify the landlord of his intentions to give up the use of the property?
   (b) Under what circumstances is a notice unnecessary?
9. Who is liable for damages if an invited guest of the tenant is injured on the property?
10. May the landlord enter the premises of a tenant at any time he wishes?

11. Who ordinarily pays the taxes and assessments on property that is rented?
12. Under what circumstances must the landlord make repairs and improvements?
13. When a tenant vacates the property, may he take with him a dishwasher which he has built into the kitchen cabinets?
14. Are oral agreements in regard to purchasing or selling real estate enforceable?
15. How is it possible to determine whether there are any claims against a piece of real estate?
16. What protection can one obtain against the possibility that the title to a piece of property may not be good?
17. What is the advantage of the Torrens System of registering land?
18. What is a deed?
19. (a) Who is the grantor of a deed?
    (b) Who is the grantee of a deed?
20. (a) What are the two general types of deeds?
    (b) In what ways do they differ?
21. (a) What is a contract of sale?
    (b) What is meant by escrow?
22. If real estate is recorded in the name of the wife only, can she sell the property without the consent of her husband?
23. Name the legal steps in buying real estate.
24. What is a mortgage?
25. Explain the difference between a mortgage and a deed of trust.
26. (a) Who is a mortgagor?
    (b) Who is a mortgagee?
27. If the mortgagor fails to pay the claim against the mortgaged property, what right has the mortgagee?
28. After the mortgage on real estate has been foreclosed, is there any means by which the mortgagor may recover the property?
29. What is a lien? Give examples.

▪ QUESTIONS FOR DISCUSSION

1. (a) What are some of the advantages of a written lease to the lessee?
   (b) What are some of the disadvantages to the lessee?
2. (a) What are some of the advantages of a written lease to the lessor?
   (b) What are some of the disadvantages to the lessor?
3. (a) May a tenant change the property that he has leased by making physical alterations?
   (b) May he repair it without the consent of the owner?
4. Mr. Jones rented a house from Mr. Adams. Mr. White was injured on a broken step while visiting Mr. Jones. Who is responsible for the injury?

5. Is a refrigerator or a stove considered part of a house that is mortgaged? Explain your answer in detail.

6. Explain why agreements pertaining to the purchasing or selling of real estate must be in writing.

7. Discuss the conditions under which a TV and FM antenna installed by a tenant may be removed when the tenant moves.

8. If a mortgage on a home is foreclosed
    (a) Who gets the extra money if the property is sold for more than the mortgage claim?
    (b) What may happen if the amount obtained from the sale is not sufficient to pay the mortgage?
    (c) What, if anything, can be done by the mortgagor to get his property back again?

9. Mr. Whiteside made a contract with Majestic Home Builders to construct a house and arranged to borrow money from the First National Bank to pay for it. Before the bank will make the final payment to the builder, it has insisted on proof that the plumber, carpenter, and all other workers and suppliers have been paid. Explain why the bank has asked for such proof.

10. Who needs the services of an attorney in transactions pertaining to leasing and to purchasing and selling real estate?

■ **PROBLEMS TO SOLVE**

1. John Dickerson bought a lot that was 85 feet wide and 140 feet deep and paid $27.50 a front foot for it. He paid his attorney $50 for services rendered and an abstract company $185 for an opinion of the title and for title-guarantee insurance. In addition, he paid the county recording **fee of $3.**
    (a) What was the total cost of the lot to Mr. Dickerson?
    (b) How much was the front-foot cost increased by the fees charged?

2. About six months ago, Mr. Palmer bought from Mr. Johnson a lot valued at $3,200. Mr. Johnson delivered a quitclaim deed to the property. In reading tax-notice information in the local newspaper, Mr. Palmer was surprised to learn a few days ago that there is an unpaid-tax lien on the property for property taxes not paid over the past three years. Mr. Palmer, of course, must pay the $157 in taxes if he is to retain undisputed ownership of the lot. Does he have any recourse to Mr. Johnson for this unexpected cost?

3. Mr. Watkins rented a house from Mr. Olsen under a written lease extending for one year. Six months before the expiration of the lease, Mr. Olsen decided that he wanted to remodel the house to get it ready for sale. Mr. Watkins objected, but Mr. Olsen brought workmen to the house and insisted upon entering in order to begin the work. Who is right in this argument?

4. Under a five-year written lease, Mr. Cowen occupied a house owned by Mr. Carson. After two years of occupancy, Mr. Carson sold the house to Mr. Griffin. Mr. Griffin insisted upon immediate occupancy. Can Mr. Griffin force Mr. Cowen to move?

5. Two years ago Mr. Roberts obtained permission from his landlord, Mr. Andrews, to build a recreation room in the house he was renting. Now, Mr. Roberts has purchased a home, and he intends to remove the lumber, plasterboard, and other materials he used to construct the walls of the recreation room. Mr. Andrews informs Mr. Roberts that he cannot remove the walls from the basement. Who is right?

▪ COMMUNITY PROBLEMS AND PROJECTS

1. Visit the office of the register of deeds at your county courthouse. Obtain information about the procedure in your community for recording deeds and mortgages. Describe the procedure to be followed and the fees that are charged.

2. Obtain copies of the legal documents which are used in the renting and buying of homes in your community. Sources of such documents are banks, savings and loan associations, lawyers, and so forth. For each document, or type of document, prepare a brief statement regarding its general purpose, the extent of its use in your community, and other pertinent information. Then plan and prepare a bulletin board display of the documents and the related statements that you have prepared.

3. The legal vocabulary relating to the buying of a home includes terms you will seldom meet in daily life. The home buying and selling language includes such terms as earnest money, escrow, easement, lien, and tenancy, and many more that make buying, and even renting, quite complex. Following careful study of the material in this chapter, prepare an extensive list of the terms you believe relate to the buying and renting of homes. For each of the terms, prepare what you believe is an adequate definition of it. Then take your list of terms and the definitions of them to a banker, lawyer, or real-estate agent. Have him study your list, criticize your definitions, and suggest the terms that should be added to or deleted from it. Follow this activity up with consideration of the terminology in a class discussion.

4. Visit the office of an apartment building or an apartment development in your community. Find out whether a written lease is used when a new tenant moves into one of the apartments. Also find out the answers to the following questions: What is the length of the tenancy period? Who must make repairs to the property? Is the rent paid in advance? Is a deposit of a certain amount of money required before the tenant can take possession? Is there a particular manner in which payment must be made? What other conditions and agreements are stated in the lease?

Index

A

Ability-to-pay theory of taxation, 279
Abstract of title, 628
Acceptability of money, 182
Account, charge, 347; coupon or scrip, 350; open, 347; service, 347
Accounting, national income or social, 243
Add-on basis of computing finance charges, 373
Administrator, 557
Advertisements, guides in analyzing, 454
Advertising, 67; and mass production, 385; benefits the consumer, 393; consumer, 389; consumer analysis of, 392; control of, 415; control of, for consumer protection, 389; cost of, 390; cost per dollar of sales, 391; creates discontent, 387; critical views of, 386; economic benefits of, 395; economic functions of, 383; educational value of, 394; expenditures for, 390; hidden benefits of, 392; increases consumer prices, 388; kinds of, 389; objective of, 384; net effect of, on consumer prices, 392; primary, 389; product information, 394; promotes unwise choices, 388; selective, 389; social and cultural goals, 394; specific functions of, 386; stimulation of demand, 384; value of, in general, 452; wise use of, in making consumer decisions, 452
Age of majority, 430
Agency shop, 89
Agent, bargaining, 89; business, 85
Aggregate income, 236
Aggregate production, 236
Agreements, defective, 436; examples of voidable, 436
Agriculture, government aids to, 148; government aids to, that affect consumer prices and taxes, 151; protective aids to, 148; subsidies to, 149; tariffs affect, 311

Agricultural Marketing Service, 408
Agricultural production, special problems of, 51
Agricultural Research Service, 408
American Dental Association, 401
American Federation of Labor (AFL), 82; merger of, and CIO, 83
American Home Economic Association, 401
American Medical Association, 401
American Standards Association, 404
Annuities, 477
Annuity contract, 531
Appraisal, 513
Appraisals, 604
Apprentices, 81
Arbitration, 96
Arbitrator, 97
Assembling, 65
Assets, 467
Assignment, of insurance policy, 509
Attachment, 356
Auction market, 72
Auctioneer, 72
Automation, 49
Automobile Information Disclosure Act, 417
Automobile insurance, 516; bodily injury liability, 516; collision, 518; comprehensive physical damage, 518; factors affecting the cost of, 519; medical payments coverage, 517; property damage liability, 516; protection against uninsured motorists, 518

B

Bacon-Davis Act, 169
Balance of payments, deficits and gold outflow, 304; definition of, 303; U.S., 303
Balance of trade, 302
Bankruptcy, 356; involuntary, 357; voluntary, 357
Bank savings, 200
Bank credit, control over, 210
Bank drafts, 320
Bank money order, 322

Bank reserves, excess, 208, 210; free, 208; maintaining centralized, 207; required, 207, 210
Bank statement, reconciliation of, 319
Banking institutions, 199
Banks, 199; a source of real estate loans, 606; and their functions, 199; bankers, 207; borrowing from, 330; charge account services by, 325; commercial, 200, 473; economic functions and services of, 202; financial and tax advice by, 324; industrial, 200, 474; instant credit by, 325; kinds of, as to organization, 201; making loans to member, 208; Morris Plan, 200; mutual savings, 473; national, 201; revolving credit by, 325; savings, 473; state, 201; travel service offered by, 324; trust functions of, 323
Bargain sales, 448; examples of, 449
Bargaining agent, 89
Base period, 231
Beneficiary, 527; changing the, 536
Benefit taxes, 287
Better business bureaus, 404
Bill of sale, 435
Blank indorsement, 327
Blue-sky laws, 419
Board of directors of a corporation, 132
Bodily injury liability, 516
Bonds, at discount or premium, 488; callable, 488; comparisons of corporation, and stocks, 489; convertible, 488; corporation, 487; coupon, 487; debenture, 488; foreign, 482; government, 481; mortgage, 488; municipal, 482; real estate mortgage, 493; registered, 487; Series E savings, 474; Series H savings, 474; U.S. government, 481
Borrowing, from banks, 330; from consumer finance companies, 333; from credit unions, 335; from life insurance companies, 331; from pawnbrokers, 337; from sav-

641

ings and loan associations, 331; from unlicensed lenders, 337
Boycott, 94; primary, 95; secondary, 95
Brand name, 453
Breach of warranty, 438; remedies for, 438
Broker, 72; investment, 496; stock, 496
Budget, 463; deficit, 263
Budget charge account, 349
Budget spending plan, advantages of a, 448
Budget surplus, 263
Budgeting, first step, 463
Building and loan associations, 331
Bureau of Labor Statistics, 419
Bureau of Standards, 148
Business, assists in paying the cost of government, 44; characteristics of, 125; classes of, 126; creates jobs, 43; definition of, 125; develops new products, 42; functions of, 40; government aids to, 148; government aids to, that affect consumer prices and taxes, 151; government engages in, 146; government regulation of, 151; growth, 128; how we benefit from, 50; in the production process, 40; making decisions in, 242; number of, establishments, 127; objective of, 126; people employed in, 127; performs complex tasks for consumers, 42; protective aids to, 148; provides organized markets, 45; provides tools and equipment for production, 43; raises the level of living, 42; size, 128; types of information on, 243
Business activities, fluctuations in, 235
Business activity, measuring, 242; sources of information on, 243
Business agent, 85
Business cycle, 236; causes of the, 237; characteristics of the, 238; phases of the, 236
Business conditions, problem of fluctuating, 235
Business enterprise, legal forms of, 129; organization of, 125
Business firms, profits of, 128
Business fluctuations, controlling, 256; effect of extreme, 257; role of government in controlling, 256
Business organizations, 125; legal types of, 129
Business success, factors affecting, 242

Business taxes, 287
Buyer, remedies of, when seller fails to perform, 440
Buying, 65; cash and credit, 459; is choice making, 446; quantity, 451; safety factor in, 597; specific guides in, 452
Bylaws, of a corporation, 132

C

Callable bonds, 488
Capital, 36, 37, 108, 353; foreign, 307; needed to create jobs, 108; net outflows of U.S. private, 306; sources of new, 111; taxes affect new, 111; working, 109
Capital goods, 2, 37; function of, 109
Capital outflows, U.S., 306
Capitalist, 129
Carte Blanche, 350
Cash, 185; estimating available, 464
Cash record, daily, needed, 466
Cash value, of a life insurance policy, 528, 535
Cashier's check, 321
Certificate of deposit, 323
Certificate of title, 628
Certified check, 321
Certified Life Underwriter (C.L.U.), 549
Charge account, 347; budget, 349; credit-bank plan of, 349; depositor's, 350; divided, 349; cost of, 351; revolving, 349; types of, 349
Charge account service offered by banks, 325
Charter, of a bank, 199; of a corporation, 132
Chattel mortgage contract, 363
Check, 318; cashier's, 321; certified, 321; postdating, 320; register, 322; stopping payment on a, 319; traveler's, 322; treasurer's, 321
Checkbook money, 184
Checking account, joint, 318; service charges on a, 320; survivorship, 318
Checking accounts, 318
Checking account service, 318
Checkoff system, 89
Checks, clearing, between local banks, 204; clearing out-of-town, 205; special, 320
Choice, and real cost, 8
Choices, 4
Civil liberties, as goal, 10
Civilian labor force, 101
Clearinghouse, 204
Close corporation, 133, 486
Closed-end investment company, 491

Closed shop, 89, 166
Coins, 183
Collateral, 208, 329
Collective bargaining, 86; and industrial conflict, 88; arguments against, 87; arguments for, 87
Collision insurance, 518
Comaker, 329
Commercial bank, 300
Commercial banks, 473
Commercial Standards Recommendations, 408
Commission, 72
Commission man, 72
Commission market, 72
Committee on Industrial Organization (CIO), formation of, 83
Commodity market, 73
Commodity taxes, 286
Common stock, 482
Company union, 96
Compensation, of employees, 247
Competent parties, 429
Competition, 24; and prices, 223; and profits, 171; definition of, 25; factors in export, 297; nonprice, 223; promotion of free and fair, 413
Comprehensive personal liability insurance, 514
Comprehensive physical damage insurance, 518
Conciliation, 97
Conditional sales contract, 364; illustration of a, 365
Congress of Industrial Organizations, merger of AFL and, 83
Consumer, tariffs affect the, 312
Consumer advertising, 389
Consumer cooperatives, by type of association, 137
Consumer credit, 189, 244, 345; outstanding, 190
Consumer-credit insurance, 373
Consumer finance companies, borrowing from, 333
Consumer finance company, 367
Consumer goods, 2
Consumer prices, 243; net effect of advertising on, 392
Consumer protection, by professional associations, 401; city and state, 406; consumer-sponsored services, 399; consumers' need for information, 398; control of advertising for, 390; government sources of, 406; labeling for, 402; private sources of, 398; testing for, 402; U.S. Department of Commerce, 406
Consumers' Research, Inc., 399
Consumers Union of United States, Inc., 400

Consumption, 39, 40, 64; curtailment of, 113; influenced by prices, 220
Contract, carrying out the, 437; definition of a, 425; land, 631; legal purpose of, 432; sales, 631; to convey, 631
Contracts, consideration, 433; essentials of written, 434; express, 436; implied, 436; land, 609; oral, 434; proper legal form of, 434; voidable, 430, 436; written, 434
Convertible bonds, 488
Convertible preferred stock, 486
Cooling-off period, 97
Cooperative, 135; characteristics of a, 136
Cooperative apartment, buying a, 597
Cooperative banks, 331
Cooperatives, consumer, by type of association, 137
Corporate profits, 248
Corporation, 132; advantages of the, 134; characteristics of a, 135; chart of the organization of a, 132; close, 133, 486; closely held, 133; disadvantages of the, 135; open, 133, 486; public, 134, 486; publicly held, 134
Corporation bonds, 487; callable, 488; comparisons of, and stock, 489; convertible, 488; coupon, 487; debenture, 488; mortgage, 488; registered, 487
Corporation income tax returns, 285
Cosigner, 329
Cosmetic standards, 412
Cost, choice and real, 8; of distribution, 75
Cost-of-service-received theory of taxation, 279
Council on Consumer Information, 400
Counteroffer, 429
Coupon bonds, 487
Craft guild, 81
Craft union, 81
Credit, 186, 344; affects prices, 226; and debt, 194; application for, 353; business, 189; classification of, 345; consumer, 189, 244, 345; commercial, 189; economic problems of, 357; effect of, 188; essentials of, 344; expanding purchasing power with, 192; forms of, 345; functions of, 187; government, 189; government regulation of, 229; home mortgages, 191; importance of, 344; increases purchasing power, 187; installment, 346; 361; instant, 325; instruments

of, 188; intermediate-term, 345; kinds of, 188; line of, establishing a, 353; nature of, 186; noninstallment, 346; revolving, 325; short-term, 345
Credit buying, 459
Credit cards, 350
Credit life insurance, 373
Credit rating agencies, 354
Credit standing, establishing, 351
Credit terms, 347
Credit unions, 201, 476; borrowing from, 335; interest rates charged by, 336; membership and operation of, 336
Cumulative preferred stock, 485
Currency, 183; managed paper, 186; paper, issuing, 207
Curtesy, 632
Customer protection, 203
Customs duties, 310; ad valorem, 310; specific, 310
Cycle billing, 348

D

Death taxes, 287
Debenture bonds, 488
Debt, 345; installment, 346; noninstallment, 346
Debts, responsibility for, 355
Deed, 628; grant, 628; quitclaim, 628; warranty, 628
Deed of trust, 633
Deficiency judgment, 636
Deficit, 307; solving the, problem, 307
Deficits, and liquid liabilities, 304
Deflation, 209, 239; ways to halt, 241
Demand, 40, 220; a farm problem, 52; determines production, 39; effective, 39; elastic, 221; for labor, 166; for labor, factors affecting, 166; inelastic, 221; price and, 220; stimulation of, 384
Demand deposits, 318
Department of Health, Education, and Welfare, 409
Deposit, certificate of, 323; time, 323, 473
Depositors, insurance protection of, 203
Depositor's account, 350
Deposits, demand, 318
Depreciation, 595
Depression, 236
Descriptive labeling, 457
Direct marketing, 75
Direct taxes, 280
Direct-reduction loan, 611
Direct strike, 93

Discount, 209; bonds at, 488
Discount houses, buying from, 451
Discounts, 348
Disposable personal income, 174
Distribution, channel of, 74; cost of, 75; problem of, 120; production and, 117
Distribution system, marketing, 61
Diversification, 53
Divided charge account, 349
Dividend patronage, 136
Dollar-averaging principle, 497
Dower right or interest, 632
Drafts, bank, 320
Drawee, of check, 318
Drawer, of check, 318
Drug standards, 411
Durable goods, 157

E

Economic activity, 6
Economic freedoms, 10; as goals, 10; of citizens under a free-enterprise system, 12
Economic goals, 7; in America, 7; national, 9; personal, 7
Economic goods, 2
Economic growth, 112; cost of, 113; curtailment of consumption, 113; factors in, 112; meaning of, 112; national, 108; population and, 112; sacrifice of leisure, 113
Economic independence, American's desire for, 564
Economic indicators, examples of, 248
Economic rent, 163
Economics, definition of, 3; simple truths of, 1
Economic services, 2; performing, 38
Economic stability, conditions favorable to, 256
Economic system, role of government in our, 143
Economic value, 215
Economic vote, 12
Economic wants, 3; satisfying our, 5
Economy, 450; national, 157; private sector of the, 259; public sector of, 259
Effective demand, 39
Elastic demand, 221
Emergency Price Control, 229
Employees, compensation of, 247
Employers, methods used by, in industrial conflict, 95
Employment, full, 103; problem, 101; technology and, 106
Employment status and wages, 244

Endowment insurance, 476, 530
Enterprise, individual, 129
Entrepreneur, 36
Equipment, business provides, for production, 43
Escrow, meaning of, 631
Estate, administering an, 324; creating a cash, for investment, 555, defined, 536; insurance as a factor in a person's, 556
Estate tax, 287
European Atomic Energy Community, 310
European Coal and Steel Community (ECSC), 309
European Common Market, 309
European Free Trade Association (EFTA), 309
Exchange, 73
Exchanges, stock, 134
Excise tax, 281
Exclusive deals, prevention of, 413
Executor, 557
Expenditures, 464; estimating, 465
Exports, 159; foreign nations need our, 295
Express contracts, 436
Express warranties, 437
Extended term insurance, 535

F

Fair Labor Standards Act, 169
Fair-trade laws, 414; arguments against, 414; arguments in favor of, 414; provisions of, 414
Family housing, 581; obtaining, 586
Farm aids, 53
Farm controls, 53
Farm production problems, 51; aids and controls, 53; efficiency, 51; natural hazards, 53; soil and climate, 53; supply, demand, and price, 52
Farms, classified by acreage, 51
Featherbedding, 92
Federal budget, 262; deficit, 263; reflects fiscal policy, 264; surplus, 263
Federal Credit Union Act of 1934, 476
Federal Deposit Insurance Corporation, 474
Federal Food and Drug Administration, 410
Federal Food, Drug, and Cosmetic Act, 410
Federal Home Loan Bank, 474
Federal Housing Administration (FHA), 614

Federal reserve note, 207
Federal Reserve System, 205; buying short-term securities, 211; control of speculation, 212; functions of the, 207; making loans to member banks, 208; open-market operations of, 211; organization of the, 205; regulating business activity, 209
Federal Savings and Loan Insurance Corporation, 474
Federal Social Security Act, 565
Federal taxes, a stabilizer, 261
Federal Trade Commission, 139, 412
Federal Wage-Hour Law, 169
FHA loans, regulations, 615; secured, 333; where and how to apply for, 615
Finance charge, on installment sale, 372
Finance charges, add-on basis of computing, 373; computing, 373; percent-per-month basis of computing, 375
Finance companies, 366; banks and other lending agencies, 368; consumer, 367; sales, 366
Financial advice, by banks, 324
Financial institutions, other, 201
Financial management, savings and, 470
Fiscal policy, control through, 259; type of government control, 257
Flammable Fabrics Act, 417
Fluctuations, in business activities, 235
Food standards, 411
Foreclosure, mortgage, 635
Foreign bonds, 482
Foreign exchange, 299; a simple illustration in, 299; involving several exporters and importers, 300
Foreign investments, income on, in the U.S., 306
Foreign purchasers, 159
Foreign, trade, see International trade, 294; position of the U.S. on, 308
Form utility, 40
Franchise, 138, 287
Fraud, preventing, 437
Free enterprise, essential characteristics of, 19
Free-enterprise system, 9; American, 19; economic freedoms of citizens under, 12; nature of the, 19
Free good, 2
Free market system, 21; distribution in, 26; how government influences the, 30, 31; production in the, 26
Fringe benefits, 91

Full employment, 103
Fur, used, 416; waste, 417
Fur product, 416
Fur Products Labeling Act, 416

G

Garnishment of wages, 356
Gasoline taxes, 281
General Agreement on Tariffs and Trade (GATT), 309
General medical expense insurance, 539
General sales taxes, 286
Gift taxes, 288
Goods, capital, 2, 37; capital, function of, 109; consumer, 2; control of prices of, by government, 228; durable, 157; economic, 2; entrusted to others, 441; final, 157; free, 2; nondurable, 157; not ordered, 441; producer, 2
Goods and services, receipts for, 306; U.S. expenditures for, 306
Government, 38; business assists in paying the cost of, 44; engages in business, 146; financial operations of, 264; financing the functions of, 264; purchaser of goods and services, 159; role of, in our economic system, 143
Government aids, for industrial development, 149; to business and agriculture, 148; to business and agriculture that affect consumer prices and taxes, 151; to management, 148
Government bonds, 481; foreign, 482; municipal, 482; sale of, by banks, 325; U.S., 481
Government control, fiscal policy, 257; monetary policy, 257; types of, 257
Government credit, 189
Government expenditures, 265; federal, state, and local, 265
Government finance, 264
Government grants, U.S., 306
Government loans, repayments in U.S., 307
Government receipts, 265
Government regulation, of business, 151; of business, why imposed, 152
Government-secured real estate loans, 614
Government services, control of, 144; dependence upon, 146; for special groups, 146; for the public, 146; growth of, 143; issues of, 145; who pays for, 144

Government spending, 259; effect of, 260; payments for pensions, subsidies, and interest, 260; total, 261
Government surveys and statistics, 243
Grace period, of life insurance policy, 535
Grades, 455; using, as guides, 455
Grading, 66
Grantee, 628
Grantor, 628
Grievance procedure, 96
Gross national product (GNP), 112, 157, 243, 244; as an indicator of business conditions, 245; population and, 112
Group insurance, 532; permanent, 532; term, 532
Guild, craft, 81; merchant, 81

H

Health insurance, 538; and medical care for the aged, 572; general medical expense, 539; hospital expense, 538; loss-of-income, 540; major medical expense, 539; purpose of, 538; surgical expense, 539; voluntary supplementary plan, 573
Hidden taxes, 281
Home, advantages of owning a, 582; amount of loan on, 591; amount of yearly payments on, 591; analysis of financing costs, 589; buying for cash, 587; cautions in building a, 584; choices of ways to build a, 584; cost of, and annual income, 588; deciding on kind of, 583; disadvantages of owning a, 582; down payment on, 588; first-year cost of financing a, 590; initial occupancy costs, 589; insurance on, 592; legal aspects of leasing or renting a, 622; legal aspects of purchasing a, 627; legal problems of obtaining a, 621; monthly payment on, 589; paying for the, 587; renting or leasing, 592; selecting a, 585; taxes and assessments on, 592; upkeep of, 592; value of house and lot, 591; when to buy a, 585
Home mortgages, 191
Home ownership, comparison of, and renting, 594; first-year cost of, compared with renting, 595; fitting cash outlay into the budget, 596

Homeowners policy, 511; amount of coverage, 513; comprehensive personal liability provision of, 514; liability insurance under the, 514; medical payments provision of, 515; perils not covered, 513; physical damage to the property of others clause in, 515; property covered, 512; property insurance under the, 511; need for inventory, 513
Homestead associations, 331
Hospital expense insurance, 538
Household inventory record, 514
Household products labeling, 412
Housing, providing, for the family, 581

I

Implied contracts, 436
Implied warranties, 437
Imports, 159; of essential commodities by U.S., 295
Impulse items, 448
Income, 464; aggregate, 236; as a goal, 8; buying sufficient insurance to yield, 555; claim of government on, 173; definition of, 13; disposable personal, 174; distribution of, among producers, 163; distribution of, an illustration of, 163; earned by labor, 165; earned by landowners, 163; earned by owners, 171; from investments, 495; from U.S. investments abroad, 306; insurance as a source of future, 555; national, 160, 161, 243, 247; national, shares in, 161; personal, 174; proprietors', 247; real, prices affect our, 116; relation between, and wealth, 14
Income tax, federal, who files return, 284; withholding wages for federal, 284; records needed for, 469
Indemnity clause, double, 537
Index number, price, 191
Index numbers, 229
Indirect marketing, 75
Indirect taxes, 280
Individual enterprise, 129
Individual income tax returns, 285
Indorsee, 326
Indorsements, blank, 326; forms of, illustrated, 327; in full, 326; qualified, 327; restrictive, 327
Indorser, 326

Industrial bank, 200, 474
Industrial conflict, collective bargaining and, 88; methods used by employers, 95
Industrial development, government aids for, 149
Industrial insurance, 532
Industrial production, 244
Industrial unions, 82
Industry standards, for informative labeling, 457
Inelastic demand, 221
Inflation, 120, 210, 238; ways to halt, 240
Informative labeling, 457; industry standards for, 457
Inheritance tax, 287
Injunction, 95
Insolvent, 356
Installment buying, 361; advantages of, 370; disadvantages of, 370; economic problems of, 362; importance of, 362; terms of payment, 371
Installment contracts, characteristics of, 366; types of, 363
Installment credit, 346, 361; economics of, 379
Installment debt, 346
Installment plan, buying on the, 368
Installment purchase, cost of an, 376
Installment service, finance charges for, 371
Instant credit, 325
Insurable interest, 508, 527
Insurance, as a form of saving, 534; as a source of future income, 555; automobile, see Automobile insurance; buying sufficient, to yield income, 555; comprehensive personal liability, 514; contracts, 507; endowment, 476; factors affecting the cost of property and liability, 515; for the home, 510; general medical expense, 539; health, 538; hospital expense, 538; life, see Life insurance; loss-of-income, 540; major medical expense, 539; medical payments provision in homeowners policy, 515; nature of property and liability, 506; need for, 506; on home, 592; old-age, nature of, 567; physical damage to the property of others clause, 515; private, 565; property, under the homeowners policy, 511; social, see Social insurance; surgical expense, 539; unemployment, 566

Insurance agent, using the, 549; factors in selecting, 547

Insurance companies, bear the risk, 507; mutual, 509; state regulation of, 510; types of, 509

Insurance company, bases for selecting, 545; legal reserve of, 528; selecting a property and liability, 521

Insurance policies, comparing costs of, 546; nonparticipating, 509; participating, 509

Insurance policy, 507; cash value of, 508; face value of, 507; transfer of, 508

Insurance premium, 507

Insurance protection, of depositors, 203

Insured, 527

Intangible wants, 3

Interest, definition of, 169; income earned by lenders, 169; net, 247; why paid, 170

Interest rate, 169; maximum, 330

Interest rates, 329; charged by credit unions, 336; legal, 330; on small loans, 334; regulation of, 229

Intermediate-term credit, 345

International markets, 73

International trade, 294; affects relationships among nations, 294; basis for, 297

International trade, essential to U.S. economy, 296; importance of, 294; low cost, a competitive advantage, 297

International trade agreements, 308

Inventory record, household, 514

Investing, 494

Investment, creating a cash estate for, 555; in a small business, 491; in real estate, 492

Investment broker, 496

Investment clubs, 501

Investment companies, 490

Investment company, closed-end, 491; open-end, 491

Investment information, sources of, 495

Investment procedure, 491

Investment trusts, 490

Investments, growth of, 495; growth possibilities of, 497

Investments, income from, 495; kinds of, 481; margin of safety of, 498; rate of return on, 498; regularity of income from, 498; safety of, 495; safety of principal of, 496; satisfactory income from, 498

Investors, business, 158

Involuntary bankruptcy, 357

J

Jobber, 74

Jobs, business creates, 43; capital needed to create, 108

Joint checking account, 318

Joint ownership, 632

Journeymen, 81

Judgment deficiency, 636

Jurisdictional strike, 94

L

Label, defined, 456

Labeling, informative, 457; descriptive, 457; for consumer protection, 402; informative, industry standards for, 457

Labels, how to read, 458; self-certifying, 408; using, as guides, 456

Labor, 36, 79; central ideas about, 79; demand for, 166; division of, 47; factors affecting supply of and demand for, 166; income earned by, 165; legislation affecting the wages of, 167; methods used by organized, 93; restricted definition of, 80; supply of, 165; tariffs affect, 311; wages of, 165

Labor and management, public policy on, 96

Laborer, 129

Labor force, civilian, 101

Labor movement, 79, 80

Labor organizations, development of national, 82

Labor relations, management and, 86

Labor turnover, 103

Labor unions, company, 96; craft, 81; early, 81; industrial, 82; international, 85; local, 85; national, 85; trade, 81

Land, 36, 163

Land contracts, 609, 631; illustration of, 609

Landlord, 622; relations of, and tenant, 622; rights and duties of the, 625

Lease, 622; illustration of a, 623; length and expiration of, 593; tenant's notice of intention to terminate a, 625; usual content of a written, 622

Leasing, 622; distinction between and renting, 624

Legal advice, when to use, 423

Legal aid societies, 402

Legal rate of interest, 330

Legal reserve, of insurance company, 528

Legal tender, 207

Lenders, protection for, 616

Lessee, 622

Lessor, 622

Level of living, 113; business raises the, 42; elements determine the, 113; raising our, 114; value of a dollar affects, 115

Level-premium insurance, 528

Liabilities, 467

Liability, liquid, 304; unlimited, of a partner, 131

Liability insurance, bodily injury, 516; property damage, 516; under the homeowners policy, 514

Licenses, 287

Lien, 637; mechanic's, 637

Life insurance, 525; annuity contracts, 531; as a factor in a person's estate, 556; buying, 545; cash value of, 528; combination, 531; defined, 527; economics of, 537; endowment, 530; group, 532; group permanent, 532; group term, 532; how families use, 526; industrial, 532; level-premium, 528; limited-payment, 529; ordinary, 529; ordinary, types of, 528; purpose of, 525; savings-bank, 533; straight, 529; term, 529; using proceeds to provide fixed income for dependents, 556

Life insurance companies, a source of real estate loans, 605; borrowing from, 331

Life insurance expenditures, relationship of, and personal income, 554

Life insurance policies, assigning, 537; cash value of, 535; extended term, 535; features of, 534; grace period of, 535; incontestable clause in, 534; limitations on, 537; nonforfeiture values of, 535; paid-up insurance plan, 535; paying premiums on, 535; riders, 537; use of dividends paid on, 535

Life insurance program, developing a, 549; planning for the readjustment period, 551; planning the initial, 549; examples of, 551

Limited partnerships, 131

Limited-payment life insurance, 530

Line-o-credit, 325

Line of credit, establishing a, 353

Liquid liability, 304

Loan, direct-reduction, 611; revolving, 330

Loan application and appraiser's report, illustration of a, 608
Loans, intermediate-term, 328; long-term, 328; mortgage, 603; obtaining, 328; real estate, see Real estate loans
Loans, secured, 329; short-term, 328; types of, 328; unsecured, 329
Loan sharks, 337
Local markets, 73
Local unions, 85
Lockout, 95
Loss-of-income insurance, 540

M

Machinery, effects of new, on production, 49
Machines, 47; use of labor-saving, 92
Maintenance of membership, 89
Major medical expense insurance, 539
Maker, of note, 326
Management, 37; and labor relations, 86; financial, savings and, 470; government aids to, 148
Management and labor, public policy on, 96
Manpower, 102; resources, 102
Manufacturing, tariffs affect, 311
Margin, buying on, 500
Market, auction, 72; buyer's, 219; commission, 72; commodity, 73; organized, 73; retail, 72; security, 73; seller's, 220; wholesale, 71
Marketing, definition of, 64; direct, 75; economic functions of, 61; economics of, 61; functions of, 64; indirect, 75; methods of, 74; nature and costs of, 71; significance of, 62
Marketing distribution system, 61
Marketing institutions, 71
Marketing services, 62
Marketing utility, 62
Market prices, 54
Markets, business provides organized, 45; free, 21; geographical range of, 73; international, 73; kinds of, 71; local, 73; national, 73; regional, 73; tariffs affect, 310; world, 73
Market system, free, 21
Mass picketing, 94
Mass production, advertising and, 385; principle of, 46
Maturity, of note, 209
Maximum interest rate, 330
Mechanic's lien, 442, 637

Mediation, 97
Mediator, 97
Medical payments coverage, 517
Medical payments provision of homeowners policy, 515
Medicare, 572
Merchandising, 68
Merchant guild, 81
Middlemen, place of, 74
Minors, 356, 430
Model Consumer Finance Act, 334
Money, 182; acceptability of, 182; affects prices, 226; and credit, effect of, on purchasing power, 190; as a measure of value, 182; as a medium of exchange, 182; as a standard of future payments, 182; as a store of value, 182; checkbook, 184; effect of supply of, on total spending, 258; functions of, 182; kinds of, 183; making, work for you, 471; nature of, 182; U.S., backed by credit reserves, 186; U.S., backed by silver and gold, 185; U.S., in circulation, by denomination, 185; U.S., managed paper currency, 186
Money order, 322
Monetary policy, control through, 257; defined, 258; type of government control, 257
Monopoly, 26, 138, 225; affects prices, 225
Moonlighting, 108
Mortality tables, 527
Morris Plan bank, 200
Mortgage, 494, 633; illustration of a, 634; package, 613; partial-payment, 603; renewing a, 610
Mortgagee, 635; rights and duties of the, 635
Mortgage bond, 488, 633; real estate, 493
Mortgage companies, real estate loans from, 606
Mortgage contract, 633
Mortgage foreclosures, 616, 635
Mortgage loans, 603
Mortgage note, 493; illustration of a, 493
Mortgage redemption insurance, 614
Mortgages, 603; home, 191; open-end, 603; package deal, 603; real estate, 603
Mortgagor, 635; rights and duties of, 635
Municipal bonds, 482
Mutual assent, 426
Mutual funds, 490
Mutual insurance company, 509
Mutual savings bank, 473

N

National bank, 202
National Bureau of Standards, 407
National Canners Association, 404
National Consumer-Retailer Council, Inc., 405
National debt, 266; concern about, 269; essential facts about, 270; growth in, 267; management of, 270; per capita, 268
National economic goals, 9
National economic growth, 108
National income, 160, 161, 243, 247; distribution of, 156; person's share in, 174; shares in, 161
National income accounting, 243
National Industrial Recovery Act, 86, 228
National Labor Relations Act, 86
National markets, 73
National output, 112
Natural hazards, farm production problems, 53
Natural resources, 36
Negotiable instrument, 326
Net interest, 247
Net profit, 171
Noncumulative preferred stock, 485
Nondurable goods, 157
Nonessential wants, 3
Noninstallment credit, 346
Noninstallment debt, 346
Nonparticipating insurance policies, 509
Nonprice competition, 223
No-par-value stock, 484
Notes, issuing, by Federal Reserve System, 207, rediscounting, 209

O

Offer, 426; essential characteristics of an, 426; keeping an, open, 429; terminating an, 429
Offeror, 427
Office of Price Administration, 229
Office of Technical Services, 408
Old-age insurance, benefits, 569; benefits for a wife, 570; benefits for other survivors, 570; meaning of full coverage, 570; nature of, 567; rules for benefits after age 65, 572; single lump-sum death benefit, 571; special provision for disabled workers, 571; summary of benefits to survivors, 571;

those covered, 568; those not covered, 568; wages and taxes, 567
Old Age, Survivors, and Disability Insurance, 573
Open account, 347
Open corporation, 133, 486
Open-end investment company, 491
Open-end mortgage, 603
Open-market operations, 211
Open shop, 89
Opinion of the title, 628
Option, 429
Oral contracts, 434
Organized market, 73
Organized markets, business provides, 45
Output, national, 112; restriction of, 92
Overexpansion, 210

P

Package mortgage, 613
Paper currency, issuing, 207; managed, 186
Parity, 229
Parity price, 54
Partial-payment mortgage, 603
Participating insurance policies, 509
Participating preferred stock, 486
Partner, unlimited liability of, 131
Partnership, 131
Partnership income tax returns, 285
Partnerships, limited, 131
Par-value stock, 484
Patronage dividend, 136
Pawnbrokers, borrowing from, 337
Payee, of check, 318; of note, 326
Payments, fixed, 465; U.S., to foreign countries, 305; variable, 465
Pensions, 306
Percent-per-month basis of computing finance charges, 375
Permits, 287
Personal economic goals, 7
Personal income, 174; by years of education completed, 168; differences in, 174; disposable, 174; relationship of life insurance expenditures and, 554
Personal loans, characteristics of, compared by sources, 332
Personal property, 512
Personal selling, 67
Physical damage to the property of others clause in homeowners policy, 515
Picket, union, 94

Picketing, 94; cross, 94; mass, 94; secondary, 94
Piecework, 89
Place utility, 40
Policy insurance, 507, 527
Policyholder, 507
Political freedoms, as goals, 10
Poll tax, 281
Population, and economic growth, 112; gross national product and, 112
Possession utility, 40
Preferential shop, 89
Preferred stock, 485; convertible, 486; cumulative, 485; noncumulative, 485; participating, 486
Premium, bonds at, 488; insurance, 507, 527
Premiums, 451
Premium waiver, 537
Prepayment without penalty clause, 613
President's Committee on Consumer Interests, 419
Price, 216; a farm problem, 52; and demand, 220; and supply, 218; economic factors related to, 224; parity, 54
Price ceilings, 229
Price competition, 223
Price discrimination, prevention of, 413
Price index number, 191
Prices, 217; consumer, 243; consumer, net effect of advertising in, 392; consumption influenced by, 220; control of, 228; credit affects, 226; money affects, 226; monopoly affects, 225; nature and significance of, 215; rent and, 164; tariffs affect, 310; taxes affect, 227; wholesale, 243
Price supports, and limitations on production, 150
Price system, 216
Primary advertising, 389
Primary boycott, 95
Primary wants, 3
Private insurance, 565
Private property, 19
Producer goods, 12
Production, 15, 217; aggregate, 236; agricultural, see Agricultural production; and its distribution, 117; business provides tools and equipment for, 43; characteristics of our, 45; demand determines, 39; effects of new machinery on, 49; elements and functions of, 35; factors of, 35; farm, see Farm Production; how shared, 29; industrial, 224; mass, principle of, 46; must create value or utility, 40; must in-

crease, 119; price supports limitations on, 150; solves problem of scarcity, 117; specialization in, 46; wheat, 55
Production efficiency, 46
Production process, business in the, 40
Production system, our, 35
Productivity, 47; and real wages, 119; and wages, 119
Profit, definition of, 171; income earned by owners, 171; net, 171; pure, 171
Profit motivation, 22
Profits, 217; competition and, 171; corporate, 248; of business firms, 128; owner's right to, 172
Promissory note, 326
Property, improvements and fixtures, 626; insurable interest in, 508; personal, 511; private, 19; public, 20
Property damage liability, 516
Property insurance, under the homeowners policy, 511
Property taxes, 282; advantages and disadvantages of, 284; assessment of property, 283; exemption of property, 282; rates, 283
Proprietorship, individual, 129; sole, 129
Proprietors' income, 247
Prosperity, 236
Proxy, 133
Public corporation, 134, 486
Public finance, 264
Public Health Service, 409
Public property, 20
Public utilities, 137
Pump priming, 105
Purchasing power, 190; changes in, of consumer's dollar, 117; effect of money and credit on, 190; expanding, with credit, 192
Pure profit, 171

Q

Qualified indorsement, 327
Quantity buying, 451
Quitclaim deed, 628; illustration of a, 630

R

Railroad Retirement Act, 573
Real cost, 8
Real estate, claims against, 637; economics of buying, 616; investing in, 492; points to investigate in buying, 636; title to, 627
Real estate agreements, 627

Real estate loan, other factors to consider in obtaining, 613; prepayment without penalty clause, 613

Real estate loans, 604; closing costs, 613; extra charges on, 611; factors about, 607; FHA, 614; from banks, 605; from life insurance companies, 605; from mortgage companies, 606; from private lenders, 606; from savings and loan associations, 604; from trust companies, 606; government-secured, 614; payments and rates on, 611; protection on, through life insurance, 613; sources of, 604; VA, 615

Real estate mortgage, 603

Real estate mortgage bonds, 493

Real estate tax, 280

Real income, prices affect our, 116

Real property, legal steps in buying, 632

Real wages, 116; and productivity, 118

Reconciliation of bank statement, 319

Recovery, 237

Receipts, U.S., from foreign countries, 305

Receiver, 357

Recession, 236

Rediscounting notes, 209

Regional markets, 73

Register check, 322

Registered bonds, 487

Remittances, 306

Rent, 163; and prices, 164; economic, 163; of land, regulation of, 164

Rental income of persons, 247

Renting, comparison of home ownership and, 594, distinction between leasing and, 624

Renting a house or apartment, 592; points to investigate in, 593; with or without a written lease, 593

Replevin, 379

Repossession, 379

Resources, 36; changes in the use of, 39; choice in the use of, 38; government decisions in the use of, 39; natural, 36; productive use of our, 36

Restriction of output, 92

Restrictive indorsement, 327

Retail market, 72

Revolving charge account, 349

Revolving loan, 330

Risk, 507; in lending money, 170

Robinson-Patman Act, 414

S

Sabotage, 95

Safe-deposit boxes, 324

Sales, special, and bargains, 448

Sales contract, 631

Sales finance company, 366

Sales tax, 280, 286; general, 286

Saving, insurance as a form of, 534; rewards of, 471

Savings, and financial management, 470; come from individuals, 110; growth of regular, 472; setting goals for, 471; taxes affect, 111; where to put, 472

Savings-bank insurance, 533

Savings accounts, 323

Savings and loan associations, 474; a source of real estate loans, 604; borrowing from, 331

Savings bank, 200, 473, mutual, 200, 473; stock, 200

Savings bonds, Series E, 474; Series H, 476

Savings programs, economic problems of, 477

Scarcity, problem of, 3

Services, importance of, in buying, 450

Shares of stock, 132, 483

Shop, agency, 89; closed, 89, 166; open, 89; preferential, 89; union, 89

Shop stewards, 85

Short-term credit, 345

Short-term securities, buying, 211

Simplified practice, 408

Sit-down strike, 94

Second-mortgage borrowing, 607

Secondary boycott, 95

Secondary picketing, 94

Secondary wants, 3

Secured FHA loans, 333

Secured loans, 329

Securities, buying and selling, 499; buying on margin, 500; federal and state regulation of, 419; installment purchases of, 500; listed, 500; pay-as-you-go method of buying, 500; short-term, buying, 211; unlisted, 500

Securities and Exchange Act, 212

Securities and Exchange Commission, 419

Security, 495; union, 88

Security market, 73

Selective advertising, 389

Selective taxes, 286

Self-certifying labels, 408

Self-employment tax, 288

Seller, remedies of, when buyer fails to perform, 439

Selling, 67; personal, 67

Severance tax, 287

Service account, 347

Service taxes, 287

Services, economic, 2; control of prices of, by government, 228; marketing, 62; on a checking account, 320

Slowdown strike, 94

Small business, investing in a, 491

Social accounting, 243

Social insurance, 565; economics of, 577; need for, 564

Social legislation, 564

Social security account, verifying, 575

Social security card, 575

Social security coverage, applying for, 574

Social security number, application for, 575

Social security taxes, 288; employer-employee, 288; schedule of, including medicare, 568; self-employment, 288

Soil, a farm problem, 53

Sole proprietorship, 129

Specialization, advantages of, 47; disadvantages of, 47; principle of, 46

Speculating, 494

Speculation, control of, 212

Spending, a plan for, 448; general guides in, 446

Stamp taxes, 289

Standard of living, 114

Standardizing, 66

Standards of identity, 456

State bank, 201

Statement of assets and liabilities, 467

Statutes of limitations, 356

Stewards, shop, 85

Stock, shares of, 132; common, 482; convertible preferred, 486; cumulative preferred, 485; noncumulative preferred, 485; no-par-value, 484; participating preferred, 486; par-value, 484; preferred, 485; shares of, 483

Stockbroker, 496

Stock company, 509

Stock exchanges, 134, 499

Stock rights, 484

Stock splits, 484

Stockholder protection, 203

Stocks, comparisons of corporation bonds and, 489

Stockholders, 132

Storing, 65

Strike, 93; direct, 93; general, 93; industry-wide, 93; jurisdictional, 94; sit-down, 94; slowdown, 94; sympathetic, 93; wildcat, 94

Strikebreaker, 96

Straight life insurance, 529
Subsidies, to agriculture, 149
Subsidy, 149
Substitution, principle of, 223
Supply, 218; a farm problem, 52; and demand, 218; of labor, 165; of labor, factors affecting, 166; price and, 218
Surgical expense insurance, 539
Surplus, 4

T

Take-home pay, 465
Tangible wants, 3
Tariffs, 310; affect agriculture, 311; affect labor, 311; affect manufacturing, 311; affect markets, 310; affect prices, 310; affect the consumer, 312; conflicting theories of, 312; purposes of, 310
Taxes, affect prices, 227; affect savings and new capital, 111; benefit, 287; business, 287; claim of government on income, 173; commodity, 286; control over, 276; corporation income, 284; death, 287; direct, 280; estate, 287; excise, 281; for unemployment insurance, 288; gasoline, 281; gift, 288; hidden, 281; in home, 592; income, records needed for, 469; indirect, 280; individual income, 284; inheritance, 287; kinds of, 28; nature of, 276; poll, 281; property, 282; real estate, 280; sales, 280, 286; selective, 286; service, 287; severance, 287; share, 287; social security, 288; special, 289; stamp, 289
Tax advice, by banks, 324
Tax revenue, federal, state, and local, 265
Tax system, 278; essentials of a, 278
Taxation, 275; ability-to-pay theory of, 279; cost-of-service-received theory of, 279; fairness in, 278; principles of, 275
Technology, 49; and employment, 106
Tenant, 622; relations of landlord and, 622; rights and duties of the, 624
Tenant by entirety, 632
Term life insurance, 529
Terms, credit, 347
Textile Fiber Products Identification Act, 417
Time balance, on an installment sale, 372
Time deposit, 323, 473
Time utility, 40

Timework, 89
Title, abstract of, 628; certificate of, 628; deed, written evidence of, 628; defined, 627; examination, 627; opinion of the, 628; passing the, 439
Title-guarantee policy, 628
Tools, business provides, for production, 43
Torrens System, 628
Trade, balance of, 302; how nations control, 308
Trade agreements, 309; international, 308
Trade channel, 74
Trust company, 201
Trust deed, 633
Trade Expansion Act of 1962, 312
Trade names, 457
Trade puff, 438
Trade union, 81
Trade unions, AFL, a federation of, 82
Trading stamps, 451
Trademark, 453
Transportation, 69
Traveler's check, 322
Travel service, offered by banks, 324
Treasurer's check, 321
Trust companies, a source of real estate loans, 606
Trust indenture, 633
Turnover, labor, 103

U

Underemployment, 103
Underwriter, 507
Unemployment, general solutions to, 103; proposed specific solutions, to, 104; solutions directed primarily by business and individuals, 104; solutions directed primarily by government, 105; supply and demand determine, 103
Unemployment compensation, 566; causes for denying or forfeiting, 566
Unemployment insurance, 566; taxes for, 288; those covered by, 566
Uniform Commercial Code, 363, 364, 426
Uniform Small-Loan Law, 334
Union picket, 94
Union recognition, 88
Unions, craft, 81; company, 96; early, 81; industrial, 82; international, 85; local, 85; national, 85; trade, 81
Union security, 88
Union shop, 89
Unlimited liability, of a partner, 131

Unsecured loans, 329
United States Department of Agriculture, 408
United States Department of Labor, 419
United States Post Office Department, 419
Usury laws, 432
Utility, 40; form, 40; marketing, 62; place, 40; possession, 40; production must create, 40; time, 40

V

Value, 450
Veterans Administration (VA) loans, 615
Voluntary bankruptcy, 357

W

Wage differences, factors causing, 166
Wage plans, 89
Wage-price spiral, 239
Wage rates, regulation of, 229
Wages, 165; garnisheeing of, 356; of labor, legislation affecting the, 167; productivity and, 119; real, 116
Waiver, premium, 537
Walsh-Healey Act, 169
Wants, 40; and their satisfaction, 1; economic, 3; economic, satisfying our, 5; essential, 3; intangible, 3; many, but limited supply, 4; nature of our, 3; nonessential, 3; primary, 3; secondary, 3; tangible, 3
Warranties, 437; express, 437; implied, 437
Warranty, breach of, 438; breach of, remedies for, 438
Warranty deed, 628; essential provisions of a, 631; illustration of a, 627
Wealth, definition of, 13; relation between income and, 14
Wheat, planting and production, 55
Wheeler-Lea Act, 415
Wholesale market, 71
Wholesale prices, 243
Wildcat strike, 94
Will, defined, 557
Wool product, 416
Wool Products Labeling Act, 416
Work, reduction of hours of, 90
Work force, 102
Working capital, 109
Workweek, shorter, 107
Workmen's compensation, 576
Workmen's compensation laws, 564
World markets, 73
Written contracts, 434

Tracey
x
Bobby

Tracy
&
Joe